IN THE SPIRIT OF CRAZY HORSE

ALSO BY PETER MATTHIESSEN

NONFICTION

Wildlife in America
The Cloud Forest
Under the Mountain Wall
Sal Si Puedes
The Wind Birds
Blue Meridian
The Tree Where Man Was Born
The Snow Leopard
Sand Rivers

FICTION

Race Rock
Partisans
Raditzer
At Play in the Fields of the Lord
Far Tortuga

PETER MATTHIESSEN

IN THE

SPIRIT OF CRAZY HORSE

THE VIKING PRESS • NEW YORK

First published in 1983 by The Viking Press
40 West 23rd Street, New York, N.Y. 10010
Published simultaneously in Canada by
Penguin Books Canada Limited

An excerpt from this book originally appeared
in *The New York Times* in different form.

LIBRARY OF CONGRESS CATALOGING IN PUBLICATION DATA
Matthiessen, Peter.
In the spirit of Crazy Horse.
Includes index.
1. Indians of North America—Government relations—1934– . 2. American Indian Movement. 3. Oglala Indians—Government relations. 4. Peltier, Leonard. I. Title.
E93.M46 1983 305.8'97'073 82-8466
ISBN 0-670-39702-4 AACR2

Maps by David Lindroth

Printed in the United States of America
Set in CRT Garamond

For all who honor and defend those people
who still seek to live in the wisdom of Indian way

We did not ask you white men to come here. The Great Spirit gave us this country as a home. You had yours. We did not interfere with you. The Great Spirit gave us plenty of land to live on, and buffalo, deer, antelope and other game. But you have come here; you are taking my land from me; you are killing off our game, so it is hard for us to live. Now, you tell us to work for a living, but the Great Spirit did not make us to work, but to live by hunting. You white men can work if you want to. We do not interfere with you, and again you say, why do you not become civilized? We do not want your civilization! We would live as our fathers did, and their fathers before them.

Crazy Horse (*Lakota*)

ACKNOWLEDGMENTS

Many people, past and present, Indian and white, have made important contributions to this book; I wish to thank the following for useful interviews and/or information, with apologies to anyone I may have forgotten.

Dennis Banks
Clyde Bellecourt
Evelyn Bordeaux (deceased)
Jean Bordeaux
Dino Butler
Nilak Butler
Jim Calio
Pete Catches
Mary Cornelius
Sheriff Don Correll
Leonard Crow Dog
Paulette d'Auteuil
Vine Deloria, Jr.
Roque Duenas (deceased)
Joe Eagle Elk
Bruce Ellison
Chief Eagle Feather
(Bill Schweigman)
(deceased)
Richard Erdoes
Archie Fire Lame Deer
Joe Flying By
Judi Gedye
Madonna Gilbert
Bill Hazlett
Jacqueline Huber
Evan Hultman
Roslynn Jumping Bull
Sidney Keith
June Little
Russell Loud Hawk
John Lowe
Janet McCloud
Kevin McKiernan
Bill Means
Lorelei Means
Russ Means
Ted Means
Ellen Moves Camp
Sam Moves Camp
Karen Northcott
SA George O'Clock
Leonard Peltier
Ernie Peters
Dr. Garry Peterson
SA David Price
James Roberts
Bob Robideau
Steve Robideau
Kenneth Tilsen
Al Trimble
John Trudell
Robert Hugh Wilson
"Standing Deer"

Dennis Banks, Vine Deloria, Jr., Richard Erdoes, Bill Hazlett, John Lowe, Kevin McKiernan, and Kenneth Tilsen have been kind enough to review particular sections of the manuscript; Nilak Butler, Bruce Ellison, Leonard Peltier, Bob Robideau, and Al Trimble have inspected the entire book. All have contributed important corrections, comment, and advice and none is responsible for any errors of fact or emphasis that may remain.

Dennis Banks, Dino Butler, Russell Means, Kenneth Tilsen, and Robert Hugh Wilson "Standing Deer" contributed lengthy interviews and/or correspondence; an extensive interview was also provided by Special Agent David Price. Bill Hazlett and Kevin McKiernan have been generous with their own research material; Paulette d'Auteuil was kind enough to make available a series of letters from Leonard Peltier in prison. Steve Robideau and the Leonard Peltier Defense Committee as well as the staff of the Black Hills Alliance have also been very helpful.

Particular thanks are due to Bruce Ellison, Leonard Peltier, and Bob Robideau, who provided extensive research material, information, and support from the very beginning of this project.

Finally, I wish to thank Elisabeth Sifton and Jennifer Snodgrass of The Viking Press for their cheerful and intelligent dedication in the face of a sometimes overwhelming project.

CONTENTS

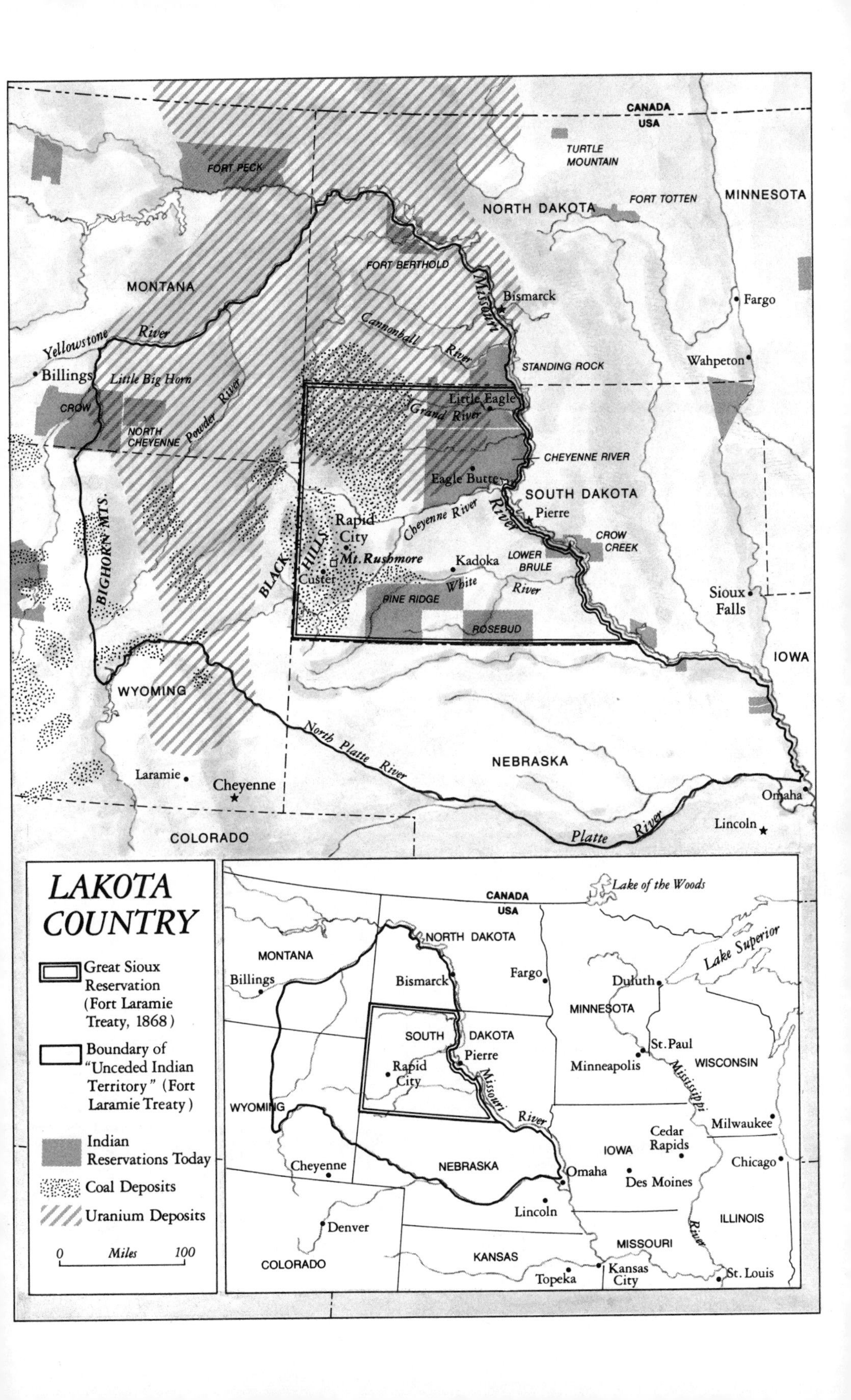

CANADA
USA
TURTLE MOUNTAIN
FORT PECK
FORT TOTTEN
MINNESOTA
NORTH DAKOTA
FORT BERTHOLD
MONTANA
Missouri
Bismarck
Fargo
Cannonball River
Yellowstone River
Wahpeton
STANDING ROCK
Billings
Little Big Horn
Powder River
CROW
Little Eagle
Grand River
NORTH CHEYENNE
CHEYENNE RIVER
Eagle Butte
SOUTH DAKOTA
BIGHORN MTS.
Rapid City
Cheyenne River
River
Pierre
CROW CREEK
BLACK HILLS
Mt. Rushmore
Kadoka
LOWER BRULE
Custer
White River
Sioux Falls
PINE RIDGE
ROSEBUD
IOWA
WYOMING
North Platte River
NEBRASKA
Laramie
Cheyenne
Omaha
Lincoln
COLORADO
Platte River
LAKOTA COUNTRY
Great Sioux Reservation (Fort Laramie Treaty, 1868)
Boundary of "Unceded Indian Territory" (Fort Laramie Treaty)
Indian Reservations Today
Coal Deposits
Uranium Deposits
0 Miles 100
Lake of the Woods
CANADA
USA
NORTH DAKOTA
Lake Superior
MONTANA
Fargo
Billings
Bismarck
Duluth
MINNESOTA
SOUTH DAKOTA
St. Paul
Pierre
Minneapolis
WISCONSIN
Rapid City
Missouri River
Mississippi River
WYOMING
Milwaukee
Cedar Rapids
IOWA
Chicago
Cheyenne
NEBRASKA
Omaha
Des Moines
Lincoln
ILLINOIS
Denver
MISSOURI
KANSAS
COLORADO
Topeka
Kansas City
St. Louis

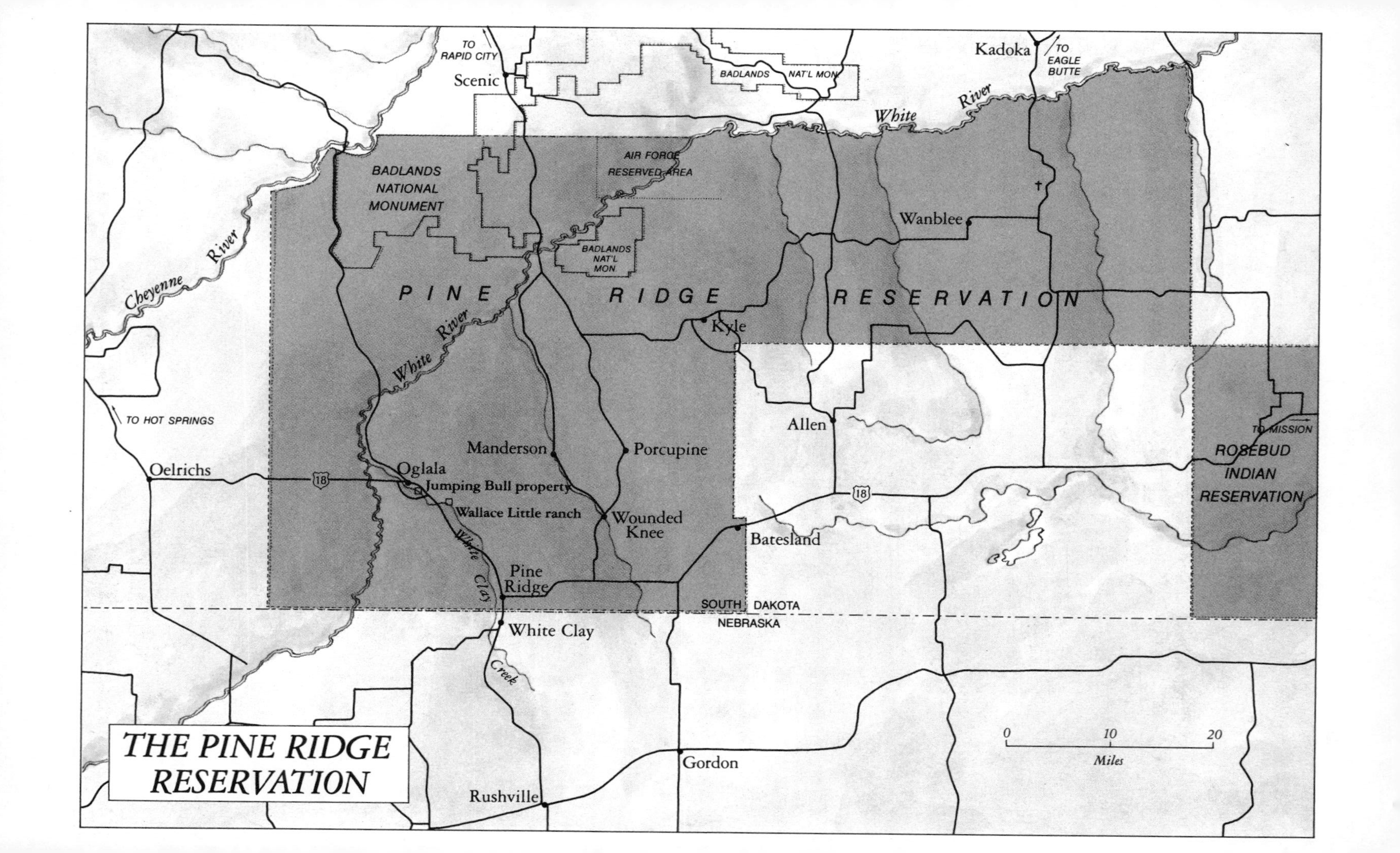
THE PINE RIDGE RESERVATION
PINE RIDGE RESERVATION
TO RAPID CITY
Scenic
BADLANDS NAT'L MON
Kadoka
TO EAGLE BUTTE
White River
AIR FORCE RESERVED AREA
BADLANDS NATIONAL MONUMENT
BADLANDS NAT'L MON
Wanblee
Cheyenne River
White River
Kyle
TO HOT SPRINGS
Allen
TO MISSION
ROSEBUD INDIAN RESERVATION
Manderson
Porcupine
Oelrichs
Oglala
Jumping Bull property
Wallace Little ranch
Wounded Knee
18
Batesland
Pine Ridge
White Clay Creek
SOUTH DAKOTA
NEBRASKA
White Clay
Gordon
Rushville
0
10
20
Miles

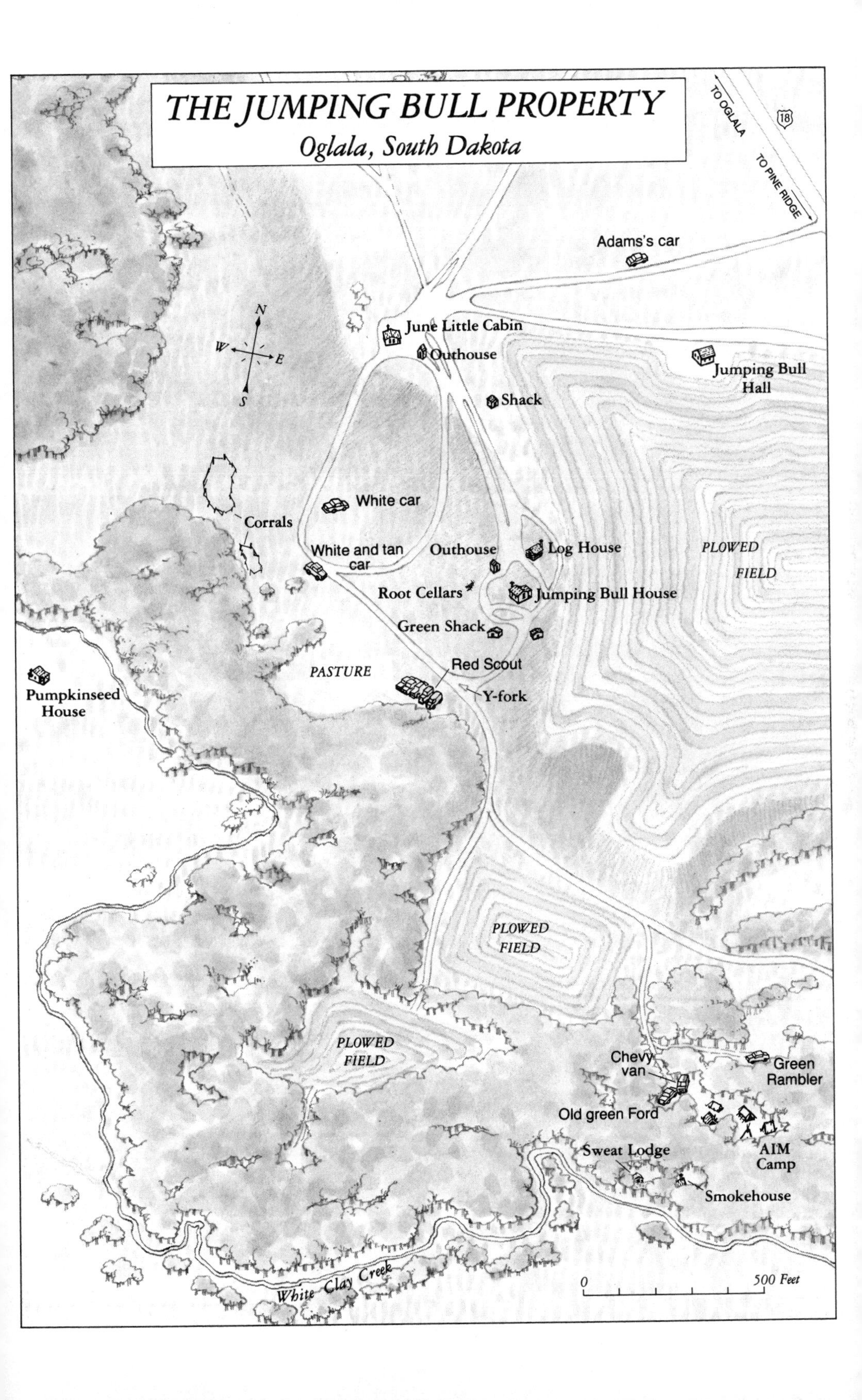

THE JUMPING BULL PROPERTY
Oglala, South Dakota
TO OGLALA
18
TO PINE RIDGE
Adams's car
N
W
E
S
June Little Cabin
Outhouse
Jumping Bull Hall
Shack
White car
Corrals
White and tan car
Outhouse
Log House
PLOWED FIELD
Root Cellars
Jumping Bull House
Green Shack
Red Scout
PASTURE
Y-fork
Pumpkinseed House
PLOWED FIELD
PLOWED FIELD
Chevy van
Green Rambler
Old green Ford
Sweat Lodge
AIM Camp
Smokehouse
0
500 Feet
White Clay Creek

INTRODUCTION

The buffalos I, the buffalos I . . .
I am related to the buffalos, the buffalos.

Clear the way in a sacred manner!
I come.
The earth is mine.

The earth is weeping, weeping.

On June 26, 1975, in the late morning, two FBI agents drove onto Indian land near Oglala, South Dakota, a small village on the Pine Ridge Reservation. Here a shoot-out occurred in which both agents and an Indian man were killed. Although large numbers of FBI agents, Bureau of Indian Affairs (BIA) police, state troopers, sheriff's deputies, and vigilantes surrounded the property within an hour of the first shots, the numerous Indians involved in the shoot-out escaped into the hills.

The death of the agents inspired the biggest manhunt in FBI history. Of the four men eventually indicted for the killings, one was later released because the evidence was "weak," and two others were acquitted in July 1976 when a jury concluded that although they had fired at the agents, they had done so in self-defense. The fourth man, Leonard Peltier, indicted on the same charges as his companions but not tried until the following year, after extradition from Canada, was convicted on two counts of murder in the first degree, and was sentenced to consecutive life terms in prison, although even his prosecutors would dismiss as worthless the testimony of the only person ever to claim to have witnessed his participation in the killings. This testimony was also repudiated by the witness, who claimed to have signed her damning affidavits under duress, as part of what one court of appeals judge would refer to as a "clear abuse of the investigative process by the FBI."

Whatever the nature and degree of his participation at Oglala, the ruthless persecution of Leonard Peltier had less to do with his own actions than with underlying issues of history, racism, and economics, in particular Indian sovereignty claims and growing opposition to massive energy development on treaty lands and the dwindling reservations. In the northern Plains, the opposition was based on a treaty, signed in 1868 between the United States and the Lakota nation at Fort Laramie, in Dakota Territory, which recognized Lakota sovereignty in their Dakota-Wyoming homelands and hunting grounds, including the sacred Paha Sapa, the Black Hills. With the discovery of gold in the Black Hills a few years later, this treaty was illegally repudiated by the U.S. government; not until the 1970s was the justice of the Lakota treaty claim recognized in court.

In the year of the 1868 Treaty, a former Governor of New York State named Horatio Seymour was nominated as the Democratic candidate for President of the United States; and the history of the Lakota people might possibly have been less tragic had the Democrats won, since

Governor Seymour held strong convictions that Ulysses S. Grant did not share about the offense to its own Constitution in the young nation's shameful treatment of the native peoples.

> Every human being born upon our continent, or who comes here from any quarter of the world, whether savage or civilized, can go to our courts for protection—except those who belong to the tribes who once owned this country. . . . The worst criminals from Europe, Asia, or Africa can appeal to the law and courts for their rights of person and property—all save our native Indians, who, above all, should be protected from wrong.

Seymour's unpopular opinion appeared on the title page of Helen Hunt Jackson's *A Century of Dishonor* (1881), one of the first books to deplore the wrongs inflicted on "the tribes who once owned this country":

> There is but one hope of righting this wrong. It lies in appeal to the heart and the conscience of the American people. What the people demand, Congress will do. It has been—to our shame be it spoken—at the demand of part of the people that all these wrongs have been committed, these treaties broken, these robberies done, by the Government. . . .
>
> The only thing that can stay this is a mighty outspoken sentiment and purpose of the great body of the people. Right sentiment and right purpose in a Senator here and there, and a Representative here and there, are little more than straws which make momentary eddies, but do not obstruct the tide. . . .
>
> What an opportunity for the Congress of 1880 to cover itself with a lustre of glory, as the first to cut short our nation's record of cruelties and perjuries! the first to attempt to redeem the name of the United States from the stain of a century of dishonor![1] *

The Congress of 1880 did not redeem the name of the United States, and that "century of dishonor" was followed by another—less violent, perhaps, but more insidious and sly—as the "frontiersman" gave way to the railroadman and miner, the developer and the industrialist, with

* Source notes and additional material can be found in the Notes section, beginning on p. 577.

their attendant bureaucrats and politicians. And the Congress of the 1980s will do no better, to judge from the enrichment of the powerful and the betrayal of the poor to which it has reduced itself under President Reagan.

The poorest of the poor—by far—are the Indian people. It is true that in our courts today the Indian has legal status as a citizen, but anyone familiar with Indian life, in cities or on reservations, can testify that justice for Indians is random and arbitrary where it exists at all. For all our talk about suppression of human rights in other countries, and despite a nostalgic sentimentality about the noble Red Man, the prejudice and persecution still continue. American hearts respond with emotion to Indian portraits by George Catlin and Edward Curtis, to such eloquent books as *Black Elk Speaks* and *Bury My Heart at Wounded Knee,* to modern films and television dramas in which the nineteenth-century Indian is portrayed as the tragic victim of Manifest Destiny; we honor his sun dances and thunderbirds in the names of our automobiles and our motels. Our nostalgia comes easily, since those stirring peoples are safely in the past, and the abuse of their proud character, generosity, and fierce honesty—remarked upon by almost all the first Europeans to observe them—can be blamed upon our roughshod frontier forebears. "The tribes who once owned this country" were simply in the way of the white man's progress, and so most of the eastern tribes were removed to Indian Territory (now Oklahoma), and the western tribes mostly banished or confined to arid wastes that no decent white man would want. By a great historical irony, many of these lands were situated on the dry crust of the Grants Mineral Belt, which extends from the lands of the Dene people in Saskatchewan to those of their close relatives, the Dine, or "Navajo," in New Mexico and Arizona, and contains North America's greatest energy resources. More than half of the continent's uranium and much of its petroleum and coal lie beneath Indian land, and so the Indians are in the way again.

After four hundred years of betrayals and excuses, Indians recognize the new fashion in racism, which is to pretend that the real Indians are all gone.[2] We have no wish to be confronted by these "half-breeds" of today, gone slack after a century of enforced dependence, poverty, bad food, alcohol, and despair, because to the degree that these people can be ignored, the shame of our nation can be ignored as well. Leonard Peltier's experience reflects more than most of us wish to know about the realities of Indian existence in America; our magazines turn away from articles about the Indians of today, and most studies of Indian history and culture avoid mention of the twentieth century. But the Indians are still among us—"We are your shadows," one man says—and the qualities they were known for in their days of glory still persist among many of these quiet people, of mixed ancestry as well as full-blood, who still abide in the echo of the Old Way.

⊡

My travels with Indians began some years ago with the discovery that most traditional communities in North America know of a messenger who appears in evil times as a warning from the Creator that man's disrespect for His sacred instructions has upset the harmony and balance of existence; some say that the messenger comes in sign of a great destroying fire that will purify the world of the disruption and pollution of earth, air, water, and all living things. He has strong spirit powers and sometimes takes the form of a huge hairy man; in recent years this primordial being has appeared near Indian communities from the northern Plains states to far northern Alberta and throughout the Pacific Northwest.

In 1976, an Indian in spiritual training took me to Hopi, where traditional leaders told us more about this being. Over several years, we visited the elders in many remote canyons of the West, and eventually I traveled on my own, from the Everglades and the Blue Ridge Mountains north to Hudson Bay and from the St. Lawrence westward to Vancouver Island. Along the way I learned a little of the Indians' identity with land and life (very different from our "environmental" understanding) and shared a little of their long sadness about the theft and ruin of ancestral lands—one reason, they felt, why That-One-You-Are-Speaking-About had reappeared. From these journeys came a series of essays attacking the continuing transgressions against these lands by corporate interests and their willing allies in state and federal government.[3]

Like most people with more appreciation than understanding of the Indian vision, I clung to a romantic concept of "traditional Indians," aloof from activism and politics and somehow spiritually untouched by western progress. This concept had a certain validity in the old Hopi nation, which was never at war with the United States and never displaced from its stone villages on the desert rimrock north of the sacred San Francisco Peaks, in Arizona; the Hopi traditionals are looked to by other Indians all over the continent for guidance in the quest to rediscover and maintain those roots of the Old Way that might still nourish the Indian people. In most Indian communities, however, romantic concepts were difficult to sustain. While it was true that, here and there, a few "old ones" still existed, it was clear that most reservation traditionals had resumed their traditions only very recently, and that many, as one Indian writer has observed, were "conservative Indians whose cultural tenacity somehow got confused with a sadly-compromised grasp of their own heritage. . . . A decline in their firsthand experience in Native American customs has resulted in a reactionary mentality that poses as traditionalism . . . and . . . a degraded and stereotypical 'pow-wow' view of themselves."[4] Such people were especially wary of the new activist organizations, in particular the American Indian Movement (AIM) and its young "warriors" from the cities with their red wind bands, guns, and episodes of violence, who were sure to bring down further grief on a desperate people. I had absorbed some of this attitude, having failed to perceive that whatever AIM's origins, excesses, and mistakes, that warrior spirit had restored identity and pride to thousands of defeated people and inspired attempts to resurrect the dying languages and culture.

Then, in the spring of 1979, while investigating the proposed construction of a vast fuel terminal on Indian sacred grounds at Point Conception, California, I took part in a sweat-lodge ceremony* led by Archie Fire Lame Deer, a Lakota of the Minnecojou band who had married among the coastal Chumash and was a leader in the Point Conception struggle. During a walk into the hills to the vision-quest pits that he maintains in the mountains of the Coast Ranges above Point Conception, Lame Deer spoke of the sweat lodge he had established at Lompoc Federal Correctional Institution, on the far side of these Santa Ynez Mountains; just recently, he said, the AIM leader Leonard Peltier had been transferred to Lompoc, to the great relief of Indians all over the country, who had feared that he would be assassinated in the federal penitentiary at Marion, Illinois. At first, I resisted the police-state implications in this idea, discounting it as Movement rhetoric and paranoia. But a few weeks later, when Peltier made a desperate escape from Lompoc in which a young Indian named Dallas Thundershield was killed, I had to take what Lame Deer had said more

* An ancient ceremony of spiritual purification and renewal.

seriously. I began to make inquiries about Peltier's case, and I have been making inquiries ever since.

Lame Deer made a firm distinction between a true leader such as Peltier and the self-appointed AIM spokesmen who turned up at every political confrontation and split the local Indians by demanding leadership and encouraging divisive factions, or brought discredit on the Movement through drink and violence. Many Indians had now concluded that AIM had been infiltrated from the start by the FBI, and the Chumash people were wondering if one of the AIM men involved in a Point Conception shooting had been sent in to damage the Indian cause with bad publicity. But Lame Deer doubts this. "Guys like these, every time they mess up, they start hollering about the FBI—well, that is bullshit. The FBI has no time to fool with every loose Indian who comes along. But Leonard is different, he is a real leader; they are afraid of him, and they're out to get him."

A very big man with a bearish walk, Archie Fire is a descendant of that Lame Deer who in the winter of 1835–36 (according to the "winter count" marked on buffalo hide by an Indian called the Swan) "shot a Crow three times with the same arrow," and also of the Minnecojou chief of the same name who joined forces with Sitting Bull's Hunkpapas and the Oglalas of Crazy Horse in the great battle of June 25, 1876, in which Colonel George Custer's Seventh Cavalry company was destroyed. At the death of his father, John Fire Lame Deer, in 1976, Archie Fire became chief, and one day he intends to return to the Dakotas. Lame Deer himself was raised on the Rosebud Reservation, but most of his Minnecojou people—the most traditional of the seven Lakota bands—live farther north on the Cheyenne River Reservation, and also on Standing Rock, on the North Dakota border.* "There's a lot

* "It is important for the reader to understand that the Sioux, in traditional times, formed three major geographical groups. The Santees, largely in Minnesota; the Yanktons (including the Yanktonais), on the prairies of western Minnesota and eastern North and South Dakota; and the Tetons, west of the Missouri River on the plains of North and South Dakota and Nebraska. These locations are only approximate, for there was much travel and movement, and bands from any of the three major groups might at any given time be living with another of the major groups.

"Each of these three major groups represented a distinctive dialect of the Sioux language, though they were all mutually intelligible. The Santees and Yanktons called themselves Dakota, whereas the Tetons called themselves Lakota. We use *Sioux* as the designation for all these groups, *Lakota* for the Teton or Western Sioux (divided into seven tribes: Oglala, Brule [*Sicangu*], Minneconjou, Sans Arc [*Itazipco*], Two Kettles, going on up in that country now," said Archie Fire, referring not only to the threat to the Great Plains from widespread mining but to recent appearances of the big hairy man at Little Eagle, on the Standing Rock Reservation, who came in sign, some people said, of those days at the world's end "when the moon will turn red and the sun will turn blue" and the Lakota people will resume their place at the center of existence.[5]

Opening his tobacco bundle, he purified the vision pit with smoke from a braided hank of sweetgrass, after which he assembled the stone pipe.* We smoked the pipe together, facing successively in the four directions, giving thanks in our own ways to the Creator, to Wakan Tanka (literally, the Unknowable Great; loosely, the Great Mystery).[6] Lame Deer stood for a long time against the California sky, chanting in the Siouan tongue, his big voice rolling down the mountains to the grasslands that today reminded him of spring on the Great Plains: *Mitakuye Iyasin!* (All Our Relations!), which signifies not merely our own kin but our identity with all things on this splendid Earth.

⊡

A few weeks later, on my way to the Black Hills, I passed through the Turtle Mountain Reservation in North Dakota, in the wooded lake country just south of the Canadian border. Indian friends had given me names of people on Turtle Mountain, and a lively evening was spent

---

Hunkpapa, and Blackfeet Lakota) and *Dakota* to refer generally to the Santee and Yankton groups. The reader should note that this is an English convention only; the Sioux themselves used the terms *Dakota* or *Lakota,* depending on the dialect of the speaker, to refer to *all* the Sioux groups. To differentiate the three groups, the terms *Titonwan,* 'Teton'; *Isanati,* 'Santee'; and *Ihanktonwan,* 'Yankton,' were used." (Walker, *Lakota Belief and Ritual,* pp. xxiv–xxv)

"Our people don't call themselves Sioux or Dakota. That's white man talk. We call ourselves Ikce Wicasa—the natural humans, the free, wild, common people. I am pleased to be called that." (John Fire Lame Deer)

* "In filling a pipe, all space (represented by the offerings to the powers of the six directions) and all things (represented by the grains of tobacco) are contracted within a single point (the bowl or heart of the pipe) so that the pipe contains, or really *is,* the universe. But since the pipe is the universe, it is also man, and the one who fills a pipe should identify himself with it, thus not only establishing the center of the universe but also his own center; he so 'expands' that the six directions of space are actually brought within himself. It is by this 'expansion' that a man ceases to be a part, a fragment, and becomes whole or holy; he shatters the illusion of separateness." (Black Elk, in Brown, ed., *The Sacred Pipe,* p. 21)

with the family of Mary Cornelius, the traditional spokesman for the Pembina Ojibwa band since the death in 1976 of Chief Keyon Little Shell. In 1864, an ancestral Chief Little Shell signed a treaty with the United States that assigned to the Pembina band 8 million acres of this wooded lakeland; in the next thirty years, the reservation was drastically reduced, as white settlers pushed out the Indians, and today perhaps 72 square miles are left of the 1,150 or more to which the Pembina had held aboriginal title. (They also held territories farther east and south, from which they were pushed out by the Dakota people who were spreading westward; some of that land is now the Fort Totten Reservation, where Leonard Peltier's Ojibwa-Sioux mother was born.) Most of the treaty land was seized from the Pembina without payment, and only recently, with the discovery of oil, has the band been offered a government "recompense" of $52 million. Mary Cornelius was trying to persuade her people to refuse, since if they accepted this money, they would waive all future claims to the lost land and permit its exploitation by the oil companies. "I'm getting kind of tired of politics," Mary Cornelius said. "The only reason I was chosen for spokesman was because I can still speak my own language: I guess I'm the first woman chosen as spokesman in the history of the band."

Like many traditional families, the Corneliuses have been harassed by the federal agencies that administer all Indian reservations. In 1969, Mary Cornelius's daughter lost her unborn child after a beating by Bureau of Indian Affairs police; the FBI covered up the episode and Mrs. Cornelius has been an energetic AIM supporter ever since. She is a second cousin of Leo Peltier, and is proud to have Leo's son Leonard in the family. "I've known him since he was a little boy. He was kind of an excitable child, he was not the kind who would sit around and wait; when Leonard saw something that he thought should be done, he did it. Even at powwows, that boy was never sitting still. Indian children are not really children after the age of ten: they take care of the house and take care of the smaller kids, and they all know how to cook, and Leonard was the same. I can't honestly say that I ever remember him in trouble, and he was never a bully. He was like a big brother to the other boys, breaking up fights instead of encouraging them, the way some kids do. And if you had started something you couldn't finish, or if you were an elder person, that boy was always there, ready to help."

Turtle Mountain was among the many Indian communities that had been visited in recent years by the "rugaru,"[7] as the Ojibwa call the hairy man who appears in symptom of danger or psychic disruption in the community. Mary's son Richard talked a little about the appearance of these beings in recent years to Lakota people at Little Eagle, South Dakota. "There were just too many sightings down there to ignore. I mean, a *lot* of people saw it. Around here, we didn't have very many reports; most of them were right here where we live now." He waved his hand to indicate the woods outside, where I camped that night along the lake edge.

From Turtle Mountain, south and west, the Ojibwa woodlands open out onto the buffalo grasslands that roll south all the way to Comanche and Kiowa country in northern Texas. Ohiyesa, a Santee Sioux boy whose band was hunting in this country in the late 1860s, refers repeatedly to the ancient enmity between Dakota and Ojibwa that made travel in this country dangerous for both. "Hush," says his grandmother, alarmed by a bird's song. "It may be an Ojibwa scout." And her lullaby begins, "Sleep, sleep, my boy, the Chippewas are far away."* Ohiyesa, who as "Charles A. Eastman" was to become a Dartmouth graduate, a doctor, a Christian, a friend of presidents, and the author of several notable books on Indian life, describes the wonderful bounty of this country at the edge of the Great Plains:

> Our party appeared on the northwestern side of Turtle mountain; for we had been hunting buffaloes all summer, in the region of the Mouse [Souris] River, between that mountain and the upper Missouri. As our cone-shaped tepees rose in clusters along the outskirts of the heavy forest that clothes the sloping side of the mountain, the scene below was gratifying to the savage eye. The rolling yellow plains were checkered with herds of buffaloes. Along the banks of the streams that ran down the mountains were also many elk, which usually appear at morning and evening, and disappear into the forest during the warmer part of the day. Deer, too, were plenty, and the brooks were alive with trout. Here and there the streams were dammed by the industrious beaver. In the interior of

* "Chippewa" is a distortion of "Ojibwa," in use mostly south of the Canadian border; and not to be confused with Chipewayan, an Athabaskan tribe from the spruce muskeg country, farther north. Some Ojibwa call themselves "Anishinabi," the Original (Woodland) People.

> the forest there were lakes with many islands, where moose, elk, deer, and bears were abundant. The water-fowl were wont to gather here in great numbers, among them the crane, the swan, the loon, and many of the smaller kinds. . . . This wilderness was a paradise, a land of plenty . . . and . . . we lived in blessed ignorance of any life that was better than our own.[8]

I headed south on long straight roads of the Great Plains, past glittering reed ponds of the prairie sloughs and over the soft rolling hills and flowing grasslands of the buffalo peoples. Widgeon and teal rose from the reeds, and to the west, a cloud-colored flight of pelicans turned bone-white, catching the sun, as the wings banked in widening far circles; the huge birds sailed westward into infinities of summer blue. At Mandan, the road crossed the wide Missouri and, in early afternoon, the Cannonball River. Here, in 1883, Cree mercenaries and the U.S. Army slaughtered the last great herd of northern bison, to help in the final subjugation of the Lakota (or western Dakota), known to their many enemies as Sioux.

The Little Eagle settlement on the Standing Rock Reservation, not far south of the South Dakota line, sits between low buttes of the Grand River, just west of its confluence with the Missouri. According to Joe Flying By, a small, mild-mannered man whom I found standing outside his house, enjoying the late-afternoon light of early summer, the Grand River had once been called the Mandan, for in the old days, before the coming of the Lakota, these grassy hills of the buffalo country had been the territory of the Mandan and Arikara, or "Rees," who were driven northward by the seven bands of the Lakota. The people here at Little Eagle are mostly descendants of the Hunkpapa band once led by Sitting Bull, who was killed just west of here, up the Grand River. The trail to his grave dies out in a graveyard of wrecked autos without tires, windshields shattered; beyond this place it disappears into the undergrowth, and the grave is lost. The once mighty Hunkpapa, who had held the place of honor in the Indian camp on the Greasy Grass Creek before the great fight with Longhair, fell on bitter times after the death of Sitting Bull, and are considerably reduced in number.

Joe Flying By pointed to the highest hill, a flat-topped eminence off to the north. "That is Elkhorn Butte," he said. "That is where we go to make medicine, that is our medicine place. All I do myself are the pipe ceremonies, but other medicine men who go out into the hills, maybe they don't talk Lakota anymore, so they use me."

Joe's father had been a preacher, he said, and his older brother was an ordained minister. He shrugged. "I talk both ways, Indian way and Bible way; if you *really* know about them, they are the same. But people today don't know about either, and these are the ones causing trouble. Drinking so much, and using that weed—that used to be only for the medicine men. They don't know how to handle it, and they go crazy with it, and kill each other!" he exclaimed suddenly, with real pain.

A few weeks before, the big, hairy man had appeared in Little Eagle for the third straight year, and more than forty people had seen him. "I think that the Big Man is kind of the husband of Unk-ksa, the Earth, who is wise in the way of anything with its own natural wisdom. Sometimes we say that this One is a kind of big reptile from the ancient times, who can take a big, hairy form; I also think he can change into a coyote. He is very powerful. Some of the people who saw him did not respect what they were seeing, they did not honor him, and they are already gone."

⊡

Not long before my arrival, the community had received an open letter from one of its young men, Dallas Thundershield, who was much impressed by his meeting with Leonard Peltier in prison:

> I like to express my inner feelings to all my people on Standing Rock. . . . We realize the importance of our culture, and the keeping of our ancestors' teaching, but we are so much into the white man's way of thinking that we too are beginning to think as them. What means more to your children and all the unborn, "land or money"? Myself, I believe that this land is not to be sold, but to live upon by all people. If this land is sold, where would all your children live when the money is gone? People have died for these lands, so we too must at least show respect and keep the land or die.
>
> *"In the spirit of Leonard Peltier,"*
> *Thundershield D.* (*Dog Soldier*)

Joe Flying By was very pleased that the first sun dance in thirty-five years had been held at Little Eagle just the week before. "Four people dragged the buffalo skulls," he said, suggesting that I go up to the sun-dance grounds and look it over.

On a flat grassy mesa high above the south bank of the river stood the sacred tree—a young cottonwood, forty or fifty feet high, with a bundle of cherry branches at the fork—which had been taken to this treeless place and placed in the consecrated ground with ancient ceremonies. White, yellow, red, and black cloths flew like pennants from the pole; strings of tobacco packets dedicated to the spirits, and broken thongs that had tugged and torn the breast and back skin of those sun dancers who had been pierced, ta-tacketed softly on the early-summer wind that stirred the grass beneath the skeletons of tipis and sweat lodges. In the quiet of the evening mesa, acknowledging the sacred ceremony and the courage and pain of those who had circled under the sun, I stood at a distance in the twilight.

". . . It is not possible to know and understand our traditional way of life without knowing and understanding the Sun Dance . . . [which] . . . is, among other things, a ceremony of renewal and restoration," says Chief Frank Fools Crow, the Lakota medicine man who restored the sun dance to the Pine Ridge Reservation in the 1950s. "The sun knows everything. To us it is like the Sacred Pipe. They are both instruments used by *Wakan-Tanka,* and they are the greatest instruments of service he has, next to the directions. But the sun is not God. The sun is something he created for the rest of creation. We respect it and pray to it because it watches over the world and sees everything that is going on. It also serves God by bestowing special gifts that it has upon the world. . . .

"We do face the sun and pray to God through the sun, asking for strength to complete the Sun Dance, and that all our prayers will be heard. As [we] continue to do this, we are able to see the sun with our eyes completely open. It doesn't blind us, and in it we see visions. No one should be surprised about this. Wonderful and mysterious things happen at the Sun Dances to prove that *Wakan-Tanka*'s . . . powers are active in our midst. . . . What makes the real difference is that the pledgers are dancing, praying very hard, concentrating, and calling for God's pity. People forget that, but what we do brings us great power."[9]

Soon a pickup truck appeared, driving right up to the tree, and an Indian family in Sunday dress emerged, talking loudly and laughing; the man of the family wore his hair short like a white man's, and his four children ran around the sun-dance grounds, uncomprehending. Finally they drew near the tree itself, with its pennants and broken thongs lifting and falling on the evening breeze over the prairies. They fiddled and joked, then tugged the pennants and hide strings, until finally the mother, who had kept her distance, called out, alarmed, "You're not supposed to touch those things!" But the grinning father, ignoring the woman's warning, encouraged his children to poke fun, and said nothing at all when the oldest girl and loudest giggler grabbed the broken thongs that had fastened the circling dancers to the tree.[10]

Again the mother cried, more urgently, "You're not supposed to touch those strings that are broke off—that's where they pierced themselves!" Her family paid her no attention. "They're all Christians up there now," Lame Deer had told me. And Joe Flying By, asked how the old people of Little Eagle accounted for the Big Man, had said shortly, "There are no more old people."

That night I slept on a high hill above the sun-dance grounds, where a prairie-dog town sloped down toward the river; not far to the west, in the dark bend of cottonwoods, was the site of the old Indian Agency where Sitting Bull was killed. At daylight, upland sandpipers flew overhead, their melodious dawn voices mixing with the sharp squeaks of the prairie dogs, which have mostly been poisoned on white man's lands but are still found on the Indian reservations.

⊡

From Standing Rock, the road led south and west to the Cheyenne River Reservation, coming down into Eagle Butte out of the high, open hills. From the top of a rise, a pickup could be seen in the far distance, perhaps five miles away, a bright metal glint at a T-fork where the road turned west toward the town. It was still there when I reached the top of the next rise, and again when I came over the last hill and rolled down to the crossing. Coming up behind, I stared into the back of the truck in disbelief. The old shoe soles and soiled clothes of a dozen bodies, tossed in like logs, filled the wooden truck bed; there was no visible twitch of life. Then the pickup door creaked open, and an Indian sagged out, as drunk as any man I ever saw who was still moving. He could not focus and he could not speak, just clung to the door window with both hands; behind him, three more bodies, as motionless as all the others, had been wedged between the front seat and the windshield.

After a moment, at a loss, I kept on going. Possibly the truck was broken down or out of gas or stalled, but it seemed more likely that the driver, ordered to halt by the stop sign at the crossroads, had simply run out of momentum, losing all track of where he was headed or why.

Eagle Butte is a dusty and decrepit settlement on a windswept plateau of old fields, abandoned farms, and defunct autos; the people here mostly belong to the smallest of the Lakota bands—the Two Kettle, Sans Arc, and Blackfoot. Sidney Keith, a spiritual leader, accepted a small offering of rough tobacco, saying, "Good! Now we can talk!" He told me that the Fort Laramie Treaty of 1868 had been sanctified and sanctioned by Wakan Tanka because of the sacred tobacco smoked in the pipe; the white man had also smoked the sacred pipe, and therefore "our Treaty" (as it is known throughout the Lakota world) was inviolable and still valid, despite the white man's transgressions ever since. Of course, he said, there would always be Indians who wanted money for the land, who wanted to live like white men, and who would be favored by the Bureau of Indian Affairs. "But the old traditional people who want to be Indians, they get nothing. You go south of here to those last real traditional full-blood communities like Cherry Creek, like Bridger, you can still find people living in old cars. They keep quiet, so they get nothing. North of here—well, you saw all that good range when you came through, all those breeds in their pickups; they get that good land for next to nothing because they cooperate with the BIA. When they get together, they don't even have powwows, they have rodeos; those people aren't Indians anymore, they're cowboys."

Sidney Keith shook his head, disgusted. "Now the BIA is trying to eliminate our rural day schools; all the kids would have to come in here to Eagle Butte and sleep in dormitories, just like we had to do in the old days, when they were breaking up Indian families." He gazed at me, tired. "Wouldn't let you speak your own language—they would soap your mouth."

Sidney Keith said that the Big Man seen at Little Eagle might be Unk-cegi, which means literally "Earth Brown" or "Brown Shit"—the filth of Creation. Unk-cegi lived long, long ago, in the time of the great animals, but he had been covered up in the Great Flood, with all the other giants. "He was down there too deep to be saved by Noah," Sidney Keith observed dryly. But all the mining, all these underground explosions of the white man's bombs, had made fissures in the earth and released not Unk-cegi but his spirit. "His bones are still down there. That's why Indians get so upset when burial grounds are disturbed, when the whole burying ceremony is interfered with; it isn't just a matter of disrespect. Disturbing the burial grounds the way the white man does releases those spirits.

"Unk-cegi was here when Indian man first came here. He seeks out Indian communities because he knew Indians in the Old Days, and he sought out Little Eagle because that is the worst place for drinking in Standing Rock, and maybe Cheyenne River, too. We drink too much in Eagle Butte, but not like that: even their old people are all drunk over there. Unk-cegi appeared to kids who smoke grass, and drunks and hotheads"—his shrug suggested that what he meant were people not taken seriously in the community—"nice people, some of 'em, but they do bad things. He won't appear to the good people; that's why Joe Flying By didn't see him. And he won't appear at the sun dance—that's a good circle."

⊡

Cherry Creek, perhaps fifteen miles off the main road, is so broken and scattered by poverty and neglect that it seems to have fallen from the high bluff on the north side of the Cheyenne River. The remnant full-blood Minnecojou here are descended from the people of Chief Big Foot, who was in Cherry Creek in December 1890 when fugitive Hunkpapa warriors arrived with the news of Sitting Bull's murder; from this place, Big Foot set out with his people on the winter trek of more than 150 miles across the Badlands toward the safety of the Oglala stronghold on Pine Ridge.

East of Cherry Creek, I swam in the Cheyenne River, not yet aware of its contamination from uranium-mine-tailings piles at Edgemont, in the southern Black Hills; from there I went south to the Rosebud Reservation to see Joe Eagle Elk, a *yuwipi** healer whom I had met the year before at a sweat-lodge purification and healing ceremony near Salt Lake City. At Rosebud, a broad highway much too large for the village was under construction, and Joe Eagle Elk commented sadly on the BIA's foolish use of federal money. "Blacktop would have been good enough. We don't need all that heavy concrete; we need jobs around here, something to do. That money could have been so much better spent." He shrugged his shoulders. "The people here, they've grown used to saying

* *Yuwipi:* "a ceremony in which the medicine man is tied and wrapped up like a mummy." (John Fire Lame Deer, in Erdoes, ed., *Lame Deer,* p. 288) During this ceremony he may hold a sacred stone, *yuwipi wasicu;* see note on *wasicu,* p. 581.

nothing; they just accept what is done for them—or *to* them, maybe—and they don't complain no more."

It had been raining off and on all day, and at his house in the Grass Mountain community, Joe Eagle Elk spoke of the unseasonable summer floods that were expected to rise again that evening; the river road was now impassable, and the road I had taken from St. Francis was already half washed away. Up on the mesa to the southwest, lightning appeared as fiery cracks in a heavy blackness, and soon an Indian policeman came to warn the community that torrential rains were expected in the next few hours. To avoid being trapped, I considered leaving the car on the far side of the low place in the road, but Joe Eagle Elk advised against it; not long before, a local Indian whose car had broken down returned to it only half an hour later to find its headlights and windows all smashed in. "It is not a good place here now, I tell you that," Joe Eagle Elk said mildly; he is a very gentle and soft-spoken man, with burn scars on his neck and face and nervous hands. "I don't blame the young people; it's not their fault. They want a lot of things that they see on TV, but there are no jobs for them anywhere, nothing for them to do, and meanwhile everything is so expensive. All they have is their anger. It's not their fault. I don't know whose fault it is," he concluded, in that gentle, shy, remorseless voice of Indians. "Maybe the government."

Uneasy, he lifted his cap to scratch his head. "This has been a bad summer. These bad floods—I never seen anything like that before. And they change everything along the river. Before, every tree looked familiar, everything I saw. I used to say to myself as I passed along here, That's where so-and-so is buried; and I'd know everything was in its place. But since the floods, everything here looks different, it's like I was in a new country." Joe shrugged again, trying to laugh. "Maybe that's okay. All these old places that my eye remembered had sad memories of the people who were gone. Maybe it's a good thing that Nature would come along and change everything, clear all that away, and start again." Of the Big Man, Joe Eagle Elk said, "It seems maybe he has got a good heart. He has never hurt nobody. A lot of people over there at Little Eagle, they been shooting at him instead of trying to exchange words and ask *why* he is coming around. Maybe he is trying to tell us what he wants and where he comes from; maybe he is bringing news for us, a warning."

With the thunder and forked lightning ranging all over the night horizon, I made my way through rain squalls to the town of Mission, where I spent the night in an Indian motel. At Mission the streets were full of puddles, but the big rains had already rushed through and the night was clearing, and the next morning early, the sun rose on empty streets; the few human figures were lone Indians. One young woman in tight black sateen and heavy makeup was yowling angrily and pounding at the door of a ramshackle big building, and as I walked past, a man seated peacefully on a curb at the street corner looked up at me, shrugging his shoulders. "She lost her key," he explained to me gently, concerned and embarrassed for the girl at the same time.

⊡

A sun dance was being held that day in a hidden valley between hills, west of Rosebud village. The sky was fresh and blue after the black rainstorms of the night before, and a clear breeze dispelled the heat from the pine-bough shade built around the sun-dance circle. In the center of the circle stood the sacred tree, a sapling cottonwood ceremonially decorated with the red, black, yellow, and white colors that represent the four directions and also the four races of man, each placed on the continent where it belonged by the Creator. An old man in a blue shirt stood with his back to the tree, addressing the twelve dancers in Lakota; the line of painted dancers included two or three young children and two old women. In the shade, four men were beating on the big Plains drum, as the sun dancers stamped forward and back, blowing eagle-bone whistles; the women wore buckskin, the men, bare to the waist, were in colored skirts, and all wore thong anklets and sage crowns in their hair.

In midmorning on this first day of the four-day ceremony, less than fifty people had turned up. There were no white people among them, and because strangers might not be welcome, I stood back a little from the gallery where the Indians were sitting in the shade. Soon a big old man with a big-nosed Lakota face and a long braid of gray hair waved me in closer, and after a moment, asked bluntly what had brought me. When I told him why I was traveling on the reservations, the old man nodded, then politely explained certain details of the sun dance, which was being led by a portly, powerful young Indian in red neckerchief, blue singlet, and faded jeans, pulled together by a beaded belt and bracelet.

After a little while, the old man said, "My name is Chief Eagle Feather, Bill Schweigman. I'm the last living traditional chief." Between dances, we were approached by the sun-dance leader, and Bill Schweigman introduced Chief Leonard Crow Dog, whom he said he had ordained as a medicine man. Crow Dog's shy grin and self-effacing manner did not go with the hard squint that looked me over. He is admired by most supporters of AIM, which he was the first medicine man to endorse, but he is criticized by other spiritual leaders for using his healing power the wrong way. However, the atmosphere felt good, and besides, I had learned that these days, at least (Fools Crow says it was not always so), Indians often bad-mouth one another with such brutal gossip that two groups rarely work together very long. Praise of one medicine man by another is almost unheard of, especially if the man becomes well known; even Black Elk, the revered Oglala prophet, was dismissed as a "catechism teacher" and "cigar-store Indian" by the late John Fire Lame Deer, and John Fire himself was widely criticized for his dedication to hard drink and stray women, which he pursued to the very end of his long life. "They respect me not because I'm good but because I have power," he once said.[11]

In the pine-bough shadows, Crow Dog and Eagle Feather sat surrounded by young disciples of both sexes. Speaking in English with scraps of Lakota, they cracked sexual jokes, jeered at "bobtailed" Indians who wore their hair short, and laughed about a white friend of Crow Dog who tended to faint in the sun dance at the sight of blood. "What's the matter, I told her," Eagle Feather said. "You see your own blood every month, don't you?" Everyone laughed. Such joking is expected at a sun dance, which has aspects of fertility and renewal, and there was a lot more talk about blood, together with rough teasing of the young acolytes, most of whom, despite long hair, wind bands, and beads, appeared to be whites.

Now Crow Dog turned to give me a bad smile; his shy manner had disappeared entirely. Soon the dancing resumed, and Crow Dog returned into the circle. This first day of the sun dance, Eagle Feather said, would be dedicated to one of the most sincere of his young sun dancers, who had returned here a few months ago on leave from the Navy, only to be murdered by three drunks in St. Francis. "They bashed his head in," Eagle Feather said disgustedly. "White men?" I asked before I thought, and he stared at me, surprised. "No, no," he said. "Injuns." We fell silent awhile, watching the dancing. Despite the small crowd and the small, uneven line of dancers, the ardor of the participants was stirring. In these sunny hills, under the blue sky of the prairies, the chanting dancers moved back and forth in pounding step, raising fingers to the sun on extended arms, the drums and wistful voices pierced by the shrill eagle-bone whistles. One of the young men had scars over his nipples, the marks of flesh offerings made to Wakan Tanka in other years. "They'll be pierced on Sunday," Chief Eagle Feather told me.

⊡

From Rosebud, I headed west into the Pine Ridge Reservation, a tract of dry country just north of the Nebraska border that is one of the largest Indian reservations in the United States. There I visited with Petaga, or Pete Catches, a respected holy man who has strongly supported the fight of the traditional Lakota people to regain their treaty land in the Black Hills. Pete Catches lives in a small cabin on an open hillside north of Pine Ridge village. A gaunt man in a lavender shirt with an intelligent, sensitive face, he regarded me peacefully for a time before inviting me into the disheveled room with the dartboard on the wall and the monastic iron cot that stood out away from the wall over toward one corner. Next to the cot sat a small traveling bag, not so much packed as not-unpacked, as if Pete Catches were ready to depart Pine Ridge with the first person who made the suggestion. "This nation," he said, and stopped to glare at me. "This nation—I can't say *my* nation, because they stole it away from me." He waved his arm in sudden anger. "They cheated and lied, and broke every treaty, even the sacred treaty that protected the Black Hills." The medicine man subsided suddenly and became silent, composing himself.

"We've come to an age when we should know better what we are doing," Pete Catches resumed softly, in a silence that followed some meditations on the Big Man, who was trying to save mankind, he said, from the great cataclysm the Indian people knew was coming. "We must now try to understand what is wrong with us, why we have to tamper with and change the forests and the land. We have done this too long—not us, but the white man. Let's not walk on the moon, then fail to understand what this Creation is all about. This is life, this is beautiful, everything is the way it should be."

That night I camped on a mesa north of the Badlands, where at daylight a flock of sharp-tailed grouse scratched the dew-softened dirt that with a dry sun would turn to the color of sand; in the western distance, sharp in the early sun, the Black Hills rose in a dark wall from the golden rises of the Plains.

> This beautiful region, of which the Lakota thought more than any other spot on earth, caused him the most pain and misery. These hills were to become prized by the white people for reasons far different from those of the Lakota. To the Lakota the magnificent forests and splendid herds were incomparable in value. To the white man everything was valueless except the gold in the hills. Toward the Indian the white people were absolutely devoid of sentiment, and when a people lack sentiment they are without compassion. So down went the Black Forest and to death went the last buffalo, noble animal and immemorial friend of the Lakota. As for the people who were as native to the soil as the forest and the buffalo—well, the gold seekers did not understand them and never have. The white man will never know the horror and the utter bewilderment of the Lakota at the wanton destruction of the buffalo. What cruelty has not been glossed over with the white man's word—enterprise![12]

I headed westward to the original homeland of the Minnecojou, that valley of the Rapid River on the eastern slope of the Black Hills where the concrete and neon conglomerate called Rapid City squats today. From Rapid City, a road climbs into Nemo Canyon, a beautiful steep-sided valley where the recent discovery of uranium-bearing rock had set off a whole new wave of mining claims on national forest land that by the terms of the 1868 Treaty belonged to the Lakota nation. From the upper canyon, in the heart of the Black Hills, a ridge route winds southward around high blue lakes that freshen the dry piney forests; on the higher ridges, a few mountain goats persist, and the rare cougar. It was now July, and the highways were churning with tourists, drawn from near and far to such scenic wonders as Sitting Bull Crystal Cave, Wonderful Wonderland Cave, Black Hills Holy Land, Inc. ("Approved Attraction"), and "Crazy Horse: A Mighty Monument in the Making" (where a man for whom no likeness exists—he never let himself be photographed or painted[13]—is being "portrayed" on a huge and vulgar scale above the rubble of a sacred mountain). Keystone, a honky-tonk town with loudspeaker tin music and billboard facades, is tacked together by fast-food emporiums and Golden West "trading posts" stuffed with Indian-type art made mostly in Hong Kong, Taiwan, and New Jersey. Beyond Keystone, the road climbs through the ancient forest to a vast parking lot and shopping and tourist center, from which the pilgrim may elevate his gaze to the mountain home of the great thunder beings, now "Mount Rushmore," home of the most enormous novelties in the whole world. What does this Mount Rushmore mean to us Indians? asked John Fire Lame Deer.

> It means that these big white faces are telling us, "First we gave you Indians a treaty that you could keep these Black Hills forever, as long as the sun would shine, in exchange for all of the Dakotas, Wyoming and Montana. Then we found the gold and took this last piece of land, because we were stronger, and there were more of us than there were of you, and because we had cannons and Gatling guns, while you hadn't even progressed far enough to make a steel knife. And when you didn't want to leave, we wiped you out, and those of you who survived we put on reservations. And then we took the gold out, a billion bucks, and we aren't through yet. And because we like the tourist dollars, too, we have made your sacred Black Hills into one vast Disneyland. And after we did all this we carved up this mountain, the dwelling place of your spirits, and put our four gleaming white faces here. We are the conquerors." . . .
>
> One man's shrine is another man's cemetery, except that now a few white folks are also getting tired of having to look at this big paperweight curio. We can't get away from it. You could make a lovely mountain into a great paperweight, but can you make it into a wild, natural mountain again? I don't think you have the know-how for that. . . . Maybe it's not too late to put an elevator under this whole shrine of democracy—press a button and the whole monument disappears. And once a week—say, every Sunday from nine to eleven—you press the button again and those four heads come up again with the music going full blast. The guys who got an astronaut on the moon should be able to do this much for us Indians, artists and nature lovers.[14]

At the visitors' center, postcards of "Black Elk at Mount Rushmore" are available to historically inclined tourists; the postcards suggest Indian approval of this desecration of Indian sacred grounds and neglect to say that the sad-faced man in movie-Indian regalia with the four huge faces of Washington, Jefferson, Lincoln, and Theodore Roosevelt looming behind him is not the renowned spiritual leader, but his son Ben. The alert visitor may notice that Mount Rushmore is unusually well guarded, due to the recurrent fear that redskin terrorists or other unpatriotic types might try to obliterate this monument to the westward course of empire.

I found a soft pine-needle bed in a ponderosa pine grove under Harney Peak, the highest in the Hills, named in honor of Lieutenant General William S. Harney, who fought against the Seminoles in Florida, then traveled west to war on the Lakota; General Harney was among the U.S. commissioners who signed the treaty that reserved these Hills for the Indians forever.

As an old man, in 1931, Black Elk had climbed to Harney Peak to offer prayer: "Hey-a-a-hey! Hey-a-a-hey! Hey-a-a-hey! Grandfather, Great Spirit, once more behold me on earth and lean to hear my feeble voice. . . . Hear me in my sorrow, for I may never call again. O make my people live!"[15]

To Harney Peak came a wild wind and rain, and hollow reverberations of heat lightning, with mountain spirits roaring through the pine tops, but in the morning, two deer waited, expectant, on the woods road down the far side of the mountain. Where the foothills leveled gently westward into the sage plains of Wyoming, pronghorn antelope drifted like cloud shadows on the grass, and a young golden eagle—the sacred "spotted eagle" of the Lakota—sailed on straight strong wings down the warm wind, toward the old Powder River hunting grounds and the Big Horn Mountains.

BOOK I

CHAPTER 1

THIEVES ROAD

The Oglala Lakota, 1835–1965

Hear ye, Dakotas! When the Great Father at Washington sent us his chief soldier [Colonel William Harney] to ask for a path through our hunting grounds, a way for his iron road to the mountains and the western sea, we were told that they wished merely to pass through our country, not to tarry among us, but to seek for gold in the far west. Our old chiefs thought to show their friendship and good will, when they allowed this dangerous snake in our midst. . . .

Yet before the ashes of the council fire are cold the Great Father is building his forts among us. You have heard the sound of the white soldier's axe upon the Little Piney. His presence here is an insult and a threat. It is an insult to the spirits of our ancestors. Are we then to give up their sacred graves to be plowed for corn? Dakotas, I am for war!

Red Cloud (Lakota)

Then another great cry went up out in the dust: "Crazy Horse is coming! Crazy Horse is coming!" Off toward the west and north, they were yelling "Hóka Hey!" like a big wind roaring, and making the tremolo; and you could hear eagle bone whistles screaming.

Black Elk (Lakota)

In 1835, five white prospectors who entered the old silences of the sacred mountains were attacked by Indians; their fate was scrawled in a last note, "All kilt but me." Probably Ezra Kind's small expedition was the first to pursue the sunny glint of gold in the earth and streams of the Black Hills, an isolated ridge of pine-dark peaks and high blue lakes that rises strangely from dry plains on what is now the Wyoming–South Dakota border. This outcropping of ancient limestones and granite, roughly 40 by 120 miles, is considerably older than Mount Everest; it is as old, perhaps, as any geological formation in North America. Like any isolated mountain in flat country, it has a mystery and power, as if placed there as a sacred place at the center of the circle of the world.

Or so it was perceived by the Cheyenne and the Arapaho, and later by the seven bands, or council fires, of the Lakota Oyate, or western Dakota nation, which was moving westward out of Minnesota, the Land-of-Many-Waters, in the course of a two-hundred-year dispute with the woodland Ojibwa and the Cree. When the Lakota crossed the Missouri River, they abandoned the woodlands for a great, free life on the open plains, hunting the buffalo with other Indian nations that had captured or stolen the horse.[1] All of these people were drawn to the dark hills, a shelter and a hunting place for deer and birds and buffalo in winter, a source of stone implements and medicine plants and sparkling clear water. In the summer, in the time of the great tribal gatherings and renewal ceremonies such as the sun dance, the young men would go to sacred points in Paha Sapa on the four-day vision quest that would form and guide their lives—"the decision to meet one's self," a Lakota has said.

> Of all our domain we loved, perhaps, the Black Hills the most. The Lakota had named these hills *He Sapa,* or Black Hills, on account of their color. The slopes and peaks were so heavily wooded with dark pines that from a distance the mountains actually looked black. In wooded recesses were numberless springs of pure water and numerous small lakes. There were wood and game in abundance and shelter from the storms of the plains. It was the favorite winter haunt of the buffalo and the Lakota as well. According to a tribal legend these hills were a reclining female figure from whose breasts flowed life-giving forces, and to them the Lakota went as a child to its mother's arms.[2]

To westward, the Black Hills overlooked the great hu
along the Powder River, stretching away across Wyom
Horn Mountains; the hunting grounds, shared with th
Northern Cheyenne, were disputed by the Crow, or
sometimes the Shoshone, or "Snake Indians"; these enem inter-
mittently assisted by white mountain men, the prospectors and fur trappers, in running skirmishes with the fierce Lakota.

The first white men to appear from the north and east in the eighteenth century were tolerated, if not welcomed, by the strong and warlike buffalo people of the Plains. "All-the-Indians-See-the-Flag-Winter," when a U.S. flag was seen near the Missouri, was 1791;[3] in the winter of 1802, some horses stolen from the whites were found to be wearing shoes. By 1809, an English trapper had a cabin on the White River, and in 1819, many Indians died of measles or smallpox, strange awful plagues that were later explained to them as the work of God, clearing the way for His own people in the wilderness. In 1822, a trading post was established at the mouth of the Bad River by a white man known as "Big Leggins," and the following year, some Lakota joined their Dakota kinsmen and a company of the Sixth U.S. Infantry in an attack on two Minnetaree villages, in an early example of War Department policy of setting one Indian against another. But bad feeling against the fur traders' dishonesty, fired by their alcohol, had already worsened when in 1837 a smallpox epidemic destroyed the Mandan people, decimated the Ḥidatsa and Arikara, and killed thousands of Indians all over the Great Plains. The white man's plagues intensified the Indians' growing resentment and dread of the thousands of migrant "pioneers" who were forging muddy tracks across their hunting grounds on the way to Oregon and California, slaughtering buffalo and elk along the way; the stream of wagons on the Oregon Trail, marked out in 1842, thickened and widened with the discovery of gold in California six years later.

Having scarcely concluded unpopular and costly wars with the Creeks and Seminoles in the Southeast, the U.S. government was eager to adopt a friendship-treaty policy that would permit safe passage of pioneers and fur trappers, as well as the boats trading on the Missouri River. The first major treaty with these western "Sioux" (a French distortion of an Ojibwa word for "cutthroat,"* given to the Dakota† by

* Sometimes translated as "little snake."

† Sometimes translated as "allies."

their old enemies and adopted by the whites on their way west) was signed in 1851 at Fort Laramie, which had been made a military post two years before; the treaty permitted the pioneers to pass through Indian territory unharmed. Almost immediately this treaty was transgressed by the construction of fortified trading posts on the Platte River and along the Oregon Trail. In 1854, Colonel William Harney responded to a bloody skirmish over a Mormon cow by killing more than one hundred warriors and marching the rest into Fort Laramie in chains; four years later, a party of soldiers reconnoitered the Black Hills.

A council with Harney held at Fort Pierre in the winter of 1855–56 was conspicuously avoided by the westernmost, largest, and most powerful band of the Lakota, the Oglala, the heart of whose territory was the hunting grounds that lay between Paha Sapa and the Powder River. With the discovery of gold near Virginia City, Montana, in the early 1860s, public clamor increased for a safe trail from Cheyenne northwest across the Powder River. Most of the soldiers were withdrawn to the Civil War, but military forays into Indian country recommenced soon after the war ended. In 1866, an expedition sent to open up the Bozeman Trail into Montana—called by the Indians "Thieves Road"—was disputed at a council held at Fort Laramie, where Red Cloud, the Oglala war leader, refused to be presented to the officers, then stalked out in the midst of the discussions: "The Great Father sends us presents and wants us to sell him the road, but the White Chief comes with soldiers to steal it before the Indian says yes or no! I will talk with you no more! I will go—now!—and I will fight you! As long as I live, I will fight you for the last hunting grounds of my people!"[4]

The irascible ambitious Red Cloud had been repudiated by many of his people because he had killed the head chief of the Oglala, declaring that Bull Bear was too friendly with the whites, but no one questioned Red Cloud's abilities as a war leader or as a statesman. His foremost ally was Spotted Tail, chief of the Brule band, who had led a great raid in 1864 on Julesburg, Colorado; this raid reflected the widespread outrage among Plains Indians caused by the slaughter at Sand Creek of an unsuspecting Cheyenne camp by an armed mob of Colorado irregulars, with subsequent gross sexual mutilation of men, women, and children. ("Cowards and dogs!" declared Kit Carson, whose own regular soldiers, known to the Navajo as "Long Knives," had sometimes played catch with the severed breasts of young Navajo women.)

Crazy Horse, a young Oglala warrior who had ridden with Spotted

Tail to Colorado, led the skillful ambush and destruction of a cavalry detachment in late 1866 at Big Piney Creek on the upper Powder River. The following year, when the Oglala were routed by the U.S. Army's new breech-loading rifles near the Big Horn River,[5] the government had already had enough of "Red Cloud's War" and sued for peace with the Sioux nation. But not until the soldiers had abandoned the wagon roads and forts on the Bozeman Trail would Red Cloud come in to negotiate with a U.S. peace commission dominated by soldiers, including General William Tecumseh Sherman.[6]

According to the terms of the treaty signed by Red Cloud at Fort Laramie on November 6, 1868, the Indians were guaranteed "absolute and undisturbed use of the Great Sioux Reservation. . . . No persons . . . shall ever be permitted to pass over, settle upon, or reside in territory described in this article, or without consent of the Indians pass through the same. . . . No treaty for the cession of any portion or part of the reservation herein described . . . shall be of any validity or force . . . unless executed and signed by at least three-fourths of all the adult male Indians, occupying or interested in the same." That clause in the Fort Laramie Treaty was still critical a century later. Clothes, goods, education, a sawmill and gristmill, a warehouse, a doctor, and instruction in the white man's agriculture and technology from resident farmer, carpenter, blacksmith, and engineer would be provided for the Indians, who pledged:

> That they will withdraw all opposition to the construction of the railroad now being built on the plains.
>
> That they will permit the peaceful construction of any road not passing over their reservation as herein defined.
>
> That they will not attack any persons at home . . . nor molest or disturb any wagon-trains, coaches, horses, or cattle. . . .
>
> That they will never capture or carry off from the settlements white women or children.
>
> That they will never kill or scalp white men, nor attempt to do them harm.

Seven years before the Fort Laramie Treaty, Congress had established the U.S. Territory of Dakota for the white man's use, and this prior legislation was taken a lot more seriously than the 1868 Treaty, to judge from the continuing transgressions in Lakota country. For a brief period, Congress protested its honorable intentions toward the Sioux as well as its commitment to the treaty, which as ratified by Congress and signed by President Ulysses S. Grant in 1869 was in effect the supreme law of the land, equal in stature to the Constitution. In 1871, a rider attached to an Indian Service appropriation bill provided that "hereafter no Indian nation or tribe within the United States shall be acknowledged or recognized as an independent nation, tribe, or power with whom the United States may contract by treaty," and although the Fort Laramie Treaty was not affected, it continued to rankle Congress not only as an impediment to Manifest Destiny but as the only recognition of unconditional defeat ever signed by the U.S. government.

In 1870, on the first of several trips to the East, Red Cloud and Spotted Tail became dismayed by the sheer numbers of the whites; the two leaders perceived that the defeat of their people was inevitable. Because both let themselves be photographed (which Crazy Horse, throughout his life, refused to do), it was said of these leaders that they had "let their spirit be captured in a box," and despite all the angry rhetoric with which they would greet the betrayal of the great Treaty of Fort Laramie, neither man would counsel war ever again. "When we first had this land, we were strong, but now are melting like snow on a hillside, while you are grown like spring grass," Red Cloud said at Washington. "I have two mountains in that country, the Black Hills and the Big Horn Mountains. I want the father to make no roads through them. . . . I do not want my reservation on the Missouri."[7] The following year, he agreed to move his people to the "Red Cloud Agency," under the shadow of Fort Laramie.

The Congress, in its Christian duty, had set forth to "civilize" the Indian in the same way that the European nations, in this high colonial period, were "civilizing" the nonwhite natives of South America and Africa and Asia, using the same trusty mix of bibles and bullets. The government had long since perceived that the way west depended on the transcontinental railroad. In the southern Plains, the Union Pacific had forged its way westward on timber and coal seized or swindled from obliging chiefs in the Indian Territory; it was completed in 1869. As the Commissioner of Indian Affairs remarked in 1872, "The progress of two years more, if not of another summer, on the Northern Pacific Railroad will of itself completely solve the great Sioux problem, and leave the ninety thousand Indians ranging between the two transcontinental lines as incapable of resisting the Government as are the Indians of

New York or Massachusetts." (In the same year, Commissioner Francis Walker also commented, "There is no question of national dignity . . . involved in the treatment of savages by a civilized power." He went on to say that the purpose of the reservation system was to reduce "the wild beasts to the condition of supplicants for charity."[8]) Already, white mountain men and prospectors were passing through the Black Hills without the Indians' consent, and the rumor of plentiful "gold in them thar hills," reported by a military party in 1858, was confirmed in August 1874 by a huge reconnaissance expedition led by a jubilant George Custer. The politically ambitious Colonel Custer, who had been condemned by his superior officer on a railroad survey expedition along the Yellowstone in 1873 as "a coldblooded, untruthful and unprincipled man . . . universally despised by all the officers of his regiment,"[9] was a champion of the view that the nature of the aborigine was far more "cruel and ferocious" than that of any "wild beast of the desert," and that in no way did the red man deserve to be treated like a human being; and he was already notorious among the Indians for his attack on a peaceful Cheyenne camp on the Washita River in the same year that the Fort Laramie Treaty had been signed.

The tracks into the Black Hills left by the supply wagons of Custer's expedition of one thousand pony soldiers were later used by the gangs of gold-crazed miners who shot their way into the Hills in defiance of the Indian war parties, burning the timber, muddying the streams, and killing off the game. The white man, as one Indian said, "was in the Black Hills just like maggots";[10] *wasicu,* or "the greedy one" (literally, "he-who-takes-the-fat"),[11] was the term the Lakota used to describe the miners, and it later became their term for whites in general. "The love of possessions is a disease with them," said Sitting Bull, who was never behindhand in his contempt.

President Grant sent word to Red Cloud that the Black Hills would be respected "so long as by law and trea, it is secured to the Indians," and although a large party of white men (the Gordon party) was removed in November 1875, the Secretary of War predicted trouble in the Black Hills "unless something is done to gain possession of that section for the white miners."

> Cheyenne was then wild with excitement concerning the Indian war, which all the old frontiersmen felt was approaching, and the settlement of the Black Hills, in which gold in unheard of sums

> was alleged to be hidden. No story was too wild, too absurd, to be swallowed with eagerness and published as a fact in the papers of the town. Along the streets were camped long trains of wagons loading for the Black Hills; every store advertised a supply of goods suited to the Black Hills' trade; the hotels were crowded with men on their way to the new El Dorado; and bell boys could talk nothing but Black Hills—Black Hills. So great was the demand for teams to haul goods to the Black Hills that it was difficult to obtain the necessary number to carry the rations and ammunition needed for [General] Crook's column.
>
> Much of our trouble with these tribes could have been averted had we shown what would appear to them as a spirit of justice and fair dealing in this negotiation. It is hard to make the average savage comprehend why it is that as soon as his reservation is found to amount to anything he must leave and give up to the white man. Why should not Indians be permitted to hold mining or any other kind of land? The policy of the American people has been to vagabondize the Indian, and throttle every ambition he may have for his own elevation.[12]

That year (1875), a commission was sent out from Washington to "treat with the Sioux Indians for the relinquishment of the Black Hills." Use of the name "Sioux" (eventually adopted by the Indians themselves) was by now symbolic of U.S. relations with the Dakota nation,[13] and clearly the white man had only the crudest concept of what Paha Sapa represented to the seven Lakota council fires of the Oglala, Brule, Minnecojou, Hunkpapa, Sans Arc, Two Kettle, and Blackfoot. Even Spotted Tail, the tamed Brule chief who was trying to accommodate the invaders, was appalled by the desecration implicit in the commissioners' suggestion that the sacred earth of Paha Sapa might be looted and stripped of its minerals, then returned to the Indians to do with what they pleased. Red Cloud and Crazy Horse of the Oglala refused to attend the proposed meeting, and so did Sitting Bull of the Hunkpapa, who had harassed the railroad survey expedition in the Yellowstone Valley two years before. "We want no white men here. The Black Hills belong to me. If the whites try to take them, I will fight," said Sitting Bull, sending word that he would sell no land to the white man, "not even a pinch of dust." Crazy Horse, who had had his great vision quest in the Black Hills, sent Little Big Man as a witness for the "wild" Oglala who refused to come: "One does not sell the land on which the people walk," said Crazy Horse, who, unlike the loquacious Sitting Bull, spoke briefly when he spoke at all. Perhaps impressed by Little Big Man, who rode up and down between white men and red, threatening death to the first chief who spoke in favor of selling Paha Sapa, Spotted Tail (who, with Red Cloud, had once been willing to sell at a fair price) decided not to sign the document.[14]

Since the Sioux were being so unreasonable, President Grant withdrew the soldiers who were supposed to keep the whites out of the Hills; by the winter of 1876, more than ten thousand whites were jostling for advantage in the raw mud streets of Custer City, the new frontier town in the southern Hills. It was now widely proposed that the Black Hills be purchased from the Indians whether they liked it or not; if they chose to refuse $5 million, that was their affair. Early in 1876, in open contravention of the Fort Laramie Treaty, in which the government had pledged its honor to keeping peace, troops were sent into the Great Sioux Reservation in pursuit of those "hostiles" most likely to resist the voice of reason, especially Sitting Bull's Hunkpapas and the "wild" Oglala under Crazy Horse, who was camped that winter not far from Custer's trail to discourage trespassers in Paha Sapa. By spring, Crazy Horse had joined forces with Sitting Bull, who said that year, "Tell them at Washington, if they have one man who speaks the truth, to send him to me, and I will listen to what he has to say." The one man who met this description was George Crook, the greatest Indian fighter in American history in the opinion of General Sherman, and also the only leader of the whites whom the Indians could trust to keep his word. But General Crook had been sent not to speak truth but to wage war. (Before leaving Apache country in March 1875, he was asked if it was not hard to go on another Indian campaign, to which he made the famous answer, "Yes, it is hard. But, sir, the hardest thing is to go and fight those whom you know are in the right.")

By late spring, the "hostiles" had been joined by numerous Cheyenne and Arapaho, and also bands of Minnecojou led by Hump and Lame Deer, together with a number of Blackfoot and Sans Arc; though Indians question it, white historians declare that this was the greatest gathering of Indian people ever assembled.

In the second week of June, a great sun dance was held at Medicine Rocks, in what is now Montana. Here Sitting Bull sacrificed, then stood all day staring at the sun before he fell; in his vision, he saw the blue-jacketed soldiers falling backward into the Indian encampments. On

June 16, inspired by this vision, Lakota and Cheyenne warriors led by Crazy Horse made a successful raid upon Crook's forces—the only defeat by Indians Crook ever suffered—and on June 25, 1876, on the windy ridge east of the Greasy Grass Creek, known to the Blue Coats as Little Big Horn, Crazy Horse and his men drove off an attack by Major Marcus Reno, then surrounded and exterminated another attacking column led by Colonel Custer, who had ensured this fate two years before by his transgressions on the sacred ground of Paha Sapa. More than two hundred pony soldiers, together with a number of Crow and Shoshone scouts, lost their lives on a hot early-summer morning because Custer had disobeyed his orders and ignored the good advice "Now, Custer, don't be greedy. Wait for us."[15]

Within ten years, the Oglala Lakota led by Red Cloud and Crazy Horse "had been responsible for two of the three greatest defeats ever inflicted on the United States Army by Indians,"[16] and this last great Indian triumph in American history won the victors a cold retribution that has not relented to this day. Although forcible and illegal seizure of the Black Hills, already under way, had invited the disaster at Little Big Horn, the U.S. government now declared that the Fort Laramie Treaty was no longer valid, due to the Indians' warlike behavior; two weeks after the defeat, *The New York Times* reported (July 7) that certain high officers in the War Department were advocating a "policy of extermination of the Indians" and "the speedier, the better." Within two months, it was formally decreed that the Sioux must relinquish all claim to the Black Hills; they were rounded up and confined to the vicinity of the Blue Coats' forts, where their ponies and rifles were confiscated by the soldiers. In August, yet another commission was sent out with documents designed to establish United States ownership of Paha Sapa in an orderly and legalistic manner; this time, even Spotted Tail protested. Accusing the government of lies and broken promises, he declared that hostilities had been caused by those "who came to take our land from us without price, and who, in our land, do a great many evil things. This war has come from robbery—from the stealing of our land." The Indians protested that these documents were meaningless, since most of the adult males whose signatures were required before the Black Hills could be legally relinquished were off with the war parties of Crazy Horse and Sitting Bull. To this argument, the commission responded that the "hostiles"—those, that is, who wished to see their treaty honored—were no longer covered by the treaty; anybody who wished to sign this "agreement" would do nicely for the purpose that the commissioners had in mind. That purpose included the cession of much reservation land, including the Black Hills, together with three rights-of-way across the much-reduced Great Sioux Reservation, all of which led straight to Paha Sapa; from now on, all hunting rights outside the reservation were ended, and all food and other goods on which the increasingly restricted people had been made dependent would be distributed far to the east of the Black Hills, on the Missouri River. It was further suggested that failure to sign the official documents would lead to delay in the delivery of supplies and therefore to starvation, since the new "agreement" was part of a law that authorized funds for Indian rations.

Thus, in September 1876, eight years after the Indians had secured the Black Hills "in perpetuity," and three months after their great victory at the Greasy Grass Creek, Red Cloud of the Oglala was forced to sign a document that abrogated the Treaty of Fort Laramie and awarded Paha Sapa to the white man. ("Which God is our pious brother praying to now?" asked Red Cloud after the invocation. "Is it the same God whom they twice deceived, when they made treaties with us which they afterward broke?"[17]) Spotted Tail signed, also; and the other chiefs of the southern bands shortly capitulated. The event was made "legal" in the Black Hills Act of February 28, 1877, when all of Paha Sapa, together with 22.8 million acres of surrounding territory, was appropriated by the U.S. government in exchange for subsistence rations for an indefinite period. The Oglala and Brule were sent to live on barren lands on the Missouri that the *wasicu,* building their railroads, had already stripped of trees as well as game, and although they were permitted to return the following year (Red Cloud settled on Pine Ridge, while Spotted Tail stopped farther east at Rosebud), the Lakota were forbidden to trespass on the 40 million acres of unceded land that supposedly was still a part of the Great Sioux Reservation.

Farther west, Sitting Bull's hunting grounds on the Tongue River had been invaded by soldiers under General Nelson Miles, who had tracked down and killed Chief Lame Deer that same year. In the knowledge that he and Crazy Horse had been abandoned by the reservation chiefs, Sitting Bull, with the Oglala war chief Gall and several hundred people, retreated northward and crossed into Canada in February 1877.

The Northern Cheyenne and their Arapaho allies were defeated in the same period, after an attack on Dull Knife's village near the head of

Crazy Woman Creek. The great Cheyenne leader surrendered in the spring of 1877 and was sent south to Indian Territory, but preferring death to this barren place so far from home, he led his remnant people in a desperate trek northward in September of the following year, pursued all the way by soldiers, oncoming winter, and starvation. Dull Knife himself was one of the few survivors of this doomed, heroic journey;[18] he eventually found shelter with Red Cloud's people on Pine Ridge, where he died in 1883.

With Sitting Bull in Canada, Crazy Horse became the last great figure of resistance. In late 1876, Spotted Tail was sent to plead with him, carrying the promise of General Crook that Crazy Horse would be permitted to hunt buffalo and wander on the Powder River hunting grounds as in the old days. Crazy Horse ignored Spotted Tail, who returned instead with a Minnecojou band under Chief Big Foot.

In January 1877, the wild Oglala survived an attack by Bearcoat Miles, who pursued Crazy Horse all the way to the Big Horn Mountains. Crazy Horse understood quite well that the victory at Greasy Grass Creek had hastened the day of ultimate annihilation, and in May 1877, to spare his followers another winter of misery and privation, he rode into the Red Cloud Agency of his own accord. But the great war leader never received the Powder River reservation offered by Crook; once Crazy Horse had led his warriors into captivity, the U.S. government forgot its offer.

> Crazy Horse was a man of his word and was furious at the duplicity of the white man. . . . Crazy Horse saw Red Cloud and Spotted Tail both betrayed by the white man as well as Sitting Bull. They had all signed treaties with the white man in solemn council and the words of the white man had been broken. . . .
>
> Crazy Horse foresaw the consequence of his surrender. It meant submission to a people whom he did not consider his equal; it meant the doom of his race.[19]

Crazy Horse could never be prevailed upon to accompany Red Cloud and Spotted Tail to Washington to hear the Great White Father. "My father is with me, and there is no Great Father between me and the Great Spirit." In September 1877, he was summoned to Fort Robinson (Nebraska), where he was fatally stabbed under disputed circumstances involving that Little Big Man who had once declared that he would kill the first Indian to speak of selling the Black Hills. In the months that followed, the Indians were lined up by the soldiers and marched eastward to the barren lands on the Missouri. That same year, George Hearst's Homestake gold mine was established at Lead, in the northern Hills; within two years, Homestake appeared on the New York Stock Exchange, and within ten, an investment of $10,000 was worth $6 million—a million dollars more, that is, than had been offered by the commissioners for all of the Black Hills. "An idle and thriftless race of savages cannot be permitted to stand guard at the treasure vaults of the nation which hold our gold and silver. . . . The prospector and miner may enter and by enriching himself enrich the nation and bless the world by the results of his toil."[20]

As General Sherman had noted, the most important factor in "making peace" with the Indians was the completion of the transcontinental railroads. The ambitions of miners, trappers, and traders, as well as of the cattlemen and settlers who would follow, all depended on the expanding railroad systems, as shipments of beaver pelts and buffalo hides gave way to timber and packed meat and minerals. And as among the eastern Indians, innocent or greedy "chiefs" appointed by the white man were soon selling or leasing ancestral lands that did not belong to them, in dishonest arrangements that were duly endorsed in the white man's courts. Despite their records as great war leaders, Red Cloud and Spotted Tail are now included among such chiefs by their own people.

Four years after the murder of Crazy Horse, Spotted Tail was shot down by his cousin Crow Dog, a brave warrior who had ridden with his friend Spotted Tail in the old days but who now believed—as did many of the Brule—that this fierce old war leader had been paid off by the enemy. Although Spotted Tail protested against government policies as much as he thought he could get away with, the government had set him up as "paramount chief" over his people and presented him with a three-story house. To make matters worse, this white man's chief wished tributes to his high position that traditional chiefs had never wanted, including possession of any woman who pleased his eye. One of his unwilling women was in the Crow Dog family. After his death, the agency officials belittled the whole episode as a quarrel over a woman, and the Brule band resolved the matter in the traditional way, but the white public, for whom the handsome Spotted Tail had become a hero, had taken an interest in justice for Indians and was clamoring for Crow Dog's execution; eventually he was sentenced to death by a

Dakota circuit court sitting in Deadwood, in the north Black Hills. In a tribute to Crow Dog's reputation (and the good sense of the court), he was granted permission to return home to prepare his death song, and also the white buckskin suit that he wished to die in. On the appointed day, as promised, Crow Dog, accompanied by his wife, drove himself in his own buckboard back to prison.[21] The episode excited a new interest in the case, and eventually the death sentence was overturned by the Supreme Court, which held that an Indian nation had full jurisdiction over its members. Congress was outraged by this decision, and also, perhaps, by its recognition of Indian sovereignty ("It is infamy upon our civilization, a disgrace to this nation, that there should be anywhere within its boundaries a body of people who can, with absolute impunity, commit the crime of murder"[22]), and the result was the Major Crimes Act of 1885, which authorized federal jurisdiction over any major offense on the reservations, whether the Indians considered it "major" or not.

The government had meanwhile set about the extermination of the sacred buffalo, which the Indian saw as the comrade of the sun and which was thought to have numbered between thirty and sixty million when the first horse Indians hunted the Plains. As early as 1859, the great Chief Lone Horn, father of Chief Big Foot, had made medicine to bring about the return of the vanishing buffalo, but the great shaggy animal on which the Plains peoples depended for food, shelter, clothing, and utensils had been much reduced by the rifles of the pioneers and later the buffalo hunters for the railroads, and after 1862 was never plentiful again. (A bill to protect the remnant bison had been passed by Congress, but President Grant, a military man, never got around to signing it.) In 1883, when the last herd of northern bison was wiped out by soldiers and mercenaries on the Cannonball River (with the assistance of the Lakotas' old woodland enemies, the Cree),[23] a century of utter dependence on the white man had begun.

"There is a time appointed to all things," Spotted Tail had said, not long before his death. "Think for a moment how many multitudes of the animal tribes we ourselves have destroyed; look upon the snow that appears today—tomorrow it is water! Listen to the dirge of the dry leaves, that were green and vigorous but a few moons before! We are a part of that life and it seems that our time has come."[24]

It was recognized that the loss of their life-way would weaken the warlike spirit of the Indians, as would conversion to the Christian

Church, and the Indian agents worked closely with their black-frocked brethren at the missions, whose interests were very much the same. As early as 1878, an Episcopal church had been set up at the Pine Ridge Agency, and in 1881, the "savage rite" known as the sun dance was forbidden on all of the Sioux reservations; suppression of other religious ceremonies soon followed. The missionaries decried the "cruel" and "sadistic" nature of the sun dance, perhaps not wishing to understand that participation was an honored and joyful act. "The Sun Dance is the greatest ceremony that the Oglalas do. It is a sacred ceremony in which all the people have a part. . . . If one has scars on his breast or back that show he has danced the Sun Dance, no Oglala will doubt his word."[25]

At the Indian agencies, the condition of the Lakota people declined rapidly. The proud horsemen who, less than twenty years before, had decreed their terms to the chastened white men at Fort Laramie were already sedentary, half-starved dependents of the U.S. government, despised by these *wasicu* for whom they had no respect. In *A Century of Dishonor* (1881), which deplored the mistreatment of the Indians, Helen Hunt Jackson also argued that the native peoples should be "civilized" by assimilation through land ownership and education into the nation's economic life, a well-meant idea that was seized upon by those who wished to assimilate the reservation lands as well. As General Sherman, never an Indian lover, had long since noted, a reservation was "a parcel of land inhabited by Indians and surrounded by thieves," and a few congressmen, at least, saw through the General Allotment Act, which was, one said, "in the interest of men who are clutching up this land, but not in the interest of the Indians at all." Another said, "The provisions for the apparent benefit of the Indian are but the pretext to get at his lands. . . . If this were done in the name of greed, it would be bad enough; but to do it in the name of humanity, and under the cloak of an ardent desire to promote the Indian's welfare by making him like ourselves, whether he will or not, is infinitely worse." These voices were lost in the general clamor of a nation hell-bent on westward progress. "They must either change their mode of life or they must die!" one senator cried. "They have got as far as they can go, because they own their land in common," sniffed another Indian well-wisher, Senator Henry L. Dawes of Massachusetts, in precocious disapproval of the Indians' "communism" (observing also that, among Indians, "There is no selfishness, which is at the bottom of civilization").[26] And it was precisely that communal attitude toward land that had to be destroyed before the buffalo plains could be domesticated and the huge railroad, oil, and cattle empires could rule the West. In 1887, after years of fierce debate, Congress passed the General Allotment Act (the Dawes Act), yet another in the long series of "reform" laws designed to assist the Indian into the American mainstream by breaking down his traditional means of existence (the act was "a mighty pulverizing engine to break up the tribal mass," cheered Teddy Roosevelt, who with the help of his friend J. Pierpont Morgan would later sponsor Edward Curtis's photographic portraits of "The Vanishing Redman"). Each male Indian in those tribes coerced by the Indian Bureau into accepting allotment would be given 160 acres, with any "surplus" land to be purchased inexpensively by the government and turned over to white settlers at its own discretion, according to the rules set out by the Homestead Act of 1862. This "surplus," as it turned out, comprised most of the remaining Indian land.

By destroying communal guardianship of land, the Dawes Act—first aimed at tribes in western Indian Territory but eventually affecting more than one hundred Indian groups—destroyed not only the unity of Indian nations but the people's tradition of generosity and total sharing for the common good. Since according to their sacred instructions the Indians could never "own" a Mother Earth of which they felt themselves to be a part, and since even those willing to go against the Indian life-way—*wouncage,* "our way of doing," as the Lakota say[27]—had no experience of the white economy, most of those who tried to adjust to the new system were sooner or later relieved of their land due to innocence, drink, inability to pay off mortgages and taxes, and, finally, the hard exigencies of starvation; for by this time the people had been reduced to irregular handouts of flour and lard, the ration of which depended largely on their willingness to cooperate with the agents sent out by the Indian Bureau and their accomplices in the reservation missions. In short, the Dawes Act legalized an arrangement in which, during the next half century, the native people all across the country would lose two thirds of their remaining lands by sale and swindle.[28]

Until World War I, the Lakota managed to resist allotment, but in 1889—the year of the great Oklahoma land rush inspired by the Dawes Act—General Crook was dispatched to the Lakota with the proposal that 9 million acres of their remaining land should also be turned over to white settlement. The aging Red Cloud refused to sign such an agreement, and so did Sitting Bull, who had returned from political asylum in Canada in 1881 (for a time he appeared in "Wild West" shows with the old railroad hunter Buffalo Bill Cody) and was living at Standing Rock on the Grand River, not far from the place where he was born:

> Friends and Relatives: Our minds are again disturbed by the Great Father's representatives, the Indian Agent, the squaw-men, the mixed-bloods, the interpreters, and the favorite-ration-chiefs. What is it they want of us at this time? They want us to give up another chunk of our tribal land. This is not the first time nor the last time. They will try to gain possession of the last piece of ground we possess. They are again telling us what they intend to do if we agree to their wishes. Have we ever set a price on our land and received such a value? No, we never did. What we got under the former treaties were promises of all sorts. They promised how we are going to live peaceably on the land we still own and how they are going to show us the new ways of living, even told us how we can go to heaven when we die. . . .
>
> When the white people invaded our Black Hills country our treaty agreements were still in force but the Great Father ignored it. . . . Therefore I do not wish to consider any proposition to cede any portion of our tribal holdings to the Great Father. . . . My friends and relatives, let us stand as one family as we did before the white people led us astray.[29]

Due mostly to the stubborn resistance of Sitting Bull and Red Cloud, the signatures required for the cession of Indian land were not obtained, and as in the seizure of the Black Hills, it was recommended to the government that it simply ignore the 1868 Treaty, which it did. A few months later, President Benjamin Harrison proclaimed an act that dismantled the Great Sioux Reservation established at Fort Laramie and created the seven reservations that exist today; the Oglala band, which had been the most hostile, was given the dry rolling hill country between the Dakota Badlands and the Sand Hills of Nebraska, now known as the Pine Ridge Reservation. All the rest of the Lakota land was turned over to the new states of North and South Dakota, which had been created just one month before.

In that same year, a "peace and prosperity" ritual known as the ghost dance—seen in a vision by a Paiute holy man, Wovoka—was transformed by the desperate Lakota into a purification ceremony that would restore the vanished buffalo and banish the *wasicu* from the Plains. "The world was shortly to come to an end . . . and the dead Indians would return with the buffalo. The white man would be destroyed, and the earth which he had corrupted would be renewed."[30] Besides Short Bull and Kicking Bear, who carried this version of Wovoka's vision to the Lakotas, the ghost dance was taken up by such chiefs as Crow Dog on Rosebud, Sitting Bull on Standing Rock, and Big Foot on Cheyenne River, as well as by Red Cloud's son and others on Pine Ridge; Red Cloud himself, now an old man, maintained an ambiguous silence. A number of Indians, believing that wearing the ghost-dance shirt made them impervious to bullets, had acquired arms; then, on December 15, 1890, Sitting Bull, like Crazy Horse before him, was killed while "resisting arrest" for fomenting trouble. Big Foot, now the leading traditional chief, set out with his people on a long winter trek across the Badlands, seeking safety with Red Cloud's people on Pine Ridge; two weeks later, on December 29, when Big Foot and two hundred or more Minnecojou men, women, and children, with a few fugitives from Sitting Bull's Hunkpapa band, were slaughtered by the Seventh Cavalry at Wounded Knee, Custer's avenged regiment received twenty Congressional Medals of Honor from a grateful government, despite a bungled maneuver in which at least twenty-five Blue Coats perished in the cross fire from their own guns. General Crook, who had died earlier that year, would surely have had contempt for the whole business.

Dr. Charles Eastman (formerly Ohiyesa), the young Santee Sioux physician on Pine Ridge, went out in search of survivors:

> Fully three miles from the scene of the massacre we found the body of a woman completely covered with a blanket of snow, and from this point on we found them scattered along as they had been relentlessly hunted down and slaughtered while fleeing for their lives. Some of our people discovered relatives or friends among the dead, and there was much wailing and mourning. When we reached the spot where the Indian camp had stood, among the fragments of burned tents and other belongings we saw the frozen bodies lying close together or piled one upon another. I counted eighty bodies of men who had been in council and who were almost as helpless as the women and babes when the deadly fire began, for nearly all

> their guns had been taken from them. A reckless and desperate young Indian fired the first shot when the search for weapons was well under way, and immediately the troops opened fire from all sides, killing not only unarmed men, women, and children, but their own comrades who stood opposite them, for the camp was entirely surrounded. . . .
>
> All this was a severe ordeal for one who had so lately put his faith in the Christian love and lofty ideals of the white man. . . .
>
> After some days of extreme tension, and weeks of anxiety, the "hostiles," so called, were at last induced to come in and submit to a general disarmament. . . . The troops were all recalled and took part in a grand review before General Miles, no doubt intended to impress the Indians with their superior force. . . .[31]

Custer's regiment was harshly chastised by old "Bearcoat" Miles, an Indian fighter since the Civil War, who had sent out that Seventh Cavalry detachment in response to the unwarranted panic of an Indian agent, caused by the ghost dances. As an old man in 1916, General Miles was still bitterly repudiating the massacre as "most reprehensible, most unjustifiable, and worthy of the severest condemnation."[32]

After Wounded Knee, the soldiers were replaced by bureaucrats, including "educators" whose official task was to break down the cultural independence of the people. On pain of imprisonment, the Lakota were forbidden the spiritual renewal of traditional ceremonies; even the ritual purification of the sweat lodge was forbidden. They were not permitted to wear Indian dress or to sew beadwork, their children were seized and taken away to government boarding schools at the Pine Ridge Agency, and use of their own language was discouraged. They were, however, invited to celebrate American Independence Day on the Fourth of July, which they used at first as a secret memorial to Wounded Knee and later adapted to their own giveaway festivals and powwows. "We felt mocked in our misery," old Red Cloud said. "We had no one to speak for us, we had no redress. Our rations were reduced again. You who eat three times a day and see your children well and happy around you cannot understand how starving Indians feel."[33] The despairing Red Cloud was converted in the 1890s by the Holy Rosary Catholic Mission, established on Pine Ridge in 1888 (and often called the Red Cloud Mission); later he asked to be buried in a priest's black robe.

When first penned up on the reservations, a great many Indians had weakened and died of tuberculosis, for which their dispirited medicine men had no cure. The health care offered by the government (after 1878) was entirely inadequate until 1890, when young Dr. Eastman arrived on Pine Ridge and sharply criticized the shameful lack of medicines, surgical instruments, competence, and even concern. By the time Eastman was forced out of the Indian Service by hostile bureaucrats, in 1892, the Pine Ridge Hospital was already under construction, and in 1896 a remarkable doctor named James R. Walker was transferred to Pine Ridge from Leech Lake on the White Earth (Ojibwa) Agency in Minnesota. Recognizing that the medicine men achieved real results in a variety of ailments,[34] Dr. Walker worked closely with them and won their trust; endorsed by many spiritual leaders, including Short Bull (who, with Kicking Bear, had brought home the word of Wovoka's ghost-dance vision from Pyramid Lake, Nevada) and Little Wound (son of Bull Bear, the head chief killed by Red Cloud), Walker himself was eventually accepted as a medicine man and was also entrusted with the shamans' secrets. His invaluable data on Lakota customs and religion, acquired in eighteen years of study with the last great medicine men of the nineteenth century, were to become the foundation of Lakota anthropology.

⊡

On Independence Day in 1903, Red Cloud offered his farewell address to the Lakota people:

> My sun is set. My day is done. Darkness is stealing over me. Before I lie down to rise no more, I will speak to my people.
>
> Hear me, my friends, for it is not the time for me to tell you a lie. The Great Spirit made us, the Indians, and gave us this land we live in. He gave us the buffalo, the antelope, and the deer for food and clothing. We moved on our hunting grounds from the Minnesota to the Platte and from the Mississippi to the great mountains. No one put bounds about us. We were free as the winds, and like the eagle, heard no man's commands. . . .
>
> I was born a Lakota and I shall die a Lakota. Before the white man came to our country, the Lakotas were a free people. They made their own laws and governed themselves as it seemed good to

them. . . . The priests and the ministers tell us that we lived wickedly when we lived before the white man came among us. Whose fault was this? We lived right as we were taught it was right. Shall we be punished for this? I am not sure that what these people tell me is true. As a child I was taught the Supernatural Powers (*Taku Wakan*) were powerful and could do strange things. . . . This was taught me by the wise men and the shamans. They taught me that I could gain their favor by being kind to my people and brave before my enemies; by telling the truth and living straight; by fighting for my people and their hunting grounds. . . .

When the Lakotas believed these things they lived happy and they died satisfied. What more than this can that which the white man offers us give?

Taku Shanskan is familiar with my spirit and when I die I will go with him. Then I will be with my forefathers. If this is not in the heaven of the white man, I shall be satisfied. *Wi* is my father. The *Wakan Tanka* of the white man has overcome him. But I shall remain true to him.

Shadows are long and dark before me. I shall soon lie down to rise no more. While my spirit is with my body the smoke of my breath shall be towards the Sun for he knows all things and knows that I am still true to him.[35]

Frank Fools Crow, who was born about the time of Wounded Knee, recalls being told how a woman survivor of the massacre, her arm shot off, reached his community at Porcupine (named for his grandfather, Porcupine Tail), but already he perceived things differently from the old warriors who could still remember the long days on the Great Plains. The decade that followed Wounded Knee, he says, was a time of great melancholy and deprivation, but after the turn of the century, when the old wounds had been scarred over, if not healed, his people had made a great effort to adjust to the white man's way, and probably more than half of them were baptized, including his uncle, the great medicine man Black Elk, who was dubbed "Nicholas" by the Red Cloud Mission. Black Elk told his nephew that "the Sioux religious way of life was pretty much the same as that of the Christian churches. . . . We could pick up some of the Christian ways and teachings, and just work them in with our own, so in the end both would be better." According to Fools Crow, Black Elk prayed constantly that all peoples would live as one and would cooperate with one another. "We have both loved the non-Indian races, and we do not turn our backs on them to please even those of our own people who do not agree. . . ."[36]

> Most people think that our early years on the reservation were our most difficult ones, but that is not actually the case. First there was a period of comparative happiness, and then later on the tragic times came. . . . It was especially hard to have the children sent away to school, and that was resisted, as was the order to cut our hair short. People were also unhappy about relatives being moved to reservations some distance away. And we were not pleased about the interference in our religious ceremonies.
>
> But at the same time, the new life proved before long to be challenging and interesting. . . . We now had new things to talk about and to do, and we made progress, quickly. By 1909, we were already well into the farming life. . . . In some ways, conditions were even better than the old buffalo-hunting days. In the fall of each year we helped one another to gather the harvest, and to store it in root cellars. Winters in our country had always been difficult to live through, and being able to store food like this was a proud and comforting achievement. . . . I feel it was important that the men had work to do that occupied their minds and bodies. In former days the women did most of the work around the camp, while the men hunted, made their weapons, defended their territory, and went on horse raids and war parties. When this life-way ended, the men were restless, frustrated, and felt unproductive. Now everyone had something valuable to do. . . . Besides our farm produce and the agency supplies, fish were plentiful and so was wild meat. The year-round hunting was great, even though we had to do it with bows and arrows. The women could obtain permission from the agent to purchase the knives they needed for housework and tanning. But there was a federal law forbidding Indian men to have firearms, knives, or liquor. Usually, four or five of us young fellows would get together, obtain authorization from the agent, and go hunting anywhere we wanted to on the reservation. Sometimes we would be away from home as long as two weeks. We brought home deer, antelope, prairie dogs, and all of the wild animals you can name that Indians ever ate. . . . After 1915, we began to go over to Custer, to the buffalo park there. They had a small buffalo herd,

> and since a lot of townspeople and National Parks Service personnel wanted to see Indians on horseback killing buffalo, they let us shoot a few of them with our bows and arrows.[37]

Before the days of immense farm operations and irrigation, when the White River "still had lots of water in it," the Oglala could earn most of their needs from their arable land. Also, Pine Ridge was benefited by an Indian agent who was both honest and intelligent (in the graft-ridden Indian Bureau, such agents were rare),[38] and who fought hard to keep liquor off the reservation; a person caught drinking was fined $500, and since there was little or no cash in the Indians' barter economy (the government supplied allotments or "rations" of tools, livestock, and clothing, as well as supplementary food), the usual result of drunkenness was a year and a day in jail. The Pine Ridge Reservation (which until this period had been able to resist allotment) had enough good cattle range to support a number of Oglala ranchers, who had built up large herds, but in 1916 a new Indian agent pressured them to sell off their cattle for the war effort and to lease their land to white ranchers in the region;[39] many of these Indians, lacking employment, began to gather at the agency village of Pine Ridge. Later, Indian soldiers home from the European war, who had learned the purposes of money and liquor without learning how to handle either one, encouraged the leasing of the land and the sale of livestock to obtain money for liquor and possessions. The situation worsened when allotment was forced through, and again after 1920, when the ration system and barter economy were replaced by new government programs of financial handouts. Within a few years,

> there were hardly any milk cows, chickens, ducks, or pigs left. The once beautiful gardens were nothing but dry brush, and the chicken coops were broken and falling down. Even the corrals had weeds in them, because the horses were gone. Gone also were many of the farm residents. Stores and schools were being built by the government, and the people were abandoning their farms and settling down around these. Towns were coming into being. But what pitiful towns they were. The government had taken advantage of us once more. At the same time, problems were coming from another direction. The white population around the borders of the reservation was growing and expanding. They decided we

owned more land than we needed, and they figured out a way to get it. It was easy. They encouraged the destitute Oglalas to sell or to lease their allotments to them and then to move into towns, which they did, for the money, naturally!

So people left their once fine log homes and storage cellars and settled down in tents and shacks. They exchanged their freedom for money and liquor, and as it turned out there would be no end of this curse. The flood had begun, and the traditional life-way dam was so weakened it could not hold it.[40]

Because thousands of Indians had done their best to act as citizens (ten thousand died as American soldiers in World War I), American citizenship was bestowed upon the first Americans in 1924, with a great patriotic fanfare heralding the event as a "righting of the wrongs" done to the Indian; in fact, this hollow citizenship broke ground for subsequent legislation that further undermined the Indians' hold on their last lands. Almost invariably, such legislation was endorsed by the Indian Bureau (later the Bureau of Indian Affairs) established in 1832 and transferred from the War Department to the Department of the Interior in 1849; from the beginning, this weak and ambivalent bureau was manipulated by special interests that coveted Indian grazing land, with its timber, water, and the minerals beneath. "The Indian today is not only unheard and unheeded, but robbed, pillaged, denied his heritage, and held in bondage. The greatest hoax ever perpetrated upon him was the supposed citizenship of 1924 [that] supposedly gave the Indian the same rights enjoyed by other men. The reservation still remains, the agent is still on the job . . . the Indian Bureau politicians still fatten on Indian money and the Indian is still being robbed. My people of South Dakota have been in dire straits . . . and have slowly become undermined in health by starvation while the public sleeps on the thought that 'the Government takes care of the Indian.' " So the Oglala chief Luther Standing Bear told his niece in 1932, by which time a pantheon of great pale faces was being hacked out of the sacred rock of Paha Sapa, to "endure"—in the sculptor's own reverent words—"until the wind and the rain alone shall wear them away." According to the dedication of Mount Rushmore by President Coolidge, in 1927, "The union of these four presidents carved on the face of the everlasting hills of South Dakota will contribute a distinctly national monument. It will be decidedly American in its conception, in its magnitude, in its meaning, and altogether worthy of our country." The Indians agree, in profound bitterness and disdain.

"The Lakotas are now a sad, silent, and unprogressive people suffering the fate of all oppressed," Standing Bear said. "Today you see but a shattered specimen, a caricature . . . of the man that once was. Did a kind, wise, helpful and benevolent conqueror bring this about? Can a real, true, genuinely superior social order work such havoc?"[41]

⊡

In 1928, the Meriam Report (commissioned by the government) attributed the wretched state of the Indian people to such mistaken legislation as the Allotment Act of 1887, and blamed the Bureau of Indian Affairs for its role in suppressing Indian culture. The report opened the way for a former social worker and energetic new Indian Commissioner named John Collier, who pressed fiercely in Congress for reforms; it was Collier[42] who put together the Indian Reorganization Act of 1934, which restored to Indians the right to live and worship in a traditional manner, as well as a certain measure of self-government. Under the IRA, the Allotment Act was abandoned and a small amount of land was reacquired; improvement loans were made to certain communities, and schools were established on certain reservations.

Collier and the IRA were well-intentioned, but as with all the earlier reform acts, the IRA cost the Indians more than they gained. The traditional forms of tribal government were replaced by "Indian chartered corporations," complete with constitutions, set up for their benefit under the auspices of the Bureau of Indian Affairs, and an intensely democratic people was subjected to the undemocratic decisions of so-called tribal councils that mostly reflected the wishes of the white man's church and state. According to widespread Indian custom, those who oppose a certain course of action register disapproval of it by staying away, and the councils promoted by the BIA in the Hopi nation and many other places were supported by hollow "majorities" of acculturated Indians, without any real approval from their people. These tribal-council governments could count on federal assistance so long as they deferred to the BIA; those who resisted tribal-council policies could count on nothing. While some tribal councils were (and are) strong and constructive in forwarding the best interests of their people, too many others become tame "puppet governments" for the BIA. Intended or not, the ultimate effect of the Indian Reorganization Act "was to use tribal culture and institutions as transitional devices for the complete assimilation of Indian life into the dominant white society."[43]

The conflict between "the BIA progressives" and the traditionals became increasingly bitter with the creation in 1946 of the Indian Claims Commission, which like the IRA was considered a well-meaning measure to most of those congressmen who voted for it. Ostensibly designed to "right a continuing wrong to our Indian citizens for which no possible justification can be asserted,"[44] the ICC in fact extinguished existing and potential Indian land claims by monetary settlement (the Claims Commission had no authority or wish to return land) before the tenuous or illegal nature of many of the white man's land titles could be challenged; the chief beneficiaries of this commission were not the Indians but the Washington law firms that represented them before the U.S. Court of Claims.

Predictably, the arch-conservative reformers claimed great moral credit for such legislation. A leading advocate, Senator Arthur Watkins (R, Utah), later chairman of the Claims Commission, was pleased to refer to it as "freedom legislation"; as South Dakota's Senator Karl Mundt remarked in regard to the Claims Commission Bill, "If any Indian tribe can prove that it has been unfairly and dishonorably dealt with by the United States, it is entitled to recover. This ought to be an example for all the world to follow in its treatment of minorities."[45]

The Indian Claims Commission's work was a necessary prelude to the so-called termination legislation, first passed in the 1930s but not enforced until the 1950s, a period which, by no coincidence, was noted for its organized attacks on civil liberties. (An early advocate of termination was Dillon Myer, Indian Affairs Commissioner under President Truman; Myer's apparent qualification for his job was his previous experience as head of the War Relocation Authority, which ran the bleak internment camps for American Japanese.) Like the Claims Commission, the termination policies were designed "to get the government out of the Indian business" and thereby end the vast, wasteful, and unproductive public expenditure on the nation's wards. With land claims extinguished and federal responsibility withdrawn, the Indians could be scattered in "relocation programs" into the cities, thereby conferring "independence" on a people trained to total dependency for almost a century. Another important benefit, less often mentioned, was the transfer of the reservations into the hands of sensible Americans who would "do something with the land," such as stripping off the last of its good timber and ripping out the minerals beneath.[46] As independent citizens and taxpayers, without good education or experience, most "terminated" Indians were reduced within a very few years to widespread illness and utter poverty, whether or not they were relocated in the cities. Meanwhile, bitterness increased between those people who were trying to live like whites and those still committed to "our way of living."

Among the Lakota, the grievous split between these factions (encouraged as part of the colonial strategy all over the world) dates back to the days when "loafer" Indians around the forts on the Bozeman Trail first got a taste of the white man's liquor and molasses; when Spotted Tail and Red Cloud were flattered and manipulated by trips to Washington; when Crazy Horse and Sitting Bull, "resisting arrest," were killed with the help of their own Indians, who served the whites as Indian Agency police. ("These people on the reservations are fat from the white man's food and foolish from his religion," the acerbic Dr. Eastman observed at the turn of the century, in the first of his several valuable books about his people. "They are only a shadow of what it really means to be an Indian."[47]) From the beginning, those Indians willing to obey the government agents and the missionaries fared much better than those who held to traditional Indian ways.

Full-blood traditionals sometimes refer to the mixed-bloods as "breeds" and to themselves as "skins" (short for "half-breeds" and "redskins," respectively), but since many mixed-bloods resist the BIA, while certain full-bloods have reason to endorse it, these terms refer less to actual blood ratios than to cultural attitudes. Older traditionals who speak Lakota call the mixed-bloods *iyeska,* or "those-who-speak-white," the name given to the scout-interpreters of the nineteenth century, most of whom had a "squaw man" for a father. Many traditionals (who were already expressing fear of domination by the mixed-bloods at a meeting with John Collier on Pine Ridge on March 2, 1934[48]) lived "out in the districts," in small outlying communities far from the bureaucratic trough, which was all but empty for those people who did not wish to send their children to government or mission schools, where the Lakota language and customs were forbidden. Despised and exploited, the traditionals—many of them full-bloods who spoke little English—were the people who suffered most from despair and apathy, poverty and unemployment, alcoholism, and the random angry violence that besets depressed Indian communities to a degree almost unimaginable to most Americans, who still suppose that "the government takes care of the Indian." In truth, the government takes care of the "progressive" Indian who does not resist the assimilating policies of the BIA. Among traditionals, it would be difficult to find a family without an alcoholic or a member in jail, a recent suicide or car-wreck victim, a woman sterilized by the Indian Health Service without her consent, or a child removed to a government boarding school or foster home against the family's will. And almost everywhere, these people have been subjected to vicious racism that would not be tolerated by the public or the courts toward any other minority in the country.

⊡

On Pine Ridge, most of the Tribal Council families were mixed-blood Christians, well indoctrinated with the "European" values acquired originally from the traders, half-breed scout-interpreters, and trading-post Indians of the nineteenth century. Some of these people did their best to live like whites, and others wandered between two very different societies, in neither of which did they feel welcome or at home. Together, these groups formed a dependent and therefore dependable voting bloc which the tribal governments used to their own advantage. "Today the popular interpretation is that tribal councils are corrupt and have been the major oppressors [of the so-called traditionals]. That is true only in the vaguest terms and only when the whole context of how tribal government evolved is properly understood. The mixed-bloods do dominate things, but that has been true for the better part of two centuries. There has been a continuing tradition—maybe almost from the Pilgrims—that mixed blood peoples have acted as *brokers* between the two societies, and in this capacity they have not always thought about the best interest of the tribe as a whole."[49]

On Pine Ridge, at least, Tribal Council administrations have been regularly accused of acting exclusively in their own best interests by carrying out the wishes of the BIA, which tends to ignore nepotism, incompetence, and corruption as long as its own policies are carried out. In recent years, Indian activists have dismissed the tribal-council system as "neocolonialism" in which a favored indigenous group implements the wishes of the colonial administration.

Although chartered to protect Indian people and Indian lands from exploitation, the BIA has accomplished just the opposite. On Pine Ridge and elsewhere, its land-tenure rules provided that each family's allocated land be divided in equal interests among the heirs, with the result that after a few generations the holdings consisted of numerous small parcels, insufficient to support a family; at this point, the BIA, as "trustee" of Indian land, would take over its administration and lease it out at nominal cost to the white ranchers who today control most of the good land on the reservation.[50] By 1942, nearly 1 million of the 2,722,000 acres assigned to Pine Ridge when the reservation was created in 1889 had passed into other hands, and by the 1970s, over 90 percent of reservation lands were owned or leased by white people or people with a low percentage of Indian blood, not because these people were more able but because the dispossessed traditionals had no money or means to work their land. Sadder still, these "red niggers," as the ranchers sometimes called them, had all but accepted the poor opinion in which they were held by the *wasicu* and the *iyeska.* Nevertheless, there was still a wistful faith that under the U.S. Constitution their educators had described to them, under the great legal system of justice for all, regardless of race, creed, or color, the wrongs perpetrated on the Lakota peoples would one day be made right, and the benefits of "our Treaty" restored to them.

After 1904, additional tracts of Lakota land had been "alienated" for white use, mostly through proclamations issued by President Theodore Roosevelt, whose bespectacled face, completed in 1939, was the last vast adornment of Mount Rushmore. In 1909, during the years of widespread farming, a Lakota delegation had petitioned South Dakota congressmen for compensation for the pony herd that had been confiscated from the Indians in the aftermath of the Custer battle; when the Pony Claim was refused, the people determined to pursue their land claims under the Treaty of 1868. In 1918, an attorney was hired, and in 1923—although aware that his clients sought the return of Paha Sapa—this man filed a money claim to the Black Hills. In those bitter years, such a claim could have been no more than a symbolic protest, yet it served the traditional people as a spark of hope: the "Black Hills case," as it was known, has dominated politics on the Lakota reservations ever since. Although the courts eventually got around to denying the claim in 1942, it reemerged in 1950, after the creation of the Indian Claims Commission. Most of the people, demoralized and desperate, were now interested in a monetary settlement, but a few traditionals, seeking a social and economic means of preserving traditional culture, held out for the return of the land itself.

In 1952, uranium was discovered near Edgemont in the southern Hills, and a new uranium "gold rush" now began; in the same period, vast deposits of surface coal accessible to strip-mining were located on reservation lands in Montana (Northern Cheyenne and Crow) and Wyoming (Shoshone) as well as in the Dakotas. Not surprisingly, the pressure for termination intensified, as what President Eisenhower called "the military-industrial complex" laid plans for a great energy empire in the western states. The Tribal Council claims for money compensation were ignored until the late 1960s, when the American Indian Movement, dramatizing the efforts of earlier Indian activist organizations, demanded the revalidation of Indian treaty claims around the country. Insisting upon land, not pay-off money, AIM drew particular attention to the Fort Laramie Treaty of 1868 and the lawless seizure of the Black Hills nine years later, and in this way—unwittingly, at first—it placed itself directly in the path of the huge energy consortiums that were already moving quietly into the Hills.

CHAPTER 2

THE UPSIDE-DOWN FLAG

The American Indian Movement, 1968–73

Tell the people it is no use to depend on me any more now.

Crazy Horse, dying (*to his father*)

What treaty that the whites have kept has the red man broken? Not one. What treaty that the white man ever made with us have they kept? Not one. When I was a boy the Sioux owned the world; the sun rose and set on their land; they sent ten thousand men to battle. Where are the warriors today? Who slew them? Where are our lands? Who owns them? What white man can say I ever stole his land or a penny of his money? Yet, they say I am a thief. What white woman, however lonely, was ever captive or insulted by me? Yet they say I am a bad Indian. What white man has ever seen me drunk? Who has ever come to me hungry and unfed? Who has ever seen me beat my wives or abuse my children? What law have I broken? Is it wrong for me to love my own? Is it wicked for me because my skin is red? Because I am Lakota, because I was born where my father died, because I would die for my people and my country?

Sitting Bull (*Lakota*)

In 1962, in Minnesota's Stillwater State Prison, two Ojibwa inmates, Clyde Bellecourt and Eddie Benton Banai, excited by the Indian protest that was being heard here and there around the country, concluded that government supervision was destroying the Indian people and that Indians had to deal with their own problems if they were to survive. While still in prison, they organized forty-six Indian prisoners, offering them, as Bellecourt says, "education about being Indians, instead of just rotting in prison making license plates. I guess we had the first real Indian Studies Program in the country."

In Minnesota, less than 1 percent of the state population is Indian, as opposed to 8 percent of the prison population; in South Dakota (where the rate of Indian recidivism is three times that of whites), Indians make up 6.5 percent of the general population and somewhere between a quarter and a third of all prison inmates. These ratios, typical of many western states and Canadian provinces, are less a reflection of antisocial tendencies than of the racism and punitive attitude toward Indians, whose "crimes" mostly relate to alcohol, who are jailed regularly because they cannot afford bail, and who are often convicted because—until recently—they rarely attempted to defend themselves in court.

Out on parole in 1964, after three jail terms for burglary and armed robbery, Bellecourt tried to organize the large "red ghetto" population in Minneapolis. What Bellecourt and his friends had in mind was a typical civil-rights program of the 1960s, increasing the opportunities for the city Indian to "enjoy his full rights as a citizen of these United States." Not until later was it realized that the Indians' citizenship meant nothing and that therefore "civil rights" was the wrong approach. "I tried to work within the System for four years, demanding a fair share of it for my people," says Bellecourt, a tall, thoughtful man in braids, who now wears spectacles and a mustache, "but all the money was controlled by the churches and bureaucracies, and they weren't interested in any programs that might have led toward real economic independence for the Indians." In July 1968, with Eddie Benton Banai, George Mitchell, and another ex-convict named Dennis Banks, Bellecourt founded the "Concerned Indian Americans"; this name, because of its acronym, was speedily changed to the American Indian Movement (AIM). "There has always been an American Indian Movement," Bellecourt has said. "For hundreds of years there have been people like Crazy Horse who stood up and fought for us."

Dennis Banks, who would soon become the best known of the AIM leaders, was an Anishinabi ("Chippewa") from Leech Lake, Minnesota, where he was born in 1935. Taken from his family at the age of five, he lost his language during fourteen years in BIA boarding schools in North and South Dakota and Minnesota. In 1953, he joined the Air Force and for three years was stationed in Japan; for the next ten years, he "bummed around between the reservation and Minneapolis and St. Paul—there were no jobs, no nothing." In 1966, he was sent to jail for five years on a charge of burglary; released, he was jailed again in 1967 for violation of parole. As soon as he got out of jail, he joined forces with Clyde Bellecourt, whom he had known slightly since the mid-1950s; "I organized a mass meeting to create a coalition of Indian people willing to fight for Indians," Banks says. A handsome man with an intense, brooding expression, Banks was quickly established as the most thoughtful and articulate leader in the new Movement.

Although much of its inspiration derived from Indian fishing-rights battles* already under way in Washington and Oregon, from Six Nations ("Iroquois") land protests in Ontario and New York, and from the "Red Power" activity that had evolved out of civil-rights activism on the West Coast, AIM came into existence as a direct result of the termination and relocation programs that dumped thousands of bewildered Indians into the cities. Even those who received job training found themselves faced with open racism and discrimination (from

* The Puyallup-Nisqually peoples of the south end of Puget Sound (followed by the Yakima, Nez Perce, and many smaller Indian nations in Washington, Oregon, and Idaho) challenged a half century of attempts by the state of Washington and its courts to deny them the fishing rights guaranteed by the Treaty of Medicine Creek (1853), in which their peaceable forebears had signed away most of the Pacific Northwest in exchange for permanent access and a fair share of the river-running salmon; like the buffalo of the Plains tribes, the salmon was a sacred creature that carried within it the very life and spirit of their culture. In the next century, as the white population took over the region, several salmon species (and the steelhead trout, as well) were drastically reduced by overfishing, hydroelectric dams that blocked the spawning runs, and logging and industrial pollution that poisoned the rivers; and inevitably it was the Indians (taking less than 1 percent of the annual harvest) who received the blame. The state courts refused to help them even when the police, under pressure from white fishermen, confiscated their nets and boats, until finally, in 1963, they acted on their treaty rights in a series of confrontations that began at a fishing place known as Franks Landing. The "fish-ins," joined by the National Indian Youth Council and other organizations, attracted the support of Indians from all over the country. The NIYC, founded by Vine Deloria, Jr., and other educated young Indians in 1960, was the first all-Indian protest group.

trade unions as well as from employers), "receiving the lowest wages for the dirtiest, most onerous work, and living in the worst conditions of urban blight and official neglect."[1] In its first year, AIM's main concerns were jobs, housing, and education; in addition, Bellecourt set up a street patrol to protect Indians from police abuse and violence, filming arrests and advising those taken into custody that they did not have to plead guilty, that they were entitled to an attorney and a jury trial ("We just showed the people that somebody cared"). Very quickly the patrol reduced the number of Indians arrested, but Bellecourt was beaten at least thirty times by outraged law-enforcement officers and still has a broken mouth to show for it.

The termination policies carried out by the Eisenhower administration had not been pursued under President Kennedy and were finally repudiated by President Johnson ("We must affirm the right of the First Americans to remain Indians while exercising their rights as Americans. We must affirm their rights to freedom and self-determination"[2]), and as a result, AIM's social-service and legal-rights programs attracted help from community-action groups funded by the federal Office of Economic Opportunity as well as from church groups and foundations; Bellecourt himself, endorsed by his parole officer, was given a full year's salary by the Northern States Power Company in order to develop his ideas. With the support of Minnesota's judiciary, AIM started a program to assist juvenile offenders as an alternative to reform school, and in 1970 it began its own "survival school," the first three students of which were children of people in the workhouse: the survival-school concept, which spread to other states, was an attempt to help young Indians adjust to the white society without losing what was most valuable in their own culture, and to offset the distorted information about the Indian role in American history that has been disseminated by school textbooks since the nineteenth century. "We wanted to teach our kids the truth about Indian people," Bellecourt says, "who our real leaders were and what they said and did, and also the contributions that they made, and that some old white man in lace shirt and powdered wig was not our 'Great White Father.' " In this period, at a meeting at Cass Lake (to support Chippewa fishing rights against incursions by the state of Minnesota), the fundamental principle of tribal

sovereignty was endorsed, arms were publicly brandished, and the American flag, flown upside-down, was formally adopted as AIM's sym-

bol. "Some ex-Navy guy suggested it," Banks recalls. "White people protested, of course, and a lot of our Indian people protested, too; a lot of the guys there had been in the military, and in some way they were still Americans, and it made 'em uneasy to see that flag flown upside-down. We had to explain that this was the international distress signal for people in trouble, and no one could deny that Indians were in bad trouble and needed help."

Inevitably, AIM was accused by disillusioned state and municipal authorities of teaching a "hate whitey" attitude in its school, and meanwhile the John Birch Society attacked the new Movement as a nest of ex-convicts, and Commie ex-convicts at that. But AIM had caught the imagination of young Indians in a way that the earlier activist groups had not, and soon AIM organizers and local partisans were turning up at demonstrations from coast to coast. One of these was the "Indians of All Tribes" occupation of the abandoned federal penitentiary on Alcatraz Island, in San Francisco Bay, led by a young Mohawk, Richard Oakes,[3] Grace Thorpe (daughter of the great Olympic athlete Jim Thorpe), and the Tuscarora medicine man Mad Bear Anderson;[4] this action by perhaps two hundred Indians, supported by white liberals in San Francisco, lasted from November 1969 until June 1971.

PROCLAMATION: TO THE GREAT WHITE FATHER AND ALL HIS PEOPLE

We, the native Americans, reclaim the land known as Alcatraz Island in the name of all American Indians by right of discovery. . . . We feel that this so-called Alcatraz Island is more than suitable for an Indian Reservation, as determined by the white man's own standard. By this we mean that this place resembles most Indian reservations in that:

1. It is isolated from modern facilities, and without adequate means of transportation.
2. It has no fresh running water.
3. It has inadequate sanitation facilities.
4. There are no oil or mineral rights.
5. There is no industry, and so unemployment is very great.
6. There are no health care facilities.
7. The soil is rocky and unproductive; and the land does not support game.

8. There are no educational facilities.
9. The population has always exceeded the land base.
10. The population has always been held as prisoners and kept dependent upon others.

> Further, it would be fitting and symbolic that ships from all over the world, entering the Golden Gate, would first see Indian land, and thus be reminded of the true history of this nation. This tiny island would be a symbol of the great lands once ruled by free and noble Indians.[5]

The occupation "took place because we wanted to draw attention to the fact we had no education and we had no housing and so on," says John Trudell, a young Santee Sioux (and Alcatraz leader) who joined AIM in the spring of 1970 and became a national spokesman soon thereafter. "Alcatraz was occupied for an educational and cultural center, but we never got it."

Another AIM recruit that year was Russell Means, a young Oglala born at Porcupine, on the Pine Ridge Reservation, but raised mostly in Oakland, California, where he was trained as an accountant. In the late 1960s, he found work in the tribal offices on the Rosebud Reservation, where the white owner of the Maverick Motel in Mission remembers the 6′1″ 185-pound Means as a "good-looking, hardworking boy" who went wrong due to overexposure to liberal thought. Means bitterly resented the loss of his culture and language, "stolen from me by the white man." As head of Cleveland's Indian Center in 1970, he went to Minneapolis for an Indian conference; upon his return, he established Cleveland AIM.

In the fall of 1970 and again in the spring of 1971, AIM established a camp at Mount Rushmore, in symbolic enactment of Lakota claims to the Black Hills. Means participated in the demonstrations at Mount Rushmore and also in the National Day of Mourning at Plymouth, Massachusetts, on Thanksgiving Day. A former rodeo rider and Indian dancer, he wore traditional long braids and bone neck choker, red wind band, black shirt, and embroidered vest, together with a beaded belt and turquoise jewelry, jeans, and boots; in this outfit, he looked like a modern version of the tall and striking Lakota leaders of the nineteenth century, which made him all the more effective as a symbol. Like Dennis Banks, he was eloquent and charismatic, with an instinct for inflammatory statements, and "Banks and Means" were soon synonymous with the AIM cause all around the country. Banks, who was older, was more thoughtful and reserved; in the Plains states it was Russell Means who came to stand for almost everything that local white people and the authorities feared and resented about AIM. "Russ Means's name was everywhere," says a young Iowa white woman raised in a family ashamed of its Indian blood. "Back in Sioux City, used to be that drunken Indians were thrown in jail a couple of days and nobody said a thing; pretty soon they were all hollering for AIM. Before Russ Means showed up, we never *saw* any Indians, hardly, never knew they existed; they all lived over in some bad part of town. We just . . . well, we just *overlooked* 'em, I guess."

John Trudell, a small catlike man with a big voice that was merry and harsh at the same time, was also an incendiary talker, and inevitably these AIM spokesmen were regarded with suspicion not only by BIA Indians and Christian converts but by other Indian activist organizations and by many traditionals as well. The loud aggressive "AIMers" were dismissed as "city Indians" with white-man manners who had lost touch with Indian way; the brandished weapons and warrior talk, the red wind bands and long hair and feathers, were more exciting to the white people than they were to the quiet people on the reservations. The Movement found no significant acceptance in the last strongholds of traditional culture, such as Hopi (which had asserted its rights as a sovereign nation in a letter to President Truman in 1949, and had sent a delegation to the United Nations ten years later). Similarly, the Six Nations ("Iroquois") had reaffirmed the principle of sovereignty as early as 1924, when they formally declined American citizenship; they were experts on treaty law and had never abandoned their concept of themselves as an equal nation. In the Pacific Northwest, where AIM had endorsed the fishing-rights struggle, the Puyallup-Nisqually had been fighting state transgressions of their treaty rights for fifty years before AIM was born, and their recent confrontations with the authorities, supported by the National Indian Youth Council and by civil-rights celebrities such as Marlon Brando, Jane Fonda, and Dick Gregory, had become the first well-publicized treaty defense of modern times; here as elsewhere, many of the local leaders remained suspicious of AIM's "radical" element with its seeming tendency toward violence. Nevertheless, AIM warriors were approached for help by many Indians and Indian organizations in the region, and the Movement was eventually endorsed by spiritual leaders of many Indian nations who saw these young militants as the last desperate hope of their people.

> . . . a different force began to assert itself in Indian affairs as the discussions of treaties grew. Each reservation had a number of traditional Indians, largely full-bloods, who had preserved the tribal customs and had generally boycotted the tribal governments. . . . These people represented the Indian traditions in the best sense, were generally leaders in the tribal religious ceremonies, and were eager to see something done about the treaties. . . .
>
> The overtures made by the traditional Indians came at an opportune time for many of the new Indian leaders. Many had been taken from the reservations when they were children and had never lived in an Indian community. They had grown up in the slums of the cities of the West Coast and Midwest and were toughened in the ruthlessness in which urban America schools her poor and disadvantaged. As more and more urban Indians joined the three major protest organizations—the American Indian Movement, the United Native Americans, and the Indians of All Tribes—they came into contact with young people who had grown up on the reservations and spoke the tribal language . . . and many of the urban Indians began to show up on the reservations, seeking the tribal heritage which they had been denied. They became the most militant of the advocates of cultural renewal. . . . By mid-1972 the middle ground of progressive ideology in Indian affairs was fast eroding, and desperate confrontation was in the air.[6]

Among the first religious leaders to endorse AIM was a young Lakota medicine man named Leonard Crow Dog (the great-grandson of that Crow Dog who killed Spotted Tail on the Rosebud Reservation). Crow Dog was a leader in the Native American Church, which used peyote in its ceremonies and had a growing following among Indians throughout the West, including Christians disillusioned by the white man's churches.

"We started here in the Twin Cities," Bellecourt says, "but from the start, our Movement was based on the guarantees to Indians in all the treaties; we didn't want to get caught up in the civil-rights struggle because that was between blacks and whites; it was within the System, and the System had nothing to do with Indians. And we always felt we had to have a spiritual foundation, a spiritual direction. In 1970, we heard about Crow Dog and went out to see him; he had had a vision, and he knew that we were coming, and he became our spiritual adviser. Today we have regular ceremonies, wherever we go. The drum had been silent for so many years; now, every day in our survival schools, the children hear it."

Already, the AIM drum had been heard by many Indians around the country who were struggling to find some meaningful existence. Among them was Leonard Peltier, a young Ojibwa-Sioux from Turtle Mountain, North Dakota, whose wandering life, from the bleak reservations and BIA boarding schools to the interstate highways and slum outskirts of the cities, was typical of many if not most of the dispossessed young Indians of his generation.

⊡

Peltier was born on September 12, 1944, in Grand Forks, North Dakota, "during harvest season, when my whole family—grandparents, aunts, uncles, and children—would migrate from Turtle Mountain to the Red River Valley to work in the potato fields. In those days, potatoes were picked by hand, and Indians would be hired to pick spuds at three to four cents a bushel, while Mexican Indians worked the sugar beets. When I was old enough to go into the fields, I would work ahead of the pickers, shaking the potatoes loose, which made it faster."

Peltier's maternal grandmother was "full-blood Sioux, my father was three-quarters Ojibwa, one-quarter French. My dad and my uncle Ernest Peltier were in the Army; Ernest got killed in Germany, and my dad was machine-gunned in the legs. My folks separated when I was four, and me and my younger sister Betty Ann lived with my grandparents, Alex and Mary Peltier; Grandma was originally from Canada. In those days a lot of Indian grandparents were still raising their grandchildren. It's an old Indian tradition, still being practiced in some Indian nations. Our land on Turtle Mountain was about four miles northeast of Belcourt. With the help of my uncles, Grandpa built a small ranch with a few head of cattle, horses, pigs, and chickens, on forty acres of bush and hilly land. I remember running through them woods at night when I was late, because I was real frightened of them rugarus! The old people said we would see one if we were bad. My first real memory of this home was when us younger kids used to watch and wait for Grandpa returning from town with our monthly issue of government commodities. About a mile from our house there was a large hill and on the other side was the main road where they would get off to start walking home. Very few people on the res owned automobiles in those times; I can remember buckboards on my mother's Sioux reservation at Fort Totten. Anyway, as soon as we spotted them, we would take off and go meet them and help carry the groceries home, usually in burlap sacks.

"Sometime around 1950, Grandpa decided to move the family to Montana to look for work in either the logging camps or the copper mines. I remember Gramps sold everything we owned—land, livestock, and all. One day he drove up into the yard with a large red-and-black Chevy truck, I think it was a 1940, '41, and someone said the previous owners was some Mexican migrant workers because of the way it was hand painted, which was their style of decorating their vehicles. On our way to Montana our right front wheel come off and we were stranded on the road most all that day. Traveling together was two, three of my uncles and their wives and children, and I remember us older kids sitting alongside of the road in the ditch telling ghost stories and about all the wild animals that were waiting for darkness to come down from the hills and get us.

"We arrived at some logging camp; there was a lot of snow, and we were living in a log cabin. One day we ran over a moose, and my uncle and grandfather attempted to load it in the back of the truck, but the moose was so large and heavy, we rushed home to get the rest of the men to help. My main memory in this camp was receiving my first Christmas present. My mother sent me a toy cap gun (gold-plated) and white holster with multicolored spots. My sister Betty Ann received a doll. (Our other sister, Vivian, was not with us because she was being raised by our mother.)

"Because more money could be made from working in the copper mines than in a logging camp, we moved to Butte, Montana. There was a lot of Indian families living there. One day three white kids about my age started yelling, like, Hey, you dirty Indian, go home! and started throwing rocks at me. I was wondering what they were talking about and why, and attempting to pay no attention and avoid being hit, but then a larger and older kid came along, and the others told him, There's a dirty Indian! This older kid was pretty accurate in his rock throwing—it was impossible to avoid being hit—but I did not start throwing rocks until I was hit hard and almost crying. I remember picking up a rock about the size of a marble, and I hit him on the temple. I seen blood, and with his screaming, I panicked and ran straight to our house. It must have been about one, two hours later this kid and his mother came over. She parked in the yard and was hollering for my parents to come outside. In those days, anyone who owned or drove a new automobile was considered someone of authority. When Grandma came out to see what all the commotion was about, this woman started screaming that I tried to kill her son with a rock and she was going to have me put in a reformatory. Since Grandma couldn't speak but a few words of English, she was unable to answer, which made the woman very angry. She started screaming again, calling Grandma 'you stupid Indian bitch'! My aunt heard this and went outside and told this woman if she continued cussing her mother she was going to beat the shit out of her. The woman then backed up into her car, but before she did, she said she was going to have us all put into jail.

"When Grandma asked me what was *that* all about, I refused to say anything, mainly because I did not understand what the hell was going on, I was still trying to figure out what 'a dirty Indian' was. Naturally, because of my silence, I was given a spanking. I was very seldom disciplined with a spanking of any kind, but Grandpa did have two lengths of horse bridle that were pointed to when the children were bad. When the men returned from work, there was a big discussion, there was a lot of hysteria because I would have to go to the reformatory. Grandpa took me aside and asked me what happened. I told him. He rubbed me on the head and said, All those white people are like that. So Grandpa made a decision to pack up everything and we would go home to North Dakota. Most of the family left that evening. The men stayed until the next day to pick up their paychecks and caught up to us on the road the following day.

"After we returned to Belcourt, Grandpa bought the thirty acres which is still our land, hilly and wooded with a lot of oak and poplar, supposed to be on the highest hill on the reservation. I became very close to my grandpa. He used to take me hunting with him and sit around and tell me stories about the old days, about the Indians, mainly about what life was all about in his youth."

Leonard spoke Ojibwa as a child, since his paternal grandmother spoke no English at all; it was she who introduced him to traditional medicine. "When I was six or seven, I guess, my grandmother was suffering from a swollen jaw, so she took gifts to the *mijin,* and we had a ceremony with drums and praying, and next morning her jaw was still wrapped up, but you could see how the swelling had gone down.

"One winter I remember being allowed to go to town—Rolla, which is seven miles from Belcourt—and just before we went into the store, Grandma said, Now don't touch anything or you can't come to town again. So I thought, Okay, I'll put my hands in my pockets, which I did. I went through the whole process of being fitted for shoes, and when Grandma was paying for them, and I was staring and checking out everything, big-eyed, the man said, What do you have in your pockets? Man, I panicked. Remember, I was warned if there was any trouble, I would never be allowed to come to town with them, it would be years before I would ever get to see any of the things in these stores. I froze. When Grandma understood what the man said about wanting to search me, she told me to empty my pockets. I would not move, so Grandma cuffed me once or twice. I emptied my pockets. Of course there wasn't anything in them but personal kid junk—a ball of string I collected to use for the bows I used to make, and stuff like that. I never asked to go to town again, because my experiences with these white people were not so great.

"We used to go to the clothes sales the Catholic sisters had every week at the Belcourt Catholic Mission. Indians called it Bundles Day because they sold mostly rags for twenty-five cents a bundle. The rags were popular with the women, who made quilts. Many of us kids went to school at the mission, and we all hated them sisters—damn, but they were mean! I'm seven or eight by now and beginning to understand the meaning of hate and racism. It seemed as if all white people hated us, and I was beginning to hate just as much.

"In the winter of '52, my grandfather got sick with pneumonia and went on to surely a better life than we had been leading. Although these were happy times for me and we seemed to feed regularly, life was rather hard. It seemed as if Grandpa was always working hauling wood to sell around the res; if he wasn't cutting wood, he was out hunting, and he never seemed to come back without at least a rabbit. After Grandpa died, it seemed to get worse to try to feed ourselves. I remember Grandma telling us to go hunt for some ground squirrels or anything eatable for meat. We would first locate a squirrel stronghold, then load our kids' wagons—all homemade, by the way—with all the water cans we could find, pull them downhill to a big lake, pull them back up, and flood the squirrels and stone them as they came out. We had meat on the table if we were successful; if not, and we were only able to get one or two, it was mainly used to flavor the soup.

"Many of us kids knew how to trap muskrats and when the berries were just ripe enough—things like that. Every day after I helped with the chores, hauling wood and water, we would all get together and plan a hike to some lake and swim; what we thought was a long hike was really only a mile or two from our houses, but we would sharpen our pocketknives, make certain we had a pocketful of the correct-size rocks for our slingshots, and off we would go. We always seemed lucky enough to bag us some kind of bird, which we would roast over a little fire while we were swimming, and we always stopped in a berry bush, or whatever was in season. To us kids the summer months were the greatest because of what Mother Nature provided for us to eat. The winter season was hardest. Rabbits were about the only animals that did not seem hunted out, but they were harder to hit with slingshots; you really needed a .22 or shotgun to have rabbit stew.

"In 1953, when my grandfather had been buried about a year, my grandmother was attempting to get some kind of assistance for raising my sister, my cousin Pauline, and me. The BIA suggested that we would be better off in a welfare home or foster home. We were put in a foster home for one day, and my grandmother came after us that night, and we were taken back home. That fall a government car drove up while I was outside playing. My grandmother started crying and went into the house. She called us in and told us this man was here to take us to Wahpeton Indian School. We did not own any suitcases, so she put our belongings in a bundle and off we went to Wahpeton, North Dakota.

"At the school we boys were lined up military-fashion and marched to the dorm. We were told to stand in line until we were processed. When our names were called, we were taken into the barbershop and our heads were cut military-style. Next we were stripped and DDT was poured on us (powdered) and then we marched in a line to wait for our turn to shower. If there was any dirt or dead skin left when we were finished, we were turned around and given a few hard whacks with a school ruler on the seat and told to go rewash ourselves. The sound of the ruler hitting the boys and their screams is something that still affects me whenever I see someone striking a child.

"In my later years there, I was considered a elder boy, and I was assigned a little boy to wash. His name was White Cloud. He was a very small little guy who had very tender skin, and if I rubbed too hard, he would start crying. I used to scrub him very gently until one time, when we were going to the checkpoint, dead skin, *not dirt,* was taken off him. I was given a few hard whacks on the ass and told to wash him right. I was very angry and took this little guy in the shower and used the scrub brush I was told to use on him, and I admit I scrubbed very hard on his inner arms and small amounts of blood came out, because the brush we were given was the same kind used to scrub floors, only smaller, with very stiff bristles.

"It's really difficult for someone who comes from a low level of poverty to describe a situation like this. I mean, the disciplinary measures used was very harsh, but we had a clean bed and a regular meal every day. My sister, cousin, and I became very close to one another; all we had in the world was ourselves. I used to lay in bed at night thinking, What the hell happened? It seemed as soon as Grandpa died our world came to an end.

"I heard this new BIA Superintendent was letting everyone go home whose parents came after them. I shot a quick letter off to my mother and said, Come after us right away. I do know as soon as our mother could afford it she came right after us. Our mother was trying to make another life for herself after she and my father separated. Our dad was doing the same thing. We knew they loved us—they told us so—but I guess we just couldn't understand why they couldn't take care of us. Hell, they had a hard time feeding themselves!"

The following year, while living with his mother in Grand Forks, Leonard had his first experience with the law. "That day my ma had sent me out to check the fuel tank—she was worried we might run out during the storm that was coming, and it was still a couple of weeks before our welfare check arrived. A friend of mine's house was also out of fuel, and it was colder than ol' holy shit outside, so we decided to go out and rip some off." Waiting until midnight, Leonard and his friend climbed into an Army Reserve depot and siphoned diesel fuel from trucks, then lugged their cans almost a mile through snowdrifts to their car. Because of the bitter cold and their fatigue, "we got a little bold and parked our car right on the road by the armory for the last load; we jumped the fence and proceeded to fill my cans, and when we got back to the car, the cops were waiting for us, and we were trucked off to jail. I think I spent two weeks in there. When my mother was finally allowed to take me home, she asked me in front of the juvenile officer why I had done it, but I could see the look on her face, and she knew why. Shortly after that, my dad came after me, and I went back to the Turtle Mountain Reservation."

Leonard recalls how as a teenager on Turtle Mountain he used to run from house to house to warn the people to hide their food from the social workers who were making rounds, in order to be eligible for more, and how "the people would all look bewildered, saying, Food? But we ain't got any. The younger children would be begging for scraps of bread—baking-powder bread, because yeast bread was a treat for many of us. What hurt most was to see the look on the mothers' and fathers' faces when there wasn't even bread to give the kids."

In this period, he attended his first Indian meeting. "At first my only reason for going to these meetings was to get some food, because most of us had nothing to eat, and there was hunger for everybody every day. After these meetings we would all sit and eat together what little groceries the people had been able to collect. One day I got bored just fooling around outside with other teenagers, and I went in and seen and heard this old Ojibwa woman—she was my relative, Celia Decoteau—raise up to speak with tears in her eyes, pleading for someone to help because her children were at home slowly starving to death. She asked if there were no more warriors among our men. She said if there was, why did they not stand up and fight for their starving children? That day was very educational for me, and I vowed I would help my people for the rest of my life. I began to learn why my people were not employed and why we never had any food to serve at mealtimes."

In 1958, Leonard attended his first sun dance on Turtle Mountain. "It was against the law, you know—and it's *still* against the law in some respects; I mean, you're not allowed to pierce real deep in the old traditional way—so it was held secretly, at night, about five miles from where we lived. There was a lot of talk in my family about who was piercing and all, and some of us kids decided to sneak down and have a look. It was held in a tipi, and we just looked through the flaps. I expected a lot of blood and a lot of screaming because of the pain, and I was amazed when there wasn't any—just a little blood, you know, and nobody hollering at all. That's when I knew there was real spiritual power there, and that one day I would be a sun dancer myself. But anyway, the Indian cops had heard about it; they wouldn't dare go onto private property to bust it up, but when us kids came out of there, maybe three or four in the morning, they arrested us as drunks, and we weren't even drinking. I didn't really understand the politics of it, but the next thing we knew, we were in jail."

Although Leo Peltier remained at Turtle Mountain, Leonard's mother, Alvina Robideau, left for the West Coast about 1959, when the government's termination program gave many reservation people the choice, as Leonard says, between urban slums and starving to death on the reservations. On one occasion, he recalls, the BIA Superintendent announced a policy of no food for those who were resisting termination, and one day the starving people refused to let him leave his office until something was done. "They held him hostage," Peltier says, "and he's hollering, Hey, I gotta go home, that was my wife who just called, and she says my lunch is getting cold! Well, them people nearly lynched him. His lunch is getting cold, and *our* kids been hungry for *weeks!*" Since then, Peltier has had no use for the BIA; nor has he forgotten how his cousin Patricia Cornelius lost her baby after being beaten by the BIA police.

The BIA was now proposing total termination of the "Turtle Mountain Chippewa"; it reconsidered when the state of North Dakota threatened to refuse all help to its own Indians. Nevertheless, relocation was strongly encouraged. Most of the affected families moved into the "red ghettos" of cities such as Minneapolis, where a few years later the American Indian Movement would begin, but Alvina Robideau joined her brothers' families in the stream of migrant agricultural harvest workers traveling up and down the West Coast between Seattle and Portland, where she lives today. Of her son, who eventually followed her to the West Coast, his mother says, "As far as I've seen, Leonard has always been fighting for justice, for the rights of the Indian people, so they will be treated like human beings. He has never started fights; he is always joking and laughing and a good worker, and helping people in a good way."

When he was fourteen, Leonard took off for the West Coast, where his mother's Robideau brothers were struggling to survive. "I was born just one week after Leonard," says his cousin Steve Robideau, "at the Red Lake center for unwed mothers in Minnesota. My grandmother raised me in Grand Forks, and I was sent to the government boarding school at Turtle Mountain, but I didn't really know Leonard well until he showed up in Oakland with Bob's family. It was Bob's father, Bill, who taught all of us about machine work and carpentry, and later me and Leonard worked as welders in shipyards up in Portland. Leonard always had girls, and money in his pocket, because he's a real good worker, and people liked him. He was just Leonard. He's always been just who he is, and he's always been good-hearted, he just liked to laugh and tease. Leonard really wanted to be in the Marines, go off to war in Vietnam, but they gave him a medical discharge because of a shallow bite. He was disappointed but he could still laugh about it. I wasn't in the Marines to bite people, he said, I was in there to shoot people!"

("I was seventeen then," says Peltier with a grin, "and still raising a lot of hell. A couple of years before, I got my jaw busted in a fight; I was supposed to wear this brace for it, but I didn't. So one night I'm partying, and damned if I don't get in another fight and bust it again! But this time the muscle didn't heal properly, and my jaw came out kind of stiff." Saying this, he tries his jaw out in a comic way. "It's true, I guess. I ain't got much of a bite.")

In 1965, at the age of twenty, Peltier was part owner of an auto body shop in Seattle; the second floor of the building served as a kind of halfway house for Indian alcoholics and ex-convicts who were trying to find work in the community. In those years Leonard won a reputation for kindness and dedication to his people: in the words of Ramona Bennett, a Puyallup elder and a leader in the fishing-rights fight, Leonard was "never a cruel person. . . . I never saw him mad at anyone."

"Along about the time he was getting his auto shop started," Steve Robideau says, "me and my brother Jim got sent up for armed robbery of a supermarket. In Walla Walla they took us for Chicanos because our family—Leonard, too—looks kind of Mexican when we wear our hair short. We said, No, we are Indians! But we were like a lot of Indians back then: we had been relocated to the cities and we didn't really know what Indians we were—it was pretty embarrassing! So when I got out, I went to Leonard's shop, and it was Leonard who straightened me out about who we were."

Peltier's first experience with AIM-style confrontations was the 1970 takeover of Fort Lawton,[7] outside Seattle, which, like Alcatraz, was on "surplus" federal land to which the Indians had first right under the law. "The Indians on Alcatraz sent some delegations to help us keep from making the mistakes they made, and that's when I met Richard Oakes. He was a gentle, soft-spoken person, very big, very muscular, and had quite a reputation as being pretty good with his dukes, but he was very pleasant to speak to. When they murdered him, that really inspired us to keep on going in the struggle. And that's when I met Mad Bear, too—I love that guy, he's funny and he's effective. Later I traveled with him for a while down around New Mexico, Arizona, working mostly with Navajo civil-rights violations."

The Chicano community in Seattle was also supporting the fishing-rights fight, and at Fort Lawton, Peltier met an activist from Texas named Roque Duenas, who remembers well how the fourteen people taken into custody at Fort Lawton were beaten by the police at the time of arrest and beaten again when taken to their cells, and how Peltier, when finally released, refused to leave the Army stockade until all the others had been freed. "Leonard was already a leader," recalls Duenas, a tall, slim, soft-voiced man with mustache and glasses. "And I remember a benefit he set up there in his auto shop. But he was pretty quiet around the action at Fort Lawton, just doing what he could. It was the first time he had been involved in that kind of confrontation—it was the first time for most of us, I guess—and we were still kind of in awe of what we had gotten ourselves into. When they marched us out of the stockade, they done it two at a time, and one guy who had given the MPs hell never showed up. Well, some of the brothers seen what was coming down, but it was Leonard who took responsibility right away and made sure that all of us stuck together. He decided that we all would stay right there, refuse to leave, until that last guy was released. Leonard was always for taking action like that before things got serious, out of control."

After Fort Lawton, Peltier wandered south to Arizona "at the time of the Flagstaff Fair. There was a lot of white people and Indians in town, and the cops were beating on Indians all over the place. So I couldn't take that, and got the hell out of there, took a job as a carpenter over at Page, on the Colorado—that new power plant was under construction, the one using the strip-mined coal off the Navajo land up on Black Mesa. Anyway, the scene was just as bad down there. Soon's they found out I was some other kind of Indian, all they could talk to me about was how lazy them goddam Navajo workers were—trying to set Indians against Indians, you know, the same as always. And all this time I was hearing on the radio about AIM, which in those days was really making news. After a month, I couldn't take Page no more, so I headed north and checked out the AIM office in Denver. Vernon Bellecourt was there, and he explained to me what AIM was trying to do for the

Indian people, and not long after that he took me with him to an AIM meeting at Leech Lake, Minnesota.

"In those early days, it only took one Indian to raise a protest somewhere, and we sent people in; we did that once at my mother's Sioux reservation up at Fort Totten, North Dakota. We never bothered with invitations from the traditional leaders the way we should have. After the Leech Lake meeting, all that changed; we never went anyplace again without being invited by the elders. There was a lot more discipline in every way, mainly because of Dennis Banks and Herb Powless. At Leech Lake, Dennis told the leadership, including the AIM chapter heads from around the country, that the Movement had to get more serious if people were going to take it seriously, that it had to cut down on all the drinking and drugs and partying, the groupies and the 'Saturday-night warriors.' He was right, and I quit drinking there and then. But what he said was resented by the other leaders, the Means group especially, and we got outvoted; they didn't want no national office telling 'em what to do. So we went back to Dennis's cabin and we decided that we had to resign from AIM and start our own Indian organization. Trouble was, a lot of the chapter heads wanted to come with us. So finally Russell and Ted Means and the Bellecourts persuaded us to stay on, come to a compromise. The compromise never really worked, and later on, when Dennis wasn't there, those guys tried to vote him out as national director.

"In '71, I went back to Turtle Mountain, worked in potato houses for a while, then got fired from a job up there with missile-site construction; I blew the transmission on my car, coming up from Grand Forks, and couldn't get there. That was one of those government-funded projects on the res that required the contractor to hire a certain percentage of Indians; well, as soon as they hired 'em, they started looking for excuses to lay 'em off, and being late for work was good enough. In '72, I traveled with Banks to Arizona, and then to Hollywood, trying to raise support among the movie people. I didn't like L.A.—it seemed to me like some kind of a jungle—and when Herb Powless showed up, I went back with him to Milwaukee to work on alcoholic problems in the Indian community there." In 1970, Powless had founded AIM's Milwaukee chapter and in 1971 he led the AIM takeover of that abandoned Coast Guard station on the Great Lakes. "The following year, we went on the Trail of Broken Treaties. My cousin Steve Robideau went, too; he was a leader in the car caravan out of Seattle that was led by Russ Means, Hank Adams, and Sid Mills, a young Yakima leader in the fishing-rights fight."

Like many young Indian activists, Sid Mills was a decorated veteran, seriously wounded in Vietnam, and still bitter about his enforced participation in a white man's war against a native people; of his own accord, he had "resigned" from the U.S. Army to offer his full commitment to the Indian struggle. In early October 1972, Mills, Means, and Adams had held a press conference in Seattle to denounce the murder of Richard Oakes[8] on September 20, in Santa Clara, California, and to demand protection of Indians against the widespread vigilante action that had been inspired by AIM's insistence on Indian treaties. Adams, an Assiniboine-Sioux, had been shot in the stomach the year before, while working with fishermen on the Nisqually River—the Tacoma police claimed he shot himself—and four attempts on Means's life would be made in the years to come.

The murder of Oakes had unified the various Indian protest groups, and gave impetus to the Trail of Broken Treaties march—first discussed that summer on the Rosebud Reservation—that was scheduled to arrive in Washington, D.C., in time for the presidential election. A car caravan from San Francisco led by Dennis Banks and Mad Bear Anderson joined the Seattle caravan and others from around the country. The four-mile-long procession arrived early on the morning of the Friday, November 3, just before Election Day, and although seven other Indian organizations helped in the planning, it was AIM that became notorious across America. The Indian groups had notified the authorities of their plans, which included a twenty-point proposal for improving U.S.-Indian relations.

"There is a prophecy in our Ojibwa religion that one day we would all stand together," said Eddie Benton Banai of AIM. "All tribes would hook arms in brotherhood and unite. I am elated because I lived to see this happen. Brothers and sisters from all over this continent were united in a single cause. That is the greatest significance to Indian people—not what happened or what yet may happen as a result of our actions."

The BIA Commissioner, Louis Bruce, was a Sioux-Mohawk who was mainly sympathetic with the marchers, but he was instructed by Assistant Secretary of the Interior Harrison Loesch to withhold all support from the demonstrators. Loesch, the head of the Bureau of Land Management (BLM), which supervises the BIA, was highly regarded by the private mining and timber interests that coveted the public lands under his care. The year before, in approving oil and gas leases on 89,535 acres of Apache land, Loesch had ruled that the environmental impact statements required by the National Environmental Policy Act were not needed for Indian territory "because it was not public land"; similar determinations were made on land of the Tesuque Pueblo, Northern Cheyenne, and elsewhere, in graphic illustration of the Indians' claim that in the inevitable conflict of interest between the BLM and the BIA, the Indian people invariably lost.

"We had our chiefs with us—Frank Fools Crow and Charlie Red Cloud and many others," says Leonard Peltier. "Lodging had been promised for these elders, but the church where they were supposed to stay was full of rats; Dennis and me seen a rat right in the street where a car run over it! And these were the chiefs of our nation; we felt they should be treated with respect. So we decided to go over to the BIA and speak with Louis Bruce, and if we were denied decent housing for our chiefs, the plan was to hold a sit-in in the building until we got results. We certainly never planned no occupation! Well, first they stalled us, and then, about six p.m., the riot squads start busting down the doors, trying to evict us, and they grab one of our guys and beat the hell out of him. We had a lot of youngsters with us, and we couldn't control them after that, they went kind of crazy and tore everything apart, and you couldn't blame 'em: I was right there, I seen the attitudes toward Indians those people had, and I seen it all come down."

With a young Bad River Chippewa named Stanley Moore, Peltier was chosen to direct security in Washington. "I'd been around awhile, I was well known and well trusted, so they asked me to do it. The first time they asked me, I wouldn't get up and volunteer; it was a heavy job, and a lot of responsibility. But Russ Means and Carter Camp kind of insisted, so me and Stanley got appointed whether we wanted it or not. And after the Trail, I kind of got called on whenever someone was needed for security."

Richard Nixon had followed Lyndon Johnson's lead in advocating "self-determination" for the Indians (his relatively good administration record had included restoration of the terminated Menominee to tribal status and the return of their sacred Blue Lake to the people of Taos Pueblo) though he later relapsed into standard Republican policies, in which a new facade of "self-government" was used to camouflage the continuing exploitation of Indian land. Neither President nor Vice-President had time to meet with unruly militants. Confronted with the usual evasion and broken promises, the marchers occupied the BIA building for five days, causing considerable damage to the premises by trying to barricade themselves against the riot squads that kept threatening them with ultimatums, and making off with a number of documents that (it was claimed) established discriminatory government attitudes toward their people. Despite the fact that Robert Burnette, head of the Rosebud Tribal Council, had been one of the leaders on the march, tribal-council chairmen from all over the country issued dutiful protests on behalf of "dignified reservation Indians," and newspaper editorials recalled the damage done at Alcatraz and made stern distinctions between good Indians and bad. Secretary of the Interior Rogers Morton said, "It is a shame that a small, willful band of malcontents should try to wreck the headquarters of the government's chief instrument for serving the Indian community." The real shame was that the "Twenty Points"[9] of the Trail of Broken Treaties were lost in the clamor of bad publicity.

Carter Camp, the young Ponca head of Oklahoma AIM, advised the press that a polite reception, as promised in advance by Washington officials, could have avoided the whole confrontation. "Instead, Secretary Loesch laughingly told us that the Bureau was not in the housing business, and threatened to have us thrown out. We were only in here talking to Bureau officials; there was no occupation at all. Then someone . . . called the riot squad and they just came in, busted a bunch of windows . . . and attacked us. As soon as our Indian warriors saw what was happening, well, they just kicked their asses out, then barricaded the doors and windows. Most of the damage had been done by the police."[10]

Later reports of looting and vandalism by frustrated and angry Indians that caused damage "in the millions" were termed "grossly exaggerated" by Secretary Morton. The real damage was suffered by AIM's reputation, and in the newspapers, the Indians' behavior was compared unfavorably with the "restrained" performance of the police, the main reason for which was Nixon's reluctance to authorize a massacre on the very eve of the elections; clearly these young Indians meant business and were not going to be removed without a fight. Morton extolled Nixon's good will toward his red brothers, adding for good measure his own "prayer that soon he [the Indian] will sit at his table and in truth be thankful for the bounties of this land—his land—our land. I want his heart to swell with pride that he is an American and that for him there is an American dream."

At the same time, an angry and embarrassed U.S. government attempted to belittle the whole episode, giving $66,000 to the Indians to pay for their transportation out of town; the BIA Commissioner and his staff were fired or forced to resign. According to a "white paper" put out by the Justice Department, "An Indian seated behind a bureaucrat's desk did not look like a civil rights protester. He looked like a burglar. And when the Government signaled that it might be willing to take a gentle attitude if the whole silly exercise were ended, A.I.M. and its followers departed expeditiously." But the FBI took a harsher view of red wind bands and upside-down flags. Mad Bear Anderson, after all, had visited the Cuban Communists as early as 1958; Sid Mills, Hank Adams, and Russell Means, it was said, had been welcomed by Communists in Hanoi just the previous spring. For the FBI, as for the John Birch Society, the term "red Indian" meant precisely what it said.

For all its scare talk of terrorists and reds, even the FBI cannot have imagined that AIM Indians—or the Black Panthers, or the puny U.S. Communist party, for that matter—were ever a real threat to national security; what was being protected was the "American Dream" in which the Secretary of the Interior wished Indian hearts to swell with pride, the swollen "System" of conspicuous consumption, waste, and gross pollution that was so profitable to the big corporations and so destructive to the long-term prospects of humankind. In the narrow vision of the FBI, there was no place in the American Dream for these ungrateful aborigines who dared to state that all national boundaries in the Western Hemisphere, from Alaska to Argentina, were entirely meaningless, since "Americans" were really Europeans, and the Americas were Indian country from end to end.

The first of the Indians' Twenty Points demanded the restoration of their constitutional treaty-making powers, removed by the provision in the 1871 Indian Appropriations Act, and the next seven concerned recognition of the sovereignty of Indian nations and the revalidation of treaties, including the Fort Laramie Treaty of 1868: the fundamental demand was that Indians be dealt with according to "our treaties." Other points were addressed to such related matters as land-reform law and the restoration of a land base, which would permit those Indians who wished to do so to return to a traditional way of life. From the

U.S. government's point of view, to recognize or negotiate treaty claims all over the country might necessitate the return of vast tracts of America to the true owners, a very dangerous idea indeed.

After the Trail of Broken Treaties, government support through the Office of Economic Opportunity was withdrawn from the AIM survival schools in St. Paul, Minneapolis, and Milwaukee.* AIM was classified "an extremist organization" by the FBI, and on January 8, 1973, the leaders on the Trail were added to the Bureau's list of "key extremists." On January 11, the White House in effect rejected the Trail of Broken Treaties' Twenty Points as a "wholly backward step. . . . A government makes treaties with foreign nations, not with its own citizens," the Indians were informed by a Nixon aide.

Meanwhile, thirty-two men had been listed for prosecution, but despite the seriousness of the charges—mostly grand larceny and arson—not one was ever indicted in the East, where public sympathy was traditionally with the Indians. It was safer to go after AIM in South Dakota, an impoverished state where anti-Indian prejudice was epidemic, where local politicians and law-enforcement officers could be counted on for enthusiastic cooperation, and where vast economic considerations were at stake: uranium leases on treaty land in the Black Hills that were being issued quietly if not secretly to the huge energy consortiums might be delayed by prolonged treaty hearings in the courts. To camouflage the role of the U.S. government, units of the BIA's Indian police would be trained in paramilitary tactics; at the same time, the focus of the still-secret FBI counterintelligence program (COINTELPRO) was turned from the Black Panthers onto AIM, and an organized "neutralizing" of AIM leaders was begun.

On November 22, 1972, a few weeks after his return to Milwaukee from the BIA building takeover in Washington, Leonard Peltier and two Indian friends were badgered in Tex's Restaurant on Fifth Street by two other customers. "These two guys at another table—we didn't know they were plainclothes cops at the time, because one of 'em had on a black leather jacket and the other one was in a windbreaker—anyway, they were looking over at us, pointing and laughing, you know, really cracking up. Well, one of the brothers, he's a pretty good fighter, and I guess I am, too, and he says, If they give us any more of that, we'll

* OEO funds were later released by federal judge Miles Lord, who recognized the "community need" met by the schools.

kick the shit out of them. So when I had paid up and was starting out, here are these two guys right in the doorway, like they were waiting for us, and they're still pointing at us and cracking up. So I say, What the fuck's so funny? I knew me and this other bro could take 'em, see. Why, hell, they pull *guns* on us, right then and there, before we could get it on; one of 'em had his piece strapped to his leg. And them .357s look pretty goddam big; when this guy in the black leather jacket put that thing to my head, it come up at me like a goddam *cannon*."

Remembering, Peltier raises his eyebrows and laughs ruefully, shaking his head. "When they saw them guns, my friends just split, and I don't blame 'em. As for me, I'm backing up fast into the restaurant, figuring they might not kill me in front of witnesses. Once I'm in there, I say in a loud voice, Okay, I give up! So they call a paddy wagon and handcuff me and drag me outside and shove me in, hands cuffed behind my back, and once I'm in there, this cop Hlavinka, he starts beating on me like a stepchild! And in all the skirmishing around, my coat gets ripped open and this old piece falls out—hell, it was an old busted Beretta, couldn't fire at all, I had just given a guy twenty bucks for it as a favor, figuring I might get it fixed sometime. Well, that gun was just what them pigs needed; they busted me for attempted murder, and here Hlavinka is hitting me so hard that I had to jam my head under the wagon seat to keep my brains from being beat out. Finally the other one, James Eckel—the one who later admitted in court that he had kicked me 'four or five times' while I was laying handcuffed in the paddy wagon—this Eckel tells Hlavinka he'd better take it easy. By that time, Hlavinka had busted all the blood vessels in his right hand, he had to take sick leave for three days—that come out in court, too.

"So after they brought me to the jail, one of the black cops says to me, We know what you're involved in: your people and mine have a real grievance in this country. How did he know what I was involved in, unless Hlavinka and his partner knew it, too, before they started trouble in that restaurant?"

Officer Hlavinka stated that Peltier had taken out a loaded gun and pulled the trigger twice in an effort to shoot him; the gun had failed, it was said, and before a third shot could be attempted, Hlavinka's partner had thrust his hand between the hammer and the firing pin. Officer Eckel received a citation for having saved Hlavinka's life, although the state crime lab would conclude that Peltier's gun was "incapable of being fired."

The young Indian's claim that he had been set up by the police was eventually supported by several witnesses who described the episode in the restaurant, and also by Hlavinka's former girl friend, Bell Anne Guild, who said that Hlavinka, in this period, had waved around one of Peltier's pictures, sent to the local police from Washington, announcing his intention of "catching a big one for the FBI." Meanwhile Peltier spent five months in jail before Milwaukee AIM could raise bail. Seeing no reason to expect justice in a trial in which the word of an AIM Indian would be pitted against the testimony of two policemen, Peltier went underground soon after he was released. In July 1973, when due to appear for a pre-trial hearing, he had already headed west for the Dakotas.

CHAPTER 3

TO WOUNDED KNEE

February–May 1973

The whites are crazy!
The whites are crazy!
ghost-dance song

By now many other Lakotas, who had heard the shooting, were coming up from Pine Ridge, and we all charged on the soldiers. They ran eastward toward where the trouble began. We followed down along the dry gulch, and what we saw was terrible. Dead and wounded women and children and little babies were scattered all along where they had been trying to run away. The soldiers had followed along the gulch, as they ran, and murdered them in there. Sometimes they were in heaps because they had huddled together, and some were scattered all along. Sometimes bunches of them had been killed and torn to pieces where the wagon-guns hit them. I saw a little baby trying to suck its mother, but she was bloody and dead. . . . Men and women and children were heaped and scattered all over the flat at the bottom of the little hill where the soldiers had their wagon-guns, and westward up the dry gulch all the way to the high ridge, the dead women and babies were scattered.

Black Elk (*Lakota*)

In February 1972, an Oglala from Pine Ridge named Raymond Yellow Thunder was severely beaten for the fun of it by two white brothers named Hare, then stripped from the waist down and paraded before a patriotic gathering at an American Legion dance in Gordon, Nebraska; the merry crowd was invited to join the Hares in kicking the Indian, after which the brothers stuffed him into a car trunk, where he perished. When his body was found, the Hares were arrested, then released without bail while awaiting trial for second-degree manslaughter; even this charge might have been dismissed had not Raymond Yellow Thunder's family, in the absence of meaningful interest or help from local authorities or the FBI, made the decision to call on AIM. Severt Young Bear says:

> Raymond Yellow Thunder was an uncle of mine, and his sisters all live in Porcupine. When that happened, they went to the BIA for help, they went to the Tribal Government for help, they went to some private attorneys for help, because they wouldn't let them see the body, they wouldn't let them see the autopsy report, and they sealed the coffin when they brought it back. This is what really hurt his sisters.
>
> So after they ran into all these brick walls, they had no place else to go. That Friday evening, I came back from work . . . and a car pulled up and there's my three aunts, all three of them. They came in crying and said, "Sonny, we don't have no place to turn. So we came over—maybe you could help us." They said, "You have some friends that are with AIM. I wonder if you could go to them, ask them that we want something to be done to the people that killed our brother, and we want a full investigation."[1]

The AIM leaders, who were meeting with other Indian groups in Omaha, went straight to Pine Ridge with red flags and drums to organize the people, then led an enormous caravan of two hundred cars across the Nebraska line to Gordon, where a large force of sheriff's deputies, state troopers, and FBI agents capitulated to the Indian demands that serious charges be filed against the Hares, that the local police chief be dismissed, and that long-standing grievances about the rampant racism in Gordon be discussed. The victory gained AIM the lasting respect of the Pine Ridge traditionals, who until then—like most reservation Indians around the country—had regarded these "city Indians" with great suspicion. Young Bear continues:

> People here still talk about Yellow Thunder and what happened in Gordon. When A.I.M. came in and helped the family look into the death, that made the older people that are living out on the reservation, out in the country—they kind of lifted up their heads, and were speaking out then. And they been talking against BIA, tribal government, law and order system on the reservation, plus some of the non-Indian ranchers that are living on the reservation and been abusing Indians.

Even before the Trail of Broken Treaties, the showdown in Gordon had alerted the authorities to a radical new element among the Indians, the great majority of whom had remained peaceable throughout the civil-rights tumult of the 1960s; without AIM agitators, it was felt, those Sioux would subside once again into listless dependence on BIA and tribal-council handouts. Therefore a tougher policy was needed, not only toward AIM but toward those who had dared to support it. As luck would have it, the right man for the job took over in the spring of 1972 as the new president of the Pine Ridge Tribal Council, despite a long history of previous exploitation of his people as a bootlegger, and also a near-indictment three years earlier on charges that he had "misused" $6,000 of federal funds.

A paunchy pale-skinned man with dark glasses, a military haircut, and a heavy drinking habit, Richard "Dick" Wilson was violently anti-AIM; with nothing else to recommend him, his main attraction on the poverty-stricken reservation was his lavish campaign spending, the real source of which has never come to light. No sooner was this man in office than he handed out fat Tribal Council salaries to his wife, brother, cousin, sons, and nephew ("There's nothing in tribal law against nepotism,"[2] Dick Wilson said), as well as to as many of his supporters (about nine hundred) as could be piled onto the government payroll. Dr. Jim Wilson, the president's brother and head of the planning committee, was paid $25,000, which compared very well with the median annual income of $800 among his tribesmen, most of whom lived in tarpaper shacks without electricity or running water. "I'm not one of those Indians who sets on his tail waiting for a government handout," announced Dick Wilson, who was raising stock, operating a trucking business, and occupying federally subsidized housing, in addition to his $15,500 government salary.

Meanwhile, Russell Means, fed up with city life, decided to return to the reservation, where he announced plans for a food co-op for people in the traditional village of Porcupine. After the Trail of Broken Treaties, when Means and Banks proposed a victory celebration on Pine Ridge, Wilson banned all AIM activities and called for U.S. marshals to protect the BIA building from another occupation like the one in Washington. He also commenced an open war against those who supported AIM, including his own vice-president, whom he fired. "If Russell Means sets foot on this reservation, I, Dick Wilson, will personally cut his braids off," Wilson declared, aware that Means, his main political rival on Pine Ridge, intended to run for his own job. Means, who had led the Yellow Thunder protest, was arrested by BIA Special Officer Del Eastman when he attempted to tell the traditionals of the community at Oglala what had taken place on the Trail of Broken Treaties; Banks was subsequently arrested by BIA Officer Duane Brewer. Both Eastman and Brewer would become notorious in the next three years.

Using federal highway funds assigned to a "Highway Safety Program" and "Tribal Rangers," Wilson augmented the BIA police by outfitting and arming a private police force, composed mostly of out-of-work supporters who had become dependent on Tribal Council handouts. Due to the drunken brutality of its repressions, this force was soon known as the "goon squad"; in its arrogance it adopted this name as an acronym for "Guardians of the Oglala Nation." Though threatened repeatedly with impeachment by his own Tribal Council because of a whole series of illegal acts (there were more signatures on one petition to impeach Wilson than people who had voted for him in the first place), Wilson was staunchly supported by the BIA and the FBI as well; the Justice Department was only too happy to endorse this serviceable Indian who requested them to attack AIM members and offered the services of his own goons to do the job.

Like most Wilson people, the goons were drawn from the eight or nine hundred mixed-bloods on the payroll of the Tribal Council, and much of their hatred toward those who supported AIM stemmed from economic fear; a precarious security would be threatened if the traditionals gained a say in tribal matters and, with it, a fair share of federal benefits, which were scarcely enough to go around.

"The past administrations all along have been pretty sly and crooked with Indian funds," said a tribal elder named Gladys Bissonnette, "but they weren't quite as hard on us as this drunken fool we got now, who hasn't got the backbone to stand up and protect his Indians." And Grace Black Elk said, "This Dick Wilson, he hates AIM people because they are doing what he should have been doing. So he's jealous of them, more jealous than anything else."

"We all wonder why it is that the government is backing him up so much," another leader named Ellen Moves Camp said early in 1973, before anyone had grasped the true nature of the government's sudden, quite extraordinary interest in local disputes on a remote Indian reservation in South Dakota. "None of our other tribal councilmen were ever backed up like this. Nothing like this has ever happened before, where we have guns all over the reservation. Threatening people, hitting people, putting them in the hospital—you don't have no protection at all. . . . You have to carry a gun on this reservation now, ever since he's been in there."

Tension on Pine Ridge increased when in January 1973 a young man named Wesley Bad Heart Bull was stabbed in the heart in a Buffalo Gap bar in the second attack by a white businessman named Darold Schmidt. Like the murderers of Raymond Yellow Thunder, Schmidt was charged with involuntary manslaughter, and Sarah Bad Heart Bull, the victim's mother, asked AIM to seek justice from the state authorities. The officials were uneasy when they heard that AIM was mobilizing, and brought heavy police support to a meeting with the Indians in the old courthouse in Custer (formerly Custer City), in the Black Hills. On February 6, the more than two hundred Indian people who had come there in a caravan of old cars in support of Sarah Bad Heart Bull were told by the heavily armed police that the open meeting was postponed; only their spokesmen—Means, Banks, Crow Dog, and a young Choctaw named Dave Hill—were allowed inside to talk with the nervous officials. When Sarah Bad Heart Bull attempted to enter, she was seized and beaten on the courthouse steps by two police officers, who later accused her of yelling obscenities; those Indians who tried to intervene were teargassed and beaten. A fracas between Indians and police spread through the courthouse. Subsequently, two police cars were overturned and set on fire, and an abandoned Chamber of Commerce building next to the courthouse was burned to the ground in a riot that ricocheted all over town; for the first time in a century, the white people could holler, "Injuns comin'!" Although no one was killed, the Custer courthouse riot was an historic event, the first outbreak of violence between white men and Lakota since the massacre at Wounded Knee in 1890.

"While we were talking to the state's attorneys, the mayor and commissioners and all," Dennis Banks remembers, "fighting started outside on the steps, then swept into the corridors outside the room. Next thing we knew, the door opened and a tear-gas canister came rolling in. People tried to get out, but they couldn't make it because of the fighting out there, so we tried the window. Well, this was the old courthouse building, the windows hadn't been opened in a long time, and they were stuck. I grabbed a chair and broke out a window with the legs, and some of us went out.

"The rioting must have lasted forty-five minutes, maybe even an hour, and thirty people were arrested. I went over to the police station to see about bailing people out, but there was no real communication over there, there was nothing but hate. About nineteen were released finally on low bail, but they kept the ones they thought were leaders, including Sarah Bad Heart Bull. Originally I was questioned and released—then, suddenly, three or four days later, charges of arson, burglary, and malicious damage to a public building were filed against me, not because I had broken any laws but because I was a leader of AIM."

The presence of FBI observers at the "uprising" suggested to the Indians that state and government authorities were concerned less with law and order than with the obstacle to Black Hills mining leases that AIM insistence on Indian sovereignty might represent. The Black Hills was only one of the rich mineral regions in the West that according to treaty belonged to the Indian people—Pueblo and Navajo, Shoshone, Crow, Ojibwa, and Northern Cheyenne as well as Lakota. Following the Custer riot, the Attorney General assigned sixty-five U.S. marshals to Pine Ridge: the "new Indian wars" were under way.

In late February, the traditional people, organized by the Oglala Sioux Civil Rights Organization (OSCRO), marched on the red-brick BIA building in Pine Ridge village. Originally, they had intended to protest the low land rentals encouraged by the BIA and also the illegal termination of Dick Wilson's impeachment hearing by the defendant himself; now they were challenging the recent invasion by these marshals, who had no legal jurisdiction on the reservation. According to the Major Crimes Act of 1885 (and later the Assimilative Crimes Act), the government had jurisdiction only in the case of serious felonies, and none had been committed on Pine Ridge. Finding themselves denied access to their own building by the well-armed marshals with their sandbag fortifications and machine guns, they realized that "the feds" intended to support Dick Wilson no matter what offenses he had committed, so long as he waged war on AIM; clearly, this Wilson was no different from other petty dictators around the world, propped up by weapons sent from the U.S. under the panoply of "anti-Communism" so long as they protected corporate interests. In his hatred and fear of AIM, Wilson found his strongest support among middle-aged people of his own generation, who were born at a time when the missions were strongest and the Indian traditions most despised, and whose jobs depended on the BIA and the Tribal Council; most others had nothing to lose by endorsing AIM—or not, at least, on the Pine Ridge Reservation—and AIM's strongest support came from older people with family memories of the Indians' great days, and from the many embittered young men who had served time in the armed services or in jail.

For their part, the AIM leaders were eager for more confrontations, persuading themselves that militancy (and publicity) could accomplish what traditional patience and stoicism had not. On February 26, the Oglala chiefs, with Frank Fools Crow as their spokesman, decided once again to ask AIM's help, and a meeting was called for February 27 at Calico Hall, a community log house not far west of Pine Ridge village. Gladys Bissonnette has estimated that six hundred Indians turned up at Calico, and all of them, by Indian custom, had to be fed; when help with money for the food was asked from the Holy Rosary Catholic Church, whose Red Cloud mission school Mrs. Bissonnette had attended as a child, it was refused by Father Paul Steinmetz, who explained to the Indians that the church was afraid to jeopardize its financial support from all those good Christians on the Wilson side. (After ninety years of missionary zeal, an estimated 163 churches of seventeen denominations had fastened on Pine Ridge, and almost all of them preserved an unholy silence during the next three years of violence and terror on the reservation.) "It has been said of missionaries that when they arrived they had only the Book and we had the land," says Vine Deloria, Jr., a Standing Rock Sioux lawyer and writer, and a longtime caustic spokesman for his people. "Now we have the Book and they have the land."[3] The Holy Rosary Church, with eighteen square miles, is by far the largest landowner on the reservation.

At Calico, OSCRO decided upon a symbolic confrontation. In the words of Dennis Banks, who joined Russell Means at the meeting, "We had reached a point in history where we could not tolerate the abuse any longer, where these mothers could not tolerate the mistreatment that goes on on the reservations any longer, they could not see another Indian youngster die.

"They asked A.I.M. what we were going to do about the injustices that were going on at that very minute, allowing the federal officers, the FBI, the marshals to turn the village of Pine Ridge into an armed camp. These women asked that the fighting spirit return. One by one, the chiefs stood up."[4]

Ellen Moves Camp, mother of six children and a Community Health representative on the reservation for eight years before Dick Wilson had her removed for her AIM sympathies, was one of these strong women. With her son Louis, Mrs. Moves Camp joined the caravan of several hundred people who on February 28 traveled to Wounded Knee and took over the community as a gesture of protest:

> We decided that we did need the American Indian Movement in here because our men were scared, they hung to the back. It was mostly the women that went forward and spoke out. . . . All of our older people from the reservation helped us make the decision. . . . There were only two members from A.I.M. that was with us when we had that meeting, and that was our brother Russell Means and about an hour later Dennis Banks came in and set by the door and listened to us. And when we kept talking about it then the chiefs said, "Go ahead and do it, go to Wounded Knee. You can't get in the BIA Office and the Tribal office, so take your brothers from the American Indian Movement and go to Wounded Knee and make your stand there." . . . With our brothers and sisters of the American Indian Movement, we feel stronger. We're not scared of them. This is what we needed—a little more push. Most of the reservation believes in the A.I.M., and we're proud to have them with us. And now that we've done it, my feeling is, "What did I get them into?" I hope that they don't get punished as severely as we do—I don't care how *I* get punished—because our people need these men.[5]

A meeting held at Wounded Knee on that first evening was addressed by Means, Banks, and Pedro Bissonnette, a small scrappy boxer who became the main spokesman for the traditionals. "OSCRO was largely put together by Pedro Bissonnette," Dennis Banks recalls. "He was a truly spiritual man, I think—one of the few men of that quality I have ever met—and he was also very fair, very generous, trying to take care of his people, with a lot of humor even in hard times. As soon as he walked into a room, he was in charge—a natural leader. He spoke English as well as his own language and he had real energy; more than anyone else, he organized the Oglala people behind AIM."

The Indians issued a public statement demanding hearings on their treaty and an investigation of the BIA: "The only two options open to the United States of America are 1) They wipe out the old people, women, children, and men, by shooting and attacking us. 2) They negotiate our demands." The intractable tone of this release was caused by the government's outright rejection of the Trail of Broken Treaties' Twenty Points; this time the Indians had no intention of emerging empty-handed. The Oglala statement was signed by Bissonnette, Vern Long, and Eddie White Wolf, followed by AIM leader Means; it was endorsed by the eight leading chiefs and medicine men of the Oglala band, including Frank Fools Crow, Edgar Red Cloud, and Pete Catches, and was therefore the voice of the Lakota nation that had won the Treaty of 1868. "We want a true nation," Carter Camp declared, "not one made up of Bureau of Indian Affairs puppets."[6]

When Wounded Knee was surrounded the next day by the FBI, the U.S. Marshal Service, and the BIA police, the most powerful nation in the world had been challenged by a tiny Indian nation that dared to demand restoration of its sovereignty according to the terms of its great treaty. The AIM people who supported it were mostly volunteers from other tribes, and the inter-tribal spirit at Wounded Knee inspired a revival of Indian sovereignty claims all over the continent. Yet AIM had always attracted more support from the Lakota than from most other Indian nations. "The Lakota aren't the same people as the Pueblo, or even the Navajo," says Madonna Gilbert, a cousin of Russell Means. "The Lakota were always a warrior people, and taking up arms to defend the nation is the traditional way. And it was the traditional people who invited us down to Pine Ridge to help out in 1972 and 1973. At Calico, the elders said, What can we do to wake these Indians up? We have to take a stand *some*where! So we decided that the symbolic place would be Wounded Knee. What happened there was never expected; we figured we'd be there just two or three days, we were never told to bring food or anything, I just had my jacket and my purse! And my two kids! We didn't realize what was happening until we were surrounded. We never broke the law in any way or did one thing wrong; it was the feds who were breaking the law by being on the reservation without jurisdiction, without any real permission from the people. But the FBI made *us* out to be the criminals right away, and a lot of the agents they had out there believed all that scare talk themselves! The first time me and Lorelei [Lorelei Decora, a young leader of AIM's Iowa chapter] went out, we ran into a whole army of tribal police, sheriffs, U.S. marshals, FBI, and those guys were scared shitless—you could see it. They handcuffed us, threw us in vans, called us 'gooks' and a lot worse—derogatory dirty stuff, you know, because we were women. And that was America's elite with all their war toys—I mean, helicopters, APCs [armored personnel carriers], the whole Vietnam number, blue jump suits, infrared lights, guns everywhere you looked; it was Wounded Knee and the Seventh Cavalry all over again."

"We didn't know we were going to be crowded in there by a bunch of guns and stuff, military and FBIs and marshals and goons," Ellen Moves Camp recalls. "We didn't talk about going in there and taking over Wounded Knee. That was the furthest thing from our minds. But what choice did the government give us?"

In fact, a makeshift federal army had been created by the Justice and Defense departments by training civilian law-enforcement officers in paramilitary units and equipping them with armored personnel carriers, automatic weapons, and enough ammunition (133,000 rounds for the M-16 rifles alone) to wipe out every Indian in the Dakotas. The excuse offered for this exercise was the brief detention of a few "hostages," mostly at the white trading post, which has prospered for years from tourists attracted to the site of the 1890 massacre ("Wounded Knee Massacre Historical Site—Mass Burial Grave—Authentic Arts and Crafts—51 Miles"), and which was emptied of food, clothes, guns, and ammunition by the occupying Indians. When Senators George McGovern and James Abourezk arrived at Wounded Knee on March 1, deploring AIM's seizure of white hostages, they were told by one of the victims, Father Paul Manhardt, that those who wished to depart had already gone; those who stayed on had done so voluntarily, not only to protect their property but because this village was their home. Unlike most of their predecessors, both South Dakota senators were among the Indians' few sympathizers in Congress, and their visit had a calming effect on the federal policemen, who were all for assaulting Wounded Knee. "We as a group of hostages decided to stay on to save A.I.M. and our own property," said Wilbur Riegert, eighty-two years old. "Had we not, those troops would have come down here and killed all of these people. The real hostages are the A.I.M. people."

Many Indian residents stayed on as well. An old lady named Rachel Hollow Horn (who was beaten by goons and hospitalized a few years later) said she had stayed "because I have a wound that was never healed. Back in 1890 my grandfather was in that massacre. And my dad's three older brothers were shot and killed. My grandfather escaped with wounds. He died later. I wasn't actually in the fighting but I stayed because I didn't want to see them die alone. 'If they are going to be wiped out,' I said, 'I want to be one of them.' "[7]

Senator Abourezk, as chairman of the Senate Subcommittee on Indian Affairs, and Senator McGovern, who had fought for Indian land rights in the 1960s, promised the Indian leaders that there would be hearings to investigate their grievances, and on March 4, during preliminary talks with the Justice Department, the leaders agreed to abandon Wounded Knee if the government withdrew its forces from the reservation and let the people work out their own problems. According to a Pentagon intelligence report on that same date,

> The Indians do not appear intent upon inflicting bodily harm upon the legitimate residents of Wounded Knee, nor upon the federal law enforcement agents operating in this area, even though small arms fire has been exchanged between opposing forces. Because of its isolated geographical location, the seizure and holding of Wounded Knee poses no threat to the Nation, to the state of South Dakota or the Pine Ridge Reservation itself. However, it is conceded that this act is a source of irritation, if not embarrassment, to the Administration in general, and the Department of Justice in particular.[8]

This sensible assessment was ignored by the Pentagon, which wished to try out its "Garden Plot" operation (designed in 1968 for use against civil disorders such as protests against the Vietnam war) and therefore contributed a vast amount of lethal hardware. The FBI was intent on "neutralizing" its "key extremists," and the Attorney General's office was already threatening prosecution; the occupiers were ordered to turn themselves over to the law. Although the Indians ignored it, this ultimatum, with its hint of violence ("I call upon them to send the women and children out of Wounded Knee before March 8"), persuaded the last white residents to depart. Meanwhile, the National Council of Churches announced that its emissaries would post themselves between the firing lines in the event of a government attack.

On March 8, the Justice Department approved a cease-fire agreement worked out by John Adams, a minister from Washington, D.C., whose United Methodist Church supported the Indian cause. "They had delivered an ultimatum," Adams said, "and they had to get out of the box they had created for themselves."[9] On March 9, as rumor spread that the government was planning a full-scale attack, hundreds of Indians—many of them Wilson supporters who bitterly resented those who had taken part in the occupation—jammed all roads into the settlement to try to prevent a second Wounded Knee. That evening, heavy fire broke out that both sides claim was started by the other as a provocation, and a young Oglala, Milo Goings, became the first Indian to be wounded in the siege. This "firefight" presented the government with its last chance to end the occupation by a quick military strike while it still had the support of the general public: already the public reaction, maneuvered by the media, was veering from outrage over the hostages to sympathy for the beleaguered Indians (one poll declared that 51 percent of the American people sympathized with the Indians, with only 21 percent against). However, the "Friendly Forces"—FBI agents, U.S. marshals, and BIA police, supported irregularly by goons and vigilante ranchers who threatened to "declare war" on Wounded Knee—not only received conflicting instructions from their leaders but rarely agreed on anything among themselves. The FBI, for example, endorsed Dick Wilson's goons and helped to arm them, while the U.S. marshals dismissed these often drunken allies as a dangerous nuisance.

The FBI agents, all suited up in war-games costumes, and the marshals in their bright blue jump suits and orange neckerchiefs (with large gold Special Operations Unit patches on their sleeves and large silver stars upon their chests, just like the old-time marshals in the movies), had no more idea of how to deal with the long-haired "hostiles" than the Blue Coats had had at the battle of Greasy Grass Creek. The most visible and vocal Indian spokesman was Russell Means, but

Means, who had lived most of his life away from the reservation and had lost most of his Oglala tongue, felt responsible to the traditionals who had invited AIM to help, and these people, whose spokesman was Pedro Bissonnette, rarely acted without painstaking consultation with their medicine men and elders, who were not resident in the camp. (One medicine man, Wallace Black Elk, with Leonard Crow Dog from the Rosebud Reservation, remained at Wounded Knee through most of the occupation.) To the white men, the "hostiles" seemed to have no spokesman with the authority to make decisions (or not, at least, in the orderly western way), and the early meetings, as they saw them, were mostly exercises in fiery rhetoric from Means and Banks that attracted unwelcome publicity to the whole business, and perhaps stirred up trouble among other Indians as well; on March 5, the Northern Cheyenne, followed soon after by the Crow, canceled all the mining leases on their reservations.

With the cease-fire agreement of March 10, federal officials decided to lift the heavy roadblocks and permit free access to the village; from their informers they already had the names of those they wished to prosecute, and apparently they had convinced themselves that these AIM Indians were just rabble-rousing loudmouths who would sneak away as soon as they could do so, just like those treacherous redskins in the history books. Instead, the defenders used this opportunity to consolidate their fortifications and supplies, and on March 11, after an all-day meeting of the elders, the Oglala traditional leaders proclaimed the revival of the Independent Oglala Nation, which proposed to discuss its treaty with the United States on equal terms.

The elders and chiefs were quite aware of the significance of the brave stand that they were taking on behalf not only of the Oglala but of traditional Indians all over North America and traditional peoples all over the world; "Wounded Knee II" was immediately taken up in the European press, giving the Indian cause an international notoriety that it had not achieved since the great days of Red Cloud. The Indians knew that they were risking an angry reprisal from the U.S. government. "Indian people, the smallest number of people in the country, the poorest people in the country, are making a stand here and are ready to die," declared Lorelei Decora of Iowa AIM.[10]

On the day of the cease-fire, four government postal inspectors, accompanied by two ranchers, attempted to enter Wounded Knee; a group of defenders, including Carter Camp, Leonard Crow Dog, and a young Wichita Indian named Stan Holder, a former Marine and Vietnam combat veteran who was head of Wounded Knee security, assumed that these white men were there to spy out the defenses; they arrested, disarmed, and detained them for about six hours. Later that day, a van attempting to return to the village was intercepted by the FBI, and an agent was wounded in the hand in a brief exchange of fire before the van made it through (later an FBI informer would allege that a man named Frank Black Horse had winged the agent, and that Black Horse had been awarded an eagle feather for this feat by Russell Means). In any case, the cease-fire had failed. That evening, the roadblocks were reestablished, and the government forces, which now numbered at least three hundred men, began the construction of permanent bunkers; once again, Indian supplies had to be packed in at night by men and women who knew how to travel the rolling plains and creek gullies on foot. On March 13, a federal grand jury in Sioux Falls issued its first indictments in the Wounded Knee case, against Clyde Bellecourt, Banks, Camp, Russell Means, and Pedro Bissonnette. The head of the U.S. marshals, pointing out to the press that until now the government had permitted the flow of food, medicine, and utilities to the besieged village, vowed to "change their lifestyle."

On March 22, a group of attorneys and volunteers led by Kenneth Tilsen of St. Paul, Minnesota, had formed the Wounded Knee Legal Defense/Offense Committee (WKLDOC) to fight what they saw as an illegal invasion of the reservation by government forces and to defend those already arrested or indicted; the committee members were unpaid, receiving only room and board through private contributions, which perhaps explains why the FBI would later refer to them as a "revolutionary organization." Contesting the legality of the blockade, "Wickle-dock," as it was known to its members, won a temporary restraining order in federal district court in Rapid City that permitted six lawyers (with six carloads of food) to enter Wounded Knee each day between March 26 and March 31. Dick Wilson, proclaiming his fear that the U.S. government might be negotiating with the Independent Oglala Nation, set up roadblocks outside those of the U.S. marshals, where his goons stopped the lawyers' cars and ransacked them; despite the court order, this activity was not discouraged by the "Friendly Forces."

The Indians' contempt for the military might that had been mustered to put down a spontaneous protest against Dick Wilson and the BIA was shared in part by Lieutenant Colonel (now Brigadier General) Volney Warner, who in February 1973 was Chief of Staff of the Eighty-second Airborne, a full fighting division with special training in putting down civil disturbances; Colonel Warner, in civilian clothes, arrived in the area on March 3 with orders to determine whether U.S. troops should be committed—a serious decision, since an executive order from the President would be required. Joseph Trimbach, Special Agent in Charge (SAC) of the regional FBI office in Minneapolis, who met him at Ellsworth Air Force Base, near Rapid City, assured him that this was a case for the U.S. Army: the FBI requested that two thousand soldiers seize the reservation and restore order, after which the FBI would move in and make arrests. Colonel Warner recommended that SAC Trimbach's request be refused, and also that the FBI change its standing orders from shoot-to-kill to shoot-to-wound, in light of the fact that the Indians were not trying to harm anyone. The symbolic presence of the U.S. Army, in the person of Colonel Warner, is credited with blocking the all-out attack that the FBI and its allies had in mind.

Warner stayed on as an observer in case intervention later seemed desirable, and what he observed apparently filled him with impatience, not so much because the overwhelming military presence was unjustified (at one point he himself ordered up twelve rocket launchers, only to have the order countermanded in Washington) as because it was all so wasteful and inefficient in the hands of this damned civilian army. The knowledge that supervision of the Indians had been taken from the War Department in 1849 and turned over to the bureaucrats may have intensified the colonel's poor opinion of the whole operation, which he observed not only in the field but from his headquarters in the BIA building in Pine Ridge; in both places, the U.S. marshals, FBI agents, BIA police, and assorted goons were mostly getting in one another's way. "I can't imagine anyone at Wounded Knee who was more hated by the FBI, except possibly Russell and Dennis," Kenneth Tilsen says, "because Warner was the only one who really knew what he was doing, and he didn't mind putting in writing that he thought the whole thing was stupid as hell."

On March 12, Colonel Warner and his colleague Colonel Jack C. Potter, who was Chief of Logistics for the Sixth Army, submitted an attack plan to General Alexander Haig; though this plan was never acted upon and though—officially, at least—the Defense Department was not present, Warner stated later that "Army representatives soon began operating in a manner similar to a Military Assistance Advisory Group and with an equal vote in the decision-making process at Wounded Knee."[11]

⊡

According to an FBI report called "Disorder by American Indians and Supporters at Wounded Knee," "The identity of individuals reportedly in or en route to Wounded Knee includes not only Indians but representatives of such revolutionary-type organizations as the Vietnam Veterans Against the War, the Students for a Democratic Society, violence-prone Weatherman associates, the Marxist-Leninist-Maoist Venceremos Organization, as well as representatives from a black extremist group." For his part, Dick Wilson issued a proclamation to "Fellow Oglalas and Fellow Patriots," which read, in part:

> What has happened at Wounded Knee is all part of a long range plan of the Communist Party. . . . There is no doubt that Wounded Knee is a major Communist thrust. . . . And when the Fed. Gov. has yielded, conceded, appeased and just short of surrender, we will march into Wounded Knee and kill Tokas, wasicus, hasapas and spiolas ["outside Indians," whites, blacks, and Mexicans; the white people, mostly noncombatant, comprised perhaps 10 percent of an estimated population of three hundred]. They want to be martyrs? We will make it another Little Big Horn!! and any of their beatnik friends can be a stand-in for Yellow Hair [Custer].
>
> The supporters of AIM come in all shades and the National Council of Churches are very vocal because the Liberal Press and the T.V. News media is right at their elbow. No news reporter or t.v. camera man has ever won a war, but they can destroy a Nation by the propaganda of lies and hate that they broadcast for every Crackpot, Screwball, and Communist-front organization who wants to take a swat at our American way of life, take a blast at the U.S. Constitution, spit at the American Flag, burn it, wear it as a poncho, or hang it upside down.
>
> Since the American Indian Movement at Wounded Knee is supported by non-Indians, we are enlisting the help of non-Indian residents of the Pine Ridge Reservation. So come on in and sign up, so we can get this show on the road.[12]

Wilson's opinions were probably shared by most white South Dakotans, who felt that AIM had attracted not only outside agitators but "bad Indians"—the drunks, the rowdies, and the chronically unemployed, "the transient bums living off the struggle," as one AIM leader says—for whom putting on a red wind band and taking part in demonstrations was only an excuse for further idleness and even a justification of their existence. To a certain extent, this charge was true. Since AIM was not an organization but a movement, with no qualification for membership other than good will, it had been plagued from the start by Indians (and would-be Indians) whose behavior hurt its name; and some of its early supporters on Pine Ridge, having discovered that the Movement had no money, eventually went over to the goons.

On the morning of March 26, when Dick Wilson's roadblock was set up, the last phone line into Wounded Knee was cut and the last news team (NBC) was ordered to leave by federal officials; a few hours later, heavy fire descended on the village, and a U.S. marshal named Lloyd Grimm was seriously wounded. The Indians claim that Grimm was hit by wild fire from the goon roadblock set up behind the marshals, and the marshals themselves seemed to agree, despite the fact that five of the defenders were charged with the shooting, and no goon was arrested. Two days after this episode, a U.S. Department of the Interior negotiator acknowledged to Kenneth Tilsen, who was in Wounded Knee that day (he estimates that the village took twenty thousand rounds, or four times the number reported by the government), that an agreement had been made with Wilson to give his goons immunity from arrest when they broke the law. As Tilsen observed at the time, "The best analogy [to Pine Ridge] is South Viet Nam. There are a lot of similarities. Most obviously, there is a corrupt government of natives, who are set up, armed, supplied, financed, propagandized for, and maintained in power by the U.S. Government. Richard Wilson, whom the Government and the press repeatedly style the elected leader of the Pine Ridge Reservation people, plays a role like that of Thieu and Ky in South Viet Nam—ruling and repressing the people of Pine Ridge in the interest of a foreign power—and in the interest of personal gain."[13]

Existence in Wounded Knee was increasingly difficult, and toward the end of March, the Indians considered serious negotiations to end the siege. The federal forces, getting wind of these discussions, presented them to the public as a dispute between AIM and the Oglala leadership, but a joint statement by Banks, Means, and Pedro Bissonnette put an end to speculation that the "hostiles" were getting ready to surrender. Asked by the press why the Justice Department had reported a showdown confrontation between AIM and the Oglala leaders, Ted Means called it "the old divide-and-conquer tactic: they are trying to pit Indian against Indian." And in fact, it was crucial to the government to persuade the public that AIM did not represent the "good Indians" of America. Unquestionably, the FBI's racism and paranoia about "reds" had curdled the attitude of the Justice Department, the Interior Department, and the Senate Interior Committee, whose opinion, set forth in a joint position paper during the siege, was that "Indian militants comprise a 'revolutionary Indian element' involved in symbolic actions arising from attempts to redress the bloody Indian past. They are not representatives of the Indian population at large, are criminally oriented, and must be stopped by criminal prosecution before they create more havoc throughout America." "It's like the old days," said Russell Means, "except now they call us 'militants' instead of 'hostiles' or 'renegades.' "

Trying to sidestep AIM, the U.S. government opened negotiations at the end of March with the local Indians, who promptly demanded that the White House appoint a commission to review the Treaty of 1868. The representative of the Interior Department doubted that any such commission would have authority to renegotiate the treaty, since according to the Congressional Act of 1871, "No Indian nation or tribe within the territory of the United States shall be acknowledged or recognized as an independent nation, tribe, or power with whom the United States may contract by treaty." Loudly and angrily, Means reminded him that the Fort Laramie Treaty preceded that legislation and was therefore still valid:

> This is our last gasp as a sovereign people. And if we don't get these treaty rights recognized, as equal to the Constitution of the United States—as by law they are—then you might as well kill me, because I have no reason for living. And that's why I'm here in Wounded Knee, because nobody is recognizing the Indian people as human beings.
>
> They're laughing it off in *Time Magazine* and *Newsweek,* and the editors in New York and what have you. They're treating this as a silly matter, just as they've treated Indian people throughout his-

tory. We're tired of being treated that way. And we're not going to be treated like that any more.

You're going to have to kill us. Because I'm not going to die in some barroom brawl. I'm not going to die in a car wreck on some lonely road on the reservation because I've been drinking to escape the oppression of this goddamn society. I'm not going to die when I walk into Pine Ridge and Dickie's goons feel I should be offed. That's not the way I'm going to die. I'm going to die fighting for my treaty rights. Period. . . .

We haven't demanded any radical changes here, only that the United States Government live up to its own laws. It is precedent-setting that a group of "radicals," who in the minds of some are acting outside the law, are just in turn asking the law to live up to its own. We're not asking for any radical changes. We're just asking for the law to be equitably applied—to all.[14]

On April 5, an agreement was signed: a Wounded Knee delegation would submit itself to arrest, post bond, and go to Washington for discussions. Russell Means, Leonard Crow Dog, and Chief Tom Bad Cob went to Washington, only to learn that the government refused to negotiate with them until their companions back in Wounded Knee were disarmed. What follows is a segment of taped conversation that occurred on April 7 between Wayne Colburn, head of the U.S. Marshal Service, and Stan Holder, the head of Wounded Knee security:

COLBURN: We just want to neutralize and sanitize the area. The marshals will appear in their blue uniforms with a sidearm—no rifles or anything like that. This is strictly a business transaction.

HOLDER: When my people are disarmed in Wounded Knee, I feel that a simultaneous disarming of your people—

COLBURN: Now wait a minute! You don't want that to happen.

HOLDER: During the time that people are being processed, I feel that nobody in Wounded Knee should have a weapon.

COLBURN: I couldn't do that. I don't even think that we could even arbitrate that because I couldn't operate without the normal sidearm. You know what that is—just a police belt with a revolver.

"People are so anxious for the Indians to disarm!" Ellen Moves Camp commented, in ironic reference to "Wounded Knee I" (1890). And

Clyde Bellecourt told the U.S. marshals, "The people are pretty uptight about the fact that there would be marshals coming in with handguns and they would be totally unarmed. And they still envision what happened to Big Foot and his band in 1890, and they totally distrust the United States government at this point. And when they're told we're running low on food, they made the statement that they would eat horses, dogs, cats, mice, or dirt before they surrendered under those terms." That same day, April 7, a small pony was gunned down by automatic fire from the marshals. "The pony got up several times and tried to make a run," Gladys Bissonnette recalled, "and it was mowed down each time. I thought that was one of the saddest days, to see a dumb animal like that get riddled down."[15]

After April 8, negotiations broke down once again, and the "hostiles" resigned themselves to a long siege. On the evening of April 12, in one of the few celebrations in a grim period, a young Micmac woman named Anna Mae Pictou was married, in a traditional ceremony conducted by Wallace Black Elk, to an Ojibwa artist named Nogeeshik Aquash. On April 16 WKLDOC filed suits against the BIA (the Department of the Interior) and the FBI (the Department of Justice), declaring that "the United States Government has established a military siege of the village. It proposes to starve the people into submission by depriving them of food and necessities of life. . . . The use of Marshals, FBI agents, and others to perform a military function . . . is a usurpation of power which brings us frighteningly close to the creation of a police state." On April 17, a firefight erupted in which a Cherokee named Frank Clearwater was fatally wounded by a stray bullet. To appease the public, the FBI later issued a statement casting doubt on the authenticity of the victim, as if to imply that he deserved death more than most: "A check of military records revealed that Frank Clear was not an Indian but a white man, dishonorably discharged from the Army, who later fraudulently re-enlisted." Meanwhile, the blockade was tightened: to undermine morale, utilities and water were turned on and off (they could not be turned off entirely without depriving the rural area for miles around), and food and medicine were soon in short supply.

On April 20, when Crow Dog returned from the useless trip to Washington, the Independent Oglala Nation requested new talks with federal officials. The FBI, goons, and vigilantes were especially impatient to get in there and "clean out" the settlement, an aim in which they were fearlessly supported by the editor of the *National Review,* who used the word "supine" to describe the government's reluctance to commit what was bound to be a second massacre at Wounded Knee. Even Senator McGovern, who for many years had been one of the Indians' few champions in Congress, was crying out for their expulsion. "We cannot have one law for a handful of publicity-seeking militants and another law for ordinary citizens," said McGovern, fluttering in the wind.[16] Colonel Warner and others who understood that bloodshed involving women and children would invite public sympathy and even support for the Indian action, wished to avoid a military solution; on the other hand, simply to withdraw the huge paramilitary expedition would make the government look foolish. In preventing a "bloodbath" between the besieged Indians and the goons and vigilantes who surrounded them, the government found its excuse to stay on.

On April 26, a heavy exchange of fire continued from early in the morning until late afternoon; it seemed as if negotiations were all over. "I remember back on days when they had unarmed our ancestors, killed them and let them freeze to death; there was no mercy for children, there was no mercy for women. That's the very first thing that had come to my mind during that firefight," Gladys Bissonnette recalled. "I knew this had to be the last. I didn't care for myself because I knew what I was standing up for; I was standing up for justice for the Indian people. But I just couldn't bear to think of the small children who still have a life—a full life ahead of them." Toward 4:00 p.m., the firing diminished. "I had crawled into this little room with my boy and several others, Lou Bean and her husband, and this fellow called me over: Do you know Lamont? I said, Yes, he's my nephew. He said, Well, he's been killed."

Buddy Lamont, the brother of Lou Bean, had been struck down by a sniper's bullet. Later, his mother, Agnes Lamont, whose grandparents were with Crazy Horse at the Greasy Grass Creek, whose great-aunt and -uncle were among those slaughtered in the snow at Wounded Knee (her mother, aged twelve, was one of the few survivors), recalled how, at Calico Hall, the people asked AIM to stay until the finish, and she remembered the line of red lights on the winter roads as the caravan moved through Pine Ridge village, then headed east. The first day that the roadblock was open, her daughter Lou had joined the occupation at Wounded Knee ("Take care of my kids till we get back!"); her son Buddy, an idealistic Vietnam volunteer who had fought for his country so that his people at home "could sleep safely at night" (and amused his mother by sending her a portrait of John F. Kennedy all the way from Vietnam), had gone to Custer, then to Wounded Knee, because "Dickie Wilson is accusing me of being AIM, and I'm not, but I can't get a job, so I may as well join them." Like Stan Holder and other Vietnam veterans, he knew just how to construct good bunkers, which the Indians credit with saving many lives. By the time his mother tried to persuade him to come home, he was truly committed. "We are here for our civil rights, and our treaty rights. I won't be back until we win this game. Dickie Wilson is not going to get me out of here alive." Reflecting on this, his mother decided that Buddy must have known something would happen, because he also said, "If anything happens to me, just bury me at Wounded Knee; I don't want to be any trouble, so just bury me in my bunker." Instead, his body was removed to Pine Ridge for autopsy, and for a few days Dick Wilson refused permission to let it be returned to Wounded Knee. At the autopsy, when Lou Bean and Agnes Lamont demanded to know what sort of bullet could have made such a huge hole, the BIA pathologist, Dr. W. O. Brown, refused to tell them, saying cynically, "I'd have to change my story." Although the family wished to prepare the corpse for traditional ceremonies, it was turned over by the BIA to a coroner in Rushville, Nebraska, who would not release it until the Indians, dead broke, had scraped together $1,800.

This first Oglala death, for which Wilson was blamed, increased the high tension on the reservation, and the traditionals vowed to breach the roadblocks, if necessary, in order to attend Buddy Lamont's funeral at Wounded Knee. Eventually a traditional ceremony was permitted, and Lamont was buried near the common grave of Big Foot and his people on the small hill west of the road.

On May 4, a letter from Washington promised that four or five White House representatives would "meet with the headmen and chiefs of the Teton* Sioux during the third week in May for the purpose of examining the problems concerning the 1868 Treaty on the condition that the Indians lay down their arms"; on May 5, the defenders agreed to do so. By this time, the trading post had burned to the ground in an accidental fire, the dry grass in the old, rolling buffalo hills

* Another name for the western Dakota: "Teton" comes from *Titonwan,* or "Dwellers of the Plains."

had been crusted black by flares, electricity in the creek settlement had been cut off when a transformer was shattered by bullets, and the lack of good water and sanitation had added to the long winter's privations. The sated press had been drawn away by the scent of Watergate, the AIM leaders were mostly off on speaking tours, trying to raise money, and the American public seemed to have lost interest—all but those red-blooded local ranchers who were threatening commando raids and bomb-drops on the village if the government failed to clean out the goddam Commies by May 4. Even the Indians' liberal supporters were eager to end the whole long guilt-inducing business. But in the opinion of AIM leader Carter Camp, it was the sadness after Buddy Lamont's death that finally persuaded the tired Indians that the occupation of Wounded Knee had served its purpose.

On May 9, the few Indians still left in the settlement submitted themselves to arrest by the U.S. government; Crow Dog recalls that with Carter Camp he was taken in chains to Rapid City in a helicopter. "And the way they treated Black Elk was really pitiful, man," said one young Oklahoma Indian. "He got out of the car, and they grabbed him like they would grab some young dude and threw him up against the car. They took his headband away from him, they took his medicine bag, everything that he had on him they took away from him. And as far as I'm concerned, those people have made an enemy for the rest of their lives."[17]

For seventy-one days, a few hundred men, women, and children—supplied by volunteer airlifts and by sympathizers who slipped in and out during the night—had challenged a large paramilitary force abetted by hundreds of short-haired vigilantes, red and white, who were eager to wipe out the "longhair troublemakers." For Dick Wilson's men, the threat posed by the occupation of Wounded Knee was economic: under an Independent Oglala Nation, the Tribal Council and its dole would end. But the threat was also psychological: what fired their hatred, in some cases, was their sense of shame. For the baffled victims of "acculturation," no longer at home in the Indian world and not accepted in the white one, there was none of the exhilaration felt by those Oglala who had risked themselves in the cause of justice for their people. "This was one of the greatest things that ever happened in my life," said Gladys Bissonnette, who with Ellen Moves Camp and Lou Bean had remained at Wounded Knee from start to finish. "And although today is our last day here, I still feel like I'll always be here because this is part of my home. . . . I hope that the Indians, at least throughout the Pine Ridge Reservation, unite and stand up together, hold hands, and never forget Wounded Knee. We didn't have anything here, we didn't have nothing to eat. But we had one thing—that was unity and friendship amongst sixty-four different tribes. . . . I have never seen anything like this. . . . We were all happy together and it is kind of sad to see everyone leave."

> Of course, you can't go back to the old Indian way of life at this point. We have to deal with the mother earth in its present condition, which is pretty bad. . . .
>
> Wounded Knee was an educational process for all Indians. Right there you had Indians from Los Angeles and San Francisco, New York and Chicago, Minneapolis and Oklahoma City—big cities where Indians live and become urbanized. They went into Wounded Knee and met there Indians who had never been off the reservations, who live in the traditional way. . . . They were still one people, still one race, and they can be together again. The urban Indians found out what it was to be able to worship their mother earth the way they want. They'll go back to their cities but they'll always have that religion in their hearts. They'll look at the city streets and buildings and cars and they're going to hate it. They're really going to hate it. So they're going to go back home to their people more and more.[18]

On May 2, the Department of the Interior's negotiator had told the Indians, "I do have the authority to insure that the government of the United States, certainly the White House, and probably Congress, will discuss anything with your chiefs—anything and everything you want to discuss about the 1868 Treaty. I think there will be congressional hearings into the 1868 Treaty. I have authority to tell you that any and all criminal violations against you by any outsiders will be prosecuted. I do have the authority to tell you that members of the tribal government will be prosecuted."

On May 17, at a meeting at Chief Fools Crow's camp at Kyle, a White House "delegation" without standing or authority met with several hundred Indians gathered for the occasion; after empty discussions, it went back to Washington, saying that it would return in two weeks with some meaningful answers. On May 31, when the hundreds of Indians reconvened at Fools Crow's camp, no White House people bothered to show up; instead, the Indians were presented with a short evasive letter from the same Nixon aide who rejected the Twenty Points presented to the U.S. government on the Trail of Broken Treaties: "The days of treaty making with the American Indians ended in 1871, 102 years ago. . . . Only Congress can rescind or change in any way statutes enacted since 1871, such as the Indian Reorganization Act [1934]." In the same spirit, Senator McGovern, who owns a vacation place in the Black Hills, said he thought it was "ridiculous to talk about the Treaty of 1868 being carried out."

"The treaty law of 1868 . . . stands firm, like the Black Hills," said Frank Kills Enemy, now in his eighties. "This law cannot be moved, like the Black Hills."

The 1868 Treaty was never seriously discussed, nor was corruption in the BIA investigated: hearings held in June by the Senate Subcommittee on Indian Affairs accomplished nothing. Despite open violations of the law, committed sometimes in the presence of FBI agents and U.S. marshals, neither Richard Wilson nor his goons were ever prosecuted. Instead, more than five hundred traditional people were indicted by the FBI in connection with Wounded Knee, and one hundred eighty-five were subsequently indicted by federal grand juries on charges of arson, theft, assault, and "interfering with federal officers." Wounded Knee II, which had already cost the nation $7 million, was at an end.[19]

CHAPTER 4
THE WOUNDED KNEE TRIALS
January–September 1974

The next morning the officer told Big Foot that they wanted all his guns. He was our chief and we looked to him to say something but he was coughing all the time. Finally he said you men better give him your guns, we are not on this trip to do any fighting. . . . I looked over and saw an officer on a sorrel horse. . . . I heard him give a command and right after the command it sounded like a lightning crash. . . . When I became conscious I was lying down. As I rose and started to go I became unconscious again. . . .

I have my old cloak and it has nine bullet holes in it. I am shot all through the body and I may die anytime. . . . I was bleeding through my nose and mouth. I want my good friends to tell the good white people what they did to us here at Wounded Knee. . . . We know that some white people are good friends of the Indians, but most of them do not like us. . . . We don't have hate in our hearts for the white people, but the soldiers tried to murder us and we want the Government to find out the truth.

Afraid of the Enemy (*Lakota*)

This Massacre is absolutely a grave injustice and [the most] disgraceful, cowardly and treacherous killing ever staged by the United States Army. Then the white people say the Indians are treacherous, but we are not, we love our families and we do not bother the white people, but they came here, killed us—women and children, we have the wounds to prove what they done.

James High Hawk (*Lakota*)

Dennis Banks and Russell Means, whose national celebrity began on the Trail of Broken Treaties and increased during the occupation of Wounded Knee, were perceived by outsiders as a team; in fact, they were different in age as well as temperament, and rarely worked together. At Wounded Knee, which was "Russ's show," since Means, as an Oglala, was AIM spokesman, an incipient rivalry was increased by differences of opinion not only about the future course of AIM but about how the leadership should conduct itself.

At AIM's national convention at White Oak, Oklahoma, from July 25 to August 5, 1973, Banks was elected national director, with Carter Camp and John Trudell as co-chairmen and the Navajo leader Larry Anderson as national treasurer. "Russ ran for office, but nobody voted him in," one AIM warrior recalls. "Nobody took him serious then, I guess. Russ had his groupies, and his little groupie chapters, but it was all Saturday-night warriors and raising hell."

At White Oak, AIM pledged to continue its campaign to repeal the Indian Reorganization Act of 1934 and dismantle not only the whole system of government-sponsored tribal councils but the Bureau of Indian Affairs itself, so that, as Banks said, "Indian people might have something to say about their lives and their destiny." AIM also endorsed the nationwide boycott of Safeway Stores by Cesar Chavez's United Farm Workers Union, and made an alliance with Mexican-American activists in the Southwest, where Indian and Chicano problems with Anglos were often the same.

Despite the seeming unity at White Oak, the leadership could not agree on how to deal with the threat of U.S. government repression. For some, armed guerrilla warfare seemed the only solution, whereas others felt that such a course was doomed: Clyde Bellecourt, for one, had always been opposed to violence, and although he repeatedly exposed himself to police beatings in Minneapolis, he had not carried a weapon at Wounded Knee. Dennis Banks, supported by Carter Camp and Herb Powless, felt strongly that the Movement needed more discipline. "At Wounded Knee, there was absolutely no drinking, but after that it was all drugs and alcohol, which weren't so much an obstacle to taking action as an impediment to an effective organization, and also something that compromised our public positions. Not that I wanted a fanatic policy, but here was a young Indian organization moving to national prominence, and people were watching us, our own people especially. I quit drinking myself in 1969, after I found myself passed out in my own car; I didn't want young Indians seeing their leaders in that kind of shape."

Means, Crow Dog, and their followers drank hard and were involved in one fracas after another. "Russ always had a low tolerance for alcohol," one Indian says. "He just didn't handle it well, that's all there was to it." Also, they were accused of arrogance and racism, not only against whites but against anyone who was not Lakota. "The trouble started way back at Leech Lake," Leonard Peltier says, "and it continued on the Trail of Broken Treaties. In Washington there was a lot of disagreement on how to deal with the Nixon administration; things got so frustrating that finally everyone was for burning down the goddam building.[1] Vern Bellecourt gave a great speech against this, explaining why we shouldn't, and Carter Camp asked him who the hell he thought he was, trying to give us orders. I guess that bad feeling continued right through Wounded Knee. Later, some of the Means people said that Carter was working with the feds, but I never believed it."

Not long after the White Oak convention, a huge sun dance was held at "Crow Dog's Paradise" on the Rosebud Reservation. For most of the AIM leadership, this sun dance was the first real experience of spiritual training, and Peltier was among those pierced for the first time. "After just four days and four nights," he recalls with gratitude, "I felt great for weeks after . . . a feeling as if my body had been thoroughly cleansed inside and out." He also remembers how the old medicine man John Fire Lame Deer walked among the dancers, touching each with a red-and-white eagle feather.

One evening in this period, Carter Camp's younger brother Craig beat up a friend of Russ Means and Clyde Bellecourt. The two leaders heaped public abuse on Craig, and he brought his older brother back to the house to settle the score. Although Carter Camp had quarreled openly with Means at Wounded Knee and was—according to one account—"out gunning for him," it was Clyde Bellecourt who opened the door and who, after an argument, was shot in the stomach. ("Carter was very eloquent," Banks remarks without irony, "but he wasn't ready for leadership.") In another version of the event, Craig Camp had been beaten up by Bellecourt after calling the leader a coward because he had not carried a gun at Wounded Knee. In a third version, rumors of FBI informers among the leadership had caused a showdown: according to Russell Means, who witnessed the shooting, "Federal officials were paying off some of the AIM leadership to turn on other leaders. Clyde thought Camp was being paid off."[2] Bellecourt (who believes that his life was saved by John Fire Lame Deer's doctoring during the emergency operation) refused to testify against Camp in a white man's court, but the dispute continued when Means and Banks went on trial a few months later. The outraged Means threatened to resign from AIM in protest when Camp was invited to the trial in a show of unity; he says he was dissuaded from this gesture by Leonard Crow Dog. (Crow Dog himself came into disfavor by permitting Camp to participate in a sun dance the next year. "I remember just who hung in there to the end of Wounded Knee," Crow Dog has said. "Camp was flown out of there in chains, along with me, so I'm not going to tell him he can't sundance."[3])

Despite the frequent charge of the John Birch Society and other right-wing aggregations that AIM was composed of hate-filled ex-convicts with a taste for violence ("the violence-prone AIM," as the FBI would call it), most of the trouble in AIM's brief history was instigated by its enemies, or derived from isolated episodes that had little to do with the history of the Movement. Nevertheless, the Bellecourt shooting worsened AIM's reputation as a violent and irresponsible organization, and anti-AIM prejudice was so intense that Dennis Banks, indicted in September 1973 on additional charges having to do with the Custer courthouse riot, concluded that he had no chance for a fair hearing; a few days later, Banks fled to Canada with Ron Petite of Iowa AIM, accompanied by Petite's wife and a young niece of Buddy Lamont named Kamook Nichols. "We went to Rae Lakes, north of Yellowknife, way up on the Arctic Circle, and we stayed there until Indian friends in Yellowknife got word to us that money for my bond had been secured. That was my plan: to leave the United States and not to surrender until I was sure that money was available, so that I would spend the minimum amount of time in jail. After maybe three weeks or so, word came that the bond money was secured, and we went back to Yellowknife. Our California supporters wanted to fly us back south to Los Angeles, but I figured I'd be busted there by Immigration, so I called Doug Durham, who had a plane up there within twenty-four hours. He flew us in over the Montana line, staying real low over the trees, and from there he went straight in to Rapid City."

Douglass Durham, big and dark-haired, "one-fourth Chippewa," had entered Wounded Knee in March with press credentials from a left-wing Des Moines newspaper called *Pax Today,* and had returned to

South Dakota for Crow Dog's sun dance as a vice-chairman of Des Moines AIM.

⊡

In the preparations for the numerous Wounded Knee trials, the female elders—the "brave-hearted women" of Oglala tradition who had restored the fighting spirit of their men—had been mostly ignored by the Justice Department, which realized that the women might not pass in court for dangerous terrorists. Pedro Bissonnette was the only indicted leader more identified with the Independent Oglala Nation than with AIM, which was unquestionably the true target of the trials. Originally, the leaders of the Wounded Knee "conspiracy"—Banks, Means, Bellecourt, Camp, Crow Dog, Holder, and Bissonnette—were indicted together. Then Means and Banks were separated from the others and burdened with $135,000 bail each, apparently to give as much publicity as possible to their alleged crimes. After hearings based on surveys showing that these two defendants could not receive a fair trial in South Dakota, their case was transferred by Judge Frederick Nichol to St. Paul, Minnesota, where it opened on January 8, 1974.

Long before it began, the Banks-Means trial was perceived as a symbolic confrontation between AIM and the U.S. government, but it was mostly non-AIM Indians who came into the Twin Cities from all over the country in a huge demonstration of support; among them were sixty-five Oglala leaders (including a few ancient survivors of the Wounded Knee massacre) whose spokesman was Frank Fools Crow. "We called our brothers and AIM to help us because we were being oppressed and terrorized," the old man said. "They answered our call. . . . If Dennis Banks and Russell Means go to jail for supporting the dignity of the Sioux Nation . . . you must be ready to send us all to jail."[4] The visitors were supported in their turn by small contributions of money and food made by thousands of other Indians too old or young or poor or sick to travel. These efforts were coordinated by an AIM national office opened in St. Paul by Dennis Banks and Douglass Durham, who was serving Banks as an organizer and administrator as well as a pilot; Durham was also a cameraman, self-trained, he said, in psychology and clandestine tactics, and he was now very close to Banks. As AIM's first national director of security—a job created for him at Banks's suggestion—Durham was coordinator of the Defense Committee office in St. Paul throughout the trial.

From the beginning, the Wounded Knee defense, based on the 1868 Treaty, sought to present Banks and Means as "political prisoners"; the prosecution, dismissing past wrongs as irrelevant to this case, portrayed the two leaders as common criminals who had invaded, terrorized, and looted a helpless community. "You should expect to pay for civil disobedience," said the prosecutor, Assistant U.S. Attorney (for South Dakota) R. D. Hurd. "We cannot permit individuals to set up their own law. . . . They put a gun to the head of the U.S. and said, Come talk to us."[5]

The prosecution evidence, which consumed six of the trial's eight and a half months, commenced with the testimony of a white rancher named William Leavitt, a member of the John Birch Society and the proud owner of thirty guns, who with the encouragement of the BIA was leasing his land from Pine Ridge people at between one and ten dollars an acre; although he had not been present in the village, Leavitt described the looting of the trading post and houses at Wounded Knee. An Indian boy named Alexander Richards testified that Russell Means had carried a gun while at Wounded Knee; this testimony turned out to be perjured, and was stricken from the record. A parade of further witnesses, red and white, declared that Means had threatened the "hostages" and encouraged stealing; that Pedro Bissonnette had given the money from a trading-post safe to Means and Banks; that Means had suggested that Senator McGovern be taken hostage at the time of his visit; that Means had fired an M-1 at an armored personnel carrier—in short, that Banks and Means were lawless, dangerous renegades who would kill God-fearing white Americans as quick as look at them.

Federal Judge Frederick Nichol (himself a former U.S. Attorney for South Dakota) seemed sympathetic to the government when the trial began, and engaged in sharp altercations with three of the defense attorneys. One of the three was Kenneth Tilsen, who was in charge of the nuts and bolts of the defense; the other two were William Kunstler, representing Means, and Mark Lane, representing Banks. (Banks, who became good friends with his attorney, recognized that Lane was "a great investigator, but he's too conspiracist; he's always trying to hook pieces of evidence together whether they fit or not.") From the very beginning, Kunstler and Lane competed for the attention of the press by causing disruptions, even shouting at the judge. On one occasion, threatened with jailing for contempt of court, Kunstler "started doing his thing," Tilsen recalls. "He all but threw himself into the arms of the

U.S. marshals, smiting his brow and crying, Take me! Take me! Well, Lane couldn't let him get away with that, he couldn't let Bill get busted and not *him,* so he went running over there yelling, Take me, too! The whole thing would have been comic if it hadn't been so childish." Tilsen became so fed up with the opportunistic Lane that by the end of the trial they weren't speaking, but he and Kunstler are still friends. "Bill Kunstler is a good lawyer," Tilsen says.

Rather early in the trial, Judge Nichol expressed irritation at the stalling and lack of cooperation from the government attorneys in obeying his discovery orders pertaining to supplying prosecution evidence to the defense. Also, there were increasing discrepancies in the prosecution's testimony. FBI Regional Director Joseph Trimbach (the man who had recommended to Colonel Volney Warner that he call in the Eighty-second Airborne at Wounded Knee) denied that he had ever applied to a court for wiretaps on the Wounded Knee telephone, despite the presence of his signature on the applications. "I don't know if that's my signature," Trimbach said. Amazed by this casual attitude, Judge Nichol mentioned greeting cards he had received over the years from Trimbach's predecessor in Minneapolis, Richard G. Held. "I am cut to the quick to realize," Nichol snapped, "that I may never have had a birthday card from Mr. Held at all." Suspecting that the FBI was withholding evidence, Nichol ordered the Bureau to produce its files, only to discover that this obsessed bureaucracy had 315,000 separate file classifications on the occupation of Wounded Knee, some of them hundreds of pages long. "If this government falls," Nichol observed, "it won't be because of subversion. It will topple under the weight of its own paperwork."

As the trial continued, the judge was less and less amused by the performance of the FBI, and he did not hesitate to express his disapproval in court. "If that's the kind of arrogance that's going to exist down there in that Minneapolis office of the FBI," he said on May 1, "I can . . . dismiss this case entirely on the ground of governmental misconduct, which apparently appears to be deliberate." Not long afterward, he was accused by prosecutor Hurd of "a hostile attitude toward the Federal Bureau of Investigation." Nichol pointed out that he had worked with and respected the FBI when he himself was U.S. Attorney for South Dakota, but that it seemed to have "deteriorated," due in part to its manipulation by Richard Nixon. Cooling off a little from this latest of what he himself called his "explosions," Judge Nichol told Hurd (who had made mention of their friendship), "I would still hope I could regard you as a friend, just as I regard Mr. Kunstler, Mr. Lane, Mr. Tilsen, Mr. Hall [Douglas Hall, a respected attorney for Banks], Mr. Means, and Mr. Banks as friends of mine."

Early in the trial, Judge Nichol had apologized to Means and Banks for the 1890 massacre at Wounded Knee, and his seeming wish to be friendly with the defendants did not surprise Kenneth Tilsen. "Nichol was trying hard to be fair and just. He had some understanding of Indians, and some guilt, but his understanding was cerebral and sometimes his guilt got in the way. Russ appeared to be unforgiving and ungrateful for rulings in his favor; he took them as his right, and to many this appeared as arrogance. Nichol would have liked him to say 'thank you' just once; instead, Russ referred to him after the trial as a 'racist.' It was a very complex relationship between two complex people. Means understood that Nichol was a liberal who had set him and others free, yet he did not want Nichol to think that now he had atoned for centuries of crimes against the Indian people, that now he could relax; in Russ's eyes, he had miles to go before he crossed the river." Recounting this, Tilsen grins. "Russ is really something. . . . There's hardly anything he hasn't tried! Russell and Dennis and Clyde aren't leaders by accident; they are tremendously powerful people, intellectually and in person—they had to be in order to survive." Tilsen, who is bright and tough, makes no secret of his admiration for these same qualities in the AIM leaders. "It's not surprising that Russ had Nichol's number. Russ has a *lot* of people's number, so this is nothing against the judge. Nichol had a strong sense of right and wrong and a strong desire to get at the truth, and he almost always made the right decision. I liked him; he's a very decent man."

Dennis Banks agrees. "Judge Nichol was very sensitive, very careful, very conservative. But he hated Nixon and everything he stood for, including his manipulation of the FBI, and he tried to be fair even though he was nervous about damaging his career."

⊡

In July 1974, after six months, the prosecution rested its case; the defense was finished in eight days in court. Among its witnesses were the authors Vine Deloria, Jr., and Dee Brown, who helped to establish some of the religious and historical background to the occupation of Wounded Knee. In regard to the recurrent charge that AIM people were outsiders, "city Indians" who knew nothing about the religious traditions of their people, Deloria, a Standing Rock Sioux, said that an Indian's religious heritage depended more on who his grandparents had been than on whether or not he was raised on the reservation. Brown, whose book *Bury My Heart at Wounded Knee,* a best-seller in 1971, was apparently one reason why "key extremists" of the Trail of Broken Treaties were not prosecuted—or not, at least, in the courts of the "bleeding-heart East"—decried the redskin stereotypes in American history books, which portrayed most Indians as cruel, treacherous, and untruthful, with a taste for killing—in short, an excellent description of the Indian experience of the whiteskins.

Next, the defense called Gladys Bissonnette, who explained the desperation of the Oglala traditionals that led them to protest at Wounded Knee. "The goons were allowed to carry high-powered rifles," she exclaimed at one point. "It's *nothing* to kill an Indian on our reservation!" Mrs. Bissonnette also explained how Wallace Black Elk or Leonard Crow Dog had held a prayer ceremony with the sacred pipe before every meeting. "The Indians are guided by the Great Spirit and our sacred pipe, so we look into whatever we think is right; we walk right in with open minds. We do not intend to break any laws. We do not intend to commit any crimes. If there's a crime against looking for justice, where do we go to find justice here in America?"

Assistant U.S. Attorney Hurd, an articulate and persuasive man with a high, boyish voice, attired in loud checks and bright trousers, did his best to discredit this eloquent old lady.

> Q: There's been a liquor problem on the reservation for many years, hasn't there?
> A: Oh yes. That's the way the white man brought us up.
> Q: And you have had some first-hand experience of that yourself, haven't you?
> A: Oh yes.
> Q: And you have drunk on the reservation, haven't you?
> A: Oh yes.
> Q: And you have had possession of liquor on the reservation?
> A: Oh yes.

Hurd was unable to shake the composure of the witness, who told the court, "While we were in Wounded Knee, we were being shot at constantly . . . but that is where we had freedom, that is where the Indians can go around . . . without anybody telling them what to do. . . . We were tired of running."

On August 16, when the defense rested, the government introduced a last-minute "surprise" witness who, in Tilsen's words, "filled in every gap in the prosecution's case, directly connecting the defendants with the alleged offenses—it was amazing!" In addition, this witness offered testimony in support of the FBI's cherished belief that the international Communist conspiracy was somehow behind AIM; he declared that agents from Russia, China, and Czechoslovakia had attended the first meeting of the AIM-sponsored International Indian Treaty Council in June 1974, at Mobridge, on the Standing Rock Reservation, where an estimated thirty-six hundred people from ninety-seven Indian nations had agreed that Indian self-government was the only hope.

As it turned out, this useful witness had been located by an FBI agent named David Price, who was already well known to the Defense Committee. In March 1973, Special Agent Price had arrived in Rapid City, where he moved in next to the Defense Committee headquarters; he later became a neighbor in Sioux Falls (the original site of the Banks-Means trial). In both places, SA Price had kept the Indians' lawyers and legal aides under open and even aggressive surveillance. "He even photographed our cats and dogs," one aide remembers, "and he took real glee in it; you can't be around Price very long before picking up that he goes far beyond the requirements of his job. He's an all-American boy, slim and trim, with freckles and an angelic nose, and reddish-blond hair combed over his bald spot. But there's a lot of aggression there, there's something *mean;* he's a very complex man. Price can be very friendly when he feels like it, and he can also look you in the face and lie—and know you know he's lying—and *still* not show a damned thing in his eyes."

David Price's surprise witness was former AIM member Louis Moves Camp, twenty-two, who earlier that year had co-authored a letter to the Rapid City *Journal* in support of Russell Means's campaign for Dick Wilson's job ("We urge the Oglala people to vote for Russ Means, and we return to the dream of Black Elk and the tribal ways"), and who had come to St. Paul as part of the AIM support group. On July 4, Moves Camp resigned from the Movement after returning to the AIM house to find his belongings out on the sidewalk; the expulsion, ordered by Dennis Banks, would have happened sooner had he not been the son of a respected elder, Ellen Moves Camp, since he had repeatedly broken the AIM house rules in regard to drugs, drinking, and creating disturbances. He had never been entrusted with responsibilities ("Louie wasn't even asked to pick people up at the airport"), and he felt bitter and ignored. Besides, he was awaiting trial for robbery, assault with a deadly weapon (two counts), and assault causing bodily injury (two counts); faced with a possible jail sentence of twenty years, he may have decided that a constructive relationship with the Federal Bureau of Investigation could not do a willing young man one bit of harm.

In cross-examination, it developed that SA Price and his young partner, SA Ronald Williams, had met daily with the witness between August 5 and August 10—at least one of these meetings took place at Ellsworth Air Force Base, the huge nuclear-weapons depot outside Rapid City—and that on August 9 the witness had provided three signed affidavits that were subsequently turned over to prosecutor Hurd. Hurd himself met with the witness three times before putting him on the stand, and apparently he had some doubts as to his truthfulness, since he requested a lie detector test that Regional Director Trimbach refused; Hurd could have insisted on the test but for one reason or another did not do so.

Almost immediately, the defense established that Price's witness had left Wounded Knee for the last time about March 11 and that he was actually in California at the time of most of the events he had described. Judge Nichol expressed astonishment that the FBI, which had been "developing" this witness for six weeks, had not verified a story that the defense shot to pieces almost overnight.

In the days before his appearance on the witness stand, Moves Camp had accompanied his new friends Dave and Ron from South Dakota to Minneapolis, where they had found lodgings at the Dyckman Hotel; Price and Moves Camp occupied adjoining rooms, with Williams in the Senatorial Suite across the hall. On August 13, these three fellows repaired to the J+R Dude Ranch, across the border in Wisconsin, where Moves Camp had his first meeting with prosecutor Hurd.

SA Ronald Williams acknowledged "drinking heavily" with Louie on at least two occasions. The occasion in question was the evening of August 14, when the three men went bar-hopping in River Falls, Wisconsin, about twenty miles from the ranch, in the course of which, by Williams's estimate, he himself consumed nine Scotch-and-waters; Price, he said, had been content with four or five. Not surprisingly,

"Mr. Price and I were ready to go back and retire for the evening" when the 1:00 a.m. bar curfew came around. By now, however, Louie had struck up a friendship with a young white woman—eighteen or nineteen years old, Williams estimated. "Mr. Moves Camp indicated to us that he wanted to accompany us back to the room and that the girl was going to join us, and I advised Mr. Moves Camp that that type of an arrangement was not possible."

As Williams repeatedly pointed out, Moves Camp was not in the custody of the agents; they were there "at his pleasure" to protect him. Since Louie and the girl felt no need of their services, the agents retired for the evening, leaving their drinking companion with the young woman and another couple. At eight in the morning, the telephone rang in Williams's room back at the ranch; it was Louis Moves Camp, asking Ron to pick him up at a River Falls café, where he was eating his breakfast.

> Q: Did you get dressed and go down and pick up Louie Moves Camp immediately?
> A: No, I didn't.
> Q: What did you do?
> A: I went back to sleep. If you've eaten with Louie, you'd understand that.
> Q: It takes Louie a long time to eat breakfast, generally?
> A: He usually eats two breakfasts.
> Q: And did you leave a wake-up call at the J+R Ranch?
> A: No, I didn't.
> Q: Did you have a little bit of a hang-over from the night before?
> A: No, I didn't.
> Q: But eventually you did get up again. . . .
> A: Yes, I did.
> Q: And what caused that?
> A: Mr. Price summoned me . . . to the door of the room I was staying in.

As it turned out, Price was distressed because Louie had gotten himself into some sort of trouble. He was, in fact, now in the custody of the River Falls police, who had interrupted his first or second breakfast to take him in for questioning, at which time he had revealed the names of his influential fellow dudes out at the ranch. The agents hurried down to River Falls, where Louie related his adventures. In the gingerly sex-handbook language peculiar to law-enforcement officers on the witness stand, Ron Williams described these as follows:

> Mr. Moves Camp advised me that he had gone to a place with a girl . . . and in the presence of two other individuals . . . I believe he said on the floor, he had sex activity with the girl which . . . because of the fact he had been drinking, he had been unable to achieve an erection; and because of that, she engaged in—she engaged in oral copulation with him, and eventually he was able to achieve an erection, and he initially set out to have what I would consider normal sexual intercourse with her, but she indicated . . . that she preferred to have anal intercourse, which he declined to do, and he subsequently requested her to again participate in oral copulation until he achieved ejaculation.

Williams went on to report that Price had seemed rather subdued after Louie's account. "Knowing Mr. Price as I do," Williams told the court, "I know that that type of conversation, those kind of details, he might ignore, because that type of thing does repulse him." (Actually, Price acknowledged on the stand that he had teased Moves Camp about his impotence.) Mark Lane, never a man to be outdone, advised the court that he was repulsed, too.

The River Falls police detained Moves Camp for further questioning, and the agents returned to the J+R Ranch; shortly thereafter, Price received a phone call. To quote Ron Williams, "He indicated it was from some type of law-enforcement-related person, but he did not specify the individual. As I recall it . . . he had been advised that a female had made an oral allegation . . . that Mr. Moves Camp had raped her." At this news, Price returned immediately to River Falls, leaving Williams back at the ranch; he telephoned in midafternoon to notify his partner that no rape complaint was going to be filed after all, and that he was on his way home with good old Louie. With Louie's whereabouts exposed, however, it seemed like a good idea to leave the J+R Ranch, since "hostile persons might find out where we were. So we located another domicile, a place for us to reside."

Curiously, despite the importance of their witness, Price and Williams failed to prepare a field report, or F.D. "302," on all of these exciting events, a standard procedure for agents when on duty. In cross-examination, the defense established that before the rape charge against Moves Camp was dropped, Price had conferred for several hours with a state prosecutor as well as with the River Falls police, and had made it clear to his fellow lawmen that Moves Camp was a crucial witness for the prosecution in the Means-Banks trial; it also turned out that prosecutor Hurd had known of the rape charge before putting Moves Camp on the stand, but that he had chosen to accept Price's reasoning that because the charge had been withdrawn, rape had not occurred. In fact, Hurd declared that he saw no reason to believe that what had happened "wasn't a consensual act between two adults. I have seen no evidence yet that there was any rape. . . . I don't think this affects his believability."[6]

After the trial—despite the vivid account of his experience as related by Williams—Moves Camp denied any memory of the young woman. The agents had gotten him drunk, he said, and when he woke up in the morning, Price and Williams, apprising him of the alleged rape, had offered to help him avoid prosecution on this charge in exchange for his testimony against Means and Banks, which he had been thinking that he might withdraw. Kenneth Tilsen, who interviewed the girl, says this is nonsense. "That girl was raped," he declares firmly, "and all those sexual details were probably made up by the agents to discredit her. She was so stunned and outraged by what had happened that she wanted to sue everyone involved in dropping the charges, not only the FBI but the local police and her own parents. And I can't ignore the fact that within the year Moves Camp was convicted and jailed on another rape charge, though you couldn't link the two cases in a court of law."

Ronald Williams, who did not accompany David Price on his consultations with the local authorities in River Falls, cannot be implicated in the alleged cover-up of the disputed rape. It is even possible that he thought Moves Camp's testimony was true. "I never knew Williams," Tilsen says, "but on the stand, he seemed pretty young and innocent, kind of an 'apple-pie' look, and I got the impression he just went along with anything Price said. Price was the senior partner, and we know him pretty well." (Dennis Banks remembers neither man. "All FBI agents strike me the same," he says. "They look like amateurs, and they look like killers.")

⊡

Ellen Moves Camp, who had gone back to Pine Ridge after the first weeks of the trial, got word while on the reservation that her son Louis was "on the stand lying," and she returned to St. Paul before his testimony had ended. "That isn't Louie Moves Camp on that stand!" she cried out, heartbroken. "You can tell by the looks of him, and the spirit he's got on his face! *That* isn't Louie Moves Camp! I think they're keeping him from me! I'll just tell him, quit his damn lying, that's what I'll tell him! He's lying about everything! Every statement that he signed is a lie! He's lying! Everything he said is a lie!"[7] At one point, she became so upset that she actually jumped up from her seat and ran down the courtroom aisle crying, "Louie, why are you lying? You weren't even there!" ("At first the judge thought I had put her up to it," Tilsen says. "He was going to jail me for contempt.") Called to the witness stand, Mrs. Moves Camp said that her son had left Wounded Knee about March 12: "Louie never stayed at Wounded Knee. Even while he was there, he was in and out." She flatly denied his account of an AIM meeting attended by delegates from behind the Iron Curtain. Asked by the defense how it felt to contradict her own son's testimony, Ellen Moves Camp said, "I feel that Louie has done something very wrong by lying, and I feel that I cannot turn against my brothers and my Indian people. I have to tell the truth."

More serious than Louis Moves Camp's lies was the all but inescapable conclusion that Agent Price and perhaps Agent Williams had knowingly prepared this man to give false testimony; at the very least, they found his story so convenient that they had not bothered to find out if it was true. More serious still was the likelihood that Assistant U.S. Attorney Hurd had also been aware that Moves Camp's testimony might be false even before he put him on the stand. Judge Nichol later concluded that Hurd did not have foreknowledge, but the whole lurid episode, which turned out to be the climax of the trial, was a fatal discredit to the prosecution.

In July, when the government had first rested its case, Judge Nichol had dismissed the burglary, arson, illegal weapons (Molotov cocktails), and theft charges—there was simply no proof to sustain them—and subsequently he dismissed two counts of "interfering or obstructing federal law enforcement officers during a civil disorder" because the government could not show that the presence of these officers was lawful in the first place. (In reference to the "unlawful military involvement at Wounded Knee," the judge commented, "We don't want the military running the civil affairs in this country, or having anything to do with the execution of the laws.") Eventually the case went to the jury on the four remaining counts of larceny, conspiracy, and two separate assaults. A not-guilty verdict on the conspiracy count had already been signed when on September 17 a member of the jury became ill. The prosecution refused to risk the verdict of the eleven remaining jurors on the other counts, and rather than declare a mistrial, Judge Nichol dismissed the remaining charges, criticizing Hurd for being "more interested in convictions than in justice."

Although he chastised prosecutor Hurd for well over an hour ("The U.S. Attorney may strike hard blows, but he is not at liberty to strike foul ones"), Nichol spoke with particular severity of the FBI. "It's hard for me to believe," he would remark, "that the FBI, which I have revered for so long, has stooped so low."

> I am forced to conclude that the prosecution acted in bad faith at various times throughout the course of the trial and was seeking convictions at the expense of justice. . . . In deciding this motion I have taken into consideration the prosecution's conduct throughout the entire trial. The fact that incidents of misconduct formed a pattern throughout the course of the trial leads me to the belief that this case was not prosecuted in good faith or in the spirit of justice. The waters of justice have been polluted, and dismissal, I believe, is the appropriate cure for the pollution in this case.[8]

The Banks-Means acquittal—contested unsuccessfully by the Justice Department, which criticized Nichol and asked for a new trial—pointed up not only the political aspect of the Wounded Knee indictments but extensive FBI manipulation, which would make it difficult to secure convictions in the "nonleadership" cases. Remarkably, seven of the jurors (and several alternates) campaigned after the trial for the cancellation of all cases that were still pending, and the U.S. attorneys, well aware of their weak position, offered at one point to dismiss one hundred thirteen of them if the defendants would plead nolo contendere in just five. This plan was sabotaged by the FBI, which was interested in harassing AIM, and in the end, although most of the cases that went to court were tried in the anti-AIM atmosphere of South Dakota, only a few minor convictions were obtained, at the cost of additional millions of the taxpayers' money.[9] In Iowa and Nebraska, almost all defendants whose cases weren't dismissed were soon acquitted; in one eight-day period in early March 1975, Judge Warren Urbom dismissed thirty-two cases before trial, noting, however, that despite the "ugly history" and the "treaties pocked by duplicity" that characterized U.S. relations with the Indian nations, Lakota claims to sovereignty (which would have invalidated U.S. jurisdiction over the defendants) were "squarely in opposition" to law and Supreme Court rulings, as developed in "an unbroken line."[10]

In the remaining "leadership" cases, the charges against Leonard Crow Dog, Carter Camp, and Stan Holder were reduced from the original eleven counts to three. They were tried eventually, in June 1975, in Cedar Rapids, Iowa, and once again the prosecutor was R. D. Hurd; this time, Hurd won his convictions. Defendants Camp and Holder failed to show up for sentencing despite the opinion of Kenneth Tilsen, their attorney, that nobody would actually be sent to jail; both later served brief sentences for having fled. Crow Dog, released on probation, was to become the only one of the leaders brought to trial who ever spent a day in prison on charges directly related to Wounded Knee; he eventually served a few months of his sentence after his probation was revoked in a separate case.

The evidence against Clyde Bellecourt was so paltry that, as in the case of the twelve indictments filed against him after the Trail of Broken Treaties, the charges were finally dismissed. (Bellecourt, who had turned up in Cedar Rapids for a pre-trial rally—he felt that Indians should stick together in the struggle, whatever his private feelings about Camp—was now devoting himself almost entirely to the survival schools in St. Paul and Minneapolis, and encouraging the spread of the survival-school idea to other states.)

Pedro Bissonnette never went to trial, either. Arrested in Rapid City on April 27, 1973, the Oglala leader had been jailed on charges of "interfering with a federal officer"; he was offered probation on a previous offense in return for helpful testimony about Wounded Knee and was threatened with a ninety-year sentence when he refused. "I will stand with my brothers and sisters. I will tell the truth about them and about why we went to Wounded Knee. I will fight for my people. I will live for them, and if it is necessary to stop the terrible things that happen to Indians on the Pine Ridge Reservation, I am ready to die for them. . . . I will never lie against my people, crawl for a better deal for myself. I stand with Russell Means, Gladys Bissonnette, Ellen Moves Camp, Clyde Bellecourt."[11]

Due to evidence of gross government misconduct, Bissonnette was set free; he returned to Pine Ridge before the Banks-Means trial. Because he knew every last detail about the Wilson regime and its dealings with the U.S. government, he would have been a crucial witness for the defense. He never testified. Dick Wilson had called for an all-out war against the traditionals and AIM, which was still forbidden on the Pine Ridge Reservation, and on October 17, 1973, Pedro Bissonnette was shot to death by BIA police, who claimed he resisted arrest; his alleged crime was to knock down a man who had insulted him in White Clay, Nebraska, in what was apparently a provocation. The following statement was released next day by his co-leaders in the Oglala Sioux Civil Rights Organization:

> All day yesterday, October 17th, there was an extensive manhunt for Pedro. The search involved about 20 police cars and several airplanes. They hunted Pedro down like an animal and murdered him in cold blood. We have not yet determined who did the actual shooting but we are quite certain that the murder was engineered by BIA Special Officer Del Eastman. Eastman is a Sioux-hating Crow Indian from Montana. . . .
>
> Last summer a little Indian girl, Mary Little Bear, was shot in the head and lost an eye from goon bullets. Later, Vern and Clarence Cross were shot by BIA police and goons. . . . And only last week the BIA police were involved in the shooting death of Aloysius Long Soldier at Kyle, South Dakota. The BIA and Dick Wilson have done a very effective job of suppressing the news coverage of any of these incidents. Now, Pedro Bissonnette has been murdered by these same outlaws and hoodlums.
>
> Because of this new wave of terror by Dick Wilson, the BIA and the F.B.I. against the traditional Oglala Sioux people, we are again extending an invitation to the American Indian Movement to come to the Pine Ridge Reservation to help us investigate the murder of Pedro Bissonnette and to take whatever action is necessary to see that his murderers are brought to justice.

Meanwhile, the BIA police had claimed that Bissonnette had reached for a gun while resisting arrest. The gun was never produced, nor was this case ever investigated, but an interesting report on it turned up a few years later. The report was given by Don Holman, former chief of the Sisseton Sioux Police and the Indian representative on the South Dakota Criminal Justice Commission—in short, a progressive who was working within the system.

> The story was told to me in Helena, Montana, in December 1975. The gentleman was Mr. Wilbur Reed . . . an employee of the U.S. Justice Department, Community Relations Service, working at the Rocky Mountain Office in Denver, Colorado. I am not sure of the date, but in early 1973 Mr. Pedro Bissonnette was shot to death on the Pine Ridge Reservation. This apparently was done by the BIA police. . . . He was killed by a shotgun blast while supposedly resisting arrest.
>
> Mr. Reed told me that he had been contacted by some members of Mr. Bissonnette's family who said that they couldn't find the body. The Bureau of Indian Affairs police, I believe at that time, Mr. Del Eastman, was in charge of Pine Ridge, and they would not release to them the whereabouts of the body. Finally, Mr. Reed went to the hospital and apparently talked to an orderly—and as I understand it—by pressure, stating he was from the Justice Department, and so on, and the orderly did take Mr. Reed to where Mr. Bissonnette's body was at. Mr. Reed was acquainted with Pedro Bissonnette. One of the remarkable things, he said, when he saw the body—again this was told to me second hand—was that Mr. Bissonnette had coal black beautiful hair. When he viewed the body, the hair had turned grey or white, and the only wound he could see was a round wound in the center of his chest. If it was true he was killed by a shotgun blast, that would make the range under two feet.[12]

"We lost a great man there," says Dennis Banks. "The federal police killed Pedro in an assassination conspiracy, and the reason was obvious: he knew too much about Wilson and about the BIA and about what their police were up to, and he intended to expose them. Also, I think they decided that if Pedro was dead, AIM could no longer function on the reservation."

A crowd of more than two thousand people turned out for the four-day funeral, which was guarded from BIA and goon harassment by AIM security patrols, including a "West Coast group" led by Jim Robideau and Leonard Peltier. Peltier had headed west in April 1973 after his release from the Milwaukee jail, taking part in Crow Dog's sun dance in the summer. From South Dakota he traveled to Seattle, where he rejoined the fishing-rights fight of the Puyallup-Nisqually. But when news came of the murder of Bissonnette, the West Coast group answered AIM's national call for support at the funeral on Pine Ridge. On October 21, a car registered in Peltier's name was involved in a shooting skirmish with the BIA police, in which two officers received minor injuries from glass flying from a bullet-shattered windshield. Peltier was never stopped for questioning, and after the funeral he returned to the West Coast. Having failed to appear for his pre-trial hearing in Milwaukee three months before, he was now a fugitive from justice.

CHAPTER 5

THE NEW INDIAN WARS

AIM Versus the FBI, 1972–75

I am now old. My day is nearly ended. I see the shadows of night coming. I will tell you of my people and of their old customs. I am a chief, and my father was the head chief of the Oglalas. He was murdered by Red Cloud in a cowardly way. . . . The spirits of old times do not come to me any more. Another spirit has come, the Great Spirit of the white man. I do not know him. I do not know how to call him to help me. I have done him no harm, and he should do me no harm. The old life is gone, and I cannot be a young man again.

Little Wound, son of Bull Bear (*Lakota*)

After World War II, uranium was discovered not far south of the Black Hills city named for Custer; in 1953, the Atomic Energy Commission established a station at Edgemont and began the reconnaissance that turned up uranium at the north as well as the south end of the Hills. In those days, the Atomic Energy Commission and the military were the only buyers of uranium, but with the creation of a domestic market for nuclear energy in the late 1960s, and a sudden rise in the price of uranium, a feverish interest in the Black Hills region was renewed. In the same period, the energy corporations were acquiring coal- and oil-mining rights to vast tracts of the western states, as billions of tons of coal from the Fort Union seam in Montana, Wyoming, and North Dakota—readily accessible to strip miners—were presented to the companies at a cost averaging about three dollars an acre, in a huge transfer of public wealth into private hands. As an agency of the Department of the Interior, the Bureau of Indian Affairs encouraged the tribal councils to share in this bounty. In New Mexico, the Pueblo and Navajo tribal councils had already agreed to widespread mining of their lands, while in Arizona, the Navajo and Hopi had accepted massive strip-mining for coal on the great sacred mountain called Black Mesa, despite the despairing protest of the traditional Hopi villages, which had never accepted the authority of the Tribal Council.[1] In Montana, the Northern Cheyenne leased mining rights to more than half of their 440,000-acre reservation; not long thereafter, 125,000 acres were leased by their old enemies, the Crow.

In 1971, the multicorporate North Central Power Study (dutifully endorsed by the Department of the Interior) decreed that Black Hills aquifers—the only real source of water in this dry country—could sustain massive exploitation of the coal, oil, and uranium resources of the region and that the Black Hills should become the nucleus of a vast multinational energy domain, producing power right in the mine fields, in forty-two huge thermal-generation plants, and exporting it eastward in a grid of power lines, all the way to Minneapolis and St. Louis; four of these highly dangerous lines (which have been fought hard by farmers and irate citizens' groups in Minnesota) were supposed to cross the Pine Ridge Reservation. Uranium prospecting intensified, with the strong interest and encouragement of the federal government and later the state government as well. Within a few years, more than a million acres had been claimed, staked, or leased by about twenty-five large corporations, including the Tennessee Valley Authority (which as a government-owned corporation was a fitting symbol of "the corporate state" which AIM spokesmen perceived as the monolithic enemy of the Indian nations) and Kerr-McGee, which today controls 33 percent of domestic uranium reserves. Best known for the Karen Silkwood scandal and the multiple cancer deaths of unsuspecting Navajo workers in its uranium mines at Red Rock, New Mexico,* Kerr-McGee is the colossus among those colossal companies whose strip mines and contamination have devastated vast tracts of Indian country in Montana (Crow and Northern Cheyenne), Wyoming (Western Shoshone), Colorado (Ute), New Mexico and Arizona (Jicarilla Apache, Navajo, Pueblo, and Hopi) and now wished to do as much for the Dakotas. With the cooperation of the state, widespread exploratory drilling was resumed in the Black Hills, with very promising results, and meanwhile the government agencies made preliminary surveys on the Indian reservations; in the beginning, they moved quietly, apparently not wishing to excite Indian opposition.

Among traditionals, however, opposition had been present all along, and in the early 1970s, even the tribal councils were forced to weigh the benefits of the mining leases against the long-term welfare of their nations, not simply because the terms arranged by the BIA were so disadvantageous but because the destruction of the land must lead to the certain destruction of the Indian people. In the first days of Wounded Knee, the Northern Cheyenne and the Crow canceled their leases, and while this probably came about due to the destruction of Black Mesa (where the Northern Cheyenne had sent a delegation), it must have seemed to those in power that those militant Indians were the cause of all the trouble. At the very least, with so much money on the line—Indian land in the western states (and in Canada and Alaska) contains most of the continent's uranium and a high percentage of its coal and oil—it could not hurt to identify AIM as a Communist-inspired terrorist organization and destroy this threat to democracy and mining profits once and for all.[2]

An FBI document issued in 1974 concerning the objectives of the American Indian Movement draws attention to a statement, made by

*Ms. Silkwood, an employee exposed to plutonium poisoning, was delivering incriminating documents to a *New York Times* reporter when her car was destroyed in an unexplained crash; the documents vanished. As for the dead and crippled Indian miners, Kerr-McGee, supported by the government, denied all responsibility and refused compensation to the stricken families.

Dennis Banks on April 16 of that year, that AIM now intended a shift of emphasis toward the prevention of continuing resource exploitation of Indian land. At this time there was little if any documentation for the suspicion that the great wealth in minerals beneath reservation lands explained the government's remorseless attitude toward militant Indians. Not that a prudent bureaucrat would put such a crass policy in writing; even so, a stronger case could have been made for organized suppression of the Indians' long hope of sovereignty based on the treaty claims, and the vast complications for the government that that entailed. Most likely, the government attitude, reflecting the needs of the great multinational corporations, was an outgrowth of both of these considerations; whatever its origins, the repression was carried out.

The Justice Department had been disappointed by its failure to obtain convictions in the Means-Banks case in St. Paul; yet it soon became clear that convictions—not to speak of justice—were beside the point. What was being accomplished, by foul means and fair, was the total disruption of the American Indian Movement, in what was emerging as a program to "neutralize" AIM leaders all over the country. In South Dakota, the local police effort was led by William Janklow, an assistant prosecutor in the state Attorney General's office assigned originally to help out in prosecuting cases arising from the Custer courthouse riot in 1973. Janklow, the bespectacled owner of a huge gun collection and a self-proclaimed "Indian fighter" in the tradition of George Armstrong Custer ("At least Longhair had style," one Indian says), had fiercely prosecuted and triumphantly jailed Sarah Bad Heart Bull, whose son's murder had led to the rioting; for joining the Indian protest against the state's failure to prosecute the killer, the upset mother received an indeterminate sentence of one to five years in prison, while the killer never served one day in jail. (The climax of her trial came well before the verdict, which in the climate of 1974 was never in doubt. As a protest against the overt racism in South Dakota, the Indian spectators in the Sioux Falls courtroom had refused to stand when Judge Joseph Bottum entered, and on April 29, the outraged judge, perceiving civil disobedience in what was merely a sincere contempt of court, limited the number of the Indian support group to twenty people. On the morning of April 30, because some sort of reprisal from Judge Bottum was expected, the twenty Indians who turned up were all men; they were not allowed to enter the court by the main door but had to pass through an adjacent room, where they were subjected to examination by a metal detector and to a frisking. When Bottum entered and the Indians refused to stand, the judge issued an order to clear the court, but nothing happened, and well over an hour passed in miscellaneous activity. Then a jump-suited tactical squad, twenty-four strong, backed up by an equal number of ordinary police out in the corridor, burst into the courtroom like an SS troop, as everyone in the place jumped up in alarm. According to three white clergymen who were present, these robot figures, clad in helmets with face shields, steel-toed combat boots, and metal-knuckled gloves, and armed with forty-inch clubs with steel-ball ends, as well as revolvers, Mace, handcuffs, and even gas masks, simply attacked the unarmed and outnumbered Indians without even bothering to order them out of the room. The first man they reached was knocked unconscious, and, trying to defend themselves, the desperate Indians fought back as best they could; a wild melee took place before the twenty were subdued. The injured included Custer defendant Dave Hill, who suffered permanent impairment of his vision in one eye, poked by a nightstick. "They were asking for it," Judge Bottum told the horrified bishops, "so I let 'em have it." Despite the word of the clergymen and others, a number of the victims, including Russell and Ted Means, were eventually imprisoned for "riot to obstruct justice"—the first people in South Dakota ever charged with this unlikely crime.)

Janklow had already set his sights on Dennis Banks, who, unlike Means, had managed to avoid trouble with the law in South Dakota; Janklow's political career would soar if Banks were punished in his own state courts. "The only way to deal with the Indian problem in South Dakota," Janklow declared, "is to put a gun to the AIM leaders' heads and pull the trigger." This silly remark and others like it, pandering to the local prejudice against AIM, were open encouragement to goon violence on Pine Ridge; they also advanced Janklow's designs on his boss's job as state Attorney General in the November 1974 election.

In July, WKLDOC called a meeting of South Dakota Indians to discuss various civil-rights complaints that it might take into court. On January 14, 1967, according to delegates from the Rosebud Reservation, a fifteen-year-old girl named Jancita Eagle Deer, who sometimes worked in the white community at Rosebud as a baby-sitter, reported to her school principal that she had been raped on her way home the night before by her employer, a young white lawyer named William Janklow who served as director of the tribe's Legal Services program. A complaint was made to a BIA investigator, who filed a report; the principal escorted the shocked girl to the hospital, where a doctor found evidence that an attack had occurred. But no help was available from the Legal Services program, and the case was speedily smoothed over by the FBI.[3] In a January 16 report, Agent John Penrod stated that "it was impossible to determine anything," and Agent Richard G. Held (later Special Agent in Charge in Minneapolis and a leading FBI official at Wounded Knee) concluded six weeks later that there was "insufficient evidence, allegations were unfounded; we are therefore closing our files on the matter." Meanwhile Jancita, ashamed when the ugly story spread, lost progress in school and finally disappeared from the reservation.

Seven years later, AIM was unable to locate either the victim or the BIA investigator of the incident, nor were supporting documents available. The impasse was resolved by Dennis Banks's bodyguard and pilot, Douglass Durham, who said he had encountered Jancita Eagle Deer in Des Moines the year before and felt confident that he could track her down again. The resourceful Durham also found the BIA investigator, whom he visited in Tulsa, Oklahoma. Durham's unusual contacts and methods, his familiarity with airplanes and electronics, firearms and cameras, not to speak of burglary techniques and clandestine tactics, had long since won Banks's admiration; also, Banks was understandably impressed by Durham's eagerness to discredit Banks's own persecutor, William Janklow.

In September 1974 Durham brought Jancita to St. Paul, where the Banks-Means trial was still under way; there the AIM leadership expressed doubts about using the young woman's story without documentation. Durham, assisted by a white AIM legal worker named Paula Giese, continued to investigate the charges against Janklow. In October 1974, in an effort to obtain the BIA reports needed to substantiate the story, Dennis Banks petitioned to have Janklow disbarred in the Rosebud Reservation Tribal Court, where Jancita Eagle Deer, now twenty-two, repeated her accusation of seven years before; however, the would-be Attorney General refused to answer his summons, the BIA refused to deliver the subpoenaed rape file, and the FBI refused to cooperate in any way.[4] Nevertheless, Janklow was charged by Judge Mario Gonzales with "assault with intent to commit rape, and carnal knowledge of a female under 16." As a white man, however, he was not subject to tribal jurisdiction; for want of any stronger measure, he was disbarred from further legal practice on the Rosebud Reservation.

Although Janklow denies the charges, two witnesses testified that he "brooded" over the episode for three days after it occurred; another witness declared that Janklow had tried to give money to Jancita's grandfather after coming around to make inquiries about her. Because Janklow refused to appear in court—and because the government did its best to thwart any investigation of the charges—no firm conclusion on this matter has been reached; nevertheless, the Indian people remain convinced that Janklow was guilty and that the alleged cover-up of a white man's crime was the other side of justice for Indians in South Dakota.

"I see no reason to doubt that these charges were true," Dennis Banks says. "I knew of Janklow as early as '70 or '71, from talks with the Rosebud Tribal Council leader; he told me that this Janklow had raped a young Indian girl while working down there for the legal service. Hell, that guy's bad name was floating around even before Custer. We had affidavits from two BIA cops on the Crow Creek Reservation who had picked him up for driving his car around dead drunk and nude. There was also sworn testimony that Janklow rode a motorcycle in a reservation residential area, shooting dogs. Anyway, he was assigned to the Custer courthouse cases, and along about this time, discussing me and Russell Means with another young lawyer named John Gridley, he made that remark that was later picked up by the wire services about putting a bullet in the heads of the AIM leaders.[5] In 1974, when we were trying to prosecute him, I saw those rape reports made out by the doctor and the BIA investigator, [Peter] Pichlin; the BIA man we subpoenaed showed them to me, but his superiors refused to release them, so we could not introduce them into evidence. In Pichlin's report, it said that he went to interview Janklow in his office, but Janklow locked himself in there for three days; he just wouldn't come out."

Meanwhile, Durham tried in vain to persuade AIM to kidnap Janklow as a protest, just before a pre-Election Day rally in Pierre. At the same time, he informed Jancita Eagle Deer, who was now his woman, that her charge against Janklow would be made public at the rally, and he also arranged for her to repeat her story on Sioux Falls television. Janklow, who could claim a good record as a poverty lawyer who had defended dozens of hapless Indians at Rosebud, successfully dismissed the charges as a poor, crude smear; in an anti-AIM climate, the rape charge rebounded against AIM, and he won easily.

⊡

One of the first AIM people to suspect that Douglass Durham was some sort of government agent was Anna Mae Pictou Aquash, the young Micmac woman from Shubencadie, Nova Scotia. An intelligent, energetic person who dreamed of assembling a whole cultural history of the Indian people, Anna Mae had attended Wheelock College, where she won a scholarship to Brandeis University which she never used. In 1969, she had helped to organize the Boston Indian Council as an aid to Indian alcoholics; she had also taught children and done social work in the black community in Roxbury, a district in Boston. In 1970, when she was twenty-five, she made her first contact with AIM when Russell Means traveled east in support of the "Mayflower II" Thanksgiving Day demonstration against white man's justice; in 1972, she participated in the Trail of Broken Treaties; and on March 10, 1973, she left her job as an assembler in a General Motors plant in Framingham, Massachusetts, and traveled west to Wounded Knee, where, in the exhilaration of the new Indian spirit, she was married to her Ojibwa friend Nogeeshik Aquash in a traditional ceremony performed by Wallace Black Elk. At Wounded Knee, Anna Mae Aquash was one of the few women to help dig bunkers and take part in the nightly patrols; because she was tough, cool, and resourceful—she regarded herself proudly as a "female warrior"—she was also used as a courier, slipping in and out of the besieged village to pack in supplies on the night trails over the hills.[6]

After Wounded Knee, the Aquashes returned to Boston, where they tried to establish an AIM survival school. Unable to find funding, they went to Ottawa, where Anna Mae, who had made herself an authority on Indian culture, set up a show at the National Arts Centre. In her researches into Micmac customs, she had rediscovered the ribbon shirt, apparently devised by a Micmac band to brighten the drab garments they received from the missionaries; it seemed to her that manufacture and sale of these colorful shirts by AIM women would help defray expenses of the Movement. (The ribbon shirts became so popular with AIM men that there were none left over; besides, some people felt that the shirts were ceremonial and should not be sold.) Meanwhile, she traveled back and forth to the Means-Banks trial at St. Paul.

She had separated from Nogeeshik Aquash, and because this was a transgression of her traditional marriage, she suffered from intermittent depression, confiding to a friend her intuition that she did not have long to live, that Indians who fought for their people would be "executed." In May 1974, after the Arts Centre show opened in Ottawa to considerable acclaim, she joined the AIM group in St. Paul, where she taught in the survival school called the Red School House. In this period she became involved with Dennis Banks, and this depressed her, since she was close to Banks's wife, the young Oglala woman Kamook Nichols.

During Doug Durham's brief visit to Wounded Knee,[7] certain AIM women, Aquash among them, had noticed that this "one-fourth Chippewa" in headband, beaded belt buckle, and turquoise jewelry was dyeing his hair black. That summer of 1973, when he attached himself to Banks, the women dismissed him as "Dennis's boy," an arrogant would-be Indian who flattered Banks and made him less accessible to his people, and who talked to no one who was "not important. He never talked to the Defense Committee staff except to give orders," a veteran legal worker named Karen Northcott remembers. "We were just too lowly. Doug Durham was full of himself—big and chunky. But there was something *soft* about him, he looked dirty in some way."

"I didn't like him because the old people didn't trust him," Leonard Peltier says. "In 1974, some of them saw him taking pictures at Crow Dog's sun dance and became suspicious. So I confronted him about it—pretty heavy, too—in the cellar of the Red School House in St. Paul, and he said, Those people were lying! and I said, Don't you tell me my old people are lying! I knew right away that he was the one doing the lying, and that there was something fishy about his entire story. I also noticed that he had been trying to get rid of me, separate me from Dennis, who was beginning to give me the cold shoulder. But by that time, nobody could talk to Dennis, you just couldn't seem to get him alone."

In the autumn of 1974, after the St. Paul verdict, Anna Mae Aquash was sent to Los Angeles to help set up a West Coast office; Douglass Durham turned up there as well. Almost immediately, in Anna Mae's opinion, Durham undermined her fund-raising efforts. Eventually she complained to the AIM national office in St. Paul, which informed her that Durham had been sent out to the Coast while his role in the Janklow fiasco and other counterproductive activity was being investigated, and that she should keep an eye on him. Despite Durham, Anna Mae (or "Annie Mae," as many people, Banks included, called her) was very effective. "She was very intelligent," says Ernie Peters, a Lakota spiritual leader who became director of the West Coast office. "Anna Mae was an operator and a real go-getter; she didn't let no grass grow under her feet. And when she went to the sweat lodge and ceremonies, you couldn't find a stronger person."

In California, Durham took particular interest in an AIM rest camp in a secluded corner of Box Canyon, a barren arroyo leading down to the coast south of Ventura that is best known for Spahn Ranch, the hideout of the Charles Manson group after the murder of the movie actress Sharon Tate. A sign put up by the religious sect that owned this property called it "a Centre of Spirituality," but it was already notorious as the site of the dynamite murder of a swami and his flock in the late 1950s. Although AIM (which took it over after Wounded Knee from a Chumash shaman named Paul "Semu" Huaute) had intended it as a wooded retreat for spiritual ceremonies and renewal, it soon attracted a fallout of non-Indians (some of them from the Hollywood community) addicted to strong drink, drugs, and kinky violence. Because of its bad reputation, the Movement withdrew support from Camp 13 (which was given this spy-novel name by Durham); yet somehow the rent continued to be paid from unknown sources through an AIM coordinator known as "Blue Dove."

On October 10, 1974, Box Canyon's bad reputation suddenly worsened when a white man was tortured, then killed, by two young Indians, Black Cloud and Rising Sun. Two days later, an unknown informant in the camp "dropped a dime" on his/her companions, notifying the police that another Box Canyon death had just occurred, this time on the AIM property. The police were led to the remains of a young white cabdriver named George Aird, who had picked up a Pine Ridge Oglala named Marvin Redshirt, his white girl friend, Holly Broussard, and a young Indian woman named Marcella Makes Noise Eaglestaff from the Hollywood Hills house of the actor David Carradine and driven them to Camp 13 . (Carradine had visited Doug Durham on Durham's birthday in St. Paul, two weeks before.) Dead of seventeen stab wounds, Aird had been stuffed into a drainpipe. All three of his passengers were drunk and bloodstained, and a bloody knife and bloodied book belonging to Holly Broussard were seized as evidence.

Within three months, all three of these blood-spattered people had been set free in exchange for testimony that a young Ojibwa named Paul Durant "Skyhorse," and Richard Billings, a young Tuscarora-Mohawk—the only two AIM people in the camp—had dragged the cabdriver outside and stabbed him repeatedly after an argument over the fare. Both "Skyhorse" and "Mohawk" (as they became known after their cause had been taken up by the liberal press) had longtime records as participants in Indian causes all around the country. They also had criminal records (both had served time for robbery), a reputation for hard drinking, and—in Durant's case—a history of mental instability.

In the week before Aird's murder, Dennis Banks had gone out to Box Canyon and found beer cans and trash littered everywhere; the whole spiritual center was a shambles. "Skyhorse and Mohawk were so drunk they could hardly talk, and I got mad," Banks says, shaking his head in disgust at the recollection. "I told them that AIM was withdrawing all support from this fucking camp right there and then. When the murder occurred, we had a thorough investigation right away; on the night it happened, Mohawk was passed out—he couldn't even move—and Skyhorse wasn't much better. He was called down to the scene because the guy was still alive, and the people who had stabbed him—they were all drunk, too—didn't know what to do; they realized they had to get rid of him, and so they killed him. Didn't even bury him, just stuffed him down a hole. At the National Indian Education Association meeting in Phoenix, two days later, Skyhorse and Mohawk told me they were on the run; I told them not to mention their real names to anybody. Just then Durham walks in, and Skyhorse, who is drunk, as usual, asks him if he can get a plane to fly them the hell out of there. Needless to say, they were picked up right there in Phoenix, after one of 'em—Mohawk, I think—got shot up in a local dance hall."

According to a civil-rights attorney in Los Angeles (who says he would not defend Skyhorse and Mohawk because of AIM's own refusal to support them),[8] Douglass Durham, usually accompanied by the West Coast AIM director, Ernie Peters, attended all of the strategy meetings after the arrest, declaring that AIM should disown these two entirely, even though Peters thought AIM should support them. At a pre-trial hearing, where he identified himself as a "psychotherapist" from Iowa, Durham testified to Skyhorse's mental instability. He also said that the defendants were not really AIM people, although they had been co-founders of the Illinois AIM chapter in January 1973. Since then, Skyhorse had attended AIM's national conference at White Oak, Oklahoma (August 1973), and Mohawk had been present at the first International Indian Treaty Council meeting at Mobridge, South Dakota (June 1974), just a few months before the killing at Box Canyon.

"For a year and a half," Banks remembers, "I would not give those guys support. Skyhorse and Mohawk didn't start the killing, and they didn't finish it, but they were the ones who were bringing in all the booze and drugs, and they had a lot of responsibility for what had happened. AIM had closed that camp, and I just couldn't condone what they were doing; the liberals, the whole Indian community, were making them into heroes, and they weren't. Then one of the prosecution people told me, Dennis, if you repeat this, I'll call you a liar, but we gave immunity to the wrong people. I changed my mind about AIM support when I realized that they were going to nail Skyhorse and Mohawk not because they were guilty but because they were AIM."

The trial began on June 1, 1977, after one of the longest pre-trial proceedings in the history of U.S. justice; it ended on May 24, 1978, with the acquittal of both defendants, by which time almost everyone had been convinced that the two had been set up by FBI provocateurs.

On the day of Aird's murder, Skyhorse and Mohawk had been driven to the Los Angeles federal building by Blue Dove (a would-be Indian in the AIM office who claimed she was given this name by Mad Bear Anderson during the Alcatraz occupation); while awaiting a nonexistent protest rally on behalf of Sarah Bad Heart Bull, Blue Dove secretly took their pictures, and after the murder, these photographs were used by informers to identify the pair at the Phoenix convention, which Skyhorse, a few days before the murder, had told Durham he planned to attend. In 1976—after being thrown out of AIM by Ernie Peters because she was white and because she was disruptive—Blue Dove was exposed as an FBI operative named Virginia DeLuce, erstwhile actress and a friend of the Barry Goldwaters.

AIM leaders believe even today that the FBI (through Durham, DeLuce, and probably others) had promoted "AIM Camp 13" from start to finish as part of a COINTELPRO plan to discredit the Movement, which was said to have lost 95 percent of its financial support in California after Aird's murder. It turned out, for example, that Marvin Redshirt had driven Aird's cab into Box Canyon (presumably, poor Aird himself was already disabled, though not dead) and that he had parked it right beside Durham's new AIM CAMP 13 sign; therefore this sign was prominent in the lurid photo stories on this case, which included accounts of torture, scalping, and ceremonial murder, all to the beat of the AIM drum. Although Redshirt insisted that he had seen Skyhorse and Mohawk stab George Aird, he also admitted that he himself had struck the first blow against Aird and had also participated in the orgy of stabbing that finally killed him. And although he acknowledged lying "about a thousand times," this man was released less than four months after the murder.[9]

After Redshirt's collapse on the witness stand, the discouraged prosecutors offered a plea bargain based on the two and a half years that the defendants had already spent in prison. Although the deal was acceptable to the defendants, it was prohibited by Judge Floyd Dodson, who appeared eager to prolong his last trial as long as possible; the trial wandered on for another ten months before the whole travesty came to an end. As for Redshirt, he was sentenced to five years on probation, during which time he received government aid for going to college. Black Cloud and Rising Sun, whose torture-killing in the same locality just two days before the Aird murder had helped to destroy AIM's reputation in the West, received similar understanding and consideration.

Archie Fire Lame Deer, who had been spiritual adviser to the Box Canyon camp, believes that Skyhorse and Mohawk deserved to be acquitted, but he wasn't surprised that both of them were in trouble soon again: Mohawk was one of the AIM "security men" ordered out of the Indian camp at Point Conception by the Chumash elders after a drunken shooting, and Skyhorse was arrested on new charges in Chicago. Marvin Redshirt, the government's star witness, had also been rearrested; in 1978, his college career was interrupted in his hometown of Hot Springs, South Dakota, where he was charged with the near-fatal stabbing of his Box Canyon consort, Holly Broussard.

⊡

Among the people who assisted Anna Mae Aquash in the West Coast office (located on Pacific Avenue, in Venice) was a young AIM warrior named Darrelle Dean Butler. "Dino" Butler had been in the AIM office in St. Paul when the news came in about a murder in California, and he recalls how Douglass Durham, who happened to be there on that day, had immediately taken over all contact with the media, creating as much bad publicity as possible under the pretense of absolving AIM of any guilt. "This wasn't too long after the St. Paul acquittal," says Butler, "and AIM was really going strong, with a lot of acceptance from the public. There's no doubt in my mind that Durham set up all that trouble out there. He was undermining Anna Mae by turning off all her contacts, abusing their help, you know, by exploiting their offices, using their telephones, telling them not to trust their money to Anna Mae but to give it to him."

Another assistant in the West Coast office was a pretty young Inuit woman who had been raised by a white family in the Pacific Northwest. As Kelly Jean McCormick, she had gone to college and become an actress, playing the young romantic lead in the film *White Dawn.* ("I'm the one who died.") In the late summer of 1974, Kelly Jean was acting in the stage play *Savages,* which concerned the ongoing slaughter of Brazilian Indians, and one performance was attended by Dennis Banks and Ernie Peters, who told the audience that genocide against Indians was not limited to Brazil, "It's still going on here." The remark made a strong impression on Kelly Jean, who had not realized the full effect of the white culture on traditional people until she had gone on location with *White Dawn* to the depressed Inuit community at Frobisher Bay on Baffin Island. When Banks spoke, she listened carefully ("I wanted to know what AIM was trying to do, I wanted to help, but I didn't know how to begin"), and subsequently, she attended sweat-lodge ceremonies run by Peters. "It was in the sweats that I realized there was something I *needed* to know. And it was then that Anna Mae showed up to help Peters establish that West Coast office. Then Dino Butler came, not long after Box Canyon, and I thought he was bossy as hell. I guess it was arrogance versus arrogance. He was with another woman then—I had no thought of snagging him—but I had a lot of respect for him right from the start: he had a lot of power and a lot of heart."

Kelly Jean, who soon adopted the Inuit name Nilak, was still very young and sheltered, and she wished to give Douglass Durham the benefit of the doubt, despite the fact that his disruptive behavior had sabotaged a proposed benefit that the cast and company of *Savages* had offered. "I was one of the few people—*very* few people—who wasn't suspicious of old Doug," she says, eyes rolling at her own naiveté. "I don't mean I *liked* him—nobody liked him, and they were avoiding Dennis just because of it—but he seemed to be pretty effective, so I kept saying, Let's give old Doug a chance. Then one day I flashed on something, and I said to him, You don't like me, do you? I said it suddenly like that, just blurted it out, and I guess it caught him off guard.

He said, I *do* like you; you're intelligent and therefore dangerous. And *that's* when this Eskimo finally caught on that something was very very wrong. We already knew that Durham wouldn't come to sweats with Ernie, because the truth comes out in sweats, you just can't lie in there; and Anna Mae hated him because he had lied, telling Indians he had smoked the sacred pipe with her. But what he was really doing was telling the white people who wanted to help that Dino Butler was a criminal and the rest of us weren't really AIM at all, just a gang of rip-off artists who were stealing their money. Soon the national office was getting complaints and asking suspicious questions about what was happening to all the donations, because the donors were getting so uptight. Well, that money was going into a second account under the name of Douglass Durham. . . .

"Anna Mae just couldn't stand Doug: she was on to him. She was a smart woman. She'd just kick him out of the office: Go sleep in your van! You're not coming in here! She kicked Blue Dove out of the office, too. She was very smart about people. She knew a lot about people. She knew a lot about natural creation. She just shared it all."

In November, Nilak traveled to South Dakota for a rally for Sarah Bad Heart Bull in Pierre (pronounced *Peer*). On the return trip to Pine Ridge, the car hit an ice patch and turned over, and one of the passengers was nearly killed. Though still breathing, he was unconscious, "with the whole top of his head peeled back, and bleeding like anything," Nilak remembers. "I didn't know his name, but when the BIA cops came, they knew him: Hey, one says to the other, that's June Little! Right away, they want to arrest us all for dangerous driving, instead of offering help, and I really let them have it before they backed off. When the BIA ambulance finally showed up, I didn't like the way they handled this June Little, so I insisted on riding in the ambulance. They didn't go for that, but it's a damn good thing I did. As it was, we'd hardly got started for the Pine Ridge Hospital when the goddam guys pull over at somebody's house for a cup of coffee, with this man bleeding to death out in the ambulance! And when I hollered, they said, If you're so concerned, go out there and hold the top of his head on." As she describes this, Nilak's round eyes narrow to a fierce slit, and her voice deepens. "They were trying to murder that man. And at Pine Ridge Hospital, they told us they didn't have no facilities to take care of him, so we finally ended up in Gordon, Nebraska. That episode gave me my first understanding of the evil on the Pine Ridge Indian Reservation."

In late December, Dino Butler accompanied Nilak and Anna Mae to Gresham, Wisconsin, where early in the morning of January 1, 1975, the Menominee Warrior Society occupied an unused abbey of the Alexian Brothers Novitiate, with the idea of making it a health center. Outraged by this threat to private property, the white community threw off its New Year's Day hangover and besieged the abbey, which was soon surrounded and under fire from hundreds of law-enforcement officers. There were also large numbers of vigilantes of a self-styled Concerned Citizens Committee (later the White America Movement [WHAM]), who were held at bay by detachments of the Wisconsin National Guard; although the Guardsmen shared vigilante suspicions that some of those terrorists in the abbey had been "flown in from Europe," they were under strict orders from Governor Patrick Lucey to prevent an attack. The occupation ended inconclusively in early February, after which the Indian leaders were prosecuted; one of them, John Waubanascum, was slain a year later by a deputy sheriff.[10]

At Gresham, Dino Butler served as a courier, traveling in and out of the besieged abbey, and on one of these journeys he ran into Leonard Peltier and Frank Black Horse, who were trying to reach the abbey in a pickup truck. "I had talked to Leonard a few times in '74, but we never really became friends until the abbey takeover," Butler says, and Peltier agrees. "I never seen much of Dino before Gresham. In 1974, I was living mostly on Rosebud. When I came down to St. Paul, Dino was head of security and bodyguard for Dennis, and when I walked in, he didn't know who I was. We just looked at each other like this," Peltier says, rearing back a little, scowling, "like, Who the hell are *you,* walking right in here like you owned the place? and, Who the hell do you think *you* are, questioning *me?* We were really leery of each other. My attitude was suspicious because of that episode in the cellar of the Red School House with Doug Durham—I had *him* figured for an informer or an agitator of some kind, and after that, I was more or less checking everybody out. Not that Durham was as big as he portrayed himself—to listen to Durham, you'd think he was Dennis Banks the Second! But he couldn't tell me what to do, or Dino, or anybody else—he knew we'd just tell him to fuck off. That understanding was there out front—I don't think nobody ever had to tell him. But Durham had made everyone suspicious—that was the real damage that he done, he really caused a lot of paranoia. People started calling each other 'pigs,' and if you went to town too long, people wanted to know why.

"Anyway, I had heard a lot about this Dino Butler, who he used to drink with and all, and everybody said he was all right, but we never really sat down and talked, and got to know each other. Maybe we didn't have to. I think we both understood . . . it's hard to explain, but we communicated just by sitting quiet. Dino is very quiet, and he's got a protective shell. I'm not quiet, but I'm leery of everybody until I know different; the only ones I really trust are family like Bob and Steve Robideau, people I've known all my life."

At Gresham, Douglass Durham was no longer permitted to join the AIM support group or enter the abbey. Nevertheless, he presented himself to the press and the white community as AIM's public-relations man, operating a radio from his motel room after telephone lines to the abbey had been cut. This job was assumed by Anna Mae Aquash not long thereafter, when Durham, realizing he had run out of time, departed one night, taking Jancita Eagle Deer with him. The next day, the AIM leadership confirmed the rumors that Durham had been an informer for the FBI.

⊡

From Wisconsin, Durham and Eagle Deer returned to the AIM office in St. Paul; from there, apparently, they went on to South Dakota, then disappeared. For the next two months, according to her friend Paula Giese, Jancita called her husband's family every Saturday, saying, "I love you all so much, I hope I can get away soon and come home."

On the last Saturday of March, there was no phone call, and in early April, Mrs. Scheldahl and her son Eric traveled to Aurora, Nebraska, where they identified Jancita's body in the local mortuary. According to Alfred Eagle Deer, Jancita's brother, "a dark-haired man in a blue Chevy" had picked her up at Alfred's house near Valentine, Nebraska, just south of the Rosebud Reservation, about 1:00 p.m. on April 4. She was last seen alive early that evening on a long stretch of deserted road outside Aurora. Semiconscious or drunk—in any event unsteady—she seemed to be trying to flag down the car that caused her death. (It interested Alfred Eagle Deer, who once served time in jail for running a stoplight, that no charges were ever filed against the young white driver, although he was traveling at such high speed that the young woman was hurled some distance by the impact.) The coroner told an AIM investigator that Jancita Eagle Deer might have been previously beaten, or perhaps injured by jumping from a moving car, but that no autopsy could determine this for certain, due to the massive nature of her injuries.[11]

Jancita was "a confused person," Dino Butler recalls. "She tried hard to believe in her people's ways, but she couldn't help partying around. She told me her confusion started when Janklow raped her." Nilak agrees. "She was nice, you know, she really wanted to learn, help out, but she'd been through *a lot*; she'd had a very hard time, and she was broken—that's the only word."

After her death, Jancita's stepmother, Delphine Eagle Deer, swore that she would not give up the fight to prove that her daughter had been raped by William Janklow; the following December, Mrs. Eagle Deer, who was Leonard Crow Dog's sister, died after a beating by the BIA police, who left her unconscious in a winter field.[12]

⊡

The death of Jancita Eagle Deer occurred a few weeks after Durham's public exposure, and several months after AIM acquired certain documents confirming his connection with the FBI. (Bill Means says that the AIM staff found some microfilm in the St. Paul office which Durham had mislaid.) Understandably, Dennis Banks sighs when asked why Durham was not denounced earlier. "Douglass Durham was recommended to me and Clyde by Harvey Major and Ron Petite of Iowa AIM—they're both dead now—during the big '73 sun dance after Wounded Knee. They told us that he was a former pig, busted for burglary and dismissed from the police force, and Durham admitted this; the only thing he did not admit was that he was working for the FBI. Vern Bellecourt didn't trust him, Russell and Bill Means didn't trust him; in fact, eight out of the ten leadership people present didn't trust him. But AIM had nothing to hide, we were up front about everything, so I said, He can't harm us, let's put him to work, see if he can *help* us. And he did. Doug was very able; I could depend on him. After Wounded Knee, I was demanding complete security, and as my bodyguard he was armed and I wasn't, and he had a couple of chances that he didn't take to do away with me in far-off places." At the suggestion that, with Durham in his confidence, he was more useful to the FBI alive, Banks nodded, looking worried and unhappy. "Anyway, some people suspected him from the start, and a lot of people suspected him a year later. In the fall of '74, while we were investigating him, he was sent to California, and Annie Mae was sent along to keep an eye on him. In November, Ken Tilsen found hard evidence against him, but besides Tilsen, only Clyde, Russell, and myself were aware of it, and Doug was allowed to stay in the Movement for three months, to see where he might lead us. We even had him tailed when he went to a fed debriefing in Miami—that was December '74—and I remember teasing him about his Des Moines tan when he came back; he said he had gotten burned under a sunlamp."

On March 5, 1975, Durham was confronted by AIM leaders in a Des Moines hotel room, where, after a brief protest, he acknowledged his identity as an informer. Subsequently, he submitted to a three-day interview with Tilsen and the Methodist minister John Adams, who was invited to be present as an impartial observer. Tilsen, who says he was leery of Durham from the very start ("From day one, I never told Doug Durham anything I didn't want the FBI to hear"), had earlier urged the AIM leaders not to use Jancita Eagle Deer's story, which would not be persuasive without thorough documentation and which might backfire in Janklow's favor; he still believes that it got Janklow elected.[13] Of the three-day interview, Tilsen says, "There was so much lying, bombast, and distortion that it's just impossible to sort out the truth; you could listen to all those hours of tapes and not be sure of a single thing you heard." One of Durham's peculiar boasts was that he was regarded by the Des Moines police as "head of the largest criminal organization in Iowa," and apparently he kept up his criminal career even while working for the police and the FBI.

On March 12, 1975, AIM held a press conference in Chicago at which Durham was publicly identified as an FBI informer. Durham himself was produced in order to confirm this; he identified the agents in the Minneapolis FBI office to whom he had reported, and went on to express regret about his role, praising AIM as "an organization attempting to effect social change in America." In a press interview Durham claimed to be an ex-Marine and an ex-policeman in Des Moines, where he had underworld connections; although acknowledging that he had been dismissed from the police force, he said his expulsion was intended to give him credibility in criminal circles in preparation for his subsequent career as a police undercover operative or "loaned agent" in other cities of the Midwest. (One of these cities was Chicago, where,

Durham claimed, he had Black Panther contacts that were used by the FBI, and where he was well known as a police agent even at the time he worked for AIM.) Before going to Wounded Knee, he got in touch with the FBI, to which he later sold information used in the prosecutions, as well as photographs of Wounded Knee defenses. Apparently his special mission was to keep an eye out for "involvement of representatives of foreign governments in AIM activities," of the sort reported at the Means-Banks trial by Louis Moves Camp. (Whether this concern with foreign agents was FBI paranoia or merely an excuse for COINTELPRO activity remains unclear.)

Making the most of his celebrity, Durham gave a number of boastful interviews to the press in regard to the power he had wielded as national security director of AIM. "I traveled all over with him, first as bodyguard, then as adviser," Durham said. "I exercised so much control you couldn't see Dennis or Russell without going through me, and if you wanted money, you had to see me." However, he was still perplexed about his exposure, intimating that the FBI must have been infiltrated. "At first I denied everything," he confided to his hometown newspaper in late April, "but they kept pulling more documents out. Sure would like to know how they got them." Durham said he had refused an interview with the Washington *Star,* which claimed that it had "documentary proof that I work for the CIA and I had CIA cooperation in flying Banks past radar defense without detection in bringing him back here from Canada."[14]

As the person in charge of the WKLDOC office during the Banks-Means trial, Durham had been the only person besides the defendants and their lawyers who listened regularly to defense strategy. "There was no person other than defense counsel and the defendants themselves who knew more about the total plans, concerns, and stratagems of the defense than Douglass Durham," Kenneth Tilsen said. In appreciation of the information that he passed to a special contact number in Minneapolis throughout the trial, the FBI raised his salary from $900 to $1,100 a month; this money was in addition to the $100,000 that AIM people estimate he stole from the Movement while in charge of all incoming contributions.

Among those shocked by these revelations was Judge Frederick Nichol, who became convinced that the prosecutors of Russell Means and Dennis Banks had known about Durham's infiltration all along. Ten days before Durham's exposure, the Justice Department had asked

Nichol to disqualify himself from further trials in the matter of Wounded Knee on the grounds that he was unfairly biased against the FBI. Nichol, disputing this charge, had intended to refuse the request, but after Durham's revelations he was so disillusioned that he no longer felt he could preside impartially in the forthcoming trial of Crow Dog, Camp, and Holder. "I believe I was deliberately misled by R. D. Hurd and Joseph Trimbach," the judge said, referring to Trimbach's testimony that the government had no informers infiltrating the defense, and also to a sworn affidavit filed in his court during the Banks-Means trial in which the Justice Department denied the presence of any informer among the members of the defense team. (At Crow Dog's trial two months after Durham's exposure, Trimbach would declare that he had no idea that Durham had been an informer, although one of the three agents in his own Minneapolis office, who followed him to the stand, acknowledged that Durham had contacted him at a special phone number at least thirty times during the Banks-Means trial; this agent said that Durham had been known to Trimbach from the start, and that he had notified Hurd and the other U.S. attorneys about Durham.[15]) Judge Nichol later accepted Hurd's excuse that although the FBI had told him that an informer "very close to one of the defendants" was attending the defense's strategy meetings, he had taken the Bureau's solemn word that this "informant" had been instructed not to listen to or inform on anything except potential violence. (Durham himself refuted this tomfoolery: "If Dennis and I were sitting in the room and an attorney would walk in and start talking, I couldn't jump up and say, 'I can't be here! The FBI won't allow it!' ")

Unlike Judge Nichol, R. D. Hurd was commended by the Justice Department for "superior performance" in the Banks-Means trial and received an award as one of the outstanding young prosecuting attorneys in the country.

While subverting the AIM national office, Durham had also remained active in Iowa; by encouraging rash, inflammatory acts, he had all but destroyed Iowa AIM. His South Dakota activities are more ambiguous. For one thing, it is difficult to believe that his FBI superiors would approve the public discrediting of a spiritual ally such as William Janklow (unless they were certain that the "smear" would rebound in Janklow's favor, as it did). Not only was Janklow elected Attorney General of South Dakota, but he was also nominated by President Gerald Ford as national director of the Legal Services Corporation (for which he had worked on the Rosebud Reservation) due to his well-known expertise in Indian matters. At his confirmation hearing in Washington, D.C., in May 1975, the rape charge surfaced once again, and once again he dismissed it successfully as an AIM calumny.

In Douglass Durham, it appeared, the FBI had chosen very well; no one can say that this man failed to earn his salary. Durham's history as a blackmailer, thief, and cheat was readily available to the FBI from the Des Moines police, which in the 1960s had dismissed him from the force; a police psychiatrist had diagnosed him as a "paranoid schizoid" personality with "violent tendencies" and termed him "unfit for employment involving the public trust" after the unexplained death of his first wife, in 1964. Despite his claim that his criminal record was constructed for police undercover purposes, he was the major culprit in a police corruption scandal in 1972, according to the findings of a Des Moines grand jury.

Russell Means does not acknowledge the damage done by Douglass Durham; he feels that the importance given to Durham insults the intelligence of the AIM leadership. "Durham was a gofer, a *nothing*! He was like a woman, *worse* than a woman; we used to give him pocket money, send him out for coffee! When he told people he was dying of leukemia, we just laughed at him. Banks needed a flunky, but even Banks used to chew him out in public, over and over, for being such a fuck-up. If he did anything, he did it on Banks's orders; he just bossed around the other white people in the office when none of the leadership was there. Whatever mistakes Banks may have made, he is very intelligent and organized and together, and he would not let an inefficient flunky like Durham take control. Durham never attended any important strategy meetings in St. Paul; we just *used* him, that's all, blew him up way out of proportion to publicize FBI infiltration, and of course he made the most of that, and bullshitted the feds to justify his salary."

John Trudell, who was AIM co-chairman at the time, more or less agrees. "Doug had a set of lies to produce for the FBI; he had to play his little game out, and he did. But he was a joke; he was never anything to get excited about, even in the beginning. All he really accomplished was to embarrass a few AIM people. The one thing I *do* hold him on was murdering Jancita: I *know* he did it. He brought her in and used her to seal a permanent enmity between Janklow and AIM, but she had evidence against him, and he got rid of her."

Ernie Peters, who worked with Durham on the West Coast, says loyally, "Doug was a good person, but he was on their payroll; he had been deceived by the System. No man who had not been deceived would act that way." Others, including minister John Adams, feel that Durham's seeming ambivalence about AIM and its social purposes was not entirely feigned. Durham won a reputation as a hard worker, willing to put up with hard conditions, Adams says, and occasionally he made exceptional contributions, such as the disputed "rescue" of Dennis Banks from Canada. (One WKLDOC attorney says that the rescue was a cover story, that because Banks refused to go to jail and would not leave Canada until bond money had been posted, the church groups put up some of the money for the flight and the FBI apparently supplied the rest.) There were also undisputed flights in search of gamma globulin supplies to contain a serious hepatitis outbreak during the International Indian Treaty Council in 1974. At moments, at least, Durham expressed real admiration for Banks, whom he described to Adams as "a viable, logical, and peaceful leader of a necessary social protest movement."[16] But Adams concedes that Durham extorted money from the churches while posing as an AIM leader, and stole a good deal of what was donated.

⊡

After two years of disruption and harassment by Durham and other informers, AIM was fragmented by fear of infiltration; as a national organization, it was virtually defunct. Just before Durham's exposure, twenty-eight AIM people were arrested on a single weekend, among them Leonard Peltier's old friend and partner Herb Powless, of Milwaukee AIM, seized in Hot Springs, South Dakota. Powless was booked on charges of "criminal syndicalism" as well as arms and explosives offenses; he was sentenced to three and a half years in prison.[17] That same weekend, Bill Means was arrested in Denver on a marijuana charge, and Russ Means and his friend Dick Marshall were arrested for assault with intent to kill. In the same period Means and his brother Ted were being prosecuted for defending themselves in the riot in Sioux Falls during the trial of Sarah Bad Heart Bull, and Russ Means, Powless, Stan Holder, and Ron Petite were under indictment in Phoenix, Arizona, for conspiracy to buy arms for Wounded Knee. As for Banks, he was being prosecuted by the new Attorney General, William Janklow, who was already eager to be Governor of South Dakota and was jailing Indians all over the state.

Whatever the real nature of Durham's effectiveness, his exposure as an agent provocateur attracted the attention of a Senate Select Committee on Intelligence, headed by Senator Frank Church. The Church Committee, created in January 1975 to investigate reports of domestic spying and counterintelligence programs in both the FBI and CIA, had already decried such vicious activities as the sexual blackmail of Martin Luther King and the actress Jean Seberg, allegedly pregnant by a Black Panther lover (before his murder, FBI operatives suggested to King that he commit suicide, and the harassed Seberg eventually did so); it was also interested in the role of FBI informants in the Chicago police raid of 1969 in which Black Panther leaders Fred Hampton and Mark Clark were assassinated. The Church Committee, which eventually condemned COINTELPRO as "a sophisticated vigilante operation" directed at those whom the FBI considered threats "to the existing political and social order," had its staff investigators question Durham on May 2, 1975; he was then subpoenaed to appear before the full committee, but he never did so. The tension accumulating on Pine Ridge exploded on June 26, 1975, and the committee's investigation of COINTELPRO and AIM came to a sudden and unfortunate end.

> Attached is a letter from the Senate Select Committee (SSC), dated 6-23-75, addressed to [Attorney General] Edward H. Levi. This letter announces the SSC's intent to conduct interviews relating to Douglass Durham, a former Bureau informant. The request obviously relates to our investigation at "Wounded Knee" and our investigation of the American Indian Movement (AIM). This request was received 6-27-75, by Legal Division.
>
> On 6-27-75, Patrick Shea, staff member of the SSC, requested we hold in abeyance any action on the request in view of the killing of the Agents at Pine Ridge Reservation, South Dakota.

CHAPTER 6

THE U.S. PUPPET GOVERNMENT

Pine Ridge and Dick Wilson, 1975

We see the change in our ponies. In the old days they could stand great hardship and travel long distance without water. They lived on certain kinds of food and drank pure water. Now our horses require a mixture of food; they have less endurance and must have constant care. It is the same with the Indians; they have less freedom and they fall an easy prey to disease. In the old days they were rugged and healthy, drinking pure water and eating the meat of the buffalo, which had a wide range, not being shut up like cattle of the present day. The water of the Missouri River is not pure, as it used to be, and many of the creeks are no longer good for us to drink.

Okute, or "Shooter" (*Lakota*)

Before his trial in St. Paul, Russell Means had entered his name against Dick Wilson's for the job of tribal chairman (who is also president of the Oglala Tribal Council). Wilson vowed that if reelected he would continue his ban on AIM "rabble-rousers" on the Pine Ridge Reservation: "I won't tolerate 'em, and I won't call the marshals this time, either; we'll handle 'em ourselves." Wilson's men went out marauding, and on election night (February 7, 1974) the sound of gunfire ricocheted all around the reservation, in an ominous atmosphere that reminded people of the night that Pedro Bissonnette was killed. Though he did not campaign in person, Means was barely defeated.[1] ("To tell you the truth, it's better I lost," he says today. "The System is just too powerful, it's like quicksand, and I would have been sucked in.") In the opinion of Ted Means's wife, Lorelei Decora, "The government can't afford to have a man like Russ Means in charge of the reservation. AIM is down there telling Indians they don't have to lease their land for two dollars an acre. AIM is telling them they can get their own cattle, that they can start their own economic base and won't have to be dependent on the government."

Eventually, the U.S. Commission on Civil Rights declared Wilson's reelection "invalid," since nearly one third of the votes were somehow tainted. The Justice Department took no action, and Richard Wilson, restored to office, dismissed the Civil Rights Commission as "a bunch of hoodlums." Without noticeable protest from U.S. authorities, he ordered all those who had voted for Means off the reservation, and his goons embarked on a new reign of terror; increasingly, the AIM supporters, their families, and their friends were attacked, beaten, and run off the road in an ongoing series of "accidents," many of them fatal. Despite the open lawlessness and violence he encouraged, Wilson seemed entirely confident of state and federal support, to judge from the fact that nearly one hundred people, most of them AIM members or traditionals, were victims of unsolved murders or "accidents" during his terms of office, in a feudal nightmare that Senator Abourezk would describe as "total anarchy." By 1975, almost everyone on the reservation went armed, and few dared to walk around outside even in daylight.

The mass dismissals of the Wounded Knee indictments had increased the resentment felt by Wilson and his goons, and the violence on Pine Ridge was intensified by the feud between Wilson and Means. On February 26, 1975, Means, the young AIM leader Dick Marshall, and others were assaulted in Pine Ridge village by a goon gang led by Richard "Manny" Wilson, Jr., and Duane Brewer of Dick Wilson's "Highway Safety Committee," which pursued them in a running gunfight down the road toward Wounded Knee; Marshall and his friends escaped by running a goon roadblock. The frustrated goons, who later claimed they had been assaulted by machine-gun fire, proceeded to the Pine Ridge airstrip, where they shot up a Cessna airplane that had brought a Wounded Knee defendant and a legal team from WKLDOC to the reservation.[2] When the lawyers returned, they realized that the plane was too damaged to fly, but before they could drive away, they were surrounded by more than twenty men brandishing shotguns, who jumped all over their car and kicked in the windshield. ("You want to be a Indian? Now you got a Indian car!") All six victims testified that Dick Wilson himself presided over the assault, coming to the window of the car and looking in, then telling his men, "Stomp 'em." One goon yelled at them, "Want to see a Means? Well, I'm a Means, and I ain't no Communist!" Three of the lawyers were given severe beatings, and one of them was knifed along the scalp. They were chased away in their damaged car, having been told not to come back or they would be killed.

Advised of this episode, the FBI gave lie detector tests not to the goons but to the victims. In the same spirit, a federal grand jury of twenty-one South Dakota citizens, convened not long thereafter to investigate reports of increasing mayhem on the Pine Ridge Reservation, indicted not Wilson and his goons but Dick Marshall and three AIM people, who were charged with assaulting Manny Wilson and Duane Brewer with a gun. After days of heated protest from the attorneys, the grand jury also indicted Dick and Manny Wilson, three Brewers, and two others for their actions at the airport; for the first time in his reign, the Tribal Council president was taken into court, mostly because—as the Indians noted—the victims had white skins. "When AIM complains, the government comes running; we have been ignored while the AIMers get response!" Dick Wilson cried, at a time when the U.S. government was investing $24 million a year in his administration. The outraged Wilson immediately created his own twenty-one-member Presidential Committee on Law and Order, to be convened on the same day as the twenty-one-member grand jury. "During the past 36 months, as president of the Oglala Sioux Tribe, I have endured every form of harassment believable and now I find myself in the ironic position of going from defender of my family, my home, and my tribe to defender of myself before a federal grand jury. I seriously suspect that there is a concerted effort to eliminate me as an obstacle to those individuals and groups who would rule by threat, violence, armed occupation and extortion."[3]

Having had himself fined $10 in his tribal court for the same actions, Wilson now pleaded double jeopardy on the federal charge of simple assault. Although he did not escape federal trial, he was promptly acquitted, at which point he boasted of the "justifiable stomping" of these "agitators."

Except for a tourist carnival of that name promoted by his smart rich brother Jim, Wilson had outlawed the sun dance. He also jeered at the sovereignty claim that was the main hope of the traditionals, doing his best to persuade his Tribal Council to accept the cash settlement for the Black Hills that was being sought before the Indian Claims Commission by a Washington lawyer named Arthur Lazarus. Meanwhile, he tried hard to depose the new BIA Superintendent, Al Trimble, who had flown in from Rapid City on the same day as the airport episode, and still remembers how Duane Brewer pounded on his car roof with a gun butt, shouting threats; eventually the Superintendent felt obliged to acquire a gun of his own.

A mixed-blood Oglala from Wanblee and a longtime BIA bureaucrat, Al Trimble had been in Washington at the time of the Trail of Broken Treaties. ("Dennis Banks and Trudell helped me get out of the building by a fire escape," recalls Trimble, a mild-mannered but outspoken man who now runs the Indian Center in Rapid City. "Since then, Dennis has always been a friend of ours. He was a quiet, easygoing guy even when I worked with him in Washington.") One of the rare BIA superintendents who took seriously their sworn duty to protect the best interests of the Indian people, Trimble had sought to cancel land leases with ranchers who failed to deal with diseased cattle or pay the absurdly small land-lease fees on Pine Ridge. Although a "moderate," he found himself increasingly opposed to Wilson, who had supported him until he offered help to the traditional people "out in the districts." "The real victims of law and order on this reservation," Trimble has said, "are the full-blood Indians who are cycled and recycled through this damned jail for the most trivial violations. If you're a mixed-blood and are aggressive enough to tell a policeman to go to hell, you can do anything you want. If you're a friend of Wilson's, you can do anything."[4]

As Trimble recalls, "Things started to come apart in the fall of 1974, when Wilson tried to get around the law by trying to sell beer and liquor at a rodeo on the reservation. We confiscated three hundred cases of beer, but the feds refused to prosecute anybody, and we think they gave him back his beer, as well. Then there was the murder of Jess Trueblood, when Manny Wilson and Duane Brewer concealed the evidence and the FBI cooperated, even though Brewer later hinted that Manny was involved in the killing. Hell, those goons were in complete charge, with their car caravans, squealing their tires around, intimidating people. Dick Wilson is not the most courageous person in the world; despite all the smoke that he was blowing, he never moved without a big gang of his goons. And half of our BIA cops were Wilson people, and they had our tribal judge in their pocket, too, and those white cowboys in the area were boasting about all their guns and about how they were going to shoot those 'longhairs' first and let the court ask questions later because they knew they could get away with it in South Dakota. It was a totally lawless situation, the traditional Indians just couldn't count on any law enforcement to protect them."

Al Trimble's son was pistol-whipped by goons, and the Superintendent himself was warned to "get a bodyguard because we're going to get you." The Bureau of Indian Affairs got to him first; Al Trimble was removed from office on March 20, 1975. "I really thought we were turning the corner at Pine Ridge when Wilson got them to remove me. Washington backed up a guy who has spent his whole life exploiting the Indian people."

Meanwhile, "Wounded Knee II," which had given traditionals such as Gladys Bissonnette real hope, had only produced more hatred and more violence, destroying communities as well as families even as economic conditions on Pine Ridge grew worse—or so said a spokesman for the Justice Department's Office of Indian Rights. Russell Means did not agree. "The children are wearing their hair long, wearing sacred eagle feathers," he said. "I count that an immeasurable plus. First, one has to have self-pride, then you have to have political change, then follows economic change. I don't see a really immediate change in the lifestyle on Pine Ridge, but neither do the Indian people on Pine Ridge expect it. Our concept of time, which makes up part of our reason for being Indian, is that we have no concept of time."[5]

⊡

In the dark month of March 1975, at least seven people, two of them young children, perished in the AIM–goon warfare on Pine Ridge. One of them was Pedro Bissonnette's sister-in-law Jeannette, the mother of six children, who was killed by a sniper on her way home from the wake of another AIM supporter; when her blue car had a flat tire, a friend stopped to help, at which point an unknown sniper shot Jeannette down. While attending Jeannette's funeral, Gladys Bissonnette lost her eleven-year-old grandson, Richard Eagle; the child destroyed himself while playing with the loaded rifle she kept in the house for protection. Meanwhile, harassment of traditionals continued. Bullets were fired through the house of Matthew King, an Oglala elder and interpreter for Chief Frank Fools Crow, and Fools Crow's own small house in Kyle, with a lifetime's belongings, was burned to the ground; both old men were threatened with death by marauding goons.

"The brutality and violence on the reservation is going to stop right now," Ted Means warned as AIM spokesman. Since the BIA, the FBI, and U.S. Attorney William Clayton had all ignored AIM's requests for help, the Movement would "take the necessary steps to protect Indian people on the reservation."

"We can deal with Wilson," said Ted's wife, Lorelei, later that spring. "Maybe he'll get assassinated or maybe one of us will get assassinated. We can fight like this, but what has got to change is the system of government on the reservation. People are ready to die for making that change. The hard core will probably get killed off, but I think it's going to happen. Hell, we're struggling for our life. We're struggling to survive as a people."[6]

Whether Jeannette Bissonnette had been killed by AIM hit men out gunning for Jim Wilson, near whose property she had been killed (as the FBI suggested), or by goons out gunning for Ellen Moves Camp, who drove a similar blue car (as the traditionals believe), it was clear that the traditionals were starting to shoot back. Two goons were among those who died during the bloody March of 1975, and in April, Louis Moves Camp was critically injured by a rifle bullet in Wanblee; although it might have been in retribution for his rape of a Pine Ridge woman, the attempt on his life was attributed to AIM.

The new determination of the traditionals to defend themselves was not lost on the authorities. "I'm fed up with the violence," announced state Attorney General Janklow, the man who had promised those who voted for him the year before to put "all AIM members in jail or under it"; he hated to answer the telephone, Janklow declared, for fear it would bring news of a race war.[7] Similarly, the Catholic Church, which was furnishing spiritual guidance to Dick Wilson and his goons, endorsed a "Law and Order Week." This injured the feelings of the BIA police chief, Delmar Eastman (the Crow Indian accused by the traditionals of involvement in Pedro Bissonnette's death). "There have been charges, which I emphatically refute, of a breakdown of law and order on the reservation . . . our force is very diligent, and has been doing a good job," said Eastman, apparently unaware that in 1975 the population of Pine Ridge Reservation had the highest crime rate in the United States. According to one FBI memo, the BIA police personnel were "untrained, poorly educated, and in some instances convicted felons."[8]

On April 24, the FBI circulated a six-page confidential document called "The Use of Special Agents of the FBI in a Paramilitary Law Enforcement Operation in the Indian Country." Protesting orders from the U.S. Attorney General's office at the time of Wounded Knee that they were to "aim to wound rather than kill"—not to mention the failure of other government agencies to submit to FBI authority in the Wounded Knee operation—the report made it clear that in any future confrontation "the FBI will insist on taking charge from the outset." Appearing two years after Wounded Knee, this document (signed by SAC Richard G. Held, the new head of the FBI's Internal Security Section and a longtime COINTELPRO specialist) suggests that some future confrontation was expected.[9]

In early May, the federal government announced that it was strengthening its investigative and prosecuting teams on the Pine Ridge Reservation: the U.S. Attorney's office in South Dakota would have seven more prosecutors, and the FBI would station additional agents near the reservation, in such towns as Gordon and Rushville, Nebraska. On May 10, the FBI began training a team of BIA police in Special Weapons and Tactics (SWAT) to complement its own SWAT team in Rapid City, and by the end of May, about sixty agents were posted in the Pine Ridge area, as opposed to three before the time of Wounded Knee; in addition, one thousand National Guardsmen commenced training in the Black Hills. "There are pockets of Indian population which consist almost exclusively of American Indian Movement (AIM) members and their supporters on the Reservation. It is significant in some of these AIM centers the residents have built bunkers which would literally require military assault forces if it were necessary to overcome resistance emanating from the bunkers."[10] On June 16, the Bureau called for additional agents, which supports the Indians' suspicion that an "incident" of the sort twice mentioned in Held's report was now expected. "These efforts," according to Attorney General Edward Levi, "will comprise a needed step toward enhancing the level of public safety on the reservation and show its residents we are dedicated to achieving prompt and fair enforcement." Also, additional judges were to be transferred to South Dakota to help with the backlog of Indian cases being brought into federal court by the FBI. U.S. District Judge Robert Merhige, assigned to the federal courthouse in Pierre, presided over one of the six trials at that time awaiting Russell Means, who had disturbed the peace when service to Indians was refused at a golf club in Mission built on Indian land. Judge Merhige, dismissing the case, bawled out the U.S. Attorney for bringing him all the way from Virginia to try petty police-court cases; small wonder, said he, that South Dakota had two hundred Indian cases awaiting trial.

Judge Merhige was apparently unaware of the nature of justice on Pine Ridge—where, for example, a Kadoka deputy sheriff named Ken Heltzel (a man with a reputation for disreputable dealings with Indians) made a deal with another white man to run his cattle on an Indian's land without asking permission of the owner. "He thinks he has power over the Indians because of the badge and the gun," said Sylvester Black Crow, an aspirant medicine man and AIM supporter, who impounded the cattle and prepared to slaughter them for a feast in the owner's honor. When Heltzel threatened him, "Selo" Black Crow, assisted by his dog, "shooed" the enraged lawman off his land, after which he put a call in to Pine Ridge to ask the BIA police and FBI for some protection. He was mixing paint when a large body of FBI agents and BIA and state police convened "on the BIA road," then cautiously approached his house, guns drawn. When Black Crow confronted them, he was told by Agent David Price, "I didn't come to protect you, I came because Ken Heltzel called State Alert about a heavily armed AIM camp, with Cubans." Black Crow assured Agent Price that he was harboring no Cubans, only "one Lebanese"; this was Charlie Abourezk, son of the senator, whose presence, in Black Crow's opinion, spared Black Crow from being arrested then and there for cattle rustling. Asked by Price if he understood his rights, Selo Black Crow, who went on mixing paint, said that he also understood his left. Possibly this joke and another about "cattle wrassling" in response to the threatened charge of "cattle rustling" were perceived as subversive by Agent Price; as will be seen, his preoccupation with Black Crow and Charlie Abourezk continues to this day.

In late May, at a small rodeo held in Oglala, an excited young Indian threatened a Wilson sympathizer with a gun; the traditionals in the outlying communities—at Oglala, Porcupine, and Wanblee, in particular—had had enough and were spoiling for a fight. But soon a whole column of goon pickup trucks arrived and a number of traditionals were badly beaten, including a young woman teacher who had been identified to the goons as an AIM sympathizer. In Dick Wilson's view, this was "law and order" of the finest kind. Asked by a reporter what had taken place, Wilson said, "People were shooting, so a bunch of the boys went up there and stomped hell out of 'em."[11]

The showdown that everyone knew was coming was bound to take place in Oglala, a small community in the White Clay District just twelve miles west of the Wilson stronghold in Pine Ridge village, on the road that leads northwest toward the Black Hills. Aside from the brown bare government housing, set down on a dry treeless plateau east of the road, Oglala consists of a white man's store, a scattering of old trailers, and some stripped-down "igloo" huts from the abandoned Black Hills Ordnance Depot, acquired by the BIA from the U.S. Army.

Della Star Comes Out (or Star: Oglala families often use abbreviated versions of their names) was a Community Health representative on the reservation for eight years; like Ellen Moves Camp, she had been fired from this post after Wounded Knee II because of her traditional sympathies, and she later ran an Indian store that has since closed. "For a long time," she said, "every time we start having a bingo or something, the goons and the BIA police would start coming around and, you know, start shooting around. And they'd start some kind of trouble and then we'd have to break up. . . . They were even shooting at our houses, and there's a lot of kids, you know, in some of these homes. The goons really done a lot of harassing, but there was nothing that could be done; we couldn't go to the BIA police because they were right with them. So finally the traditional, the elderly people, got together and asked, you know, that we'd have our own security around the Oglala area so we can have at least a little protection."

According to an Oglala leader named Francis He Crow, an invitation to AIM to send warriors to the community had been discussed as early as January 1975, and a general resolution in favor of it was drafted in March or April. In the same period, Dennis Banks, awaiting trial on the Custer charges, moved with his young Oglala wife into a log cabin on the property of Harry and Cecelia Jumping Bull, an elderly couple who lived a few miles southeast of Oglala on the narrow decrepit county road known locally as Highway 18. Harry Jumping Bull, a spiritual leader, gave five acres of his arid land to Banks and his infant daughter, Tasina Wanblee ("Eagle Shawl Woman"), born in August 1974. Tasina's mother, Darlene Nichols, whom Banks had met at the time of the Raymond Yellow Thunder protest in 1972 and who, as a young girl still in high school, had participated with her sister Bernardine at Custer and Wounded Knee, was called "Kamook" because, Banks says, "she was very round and strong as a baby, and her folks named her for a Japanese wrestler who was going around giving exhibitions at the time." Banks's relationship with Kamook (whose uncle was the Oglala hero Buddy Lamont) gave him a tie to the Lakota people that he had lacked at Wounded Knee.

After the abbey takeover at Gresham, Wisconsin, Anna Mae Aquash had gone back to St. Paul. With the help of figures in the entertainment world, she organized a successful benefit concert for the survival schools, which had lost all federal support after the Trail of Broken Treaties.[12] Afterward, she stayed on Rosebud for a time before joining the AIM group that was gathering at Oglala; there she lived in a small trailer house off Highway 18, between the village and the Jumping Bull property, and worked mostly with the local women. Although kept busy, Anna Mae was frustrated by the limitations of community work; she still had plans for "A People's History of the Land," compiled by researchers all over North America, which would present a true picture of Indian nations and their culture, as recorded in libraries and remembered in oral traditions.

Another member of the AIM group at Oglala was Leonard Peltier, whose West Coast group had served as security for Crow Dog's renewal of the ghost dance, in May 1974; the following month, with Jim and Bob Robideau, Peltier attended the first International Indian Treaty Council at Mobridge, on the Standing Rock Reservation—the meeting at which, according to Louis Moves Camp's testimony two months later at the Banks-Means trial, those agents from behind the Iron Curtain had been welcomed.

That summer, Peltier participated in his second sun dance, which Crow Dog dedicated to Raymond Yellow Thunder, Pedro Bissonnette, Frank Clearwater, and Buddy Lamont, and also to the vanishing bald eagle of North America. On August 9, 1974, after Peltier's failure to appear for trial in Milwaukee, a formal warrant was issued for his arrest; when the Banks-Means trial ended in September, he returned to Seattle. Earlier that year (February 1974), the fishing-rights struggle had been temporarily resolved when a courageous district-court judge named George Boldt upheld the Indian treaty, and on September 20, Peltier headed for Idaho to help the Kootenai Indians (who had declared war on the U.S. government). He had scarcely set out when he was arrested with his friend Roque Duenas and three others at Mercer Island, Washington, under the name of Leonard Little Shell (the family of traditional chiefs at Turtle Mountain), and charged with possession of illegal weapons. Because of the Milwaukee fugitive warrant, he did not show up for trial on these charges, but at the end of December he went back to Wisconsin, where he took part in the abbey takeover. By this time, an all-out search for him was under way, not only because he was a fugitive but because of his growing stature in FBI documents as an "AIM manager."

At Gresham, Peltier grew close to Dino Butler, who had taken the young Inuit named Nilak as his wife. A small, quiet man of thirty-two with a soft voice and a round, dark, unblinking gaze, Butler belonged to the remnant Tututni band from the mouth of the Rogue River.[13] "Like most Indians in Oregon," he says, "we were almost wiped out by the white people and their diseases. There are very few full-blood Indians left, and among my people, only seven or eight elders still speak our language; I am learning, but I know only a few words."

Except for brief visits to Portland and other cities, Butler never left his people's homeland until he was fifteen, when he was sent to the McLaren reform school in Woodburn, Oregon. "In those days, I used to wander a lot, and if I wanted to go somewhere, I just went. I never really did anything wrong, but if the police found me a hundred miles from home for no good reason, they'd get suspicious of a stray Indian and throw me into jail on general principles. Finally I was called 'incorrigible' and sent to McLaren. While I was there, in 1959, a guy I hung out with hit a guard, and because I was standing there, I got busted on assault charges; I didn't do nothing, so my friend got twenty months in the Oregon state pen, and I got twenty-four." At this memory, Butler smiles his strange sad-eyed smile. "That was my first felony. By the time I got out of there, I'd lost whatever spiritual instinct I had had from my grandmother, and I couldn't really relate to anything except drinking and drugs. I felt there must be something wrong with me, and I kept wandering. So pretty soon I was in trouble again, and back in the state pen—that's where I first run into Bob Robideau, sometime between 1967 and 1970, though after that I never seen him again until the Wounded Knee Memorial on Pine Ridge in '74.

"Early that year, when I was still drunk someplace in Oregon, a guy come along and asked if I wanted to help out driving some Indians in a caravan from Portland to the AIM convention down in Albuquerque. Can I drink? I said, and he said, Yup, and we went to Portland. And it was in Albuquerque that I first met Russell Means, at a big party. Banks was there, too; they had both come down for the weekend from their trial in St. Paul, and Banks said some brothers was needed up there on security. So I went on up there—that was February—and in April I traveled with Banks to a special ceremony for the Wounded Knee defendants, held at Green Grass, South Dakota. . . . I remember watching Crow Dog doctor Banks, putting a red-hot coal to his sun-dance scars; he told him he was not going to be convicted. And it was at Green Grass that I had my first sweat-lodge experience and smoked the pipe, and heard those brothers' prayers that everybody there would purify themselves of all those white-man poisons, and it was right then that I gave up drinking for good. I'd been looking for a direction like that all my life—I felt kind of reborn. After that, I went back to St. Paul, where a lot of traditional people were coming in, and those elders really opened up my mind."

In October 1974, as bodyguard to Dennis Banks, Butler had gone to Phoenix and Los Angeles, returning east for the abbey takeover in Wisconsin. In late February 1975, after the Menominees vacated the abbey, an AIM group including Peltier and the Butlers traveled south to assist John Trudell and Navajo AIM leader Larry Anderson in the eight-day takeover (February 25–March 3) of the Fairchild Corporation electronics plant on the Navajo Reservation at Shiprock, New Mexico, which had been laying off its underpaid Indian women employees for trying to protect themselves with some sort of union. (The occupation, which went off peaceably, would later cost AIM some Navajo support, since the multinational Fairchild company, transferring its operations to other desperate cheap-labor areas in Latin America and Asia, blamed the AIM people for shutting down the plant.)

From Shiprock, the group headed north for South Dakota. "Banks had called down there from Pine Ridge asking for warriors who were willing to come there and help out with the goons," Butler says. "These people were shooting into houses and throwing their bottles at cars and just running all over the traditional people, who were getting no protection at all from the police. So Leonard and me agreed to go, and we headed north with a few people, including Larry Anderson's young brother Mike. After we got there, we were joined by a few others."

"When we went up to South Dakota," Nilak says, "they sent the guys ahead and we stayed in another area and then we came. And the morning that we came, I remember the guys had been asked to pull security somewhere. They had been walking all night, and they had walked about, gee, thirty miles that night. That's when we came into Oglala. I was young and in love then; I was young and in love."

Among those who joined the West Coast group at Oglala was "Little Joe," who had been on the Pine Ridge Reservation nearly a year. Born a Coeur d'Alene Indian on Idaho's Lapwai Reservation in 1954, Joseph George had been removed to a government boarding school in Indiana at the age of seven; from there he was adopted by wealthy white people named Stuntz, who took him to New Mexico when they retired. Here young Joe Stuntz, as he was called, had a taste of affluent American life, frequenting country clubs and attending art school in Santa Fe. Eventually he married a Klallam Indian girl named Ida Charles (whom Peltier had known since 1965 and who was related to Steve Robideau by marriage), and in the early 1970s, he took a job as a forest ranger in the state of Washington. After the Wounded Knee occupation, he became restless; he joined Peltier's group for the funeral of Pedro Bissonnette, and a few months later, in February 1974, he quit his job and with his wife's young brother, Norman Charles, joined an Indian caravan from Seattle to Pine Ridge for a spiritual convention. Ida, who joined him there with their two small children, said that Joe had gone to South Dakota to relearn "what it was like to be an Indian." Looking for a "spiritual awakening," he took part in the revival of the ghost-dance ceremony at Crow Dog's Paradise, thinking that he might become a holy man, and he "pierced" in Crow Dog's sun dance later that summer. In May 1975, when he and Norman joined Peltier and Butler at Oglala, Ida Charles returned to Washington with the two children.

At Oglala, the expanding group lived at the house of an AIM supporter named Ted Lame. Here, Peltier was joined by Jean Day, a young Winnebago woman of twenty-four whose first AIM experience had been at Gresham; Day had been living with Anna Mae at Rosebud, and came with her to Oglala. "People brought us food out there, people brought us money, gas money, several times," Butler remembers. "Several times in the middle of the night, people would come to our house where we were staying and ask us to go down to their house. That their house was just shot up and that they were scared that the people who shot up their house might come back and they wanted someone from our house to go down there and spend the night. So we would go down there and we would take guns down there. I'm not denying this, you know. It would be foolish to go down there without guns.

"We met a man by the name of Francis He Crow who had some good ideals and he talked to us to help him organize in the community there, White Clay District, where Oglala is located. He said he wanted to organize the landowners there to break away from the BIA, from the United States government, and to seek help from other countries, other people. To start their own businesses in the White Clay District, where they would be self-supporting, where they wouldn't have to depend on BIA handouts.

"There were other people who came around and supported this idea. We had meetings at Oglala with the traditional people, landowners. At first, the people were kind of leery of doing this because it was done at Wounded Knee, it had been done before, and the government had come and squashed these ideals, these things that they wanted, and they knew there wasn't much chance of our pulling it off, I guess. But we kept talking and meeting with these people and finally we had sixty to seventy percent of the landowners, traditional landowners who lived on their own land out in the country. They said they would be willing to do this, and we were going to have another meeting that summer."

In March, the FBI, hunting for Peltier, had interrogated his mother, now Alvina Contreras, in Portland, Oregon. Mrs. Contreras said that she did not know her son very well, that she had no idea where he was, and that she was anxious to terminate the interview as soon as possible. On April 2, the Bureau issued a "Fugitive Alert" poster with a photograph of Peltier, describing him as "armed and dangerous."

"I remember one day we were working on the cars at Ted Lame's place, not long after Jeannette Bissonnette's death," Peltier says. "Dino was under the car and me under the hood when this David Price come in with another agent; he walks over and says, I want to talk to you guys. So I say, We don't talk to you people, and I started walking away. Well, Price grabbed me by the jacket, right above the elbow, and asked me what my name was; I jerked my arm away and gave him a made-up name, then told him to keep his goddam hands off. I told him he didn't have no right to touch me, and I wasn't going to submit to any interview or answer any questions. I guess he expected me to be docile, like most Indians; he just wasn't expecting this, and he never said a word. But maybe he remembered my face later on."

Because of increasing FBI pressure, most of the AIM people were using aliases: Anna Mae called herself "Joanna Jason," a name she had used in California. But in April she was detained and interrogated by Agent Price, who claimed to be investigating the fatal shooting of Jeannette Bissonnette. Because the FBI had shown so little interest in Indian deaths, it is now believed that Price's investigation was an FBI excuse to check out the unknown AIM people from outside the reservation who were living at Oglala, but in the paranoid atmosphere of AIM, her contact with Price, occurring within weeks of Douglass Durham's exposure, left Anna Mae open to the suspicion that she herself might be an informer, for hadn't she, too, been close to Banks? And this rumor was fed by the gossip and resentment caused by a *toka*'s, or "outside Indians," relationship with the husband of a well-liked Oglala woman. Even so, Anna Mae had many friends, including Dorothy Brings Him Back and Roslynn Jumping Bull, with whom she shared her passionate interest in Indian culture. "I tried to make myself believe in the white people's way but I couldn't," says Roslynn Jumping Bull. "Now I want to believe in the Indian way. . . . Without our ceremonies, I'd probably be just another old drunk."[14]

In May, Kamook Nichols arranged for the AIM group at Ted Lame's to occupy the log cabin on the Jumping Bull property while she and her husband were off on a trip, and in mid-May, the group moved in. The log cabin was the northernmost dwelling in a compound of three small houses with detached sheds and an outhouse; still farther north, on the dirt road that led out to Highway 18, was an outlying barn known as Jumping Bull Hall that was used for community meetings, and to the northwest, perhaps two hundred yards from the compound, was a red-and-brown frame cabin occupied by Wallace Little, Jr. ("June"), his wife, Wanda Siers, and their two children. The elderly Jumping Bulls lived in the white frame house in the compound; next door, in a very small green shack, lived their granddaughter, Angie Long Visitor, her husband, Ivis, and their three young children. As for the AIM group, most of them slept in the Bankses' log cabin, with the Butlers in their own tipi outside. The property had no phone (only one Pine Ridge house in fifty has a phone), and anyway, it did no good to call the BIA police for protection against the goons, since so many of the police were goons when not on duty. "Grandpa," who was eighty, and "Grandma," who was seventy-six, were glad to have these strangers here: they were able to teach the young Indians from other places something about Lakota spiritual traditions, and they enjoyed the protection from those breeds who had been trespassing and shooting fish with guns down at the reservoir. Over in Calico, a group of old people and young children out picking wild turnips had recently been harassed and threatened; when the terrified children ran away, the old people, including the medicine man Everett Catches, were handcuffed for no reason and forced to lie face down on the ground. Almost every night, goons roamed the area, shooting off guns and firing into the houses, but knowing that the AIM people went armed, they did not dare invade the Jumping Bull land.

In Oglala, the AIM people combined talks on the 1868 Treaty and the struggle for sovereignty with community service: they chopped firewood for the stoves of the elderly, planted trees and a community garden to offset the unhealthy welfare food, reroofed a store that had burned down, and provided counseling to alcoholics. Peltier, who had worked with alcoholics in Seattle and Milwaukee, had forbidden liquor and drug use in his group and was concentrating on young Mike Anderson's drinking. He and Butler were both good mechanics, and they offered free repairs on the worn-out local cars that were not only malfunctioning but dangerous. Peltier soon put back in service a red-and-white Chevy van belonging to Sam Loud Hawk, which came to replace Leonard's old green Ford as the group's vehicle. (All of the gear, including cars and food and guns, was owned collectively.) The women, led by Anna Mae, attended to the old people, setting up bingo games and bake sales to raise a little money for social activities that would bring people together and strengthen their resolve. In response, the Oglala community offered the outside Indians whatever food and gas money could be spared and also their respect and gratitude, particularly to Leonard Peltier, who in Banks's absence was recognized increasingly as leader.

"In Oglala, everybody knows him, respects him, especially the older people, because he doesn't drink. He is a real good man," said Russell Loud Hawk, a cousin of Sarah Bad Heart Bull and an Oglala leader whose family owned the log cabin used by Dennis Banks. Loud Hawk recognized that these Indians from other tribes had brought protection and new hope to the community, and though not an AIM member, he gave a little money to June Little to pass along to them for the group's support. Della Star Comes Out also recognized what Peltier and his people had contributed. "He has really done a lot for us. He helped us in organizing our communities, like social, you know, and he helped elderly people a lot, and he was a spiritual . . . well, in the Indian way we believe in our pipe, and we have ceremonies, and he was always there. . . . He was always good to everybody, not only me but the community. He's always helping people, you know." (In what Peltier still laughs about as "the poster caper," Della Star Comes Out, Roslynn Jumping Bull, Agnes Lamont, and other brave-hearted Oglala women made a game of tearing down the Peltier "Wanted" posters at BIA headquarters, until finally the posters were specially glassed and framed.)

"He was respected a lot," Jean Day said. "People listened to what he said, and I don't know more than that to say. For you to gain respect in the community like that is one of the highest honors you can have." Nilak Butler agrees. "I've always respected Leonard. When I met him in '74, I thought, Gee, this is a crazy guy! *Crazy* guy! But fun, *good* crazy, not nuts, really fun to be around him. We took a trip one time to Rapid, we were going down these back roads, and I mean they're barely cut out. And they're potholes and they're dirt and they're rugged. And Leonard took us at about eighty miles an hour through that road. That guy really knows how to drive! So we went up to Rapid and we all went to the movies and there was about fifteen of us stuffed in a car. . . .

"I remember one time when we were living at Oglala, we were all living in a log house at that time. The people came to visit us at our house, and one of the guys there—there was a girl who came, and Leonard was sort of checking out *that* situation, right? And he started teasing that guy about that girl. And she was a real tall girl, so Leonard was sitting there, and he's going, Yeah, in the morning, you know, we don't want to see no footprints on the ceiling! Just like that, and it really got rugged, but it was fun, you know. And when you're doing a lot of serious work like that, it's really important that you can joke around—that's what makes us different, I guess. You see all these war movies and all these dramatic situations and everybody's just always at each other's throats or having hysterics. But it was just never that way with us. We're just not that way.

"Because Oglala was so violent at that time, we were asked to be like a peacekeeping force. When there were community events, we would be asked to make sure that people, if they were drinking around, partying, that they would go somewhere else and do that. And sometimes people would come to us and their homes had been broken into and things stolen, and they would ask us to help recover that property, things like that. Part of the work we did was just helping people with funerals. We worked at a whole lot of levels. We also met with the elders and the traditional people, and many, many families, and we discussed the realities of sovereignty. What does it mean, and how can we live it? We'd talk about What Does the Treaty Mean? There was a lot of learning and teaching going on at that time. We set up a sweat lodge, and later we were living in tipis and tents, living a more natural kind of way. We didn't have electricity and we didn't have running water; we were setting up a smokehouse to dry out meat. A lot of times people talk of self-sufficiency and sovereignty, but it's more than talk, it's a way of living."

Dino Butler, though not shy, keeps silent as often as possible, with the result that when he does speak, people listen. "The stories that go out from the reservations look like Indian versus Indian—you know, Dick Wilson and his goons versus the American Indian Movement. But we know different. The Federal Bureau of Investigation, the CIA, and the BIA, and all these different organizations working for the government—they are the ones causing all the trouble. They give Dick Wilson and his goons money. . . . When AIM gathers, the FBI buys ammunition and booze and stuff for these goons so that they will start drinking. That's how they get their courage. They have to have this white man's poison in them before they can act like white people. They shot people's houses up, old people's houses. I seen a little girl at the sun dance, half of her arm was shot off, deformed. I seen a lot of people walking around with gunshot wounds and burns. . . .

"We know that the Federal Bureau of Investigation knew we were there. They knew that there was an American Indian Movement camp south of Oglala.... They knew that Dennis Banks was living there, that he had supporters there, and that we were trying to get these people to break away from the government that was doing them no good."

⊡

On June 1, 1975, a formal resolution of sovereignty based on the 1868 Treaty was signed by the Pine Ridge traditional chiefs, including Frank Fools Crow and Charlie Red Cloud, the ninety-year-old grandson of the great war leader. The document repudiated all legislation passed by the U.S. Congress since 1868, "especially the Indian Reorganization Act of 1934 and the Citizenship Act of 1924. The American Indian Movement is likewise recognized by us to reside and work here to support us in our goals."

To the traditionals, the Lakota Treaty Council, or council of chiefs, was the only legitimate government on the reservation. One signer was Frank Kills Enemy, eighty-six, an expert on treaty law, whose grandfather Red War Bonnet had been one of the eleven who made their marks on the Fort Laramie Treaty. "My grandfather, my grandson are Indian and Indian, and I got the 1868 Treaty here in my grip.... Everybody knows that everything Red Cloud was fighting for was conceded by this treaty. It was a complete great day for the Lakota."[15]

On June 5, in Cedar Rapids, Iowa, Leonard Crow Dog, Carter Camp, and Stan Holder were convicted on Wounded Knee charges after a brief trial, and Dennis Banks called for a support group to be there for the sentencing on June 27. In the meantime, the AIM group at Oglala attended AIM's eighth annual convention from June 6 to 18 at Farmington, New Mexico, a town of two dozen churches and innumerable bars that prospered on the trade of Navajos from the surrounding reservations.

The eight hundred Indians at the convention, according to a memo (June 18, 1975) to the FBI Director from the Special Agent in Charge in the Albuquerque office, "definitely had the potential of causing great harm in the form of civil violence and disorder." But great harm and the ugliest sort of civil violence had occurred in Farmington long before AIM came into town. In the preceding two years alone, ten defenseless Navajo had been tortured, sexually mutilated, then killed—in one case, by means of a large firecracker shoved up the anus—in race murders in Farmington and in Gallup, where Trail of Broken Treaties leader Larry Casuse had been shot dead by the police on March 1, 1973. Despite all their churches, both towns had made an industry of selling alcohol to Indians and declined all responsibility for the result. John Redhouse, a Navajo spokesman for the National Indian Youth Council who went to high school in Farmington, has said that assaults on Indians there were common; in his opinion, these murders were not sick isolated incidents but part of the whole pattern. Three white youths convicted of the firecracker killing as well as two other murders in the Farmington area were sentenced to two years in reform school, then released on parole outside the state well before these sentences were finished, causing the Navajo people in the region to stage the peaceful protest marches that had so alarmed the Albuquerque FBI.

At the Farmington convention, legal means of combating the illegal expropriation of mineral resources on Indian lands were discussed, and so was the damage done by Douglass Durham. Leonard Peltier, who was in charge of security at the convention, was given the responsibility of confronting Anna Mae Aquash with the spreading rumors that she was also an informer; he handled this in his own easygoing way. "I run into Anna Mae on the Trail of Broken Treaties, but we never talked hardly; we never really got to know each other until we were part of the support group for Russ and Dennis at St. Paul. She was involved in a lot of stuff, and she could have done a *lot* of damage if she was an informer. Anyway, I trusted her. So we just went over and sat in a car and bullshitted a little while, and that was all there was to it." Understandably, Anna Mae herself took the charges more seriously. Upset and disheartened, she considered going home to Nova Scotia. Instead, she stuck it out at Pine Ridge, returning to her work with the Oglala women. On June 23, accompanied by Jean Day, she left for Cedar Rapids to address a citizens' group on behalf of Crow Dog, Camp, and Holder, who were to be sentenced on the Wounded Knee charges four days later.

At Farmington, the fragmentation and dispersal of the AIM leadership was very apparent. Russell Means, for one, had not come to the convention, which had scarcely started when news came that he had been shot in the back by a BIA officer; the bullet pierced the kidney. The shooting, which occurred on June 8 on the Standing Rock Reservation, not far from the place where another Indian policeman had shot down Sitting Bull, was described as an accident by the police, who arrested Means's friends for "rowdy behavior." Means himself, when he recovered, was charged with assaulting the officer who shot him.[16]

The timing of the episode was unlucky. Perhaps in warning to the authorities, perhaps in affirmation of the desperate feeling on Pine Ridge and elsewhere that AIM had been targeted for obliteration, national secretary John Trudell passed the word at Farmington that AIM warriors were to shoot back when shot at, even by law-enforcement officers. Perhaps an informer notified the law, for on June 16—by coincidence or otherwise—the FBI office in Rapid City put in a request for additional men, citing AIM activities and potential violence on Pine Ridge.

When the Oglala group returned to the reservation in mid-June, it was accompanied by Peltier's cousin Bob Robideau, a thin, quiet man whom Leonard refers to affectionately as "Razor." (According to Butler, "Bob had had a spat with his wife, Andrea, because he wanted to come with us to Oglala and she thought he ought to come on home to Eagle Butte, up on Cheyenne River; see, they had a house up there and a young baby and everything.") Other newcomers were three young Navajo friends of Mike Anderson—Wilford "Wish" Draper, eighteen, his cousin Norman Brown, fifteen, and young Lena Funston, known as "Lynn," all of whom wished to attend Crow Dog's sun dance later in the summer—and two Lakota kids from Rapid City, Jean Bordeaux, fourteen, and her half brother, Jimmy Zimmerman, eleven, who had been at Farmington with their mother and wished to visit Peltier's camp out in the country. Jean and the little brother she called "Zimmerman," who was there to "learn the ways of the pipe" and prepare with the older boys for his first sun dance, were the only Lakota people in the group.

Young Jean, who became Norman Brown's girl friend, had full confidence in Leonard Peltier: "He was real nice and real generous, too, and teasing everybody all the time." Jean's mother had known Leonard since 1967, in the days of the auto-repair shop in Seattle. "I was really impressed," Evelyn Bordeaux remembered. "He was up front and friendly even in those days, didn't rip me off the way a lot of them do with a woman alone; he installed a new transmission for only ten or fifteen dollars, and he did it right away, didn't make me wait. Leonard wasn't into political activities at that time, he was just trying to help his own Indian people. I never seen him again until October '73, at the time of Pedro's funeral, and after that, the West Coast group stayed maybe six weeks at my house in Rapid. Leonard was sharing the leadership with Jimmy Robideau and sometimes Bob—white people never understand how Indian leadership can work that way without causing trouble. Anyway, I knew Leonard well. So when I took my kids down to the Farmington convention with our Rapid City survival school, and on the way back, they wanted to go camp down at Oglala, I didn't mind, because I figured that with Leonard there, they'd be okay."

For a few days, the enlarged group crowded into the log cabin near the Jumping Bulls' house, but eventually some tents were erected and a sweat lodge built in the woods of cottonwood, ash, and willow along White Clay Creek, perhaps four hundred yards southeast of the compound, where a slope descended from plowed fields on the plateau south of the house to the creek bottom. Three white tents, the Butlers' tipi, and an orange pup tent were set up around a clearing in the woods, and a sweat lodge of canvas draped over bent saplings of cottonwood was constructed by the water. Butler, Peltier, and Banks took turns running the sweat-lodge ceremony, in which prayer with the sacred pipe was held twice each day; there was a special ritual for the occasion when "Little Joe"—he was well over six feet tall—was given his own medicine pouch by the Oglala spiritual leaders. "It was *not* an armed military camp hatching terrorist plans," Peltier says. "It was a spiritual camp, there to support Dennis and the Oglala people."

"It was a time," Jean Day remembers, "when I really got to know myself, got to know who I was, and I really got to believe in the pipe." In addition to the daily prayers to the sun and air and earth and water and the four directions, there were prayers for the safety of everyone, even the confused Indians who wished them harm; while they all were anxious to avoid violence, Jean Day says, everyone was psychologically prepared for trouble.

Norman Brown, the youngest of the three Navajo boys, had known Peltier since 1973, when they participated in their first sun dance together. He, too, remembers the camp life on White Clay Creek as pleasant and rewarding, with plenty of firewood and good fresh water that the younger boys took turns lugging uphill for "Grandma and Grandpa" Jumping Bull. "Everybody was healthy, everybody was helping each other, and people came to visit from all over." For an anniversary party held for the old couple at Jumping Bull Hall just after the group's return from Farmington, the AIM people helped restore the ramshackle building and erect a shade to protect the guests from the June sun; that day Harry Jumping Bull, who was much respected, was presented with a rifle by Chief Frank Fools Crow, the spokesman for the Lakota Treaty Council.

Nevertheless, the boy lived with a nagging dread of goons, about whom he had been warned by some of the Oglala people and also by Bob Robideau and Anna Mae. As Brown admits, "I was scared ever since I was staying there, and we always had to look out before we went somewhere." His cousin Wish Draper was so uneasy about a goon raid on the camp that when the AIM people moved down from the compound to the creek, he remained behind, in a tent set up behind the Jumping Bulls' white house. "He's quiet, and stays to himself," Norman Brown explained.

Jimmy Zimmerman lived in an orange pup tent with Little Joe, who was changing his name from Stuntz to Killsright. "Joe was one of those real quiet persons, like Dino," Leonard says. "If he knew you, he could sit around and bullshit good as anyone, but in a group, he might sit there and say two words in two hours. Once I asked him why he decided to join the Movement, and he told me that the white family that raised him wasn't too proud of his Indian blood, but AIM had made him proud of it, and he just wanted to help the Indian people any way he could. He intended to change his name back to Joe George, the one they give him on the Lapwai Reservation, but a Pine Ridge family gave him the name 'Killsright,' and he really liked that. He was in spiritual training, too; I think it was Billy Good Voice Elk, there in Oglala, who gave Joe his medicine. I remember once I jumped on his case for leaving his medicine over at his ex-girl friend's; I warned him that it was supposed to be carried on him at all times. But I know he wasn't carrying it in June, because I remember him commenting several times about how he had to go and get it."

"Joe and Norman Charles was brother-in-laws," says Zimmerman's sister. "I didn't know Norman Charles too good; he was kind of quiet and kept pretty much to himself. Little Joe was also very shy. We had two horses, but Joe said he was scared of horses and wouldn't ride with me down to the reservoir one day when I wanted to go, so we used to tease him about being scared of women, too. One time we hid his boots, and he looked around and around, all over the place, but he wouldn't say nothing about his boots being gone, that's how shy he was."

On the early morning of June 25, Jean Bordeaux, Norman Brown, and Jimmy Zimmerman were sitting up late, down by the creek. "Maybe around three or four o'clock," Jean says, "not long before the sun, we heard something very big walking in the creek. It wasn't any animal, either, and it wasn't like somebody tossing in big rocks; it was *plunk-plunk-plunk,* like that, big steady steps. Zimmerman was so scared he just ran off, he wanted to wake up Joe, because him and Joe was living in one tent. Norman Brown said it was the Big Man, and that his people over in Arizona knew all about it, but we were all too scared to go down there and look." In the evening of that day, huge dark thunderheads gathered over the Black Hills, followed by wild angry winds and lashing rain that caused property damage all over the western part of South Dakota.

BOOK II

CHAPTER 7

THE SHOOT-OUT I

June 26, 1975

I was not hostile to the white man. . . . We had buffalo for food, and their hides for clothing, and we preferred the chase to a life of idleness and the bickerings and jealousies, as well as the frequent periods of starvation at the Agencies.

But the Gray Fox [General Crook] came out in the snow and bitter cold, and destroyed my village. All of us would have perished of exposure and hunger had we not recaptured our ponies.

Then Long Hair [Custer] came in the same way. They say we massacred him, but he would have massacred us had we not defended ourselves and fought to the death.

Crazy Horse, dying

In the late afternoon of June 25, 1975, two FBI agents came to the outlying cabin northwest of the Jumping Bulls' compound, accompanied by two BIA policemen. Insisting upon searching the cabin, they told Wanda Siers, June Little's wife, that they were in search of Jimmy Eagle, aged nineteen, who was wanted on charges of assault and theft; the BIA police had received a report that Eagle, traveling in a red vehicle, had been seen in the vicinity of this cabin. The agents were told by Eagle's friend Dusty Nelson, resting in a hammock in the small grove north of the cabin, that Eagle had not been seen for several days; Siers declared that since the agents could show no warrant, they were trespassing, and she asked them to leave. From the cabin, the agents could see a number of Indians who were watching in silence from the compound, perhaps two hundred yards away along the rim of the plateau, and apparently they decided against going closer.

By early evening, dark thunderheads rumbled all over the horizon, as the day's humidity accumulated into storm. Norman Charles, Mike Anderson, and Wish Draper, who had walked into Oglala for a shower at the end of the long hot muggy afternoon, were returning to the property along Highway 18 when a green car pulled up alongside, and the same two agents asked to see some identification. Discovering a rifle clip that Charles was carrying wrapped in his towel, they became suspicious, and when the boys could not prove their identity (all gave false names), the agents ordered them into the car and took them to BIA headquarters in Pine Ridge. There the BIA police assured the agents that none of the three was Jimmy Eagle, who was Gladys Bissonnette's grandson and the older brother of the child killed accidentally while playing with a rifle.

Mike Anderson remembered afterward that when they told the older men what had occurred, Leonard Peltier bawled them out for getting into the FBI car; he cooled down a little when the three said that the agents had not hassled them, but nevertheless he disliked the idea of FBI men hanging around the Jumping Bull property.

On the morning of June 26, after a night of heavy thunderstorms, tornado winds, and rain, Norman Brown slept late because he had been on security until 3:00 or 4:00 a.m. Awaking, he remembers seeing Jean Bordeaux and her friend Lynn preparing food. ("Oatmeal, probably," Jean Bordeaux says, " 'cause that's all we had.") The morning was sunny and pleasant, and while waiting to eat, the boy sat on the hood of

Peltier's old green Ford, the car in which they had traveled north from Farmington, New Mexico, the week before; there he was joined by Little Joe Stuntz, the tall, shy, quiet young Coeur d'Alene Indian whom Peltier had assigned as bodyguard to Dennis Banks. "Most days, Dennis picked Joe up early, took him to Custer," Jean Bordeaux recalls. "This was the one day that Joe took off."

Up the hill to the northwest, perhaps four hundred yards away, the Long Visitor family was using the white house, since Grandpa and Grandma Jumping Bull had left at daybreak for a steer auction over in Nebraska. Angie Long Visitor heard "firecrackers or something" while washing dishes, and because her small children were playing outside, she walked out onto the bluff to have a look. Two strange cars were parked in the pasture meadow west of the compound and below, down toward the horse corral, at the edge of the creek woods. One of two white men—she assumed they were lawmen because of the radio aerials and the good condition of the cars—was removing a gun case from the trunk of his car; the other was kneeling and shooting in her general direction with a handgun. Frightened, she grabbed up her kids—four, two, and nine months—and ran into the house. "We didn't know what to do at first," she says. "We just closed the door and stayed in there for a while." Then she and her young husband, Ivis, decided they'd better run: "We was so scared! We just grabbed our kids, and we just started runnin' real fast!" They fled south along the edge of the plowed field, then cut across toward Highway 18. On the way, they met a few of the AIM Indians from the camp down in the woods, who were running uphill toward the houses.

When what sounded like an exchange of shots came from the direction of the compound a quarter of a mile away, Norman Brown and Joe had jumped up to investigate. From the wood edge below the bluff, they could see nothing, but it was plain that the shooting was coming from the area of the Jumping Bull houses; they ran back downhill to arm themselves and alert the camp. Norman grabbed his single-shot .22, and Joe Killsright, a .30-30 deer rifle; then they took off again, up through the bushes. Bullets whistled overhead as soon as they appeared, Brown says; even so, he and Joe continued uphill into the compound to join Mike Anderson and Norman Charles.

"I was in the tipi with my wife," Dino Butler recalls. "We were just getting up, and I heard the firing up there. Norman Brown came down and said, There is shooting up there, there's women and children up there, we got to get up there. So I grabbed my gun and told my wife to take Jean and the other girl out of here. I went running up there with my brothers. It took me five minutes or so to get up there, and yet we were already surrounded by the time I got there. I seen Ivis and Angie and their three children run out of their house, running toward our camp, in the direction of our camp." By that time, Butler says, at least twenty shots had been fired.

From the green house in the compound, looking downhill to the west, Norman Brown saw two cars and two white men well over a hundred yards away; a gold-white car was parked behind a green one, both aimed in the general direction of the camp. The trunk of the gold-white car was open, and its driver was behind it, a rifle or shotgun at his shoulder; the other man, using a handgun, was crouching and shooting next to the green car. Brown recalls seeing Leonard Peltier lying down by a row of junked cars near the woods, rising up to fire, lying prone again.

Almost immediately, someone yelled that two more cars were coming in from Highway 18, one of them a green-and-white BIA patrol car, and Brown ran across to the log cabin to try to divert the attention of these cars with his .22. Apparently, Anderson and Norman Charles were also firing at those cars. At a distance of nearly two hundred yards, the young Indians succeeded in shooting out one tire on each of them, and the cars backed up in a wild zigzagging retreat along the rain-puddled dirt road toward Highway 18, before one of them got stuck in a muddy ditch. After a long-range exchange of shots with a big white man who jumped out of this car and began shooting, Brown returned to the edge of the bluff overlooking the meadow, in time to see the man with the shoulder gun behaving strangely. "He crawled through the front of the car and he crawled out. He was there for a while, and then he crawled back out and got in the same place where he was at." The man with the handgun, however, was still "shooting away there."

By this time, additional cars traveling at high speed were arriving from both directions on Highway 18; the Indians were astonished to see so many men arrive so quickly. At this point, or so Brown said later, his friend Joe came up "and told me they were going to kill me. This is the time to be a man; today you can be a warrior. Remember our sisters and the children at the camp." In Brown's account, Joe Killsright said that more lawmen were coming in from the southeast, and he sent

Brown and Anderson away from the compound, down along the plateau, to cover the approaches to the camp from the open fields.

⊡

"Dino and I got up late that day, and we were coming out of the tipi and the younger girls were cooking breakfast, and all of a sudden a whole bunch of shooting started. All the guys took off and went up the hill to find out what was going on, because there were about four different families living up there, and all of them had young children, and there were about, I'd estimate, eight kids up there and three pregnant women, and there were also Grandma and Grandpa Jumping Bull lived up there, and they had just celebrated their fiftieth wedding anniversary that year, so they were older people, and everybody was really concerned about someone getting hurt. . . . I took the younger girls and a young boy, and we stayed down there to see what was going to happen. We didn't know what to do. We were trying to go over this one hill and see what was going on, but we didn't want to get in the way. And a couple of people were walking out of there with their kids, and we said, Well, what's going on? They said, Oh, they're having a firefight over there. And they said that it might be police officials, and they said they were taking off. All this happened really fast: it probably takes a longer time to tell about it than it actually happened. So then we took off; we were running to this one area where we knew there was a bridge to get onto the main road and try to get the kids out of there, and by the time we hit that main road, there was already a roadblock on it, and a lot of people there. And I was so surprised because it seemed like the shooting had just barely started and already they had roadblocks up. . . . We thought about just saying we were taking a walk, but then we thought, Well, maybe not, because they looked like they were kind of eager to get it on with anybody, and I didn't want to put the kids in jeopardy. So we started walking back to camp, and at that time we saw helicopters, and I remember thinking, What the hell *is* this?!"

⊡

Although they are very careful not to mention names, the men from the AIM camp suggest that a number of Indians besides themselves and the Littles and Long Visitors ("Those are the only ones the government was sure of") were present on the Jumping Bull property that morning, and that many of them were shooting at the agents. At some point not long after noon, the agent seen crawling through the car had passed out from shock and loss of blood, and his partner, less seriously wounded, had thrown his gun down and stripped off his white shirt. Perhaps he waved it as a white flag in sign of surrender; in any case, he apparently attempted to rig it as a tourniquet on the shattered arm of the downed agent. In the next few minutes, one or more people approached the cars and killed both white men at close range with one or more high-powered rifles.

Perhaps someone panicked, though this seems unlikely; perhaps someone was settling an old score or simply had a murderous impulse, although this seems unlikely, too. In view of the virulent hostility to AIM, especially in the lawless atmosphere of Pine Ridge, the Indians present may have feared that whether or not these white men survived, anyone involved here would be shot on sight, even if they surrendered; there was no way they would ever get to trial. Even flight would probably be hopeless if anyone could be identified by the victims; their last desperate chance was to finish off the agents, one of whom seemed certain to die anyway of massive hemorrhage. And so—perhaps—one or more of these tense men, excited and angry, horrified by so much blood, and full of dread, nerved himself to finish off the white men. Whether the killing was sudden, impulsive, solitary, or whether it was done in quick consensus—and whether or not the AIM Indians were involved—it was over quickly; and after it was over, the AIM people, poorly armed and having no choice but to shoot their way out, took the dead men's arms and ammunition and moved the green car on its flat tires across the hillside and down into the woods just above the camp, where its two radios, still transmitting on the law-enforcement channels, would keep them informed of the certain death that seemed to be coming down upon them.

About forty minutes after the first shots, when the only gunfire was a long-range and sporadic exchange between the cabins and the cluster of official cars out on Highway 18, someone yelled for a cease-fire. Soon a small Datsun station wagon came bumping down the long and muddy road past Jumping Bull Hall, continuing all the way to the Little cabin before it stopped; along the bluff on foot, approaching the compound, came a young white woman whom the Indians recognized as Joanna LeDeaux, a Wounded Knee Defense Committee aide who was then living on the reservation. LeDeaux had come in to try to negotiate a cease-fire or, failing that, arrange for the safe departure from the compound of any women and children who might remain. But the women and children had already gone, and as for negotiating a cease-fire, the defenders had nothing with which to negotiate, not even live hostages; they told the young woman that the agents were dead, and they told her to leave. Their only hope for life was flight, and probably they had delayed too long already while giving the women and children in their camp a chance to flee. Shocked by the enormity of what had happened, LeDeaux eventually departed, and Peltier, Robideau, and Butler returned to the camp to load Sam Loud Hawk's red-and-white van for an escape; they left Joe Killsright and Norman Charles as a rear guard in the compound to delay anyone who tried to approach.

"By noon our defensive positions had been completely surrounded by FBI agents, some of which were SWAT-trained, BIA police, BIA SWAT teams, state law enforcement, and non–law enforcement who were comprised of local white farmers and goons," wrote Bob Robideau later.[1] "We could see some of their positions plainly, such as those to the northeast and northwest of us, but we knew that there were others in the area who we could not see because of their radio communication, which we had access to. We felt that these others were moving in on our position through the grove of trees which follow a winding stream that runs from the north to the south. The length of time that had passed was another factor that contributed to the general feeling that our position was fast becoming a very precarious one, for if they were indeed moving through the grove of trees it was essential for us to also move back toward camp and into the cover of the trees, in order for us to effectively counter their pre-planned intentions of wiping us out.

"Shortly after most of us had regrouped in camp, the message that SWAT teams from Denver and Minnesota were on their way and due to arrive in Oglala at five-thirty came through over our captured communication system. Upon hearing this, there no longer was any doubt in any of our minds and hearts that death was stalking us from all sides. We knew that we were in all probability going to die before the day was gone. There was no need for words, each one of us knew what was coming; we were mentally and spiritually prepared. . . . And although each one of us were quietly and calmly going about the camp picking out needed supplies, fear could easily be seen on each and every one of our weary faces."

Not long after LeDeaux's departure—it was now about 1:30 p.m.—a shout was heard from down in the woods perhaps eighty yards below the small green cabin. Then a big voice called, "This is the FBI!" and ordered the Indians to come out with their hands high. Joe Killsright and his young brother-in-law ran to the green shack, and one of them got off a warning shot down toward the woods. The shot was answered by a burst from several guns at once, and in the exchange of fire that followed, a bullet struck Joe Killsright in the forehead, killing him instantly.

Down in the woods, Peltier, Robideau, and Butler, assisted by Wish Draper, were loading the van with clothes, sleeping bags, CB radios, and other equipment. (Draper claimed later that he had walked the other way when the shooting began, and remained in a ravine about 150 yards south of the camp until the green car, radio squawking on the FBI frequency and full of bullet holes, had come bumping down the hill on its flat tires. His loyal cousin Norman Brown, who had known him all his life in their little Navajo community at Many Farms, near Chinle, Arizona, would support this story: "Wish is a spiritual man, and I don't think he believes in guns; that is why he did not pick up a gun.") The older men were worried about what might have happened to the three girls and Jimmy Zimmerman, and Wish Draper went back up the hill to tell Joe to hurry up. He returned with Norman Charles, followed by Anderson and Brown; Charles told the older men that Joe was dead. "We all took the news in silent acceptance of our present situation," Robideau says, "for in our hearts and minds we believed that we would be back alongside of Joe before the day was out."

Norman Brown asked Peltier what they were going to do, and Peltier said they were going to pile into the van and make a run for it. The others objected; there was simply no way they could get past all those guns out on Highway 18, even if they got that far. "I thought the only way was to *shoot* our way through the roadblocks," Peltier says, "but then I realized the van was almost out of gas, that it might quit on us even before we got to the first roadblock. Also, Dino had reconnoitered, and him and Bob thought we would never make it."

The men were still worried about the girls and Jimmy Zimmerman, but there was no more time; they got set to go. "We prayed for guidance and strength and for our brother," Butler says, "prayed that he would have a safe and good journey up to the spirit world, and that someday we would be there with him. And then we left." Each man took a rifle except Wish Draper, who was given a bag of dynamite by Bob Robideau, and an agent's shotgun.

"Our thoughts and feelings concerning our present position were discussed by all and it was agreed that if we hoped to live through the day, we would have to attempt to break free from the ring of law enforcement that surrounded us. Finally it was agreed that going south might offer the best chance for our retreat, because offensive positions seemed to be concentrated to the north, northeast, and northwest; though we knew that there were also offensive positions to the south, we felt that they were the weakest. But nevertheless, when we moved out, we moved out expecting trouble to spring up in front of us any moment. We thought that if we could get far enough south without engaging in a firefight, we would be close enough to high ground to reach it. We knew that if we could reach high ground, we might have a chance of outfighting them, at least until nightfall. We spread out in defensive positions and started moving slowly and cautiously toward the south."[2]

⊡

Meanwhile, Nilak and the children were making their way back up the creek. "We hooked up with the guys about that point—we were just crossing this little river, going across this bog, and I lost my moccasins—and that's when they told us Joe was dead, and they said he had been shot in the head. And we got growled out because they said, We didn't know where you guys were, and we were worried about you. They—you know, it was a pretty heavy firefight going on."

Nilak reported that there were roadblocks everywhere, they were surrounded, there was no way out. Not knowing what to do, they made a circle and prayed for the safety of the women and children. "Leonard told us he was real sorry me and Zimmerman were in danger," says Jean Bordeaux, "and that me and Zimmerman should try to leave them and get out safely. I thought for sure we were going to die that day, I guess everybody thought so, but I still wanted to stay. I knew what was going on on the reservation, I knew that those men had started shooting at us, and I trusted everybody I was with; they were doing what was right. So I made my decision to stick with them, no matter what."

"We all sat down together and said a prayer," Leonard remembers. "If the Great Spirit will help us, we'll get out safely; if not, we're going to die. When I said that, I saw the tears come to Jimmy's eyes—he was only a little boy and he was scared. So I decided that even *these* people wouldn't shoot down a little boy, and I asked him if he wanted to go back; I told him, If you keep your hands high and keep yelling, I'm not armed! Don't shoot! you'll probably make it. So he said he would go. Dino objected: he thought that they would kill him. Sure enough, ten or fifteen minutes later, we heard shots. And that really tore me up, because I knew I was responsible."

"I tried to tell him he had a better chance if he stuck with us," Dino recalls, "but he said he wanted to give himself up, so I led him up to the edge of the woods and wished him luck." As Nilak remembers it, "Jimmy told us that he didn't think that he could run with us. He didn't think that he was strong enough to do that yet. . . . He came and talked to each of us and we shook his hand and then he took off. And when we . . . heard them open up, we thought they'd killed him."

During the prayer, Norman Brown says, an eagle alighted in a tree above their heads and screamed. "We expected to be killed. There was no way out—we were surrounded. But an eagle came and sat in a tree above us and then flew away, and we knew that was the direction we should go in." After Zimmerman had gone, the group continued down the stream another half mile, and again the eagle appeared to Norman Brown, alighting briefly, going on; and again, he declared, they followed the eagle until they came to a culvert under the BIA school road that leaves Highway 18 west of Oglala, loops southwest behind the dam of the Oglala Reservoir, and rejoins the highway southeast of the Jumping Bull land, toward Pine Ridge. The culvert is only a quarter mile from the junction, where a big roadblock was already set up, and as they came up through a gully toward the road, three cars full of men rumbled over the culvert, then passed again; even so, this culvert was their only hope of crossing to the open hill country toward the south. (It turned out later that a BIA detachment had been posted at this place until just a few minutes before. The Indian police had heard over their radio that the assault force was "going in" to the Jumping Bull compound—it was now about 6:00 p.m.—and had decided that it was probably all right to go back out to Highway 18 for a drink of water.)

"Everybody was trying to just kind of sneak on through this great big old drainpipe," Nilak says, "and on the inside, I remember, it was all ridged, like it was just tearing up everybody's knees, and everybody was trying to get through, and I remember Leonard going, Okay, you guys, just go on through now, just go on through. And we're all looking at him, waiting for *him:* he was a little bit more *cheppah* [Lakota for "fat"] than he is today! And finally, when he went through, and we were in the middle of it, a pig car came, and everybody just froze, you know. . . . Then we got on the other side, and there were these few trees, and I mean they were scrawny little suckers, right? So all the guys went up the trees, and then this one girl and I, we wrapped ourselves around the bottom of the tree like nobody's supposed to notice. We were sort of laying there, and I remember these little ants were crawling up our noses, and these cars are going by, and we're all just trying-to-be-cool, nobody-notice-us, and they didn't. And there was a small plane above us at that time, and I thought for sure they'd spotted us because they were circling right where we were, and we all thought, Well, maybe they know we're here. But none of the police cars stopped or anything. And then this whole herd of cows came up, and they were mooing around us, which was really good, because usually if there are people around, cows take off or they act weird, but they just acted like cows, you know, roaming around us, and I think that's part of the reason nobody noticed us."

"There was a spotter plane circling overhead," Leonard says, "and there was no way we could move on up toward the ridge without being seen, and there was so little cover where we were laying in them cottonwoods that two of the younger guys had to stay back in that culvert. I told everyone, That plane has got to run out of fuel and go on back, and when it does, we'll run. We must have laid there for almost two hours when Norman Charles hollers from the culvert that Baby Aim—that's what we called Mike—is panicking in there, and Mike himself yells that he don't want to be trapped, and the next thing we know, he comes popping out! So we *had* to run then, never mind the plane."

Throughout the escape, the spotter plane had been cruising back and forth over White Clay Creek; now, suddenly, it cut away toward the south, and realizing it was probably returning to Pine Ridge for fuel, the fugitives took off for the high country. At first they hoped they had not been seen, but out on Highway 18, sixteen or seventeen cars gathered quickly. "Dino and Bob and Leonard were in the rear, making sure we got up all right," Nilak says. "But then somebody opened up on us, and it wasn't sneak anymore, it was full run. I was barefoot, running right across the cactus, and I didn't even notice."

"If we'd have headed more toward the west, we'd have been hidden from the roadblocks for quite a while," Leonard recalls, "because that country is rolling, but some of 'em took off a little too far east, and before we got it together again, the roadblock seen us. They opened up on us, and they had some real sharpshooters out there, too—it was just lucky they was a good distance off. So I hollered to the rest to keep on going, and I fired off a few rounds in that direction, just to keep their heads down. But it's still hard to believe that we got through. I felt those bullets flying close by my head a couple of times. Later we discussed it, and we all felt Something had been there. The Great Spirit helped us. He said it was not our time, and He didn't call us; He got us out of there. That's one reason we all went to the sun dance that summer, to express our gratitude; we figured that the help of the Great Spirit had been a sign to us."

"We started out at a run up the hill toward the timber 800 yards away," Robideau remembers. "Bullets immediately started flying all around us—the firefight was on—we immediately opened up on those who were firing on us from below. Even though the fire coming from government positions was right on us, barely missing, most of us stopped out of sheer exhaustion. After getting a few breaths of life back into us we would jump back up and run again for the top of the hill. We all made it to the base of the hill without getting hit."[3]

Soon two cars left Route 35 and came after them cross-country, bumping across the range; shooting now and then to keep the cars at a respectful distance, the Indians kept running. "That eagle, it took off from where the culvert was, I saw it," Norman Brown says. "It went right over us, and when the sun was going down, it flew into the sun, and from then we couldn't see the eagle no more. After it did that, I knew we would be all right, we would make it all right."

Everyone gained the ridge untouched, and Dino Butler now felt sure that the worst was over. "I did not see it, but Norman Brown told me there was an eagle. He saw an eagle come down while we were praying. There was a creek—it's really like a snake, it really winds around like that—we know how the creek goes like that but when we got done praying that day, and we left, we went in a straight line. We walked through that creek several times. We didn't know where we were going or anything, we were just going that way. We came to this road, there was a culvert there, we crawled through there and went up the hill. We got up there safely. People said, when we were going up that hill, that there was an eagle flying over us.

"If we were wrong, we would have all died there. They had us completely surrounded, yet somehow we got through all those people. . . . I could feel the bullets going through me, like, going by me. I could feel the air and I could hear their whistling noise; yet none of these bullets touched me. Going up that hill, I just knew that someone was going to get shot because there were too many bullets flying around us. And I thought about the women and I prayed for them while I was going up that hill. When we all met up there, I knew then that whatever happens, we were right, and that we would be taken care of."

Nilak Butler wasn't so sure. "I went back there since then, and it took us five minutes to *drive* up. Well, it didn't take us five minutes to run up, I'll just tell you that. It's amazing, the strength you can get. And they were opening up really hard on us, they were just all around us. One guy had a canteen on his hip which was shot off; it was automatic weapons. So . . . Dino turned to me and he goes, Yeah, I feel pretty safe now. And I remember sitting on the top of that hill and I was looking down, and all these fed cars are coming up and around to the left of us. And I said, What do you mean we are safe now? I didn't feel that same way at all. Not at *all.*

"So we were just sort of laying low then, trying to figure out what to do. The older guys like Bobby and Leonard were really concerned about everybody's safety, and the younger guys were acting like warriors that day. They were doing what they had to do.

"One fed car started to come up the hill, you know, something straight out of the movies. They were shooting at us, so people were shooting back, and these real brave guys turned around in an about-face, really fast, and scrubbed back down the hill. And there was a bunch of guys wearing black jump suits, and I *still* don't know who *those* guys were! They looked pretty serious and they were trying to sneak up the hill and they weren't sneaky. And then there were guys in green jump suits who were sneaking up the hill, too. I don't know: that was awful fast for all these guys in jump suits to be running around!"

By now it was nearly dusk; soon the shooting ceased. Two young Indians on horses who had been watching from across the valley rode over in the twilight of the long June day; they were Leon Eagle and Kenny Loud Hawk. "When them two skins showed up, I was really surprised!" Peltier says. "I asked them if they had any weapons to protect themselves, because the whole country was crawling with the law, and one says, Yeah! They had a .22 and six shells between them! The fact that they were willing to come to us and risk their lives—that was very moving to me, a very emotional moment, because I knew for sure now that the local people were behind us. And later we learned there were maybe fifty or a hundred people at the roadblocks, cheering us as we went up the hill, and that some of them Indian cops, they weren't trying too hard to hit us. And we also learned that those pigs coming up after us, they were being fired on from somewhere in the rear, not just by us."

"Them two guys was really cool," Jean Bordeaux remembers. "How you doin'? they say, like there's nothin' goin' on, nothin' at all. But they knew the country and told us how to travel; without them, we might have got killed out there."

Peltier crossed to the next summit to the south, followed by the Navajo girl, Lynn; he wanted to see if their path had been cut off, and said he would come back to warn them if anything went wrong. After a while, hearing distant shots, the others thought the worst had happened and retreated toward the southwest, away from Highway 18. But soon Leonard and Lynn caught up with them, and when dark came, a short time later, the group rested, studying a small woods not far ahead. As Nilak recalls, "Dino and Leonard and them were talking, they were saying, Well, it's possible that we're walking right into an ambush. But we really didn't have any other alternative, so we went in there, and it wasn't an ambush. We didn't have water or anything. It had been a long day. There was rainwater in ruts, and we were drinking it 'cause we were thirsty.

"And I remember we were trucking along, and got to this one spot way back in the hills, and we decided to wait until nightfall 'cause they hadn't followed us up until then. I was still trucking barefooted, and Dino said he would cut up his vest so I could have shoes, [but] a couple of the boys gave me their socks to wear. So we just waited there most of the night, and then we started trucking into somebody's house we knew. A couple of the guys went ahead to let them know that we were around. And they came out and—oh, I remember!—they brought us a little sack of carrots. We were really pretty hungry about then, too! And they brought us a sack of carrots and I think a couple of sandwiches. It wasn't very much, and we all shared."

Ted Lame, shirtless in the heat of the summer night, was waiting for them where they crossed Highway 18. He led them to his uncle's remote cabin up in the Badlands northeast of the highway; they arrived there about 1:00 in the morning.

"It was not a situation, I believe, where there would've been any captives. They were not just gonna arrest us, I know that. They were gonna kill us, that's all there was to that. And I believe that's what they were going to do when they came in there at Oglala. They just didn't expect to get return fire.

"So, we were at that old man's house and we decided we'd sleep out in the hills under trees and things, so that if anybody came up there, he wouldn't be put in jeopardy. He didn't have much food but he gave us all he had. He gave us *all* the food he had! And I remember he gave us a bag of gingersnaps!" Nilak laughs. *"That* really helped us through, I'll tell you that!"

Noah Wounded's one-room log cabin had no electricity, just one kerosene lamp, which Robideau used in drawing a sketch of a buffalo for the old man. Peltier asked Draper and Brown to stand guard; they were relieved two hours later by Charles and Anderson. At sunrise, Noah Wounded gave them food, and they hid out in the hills until dark, then headed for the small community at Manderson; they were following the old man's directions, but they did not know the country and were unsure of the way, and followed the south fork at a split in the trail.

"There was lightning and thunder all around us—the whole sky was a circle of lightning and thunder," Nilak says. "It was really beautiful and really strong. There was a lot of moonlight, moonlight and lightning. We were going through those fields single-file, and everybody was pretty quiet in their own thoughts. We were all mourning Joe. So we'd truck every night, and we'd sleep under the trees during the day. Joked around a little bit, but not that much. We were just concerned about getting out of there, getting *out* of there!

"There were a lot of coyotes, I remember that. We were headed one way and there was a bunch of coyotes, so we took a turn, and it turned out it was the wrong turn from where we thought we were going. By then we were out of food, but everybody was just really cool. Nobody ever got hysterical or growled around at each other, got ugly with each other. It was a family. Everybody was trying to just take care of each other. And when we thought we were finally in the right area, I remember we were looking at these lights, and we thought, Gee, wouldn't it be funny if we ended up in Pine Ridge! Well, guess where we ended up? We ended up in Pine Ridge, and it was right before sunrise. And we were up on this hill and we were looking out and we recognized the airport and the hospital and everything. And somebody said, Well, this is Pine Ridge. We could see police cars on every block, going around the housing. And everybody just sort of sat down for a minute. We were just stunned, everybody, 'cause the sun was coming. And right then, that's about the lowest that we got.

"Leonard—Leonard's cool that way. After we had a moment of stunned silence, he said, Well, I know some people over here and I'll truck in and see if we can all go in there. He was really good that way, he always provided—he and Dino and Bob provided leadership. I think that's a lot of what kept everybody from panicking, because they seemed to know what they were doing. Nobody *really* knew what they were doing, and we all knew that, but they had ideas on what we *could* do. They had alternatives, so nobody panicked. It was also a certain kind of a feeling you get when you know that people are willing to lay down everything for you. Be killed for you. It gives you a certain kind of feeling."

With Dino Butler, Peltier made his way to the house of Morris Wounded (an Oglala spiritual leader, and the man who was helping Jeannette Bissonnette when she was killed). "They gave us water and they gave us food and it just felt good," Nilak remembers, "and we had shelter for that night. And the next day, I remember, we were all sitting around talking I guess, visiting around, and somebody came running to the house: The feds are coming! So we all hid in this one back bedroom, and Leonard was going, *Everybody get covered.* And the person who had the house went out and talked to the feds, and it was a yellow busload full of feds. That was *another* tight moment! The guys had put themselves in the position that if anything happened they were going to be hit first; but there was more concern that nothing *did* happen, because we didn't want the people whose home we were staying in to get hurt.

"Then some people come over there and took us to another district; they split us up into two groups, because everybody couldn't all fit in the same car, and no matter what way we went out, we'd have to go through downtown. That was another hairy moment! The guys went in one car, and the younger people and the women in another, because again they figured that if it came down, it would be less dangerous for us not to be with them. So we all ended up in another district, and that's when we finally were able to kick back a little. Just a little."

The fugitives hid for a few days at Porcupine, where Oscar Bear Runner, a traditional leader at Wounded Knee, let them make camp by his wooded creek. ("I'm pretty close with Oscar—the whole family," Peltier says. "We were so close in those years, I called 'em Ma and Dad, although I don't think they ever went through the ritual of adopting me.") Soon the young Navajo Wish Draper left for Rapid City, where he stayed at the house of Evelyn Bordeaux. From there he fled to Canada; he did not go home to Arizona until December. The Navajo girl, Lynn, left for Colorado, then New Mexico. Anna Mae Aquash and Jean Day rejoined the group, but Day shortly departed for Wisconsin, where the FBI was looking for her and where in her absence—it was no coincidence, she felt—the authorities were threatening to take her two kids from their grandparents.

"We were out in the country, in a home in the country," Nilak says, "and there was this stream running through there, and it was really beautiful; we were able to just start visiting with each other again. . . . At that time, one of the girls and one guy, too, decided to leave the group, and the girl was going to Joe's funeral on the way out. And then more people joined us, I remember. Everybody, you know, was really worried about us, and when they'd come and see us, they'd just cry and be happy that we were all right, and bring food and all kinds of things. It was really something. There was nobody who ever refused to help us. And again, they were putting their life on the line by helping us. To the max.

"Anna Mae was with us then. She'd hooked back up with us. When we were at that one house in the country, over on the Ridge, Anna Mae and me and another girl, we were out picking berries, and I remember her talking to me, and she was going, I'm never gonna leave you guys again. And she hasn't. She *still* hasn't!" Nilak Butler says.[4]

CHAPTER 8

THE SHOOT-OUT II

June 26, 1975

I was told that after the battle two Cheyenne women came across Custer's body. They knew him, because he had attacked their peaceful village on the Washita. These women said, "You smoked the peace pipe with us. Our chiefs told you that you would be killed if you ever made war on us again. But you would not listen. This will make you hear better." The women each took an awl from their beaded cases and stuck them deep into Custer's ears.

Somebody who saw this told me about it. . . . Hundreds of books have been written about this battle by people who weren't there. I was there, but all I remember is one big cloud of dust.

Good Fox (*Lakota*)

On June 26, 1975—the morning after he had picked up three Indian youths on Highway 18 outside Oglala and taken them into Pine Ridge for questioning—Special Agent Ronald Williams had breakfast coffee with SA Gerard Waring at the Hacienda Motel in Gordon, Nebraska, about forty miles south of Pine Ridge village, where some of the new agents summoned to enforce law and order on the reservation had been quartered. Williams and Waring were joined by SA Jack R. Coler, a Special Weapons and Tactics (SWAT) operative who had arrived from Denver the month before with another agent, "both SWAT trained and experienced criminal investigators . . . equipped with shotgun, rifle, cuffs, binoculars and regular sidearms and [will] arrive in BuCar [Bureau Car]." Coler had just finished a long phone conversation with his friend SA Robert Bunch in the Denver office, in which he told Bunch how much he was enjoying the Pine Ridge assignment, and also how much he was looking forward to their fishing trip once this sixty-day tour of duty was at an end.

Both Williams, twenty-seven, and Coler, twenty-eight, were originally from the Los Angeles area. Coler, whose wife and two small children had remained behind in Colorado Springs, was of medium build and eager expression, with sideburns, light-brown hair balding on top, and a new mustache; Williams, a bachelor, was five ten or five eleven, trim, with dark-brown curly hair and glasses, and a young clergyman's good looks. The day before, the two agents had made an unsuccessful search of the White Clay District, northwest of Pine Ridge village, for a young Indian named James Theodore Eagle, wanted with three other AIM supporters on charges of theft and assault with a deadly weapon; Eagle, supposedly traveling in a red International Scout, was said by the Indian police to be frequenting Oglala, a traditional community that was harboring AIM agitators and was generally "uncooperative" with law-enforcement officers, Indian as well as white.

At some time after 4:00 p.m. on June 25, Williams and Coler, riding in Williams's car and accompanied by BIA Officers Robert Ecoffey, an Oglala, and Glenn Little Bird, a Nez Perce, entered the Jumping Bull property in search of Eagle; supposedly, Eagle might be found at the small isolated red-and-brown cabin where the dirt road leading west from Highway 18 made a turn back along the bluff edge toward the small houses in the Jumping Bull compound, perhaps two hundred yards away. This cabin belonged to Wallace Little, Sr., and was occupied by Wallace Little, Jr. ("June"), his wife, Wanda Siers, and their three children, as well as occasional relatives and friends such as the young Indian named Dusty Nelson who was present on that hot humid afternoon.

> LITTLE BIRD stated that the group went to the door of the residence located at the north end of the JUMPING BULL land. He advised that they were met at the door by a female who had a child in her arms and two small children standing next to her. He advised that he did not know who this individual was and did not know whether he could identify her if he were to see her again. He stated that SA WILLIAMS inquired if JIMMY EAGLE was in the house and the female replied that he was not there and that she had not seen him in quite a while. He stated that SA WILLIAMS then requested permission to search the residence and that this permission was granted by the female. . . .
>
> LITTLE BIRD advised that the search of the residence for JIMMY EAGLE was negative. LITTLE BIRD stated that the group then left the residence and went to the north side of the house where they observed an individual sleeping on a cot under a shaded area. He advised that SA WILLIAMS asked this individual if JIMMY EAGLE was in the area. He advised that this individual stated he had not seen EAGLE in several days.

Ecoffey reported later that the law officers saw two rifles on the wall upon entering the cabin, and also AIM's upside-down flag. After Siers and Nelson said that Eagle had not been around there recently, the lawmen proceeded into Oglala, where someone at the Lavete Little house suggested to the agents that he was staying at the ranch of Wallace Little, Sr., a few miles southeastward down Highway 18, toward Pine Ridge village. At the Little ranch, the four lawmen were told by a young woman (Officer Little Bird speculated later that this woman might have been the same one who talked to them earlier—that is, Wanda Siers) that Eagle had just left in a red-and-white pickup, headed for Oglala. Since the trail seemed hot, the two agents returned toward Oglala. On the way, they stopped three youths who were walking along the road and asked them for identification; one of these youths had a rifle clip wrapped in a towel. The three were ordered into the car and taken to Pine Ridge, where the BIA police informed the agents that none of these "individuals" was James Theodore Eagle.

On the morning of June 26, Williams intended to go back to Oglala, and Coler would follow him in his own car; they agreed to meet Waring and his partner, Vince Breci, back at Pine Ridge village about noon. According to Waring, Williams and Coler left the Hacienda Motel about 9:25, headed for Oglala by way of Pine Ridge village. Williams was driving a 1972 green Rambler Ambassador 401, and Jack Coler's FBI car was a two-tone four-door 1972 Chevrolet Biscayne, white vinyl over golden tan, with Colorado plates. For unexplained reasons, just before 11:00, Williams returned to Pine Ridge village, where he encountered SA Dean Hughes, head of the Rapid City SWAT team, outside the jail at BIA headquarters. Hughes was there to pick up Teddy Pourier, one of the four youths wanted in the Eagle case, who had been arrested in the Porcupine community the day before.[1] Pourier, a small light-skinned boy who would have passed for a white anywhere else, sat handcuffed in the car while the agents talked. Hughes was transferring Pourier to Rapid City, but because he apparently believed that these four young AIM supporters were "terrorists" and that the AIM people might attempt a rescue, he had arranged to be followed in a separate car by Ron Williams's former partner, David Price. While Williams conferred with Hughes, SA Price talked with SA Gary Adams, a member of Hughes's SWAT team, who passed the group on his way into the building. Hughes, Price, and Adams, who did most of their work on the reservation, were all well acquainted with Ron Williams, who was already in Rapid City when they were assigned there at the time of Wounded Knee.

According to Hughes, who glanced at his watch, Williams arrived at BIA headquarters at 10:58; they must have talked briefly, since by Hughes's own estimate he departed with Pourier about 11:00.

Not long after Hughes and Price departed the BIA building, Coler was heard trying to contact Williams on the radio, and at some point or another they joined forces. What is not clear—except perhaps to the authorities, who do not say—was what occurred between 11:00 and about 11:55, when a number of people monitoring the FBI channel heard an increasingly urgent series of transmissions. Agents Waring and Breci picked up Williams's voice while driving north from Gordon to Pine Ridge to join Williams and Coler. As Waring recalled Williams's words,

> He had observed a red and white vehicle and then almost immediately he said, "There appears to be some Indians in the vehicle, and they appear to have rifles." Then almost instantly, he said he had

> come under fire and immediately requested help from any units that were listening at that time. . . . It was basically a continuous conversation by him on the radio. . . . Another agent whose voice I recognized as Agent Gary Adams came on and he was requesting that Ron give him a location where he could be found. . . . Williams came back and said he was in the Oglala area near the Little residence. . . . He continued by indicating that "they are on the ridge above us and firing on us." Then a voice came back on the radio, again requesting help, indicating that the Indians were on the rise and that if we didn't arrive quickly that they would be dead men. I attempted at that point to make radio contact with Ron because I wanted to be sure and get an exact location and also to advise him that we were in the process of getting there to help him as quickly as possible. I was not successful. Immediately upon my stopping transmission . . . Ron's voice came back on the radio. He was noticeably out of breath at that point and his voice had a little more excitement in it and he announced that, "I have been hit." That was the termination of any radio traffic that day from Ron Williams.

Waring was beaten to Oglala by Special Agent Gary Adams, who had left BIA headquarters in Pine Ridge at some point after 11:30 a.m. and headed south across the reservation line to White Clay, Nebraska, to get something to eat. Adams was also monitoring the FBI frequency, and at about 11:45, he heard Williams say, presumably to Coler, "There are several guys around this house . . . and it looks like they're going to take off. They're getting into that pickup. I hope you have a lot of gas." A few moments later, Williams's voice said, "It looks like these guys are going to shoot at us!" Within two minutes, Adams heard gunfire on his radio. Then Williams yelled, "We have been hit!"

Adams wheeled around at the state line and took off at high speed for Oglala, about fifteen miles away. Williams was still calling for help: "Get on a high hill and give us some fire cover or we will be killed!" By this time, Agent Price had also spun his car around and was headed southeast toward Oglala. SA Dean Hughes, still going north toward Rapid City with his prisoner, heard "something like, 'Get to the high ground' "—a more likely version, since there is no "high hill" within rifle range of the spot—and then "Hurry up and get here or we are going to be dead men." Previously, he had heard Williams say, "We are being fired on. We are in a little valley in Oglala, South Dakota, pinned down in a cross fire between two houses." Agent Edward Skelly at Rapid City headquarters heard Williams say, "If someone could get to the top of the ridge and give us cover, we might be able to get out of here." During these transmissions, a number of shots were audible in the background (possibly from Agent Coler's gun). The last thing Hughes heard was Williams's voice saying "very vaguely, 'I am hit.' "

Still calling to Williams for a more precise location, Adams hurtled through Pine Ridge village at high speed. Williams radioed that he was behind the houses at Jumping Bull Hall, and a minute later he told Adams to come to a building "with an outbuilding" some distance from the main house and give them "some covering fire or they would be killed." Presumably he meant the Little cabin. According to Adams, his friend "was very distressed and excited, and I told him, 'Ron, settle down and tell me where you are at and I will come and help you.' " But Williams's prediction that they would be killed was the last word that Adams can recall receiving.

Understandably, Gary Adams was very upset: he had worked with Ron Williams on many occasions and considered him "one of my closest personal friends." He tried to call the Pine Ridge police but could raise no one; switching to the state frequency, he heard Price alerting the Highway Patrol in Rapid City, which finally got through to Pine Ridge. Since Adams had no idea where Jumping Bull Hall was located, he continued north and west on Highway 18 at speeds he estimated later at 90 to 100 mph.

> Mrs. LINDA PRICE, employed as a stenographer for the Federal Bureau of Investigation (FBI) and currently assigned to the Rapid City Resident Agency, Minneapolis Division, Rapid City, South Dakota, was interviewed at her place of employment which is room 260, Federal Building, Rapid City, South Dakota.
>
> Mrs. PRICE said that at approximately 11:50 a.m. she began to hear radio transmissions from SA RONALD A. WILLIAMS. . . . It should also be noted that at 11:50 a.m. in addition to Mrs. PRICE, SAS GEORGE D. O'CLOCK and JOHN E. MCCARTY and stenographer ANN M. JOHNSON were present in room 260 and could clearly hear radio transmissions coming into the radio monitor in that room. Mrs. PRICE advised that at approximately 11:50 a.m. she heard SA

> WILLIAMS transmit words to the effect, "we're following a red vehicle (type unknown), you want to keep an eye out for it." There was a pause for approximately 30 seconds, when SA WILLIAMS transmitted, "I hope you have enough gas."
>
> Mrs. PRICE then heard SA WILLIAMS transmit, "can you do me a favor." This was followed by a pause for approximately 30 seconds. The next transmission made by SA WILLIAMS were words to the effect, "we got a problem here." There was another pause for approximately 30 seconds, [then] "get up on the hill, we're being fired at."
>
> Mrs. PRICE then overheard SA J. GARY ADAMS, who identified himself by his call signal X2R, and SA ADAMS was inquiring about directions from SA WILLIAMS for his location.
>
> SA WILLIAMS responded by giving directions. According to Mrs. PRICE, he was talking in a loud and hysterical voice and speaking rather fast. During this series of transmissions, SA WILLIAMS said something about an outhouse and a red house and kept repeating, "Come on, guys! Come on, guys!"

Near Wallace Little's ranch, Adams stopped his car to get his rifle from the trunk and put on his bulletproof vest; while donning the vest, he heard gunfire off to the north. He sped ahead again and soon overtook a BIA police car; the Indian police led him northwest on Highway 18, then west onto the Jumping Bull property, weaving down the muddy road past Jumping Bull Hall; the two cars skidded to a halt near the Little cabin.

> After the above series of transmissions from SA WILLIAMS, SA ADAMS stated, "I'm on the hill," and advised he could not see where SA WILLIAMS was. SA ADAMS attempted to get specific directions to SA WILLIAMS' location. Mrs. PRICE stated that she overheard SA WILLIAMS respond again in the loud and hysterical voice, "Keep coming, I'm down here." SA ADAMS then transmitted, "They're shooting all around here." Mrs. PRICE added that SA ADAMS then attempted again to get locations from SA WILLIAMS.
>
> Mrs. PRICE said that there was another transmission from SA WILLIAMS, the context she cannot recall, but she can recall that this transmission was ended by a moan.
>
> Mrs. PRICE stated attempts were made from the Rapid City Resident Agency to contact SA WILLIAMS by radio. This could not be done and there was no response.

Agent John McCarty in the Rapid City office heard "something about chasing a red jeep," and FBI stenographer Ann M. Johnson heard Williams say, "There is something wrong here, we are being fired on," followed by the emergency exchange between Williams and Adams. "The last thing I heard from Ron," Johnson remembered later, "was—I didn't really hear the words, but I heard like he kind of broke off, and it sounded like a moan."

Curiously, Jack Coler's voice was never identified by anyone during the last half hour of his life, although Ron Williams seems to have been in communication with him, at least during the early part of the transmissions. According to the people in the Rapid City office, there was no further transmission from Ron Williams "after approximately 12:10," or about ten minutes after Adams's arrival. Adams pulled to a stop in the vicinity of the Little cabin, and BIA Officer Frank Two Bulls drove to the driver's side of Adams's vehicle. As Two Bulls stopped, a shot rang out; apparently the bullet hit the right front tire of Two Bulls's car. Adams yelled a warning, and both cars backed up at a high rate of speed. Zigzagging backward on the muddy road toward Highway 18, Adams slid into a ditch, where his car remained stuck for the remainder of that day. Although the Jumping Bull cabins, where the shots had come from, were at least two hundred yards away, the right front tire of the BIA car as well as his own left front tire had been shot out by a dead-eye sniper. From the ditch, Adams fired a few long-range shots, which were ineffective, he said, because his telescopic sight malfunctioned, at which point "the individuals shooting at me . . . went back into the trees and behind the houses."

Presumably, Adams had retreated at some point before 12:06, at which time Ann Johnson and Linda Price recorded his statement that he was being fired on: "Hey, we're under fire. . . . They are firing at us like crazy, they are firing at us." Had Adams gone just a little farther down the road to where it cuts back south along the bluff edge toward the compound, he would certainly have seen the green Rambler and blond Chevrolet in the pasture below; as it was, he was still unsure where the agents were. ". . . Special Agent Williams' location was later determined to be west of the house where Special Agent Adams stopped and down in a valley approximately 200 yards. This position could only be observed from the houses or the immediate edge of the plateau on which the houses were built."

Within a few minutes, more Pine Ridge police cars started to arrive, and by 12:15 there was a long-range exchange of fire with the houses. Knowing that at least one man was injured, Adams told SA Edward Skelly in Rapid City to summon an ambulance; he also called for reinforcements and a spotter plane.

At 12:18, the Rapid City office noted, "SA J. Gary Adams on the scene and he has been receiving heavy fire. . . . Red pickup leaving Jumping Bull area, going north, and Pine Ridge police instructed to stop this particular pickup." But apparently the BIA roadblocks, not well organized, were successfully run by this unidentified red pickup truck, which was to become the most controversial element in the whole case.

At 12:28, SA Waring reported a "late model Malibu gold two-door hardtop leaving area" as he and SA Vince Breci arrived on the scene; he said that the people in this car were carrying "at least one shoulder weapon"—rifle or shotgun. At about 12:45, Richard Little, June's immense brother, approached the main BIA-FBI roadblock beyond Jumping Bull Hall in "a red Ford Ranchero." Because of his size, or because of Indian police opinion that the Littles and Loud Hawks were the most hostile traditional families in Oglala, a BIA officer shouted (according to an FBI report filed the next day), "Watch out, that's Richard Little!" Little was advised to leave the area, at which point he said that the shooting had to stop because there were women and children in there and somebody was going to get hurt. Asked if he wished to go in there "to request the individuals at that location to stop shooting," Little "advised he would not. Little was then advised to leave the area, which he did."

Meanwhile, Agent David Price was howling down upon Oglala from the west; when his overheated engine blew, he flagged down the next car along to take him the rest of the way. As it happened, the car stopped by Price was driven by legal aide Joanna LeDeaux, who had been traveling southeast on Highway 18 when she was passed at high speed by a car that she came upon shortly thereafter on the road; waving a shotgun to make certain that she stopped, its driver ordered her to drive him to Oglala.

> SA PRICE advised LEDEAU [*sic*] of his official identity and she said she recognized him. SA PRICE advised her he was commandeering her car for an emergency. She replied that he could not commandeer her car. SA PRICE advised her that Agents were receiving gunfire and

> possibly had been shot at Oglala. LEDEAU immediately quit objecting and let SA PRICE into the car along with a Bureau shotgun . . . obtained from the Bureau car. LEDEAU then proceeded to JUMPING BULL Hall at about 75 miles an hour which appeared to be the fastest her car could go. SA PRICE did not urge LEDEAU to drive fast. At one point LEDEAU advised SA PRICE that when they got to Oglala he would have to commandeer another car as she could not be seen giving him a ride. SA PRICE advised her that she would give him a ride to JUMPING BULL Hall.

By the time LeDeaux's car arrived, about 12:30, police reinforcements were coming from all directions, together with BIA personnel, white vigilantes, goons, and local onlookers, and at least five roadblocks had been set up to "secure the area." Because she was known to the Indians at the Jumping Bull place, LeDeaux was given permission by acting BIA Superintendent Kendall Cummings to attempt to negotiate a truce, arrange medical assistance, or at least bring out any women and children who might be trapped by rifle fire. LeDeaux drove her small Datsun station wagon down the dirt road to June Little's house on the bluff, from where she proceeded on foot toward the compound. At the trees between the main house and the log cabin (according to Adams, observing through his sniper scope) she was met by three or four figures with long black hair who appeared to be "Indian males"; she then disappeared among the cabins. Adams says she was in the compound for about an hour, during the course of which she was seen to walk westward toward the bluff, from which she could have seen the agents' bodies; she had returned into the compound before walking back to her car at the outlying cabin and driving out to the highway, where she told Cummings that no negotiation was possible. According to Cummings, she was "frustrated and crying," and refused to talk; before the FBI agents could reach her, she had disappeared.

Adams did not join the discussion with LeDeaux because he was still pinned down near his car by sporadic fire from the houses. When the South Dakota Highway Patrol showed up a few minutes later, followed shortly by a Fall River County sheriff's posse, he managed to crawl out to the highway, where he immediately became involved in a jurisdictional dispute with the BIA.

> It was at this point that Superintendent CUMMINGS advised Special Agent ADAMS and members of the South Dakota Highway Pa-

> trol that he was in charge of the Pine Ridge Indian Reservation and would run the operation at the crime scene. Special Agent ADAMS instructed Superintendent CUMMINGS that the FBI was in charge of criminal activity and criminal investigation on the Pine Ridge Indian Reservation and that the FBI would coordinate any activity involving an assault on the location. Superintendent CUMMINGS again related he was running the operation and that he was going to clear any assault with either the area office in Aberdeen or the BIA in Washington.

At Agent Hughes's request, Agents Fred Coward and Ed Skelly were already on their way from Rapid City; they arrived at approximately 1:20 p.m. A few minutes later, Marvin Stoldt of the BIA SWAT team got reports from his men that two individuals were fleeing the area on the far side of White Clay Creek, near the house of Judy Pumpkinseed on the loop road. Accompanied by Coward, Skelly, and Breci, Officer Stoldt led a squad of BIA police to "secure a perimeter" in that area and try to cut off any more escapes. The Pumpkinseed house, which had windows on the north and east from which the Jumping Bull land could be seen over the trees in the creek bottom, was occupied as a command post.

An all-out attack on the compound was withheld pending better information as to the fate of the agents, whose location and—in Coler's case—identity were still unknown; it was possible, at least, that they were being held as hostages. At 1:26, not long after LeDeaux's departure, Adams reported that "an older model white and red pickup" driven by "an elderly Indian male" had entered the area and proceeded into the compound, departing shortly thereafter from the area of the log cabin with at least two additional passengers; like the red pickup that had left the scene at 12:18, this one passed safely through the BIA roadblocks. Adams reported this second pickup to SA Fred Coward, who had circled around the loop road behind the dam to the west of White Clay Creek, and had stationed himself at the Pumpkinseed house with BIA SWAT leader Marvin Stoldt: "Adams to Coward, south of Oglala: pickup came in here and he just left. Can't get any BIA people on it."

Besides the two pickups (and the gold Malibu noted by SA Waring) a number of people were departing the area on foot. At 2:01, according to the Rapid City office, SA Skelly reported that "a bunch of kids and a woman" fled from the log house; about 2:30, Skelly's group reported two more fugitives seen in the creek bottom.

Meanwhile, Agent Hughes had sped to Hot Springs, in the Black Hills, to dump his prisoner in the local jail; he returned to Oglala about 1:00 p.m., by which time Adams had directed the encirclement of the entire area. Price and Waring were setting out with BIA Police Chief Delmar Eastman and seven Indian officers on a route that would take them down around to the far side of the compound by way of the heavily wooded cover of White Clay Creek. According to Hughes, who took over command of this expedition as head of the FBI SWAT team, "our objective was to flanker the people who were shooting at Agent Williams and try to rescue him." On this heavy summer day, all three agents were in street clothes—Hughes recalls wearing "brown double-knit slacks, purple shirt, tie, and sports coat"—and the seven or eight Indian policemen were in uniform, and in the hot midday undergrowth and mud along the creek bottom, the going was difficult and slow, especially for heavily armed men who spend most of their working life seated at desks or behind the wheel. By Hughes's estimate, it was nearly 2:00 p.m. before they reached the edge of the trees, perhaps a hundred yards southwest of the small green shack that sits on the bluff edge at that corner of the compound. "An individual ran from the vicinity of this green house towards me with a rifle, snapped a shot at me which went by my head; I heard the whistle of the bullet by my head, because it was quite close. We dove back in the trees for cover and I regrouped the search team. At this time I made an announcement to the individuals at the green house. 'This is the FBI and the BIA. You are surrounded. Come out with your hands up. There will be no shooting.' Immediately after that announcement, heavy firing was directed at us . . . from individuals in the green house."

In the renewed exchange of fire, two figures were seen running in the vicinity of the green shack, and eventually one of the Indian police yelled something like "I think I hit one!" After that, there was silence again; as Waring recalled, this was the last shooting of the day in the compound area. After a while, Officer Eastman, who had climbed a tree, called to Waring to come have a look; through the telescopic sight on Waring's gun, they were able to identify Jack Coler's two-tone white-tan Chevrolet with its Colorado plates, parked in the low-lying pasture under the bluff that hid it from the highway. There was no sign of Williams's car or of the agents, only the heat and insect hum and heavy stillness.

Notified that Coler's car had been located, Hughes "observed that anyone trying to reach this automobile would be exposed to a cross fire between the two houses which were located on the two hills and I remembered Agent Williams's previous transmitting that 'we are being fired on. We are in a cross fire between two houses.' "

It was now, Waring recalled, that "SA Price was heard to yell words to the effect, 'The man in the white shirt, throw down your weapon and surrender' "; this command was met by a new burst of fire from the green house. For want of a better plan, Hughes, Price, and Eastman made their way west along the wood edge, followed shortly by Waring and the others. On the way, they were shot at four or five times from an unknown source—not the green house. At a point just behind a small horse corral, perhaps seventy-five yards beyond Coler's car, Hughes called out to the car but got no response. It was now 3:05 p.m. Since ten men could not assault the compound against an entrenched group of unknown size, and since the BIA radio had gone dead, Hughes sent Price back for another radio and reinforcements.

Because Hughes had no radio, the news of Coler's bullet-riddled car had not gone out yet on the FBI frequency, on which Resident Senior Agent George O'Clock was trying to determine the fate of the agents presumed missing:

2:48 p.m.

(O'CLOCK) Do you know, GARY, how many Agents are missing at this time?

(ADAMS) We have HUGHES, PRICE, two Omaha Agents, don't have Denver, Salt Lake, and WILLIAMS.

(Omaha Unit) The only temporary Agent that is not accounted for is JACK COLER, all other temporary Agents are accounted for. The only other Agent that we know that is not accounted for is X2-H (WILLIAMS). It is my belief, and belief only, that X2-H (WILLIAMS) and JACK from Denver were working together before the shooting started.

By the time that it had been established that the only two agents not accounted for were Williams and "Denver," firing from the compound itself had virtually ceased. As late as 3:48 p.m., SA Skelly reported that this group was receiving "a cross fire" involving assailants in "a red house," identified later as June Little's cabin. However, unidentified Indians had been gathering for two hours on lookout points all around the farm, and there were stray shots from unknown sources and from all directions; Marvin Stoldt would state that the Pumpkinseed house had been fired on all afternoon and from many directions, even from behind—that is, from the hills on the west side of the loop road. None of these sources of hostile fire was ever pinned down. Instead, the lawmen scanning with binoculars saw horses grazing in the uplands and small children at play in the bare yards of far, tattered shacks, and the gathering cows in the early-summer grass near the evening gates.

About 3:00 p.m., well before the arrival of David Price with Hughes's request for reinforcements, Gary Adams was notified by a state police detachment that someone was walking along the edge of the plowed field south of the compound. "I observed a young Indian male with his hands in the air," said Adams of the eleven-year-old boy who turned out to be the only Indian male to surrender that day. As the lone child drew near the silent cabins, the attention of the authorities was distracted by "another individual" who wished to negotiate with the besieged Indians. After lengthy discussions, this man received permission to enter the compound, and about 4:20, Hughes's group, waiting in the woods, saw a figure in a white T-shirt come out onto the bluff with his hands up. Hughes summoned him down the pasture slope to the wood edge, where he recognized him as a young traditional named Edgar Bear Runner. Bear Runner explained that BIA Superintendent Cummings had given him just twenty minutes to try to effect some sort of truce before a final assault in which people might be killed, but that he had seen no one around the houses. However, there were "two individuals laying alongside of that car, and he didn't know if they were alive or dead." Hughes told him to check the individuals for signs of life before proceeding to the green shack to negotiate. Returning uphill, Bear Runner passed by way of Coler's car, where he paused for a few moments before going on, hands still high in the air, giving Hughes's squad no sign of what he had seen. He mounted the bluff near the green shack, where he stood for a few minutes before he vanished.

When Edgar Bear Runner returned to the highway, he brought the young Indian boy out with him. Not long afterward, Adams radioed

Skelly that he was off "to debrief the kid," who had already told Cummings that there were thirty well-armed Indians in the creek bed. But efforts to debrief or even identify the child were thwarted by Bear Runner, a Wounded Knee veteran whose white T-shirt read REMEMBER WOUNDED KNEE and who cautioned the boy not to talk further.

Bear Runner notified the BIA Superintendent that he had seen the two agents lying in the meadow, apparently dead; at Cummings's request, he accompanied the BIA man to the death scene a few minutes later, after Cummings had left instructions that if he were taken hostage or did not reappear, an assault on the compound should be made. They walked down the road and descended the bluff to Coler's car, hands above their heads, as Hughes and Eastman, keeping their rifle barrels pointed down to signify to anyone who might be in the cabins that they weren't attacking, moved out to meet them, crossing the pasture to the gold-and-tan car with the red-and-white Colorado plates.

Crisscrossed by bullets, both front tires flat, the car sat nosed into the field, with all windows and one headlight shot to pieces. The driver's door was open, and all four of the warning flashers were still flashing. Agent Coler's papers and personal effects were scattered through the car; Agent Williams's FBI credentials sat on the hood. On the ground behind the trunk, which was also open—the lid had been pierced in nine places by large-caliber bullets—a green SWAT-team rifle case lay in the hot summer grass, which was already turning from fresh-rain green to coarse green-brown. Of Williams's car there was no sign except the broken red glass of a shattered taillight.

Near the left rear wheel, uphill, on the driver's side, screened from the woods by the car itself, lay Agent Coler in green shirt and white T-shirt, red-belted tan jeans, white socks, tan moccasins. "Both arms were bloody and had apparently been wrapped in a shirt." His upper right arm had been almost torn away by a bullet that was later determined to have splayed like shrapnel as it passed through the opened trunk lid.

A little closer to the car, shirtless and pale-bodied in blue-checkered slacks, black socks, and red-brown loafers, was Agent Williams. Side by side, the two men lay face down in the grass, feet toward the rear of the pale car. Both had been finished off by one or more shots through the head which had shattered their skulls; in the hot sun, the blood had already begun to dry and thicken. In addition, the fingers of Williams's right hand were almost severed, apparently by gunfire, as if he had held his hand up before his face just before his death. Though their weapons were gone, both men were still wearing their watches.

4:25 p.m.

(SKELLY) Do you have hand radio contact with W (PRICE).
(ADAMS) I don't think they took a port-a-mobil with them. It does not look good.
(SKELLY) 10-4. I think W (PRICE) is going to be coming around your direction. He has a MP SWAT team with him.
(PRICE) . . . en route.
Superintendent is in there now with another man trying to get those guys out. Trying to see if they were taken hostage. . . .
(O'CLOCK) I am en route to airport to pick up Number 1 (TRIMBACH), is it pretty definite that two Agents are in the house.
(SKELLY) Better check with R (ADAMS) on that.
O'CLOCK calling ADAMS with no response.
(ADAMS to PRICE) We have met with DEL and DEAN, we have two dead Agents.
(O'CLOCK to PRICE) Has someone been in there?
(ADAMS) They are both dead.
(O'CLOCK to PRICE) Can you give me their identity?
(PRICE) RON WILLIAMS and JACK COLER.

After another jurisdictional dispute with the FBI, Cummings ordered an all-out assault upon the compound for 5:30, by which time SAC Joseph Trimbach and a special sniper team from Minneapolis, as well as other units flying in from around the country, would be in place; already, armored personnel carriers and high explosives were on their way to Pine Ridge for the second time in not much more than two years. Cummings said later that the assault on the compound was triggered while it was still "on hold" by an outbreak of fire to the south.

4:51 p.m.

(SKELLY) Can you cover the south end? . . . There is some BIA people down there. . . . Can you get word to them or if we have any guys to do it. Keep an eye on creek bed . . . they have bunkers on either side of the road and they have an arms cache.

4:52 p.m.
(SKELLY) We are southwest of the houses we are interested in. Almost directly across from the houses. We are quite a ways away, probably 500 yards. We figure they will head right for that arms cache. Should block off that creek bed and make sure that they cannot get from the house to the LITTLE place. Do you copy? [Skelly refers here to the ranch of Wallace Little, Sr.]

4:54 p.m.
(SKELLY) WALLACE LITTLE's place is located south of the two houses we are now interested in.
10-4.
(ADAMS) The kid that gave himself up said there were about 20, all armed, I guess.

By late afternoon, the growing armed force on the county road had been swollen further by a squad of well-armed amateurs in office wear led by Indian fighter William "Bill" Janklow, who had rushed home to break out weapons from his large collection; he had flown from Pierre with Assistant Attorney General William Delaney to the Hot Springs airstrip, where he passed out arms to a sheriff's posse of about twenty men. (Janklow and Delaney later participated in "securing" the compound, and Janklow was apparently impressed that "the first building that he entered was very clean and that there was warm food on the stove. He stated that he thought it was potato hash.")

In an episode that would later become almost as controversial as the red pickup truck that departed from the farm at 12:18, BIA Officer Marvin Stoldt warned SA Skelly that four fugitive males he had seen fleeing the Jumping Bull houses down into the woods in the late afternoon might be making their getaway south along the creek.

At about 5:30, not long before the final assault upon the compound, the BIA police at the roadblock by the junction of the loop road with Highway 18 called for assistance, and Stoldt went down there with some of his men, arriving between 6:00 and 6:30. When more gunfire was heard, the agents at the Pumpkinseed house joined Stoldt's SWAT team, having learned from Adams that a group of fugitives had apparently crossed the loop road to the open range and was climbing toward the ridges to the southwest; two men on horseback had also been observed in the high country. Stoldt, who knew the terrain well, helped to organize the pursuit, which was hampered by a tendency among the fugitives to turn and fire a few rounds at their pursuers. Both Coward and Skelly were radioing to Adams for airplane assistance; to judge from Skelly's report, the lawmen were not eager to follow the Indians so far off the road. "During the climb of the hill," Skelly reported, "gunfire was heard, and as a result, made the climb much more difficult."

> The pursuit continued at a very slow pace due to sporadic gunfire which was being received from the area where the Indians were located. This gunfire, although sporadic, was at times at least fairly heavy and evidently accurate. Although no member of the pursuing teams was hit by this gunfire, on several occasions, shots hit very close.
>
> The Highway Patrol spotter plane was still overhead giving directions to the location of the fleeing Indian group. However, at approximately 8:00 PM, the ground teams were advised by the aircraft overhead that it had exhausted its fuel and would have to return to its base for refueling. After the aircraft left the immediate area, the pursuing teams arrived at the top of the ridge where the fleeing Indians had last been spotted, and of course, they were not at that position.

⊡

When SA Price returned to the woods by the corrals with twenty additional men, SA Hughes made final preparations for the assault upon the compound, dividing his men—FBI, state troopers, BIA SWAT, and sheriff's deputies—into three groups, each one headed by an FBI agent. The assault was delayed by the bureaucratic bickering out on the highway, and according to Hughes, who often checked his watch, it was 5:50 when "I gave the order to assault the houses."

> I ran towards the general vicinity of the green house and at approximately half-way there I received a great deal of rapid fire directed at me. I didn't know where, it was just—heard a lot of bullets go around me and I proceeded to run in a zigzag fashion and I dropped my FBI portable radio which broke, and I managed to crawl up to the vicinity of the green house and while I was proceeding up there, then I heard a lot of fire from the group that Price had that was assaulting the green house . . . a shot was heard

> and a bullet kind of whistled through the area of the green house. I don't know where it came from. Then I proceeded up to the green house, and I observed an Indian male laying on the northeast corner of the green house. . . . Agent Taubert approached me, Agent Robert Taubert, with a 30-30 caliber rifle, Marlin, lever action, and he handed it to me and said he had taken it from an Indian laying there and I walked over and observed this dead Indian male. . . . I believe he had a bullet hole in the upper part of his head, although I am not positive about that. The foremost thing I observed, he was wearing an FBI SWAT jacket which I recognized, and it had the letters "FBI" on the left breast pocket.

Bullets and tear-gas canisters shattered the last windows of the cabins as the assault teams waited for the Indians to stream out. There was only the sound of their own firing, then a dead silence. The noisy assault upon the cabins disclosed that the defenders had made a near-miraculous escape through the small army of agents and police that surrounded the compound and camp area; there was nobody left here at all. The large force of sweating, nervous men in new battle fatigues, with their sniper and chemical-warfare teams, their APCs and air support, felt frustrated and foolish; after all that shooting had subsided, all the smoke and gas had blown away, there was only this solitary Indian, killed much earlier in the day, lying beside the small green cabin on the bluff. Outraged by what looked like a cold-blooded murder of their comrades, and sickened by the two dead bodies with their shattered faces, already swelling after four hours in the sun and the thick heat, the frustrated men took out their wrath on the ruined cabins.

The death of the Indian in the FBI SWAT jacket was later credited to another Indian, BIA Officer Gerald Hill (perhaps the man who yelled, "I think I hit him!"). Or at least Hill was the only man who made this claim, which was reported by SA Gary Adams.

While Special Officer Del Eastman took crime-scene photographs and BIA Criminal Investigator Glenn Little Bird made a sketch, Hughes, Price, Waring, and two other agents searched the immediate area of the vehicle:

> Items found in or near position of SA RONALD A. WILLIAMS' body: one expended round apparently .38 caliber; one Government issue ink pen; three large pieces of skull . . .

Other items included bits of broken glass, blood spots, sunglasses, Chevrolet nameplate, empty shell boxes and expended shells, and even "vomit" on Agent Coler's shirt. Among the ninety-nine items inside the car, which was "secured" that same evening and towed away to the sheriff's garage in Hot Springs for examination, were maps and blank forms, candy, cough drops, and chewing gum, with discarded wrappers; oranges and orange peels; numerous yellow tennis balls and rubber handballs; a charcoal grill, briquettes, and starter fluid; a blackjack, a nightstick, and a table leg; a .32-caliber revolver (in the glove compartment) and live .38-caliber ammunition; one full and four empty beer cans; a bag of sunflower seeds; and suntan lotion.

Gary Adams had not joined in the assault or in the pursuit of the escaping culprits. With perhaps twenty men, he worked south along the creek with the idea of flushing out any Indians remaining. But Adams, a huge man not at home in mud and thickets, somehow cut his hand quite badly; he withdrew from the search, thrashing through the river woods in the direction of the highway in search of medical assistance. Hearing FBI radio transmissions, he made his way in the direction of the sound, coming out in a clearing that contained a number of small tents and, near the creek, a round structure of canvas and bent saplings that he later identified as a "steam unit." Not far away was a red-and-white Chevy suburban van, and also an old green '67 Ford with a crumpled grille and a .22 rifle lying on the hood, together with the plastic cups and paper plates of a meal hastily abandoned; it later appeared that this single-shot rat gun was the weapon that had shot out the tire on his own car earlier that day.

Up the slope, just by the wood edge, sat the dark-green Rambler that Adams had last seen in front of BIA headquarters that morning; as Adams put it, "monitoring of these frequencies was audible at least 100 yards from the camp"—in short, its radio was still going strong.

The injured Adams did not search the area. So far as he knew, he was the only witness to this scene until he returned with the Milwaukee and Chicago SWAT teams early next morning, at which time it was discovered that the red-and-white van was loaded with gear and food, ammunition, and explosives, including R.C. Cola bottles that turned out to be "sophisticated homemade hand grenades that our Laboratory experts feel were made by someone who had expertise in the field and who had military training." The van also contained two new spare tires from Ron Williams's car.

Warily, Adams skirted the tents, not knowing if any Indians might be present. At Williams's car, he "turned the keys in the ignition and this deactivated the radio"; he noticed that the car was ransacked, with only remnants of the dead man's clothes—hiking boots, a crumpled suit on a fallen hanger—strewn around on the backseat. Like the two-tone Chevy, the dark-green Rambler was full of bullet holes, with windows shattered, and it had three flat tires.

By this time, the firing to the south had ceased. The sun was setting over the Black Hills to westward, and the woods were silent in the summer dusk; and as Adams learned when he got back to the highway, every one of those Indians seen running up that hill toward the ridge line had gotten away into the night.

CHAPTER 9

THE "RESERVATION MURDERS" INVESTIGATION

June–September 1975

The white man does not understand the Indian for the reason that he does not understand America. He is too far removed from its formative processes. The roots of the tree of his life have not yet grasped the rock and soil. The white man is still troubled with primitive fears; he still has in his consciousness the perils of this frontier continent, some of its fastnesses not yet having yielded to his questing footsteps and inquiring eyes. He shudders still with the memory of the loss of his forefathers upon its scorching deserts and forbidding mountain-tops. The man from Europe is still a foreigner and an alien. And he still hates the man who questioned his path across the continent.

But in the Indian the spirit of the land is still vested; it will be until other men are able to divine and meet its rhythm. Men must be born and reborn to belong. Their bodies must be formed of the dust of their forefathers' bones.

Luther Standing Bear (*Lakota*)

On the day before the shoot-out at Oglala, Richard Wilson of the Tribal Council awarded custody to the U.S. government of a large tract of Indian land in the northwestern section of the Pine Ridge Reservation. Under the circumstances, the FBI "raid" has been widely interpreted as a diversion tactic to distract attention from Wilson's action, which was unlawful according to that clause in the 1868 Treaty specifying that three fourths of all the adult males had to approve any transfer of Lakota land. Others went further: the raid was an open provocation, designed to invite fire from the Indians and thereby provide the excuse to move a paramilitary force onto the reservation and make an all-out attack on AIM and its supporters.

The timing of the two events—the land transfer and the shoot-out—was certainly dramatic, but since the people did not learn of "the Wilson agreement" until later (the document was not formally approved by Wilson's Tribal Council until January 2, 1976), the alleged connection between the two events has no more foundation than the government's claim that its well-armed agents, turning up near the AIM camp and the Banks cabin two days in a row, had only gone there to inquire about Jimmy Eagle, whose offense, at worst, was the theft of a pair of cowboy boots from an old drinking buddy during a brawl.

"By coincidence," the BIA SWAT team was on maneuvers near the Jumping Bull property on the day of the shoot-out, and perhaps it was also coincidence that, according to Edgar Bear Runner, paramilitary forces had been surrounding the Oglala region all that morning.[1] In fact, he says, he had been on the way to Oglala to warn the AIM camp that something ominous was taking place when he encountered Dick Wilson and an estimated twenty Indian police and goons on Highway 18, about three quarters of a mile east of the property; within another quarter mile, he had encountered a force of 150 white men—state troopers, U.S. marshals, SWAT teams—and by late afternoon at least 250 men were surrounding the area. Bear Runner's account of the size of the operation was confirmed by *The New York Times,* which reported that FBI agents and armaments were being airlifted from Denver, Minneapolis, Chicago, and even Quantico, Virginia, within hours of the first shots fired that day. The Indians claim that part of this force was already in the area when Coler and Williams drove onto the property, and within a remarkably short time, reinforcements arrived that can only be called massive, when set against a band of untrained men and boys armed mostly with .30-30 deer rifles and .22s. Among these reinforcements was goon chief Duane Brewer, who, seeing two Indians near the compound in midafternoon—perhaps Edgar Bear Runner and Jimmy Zimmerman—took off after them, yelling, "I'm going to kill those sonsabitches!"[2]

The large detachments of Indian, state, and federal police were attended not only by idle goons but by white vigilante ranchers of the Civil Liberties Organization, a patriotic group that owned or leased most of the best reservation land; before the day was out, this small army was supplied with a spotter plane, a helicopter, a chemical-warfare team, and a special team of snipers, in addition to four more SWAT teams from outside the state. Within a few days, the FBI operation included two armored personnel carriers, a stock of high explosives, and a force of at least two hundred agents clad in battle dress and armed with automatic weapons.

The importance attached to what the FBI code-named the ResMurs (Reservation Murders) investigation is indicated by the fact that Joseph Trimbach, head of the FBI regional office in Minneapolis, was en route to Rapid City within an hour of the first shots fired. Trimbach, who had begged Colonel Volney Warner to bring the Eighty-second Airborne into Wounded Knee two years before, was soon consulting with Governor Richard Kneip about bringing the National Guard into Oglala, and meanwhile he radioed for high explosives, which arrived by Marine jet about 6:55 p.m. Next day, SAC Trimbach, who had taken command from the Resident Senior Agent, George O'Clock, in Rapid City, was replaced by Richard G. Held, SAC, Chicago, head of the FBI's Internal Security Section and a rising star in FBI counterintelligence: Held, who remained mostly behind the scenes, assigned the logistics of the case to his protégé, Norman Zigrossi.

The Reservation Murders investigation was concerned only with the killings of the agents; it did not concern itself with the dozens of murders committed in the past three years on the reservation, almost none of which had ever been investigated, far less solved.

Since the press was banned from the scene of the shooting for two days, the public had to choose between the propaganda of the authorities and the rhetoric of the AIM spokesmen, neither of which gave an accurate account of what had happened. According to the FBI's public-relations man,[3] flown in with a planeload of forty to fifty SWATs from Quantico on that first night to present the story in the right perspective to the American people, Agents Coler and Williams had been murdered in a "cold-blooded ambush" by a large force of well-trained guerrillas in "sophisticated bunkers" and "fortifications," but not before Williams had first pleaded for their lives for the sake of his companion's wife and children. How the Bureau developed this information about Williams's last words in the absence of anyone who could have heard them was not clear. Another FBI spokesman (and also state Attorney General Janklow) declared that the bodies had been "riddled with bullets"; their cars were also "riddled by machine-gun bullets." In an Associated Press report next day, "the two FBI agents were dragged out of their cars and executed"; the UPI stated that they were "taken from their cars, stripped to their waists, then shot repeatedly in their heads" and that they were "shot up to fifteen or twenty times with automatic weapons." Reports of "bunkers" and "ambush" and "bullet-riddled bodies" carried all the way back east to the pages of *The New York Times* and *The Washington Post;* a month later, on the front page of the *Washington Observer Newsletter,* the house organ of the Liberty Lobby, it was reported that the agents had been scalped.

In the opinion of the *Columbia Journalism Review,* which surveyed press coverage of this case a few months later, "The sources for the most important—and most inaccurate—parts of the wire-service reports were the Governor and the Attorney General of South Dakota. Attorney General Janklow had gone to the scene, as he said later, because he had heard that lawmen were in trouble. . . . When he left the scene, he told both AP and UPI reporters that 'it looked like an execution.' " The day after the shooting, the man who just two months before had said that he dreaded answering his phone lest it bring him news of a race war was on statewide radio decrying the killings as "assassinations" and trumpeting his view that it was time to stop being "soft on the Indians just because they were a minority group." The next day he ranted against "sob-sisters" who tried to protect "murderers and others who have no respect for society."[4]

That the FBI did nothing to damp down Janklow's self-serving exaggerations bears out Dr. William Muldrow, an investigator for the U.S. Civil Rights Commission, who stated flatly in his report that the information released to the media in regard to the shooting had been manipulated by the FBI: "It is patently clear that many of the statements that have been released regarding the incident are either false, unsubstantiated, or directly misleading." An official FBI memo submitted on June 27 to Bureau headquarters in Washington is typical: "Reports by Agents who viewed victims' bodies indicate that there can be little doubt of execution-style slayings.... Both Agents were shot in the head in a style common to execution-type killings. Both Agents were stripped from the waist up and both were laying face down with their hands raised."

Public opinion had been hardened against AIM by the time FBI Director Clarence Kelley clarified matters at a press conference on July 1, at the Century Plaza Hotel in Los Angeles, on the occasion of the agents' funerals ("I'm Clarence Kelley, Director of the FBI, and here with me are three gentlemen who will possibly assist in what will be, I hope, a very fine exchange . . . Mr. James Adams [FBI Deputy Associate Director] . . . Mr. Joseph Trimbach . . . Mr. Gary Adams"). Kelley made no mention in this fine exchange of "ambush" and "sophisticated bunkers," since the press had now seen for itself that the "bunkers" were old root cellars and horse shelters, that there were in fact no fortifications of any kind. As for the "bullet-riddled bodies stripped to their waists," Kelley acknowledged that the agents had been struck just three times each and that Coler's shirt had been in place. Williams's shirt had been stripped off while still buttoned, and possibly he had waved it in sign of surrender; in any case, he apparently made a brave effort to fashion a tourniquet for his partner, as the Director said. Despite claims to the contrary by AIM spokesmen, it seemed clear that the agents had been executed, since the fatal bullets had been fired at close range. The Director felt obliged to deny reports of FBI threats of vengeance, though the denial seemed Nixonian and legalistic: "No statements have ever been made by FBI officials that we were going to kill one-for-one."

Many if not most of the FBI agents, fired up by the sensational press releases being issued by their own superiors, were in a dangerous, vengeful state of mind. FBI DEATHS SPARK AGENTS' ANGER was the headline of a Sunday feature in the Rapid City *Journal* on June 29. " 'We'll stay here as long as it takes to round up the people who did this,' said one of the 200 agents combing the wooded hills and ravines of the reservation for the killers. 'It may take a while, but we won't rest until we have them in custody.' " " 'We lost two guys out there, and we're going to pull out all the plugs,' said one local agent."[5] A Chicago agent was quoted as saying, "Sure, I'm mentally tense. I'm glad I had several hours to cool off before I got here. But we're professionals, and revenge is the last thing we should want." Bruce Ellison, a young legal volunteer for the Wounded Knee Legal Defense/Offense Committee (WKLDOC) who flew out from the East on June 29, says that so many agents were on his flight from Minneapolis that many civilians had to be taken off; some of the agents, drinking hard, were talking loudly about "ambushes," and one man swore aloud that he would "get 'em." Clearly, these men had been led to believe that they were up against "sophisticated terrorists."

According to Dr. Muldrow of the Civil Rights Commission, the FBI agents were "deeply upset over the 'execution' of their comrades." And if the average agent was upset, one can imagine the outrage felt by men like Gary Adams, who considered Ron Williams a close personal friend, or David Price, who participated in the crime-scene investigation and helped deal with the corpse of his ex-partner; these men can be excused for vengeful feelings, if not for the pattern of activities that was to follow. Meanwhile, a warm letter of tribute to the amiable Williams appeared in the Rapid City *Journal,* signed by eleven neighbor families.

In the late evening of the Oglala shoot-out, or early the next morning, a newsletter hand-scrawled by a young legal aide of WKLDOC was circulated in the Oglala community:

> BIA spokesman Marvin Stolte [*sic*]—"We are going to get one A.I.M. for every law enforcement; we'll get one more."
>
> 4 horses around Jumping Bull Hall were tear-gassed and bullet-riddled.
>
> Ivis & Angie Long Visitor—3 kids 6 mos–3 yrs
> Harry & Cecelia Jumping Bull—over 80 yrs old
> Wanda Little—3 kids
>
> All were shot at and tear-gassed out of homes—were shot at when attempting to leave—all are OK
>
> Pigs are fingerprinting Ivis & Angie and won't release them until after complete search.
>
> Pigs are reportedly investigating 3 people—we don't know who yet . . .

Since this report is much exaggerated in regard to the people shot at and teargassed, the rest of it is suspect as well. However, the statement it attributes to BIA SWAT-man Marvin Stoldt was and is widely accepted. Its source was Calvin Jumping Bull, the principal of the local Red Cloud School, who also commented, "They planned this all along, planned to raid the place [and] it backfired. I hate to say this, but I think they [Coler and Williams] deserve what they got." This angry reaction was echoed by AIM statements, which did little to clarify the actual events. In these statements, the armed camp down by the creek that the press referred to as "Tent City" had become a "spiritual encampment," and the men who had lived there were no longer "skins" or "bros" or even "Dog Soldiers" or "warriors," but the "People's Defenders." John Trudell announced that "FBI agents armed with M-16s came onto the Pine Ridge Reservation to serve a warrant that they didn't have, on someone who wasn't there; they were accompanied by over fifty highly trained military marksmen, also with high-powered automatic weapons. These agents opened fire on a small house in which men, women, and children were asleep. Leonard [Peltier] and the others returned fire, creating cover as the people fled to safety. On that very same day, in Washington, D.C., Dickie Wilson gave one eighth of the Pine Ridge Reservation to the U.S. government. Now, common sense tells us that something very unusual is going on." Russell Means and Vernon Bellecourt told reporters that the FBI had provoked the shoot-out by forcing their way into a cabin and shooting down Joe Killsright Stuntz when he tried to defend his people, as a result of which the firefight erupted in which the two agents were killed.

The epidemic inaccuracy of most of the accounts is exemplified in those that concerned Joe Killsright's body. Even Dr. Muldrow, whose thorough report was generally levelheaded, said that the corpse had apparently been dumped into a mud hole by the frustrated FBI agents; others suggested that it had been desecrated. William Delaney, the state Assistant Attorney General who had accompanied Janklow to the scene, told an FBI man two days later that "the dead Indian was lying on his back, and when he was turned over, it appeared that he had . . . received a burst in the back and there was blood coming from the back of the jacket." (This "burst in the back" makes no appearance in the autopsy report which notes only the hole in the forehead at the hairline.) And subsequently Mike Anderson would say, "Charles told me that Joe Stuntz had been hit and was bleeding too bad to take along," an observation that appears to have no connection to instant death caused by a bullet through the forehead. Kevin McKiernan, a National Public Radio reporter and television filmmaker who was covering the

Custer trial on June 26, was called out into the corridor by Dennis Banks, who had gotten word that "they're shooting it out on the reservation." Rushing to Oglala, McKiernan managed to make his way past the roadblocks, and he got into the compound for a brief period that evening; he was the only reporter who saw and photographed the body before the press was barred from the scene, and suggested as one possibility that the jacket might have been "put on him before outside observers were allowed into the area." McKiernan declared that reports of a hole in the forehead were "false. The only blood I saw was coming down under the jacket sleeve." WKLDOC made much of the fact that Joe Killsright's death was never investigated, but it is hard to see what an investigation would have established, since he was killed in a long-range exchange of fire, not finished off while disabled, at point-blank range.

Even today, McKiernan is disturbed by the great storm on the eve of the Oglala shoot-out, which "sticks out in my mind among storms I've witnessed. . . . When I went to court that morning, people remarked on the stillness and beauty of the morning compared to the roughness of the storm. Indian people—more than a couple—interpreted the blowing off of the roof of the Custer Hotel as a 'sign' related to the legal struggle under way at the local courthouse—this observation before knowledge of the shoot-out. It had rained so much that even by the end of what became a hot day, mud puddles and troughs of water had yet to evaporate from the Jumping Bull compound."

⊡

The elderly Jumping Bulls, on their way home from Nebraska, passed through the roadblocks without difficulty on the evening of June 26; they were the first Indians to return to the grim scene.

> About seven o'clock I loaded some yearling calves from my corral and send them to Gordon, Nebraska, sale barn, and I stayed all day and then I headed back to home until I ran into a roadblock about one mile south of my house on Highway 18, about 6:30, but I don't know why nobody stop us we drive very slowly through two more roadblocks. When I reach home we seen lots of police cars and lots of policemen looking towards west where some more cars and men were. My wife asking what's going on and somebody from someplace told her two men shot and there's another body

laying in front of a green shack belonging to Ivis and then we look at our house, went closer and found out it was lots of bullet holes and strong tear gas fumes. We cannot go inside. The locks was broken with bullets and one hour later we enter the house. We found all boxes, trunks, cabinets, drawers, some even too small for a baby to hide in. Some of our clothes on hangers were left with bullet holes and some picture belonging to our boys who were killed in the war were shot showing some lawmen shot them close range with no respect. My wife went outside where the lawmen were standing watching and she ask them who gave them permission to enter the premise and one whiteman officer lawman said to her strongly roughly we will go any place anywhere anytime and enter for arrest or find what we wanted.

THE OFFICER: Don't you know two men killed?

CECELIA: Is this one of them? (Pointing to somebody laying there, in front of the Green House.)

THE OFFICER: No, down there. (Pointing towards west towards the corrals, where some men and cars there, about 300 yards or more.)

CECELIA: What is that laying there?

OFFICER: That's just an Indian.

CECELIA: Can I see it?

OFFICER: Yes. (Calls to another officer to uncover his face.)

(Cecelia walks over to the body and mourns.)

OFFICER: Do you know him?

CECELIA: No. I've seen him, but I don't know him. They call him Joe. But why do you shoot the houses and poison it?

LAWMAN: Get the hell out er here, leave me alone. I am busy. Don't bother me. [Don't] you know two men were killed here?

CECELIA: No, I don't know. We just got home. And we own this house and this is our home you ruin. And I demand my rights. If you are a killer why don't you kill me? That means all you lawmen! Go ahead, you have your guns ready, go ahead any one of you kill me. Shoot or get the hell out er here. (No answer. Some seen putting guns away and left about nine o'clock. Another lawman came over to Cecelia apologizing.)

LAWMAN: I'm sorry I just got here after this mess is over. I was told this is your place and you were not home except three little children with mother and father. I shouldn't be rude to you. I am very sorry and please forgive me. And do you have any place to stay tonight. Don't sleep in the house, it's poisoned. You can catch some sickness as you folks are old and anything can happen to your health—even T.B.

CECELIA: Yes, thank you. We have a place to stay at our granddaughter's house.

Later Cecelia Jumping Bull gave her own account:

> There are a big happening over there, to my place. . . . FBI, BIA police, goons, and marshals. They all have guns, they are still around. I get out from our car and I ask what are they doing over there. I said, "What are you doing out here? Who give you the permission to come around here? Why are you here?" . . . Nobody would answer me. They are just all standing around. Stand there and look at me. I said, "I am a Gold Star Mother, why don't you speak to me?" Nobody say anything. . . . They already shoot down all my house . . . broke screen doors and everything. The door is wide open. I just sat close to the house but I couldn't go in.

"They shot three of our pictures right through," says Roslynn Jumping Bull, the mother of Angie Long Visitor. "Right through the heart of my cousin, you know. . . . And there's another older lady, we had a picture of her. She was in . . . it was a picture of a sun dance, where she and I took part in it. And they shot her right through the head, you know. And then I got a nephew there, too, and they shot him right through. All the rest of the bullet holes were pretty big where they shot through from the outside, those holes were pretty big, but the bullet holes through those pictures, those others, they must have been from a pistol, seem to be, or a smaller gun . . . it looked like they were mad at us."

Leonard Peltier's friend Jean Day, who had gone to Cedar Rapids with Anna Mae Aquash, hurried back to Pine Ridge on the day after the shoot-out. At Oglala, she found Harry Jumping Bull trying to get back into his house. "I went in there, you know, to more or less tell him I was really sorry for what had happened, because when we moved there, we never wanted anything like that to happen. . . . When we were coming out to go into Oglala, because his wife was sick and so I was going to go over and see how she was doing, all of a sudden . . .

there was two school vans and I don't know how many cars of police and FBI agents, and they had flak, those bulletproof vests, they were carrying guns."

Cecelia Jumping Bull said, "I am going to return these United States flags and Purple Hearts to the government because they have no respect for me . . . they don't care for me." That night she got cramps and "poison stomach" from the tear-gas fumes and had to have her stomach pumped out in the Chadron, Nebraska, hospital. When Harry Jumping Bull returned to his house on June 27, he was refused permission to enter; a few days later, his wife had a nervous breakdown.

Outraged that their respected elders should be forbidden access to their property, the traditional people of the White Clay District, more than two hundred strong, marched on one of the BIA roadblocks, which rapidly dissolved. A few days later, Wallace Little, Sr.'s, house was surrounded by twelve police cars and vans and well over fifty men in battle dress; although he protested, saying that they had no right to be on his property, two FBI agents ransacked his house without a warrant. Mr. Little, seventy-five, who claimed to have been "neutral" before this event despite the pro-AIM sentiments of his sons and nephews, said, "We didn't have nothing, no protection—no guns. We just stood out in the open so they could shoot us with those powerful guns! Cut us in two! And I went over . . . and I told those boys, You hurt my feelings today! They was looking for a fella by the name of Eagle, and I don't know that boy, he never comes around here. They put my name down, gave me a black eye. How can I get my name back up there, like I had?"

The day after the shooting, Senator Abourezk wrote a letter to President Ford demanding some sort of executive decree to eliminate the mounting violence on the Pine Ridge Reservation and pointing out that his past appeals had evoked nothing more than a "bureaucratic" response—in short, "no action"—from federal authorities. "At the very least," Senator Abourezk told reporters (in what seems to have been the first recognition by an independent observer that the new Indian wars out on Pine Ridge were a lot more complex than met the eye), "they have an interest in keeping this thing stirred up."

On June 30, the war of words was intensified by John Trudell. Speaking from the steps of the Federal Building in Rapid City, Trudell declared that Indians "were tired of being the only ones killed," and said that the American Indian Movement would "not apologize for the deaths of the two FBI agents until the U.S. Justice Department apologized for the deaths of all those Indian warriors killed in the past three years."

Of more vital concern to local interests was Trudell's threat that for the Bicentennial celebrations of 1976, AIM would intensify its "See South Dakota Last" anti-tourism campaign, announced in March by Vernon Bellecourt because "the criminal justice system in South Dakota is being used as a tool against the American Indian Movement." The day after the Oglala shooting, a bomb had shattered windows in the visitors' center at Mount Rushmore (where the elusive "red pickup truck" turned up again: according to an FBI report that day, "a red pickup truck had been spotted in the vicinity of the Visitors' Center shortly before the explosion and this may have a significant connection . . . since a red pickup truck was also reported in the vicinity of the shooting on 6/26/75"). The bomb went off at 4:00 in the morning, injuring no one. The travel director of South Dakota's Division of Tourism hastened to declare that "People visiting the major attractions of Mount Rushmore, the Badlands, and the Black Hills are not going to be bothered by any troubles out there on that reservation," reassuring the merchants that tourist ad campaigns in places such as Des Moines were really paying off. "It is within easy driving distance of South Dakota, and the population traditionally has had good travel characteristics, including good income."

On July 1, AIM coordinator Ted Means announced that AIM would sponsor a July 4 march from Keystone to Mount Rushmore in honor of "our brother who died near Oglala." Means went on to say that the Black Hills still belonged to the Indians under the 1868 Treaty and that the "four faces are a desecration to our people and religion." Vern Bellecourt said, "Our ceremony will focus attention on the hypocrisy of America celebrating its Bicentennial with ceremonies at what's supposed to be the shrine of democracy [Mount Rushmore] but really is the shrine of deceit . . . a desecration of a sacred spot, stolen from us in violation of the Fort Laramie Treaty of 1868." In response, the regional FBI office in Minneapolis sent a teletype to the Director, under the heading THE THREAT TO DESTROY MT. RUSHMORE: (DESTRUCTION OF GOVT. PROPERTY), according to which an agent investigating the visitors'-center bombing at Mount Rushmore discovered that local people had been warned to

> GET ALL OF THEIR VALUABLES AND POSSESSIONS AND THEMSELVES OUT OF THE RUSHMORE AREA AS SOON AS POSSIBLE BECAUSE THERE WAS GOING TO BE A LOT OF TROUBLE. . . .
>
> ( )* SAID THAT AIM HAS A SUICIDE SQUAD WHICH IS EXTREMELY WELL TRAINED IN MILITARY AND GUERRILLA TACTICS. THE MEMBERS OF THIS SQUAD ARE MOSTLY VIETNAM VETERANS, WHO ARE HEAVILY ARMED AND WHO HAVE DISPLAYED THEIR WEAPONS AT AIM MEETINGS IN THE PAST. ( ) BELIEVES THAT THERE ARE ABOUT THIRTY MEMBERS OF THIS AIM SUICIDE SQUAD. . . . THESE INDIANS ARE THE BEST EXAMPLES OF THE INDIAN POPULATION. . . .
>
> AIM PEOPLE HAVE BEEN TELLING THE GENERAL INDIAN POPULATION THAT ON THE FOURTH OF JULY "THE MOUNTAIN WILL COME DOWN." . . .
>
> ( ) IS THOROUGHLY FAMILIAR WITH THE INCIDENT AT PINE RIDGE WHICH RESULTED IN THE KILLINGS OF TWO FBI AGENTS. HE SAID THAT AS ( ) TALKED HE COULD NOT HELP BUT FEEL THAT THE TWO AGENTS WHO WERE KILLED HAD ACCIDENTALLY WALKED INTO THE HOLDING AREA FOR THE SUICIDE SQUAD. . . . ( ) . . . FEELS THAT "SNIFFER DOGS" TRAINED TO DETECT EXPLOSIVES SHOULD BE BROUGHT TO MOUNT RUSHMORE IMMEDIATELY.

Inevitably, the agents' nerves were wound tight by the news of "suicide squads," which turned out to have no basis whatsoever. Instead of blowing up Mount Rushmore, some dead-eye Indians celebrated the Fourth of July by shooting down one of the three helicopters involved in the ResMurs search: the huge noisy bird, called *Hotel One,* was downed without casualties by small-arms fire from the hills north of Pine Ridge village.

⊡

Two days after the shoot-out, the interrogation of ResMurs suspects was well under way:

> A female witness has been located who states that she saw three of the subjects who were shooting at the police at the time in ques-

* The blank parentheses indicate where names and phrases were blacked out by the FBI before releasing the document.

tion and describes them as Number One, the subject who was killed, Number Two, Bob LNU [last name unknown], who reportedly is staying at a local residence, and Number Three, Norman LNU, who reportedly is a Navajo from Arizona visiting on the reservation. This female witness is going to be reinterviewed today for additional details. . . .

Bear Runner has been located and has been interviewed. He is an AIM supporter and refuses to cooperate completely. He refuses to say how many Indians were in the house and to identify them. . . . [The Agents], of course, will consider the utilization of a Grand Jury subpoena to compel his testimony. . . .

I inquired of ( ) as to whether she had actually identified the legal aid representative who had made an effort during the shooting to negotiate some sort of a truce during the firing. ( ) said that this woman . . . was completely uncooperative and the Agents . . . intended to reinterview her today. . . .

( ) advised that the BIA had got a call from a Ruth Stuntz of Monticello, Indiana. She had received a call from a Ida Stuntz, who is the ex-wife of a Joe Stuntz. Ida was hysterical and reported to Ruth that "Joe had been killed on the reservation." The Identification Division had located a record for a Joseph Stuntz, whose physical description generally matches that of the dead unidentified Indian. The fingerprint card of Joseph Stuntz is en route to Pine Ridge in an effort to identify the dead Indian.

Inquiry was made as to whether an autopsy was made of the body of the deceased Indian and, if so, any bullets were found. ( ) did not know, although he was reasonably certain an autopsy had been performed. It was pointed out in view of the publicity put out by AIM in that our Agents were "hassling" the Indians involved and actually shot the dead Indian, it was felt important that we determine what kind of weapon was used in killing the Indian and furthermore if he was shot from close range.

The same day this report was filed, the FBI obtained a crucial interview with their female witness:

ANGIE LONG VISITOR (She described her house as being the green house where JOE Last Name Unknown was shot and killed in a gun fight with Federal Officers) advised as follows:

Approximately 11:30 AM on June 26, 1975, she, with her three children, were inside her house when she heard shots being fired. She went outside and around her house and saw two cars in a gully behind her house. On one of the cars the trunk was open and a white male was looking around the corner of the trunk in a crouched position. She heard additional shots coming from a tree-line to the left of these cars.

By this time her husband IVIS had arrived and the five of them attempted to flee the gun fight by running across a field in front of their house toward Highway 18. Their escape was cut off, however, due to the fact that several law enforcement cars were attempting to get to the scene of the gun fight and were, consequently, caught in a cross-fire. Her, her husband, and their children then fled through the fields at the rear of their house and finally escaped.

During this gun fight, she observed three male Indians firing at these Federal officers. The first individual that she saw was a BOB, and he was firing at those law enforcement officers attempting to arrive at the scene of the gun fight via Highway 18. His position of firing was from a wrecked car immediately behind her house. He was wearing a ski mask during this shooting, but she is positive as to her identification due to his physical description and the clothes that he wore. BOB was wearing his tan cowhide vest that he always wears.

The second individual she saw firing at the Federal Officers was the now dead Indian, who she knows only as JOE. She first saw JOE near BOB and both were firing at the Agents approaching from Route 18. JOE then left his position with BOB and went over to a wood pile on the other side of her house where he laid down and began firing at the white male she saw in the gully with the two cars. The third individual she saw firing was an Indian by the name of NORMAN LNU. He was lying in a prone position alongside JOE behind the wood pile.

When she, her husband and the children, fled down the hill behind the house to safety, she noticed a white over red Chevrolet van parked on the dirt roadway in the gully approximately 100 yards from the two other vehicles. She did not see anyone around this van at that time but knows that this van belongs to LEONARD LNU.

She does not know what caliber or type of weapon these three individuals were using except that they were all shoulder-type rifle weapons.

The three individuals she saw shooting at the law enforcement officers all lived with several other individuals in a tent city which was located at the treeline along the creek which runs behind her house. . . . They came to live in the woods behind her house approximately three weeks ago.

She described these individuals as follows:

1. BOB LNU, male, Indian, 5′6″ tall, 120–130 pounds, 25 years old, medium brown hair, (This is the individual previously referred to as firing on law enforcement officers).
2. NORMAN LNU, age 17–18, male, Navajo Indian, from Arizona, 5′2″ tall, 120 pounds, brown hair, (This is the individual previously referred to as firing on law enforcement officers).
3. LEONARD LNU, age 25, male, Indian, tribe unknown, 5′8″ tall, 200 pounds, brown hair.
4. DEANO LNU, male, Indian, tribe unknown, age 23–24, 5′6″ tall, 140 pounds, dark brown hair.
5. MIKE LNU, also known as BABY AIM, male, Navajo Indian, 17 years old, 5′2″ tall, 125 pounds, dark brown hair.
6. WISH (Unknown if it is first name, last name or nickname), male, Navajo Indian, 18 years old, 5′2″ tall, 125 pounds, brown hair.
7. NORMAN LNU, male, Indian, tribe unknown, reportedly from Rapid City, South Dakota, age 18, 5′4″, 125 pounds, brown hair.

She indicated that there were four female Indians also living in the camp and described them as follows:

1. JEAN LNU, female, Indian, tribe unknown, resides in Rapid City, age 17, 5′1″, 110 pounds, dark brown, shoulder length hair. Immediately after the gun fight, her mother came from Rapid City looking for her daughter.
2. LYNN (LNU), female, Indian, from Arizona, age 18, 5′5″ tall, 110 pounds, dark brown, waist length hair.
3. NILAK (Phonetic), female, Eskimo, reportedly from Alaska, age 19, 5′1″, 140 pounds, chunky build. She added that NILAK was DEANO's girl friend.
4. JEAN LNU, female, Indian, tribe unknown, from Wisconsin, age 24, 5′7″ tall, 160 pounds, wore glasses, light brown hair, light complexion. LONGVISITOR indicated that this JEAN went home approximately one week prior to this shooting incident and that she was the girl friend of LEONARD LNU.

On June 28, Special Agent David Price came to the house of Gladys Bissonnette, saying that her grandson, Jimmy Eagle, was one of those responsible for the death of the two agents; he was looking for Eagle and also for Joanna LeDeaux. Mrs. Bissonnette, not yet recovered from the death of her cousin's son Pedro (who after the loss of his own parents had lived mostly in her house and called her "Mother"), was still shaken by the loss in March of Jimmy's brother Richard and her daughter-in-law, Jeannette. Now young Jimmy was wanted for the killings on June 26, and another agent (Gary Adams) was threatening to have Jimmy's brother Leon indicted as a suspect; the brave-hearted woman of Wounded Knee was starting to crack under the strain. Soon a WKLDOC lawyer arrived who told Price that nobody in this household wished to speak with him. (Richard Held's protégé, Norman Zigrossi, would later complain that his investigations had been seriously hampered by the meddling of WKLDOC, which he described as a "revolutionary organization.") The next day, SA Dean Hughes showed up at Mrs. Bissonnette's house on the same errand.

In the first week after the shoot-out, "Leonard LNU" had been tentatively identified as Leonard Peltier. According to a report of July 5, by SAC Richard Held ("at Command Post, Pine Ridge"):

> The one individual that appears to have been identified by more witnesses than any other is FBI fugitive Leonard Peltier, who according to the best information that we can now obtain, may have been killed during the shootout. An informant furnished us with information last night that he knows the location of a grave where he believes Peltier to be buried, and he will take Agents to that location today.

Apparently the grave did not pan out, since two days later, agents were circulating Peltier's photograph in an effort to confirm their belief that this man was present on Pine Ridge. (Bob Robideau's photo was in circulation by July 4; Jimmy Eagle's, by July 15; Dino Butler's, by July 24.) Dino Butler's half-burned draft card had been found in the camp on White Clay Creek, together with fingerprints of Leonard Peltier, Anna Mae Aquash, and many others. Already the FBI had reported that it had "a pretty good idea" who the culprits were, although it would not release any names, and in early July the Bureau had assembled a list of suspects. Besides the members of the AIM group roughly identified by Angie Long Visitor, this list included James and Leon Eagle, Hobart Horse (one of Eagle's co-culprits in the case that inspired or at least excused the agents' visits to the AIM camp area), Frank Black Horse, Ted Lame, Richard and June Little, Sam and Kenny Loud Hawk, and a number of others, including June Little's cousin David Sky (the Skys and the Littles belong to the Little Sky family). Of the whole list, the only one arraigned so far was David Sky, said to have escaped after Oglala and walked across the hills to Wounded Knee, where he allegedly boasted to friends, "You should have been there, we had fun." According to the Rapid City *Journal* for July 2, Sky's confession had been verified by "a professional tracker from Philadelphia, Pa., who . . . put a trained dog in close proximity to Sky to acquaint the dog with Sky's scent. The dog was taken to the scene of the shootings and the dog indicated to his trainer that Sky had been at the scene and vicinity of the murders. The dog tracked the escape route which was taken by a number of individuals who had been firing at the FBI agents subsequent to the deaths of Williams and Coler. The escape route was previously known and the dog indicated to the tracker the presence of Sky along the escape route within the last several days."

Despite the conclusions of this earnest dog, Sky denied the whole "fun" statement and refused to testify before a special grand jury convened later in the month at the request of the FBI's SAC Richard Held and U.S. Attorney William Clayton of South Dakota. Subsequently, according to his half brother, Bruce "Beau" Little, Sky became pitifully frightened and disoriented by FBI harassment, and has never fully recovered to this day.

An interesting detail of the Sky case had nothing to do with Sky at all. In an affidavit used to justify his arrest, the government mentioned that just prior to their deaths, the agents had been pursuing a red Scout that "matched the description" of the vehicle in which James Eagle had allegedly been riding; since the agents' bodies were found less than a half mile from the highway, the FBI said, it was not clear whether the chase had taken place on the main highway and had led onto Indian land, or whether they had been on Indian land when they saw the red Scout depart, then started to follow it. This was the first official mention of the red vehicle that was to become so important in the case, and also of the alleged "chase" that led to the shoot-out.

On July 8, when Agent Price led a helicopter raid on the spiritual camp of his old nemesis Selo Black Crow, in Wanblee, in apparent pursuit of Eagle or his vehicle, the FBI was extending its search all over the reservation. "We know who they are," Dick Wilson announced, "and the FBI knows. If the FBI doesn't get them, we will." On July 12, Agent Adams led a raid on Oscar Bear Runner's place in Porcupine, and entered his house without a warrant; he was approximately ten days late. Bursting into houses and threatening and scaring people had caused the death of an old man named James Brings Yellow, in Oglala, and as these searches spread across Pine Ridge, the Indians signed a general petition demanding that the FBI leave their reservation.[6] Eventually the Bureau instructed its agents to take off their war zone camouflage fatigues, and FBI headquarters was moved off the reservation, but the intensity of the operation did not diminish. The breaking-and-entering, threats, harassment, and many other illegal procedures entirely alienated the Lakota, even Wilson supporters who might otherwise have helped; the Sioux Tribal Council chairmen, after a special meeting on July 12, demanded an immediate withdrawal of most of the FBI agents and U.S. marshals from Pine Ridge and other reservations; they suggested that Oglala tribal officials, Dick Wilson included, be removed from office if they failed to reinstate constitutional procedures, and they also asked Governor Kneip to reprimand state Attorney General Janklow for his inflammatory statements. For once, the BIA's Indian governments were supporting all of the Indian people they were supposed to represent.

The U.S. Civil Rights Commission called the ResMurs investigation "an over-reaction which takes on aspects of a vendetta," and the commission's chairman, Arthur Flemming, in a letter to the U.S. Attorney General on July 22, protested "the full-scale military-type invasion. . . . Their presence has created deep resentment on the part of many reservation residents who feel that such a procedure would not be tolerated in any non-Indian community in the United States. They point out that little has been done to solve numerous murders on the reservation, but when two white men are killed, 'troops' are brought in from all over the country at a cost of hundreds of millions of dollars." For example, a woman named Rose Weasel Bear, interviewed in July by NBC News, said that when her brother and nephew were found dead, earlier that year, the authorities had informed her that the deaths had been accidental, although one man had been hanged and the other chopped up with an ax. "Couldn't there be just a little justice in there with the law?" Mrs. Weasel Bear asked. She feared for Pine Ridge children in the future: "We are living in a prison camp, the way we are now."

Flemming's letter received no response, perhaps because the Attorney General was so busy defending his government's heavy presence on Pine Ridge, which was being questioned all over the country; Americans wanted to know just why, for the second time in two and a half years, the U.S. government was spending millions of dollars in paramilitary operations on a remote Indian reservation in South Dakota. Others asked why the doomed agents had been trespassing on the Jumping Bull land, since the Indians claimed that they were ordered off the place on June 25 when they could not produce a warrant for Eagle's arrest. When early reports that the agents had been carrying a warrant on the twenty-sixth turned out to be untrue, the Bureau explained that agents were not required to carry warrants in order to make arrests so long as they knew that a warrant was outstanding.

What was much harder to explain was the triviality of the offense for which a federal warrant had been issued in the first place. On June 23, Jimmy Eagle and the other three youths sought—Teddy Pourier, Hobart Horse, and Herman Thunder Hawk—had been drinking at Pourier's house with two young white ranch hands whom they had known most of their lives.[7] A friendly party had turned into a free-for-all, in the course of which Horse got into a wrestling match with one of the whites while Eagle removed a pair of cowboy boots from the feet of the other. Though he carried a clasp knife, Eagle denied that he had taken it out, or committed the robbery and assault with a deadly weapon with which he was charged; if the victim had been an Indian, it is very unlikely that any charges would have been filed at all. The white youths registered a complaint, which was probably justified; what perplexed the Indians was why warrants were issued without any investigation, and why a BIA patrolman had not been sent out on this errand, which was a matter for the tribal court, and why a petty misdemeanor had been transformed overnight into two felonies. For want of a better explanation, one must suppose that a felony was needed to give the agents jurisdiction on the reservation. The press (and the FBI field agents as well) were led to believe that a kidnapping (a capital crime) had occurred, when in fact this allegation had no substance whatsoever, and was dropped quickly without explanation. In fact, the whole episode was so inconsequential that all but Eagle were eventually released on nonsecured bonds or in the custody of others, and Eagle himself was tried only on the robbery charge and then acquitted. Understandably, the Indians concluded that the felony charges and the "search" were a cover for FBI snooping in the area of the AIM camp.

The keen FBI interest in the Oglala area is borne out by the memo prepared three weeks before the shoot-out by FBI inspectors from regional headquarters in Minneapolis, entitled "Law Enforcement on Pine Ridge Indian Reservation" ("There are pockets of Indian population which consist almost exclusively of American Indian Movement [AIM] members and their supporters on the Reservation. It is significant in some of these AIM centers the residents have built bunkers which would literally require military assault forces if it were necessary to overcome resistance emanating from the bunkers").

A notation on this memo reads as follows:

> According to the Agents it had been determined that the Indians were prepared to use these "bunkers" as a defensive position and it was believed they were constructed in such a fashion as to defend against a frontal assault. To successfully overcome automatic or semi-automatic fire from such "bunkers" it appeared as though heavy equipment such as an armored-personnel carrier would be required. The Inspectors observed no other "bunkers" and no "dug ditches."
>
> The "bunkers" in question were observed from a moving automobile for approximately one to two minutes. The Agents recommended no attempt be made to obtain a closer view as the people residing in the area were AIM members who were known to be unfriendly to the FBI.

The property in question was Wallace Little's ranch, a couple of miles southeast of the Jumping Bulls', toward Pine Ridge village, and the "bunkers" are the ones later referred to in Agent Edward Skelly's radio transmissions on the day of the shoot-out.

The degree of FBI paranoia about AIM was well demonstrated by a map found in Agent Coler's car, which indicated these (nonexistent) "bunkers" on the Little ranch, and by the fact that SA Hughes, transporting a small, solitary, handcuffed teenager (Teddy Pourier), asked SA Price to provide escort in a separate vehicle on the two-hundred-mile round trip to Rapid City, in case someone decided to set this "terrorist" free. This precaution by Hughes *before the shoot-out* is mystifying:

there was simply no precedent or cause for his stated belief that Pourier's young friends, let alone the fragmented American Indian Movement, might attempt the armed rescue of a young culprit in a nonpolitical and uncontested case. Apparently Hughes had actually been convinced by Bureau propaganda that AIM "terrorists" might seize Teddy Pourier; and if Hughes believed this, then Jack Coler believed his "bunker" map, as well. In the absence of any information about how the shoot-out actually began, the possibility was emerging that Coler and Williams might have invited their own deaths by nervous and aggressive behavior, beginning with repeated invasions of hostile territory on the Jumping Bull property and ending with failure to retreat after warning shots fired by people who, at the start, were a considerable distance away.

▣

Eagle's confederate Herman Thunder Hawk was arrested on June 28; Hobart Horse was picked up a few days later.[8] Thunder Hawk informed the FBI that he had been in Rapid City on the day of the shoot-out; he also informed them that Jimmy Eagle not only had been present at Oglala but had been wounded in the shooting. This report, apparently echoed by the BIA police, was disproven by Eagle, who turned himself in on July 9 to the U.S. Marshal's office in Rapid City, prior to sentencing on an earlier conviction for shooting one James Catches on May 17. Arrested on the cowboy-boot charges, he was held on $25,000 bail until July 28, when he was arraigned in federal court on charges of assaulting a federal officer and two counts of murder in the first degree; his bond was raised to $250,000.

James Theodore Eagle was the first ResMurs suspect to be charged with murder, and the apparent basis for the charge was a series of statements allegedly made to his cellmates a few days before. According to a four-page complaint submitted by SA Hughes, Eagle had boasted of his exploits at Oglala to one Gregory Dewey Clifford, an Indian whom he had known slightly before going to prison; Clifford's testimony was taken down by SA William Wood, who had come to Pine Ridge with the large body of agents that arrived the day after the Oglala shoot-out and who would earn a certain notoriety as the new partner of SA David Price. According to Clifford, Eagle claimed that one agent had come early on June 26 to the Jumping Bull property and had been told to leave; that there were many Indians present, some of them armed with M-14 or M-16 automatic weapons; that when the two agents returned, a warning shot was fired, at which point the agents started shooting; that when they were disabled, a number of Indians, including Eagle, moved up close and killed them. Eagle, who said he was standing four feet away, described how one of the agents had begged for his life as a family man and good-friend-to-the-Indian (just as reported in FBI news releases after the deaths); that this man was shot with a Thompson .45 submachine gun, the impact of which knocked him into the air so that he came down hard, denting the car; that Eagle and his companions had taken turns shooting the agents on the ground.

Eagle's story was apparently overheard by Marion High Bull (convicted of killing two children on the reservation in December 1974) and Melvin White Wing (stabbed to death the following year in San Francisco), who had also decided to share these revelations with the agents.

> HIGH BULL advised that EAGLE mentioned the names SAM LOUD HAWK, KENNY LOUD HAWK . . . while EAGLE was talking about shooting the FBI Agents . . . in that these two individuals had something to do with a car. . . . HIGH BULL advised that he received the distinct impression that the way EAGLE was talking he was right there all the time. . . . HIGH BULL advised that EAGLE mentioned the name of FBI Agent PRICE and EAGLE said that if he ever got the chance he would blow away FBI Agent PRICE, as he didn't like Agent PRICE's tactics.

Melvin White Wing, described in one FBI document as a lead guitarist in various country-western bands, reported a similar account, except that "a JOANN and a LEONARD lived there and were shacking up and EAGLE mentioned the names of JOANN and LEONARD while he was talking about shooting the FBI Agents." Allegedly, Eagle also said that the episode involving the cowboy boots that led to the warrant for his arrest was a ruse to set up the FBI agents for an ambush. This tangled statement incriminated Peltier (and also Joanna LeDeaux, the WKLDOC aide who was the first visitor to the scene after the killings) and was used later to support the "ambush theory" of the killings.

High Bull concluded his interview with Agents Hughes and Coward by remarking that Eagle had told "the above story several times and he was excited while talking about it and seemed to enjoy talking about it." Although these accounts conflicted with hard evidence that the agents had been shot just three times each, the "confessions" attributed to Jimmy Eagle fitted a general sequence of events that the FBI was shaping into its theory of the crime.

▣

The first grand jury in the ResMurs case was convened in Rapid City on July 14, and William Kunstler turned up to contest its right to subpoena more than fifteen Indians—none of them (so far as was known) from the AIM camp—without an evidentiary hearing. Referring to the "reign of terror" on the Pine Ridge Reservation, Kunstler declared that unless the situation changed, "there's going to be bloodshed . . . which is in part initiated by the federal government as a retaliation for Wounded Knee, as a retaliation for the emergence of the American Indian Movement as a force in American affairs, and in order to set up some innocent people as the so-called murderers of the FBI agents." Edgar Bear Runner then tore up his subpoena, declaring that it had been served improperly; the law had given it to his mother to pass along to him. His action, he said, was an answer to a government under which he felt he had no rights: "I'm not a citizen of this colonial system. I'm not a citizen of this federal government."[9] On July 17, following his refusal to cooperate with the grand jury, Bear Runner's name was added to the list of those suspected of having participated in the shoot-out.

Because of a stolid refusal by local witnesses to give testimony, the first grand jury had to be disbanded; by the time it had reconvened in August, at least fifty Indians had refused to cooperate, among them June Little and Wanda Siers, a small, delicate woman who pointedly shut her mouth and refused to open it every time she was approached by the FBI. But the Long Visitors, nonpolitical, scared, and bewildered, had already talked, and one or more others had apparently talked, too, although their identities were still confidential; on the public record, no one on Pine Ridge was willing to help out except law-enforcement officers and goons. (A witness subpoenaed by a grand jury must testify without benefit of counsel, and failure to cooperate may be punished by jailing for contempt of court for the duration of the grand jury, which can last as long as eighteen months.) Even the Long Visitors would no longer cooperate; they were sent to prison on September 16 with Joanna LeDeaux, who invoked the 1868 Treaty and maintained her silence. Although pregnant, she was held in contempt of court: "The keys to your cell are in your mouth," Judge Andrew Bogue informed LeDeaux, who had her baby during her eight months in prison. Perhaps the Long Visitors and LeDeaux were treated harshly in the hope that they would crack because they were separated from young children. A number of others who refused to testify, including June Little and Edgar Bear Runner, were never prosecuted; apparently a decision had been made to concentrate on the "outside" Indians in the AIM camp.

Despite the considerable risk of exposure, Peltier and his group had participated in a sun dance held at Crow Dog's Paradise in the first days of August. In fact, an informer notified the FBI on August 1 that he (or she) had seen Leonard Peltier at Crow Dog's Paradise that day as well as the evening before.

> ( ) advised August 1, 1975, that Leonard Peltier is at Crow Dog's Paradise staying at the residence of Leonard Crow Dog's mother. ( ) Peltier evening of July 31, 1975, and day of August 1, 1975, at this location. ( ) that there are approximately 300 to 350 people at Crow Dog's participating in the "Sun Dance," an Indian religious ceremony [*fourteen lines blotted out*]. Since Peltier is participating in a religious ceremony sanctioned by the National Council of Churches and other religious groups, and the fact that there are approximately 300 to 350 people at Crow Dog's, it is not deemed advisable to attempt to arrest Peltier at Crow Dog's. If an attempt was made to arrest Peltier at Crow Dog's, there is a good chance a gun fight could break out, thus endangering the lives of innocent people. Further, it is felt that a raid at Crow Dog's at this time could be interpreted as interfering with a religious ceremony. [*More lines blotted out.*]

Sensibly, the FBI held back, not wishing an armed confrontation with hundreds of traditionals, who would resent any intrusion on the sun dance. Oddly, neither Peltier nor anyone else in the West Coast group is mentioned in a detailed report that came in later from another source; this could mean either that their participation at Oglala was still unknown to most of the Indians who were present, or that this informer felt he did not have to betray them in order to pick up his fee. On the other hand, the report claims that Marlon Brando was among those present, which Peltier says is "simply not true."

American Indian Movement (*A.I.M.*)

A source furnished the following information regarding events at the Sundance Festival held at *Crow Dog's Paradise, Rosebud, South Dakota,* July 31 through August 4, 1975.

Sundance began Thursday, July 31, 1975 with everyone present gathering for a feast and get-together, followed by extensive drinking, partying, and use of marijuana. Indian religious ceremonies, including Sundance ceremony, took place during four day event. Among those "pierced" at Sundance religious ceremony was four year old son of Russell Means, who was present at Sundance. Coincident to ceremony, persons associated with American Indian Movement (A.I.M.) . . . met and discussed future projects of A.I.M. . . .

One night former actor Marlon Brando was present, flying in via private jet to an airstrip at Mission, South Dakota and leaving the next day. Brando mingled with Indian leaders.

Numerous non-Indians (Caucasians) were allowed to be present at Sundance and Festival, in departure from prior years and against wishes of Leonard Crow Dog.

Crow Dog's Paradise was surrounded by armed guards throughout the activity, though weapons were seldom brought into the grounds.

Conversation among individuals who attended Sundance indicated that individuals present had discussed:

The burning of Catholic churches and missions on Indian reservations in South Dakota, and running off of priests, in order that the Indians can return to original Indian religion and medicine man. Legal efforts may precede this but if these fail, burnings will occur. It was claimed that white man's religion (Catholicism) was forced upon the Indians. Leonard Crow Dog, Indian Medicine Man, was proponent of this movement which is to begin in the area near Crowdog's Paradise near Mission and St. Francis, South Dakota.

Conversion of everyone on Rosebud, Pine Ridge and Lower Brule reservations to A.I.M. philosophy or expel those reluctant with eventual desire to take over the State of South Dakota.

Assassination of Bill Janklow, South Dakota State Attorney General, whom it was claimed furnished rifles to anti-A.I.M. leader Dick Wilson.

Something to do with the State of Maine where it was stated some land has been given back to Indians and where they desire to take back "the rest of their land," by fighting, if necessary. A.I.M. participation in this activity appears to be planned for Fall, 1975.

Old Leonard Crow Dog [*sic:* Henry Crow Dog] Indian Medicine Man, has predicted that all militant Indian activity will take place before the end of 1976 and because he is Indian religious leader, A.I.M. members accept this timetable.

A.I.M. claim strength in every state where there are Indian reservations. A.I.M. claims unlimited funds and that funds for bond of any A.I.M. member arrested are immediately available, no matter how high the bond. Many old time South Dakota Indians (Full Bloods) still believe in the old religion and are somewhat sympathetic to A.I.M. They desire that land be returned collectively to the Indians, who were present first. In extremely remote areas of South Dakota the hill people are afraid not to assist A.I.M. when present.

It was stated that anti-A.I.M. leader Dick Wilson has highly paid "goons" . . . to commit acts of violence and blame A.I.M. The first such act was stated to have been the burning of a hall near Oglala the weekend of August 1–3, 1975. The desire to "execute" or "exterminate" Dick Wilson was repeatedly stated.

On Sunday night, August 3, 1975, individuals associated with A.I.M. left Sundance destined for Wanblee, South Dakota, where they are receiving food by air and taking it up in the hills nearby to people there.

⊡

On August 1, at Marksville, South Dakota, two agents interviewed Andrea Skye, wife of Bob Robideau and the mother of his son, who said that on June 26, 1975, she and her husband were in Rapid City, South Dakota, visiting her father. A week later, the FBI announced that it was looking for Frank Black Horse, twenty-six, of Cherokee, North Carolina (a.k.a. "Cherokee" and Richard Tall Bull), wanted in connection with the shootings of two federal officers at Wounded Knee on March 11, 1973, and also Leonard Peltier, thirty, wanted for attempted murder in Wisconsin; although these two men were thought to have been present on Pine Ridge on June 26, the FBI would not confirm that they were on the list of sixteen suspects, which had been condensed from an earlier list of at least thirty.

Black Horse, described by one of Peltier's friends as "a loudmouth and joker who Leonard likes to kid around with," is the same man who, according to Louis Moves Camp, had been awarded an eagle feather by Russell Means for "wounding" an FBI agent at Wounded Knee. Although Black Horse himself had been heard to boast of having "dusted a fed," the eagle-feather story is not taken seriously by anybody but the FBI, which has displayed an unusual interest in him ever since. As in the case of Frank Clearwater, the Cherokee killed at Wounded Knee, the FBI claims that Black Horse is not an Indian at all, but an Italian American out of Cleveland named Frank Leonard DeLuca, and this time the Bureau may be correct; apparently this man was one of the young would-be Indians who attached themselves to AIM at Wounded Knee.[10] On May 19, Black Horse had failed to appear before Judge Bogue in Rapid City for a pre-trial hearing on the Wounded Knee charge; nor did he turn up for his trial in July. Although the FBI assumed that he had been present at Oglala on June 26, the evidence against him in the ResMurs case was scanty, since it mainly consisted of fingerprints found in the camp by White Clay Creek. However, a youth in Porcupine tentatively identified a photograph of Black Horse as that of a man who apparently sold Agent Coler's shotgun to a mutual acquaintance on July 18, warning the buyer, "It's a hot gun, hide it or get rid of it"; the seller was said to be a friend of Edgar Bear Runner. Also, BIA Officer Marvin Stoldt would inform the agents that about one week before the shoot-out at Oglala, "in the immediate vicinity of Jumping Bull Hall" he had "stopped" four Indians for unspecified reasons; one he recognized as Jimmy Eagle, and another "bore a strong resemblance to an individual whom he knows as Black Horse."

In August, the intensity of the search had eased a little, although the FBI spent an estimated $4 million on the ResMurs investigation in that month alone. On August 19, Director Kelley circulated new instructions to the regional office in Minneapolis and to Richard Held, who was still in charge of the investigation. Kelley cited "the possibility of additional A.I.M.-inspired violence in the future," and said that "all indications of the accumulation of weapons and explosives, 'hit teams' or similar groups, or the existence of safe houses or hideouts must be promptly resolved."

Late in the month, thirty leaders of the "Oglala Lakota Nation" left for Washington, D.C., to present resolutions to the U.S. government concerning the 1868 Treaty, the issue of sovereignty, and the excesses of Dick Wilson and the FBI on the Pine Ridge Reservation. On September 5, Chief Frank Fools Crow was invited to give the opening prayer in the U.S. Senate. That same morning, the FBI staged a huge commando raid on Crow Dog's property on the Rosebud Reservation.

CHAPTER 10
THE FUGITIVES I
July–November 1975

Non-Indians who find our old spiritual life-way meaningful often wish to believe and hope that much of that ancient kind of religious life still exists among our people. . . . Sometimes it seems I am the only one left who lives completely that way. Years ago, in the time of my youth, there were a lot of them. But now, even though there are others, including a few medicine men at Pine Ridge and Rosebud whom I have taught how to live holy lives, and how even to do some of the ceremonial things that I do, there are only a few. Some have tried to live completely spiritual lives, but the attempt is as far as they get. So many drink, you see, and haven't the strength or the dedication to live that way. They just give in and give up. I am not pleased to say this, nor am I boasting when I say I do better. I wish for the sake of the people that there were hundreds immersed in constant vision-seeking and prayer. But I think I am one of the very few left. . . .

The drinking problem . . . has gotten worse with every passing year. Whiskey and wine are the most terrible things the white man ever brought to the Indian people. Alcohol is the bitterest curse we have, and it has done more to weaken and destroy us than anything else. We had no strong drink, no such thing as whiskey, before the white man came to our country.

Frank Fools Crow (*Lakota*)

On Pine Ridge it was only a matter of time before the fugitives were betrayed by an informer; they were also convinced—as Peltier had told Jean Day—that they would be shot on sight. Therefore they decided to leave Porcupine and seek sanctuary on the Rosebud Reservation, where Crow Dog's Paradise, on a large wooded tract in the Grass Mountain District, had sheltered AIM fugitives ever since the days of Wounded Knee. Although aware that the choice was risky, they wanted badly to participate in the sun dance and give thanks to Wakan Tanka, who seemingly had intervened to save their lives.

On July 2, they arrived casually at Crow Dog's, as if just turning up early for the sun dance; they had not sent word of their arrival in advance, which among Indians makes the host responsible for their safe journey. To attract less attention the group split up; some stayed across the Little White River, on the property of Crow Dog's brother-in-law, Al Running. "As soon as we got there, we just played like nothing happened and we just came to visit; we didn't want to get them in trouble," says Norman Brown, who still intended to take part in the sun dance, for which he had come to South Dakota in mid-June. Scattered among Crow Dog's people, they could "kick back a little," as Nilak Butler says, and in the next few weeks they traveled back and forth as far as Denver, assembling equipment for the armed struggle to which they felt they were now fatally committed, and to which all had dedicated themselves in talks at Porcupine. At the end of July, the group was joined by Dennis Banks.

On July 26, Banks had been convicted in Custer on the charges based on the courthouse riots of 1973; he was released next day on $10,000 bond, pending sentencing on August 5, after the sun dance. State Attorney General William Janklow expressed satisfaction with the verdict and dismay at the judge's decision to set bail, since Banks, subject to fifteen years in jail, might decide to flee; a few days later, when Banks skipped bail and went underground, advising those who forfeited his bond that he feared for his life while in state custody, he gave as one reason Janklow's statement about putting a bullet through the heads of the AIM leaders.

"Leonard [Peltier] really danced that year, he really sacrificed for our people hard," Nilak Butler says. "We were together as a group in that kind of way—in ceremony and in prayer, really strong. That feeling of family was just so tight. And it was at that time that [Banks] decided to go underground, so we thought we'd all just go together.

"When we left Crow Dog's, our group had gotten considerably larger, because a lot of people joined with us as an act of solidarity. To support us, they were . . . putting their lives on the line, because the feds were crazy during that time. . . .

"When we were underground, we were staying at one place and they had a farm and a cornfield and little pigs, and the little pigs got loose and all the guys had to chase these little pigs all over this farm. They were all talking about how fast they were and everything, and there they were, running around the farm trying to grab these little pigs. It was funnier than heck, it was really good.

"We had several cars at that point, so we were together, but we weren't always together, and people traveled in different cars and stuff. Mostly, like, in groups like that, it seems like the women stay together pretty much and the guys stay together pretty much. And I'm not a man, so I remember a lot of cooking." Nilak laughs. "At that time, I was pretty naive. I had just wandered straight out of the movies, you know. As far as a lot of understanding, I just didn't have it.

"Back in South Dakota, that's when it started getting hard, because our family got broken up. When everybody was all together, they couldn't touch us. It's when people started going out in all different directions that we started getting nailed in all different directions."

"Dennis had told the court that he'd show up for sentencing the morning after the sun dance, but he decided against it," says Bob Robideau, who served as security at Crow Dog's. "They issued a warrant for his arrest, and that same night we took off for Colorado; I remember there was a big lightning storm, lit up the night sky all over Nebraska, and it seemed like some kind of a sign that nobody knew how to read.

"In Colorado, we had the support of the Chicano community, which provided safe housing all over the state. After the Custer verdict, Dennis had no place to go; Carter Camp had also skipped his sentencing in Cedar Rapids, and he joined us, too. We decided that the time had come for armed resistance against the oppression on Pine Ridge, and this time it wasn't going to be no Wounded Knee. We planned to take over the whole reservation, put in the traditional Oglala leaders, and those leaders agreed. A small group could handle it if it was done right, and we had accumulated about thirty people, which was enough to take out the police station, the courthouse, all the seats of authority; after that, we would set up roadblocks. That was going to happen as soon as we had sufficient armament and equipment. But we had an untrained and undisciplined group, with too many leaders, and things started to break down. One group split away in Colorado; then some of our Chicano volunteers got killed in a big fight down there among themselves. By the time we headed north from Colorado, we were back down to our original group and Dennis.

"The first ones to go back to South Dakota was me, Dino, and Nilak, and also Bernardine and Kamook Nichols, and I think maybe Norman Charles; we went to Oglala, to a friend's place. While we were there, Anna Mae came in—she was real happy to see us, hugging everybody. She was just back from Canada, where she tried to straighten out custody of her two kids, and she was dissatisfied with her community work among the Oglala women and didn't think she was accomplishing anything. At this time she was suspected by a lot of people of being an informer working with the feds, but at the AIM convention down in New Mexico she got confronted very strongly by an AIM security man, and he was satisfied with her explanation. Well, that security man was Leonard, and he liked and trusted her. I trusted her, too; she stuck her neck out on many occasions when she didn't have to."

Among those who did not trust Anna Mae was Leonard Crow Dog. "I and Anna Mae was cooking for Crow Dog, that was around the first day of the sun dance," Jean Bordeaux says, "and Crow Dog was coming down on me because he wanted to hold a ceremony for Joe Stuntz and I told him I couldn't do what he wanted me to do because I hadn't been Joe's girl friend, the way he thought. So Crow Dog gets mad, saying, Why can't you people get your stories straight? After that, he turned on Anna Mae and started going about her being an informer. Anna Mae didn't cry easy, but after Crow Dog got done with her, she was crying. And I guess she didn't feel welcome there no more, 'cause she left the sun dance."

Although she had been in Cedar Rapids on June 26, Anna Mae was wanted by the FBI in connection with the Oglala shooting; a 302 (field report) dated July 16—which also mentions her arrest on April 25, 1973, for her participation in the occupation at Wounded Knee—warns that she and Nogeeshik Aquash (from whom she had been separated for more than a year) were "armed and dangerous." On August 20, a teletype from Los Angeles to Washington compounded the confusion, revealing that Anna Mae, Nilak, and Ernie Peters had gone to South Dakota on some "secret A.I.M. project associated with the Tent City area."

"By now the feds weren't looking for us any harder in Oglala than anywhere else," Bob Robideau says. "We figured Oglala was the last place they would look. And the local people there always watched out for us; we knew we were relatively safe, and we set up camp in a small house in the hills. But one day a man came on horseback, hunting a stray cow; he seen us and he got away, so we had to leave. We went back to our old camp in Porcupine, and me and Bernie Nichols, Kamook's sister, went back south to Colorado to pick up the rest of the group.

"By the time I got there, Leonard and Dennis were supposed to be in California—their job was to raise ten thousand dollars for arms and supplies—and I was kind of pissed to find them hanging around down there instead of tending to business. When they were still there four days later, I got in an argument with Dennis. See, I was never tight with Dennis the way Leonard and Dino were, and I didn't mind saying what I had on my mind.

"Leonard and Dennis finally left for California, but I left Colorado before they did. For the sake of morale, I had to get back to the people who were waiting for us in Porcupine. I remember we came to the res by way of Oglala with the idea of taking the back road over the hills to Porcupine, missing Pine Ridge. This must have been about the second or third week in August. At Porcupine, we found that the group had returned to Rosebud. There had been a big gathering at Porcupine on the anniversary of Angel's death—Angel was an AIM leader, Apache, I think, who brought his group north at the time of Pedro's funeral; he got killed in a car wreck down in Arizona. Anyway, there were just too many goons and cops around, and our group had left. When we got to Rosebud, Dino was hopping mad because we were so late, and I didn't blame him; he had to move everybody—guns, equipment, and all—out in a hurry with just one vehicle, this orange Scout that belonged to a guy called Leroy Casades. Also, Bernie and Kamook felt uncomfortable at Al Running's, just uneasy somehow, and I was always one to respect that kind of feeling. So I moved 'em ten or fifteen miles away, over there near Parmelee, and set up tents back in the hills. Maybe three days later, when me and Bernie visited Dino and Nilak and Anna Mae, they were ready to join us; in fact, Anna Mae wanted to take off that night. We talked for about twenty minutes, and finally she said she would wait and go with the Butlers in the morning. That was the last time I ever saw her. Next morning I went into Rosebud, trying to reach

Leonard or Dennis on the phone. Then we went by Running's to pick those people up, and we saw a whole lot of action in there, and Bernie says, Hey! Those are feds! I kept right on driving by, and the farther I went, the faster I drove."

⊡

According to AIM people, Leonard Crow Dog had been "very strong" during the Wounded Knee occupation, and his support for AIM at a time when other medicine men had not come forward is partly explained by deep resentment of the BIA that went back to his early childhood. Because Henry Crow Dog had persevered in his traditional religion, this family was much resented by the Catholic missionaries, who in the early 1930s with the aid of the BIA police drove the Crow Dogs out of the settlement of St. Francis during a blizzard, an experience which Leonard's infant brother did not survive. Leonard's sister Delphine, the stepmother of Jancita Eagle Deer, had been beaten by BIA police and left out in a field, where she died of exposure; in recent months (on July 25) his nephew Andrew Stewart, aged eighteen, had been killed in a shooting "accident" while in the company of a goon named Robert Beck.

In early September, Crow Dog's nephew Frank Running and another boy had been assaulted by Beck and a drunken sidekick, William McCloskey. After midnight on the evening of the skirmish, Beck and McCloskey—who acknowledged later that he and Beck had been the aggressors—drove out to Grass Mountain to pick another fight; this time, the Runnings and their friends beat hell out of the goons, after which Beck lodged a complaint with the police. The Indians believe that, whether or not Beck set it up, the episode was used by the FBI in the same way it had used the cowboy-boot episode involving Jimmy Eagle—as an excuse for another paramilitary raid, which in fact occurred about thirty hours later.

That morning of September 5, an air-land-and-river operation had descended at daybreak on the Crow Dog and Running properties, in a massive racketing of helicopters that swept in over the dawn trees. More than fifty FBI agents in combat dress, with four large helicopters, military vehicles, trucks, vans, cars, and even rubber boats—presumably to prevent aquatic escapes down the narrow creek called the Little White River—surrounded the houses and tents, shouting, "This is the FBI! Come out with your hands up!" No one was given time to dress—Crow Dog himself was marched out naked—and even the small frightened children were lined up against walls as the agents ransacked and all but wrecked every house, tent, cabin, and car on both properties.

"Dino and I were staying over at the Runnings' house, and a couple other people were at Crow Dog's. Something had happened over at Crow Dog's the night before—I still don't know what all that was about. And that night Dino and I were staying in this little house outside of Al and Diane's, and Anna Mae was in the tent. There was another guy and his little baby and they were staying in a truck. Then there was the Runnings in their home. That night—like, you know, we'd gone through a lot of stuff at that point and we never got nervous. We were always concerned, but never nervous. And that night we got *nervous.* It was really strange. It was like something was gonna happen and we knew it. We were talking about, Well, let's go out and stay in the bushes tonight. And we didn't. We didn't listen to ourselves. We should have, because the next morning at dawn, the feds came in."

"These FBI agents came in like they were in Vietnam or something," Norman Brown says. "I was sleeping and somebody knocked on the door. So they called, Come out with your hands up, this is the FBI. So we all did. The one who grabbed my hair, he said, All right, motherfucker, lay down. So I laid down and they searched me and they put an M-16 to my head. They said, Who killed those FBI agents? Told him I didn't know, so they picked me up, they pushed me with the M-16 in my back, they pushed me. They said, All right, walk to where the crowd were. And I was standing over with the crowd of my brothers and sisters. And as we were standing there—these women who weren't even dressed yet, people crying and everything—they brought Leonard Crow Dog out and he had nothing on. They wouldn't let him put on his clothes; and we tried to give him his pipe, but they had to go through his bags—they said there might be a gun there. So they tied me and five other brothers to the tree, had plastic cuffs like this around that tree. And we were sitting there for a couple of hours. So we hear choppers go by, and they were calling us all kinds of names, so we do nothing."

> During the execution of a search warrant on the AL RUNNING property, a closed green, yellow and white tent was located by SA DAVID F. PRICE and SA CHARLES P. ENGAR. SAS PRICE and ENGAR called out words to the effect "FBI come out of the tent!" A female

> voice answered approximately a minute later. A person who identified herself as ANNA MAE PICTOU, Indian, female, came out of the tent by unzipping the bottom flap and crawling out. PICTOU was fully clothed with the exception of the fact that she was not wearing shoes. PICTOU identified herself at the request of SA PRICE and was advised of SA PRICE's official identity.
>
> PICTOU was advised that SA PRICE remembered her from earlier interview concerning the murder of JEANETTE BISSONETTE and was asked several questions concerning events surrounding the murder of BISSONETTE. PICTOU advised she would not answer any questions concerning the BISSONETTE murder.
>
> PICTOU was asked whether she was a Canadian citizen. PICTOU answered that she was a native American. She refused to answer whether she was a citizen of the United States.
>
> At this point SA PRICE was called back to the tent where PICTOU had come. SA THOMAS M. DUFFIN advised that he had found hand grenades, dynamite and what appeared to be a sawed-off .30 caliber carbine in the tent. SA PRICE viewed the hand grenade, dynamite and sawed-off .30 caliber carbine along with numerous .30 caliber rounds in the yellow, white and green tent. SA PRICE then walked back to where PICTOU was standing. . . . SA PRICE reintroduced himself to PICTOU. . . . Immediately after this PICTOU was advised that she was under arrest for the possession of illegal explosive devices.

Crow Dog is a medicine man, and no arms were found on his property, but on Al Running's place the agents turned up rifles, sawed-off shotguns, pistols, and explosives, including a .44 Ruger rifle allegedly used at Oglala; Running informed the agents that Stan Holder had given him the .44 after the occupation of Wounded Knee; that he, Running, had asked Black Horse about it when it disappeared earlier that year; and that Black Horse had said it would be returned to him safely at a later date. Running said that the rifle had turned up again with Leonard Peltier and his group when they arrived on the Rosebud Reservation in July.

In addition, an AR-15 semiautomatic rifle with an obliterated serial number was found abandoned on the riverbank. The only ammunition for this weapon was some .223 clips in a jacket marked "Chicano Power," found on the Running property in an orange-and-white Scout registered in the name of Leroy Casades, described in an FBI document as "an A.I.M. weapons and explosives expert." Also located in this orange-and-white Scout was a .357 service revolver issued originally to Special Agent Ronald Williams.

⊡

"I remember," says Nilak Butler, "Diane Running came to the door and she said, Get up, get up, hurry up, get out of here! By the time we got up and got to the door, it was too late. See, Dino could've gotten out of there. He could've, but he wouldn't leave me. I wasn't dressed and I was trying to get dressed. He could've gotten out of there. They always talk about how these guys are always just looking out for themselves and cold-blooded killers and all this kind of crap. That's just what it is. Because they never have left us in any positions where we'd be hurt.

"I remember walking out that door. There were two feds on their bellies with M-16s pointed at me and two standing up with M-16s pointed at me, and one around each side of the house with pistols pointed at me. They had a couple of guys spread out, spread-eagled on the ground. There was just tons of them crawling all over the place, like a bunch of flies on a piece of meat. Just all over, and all excited, too. There was a tent over there, and I remember they were tearing up the camp and throwing stuff around.

"Later I was sitting in a car, and this fed was just retarded. His name was Dave, but it wasn't David Price. My name is Dave. What is your name? Do you live on a reservation? And I wouldn't talk to him. I just put my head down. I wouldn't even talk to him. They'd gone in and torn up all the houses and everything that was sacred to our people—they just had no *respect.* And I remember Diane came out. They'd taken her son, they'd taken her husband, and they'd taken her brother that day. And she came out and she had her pipe with her, and she was praying. I just sort of prayed with her quietly while she was there. She's crying and she's praying like that, and the feds are making fun of her: Oh, are you going to make it rain? and stuff like that. That's how they act. That's the first time I talked to Dave, when she got done praying. I just turned to Dave and said, You know, you wonder why nobody will talk to you. You people have no respect. You have no respect, and you know nothing about justice, and that's why nobody will talk to you. Those people were insane, they were *crazy* that day. Anybody who terrorizes children and threatens women, you know. I don't have no time for them kind of people.

"And I remember Henry Crow Dog, Leonard's father—he was already an old man then, and he comes over to a bunch of feds, very quiet, you know, and draws a circle in the dust in front of them and then draws a line right through the middle. This is you with your guns over on this side, he tells them, and this is us over here with our sacred pipe. And then he's quiet some more while they just stare at him. The circle is turning, he says after a while, and walks away, and all their mouths are just hanging open.

"So the feds were asking us a bunch of questions, and we were just trying not to get shot, just trying not to get shot, because they were ready for it. And then they separated us, and they took Dino and they put him in a car, handcuffed him and put him in a car, and they took me and they put handcuffs on me, those plastic cuffs. And after a while, an agent comes by and saw my hands were turning black because they had the cuffs on me too tight, and he says, Hey, those cuffs are too tight, and he loosens them, and later he comes back and says quietly, You want to talk to me? No. Later, maybe? No. *Any* time? No. And he's cool about it, he just walks away—now *that* guy scares me. But this other guy is running around like a maniac, and Anna Mae says, That one's David Price. Price is not a warrior, because he freaks—he was running around, waving stuff around and yelling, Look at this! And he wasn't the only one; those feds were wiping out fingerprints right and left.

"And Anna Mae goes, Yeah, you know what that guy said to me? He said that it was AIM leadership that killed Buddy and Frank at Wounded Knee. The man's *crazy*! He's just trying to start trouble. And so they took her in one of the first cars. Then they took Dino. And I was supposed to go in the last car that day, and at some point when we were sitting there, they realized who Dino and I were, and then it got really ugly again. I was really grieving because I heard how they were talking and I saw how they were acting, and I just didn't think he was going to make it alive that day."

⊡

"I heard a bunch of cars pulling up and looked out the window. I told my wife to get up. I picked up the pistol and I walked out. Three men were coming at me and they had guns. I asked them what the hell was going on. They said they were FBI agents: Get on the ground! So I got on the ground. They came up to me and asked me if anyone else was in the house, and I told them yes, my wife was. They told me to call her out, so I called her out, and they made her get on the ground. I showed them this driver's license that I had. It said Robert Noble. They arrested me for having a gun with an altered serial number on it. They put me in the back of this FBI car. Later, all of the other agents—they were from the South Dakota area and had been working on this case ever since it had happened, I guess—they came down there and this one walked by the car and he looked in the back of the car like that. He walked over to the other agents and said, Hey, you know who you got there? That one agent told him, Yeah, that's Robert Noble. He said, No, that's that fucking Dino Butler. Why did you take him alive? The other agent came over and he looked in the car and he said, Yeah, that's that fucking Dino Butler. Did he have a gun on him? A .45, loaded. You should have shot the son of a bitch right there.

"And they all came over there and started looking at me. Pretty soon this one came by himself and he stuck his head in the car and he says, You son of a bitch, he says, one of those agents you killed was a good friend of mine. If I ever get you alone, I am going to blow your head off. He turned around and he walked off.

"We started to leave. It was three agents got in the car and they started up the car, and a couple of agents came over and they says, You leaving now? Yeah, we're taking him up to Pierre, but don't be surprised if only three of us show up. Another one comes up and says, You're leaving now? Yeah. Well, don't leave no bruises on him.

"I accepted the fact that I was going to die, and it didn't matter no more, you know. That I wasn't going to snivel and I wasn't going to cry. I made that up in my mind.

"We started out. This one agent, he said, We know pretty much what happened June twenty-sixth, but there's a few blind spots. I told them, What do you mean? I started seeing a little hope there—I thought I might get to Pierre alive. What do you mean? You know. You know what happened. Tell us what happened. We are in the position to give you a new identification. We can send you to another location, give you a good job and a car if you will just tell us what happened and fill in the blind spots. He said, If you don't do it, you will be spending the rest of your life behind bars, or else we are going to kill you. So I says, How do I know that I am going to be safe? How do I know that you guys are going to protect me? He says, We've done it before. We've got people living like this in other places now that have helped us. We gave them a new identity, set them up in another spot. All you have to do when we do this is mind your own business and don't go out and raise a bunch of heck and stuff and get yourself picked up. Don't bring no attention to you, and you will be all right.

"So I said, How do I know where you are going to send me? He says, Well, we can send you anywhere—Florida or anywhere back east, you know. So I says, Well I don't know, you know. I kept that up all the way to Pierre.

"In Pierre, they took me up to the fourth floor in the Federal Building into this room.[1] I knew then that I was pretty safe, that they wouldn't be shooting me there in the Federal Building. So that's when I told them I didn't want to talk to them no more, I wanted to call my lawyer. They really got nasty with me and started pushing me around, cussing me out.

"They said Leonard Crow Dog was a scum bag. They said that all Indians were scum bags. They said that my people weren't going to help me, why am I protecting them? They started telling me about Wounded Knee and how a few chickenshit Indians went to Wounded Knee and laid in the grass and shot from a long ways at federal forces. He said, They weren't brave, they were chickenshit. They wouldn't come out and fight in the open. They laid behind bunkers . . . and stuff like this. They told me how I was chickenshit because I laid behind a bunker at Oglala and shot these agents. They said I wasn't brave, I wasn't tough or nothing. I was just a little bitty nobody, a scum bag that didn't deserve to live. . . .

"They promised me that they would kill me if I didn't spend the rest of my life rotting behind bars. I wouldn't say anything to them. I said I wanted to call my lawyer. They kept this up for six hours and then they got mad or madder or something. The last thing they told me when they walked out was, Dino Butler, you're nothing but a worthless scum bag, and I promise you that someday I am going to shoot you. I am going to blow your fucking head off. They turned around and walked out of the room.

"They took me out and I seen Annie Mae. She was sitting out there. She smiled at me and I smiled back at her. They threw me in the holding tank. Crow Dog and the others that were arrested were there.

"I thought that I would never be free again. I knew that they was going to railroad me. There was talk that there was an ambush. There was talk that we drew the agents in there and that we ambushed them.

It was on the news that we dragged them out of their car, shot them repeatedly. I knew that if they wanted to, they could railroad me, 'cause they had done it to other people before. I didn't have much hope of ever being out again. So I was feeling pretty low down when I went in there. Crow Dog was there. He told me, Not to worry, nephew, everything is going to be all right. He said, Just remain strong. And he rolled up a cigarette and he says, I want you to pray with me. I want all my brothers in here to pray with us. So we all sat down and we prayed."

⊡

At the time of his arrest, Crow Dog was already on probation from his conviction on the Wounded Knee charges, a few months before; he was also about to be convicted (January 1976) of assault on a provocateur who invaded his house in March 1975 and made a pass at his wife in an obvious effort to provoke the skirmish that ensued. As at Cedar Rapids, Crow Dog's prosecutor in this case was R. D. Hurd, attired as always in bright sport clothes, who recoiled at the defense suggestion that Crow Dog had been set up for the assault charge. "The Government is here to protect you!" Hurd told the jury. "I am here to protect you!" At this point he placed his hand over his heart. "Would you believe, ladies and gentlemen, that the Government, your Government, would *lie* to you?"[2]

In the Beck-McCloskey case, Crow Dog was also convicted, although Indians claim he took no part in the fight. McCloskey later wrote to Judge Robert Merhige expressing regret that he had accused Crow Dog, whom he called a holy man, peacemaker, and healer who should be released. Although Beck had terrorized the region, and was already a suspect in the death of Crow Dog's nephew (he was finally jailed for the senseless killing of an Indian named No Moccasins in broad daylight in the reservation community called Parmelee), it was Crow Dog who was sentenced to five years in prison. In September 1976, this grotesque sentence was reduced; nevertheless, Crow Dog spent twenty-seven months in prison, most of the time in solitary confinement. During his absence, the Crow Dog house was burned down over his family's heads. He was eventually paroled in 1977, after intervention on his behalf by the National Council of Churches.

⊡

Because her fingerprints had been recovered at the AIM camp and because she was known to be close to that AIM group, Anna Mae Aquash was interviewed about the shoot-out at Oglala by SA Frederick Coward and a female colleague:

> PICTOU was specifically asked if she knew DENNIS BANKS, LEONARD PELTIER, FRANK BLACK HORSE and ROBERT ROBIDEAU. At this point in the interview there was a brief pause by PICTOU who put her head down on the desk to which she was sitting at and did not reply to the question. The interviewing Agents again specifically asked PICTOU if she knew these individuals that were just mentioned. PICTOU advised at this point that "you can either shoot me or throw me in jail as those are the two choices that I am taking." PICTOU was asked specifically what she meant by this to which she replied "that's what your going to do with me anyway." PICTOU was advised by the interviewing Agents that they had been very cooperative, polite, and had responded to her personal requests during the interview for cigarettes, coffee, and the use of the bathroom and this was certainly not a display or attitude to which she indicated that the Agents would do.

Aquash's own impressions of FBI behavior on that day were somewhat different. "I was awakened around—maybe around five in the morning by someone saying they were the FBI and I should immediately come out. I was in bed and I just heard a lot of voices around. Then I heard someone say, Let's just cut it. Cut open the tent, you know. And when I walked out . . . they were just all over the place, dumping things and just tearing things apart . . . and they came over and put a pair of handcuffs on me and took me in the house and searched me. . . . I could hear things crashing inside the house. They were evidently moving large objects like furniture or . . . like refrigerators or bureaus or chests because I could hear things falling off, breaking or smashing or . . . I could hear comments coming from them from inside—Oh, look at this—or they would laugh at something, or were joking with each other because one couldn't move a dresser by himself and you could hear somebody going over and helping them and something would smash. It was just like a bunch of—uh, I don't know—

they seemed to be having an awful lot of fun. They seemed to be enjoying themselves. . . .

"While I was standing there with the group of women, waiting, I was being verbally harassed by some of the agents. They were implying that they had been looking for me for a long time and that they were very pleased that they finally found me, and then they were accusing me of a number of things that I have not done. . . . They told me that I'd be in Canada by the afternoon, that they were gonna deport me, and I was in this country illegally. I tried explaining to them that I wasn't, and they just totally ignored me. Then, during this, there were two young Indians that came up to the roadblock—because they had a roadblock just past the Al Running residence on the main road. . . . We heard some loud shouting, yelling—If you keep going, we're gonna shoot you!—you know, and the other woman that was standing there, she got pretty nervous. She said, Somebody's gonna get shot, and if that ever happens, you know, everybody's gonna start shooting, and then it's gonna be called an accidental shooting! She was really scared. It turned out that there were two Indians—I could see them walking into the driveway and they were handcuffed. They were met by about four or five agents, who turned them around and started pushing them. I couldn't even watch any longer because I was being distracted on the other side by all the smashing that was going on in the house. . . . They emptied medicine bags and threw about medicine pipes and confiscated eagle feathers, and varieties of beadwork, and those objects that are used in sacred ceremonies. . . . They just didn't seem to care. . . .

"When they were trying to remove my medicine bag . . . I refused to remove it and they told me I could take it off, the boogeyman isn't going to bother me. If they're not familiar with what your beliefs are, then they use that to ridicule you, to criticize you, to make fun of you. They were making fun of a woman that was praying, snickering at her. Those FBI don't have any respect for these articles, and the people are really worried, they want to know why they want these things. . . . What do they plan on doing with these things? I think it's a very serious matter. They have absolutely no respect for a religion or a belief that another nation has, and that's . . . very racist. They don't have the ability to just allow someone to believe in something else. . . .

"In Pierre they took me to the Federal Building. . . . One agent came in and . . . started referring to the June twenty-sixth incident that happened in Oglala where two men were killed, and I told him three, and he said, Okay, three. He kept insisting that I used to live there, and I kept insisting back to him that I have never lived there, and he just wouldn't believe me. He just kept asking me questions like whether I knew Harry Jumping Bull or Cecelia Jumping Bull. You know, I've never had the opportunity of even meeting these people, let alone knowing them. Finally, I just refused to talk, so he left me alone. But they would periodically come through and ask me something. I was there about three hours, and they finally took me over to the county jail in Pierre.

"When they took me out of jail to take me over to the Federal Building that afternoon, that's when I saw the rest of them. They were all chained up at the waist and handcuffs, and they were chained together in these green—I don't know—coveralls, I guess. And we were all put in a car, and they were going to the Federal Building, too. . . . I've never gone through anything like that before, and I've never been arrested like that, and I just didn't know what was going on.

"I have seen that there is something that is disturbing the agents very much. They are very frustrated or angry or something. There is something wrong somewheres. It is not only the raid that they seemed to be interested in . . . it's not just arresting those that they went there to arrest, because they included a lot of other things, the religious items that they took, and the ridicule and remarks that they gave which are totally unnecessary. I think that they most definitely want to destroy the Indian nation if it will not submit to the living conditions of a so-called reservation. They definitely are out to destroy our concept of freedom."[3]

Released on bond pending a hearing the next day, Anna Mae decided to return to California, where Banks and Peltier were trying to raise money. Before leaving, she was joined on Pine Ridge by Nilak Butler, who had failed to make contact with Bob Robideau and decided to go with Anna Mae instead. On September 12, with Norman Brown, they were driven to Denver by a self-styled AIM supporter named John Stewart, a Crow Dog relative and the estranged husband of Anna Mae's friend Dorothy Brings Him Back; Stewart, who had turned up in Oglala in mid-June, had spent a lot of time hanging around the Jumping Bull property in the days before Coler and Williams had appeared. "All I knew about John Stewart was that he beat his woman," Nilak says. "I don't have no use for any man who does that. Nobody on the res knew

Norman's last name, but John Stewart, who drove us all to Denver, must have pinned him down, because they busted Norman right after he got home."

Some people suspect that it was Stewart whose tip led to the raid of September 5, and also to the detention of Anna Mae and Nilak by the FBI upon their arrival at Los Angeles airport on September 13. Anna Mae was permitted to go free, perhaps in the hope that she would lead the FBI to Banks and Peltier, but Nilak was arrested and threatened with a first-degree murder indictment "before the afternoon is out"; she was jailed for two weeks before being released. "They threw me in with this three-hundred-pound nut case—I mean, she was really *dribbling,* man—and they used this to try to break down Dino, telling him I was gonna be raped by this enormous dike—oh, they're *snakey!*"

Besides Kamook Nichols, her baby, and her sister, Bernardine, the group that left Crow Dog's Paradise with Bob Robideau before the raid included Mike Anderson, Norman Charles, and Jean Bordeaux; they were joined by a young Indian named Keith DeMaris. "Leroy Casades and his friend Bambi were the only ones who got away at Crow Dog's, which seemed funny to me right away," Robideau says. "I'm the kind that don't trust nobody until I trust 'em. So when they showed up at our camp over near Parmelee, I told somebody to keep an eye on them, and when Leroy told me he wanted to go into town, I told him he couldn't. Well, I guess that made him nervous, and they took off on us, and so I realized that once again we had to move, we had to leave Rosebud, and the sooner the better: in fact, they raided that place at Parmelee a few days later. We had run out of safe houses nearly everywhere, and so we headed north for Cheyenne River.

"That old '64 Merc station wagon was in good shape when we left Rosebud. But I chose the back roads, and it had rained the previous day, and there were ruts, and with all them people and the load, I hit one big rut too hard and tore off the muffler. I didn't think too much about it, because there's no law up there; you see one cop at the most, and one man ain't never going to stop a whole carload of Indians, not for no muffler. At Eagle Butte I stopped and got a clamp, got the pipe back up there some way. But after a day or so on Cheyenne River, we realized that was still too close, and we headed south for Shawnee, Oklahoma. On the way, the muffler fell off again, and at Rosebud I spent about two hours on it, really got it in there good—why shit, we didn't clear St. Francis, hardly, before the damn thing fell off again! So I said to hell with it, threw the pipe up onto the load in back, and crossed over to Nebraska, and sure enough, we were stopped by a state trooper. Keith told him the muffler had fell off, we was lookin' for a garage to get her fixed, and meanwhile he distracted this cop by tellin' him all about the sacred pipe we had layin' up on the dash, the sage for ceremonials, and stuff. Keith really got into it—we thought he would never get finished.

"So at K.C. I tried again to see if I couldn't muffle at least *some* of that damn racket; I was twistin' at it, and somehow I got her pointed *up* instead of *out.* So we're back on the Kansas Turnpike, headed south again for the Territory, when Baby Aim yells, Hey, it's smoking back here! I pulled over quick, ordered everyone out, then ran back and looked underneath, and just then the first explosion went, blew asphalt into my eyes as I rolled away and landed on my stomach in the ditch. I thought that I was gone for sure until I realized that my brain had kept on working. So I look up through this blur and there is Keith, mouth open, he's in shock, staring down at me. So I said, Let's go, and waved everybody over the fence into the field, and we started running.

"We get in there three or four hundred yards, and we see an old man on a farm road who has stopped to look. Kamook had a bad cut on her arm, from flying shrapnel, and as for me, I couldn't hardly see at all, so I asked the old man to take us to the hospital. Mainly I wanted to put as much distance as possible, and fast, between us and that white car, which was going up in multiple explosions; we were really lucky to get out alive. Small blasts first—that was the ammunition; then a big one when the gas tank blew that rolled the roof back, then fire everywhere." Robideau laughed. "We had told the old man that them first explosions come from aerosol cans, and canned food that had overheated—well, that was some powerful food that could blow the roof off! He was a nice old man, really wanted to help us, but he was country, you know, and he had been suspicious right from the git-up-and-go, and down the road a ways he pulls over where he sees some friends, and pulls out the key, and somebody telephones for the police. I had told everyone to dump any kind of evidence out of their pockets on the way to the hospital, and we got rid of most of it, but not enough; Bernie was the only one completely clean, and she was also the only one that wasn't charged. At the hospital, when they're searching the others, I'm already on a stretcher, and as I'm going out the door, one cop says, Search him, too. I struggle and yell—you know, a little theater there—demanding my rights all the way to my room; I couldn't see much, but I knew I had a crowd there. Who are all these people in my room! I yell. Am I under arrest? *No!* Then get out of my room! *You get undressed!* No! I kept demanding that they either arrest me or get out of my room, and they wouldn't do either one, and meanwhile I can't see a goddam thing. But I hear a phone ring, and one of them answers. Then he says, Okay, you're under arrest."

Robideau identified himself as Robert Lamont, but his fingerprints were on record from his long series of arrests during his youth, and he was soon identified. Discovered among the burned and damaged weapons in the white station wagon was Agent Coler's .308 rifle, and with it an AR-15 rifle which was later selected by the U.S. government as the weapon that had killed Agents Coler and Williams.

After twelve days in two hospitals, Robideau was imprisoned in Wichita's Sedgwick County Jail. Although he was the only adult male, his group was publicly identified as a front-line attack squad for some amazing raid down in Indian Territory; the plans of these women, young boys, and a baby included the assassination of the Vice-President of the United States, who was coming to Oklahoma on a visit.

Oddly, Mike Anderson was not prosecuted, although he was wanted on a burglary charge in Phoenix, and although Agent Gary Adams, who came to Wichita to interview him, informed him that the FBI knew that he had been involved in the Oglala shoot-out. Norman Charles, Keith DeMaris, and Kamook Nichols were convicted on weapons charges, then set free on probation. Bob Robideau was the only one who went to jail. Held on $125,000 bond, he was convicted in December on nine counts of illegal transport of altered and unregistered firearms and explosives, and sentenced to ten years in Leavenworth Prison.

⊡

"I was trying to hook up with Bobby," Nilak says, "and I'm kinda glad it didn't happen, as it worked out. I'm glad I missed that ride, and I only missed it by an hour. I went back to Pine Ridge to go out to L.A. . . . I was concerned about getting out there and getting that bond money. . . . The important thing about the L.A. bust was that when I went to my arraignment hearing, they told the judge that I shouldn't have any bail because in twenty-four hours they were going to have murder indictments on me for killing the two FBI agents. And that's when I knew we were getting into a time crunch, and I wanted to get Dino out.

"Anyway, they walked me through the airport with six guards because I was so dangerous. That was humiliating, man. To go through L.A. airport with these jerks all around me. Everybody was looking at me, like, did they catch Patty Hearst? You know, that was the attitude, really, and I remember the black porters—they'd sit there and shake their heads, just look at those feds, and shake their heads. That kind of thing inspired me a little. Then they took me down to the FBI headquarters in Westwood and they did fingerprints and photographs and were all running around like real hot stuff: This is a major case investigation! And I had an agent there, Gilbert Cordova, the man who Blue Dove reported to in Skyhorse-Mohawk; she was that FBI informer from L.A. He's real dark, and he looks like a skin, so Anna Mae asked him if he was Indian, and it turns out he's one-quarter Indian, one-quarter Yakima. He's just a really wonderful person. In fact, he came all the way back to South Dakota when I went to trial, to convince the judge that I was more dangerous than Ma Barker. No jive. Really. He overdid it. He got on the stand, and God, you would have thought I was packing bombs in my teeth, the way he acted. I mean, he was just *off!* He did more to acquit me than anything that happened in that trial."

▪

After the raid on Crow Dog's Paradise, Norman Brown had gone to stay with the Bordeaux family in Rapid City, after which he went to Denver with Anna Mae and Nilak; from there he went home to Many Farms on the Navajo Reservation, where Agents Gary Adams and Victor Harvey turned up on October 10. Brown had been warned by the WKLDOC lawyers that he was not to talk to agents or police under any circumstances, but he was not prepared for the enormous Adams and his abusive partner, who had been led to his mother's house by a BIA policeman. "FBI agents came walking in, told me to sit down. I sat down. My mother sat down beside me. He said, We know you were at Oglala at the time. I told them I didn't see nothing, I didn't hear nothing. He said, Bullshit. Then I gave him that paper and said, This is my lawyer, you can call him. He said, No, we can't do that. Then I kept trying to tell them that I had a lawyer, and they wouldn't listen and started asking me questions. They sat there a couple of hours, trying to question me. Then an agent by the name of Victor Harvey, he told me, Do you know what you're facing now? I said yes. He said, You're facing two counts of first-degree murder. I said, I want my lawyer. He said, You're not getting no lawyer. So we were just sitting there. He told me, We're going to haul you in right now. My mom, she didn't know what was going on. I tried to explain to her, but they told my mom they had one of the guns that I used, that that gun killed FBI agents. My mom started crying and everything. My mom said something, What do you do, you killed one of those two FBI agents! She started crying, and one of the FBI agents said, Shut up. I said, *You* shut up, you don't talk to my mom like that. They told my mom to shut up, and I said, Don't you have any respect at all? And they kept telling me they were going to haul me in right now.

"My mom was crying. She kept telling me to talk and I told her no. I kept saying no for a while. They said, Well, I guess we'll haul you in right now. They took handcuffs and handcuffed me. I was standing there and he said, We'll do everything in our power that you rot in hell. I kept saying I wanted my lawyer. Why are you protecting these cold-blooded killers, he said, they just murdered two of my friends. And I said, That's the way the ball bounces, and he got pissed off. Then he said, It's your duty as an American citizen to talk. And I told him that I'm not a citizen of this country here, America, I am a citizen of the Navajo nation and Mother Earth, is what I told them. And they started laughing and I had some peyote with me that night and they were just making fun of me about my religion. They kept telling me that Dino and Bob and Leonard—they said, Those guys are killers, why are you protecting them? They are my brothers and I didn't hear nothing and I didn't see nothing. They told me that they were going to put me away, put me away for a long time. And they told my mom that she would never see me again, never see my family, I'd never walk the earth again.

"So my mom was crying and I didn't know what to do there. She says, Son, I don't want you put in jail! They kept saying Leonard Peltier—they kept saying he and Dino killed the agents. They kept saying, Why are you protecting these cold-blooded killers? Kept saying, Going to put you away, you're going to rot. Kept calling me names. And we were there for another fifteen minutes, trying to get me talking. Then they left after about six hours. They told me they were going to see me tomorrow. So we went home. I was ready to take off; my mom wouldn't let me. My brothers wouldn't let me, 'cause they didn't want me to go to jail. . . .

"I thought they were going to kill me. They told me I would never walk the earth again. After that they kept coming over and questioning me and everything. . . . And they told me they would give me a new name, new life, told me that I could do whatever I wanted, and new car, and live somewhere else. I told them I didn't want that, so they told me that they were going to give me protection. They weren't protecting me, they were harassing me all the time, the FBI. They kept coming by my house, always coming by. My family got tired of it. Who made that escape plan? Who led you out of there? What's his name? Where's he live? So I said, You'll never catch him, you'll never get him. They kept trying to question me like that, about thirty minutes. So finally I told him, I said, Tunkashila. Then he says, Where's he live? We'll get him. We'll put him in jail. What's his last name? How do you spell that? So I told them, They are our Creator and the Grandfathers.

"They really got down on me when I was in Arizona. . . . To make things worse, it was in front of my mom there, and I didn't know what to do. Victor Harvey told me, We have the gun that killed them. And he told me that Dino and Bob said that I killed one of them, and I knew they didn't. They didn't say that. They kept trying to tell me that Dino and Bob said this and that; they told me, We have you on two counts of manslaughter against two agents.

"And I said, How about Joe Stuntz? He's my brother. Who's going to stand for *his* trial? They said, We don't know, he was caught in a cross fire. And they said about the Movement, They're all a bunch of chickenshits, they don't have anything to do but raise hell. So I told them, In an Indian way, a man gets shot and falls on his back, and he's facing the enemy. Then I said, He falls on his stomach, he's running away from the enemy. And I asked him, I said, How were those two agents lying? They didn't say nothing, so I assumed they were lying on their stomachs."

⊡

On October 4, an FBI squad led by SAC Norman Zigrossi and including SAs Price and Adams staged a raid on the WKLDOC headquarters in Rapid City. ("I did not know it formally as such," Price testified later. "We received information that a federal fugitive named Harold Goggle Eyes, who is also known as Poncho, who is listed as armed and dangerous . . . was staying at that place.") Later in the month, Price took part in a raid on a building that turned out to be the WKLDOC headquarters in Sioux Falls.

On October 13, the day after Jimmy Eagle had been convicted of felonious assault for the shooting of James Catches on May 17, Judge Andrew Bogue ordered that he be held without bail, pending formal indictment for the murder of the agents; Bogue pointed out that "since May 16, the defendant had become involved in four violent crimes with possible sentences totaling in excess of his natural life." His decision was influenced, he said, by the facts that Eagle was nineteen years old, unmarried, never employed, without property or assets or "stabilizing roots."

On October 14, a bomb went off in the BIA Law and Order Building in Pine Ridge. According to Dick Wilson, AIM was responsible. "If any more AIM members, or any others, come onto this reservation bearing arms," Wilson declared, "they will be taking their lives into their own hands. . . . I have given up on the so-called law-and-order we have had and am taking the law into my own hands."[4] Clyde Bellecourt denied that AIM had planned the bombing, which he said was the work of the John Birch Society, in a program to discredit AIM. That very day, in fact, these superpatriots had sponsored a talk in Rapid City's Alex Johnson Hotel by Douglass Durham, whose drastic revelations about AIM had made him the most popular speaker on the John Birch circuit. "AIM is a leader in the scheme to disrupt our nation's Bicentennial in 1976," Durham declared. "In preparation for the scheduled decelebration, AIM has established training camps around the country in which political indoctrination, marksmanship, and guerrilla warfare are taught." A week later, Durham informed an audience in Mitchell that AIM's intensified guerrilla activities would include "indiscriminate killings of whites." Ted Means, responding for South Dakota AIM, warned that Durham's statements could only perpetuate racism in that state. "We'll stand and give our lives, that's true," Means said, "but we're not a terrorist organization."

"The last time I saw Durham," Bill Means says, "he was giving one of his Bircher talks to a rancher audience in Valentine, Nebraska, calling us Communists and everything else. Finally we couldn't take no more, so we went up there on the platform. A friend of mine told Durham to step to one side, and he kept an eye on him while I told those people the real truth about life on Pine Ridge. We're not Communists,

I said. We're just sick of running out your grocery boxes and stacking your hay and having you think you're helping Indians that way—how about some *real* help? And I pointed right at some ranchers in the audience who were making money out of our land on the Ridge and knew just what I was talking about. So then I reminded them how many Indians have always signed up and gone overseas to fight their wars for them [Means himself is a Vietnam combat veteran] and what a disgrace it was that this country was so goddam ungrateful, and gradually the hoots and yells died down, and they were turning to each other, discussing what I was saying. So Durham knew that he was losing 'em, and he comes my way while I'm still talking, and I'm still talking when I let him have it; next thing you know, he's picking himself off the floor with a bloody mouth. And afterward, them white people come up to me, not really knowing what to say, you know, but just trying to make me feel better some way, and themselves, too."

On October 15, Melvin White Wing, the guitarist, amplified what he said he had overheard in Eagle's jail-cell revelations to Gregory Clifford. Like Clifford, he had gotten the impression that one of the agents had come alone to the property on the morning of June 26, then returned later with another agent.

> JIMMY EAGLE would look in his direction to make sure he, WHITE WING, was hearing the conversation. . . . EAGLE was heard to say that the Agent was pulled from his car and then shot. . . . "We all took turns shooting at them." JIMMY EAGLE was emotionally involved while he was telling his story and he, WHITE WING, believed that JIMMY EAGLE was not telling a story as heard from someone else but . . . as though he, JIMMY EAGLE, was actually there. WHITE WING stated that JIMMY EAGLE . . . was very proud of the fact that "they" killed the agents.

A few weeks later, Eagle was formally indicted for murder, despite a statement given to Agent Adams by Hazel Little Hawk on November 12 that Jimmy had spent June 26 indoors at the Pine Ridge house of his grandmother Gladys Bissonnette.

On October 16, Richard Held, the administrator of the ResMurs investigation, notified the Director of the FBI that his work was finished; he planned to return to Chicago two days later. "SAC, CHICAGO has been on the scene since the early morning hours of Friday, June 27, 1975. . . .

The case is in the final stages of being prepared for prosecution." But despite Held's decision that the ResMurs evidence now justified indictments, the FBI documents already showed that many more people had been involved than the four AIM men who had been singled out for prosecution.

Of these four official suspects, the only one not in custody was Leonard Peltier. On November 18, the FBI issued a twenty-page document devoted to background information on Peltier which indicates clearly how much emphasis was being placed on this "key suspect"; apparently, Peltier had also become a suspect in the death of Jeannette Bissonnette. ("In the event PELTIER is apprehended, he should be interviewed *re* his whereabouts on the evening and night of 3/25/75, at which time JEANNETTE BISSONNETTE was shot and killed."[5]) The report cited the Wisconsin "attempted murder" charge and Peltier's fugitive status; the use of Peltier's car in the October 21, 1973, shooting skirmish with BIA police during Pedro Bissonnette's funeral; the arrest on weapons charges in Mercer Island, Washington, in September 1974; and the alleged involvement of his 1967 green Ford—the one found in the camp—in a theft from a Farmington, New Mexico, radio shop of $15,000 worth of equipment, some of which later turned up in Tent City. "Peltier is very active in violent AIM activities," the report concluded.

On November 24, increasingly upset by their separation from their three children, Angie and Ivis Long Visitor, who had been in jail since September 16, came before Judge Bogue in Rapid City and agreed to testify before the ResMurs grand jury. That same morning, their lawyer had been assured by Assistant U.S. Attorney Robert Sikma that the grand jury would not be reconvened for at least two weeks; in fact, it was reconvened without warning just thirty minutes later, before those summoned to appear "forthwith" could get legal advice.[6] Apparently Sikma (who would take a prominent part in the ResMurs trials) had employed these tactics to ensure the indictments of his suspects.

Resisting arrest, the spirited young Jean Bordeaux had to be taken into custody by force after her mother's front door was broken down, and she refused to speak when dragged before the jury. "Back there in Wichita, when I wouldn't talk to the grand jury, they talked about giving me contempt of court, but the judge used a bunch of big words I couldn't understand to say that experience in jail at my young age—

I was fourteen then—might turn me against the U.S. government. So I got out with no sentence and no probation, and my mom took me home. Then in November I got in an accident, and my face was all beat up, and the very next morning—I mean *real* early, I was still in my nightshirt—them FBIs came pushing in without a warrant, carrying M-16s."

"That one called Price says, We think your kids have information about who killed our men," Evelyn Bordeaux remembers, "and my husband told 'em, That ain't no reason to yank young kids around like that." (Price, Hughes, and their colleagues reported that Evelyn Bordeaux denounced them repeatedly as "fucking pigs.")

"Them others was just as bad," Jean says. "I didn't want to go, but they grabbed me anyway, held me in a cell three or four hours before Sikma took me in to the grand jury. Sikma was the U.S. Attorney, just a yes-man; he does anything the feds tell him to do."

"They wanted to bust Zimmerman, too!" her mother laughs. "They handed a subpoena to this little friend of his, thinking he was Zimmerman!" But Zimmerman refused to speak, and since he was only eleven years old, Sikma apparently thought better of dragging him to the stand.

The two most significant witnesses to be brought before the grand jury were Mike Anderson and Norman Brown. On September 11, the day after his arrest in Kansas, Anderson had identified photographs of Peltier, Butler, and Eagle, telling Agents Adams and Harvey that all four of the main suspects had been present on the Jumping Bull land when the agents were shot. Anderson insisted in this interview that he had arrived on the scene only after the agents were dead, and was not a witness to the shooting, but later, he said, Bob Robideau had told him that he, Robideau, had taken the rifle from one of the dead agents. In his long interview, Anderson said that David Sky had accompanied the group on the first part of the escape, carrying a short-barreled gun; his report does not mention the other Navajo boys, Draper and Brown.

A few weeks later, when Adams and Harvey traced Norman Brown to Chinle, Arizona, they presumably used Anderson's evidence as a basis for interrogating Brown; despite the brave resistance described earlier, the younger boy eventually talked, too. (In their interviews with Agent Adams, both young Navajos are reported to have indicated that the first police cars arrived after the killing of the agents, too late to help;

but FBI accounts, his own included, make very clear that Adams was there well before the finish. Adams estimates that he arrived on the scene just before noon, and it was 12:10 or thereabouts before Williams's last transmission was recorded at FBI headquarters in Rapid City.)

Norman Brown declared that when the shooting started, he and Joe Stuntz, Jimmy Zimmerman, and Anderson were about to eat a meal of pancakes made by Nilak Butler, and that all but Zimmerman ran up the hill and joined Norman Charles in shooting at "two Caucasian males" down in the meadow.

> He specifically recalled that once when looking at the two cars in the meadow below him, he observed two Indian males approach these cars from the area below the Jumping Bull residence. At the time of observation, these individuals were approximately 20 feet from the target vehicles and appeared to have come from the vicinity of a white over red Chevrolet Suburban van which was parked below the woodpile from which he (BROWN) initially was shooting. BROWN knew these individuals to be LEONARD PELTIER and DINO BUTLER. In addition, he recalled specifically that PELTIER was carrying a military-type AR-15 rifle. . . . Regarding the red and white Chevrolet Suburban, BROWN referred to this as a bus belonging to PELTIER. He stated he observed this bus on numerous occasions, always being driven by PELTIER. . . .
>
> For some unremembered reason, BROWN's attention was then drawn elsewhere for a few minutes until he heard approximately three shots which sounded as if they came from the immediate vicinity of the two vehicles. Upon hearing the shots, he again looked into the meadow and observed PELTIER, BUTLER, and a third Indian male standing immediately next to the two cars . . . this person looked very much like BOB ROBIDEAU.

Brown makes no mention in this interview of having been sent with Anderson (by Joe Stuntz) to guard the southerly approaches of the camp: "he fired all of his ammunition . . . and thereafter, along with MICHAEL ANDERSON, he returned to the tent area in an effort to escape. He and ANDERSON tried various routes from the area southward but all appeared to be blocked by law enforcement officers." Like Anderson, he makes no mention of Wish Draper anywhere in his account, nor does he mention his girl friend, Jean Bordeaux, or her friend "Lynn." Except for Leon Eagle, he avoids naming any of the Oglala people who helped on the escape, and he bypasses the Bear Runners entirely by stating that the escape group went straight to the Rosebud Reservation from the house in Pine Ridge.

Nevertheless, serious damage (to Peltier and Butler especially) had been done. "Robert Sikma . . . told me to tell the jury that Leonard Peltier and Dino Butler killed those agents. I told them I wasn't going to do that. Then he goes, You could be in jail all your life. . . . I went to the grand jury. He told me I was lucky I talked there, because we could have put you away. I didn't know what he meant by that, so that day I went home."

On November 25, 1975, mainly on the basis of the two boys' testimony, the grand jury indicted James Theodore Eagle, Darrelle Dean Butler, Robert Eugene Robideau, and Leonard Peltier on two counts of first-degree murder. Later that day, in Pierre, where Butler was sentenced on the Rosebud charge of possession of a weapon by a felon, Judge Robert Merhige was preceded into court by a large group of FBI agents, who sat down near the door; when the judge entered, he said to Butler almost immediately, "I'm sorry I have to be the one to tell you this, young man, but you've just been indicted for murder." He sentenced Butler to two years in jail on the weapons charge, then ordered that he be held without bail on the ResMurs indictment. Butler had already fired his court-appointed attorney, who had heard the FBI agents threaten his client and done nothing about it; he asked the young WKLDOC lawyer Bruce Ellison to represent him.[7] "Dino was in good spirits, which just amazed me," Ellison recorded in his notes that day. "He said he was actually relieved that it had happened. For months, he had been told by the FBI that he would be indicted for the shootings. Now it has happened. Now it can be dealt with."

Although four men had been indicted, the government's case was very weak; the firearms and ballistics evidence had not been firmly linked to the defendants, and Eagle's boasting—still the only firsthand account of the actual killings—failed to establish the premeditation that is a precondition for a conviction for first-degree murder. Therefore, the hunt for witnesses continued. On January 9, Wish Draper was picked up in Arizona on charges of drunkenness and "strong-armed robbery"; he was taken to Gallup, New Mexico, where he was strapped into a chair by Gary Adams and his partner, Victor Harvey, and threatened with prosecution for the killings. Three days later, Draper returned with Adams to South Dakota, and on January 13 he testified before a special grand jury in Sioux Falls. Both Draper and his cousin Norman Brown, who also testified, would later claim that they were coached beforehand by Robert Sikma, and both would state that in their testimony for the prosecution, they had lied.

From Draper, the FBI learned who had sheltered the fugitives on Pine Ridge. Subsequently, the Bear Runner family was repeatedly harassed by police and goons. Grace Bear Runner was assaulted by a goon named Charlie Winters, and Edgar's brother Dennis was run off the road by goons in Porcupine. Edgar himself, who had been attacked in the Pine Ridge supermarket in November 1975 by Manny Wilson and two others, was seized in early 1976 by FBI agents who burst into his father's house and took him in shirt sleeves to Rapid City for questioning; although the winter day was very cold, the bundled-up agents kept all the windows of the car wide open on the one-and-a-half-hour trip, treating this as an immense joke at the young Indian's expense. The following year he was sent to prison on charges of "obstructing" a police officer who was pistol-whipping him in Gordon, Nebraska.

Adams had also traveled to Washington state to serve a grand-jury summons on Norman Charles, whose Wichita probation sentence restricted him to the area of Port Angeles. Apparently, Charles was so determined in his refusal to cooperate that he was discarded as a potential witness. Despite his known involvement at Oglala and despite his subsequent arrest with Bob Robideau on weapons and explosives charges in Kansas, this young Indian, twenty years old, was never prosecuted, while Angie Long Visitor and Joanna LeDeaux—both of them innocent bystanders and the mothers of young children—went to prison for refusing to cooperate. The Long Visitors were released from jail in early December, but LeDeaux served eight months in federal prison, mostly in San Pedro, California; she was finally released on orders from Attorney General Levi, partly because of bad publicity caused by the refusal of the women's prison authorities to let her nurse the baby born in jail.

Meanwhile, Butler was arraigned before Judge Bogue in Rapid City, and his bond was raised from $5,000 to $250,000; the same bond was set for Robideau when he was transferred from Wichita to Rapid City for the grand-jury hearing of January 13, 1976.

In the original murder indictment, no distinction was made among the four defendants; not until this grand-jury hearing did the FBI produce affidavits purporting to show that Leonard Peltier had actually pulled the trigger in the agents' deaths. With Eagle, Butler, and Robideau in custody, the ResMurs investigation could now concentrate on the only one of the four defendants who was still at large.

CHAPTER 11
THE FUGITIVES II
November 1975–May 1976

The "First People" such as myself are born running, running for a better way of life, an even chance. . . . Indian people are virtual exiles in their own country.

Dennis Banks (*Anishinabi*)

I am a part of this creation as you are, no more and no less than each and every one of you within the sound of my voice. I am the generation of generations before me and the generations to come. . . . If I have gone against this Creation—no man on this Universe holds the power to punish me other than the Creator himself. . . .

You are continuing to control my life with your violent, materialistic needs. I do realize *your* need to survive and be a part of this Creation—but you do not understand mine. . . . I have traveled through this country and I have observed your undisciplined military servants provoke those whose rights are the same as yours. . . .

I am not a citizen of the United States or a ward of the Federal Government, neither am I a ward of the Canadian government. I have a right to continue my cycle in this Universe undisturbed.

Anna Mae Pictou Aquash (*Micmac*)

On or about November 13, 1975, the Portland, Oregon, office of the FBI was notified by two "reliable informants" that Dennis Banks and Leonard Peltier were traveling eastward in "a convoy." On November 14, an Oregon state trooper named Ken Griffiths, assigned to traffic on Interstate 80 near the Idaho border, misread FBI teletype instructions to keep a certain motor home and a Colorado station wagon under surveillance: a "stop"—meaning end-of-sentence—was interpreted as "stop the vehicle," and when the motor home came by, he ordered it to pull over. Another trooper stopped the station wagon, about 150 yards behind; commanding its two occupants to lie face down on the cold asphalt, he handcuffed them with the warning that "one false move and he would blow their heads off."[1]

Approaching the motor home with a riot gun, Griffiths ordered its occupants to come out. The first to emerge was "a large Mexican-appearing person" in a red short-sleeved pullover who was ordered to lie face down on the road shoulder; the large person complied, but not without "a lot of commotion, yelling, and screaming," apparently intended to alert his fellow passengers. Soon two women and a small child got out, after which the motor home kicked back, then suddenly accelerated; a moment later, there came a flash of gunfire that Griffiths assumed was directed at himself, and in the confusion, the man spread-eagled on the road sprang up and took off on the run toward the right-of-way fence along the highway. Swinging his weapon, the patrolman got off two rounds of heavy riot buckshot in the direction of the fugitive, who vanished over the fence into the night.

Shortly afterward, a Trooper Schmeer found the empty motor home, motor still running, about two miles east on Highway 80, and the next day, a local youth found a pistol on the roadside near this place; it looked as if the escaping driver had fired a diversionary shot at the scene of the arrest, then got rid of the gun where the motor home was found. But Griffiths insisted that the shot had come from the man running for the fence, who had risked the lives of women and child in the process. To shoot at policemen, after all, was a well-known practice of this "large Mexican-appearing person," who was shortly identified as Leonard Peltier. The women were Anna Mae Aquash and Kamook Nichols, accompanied by Kamook's little girl, Tasina Wanblee, and the driver of the abandoned vehicle (registered in the name of Marlon Brando) was presumed to have been Dennis Banks. The two AIM men in the accompanying station wagon were Russ Redner, twenty-nine (a Shoshone Indian and four-year Army Airborne Division veteran, who had served in Panama and Vietnam: "We redmen have replaced the Vietnamese . . . the government is building up to another My Lai"), and Kenny Loud Hawk, twenty-one (one of the twilight horsemen at Oglala who encountered the fugitives during the escape). The vehicles were reported to contain seven boxes of dynamite, assorted detonation equipment, nine hand grenades, and fourteen firearms (including an AR-15 rifle, which does not appear in official photographs of the captured weapons, for reasons that did not become clear until much later). Under the motor home's front seat was a paper bag, allegedly bearing Peltier's thumbprint, which contained the service revolver of the late Jack Coler.

Peltier knew that the indictment of Robideau and Butler for the death of the agents was only a matter of time, and like everyone else, he thought that there was no chance at all that they would avoid conviction. Years before, he had helped his cousin Bob to escape from a juvenile detention home, and Robideau now speculates that Leonard was on his way to Rapid City to break Dino Butler out of the old cracker-box Pennington County Jail, then initiate some course of action on the plans made earlier to turn the Pine Ridge Reservation back to the traditional people.

Later that evening (November 14), a Miss Wrinkle and her boyfriend, enjoying the evening air in an auto parked by the railroad tracks south of Ontario, Oregon, were approached politely by a bushy-haired stranger who "kept saying over and over again he wasn't going to hurt us," and who asked them to give him a ride. Instead, they drove off in alarm, and this hunted, desperate, wounded man with a growing reputation as the most notorious cop-killer in the United States (well-armed, according to Officer Griffiths) made no effort to detain them. Next day, a '71 Ford Ranchero and a .30-30 rifle were removed from a house a few miles to the south; the pickup was subsequently found abandoned in Umatilla, not far from Portland.

That day, a relative in the Portland area received a phone call from Peltier, saying that he had been shot and needed help; he was taken to a doctor who had been helpful at the time of Wounded Knee. "The doc helped him," this man recalls, "but he couldn't get that riot slug out of his right shoulder; big hole, man, but he hadn't lost much blood—right in the meat." Peltier rested for three days near Portland while travel arrangements were made; then he headed north, crossing the border into

British Columbia, where he stayed for approximately a month in a cabin almost within sight of the border. It was here that Peltier learned that he and Robideau and Butler, together with Jimmy Eagle, had been accused of "aiding and abetting" in the death of Jack R. Coler and Ronald A. Williams, a charge equivalent to first-degree murder. In early December, his name appeared on the "Ten Most Wanted Fugitives" list of the FBI.

Peltier's supporters ran around finding supplies, a little money, trying to get a car. "And that's where Black Horse joined us," said Roque Duenas, Peltier's old confederate from the days of the Fort Lawton occupation in 1970. "He's a good bro, too; he knew it was dangerous to be with us, but he wanted to help out with security. Trouble is, he just talks too much, and wherever he goes, he draws the heat. Unidentified cars started to show up, drive past, you know, and people were warning us. So one night we took off out of there, and the very next day the Mounties come in with tear gas and riot guns, shot the place to pieces and asked questions later. There was a young guy who lived there, and it was just lucky he was over at his grandmother's that night, or he might have been blowed away.

"In Canada, you know, the white people live mostly near the border, but the Indians move all around up north. So from the cabin we moved north to Kamloops country. Eventually we had to leave there, too: they were all around us, we could feel 'em. [A warrant for Peltier's arrest had been sworn out in Vancouver on January 23, 1976.] And finally we moved him over the mountains to Alberta, to Smallboy's camp, way out in the bush. Black Horse was with him, and there was another guy there, too, but we don't work with him no more. Because they got there on a certain night, and the very next day the Mounties were right on top of them."

⊡

Redner and Loud Hawk, arrested in Oregon for illegal possession of weapons and explosives, were held on $100,000 bail because of Loud Hawk's association with Oglala; Anna Mae Aquash was returned to Pierre, South Dakota, for trial on the Rosebud charges; and Kamook Nichols, eight months pregnant, was returned to Kansas City for violation of her probation (her new baby, born in jail, was named Iron Door Woman). The charges against her were eventually dismissed because of "vindictive prosecution" on the part of the government attorneys.

According to a reporter who interviewed Anna Mae in the Vale, Oregon, jail after her arrest, the young woman said, "If they take me back to South Dakota, I'll be murdered."[2] A month earlier, in a talk with John Trudell in California, Anna Mae had said, "I'll talk to you through the rain," and Trudell had the feeling that in some way she was saying good-bye. In September, she had told Bernie Nichols of a dream in which she had flown as a bird to the spirit world, and she had expressed similar forebodings to Norman Brown, Nilak Butler, and Ernie Peters, with whose family she lived for a while in California.

Bruce Ellison, who represented Anna Mae at her arraignment in Pierre on November 24, says that the FBI offered her leniency on prior charges in return for cooperation in the prosecution of the Oglala suspects, which she refused; after the pre-trial hearing, Judge Merhige released her from custody on her own recognizance when she assured him she would return the following morning. During the night, Anna Mae disappeared. "She knew she was going to get indicted on the Oregon charges no matter what, and she knew there was no chance she would receive justice, so she split," Nilak Butler says. If any of her friends ever saw her again, they have been very careful not to say so.

Ellison feared that Anna Mae might be followed by FBI agents to Banks and Peltier, though he agrees with most people who knew her that she was never an FBI informer. The Butlers did not believe those rumors, either, and neither did John Trudell; Russ Means claims that he never heard about the rumors until the following year. "Banks was so paranoid after Douglass Durham," Means says, "that he thought *everyone* was an informer, even Anna Mae." Nevertheless, some people wondered why Anna Mae had been released on such low bond after the September 5 raid, why she was released so quickly in Los Angeles, and why Judge Merhige had released her on the day she disappeared; and inevitably there was speculation about who tipped off the FBI in Oregon. "She was always around when people were getting busted," one Indian says. The arrests of Banks, then Peltier, in a two-week period in early 1976, may well have confirmed the case against her among those who had suspected her in the first place.

> The key to the successful investigation of AIM is substantial, live, quality informant coverage of its leaders and activities. In the past, this technique proved to be highly effective. As a result of cer-

> tain disclosures regarding informants, AIM leaders have dispersed, have become extremely security conscious and literally suspect everyone. This paranoia works both for and against the movement and recent events support this observation.[3]

Arrested in Oakland, California, on January 23, Dennis Banks was held on $100,000 bail on the Oregon charges; he told the court that he had committed no crime, that at Custer he had been tried and convicted unlawfully, and that if he was returned to South Dakota, he would probably be killed.

Thanks mostly to the intercession of Governor Jerry Brown, Banks's bail was reduced and he was released on $2,000 bond, pending his extradition hearings. William Janklow denounced this as "absolutely absurd," describing himself as "frustrated and disgusted." On May 12, due to excessive delays by the prosecution, the Oregon charges against all defendants were dismissed "without prejudice," which means that the government could still take the defendants into court if it put together a case that it could win. In 1977, Janklow unsuccessfully sued the state of California to force Banks's extradition, but in 1982 Governor Brown is running for the Senate, and his successor may send Banks to South Dakota. "They're not even thinking about Oregon anymore," Banks says with a pained smile. "They're going to get right to the point." Banks, who has never acknowledged that he was in Oregon on November 14, 1975, is still fighting extradition. "By the time I was tried in Custer in '75," he says, "Janklow was already Attorney General, but he left his post up in Pierre and went all the way down there to spearhead the prosecution; he even accosted me in the hallway and said he was going to get me, and he did. I think the atmosphere of hate in South Dakota might fade if they got rid of Janklow, and I'd like to go back, because I have many friends there, non-Indians, too. But I wouldn't consider going back while that guy's still in charge, because there's just something missing in his sordid life until he sees me in prison." (Not long ago, the frustrated Janklow threatened to parole South Dakota convicts on the condition that they move to California.)

Today, Banks says that he "never really believed those stories about Annie Mae." He thinks she traveled to Colorado when she left Pierre, but does not know what became of her after that. It is rumored, however, that she was interrogated by AIM members in Rapid City in December and that she was seen by friends in the Oglala area not long before Christmas. Sometime in this period, she made a telephone call to Nova Scotia. "They're out to kill me," she told her sister Mary. "They'll get me if the FBI doesn't get me first." Those who assume that she was an informer also assume that the "they" referred to AIM, but it might also have referred to the hostile goons who were still roaming the bleak roads of the Pine Ridge Reservation. In a last letter to her sisters, Anna Mae wrote, "I'm Indian all the way, and always will be. I'm not going to stop fighting until I die, and hope I'm a good example of a human being and of my tribe."

⊡

In the dark winter of 1975–76, the lawlessness on Pine Ridge intensified, despite the replacement of Dick Wilson as Tribal Council president by Al Trimble, the former BIA Superintendent. Trimble soon discovered that at least 25 percent of the federal monies allocated for small businesses and job development had found its way into the pockets of "two brothers," whom he did not have to name. It was hoped by a people sick of violence that Trimble would be a moderating influence, not only on the Wilson goons but on AIM's more hotheaded supporters, but Wilson was outraged by the three-to-one vote against him, and since he did not actually relinquish office until April 1976, he made the most of the time left. After the election, on January 17, the chairman of the Pine Ridge District—Wilson's stronghold—let it be known that Trimble's hometown of Wanblee, which had worked hard against Wilson, "needed straightening out." On January 30, a Friday evening, the village was invaded by three carloads of fifteen goons, wearing GI bulletproof vests and armed with AR-15 rifles, and the following morning, shots were fired into the house of Guy Dull Knife, a descendant of the great Cheyenne chief who had taken his people to shelter on Pine Ridge after the epic and tragic flight from Indian Territory in Oklahoma in 1878. Although the culprits were identified by witnesses, the BIA police made no arrests, and later that day, in a high-speed four-mile chase, these same goons overtook a car driven by tribal attorney Byron DeSersa (a great-grandson of Black Elk) and shot it full of holes. "Oh Christ, I'm hit, I'm hit bad!" DeSersa cried; he could not control the car, which rolled into a ditch. His passengers fled across a field, all but George Bettelyoun, who tried to help him, crying,

"They're gonna kill you!" DeSersa crawled across the seat and dragged himself out of the car, but he was unable to climb the road bank. He told his passenger to save himself, which he did. DeSersa, leg nearly severed by three bullets that splayed when they passed through the car door, would have survived if he had received help; instead, he bled to death while the goons pursued his passengers through the woods.

That afternoon, the BIA police were reinforced by two FBI agents and some Jackson County deputies, but none of these lawmen did anything to discourage the shooting and fire bombing, which continued all Saturday night. Bettelyoun gave the names of the goons and descriptions of their cars to the police and the FBI agents, who questioned everyone except those involved, and never visited the house where the goons were gathered. Instead, they arrested Guy Dull Knife for disorderly conduct. The FBI agents told those who protested that they lacked "probable cause" to make arrests, and anyway, they were only in Wanblee "in an investigative capacity" (the Bureau had speedily intervened in the cowboy-boot case and the Beck–Crow Dog brawl, but apparently it drew the line at murder). The outraged Wanblee residents finally organized their own law and gave the goons until sunset to get out of town; the goons received a BIA police escort back to Pine Ridge village.

The killing at Wanblee drew the attention of the press only because one of the fired-upon houses belonged to Charlie Abourezk, whose head was narrowly missed by a goon bullet. Not long thereafter, Wilson expelled him from the reservation as an "undesirable." Senator James Abourezk blamed DeSersa's death on the BIA, which he accused of "willfully ignoring" the lawlessness on Pine Ridge, and at first, the only man arrested was that Charlie Winters who had earlier made an assault upon Grace Bear Runner and who now confessed that he had fired the fatal bullets. Charged with first-degree murder, Winters was quickly released on $5,000 bail;* eventually Winters and goon leader Dale Janis served two years for the DeSersa killing. Dick Wilson's son Billy and his son-in-law Chuck Richards (who had earlier held a gun to a woman's throat, saying that he would kill her if he couldn't find her husband) were acquitted on grounds of self-defense, although DeSersa and his friends had been unarmed.

* Compare this to the $250,000 each placed on Butler and Robideau, for whose alleged crime there were no eyewitnesses and very little evidence.

⊡

On February 17, in a phone call sometime before midnight, Selo Black Crow's wife, Irenee, told the Wanblee ambulance driver that a hit-and-run accident had occurred between Kadoka and the junction of Highway 73 with Highway 44, which runs west to Wanblee, and that an injured person might be wandering that area; according to SA William Wood, the ambulance driver informed him that this call had come from Rapid City, over a hundred miles away.[4] The sheriff's office investigated but found nothing. On February 24, in the same location, a woman's body was discovered by Roger Amiotte, a mixed-blood rancher whose big tract on Pine Ridge overlaps the northeast corner of the reservation. Dressed in a wine-colored windbreaker, jeans, and blue canvas shoes, the childlike form lay curled up at the foot of an embankment, approximately fifty yards off the west side of the road and perhaps ten miles from the nearest settlement at Wanblee.* For several years, stray bodies had been common on the reservation, and Amiotte was surprised by the unusual attention drawn to this one: numbers of deputies and BIA police, reportedly attended by four FBI agents, came to the scene, some of them from Pine Ridge village, one hundred miles away. One of these agents (according to BIA investigators Doug Parisian and Nate Merrick) was David Price, who with William Wood and an agent named Donald Dealing also viewed the body after it was removed to Pine Ridge Hospital.

Early that evening, Dr. Stephen Shanker and Nurse Inez Hodges got bloody hands from a dark flow from the base of the woman's skull. Hodges also noticed her turquoise ring and bracelet, which were heavy and distinctive; the bracelet was turned over to the FBI. "She hadn't died of natural causes," Dr. Shanker said later to Kevin McKiernan, whose excellent interviews in this period comprise most of the available evidence in a strange case. "It looked like a police matter, and I assumed a postmortem would be done."[5] But Dr. W. O. Brown, the resident pathologist at the Scottsbluff, Nebraska, hospital, reported that a small contusion on the head was the only sign of injury, and that the woman had had sex not long before her end; he ruled out the possibility of rape, citing the absence of any signs of physical violence. Dr. Brown (who had also dealt in a controversial manner with the bodies of Buddy La-

* This site is indicated by a cross on the map of Pine Ridge Reservation in the front of the book.

mont and Pedro Bissonnette) dismissed the case later as routine—just another reservation episode, presumably, of falling-down drunkenness followed by exposure, which he offered as the cause of death. On Shrove Tuesday, March 2, after a few days in the hospital morgue and a local mortuary, "Jane Doe" was buried in a Catholic cemetery on orders from the Pine Ridge police.

Despite the "routine" nature of the death, Dr. Brown had cut off both hands at the wrist and turned them over to an unidentified FBI agent—William Wood, said the BIA police. The fingerprints (which Wood claimed could not be taken at the autopsy, due to advanced decomposition) were identified in Washington on the day after the burial, and on March 5, the Pictou family on the Micmac reservation at Shubencadie, Nova Scotia, was notifed of the demise of Anna Mae Pictou Aquash, aged thirty; her sister Mary Lafford contacted Bruce Ellison the following day. Since Anna Mae did not use drugs or alcohol (neither turned up in the laboratory analysis of her blood) and since she was known to be experienced in the woods (having repeatedly brought supplies into Wounded Knee through the government lines), no one believed that she had perished of "exposure." "She had to be murdered or something," her friend Roslynn Jumping Bull said. "She's not that dumb, to be walking out there all alone."

On Monday morning, March 8, Ellison told the FBI in Rapid City that he would demand an exhumation; that afternoon, the FBI applied for an exhumation order from Judge Andrew Bogue. An affidavit signed by SA William Wood said that no X rays had been performed at the first autopsy, and that the Bureau wished to investigate the possibilities that Aquash had been a hit-and-run victim or that she had been murdered. Wood also explained that on February 19, a few days before the body had been found, he had learned from a certain Anna Mae Tonaquodle (an associate of Carter Camp, who had recently been arrested in Chicago) that the said Aquash was thought by her confederates in the American Indian Movement to have been an FBI informer, from which Wood had concluded that "she may have met with foul play." (Tonaquodle, an Oklahoma AIM supporter, denied any such report or conversation.) What interested almost everyone was the timing of this announcement, which Wood made on the morning of the second autopsy.

At the family's request, this second autopsy was performed by a doctor less intimate with the government agencies than Dr. Brown. In no time at all, Dr. Garry Peterson, resident pathologist at St. Paul Hospital, in Minnesota, discovered that Anna Mae had been executed by a "metallic pellet . . . consistent with lead" fired at point-blank range from a .38 handgun into the back of her head; the bullet's passage was traced back from the lump in the left temple to the bleeding hole at the base of the skull that had disturbed Dr. Shanker and Nurse Hodges. "The wound was consistent with homicide," said Dr. Peterson, who was "very surprised to find a bullet and would have expected it to be found the first time."[6] Dr. Peterson also said it was quite possible that Aquash had been raped.

Dr. Peterson, a soft-spoken man who takes his work seriously ("I sincerely believe there's a doctor-patient relationship between me and Anna Mae") and would prefer to think well of everyone involved, remembers the first phone call he got from Kenneth Tilsen. "He told me about a case down at Pine Ridge where there was suspicion of foul play, and he asked me to go there as an impartial observer on the second autopsy." Two days later, Dr. Peterson was driven down from Rapid City by Bruce Ellison, and he remembers noticing the exhumation activity at the Holy Rosary Catholic Cemetery outside Pine Ridge. At the hospital, it turned out that the government agencies were not providing a pathologist; if a new autopsy was wanted, he would have to perform it himself. "I thought I was there for an educational experience," Dr. Peterson says, still a little surprised. "I hadn't brought anything except my camera. I mean, you don't just go running into strange hospitals with your autopsy kit! But a young intern scouted around and dug up a few instruments; he even went over to the trading post to get a kitchen knife.

"Then the body arrived in a pine box, all covered with preservative powder—very unpleasant due to the formaldehyde, much worse than the odor of the body itself; it was like being teargassed. For some reason, no X rays had been done the first time, so we found a girl who could do that. But even before that, I found a discolored area at the temple; I ran my hand over it and found an object which the X ray showed to be a bullet.

"The FBI agents who were present—Adams and Wood are the two names that stick in my mind—well, one of them had had mortuary experience and both were fantastically helpful. There was another agent—Price?—but he stepped outside just before I began. I don't know Price, and I don't know why he didn't want to attend the autopsy, although of course it was unpleasant; I've got to hand it to the other two. They were the only people with me, and they were surprised, upset, even indignant that that bullet had been missed; they seemed pretty sincere about it, too. But later a nurse came in—I guess she must have been present the first time—and she told me she was not surprised about the bullet, because every time they had moved the body, there was fluid loss."

Confronted with the results of the second autopsy, Dr. Brown explained that he had "inadvertently" overlooked the bullet while opening the skull and removing the brain for tests; he had not ordered an X ray, he admitted, because the decomposed body was so "stinky." "Why all the interest in this case?" Dr. Brown complained. "It seems awfully routine, you know. So they found an Indian body; so a body was found." The BIA's doctor stoutly maintained that the bullet had not caused the death. "The bullet may have initiated or set in progress the mechanism of death," he said, "the proximate cause of which was frostbite."

Apart from the lack of competence or objectivity in the first autopsy, unpleasant questions had been raised. Why had such a large group of law officers come to the death scene, one hundred miles out of Pine Ridge, when reports of dead bodies on Pine Ridge, routine and otherwise, had been common for years? The body and the death scene were inspected for two hours: this being the case, how was it possible that none of the agents or police officers noticed the lump on the temple or the hole in the back of the head, or even wondered how or why this person had arrived so far out in the uninhabited winter badlands, at least ten miles from the nearest settlement at Wanblee? And how was it that no law-enforcement officer at the death scene (or at the hospital) suspected the identity of a well-known fugitive whose description had been widely circulated since November and whose appearance was well known at first hand to at least one man said to have been present? Dr. Peterson believes that any well-trained agent could have taken fingerprints from the body: why, then, had the hands been removed from the body in this "routine" death, while a routine announcement of its presence in the morgue, which might have enabled someone to come in and identify it, was never made? Why had it been ordered buried on March 2, without waiting for the fingerprint identification that became available March 3? Why, in short, did every circumstance seem to bear out the observation made by Kenneth Tilsen, lawyer for the Pictou family:

"The FBI wanted the investigation to go cold because they thought it would lead them somewhere that they didn't want to go."[7]

Tilsen, who was extremely offended by the removal of the hands ("Simple decency requires that you wait more than a day to determine if other residents or family might recognize her before you cut off her hands"), suspects that the fingerprint identification and notification of the family were never intended by the Pine Ridge agents, that the hands got into the identification system by mistake. The FBI's own report to the Canadian authorities reveals that despite the alleged deterioration of the corpse and the need for haste, the hands were not actually forwarded to Washington for identification until March 3, the day after the burial and a week after the first autopsy.

Despite his other controversial autopsies on the corpses of Lamont and Bissonnette, Dr. Brown saw himself as a scapegoat when the BIA felt obliged to end his contract. However, the U.S. Civil Rights Commission report called it "incredible" that the bullet had been missed, and cause enough all by itself to raise the suspicion of a cover-up throughout the Indian community.

In a letter to the U.S. Attorney General, Senator Abourezk said, "It is clear that the FBI has conducted their activities on the Pine Ridge Reservation in such a manner as to leave the Bureau with little or no credibility as either a law-enforcement or investigatory agency with the people whom they are there to serve." Feeling the heat of suspicious questions from Senators Abourezk and Church and other concerned individuals and groups around the country, Bureau Director Clarence Kelley felt obliged to issue a statement that "no FBI agents were present during the [first] autopsy"—a statement later contested by Dr. Brown, who says that several agents as well as a number of BIA people were "in and out during the postmortem." ("Was it because they saw the bullet wound and didn't want to find the bullet?" Tilsen asks.) Kelley acknowledged, however, that the FBI had photographed the body prior to the autopsy: "One FBI agent who assisted in the photographing did know Ms. Aquash from previous personal contact; however, he did not recognize her on this occasion due to the advanced decomposition of her facial features." The agent in charge of the investigation, Norman Zigrossi, asserted that the quick burial had been ordered for the same reason: due to advanced decomposition, no mortuary would wish to keep the body. But like the hasty orders he had received to bury the unidentified cadaver, this statement surprised the mortician,

Tom Chamberlain, who said that there had been no urgency—or not, at least, so far as he and the body were concerned; it could have stayed in his garage-mortuary another week. Neither the mortician nor the priest who buried her was shown a burial certificate or burial permit, since neither has been issued to this day. "Darnedest thing I ever saw," said Chamberlain, who has handled cadavers for over a half century. Gladys Bissonnette, who visited the mortuary in this period to pick up the remains of a relative and offered to try to identify the unknown woman, was told that according to Chamberlain's orders only "authorized" persons were allowed to view these unauthorized remains.

By general agreement, the body had lain outside about eight days in the cold Dakota winter before being transferred to unheated winter rooms, then the cold ground, and Dr. Peterson remarked that its condition "wasn't bad, even after burial and exhumation." This finding encouraged speculation that the hands had been cut off to *prevent* identification of the body, rather than the reverse. In pictures taken at the second autopsy, it was reported, the young woman's features were still distinguishable. That being the case, why didn't this body with its distinctive turquoise jewelry—not often found on a routine drunk, dead of exposure—arouse either curiosity or recognition in that agent who had allegedly been present at the death scene, who had assisted with photography at the time of the first autopsy (the FBI refused to release these pictures), and who, less than six months earlier, at Rosebud, had exclaimed to the victim, "There you are! I've been looking all over for you!" This agent, SA David Price, was later accused by a ResMurs witness of suggesting that the FBI could get away with anything on the reservation, and that failure to cooperate might bring down upon this witness the same fate that befell Anna Mae Aquash, who certainly failed to cooperate as well. The same witness would claim that William Wood—who had also seen Anna Mae before, at Rosebud—had mentioned that he knew her identity before the severed hands were sent to Washington.

Kenneth Tilsen says flatly, "No one who knew Anna Mae has failed to recognize her from pictures taken at the second autopsy." Dr. Peterson, who took these pictures, remarked at the time that the body was "not severely decomposed"; even so, he says today, he was "not as shocked as some people that identification wasn't made from the facial features; the face of a deteriorated body is harder to identify than people think. You could say she was *consistent* with someone, but not much more." Roger Amiotte, who found the body, said much the same thing: the face "was intact, but it would have taken someone who knew her pretty well to identify her." But unlike Tilsen—and unlike Price—neither Peterson nor Amiotte had ever seen Anna Mae alive.

"Basically, my opinion or maybe intuition is—well, I doubt any knowing cover-up or conspiracy in that first autopsy," Dr. Peterson says. "I think the oversight was due to haste and lack of careful observation—not that I condone the oversight." The second autopsy revealed that Dr. Brown's observations and data on the condition of the stomach and kidneys were entirely meaningless, since he had not bothered to open either one: what was left of Anna Mae's brains was found by Peterson in her chest cavity. "The primary factor here was racism," Tilsen says. "Contempt for Indians. Brown was just there to earn his fee as quickly as he could and get the hell out."

When the second autopsy was finished, the body was turned over to the Oglala people, and Bruce Ellison demanded the return of Anna Mae's hands from Agent Wood. Entirely recovered from the indignation he had displayed to Dr. Peterson at the second autopsy, Wood grinned at him, saying, "Oh, you want her hands?" Wood went to his car, returning shortly with a big open-mouthed jar packed in a box. He was still grinning, Ellison remembers. "I knew right then what I felt about him. At least Price sometimes tries to act nice; this guy doesn't even try." One day a friend of Ellison who had been working with AIM Indians heard a hard honking at a Rapid City stoplight, and glancing over at the next car, found himself gazing down the barrel of Wood's handgun; apparently Wood intended this as some sort of warning. "He wants somebody in his gunsights very bad, he's just looking for an excuse," Ellison says, "whereas Price is content to manipulate people, let somebody else do the shooting."

On the first day of mourning, the body of Anna Mae Aquash lay in a borrowed tent on the Jumping Bull land; on the second day, after an evil wind came up—the wind that blows, so the elders say, when a murder victim is removed from the grave—it was transferred to the log cabin once occupied by Kamook and Dennis Banks. On March 14, a cold day of blowing snow, Anna Mae was buried with traditional Oglala prayers on the bare ridge above the Wallace Little ranch, beside the body of Joe Killsright Stuntz; though the ceremony, led by medicine man Billy Good Voice Elk, was attended by well over one hundred mourners, it was noticed that no AIM leaders came to honor her, not even those members of the Means family who were on the reservation at the time. (Russ Means thinks he must have been on trial somewhere: "If I had been on the res," he says today, "I would have been there.")

An AIM leader interviewed that spring said, "AIM didn't kill her, the pigs got to her first. They knew we knew who she was, and they wanted to blame AIM with her death."[8] This same person thought that the FBI was trying to blackmail Anna Mae by threatening to expose her as an informer, whether she was an informer or not. A continuing lack of FBI interest in any serious investigation of her death (despite the large turnout of lawmen at the scene of the crime, the FBI did not search the area thoroughly until three weeks after the body was found, according to Roger Amiotte, who found it) encouraged rumors among the Indians that she had been killed in retaliation for the agents' deaths, and when details of the FBI's COINTELPRO operations were released to the public by Senator Church later that spring, even those AIM people who had suspected Anna Mae realized that she had probably been a martyr. In May, the Attorney General ordered an investigation of the FBI's role in the events, and a grand jury was actually convened; the results, if any, have never been revealed. That same month, Clarence Kelley announced that he could discover no evidence of FBI involvement in the death.

"If an Indian kills an FBI, by golly they'll be coming in here like fleas again," said Russell Loud Hawk. "But Anna Mae is an Indian, and the FBI never comes around about her. All the time in my mind I think that some lawmen got her and that's why they're covering it. That's always in my mind."

"The FBI lost two agents, and I think Anna Mae and Joe Stuntz made it two-to-two," John Trudell said, in a view that is still widespread on Pine Ridge. "When they saw they weren't getting any cooperation from anyone, that's what they did. . . . We see the FBI as an extension of Custer's Seventh Cavalry. The justification they use to go after us is that we're revolutionaries but . . . we are not a revolutionary group. We are a part of a race of people who have been struggling against invaders for four hundred years."

Inevitably, local suspicion focused on David Price, who was already notorious on the reservation; Price himself remarked that he had heard that AIM had put a contract on his head. "The average Indian probably won't talk to Price anymore," said Norman Zigrossi, discussing the difficulties of his investigations. "His name is synonymous with our trouble."

Another trouble was Norman Zigrossi himself. "He comes on damn sincere, but he hasn't changed anything," said Al Trimble, the new president of the Tribal Council. "The way they've undertaken their work out here, they seem damned determined to settle old scores." Zigrossi, who saw the FBI as "a colonial police force," had not bothered to conceal the Bureau's fundamental attitude toward Indians: "They're a conquered nation. And when you're conquered, the people you are conquered by dictate your future. This is a basic philosophy of mine."[9]

After Anna Mae's death, Vern Bellecourt had flown out to California to meet with Banks, Clyde Bellecourt, and Trudell. "We wanted to clear up any suspicion that AIM was in any way involved," Banks says, "and Vern organized an investigation two weeks later; he couldn't find any real evidence that AIM people were involved." But as Banks acknowledged at the time, "If it was true that AIM was involved, it would crush our Movement," and for a while, he admits, he called off Bellecourt's investigation. Zigrossi said that he shared this fear that AIM members might have eliminated Anna Mae because they believed the rumors spread against her; he denied that she was ever an informer. But to judge from his own halfhearted investigation, Zigrossi had been no more eager than Banks to learn the true identity of the killer, whose action, directly or indirectly, was almost certainly a result of the paranoia created by the FBI. As Banks's old nemesis, William Janklow, crowed to reporters, "Some of the best AIM members and leaders are our informants. They would be surprised to learn who our informants are and how many we have." Like so many of Janklow's utterances, this one seemed designed to cause more trouble.

In a public statement, Banks declared that "Annie Mae Aquash was a dear friend and a trusted friend of my wife and I. Her murder is another example of an FBI cover-up in the attempt to destroy the leadership of the American Indian Movement." Subsequently, he concluded that no AIM member was guilty of the death. "She wasn't killed by just one person. It was what she represented and what kind of person she was. What happens to a people in four hundred years? Maybe that is the answer. Maybe four hundred years killed Anna Mae."

The family's reaction to the death—and to the FBI and the AIM leadership—was quiet and bitter. "My sister's murderer, or murderers, will probably never be found," said her sister Mary Lafford. "I believe the person or persons responsible may be connected with the FBI, perhaps not directly but indirectly somehow. Anna died as a result of ignorance . . . who could she have hurt? . . . Anna was an educated person, a person with common sense. She worked for the American Indian Movement out of dedication, not for publicity or headlines. The real Indian people, those who are like her, should be controlling that Movement."[10]

"She was a bright woman," said her former husband, Nogeeshik Aquash, "spirit-minded and strong-willed. Many Micmac people knew that they could go to her for help, a place to sleep, money, or whatever she had. She loved her children very much, it was a great sacrifice for her to be away from them, but she wanted change to come to the Indian people right away. This is why she fought and struggled so hard. . . . What she was saying in her efforts was that the Micmacs faced these problems 200 years ago, and that she understood what the Western tribes were now faced with. In that way, she was years ahead of her time."[11]

"Anna Mae was very beautiful, though not in the classic way," says Karen Northcott, at that time a WKLDOC aide. "Mainly she was very strong; she was part of that core of strong women that emerged at the time of Wounded Knee." Kenneth Tilsen recalls that Anna Mae, though aloof with white people, was "warm, loving, and intelligent," and he, too, remembers her as beautiful. And Kevin McKiernan, who met her first during the Wounded Knee occupation, describes her as "a bright and friendly person who always seemed to be doing something for somebody else, helping the wounded, feeding the children, looking after the elderly. She seemed to be everywhere at once and she really made you feel like she cared."

Nilak Butler remembers her best of all. "It's always hard for me to talk about her because it's like there aren't words that express a beauty of a spirit or a strength of a spirit or a power of a person. She's a part of the rain and she is always with us. . . . She was a woman who made a person have more respect for themselves, too . . . constantly learning, always learning, there was not anything she couldn't figure out how to do, and her direction was always toward the earth, protecting the earth, and toward fighting for our people. . . .

"We did a lot of fun stuff together, we went swimming; just being around her was another way of being alive. That's the only way I know how to put it. She'd be tanning leather or be sewing, and it was beautiful work, beadwork—a very smart woman. And we went one place where there was a lot of trouble one time, and she'd pack food in and out and supplies for people. She was a hardy woman and a brave-hearted woman.

"She knew she was going to die, because when we were at Rosebud that summer, sitting in the tipi talking one night, and she—there's a book called *Voices from Wounded Knee,* and Anna Mae was married at Wounded Knee to Nogeeshik Aquash, and in there, there's a picture of their wedding. We were sitting there talking, and she goes, Well, I visited this old woman over here in Rosebud, and she was looking through that *Voices from Wounded Knee,* and she came across my picture and she told me that I didn't have much time. Because she said she saw no future for me. So she began to prepare herself for death. And another thing that *really* sticks in my head was when I hooked up with her in Pierre when we were to go to trial, and she was talking about how they fingerprinted her and everything that they did, and how they told her, like, to take off her medicine pouch she was wearing. You know, What are you afraid of—the boogeyman's going to get you? And I remember she was saying, yeah, she goes, The only way I could get away with anything, with all the fingerprints they took, would be to have my hands cut off!

"That winter, I almost hooked up with Leonard. I went north for a while, and I was supposed to go to Smallboy's camp. That was another hard period, because that's when they nailed Banks, and then they nailed Leonard, and then they found Anna Mae's body, and then I about went crazy. See, I'm still underground. Dino and Bobby have not gone to trial, Leonard's captured and they're starting extradition proceedings, and I'm up in space."

⊡

On March 1, 1976, a week after Anna Mae was found, Jimmy Eagle's old partner, Hobart Horse, was shot and killed in yet another unsolved murder. In just three years on Pine Ridge Reservation, there had been sixty-three well-documented violent deaths; many more than that, for one reason or another, were never reported. In the view of the International Indian Treaty Council (which reflects the view of AIM), the true number may be closer to three hundred.

The strange sad death of Anna Mae Aquash was the first of two important cases that were to have a bearing on the ResMurs trials; the second case involved that shooting, charged against Dick Marshall and Russ Means, which had opened the violent month of March just a year before. This episode, still unexplained, took place in Scenic, off the north border of the reservation, on the Badlands road through Wounded Knee and Porcupine toward Rapid City. Like White Clay, Nebraska, on the south border, Scenic is a hamlet of small houses clustered around the place of local commerce, which is based on the sale of liquor to the Indians. In Scenic, this place of business is the Longhorn Bar, owned by Halley Merrill, a hard old man with a reputation as a fence and bootlegger.

On March 1, 1975, in the afternoon, an Indian named Martin Montileaux, twenty-eight years old, entered the Longhorn with a woman named Marion Poor Bear and another couple. They drank all afternoon and evening, and they were still there around midnight, together with fifteen or twenty others, when a new group of thirteen or fourteen Indians arrived. This was a time of high tension on the reservation, and when Halley Merrill recognized Russ Means and a group of AIM people "milling around," he told his grandson to call the sheriff, apparently anticipating trouble. Shortly before the AIM group left, so it was said, Montileaux went to the men's room in the rear; a thump was heard, and then a shot. Investigating with her friends, Marion Poor Bear looked into the men's room and saw Montileaux sitting on the floor, shot in the neck.

Meanwhile, the AIM party, headed westward, had encountered state troopers and Sheriff Melvin Larson, who had been alerted about the shooting. After a high-speed chase, a car driven by David Clifford and containing Means, Dick Marshall, and five women, including Cleo Marshall (Dick's wife) and Evelyn Bordeaux, had to be rammed by the sheriff's car before it would pull over. Means claimed that a sheriff's deputy had hit him in the face with a rifle butt as he emerged from Clifford's car, leaving a three-inch gash under his eye that required twelve stitches to close, and that the deputies left him bleeding for three and a half hours in a Pennington County Jail cell before taking him to the hospital. Clifford was charged with drunken driving and endeavoring to elude a police officer; Means and Marshall were charged with shooting Martin Montileaux with intent to kill.

"We were drinking that evening," Evelyn Bordeaux says, "and we just stopped in Scenic to pick up some beer; we were going on, so I never got out of the car. When them guys come out, I never had any feeling they was in a rush, or anything was wrong. I was in the convertible—that was the first car—and there were three other cars, and we all headed for Rapid, but not one of them other cars was stopped, only our convertible, the one with Russ in it. When they caught up with us, they were chasing us around this tourist court, and finally the sheriff rammed us from the back so hard that Russ got hurt when his face hit the windshield or the mirror. Then we heard this bullhorn: Come on out with your hands up! They took us to jail and tried to get us to tell stories on each other the way they always do. I wouldn't say nothing, so when they let me go back out to my friends, this deputy says, right in front of them, Thanks for all you told us. And I yell at him, I didn't tell you *nothing!*"

Before leaving the car, Marshall and Means had put on each other's jackets, which the sheriff interpreted as a sign of guilt and which their lawyers explained as an attempt to protect Means, who had already been the victim of two shootings and several serious beatings, and was to be shot again just three months later: not knowing at first who was chasing them, and imagining it might be Wilson's men out gunning for Means, the two had switched jackets to confuse their pursuers. "It's the kind of thing that Dick would do," says his attorney, Kenneth Tilsen. Russ Means himself has a much simpler explanation. "It was cold," he says. "We just grabbed the wrong jackets when we jumped out of the car." At any rate, Marshall was arrested in Means's conspicuous brown-and-white cowhide, which was made much of in the subsequent trials.

Although it was a county police matter, the FBI pounced on this case involving two AIM leaders, and on the day after the shooting, its Minneapolis office sent out a memo *re* Richard Marshall that reflects the political nature of its interest:

> This investigation is based upon information which indicates the subject is engaged in activities which could involve a violation of Title 18, U.S. Code, Section 2383 (Rebellion or Insurrection) or 2384 (Seditious Conspiracy), as indicated hereafter. The subject has been identified as being actively involved in militant activities of the AIM. . . .
>
> The above individual was arrested 3/1/75 with RUSSELL MEANS, AIM Leader, after a high speed chase by members of the SD Highway Patrol and Pennington County Sheriff's Office. MEANS and

> RICHARD MARSHALL are suspects in a shooting at the Scenic, S.D. Bar in which victim remains paralized [*sic*].

A founder of the Oglala Sioux Civil Rights Organization in 1972, and a young AIM leader on the Committee for Better Tribal Government, Dick Marshall had been harassed so consistently by Wilson's men that the summer before, he and Cleo had abandoned their Pine Ridge house and returned to the small community of Allen. Only a few days before the Scenic shooting, he was charged with assault on the goon gang that had chased him and his friends out of Pine Ridge in a running gunfight, then shot up the airplane and beat up the legal team at the Pine Ridge airstrip; while he was out on bail, awaiting trial, a bullet apparently intended for Marshall had grazed the head of Winnie Red Shirt in the store at Porcupine.

That weekend of March 1, 1975, nearly twenty AIM members were arrested in South Dakota and Colorado, in what Kenneth Tilsen denounced to the press as a "coordinated attack on the American Indian Movement." Therefore it came as no surprise that among the thirty or forty people in the bar, the two AIM leaders were the only ones charged with the assault. According to the sheriff's office, the .22 revolver that had fired the bullet into the victim's neck had been located among the two rifles and three pistols found in Clifford's car; also, two witnesses—the bar owner, Halley Merrill, and the victim's girl friend, Marion Poor Bear—were willing to testify that they had seen Russ Means and another man follow the victim into the men's room and emerge again after the shot.

Halley Merrill's daughter, who worked in the bar, would declare in court that she heard the shot while returning from outside through a rear door; that she then discovered Montileaux, "a very quiet sort of person," lying on the men's room floor; that he said, "Twila, help me"; and that, a little later, she heard him give the answer "Means's friend" when being questioned by Deputy Sheriff Donald Phillips.

While in the hospital, the victim was interviewed three times by Deputy Phillips. The first of these taped interviews took place the following morning:

> Q: Martin, can you talk?
> A: Yeah.

Q: Do, do you know who shot you?
A: No.
Q: You told me last night.
A: No I didn't. I don't know. I don't know him.
Q: Could you, how many people were there in the bathroom with you?
A: Just me and that guy.

Although Montileaux made it clear that his assailant was alone in the men's room when he got there, Phillips was not satisfied with this answer.

Q: How about the other guy that was in there with him, do you know him? Do you know you're pretty serious, Martin? Can you hear me, Martin? Can you hear me?

The following day, when Phillips returned to the hospital and interviewed Montileaux a second time, he asked the patient if he would recognize the man who shot him from a photograph, and Montileaux said, "Probably." Despite this answer (or perhaps because of it), he was never shown a photograph, or a suspect, either; Phillips said this was because he thought the patient would recover. By now the dying man had come around to Phillips's opinion that there had been not one but two men in the men's room, that they had come in not before but *after* his arrival, and that one of the two was Russell Means, whom he had greeted. However, he insisted that Means had not shot him, and that he did not know the identity of the other man, who was wearing an "army coat" and who had "shaggy hair." In the course of this interview, having led Montileaux to say that he was afraid of AIM and that AIM might kill him if he testified, Phillips said, "Oh, I think we can prevent that. You're not in too good of a shape now, and I'd hate to see these guys go free, especially if it is some of the big AIM leaders, wouldn't you?" In the third and final interview, on March 5, Phillips asked Montileaux if he knew Richard Marshall, and he said he did not. Phillips also made two more attempts to get Montileaux to implicate Means, which he would not do.

Phillips's unusual persistence might suggest that he was receiving more encouragement from the FBI than from the victim; at any rate, the indictment was changed to murder after Montileaux died the following day (the bullet had severed his spine, causing paralysis and other complications, including the pneumonia that caused his death). Means's case was separated from Marshall's after pre-trial hearings, and when he finally came to court, in the summer of 1976, he was acquitted. As for Marshall, the case against him was so weak and contradictory that the state suggested he plead guilty to manslaughter, a lesser charge (without, however, any recommendation as to sentence, which could have been anything from probation to life imprisonment). Marshall refused this, saying he was innocent.

At Marshall's trial, which began March 29, 1976, in Rapid City, Marion Poor Bear and owner-bartender Halley Merrill, both of whom claimed to have known Marshall for years, testified that he and Means had followed the victim into the men's room; they heard a thump, then a shot, after which two men emerged and left the bar. "They were smiling," Marion Poor Bear said.

Curiously, neither witness had been able to identify Marshall in a police lineup of suspects arranged by the court, although Marion Poor Bear claimed she had known "Dickie" Marshall ever since grade school. Also, all witnesses agreed that Marshall had been wearing an olive-green down-filled jacket, not an "army coat," and that his hair, far from being "shaggy," had been tied in his customary neat braid, or "pony tail." The victim himself had been specific on this point.

> A: . . . a shaggy-headed guy.
> Q: Uh-huh. Was his hair in a pony tail?
> A: Yeah. No, it wasn't in a pony tail.
> Q: No pony tail?
> A: Unh-unh.
> Q: Was . . . Do you know a guy by the name of Richard Marshall?
> A: Unh-unh.

As for motivation, there was no evidence whatever that Marshall had known Montileaux was in the Longhorn, that he planned to kill him, or that he had carried a weapon into the bar. What is more, the ballistics experts could make no conclusive tie between the .22 pistol found in Clifford's car and the fatal bullet; the shearing marks scoring the slug were typical of those made by most cheap guns, due to misalignment of the cylinders.

The prosecution's dilemma was resolved when a last-minute witness, whose name had not been presented at the pre-trial hearings, was "supplied" to the state by FBI agents David Price and William Wood. For producing the perjurious witness Louis Moves Camp against Russell Means and Dennis Banks in their St. Paul trial in 1974, Price had won an outraged denunciation from the judge; this time, his witness was a Myrtle Lulu Poor Bear, a cousin of Marion from Marshall's village, who identified herself as a friend of the defendant and his wife, Cleo, and hinted that she had been Dick Marshall's girl friend. Like Louis Moves Camp, Myrtle Poor Bear filled in all the missing pieces in the prosecution's case. She testified that Marshall had the motive necessary to sustain the first-degree murder charge, namely, a beating by Montileaux suffered in a Gordon, Nebraska, bar; that Marshall had carried a gun into the Longhorn; that he shot Montileaux; and that he had admitted his crime to her on three separate occasions.

> A: He was dancing and then he stopped and he came over to the table where I was sitting and he said, "You know, that guy that got killed at Scenic?" I said, "Yeah." He said, "I asked the guy if that was the right one and he said, 'yeah,' it was," so he said, "We waited for him and we followed him in the bathroom," and then he said, "I pulled the trigger." He said, "I'll never forget the look on that son-of-a-bitch's face as he went down."
> Q: Did you say anything in response to that?
> A: No, I didn't.
> Q: Who all was present then?
> A: There was a guy named Leonard. I don't know his last name. . . .
> Q: All right, and did you have a conversation again with the Defendant about what happened at Scenic?
> A: Yeah, I did.
> Q: Would you relate that conversation as well as you can recall?
> A: He was dancing and he came over and he said, "I don't know why I shot him."

The witness testified that she had described this conversation to the FBI sometime late in 1975, which meant that the FBI delayed three months or more before notifying the sheriff's office of this crucial evidence; since she was not revealed as a witness until March 25, four days before the trial, Marshall's attorneys had almost no chance to interview her or investigate her story. Had Marshall not been an AIM leader, but simply an Indian in a crowded late-night bar where another Indian had been wounded under confused circumstances, it is very unlikely that he would have been tried at all. But in the anti-AIM climate, in a South Dakota court, this witness's word sufficed to send Dick Marshall, aged twenty-five, to jail for life at hard labor in the state penitentiary at Sioux Falls.

After the verdict, despite the FBI's official disinterest in the case, Special Agent Price sent copies of the following cable to the FBI offices concerned:

> ON APRIL 6, 1976, RICHARD MARSHALL WAS CONVICTED OF FIRST DEGREE MURDER, PENNINGTON COUNTY COURT, RAPID CITY, SOUTH DAKOTA. MARSHALL WAS IMMEDIATELY GIVEN THE MANDATORY SENTENCE OF LIFE IN PRISON AT HARD LABOR. THE RAPID CITY OFFICE OF THE FBI WAS HELPFUL TO LOCAL AUTHORITIES AS THE FBI SUPPLIED ONE WITNESS WHO HEARD MARSHALL BOAST OF THE MURDER. MARSHALL IS CURRENTLY INCARCERATED.

⊡

On February 6, 1976, a Royal Canadian Mounted Police inspector named Edward W. J. Mitchell received a call after midnight in his motel at White Core, Alberta, instructing him to go to Hinton, one hundred sixty miles west of Edmonton, to organize a search for "a Mr. Peltier." The search was unnecessary, since an informer had apparently told the police just where to go. That day, Mitchell and his Mounties proceeded to the remote camp of a Cree leader named Robert Smallboy, who had occupied this place in a peaceable "takeover" a few years before. Smallboy's camp is a makeshift congregation of small cabins and portable one-room schoolhouses donated after the occupation by the provincial government, and in one of the schoolhouses, at about three in the afternoon, the fugitive was found sitting near the blackboard, beside a suitcase containing two loaded revolvers, an M-1, and a .30-30: "At the initial point of arrest," says Corporal Dale Parlane, "I put him up against the wall, at which time he shouted at me, 'I am not going to do anything you say, I have nothing to lose!' at which time he started to struggle, at which time I had to push him harder against the wall." When he cooled off, according to Parlane, Peltier was permitted to chant a prayer, in which he invited a Cree elder to accompany him.

While in the schoolhouse, Sergeant Mitchell took note of the "scars on his chest, and he indicated he had acquired them in a sacred ritual. He referred to his strong belief that the magic in his necklace had cured his buckshot wounds after he had been gunned down, shot in the back—that was his term—on a highway in the United States. He said that he had been unable to get a doctor but had phoned Pine Ridge, and they held a prayer session for him."

The captive was placed in an unmarked police car with another Res-Murs suspect named Frank Black Horse, twenty-seven, who was later charged with marijuana possession, and later still with attempted escape from jail in Fort Saskatchewan, Alberta.[12] Mitchell asked them if a third captive, Ronald Blackman (a.k.a. Ron Janvier), was involved with them in the possession of the rifles and revolvers. "Mr. Black Horse was noncommittal. However, Mr. Peltier said, 'He was not with us. Those guns in the suitcase were mine, and the suitcase is mine, also.' " (Peltier denies making this statement, which was used to incriminate him on the Oregon burglary charges; he says that the statements attributed to him by Mitchell and Parlane were fabrications, and that the weapons he was found with were unloaded.)

On the car ride to Hinton, where they spent the night, Peltier told Parlane that he had been shot in the back by Oregon police; he also said that "he didn't want to go back to the States because he feared for his life." Because the .30-30 rifle in his possession had been taken from the farm in Ontario, Oregon, on November 15, 1975, he was charged with the theft of the gun and pickup truck in addition to his alleged murders and attempted murders. While awaiting a hearing, he was removed to Oakalla Prison, outside Vancouver, which was now subjected by the press to FBI warnings of armed escape raids and terrorist crimes against the populace. In the lurid atmosphere being whipped up to expedite his extradition, this desperate felon (never convicted of a felony in all his life) was kept in complete isolation from the other prisoners and handcuffed at all times when outside his cell except during his exercise, which was limited to less than half an hour each day; he was permitted no outside exercise at all between February and June 1976.

Friends and relatives, even attorneys, who tried to assist Leonard Peltier found themselves harassed and obstructed by the Canadian officials. In general, Indians in Canada have been spared such bureaucratic persecution as allotment, termination, and relocation, but the fundamental attitudes toward them are the same.[13] Despite a show of concern for justice—including formal demands for an investigation into the death of Anna Mae Pictou, "a Canadian citizen" who would not have acknowledged herself as such (and whose impoverished Micmac people would soon undergo their own fishing-rights struggle with Quebec police)—the Dominion was undergoing its own fever of anti-Indian sentiment, and was anxious to rid itself of Peltier, who was sure to organize Indian resistance: the Cree were protesting the destruction of their James Bay lands for hydroelectric energy; the Dene Indians of northern Saskatchewan were fighting uranium contamination of their territories, including wholesale pollution of the waters from Lake Athabaska to the great Mackenzie River; the Ojibwa of Ontario were plagued with "Minimata disease," due to mercury poisoning of their waters from huge pulp mills; and everywhere the native peoples were making land claims. The year before, in a document leaked to the willing press, the Royal Canadian Mounted Police had warned the citizens about a dangerous, AIM-inspired Indian movement, part of an international terrorist conspiracy, which sought social and economic equality for Canada's Indians as well as just recognition of their land claims: "The Red Power Movement," the police declared, "has become the principal threat to Canadian stability."

Established in the late nineteenth century as a military force to remove Indians from prairie lands coveted by the settlers, the Mounties have never outgrown the idea that Indians, in the main, are a verminous nuisance. In recent years, a Chilcotin Indian named Fred Quilt was stomped to death by two RCMP officers in British Columbia, in a killing that an all-white jury dismissed as "accidental"; a second jury, convened after an outraged protest by the Indians, agreed with the first that all those fatal kicks had been unintentional. This beefy side of Mountie nature is very familiar to Canada's Indians if not to the white public, accustomed as it is to postcard Mounties guarding the Dominion in World War I hats and red tunics, astride huge horses by the shores of Lake Louise. (An indication of the status of the native peoples, and the special attention paid to them by the police, may be had from the fact that 25 percent of the jail inmates of Saskatchewan are Indians, who represent just 2 percent of the general population.) In fact, the Mounties were only too eager to cooperate with their American colleagues in bringing to justice this cop-killing aborigine, who was sought by the United States with the same fervor that Sitting Bull had been sought a century before.

Excepting a week or so in California, Peltier says, he spent most of the fall of 1975 in Canada. "Up there in Canada, you know, That One we used to call rugaru comes up often in the conversation. You know, the people up there just take 'Bigfoot' for granted. Anyway, I have relatives up there, and I spent some time in B.C. and Vancouver, and also over in Manitoba, Portage la Prairie; used to be a reservation there where my grandmother's parents used to be."

While in prison, Peltier was adopted by the Kwikwasutainwook people of the Kwakewlth ("Quakiutl") nation on Vancouver Island at a traditional potlatch ceremony; he was given a plot of land on Kwakewlth territory and the name Gwarth-ee-lass, "He-Leads-the-People." As a Sioux-Ojibwa from the Canadian border country, he had rapidly become a hero, and when his extradition hearings came up in May, an effort was made to present him as a caged animal instead. Although an assistant referred to Peltier as "a model prisoner," the director of Oakalla described him publicly as one of the most dangerous prisoners ever confined there, a man capable of committing "any sort of act to stay in Canada—even as far as to murder or maim an inmate or prison official. . . . He is a real sociable fellow, but I would never turn my back on him."[14] In treatment condemned as "unjustifiable" by Amnesty International, which sent an observer to his trials, he was kept alone under heavy guard in an observation unit, due to the alleged escape plots he was hatching. Whenever he left his cell, he was subject to body searches, and was invariably shackled hand and foot on the short trip between his cell and the courtroom; the first sound each morning during the Vancouver hearings was the clang of the chains on the iron stair leading from the detention cells to the prisoner's dock. In what the Vancouver *Sun* described as "what surely must be one of the most remarkable occasions in the history of this country's legal process . . . entrants to the courtroom are being spread-eagled against the wall and frisked in scenes from S.W.A.T. A policewoman runs her hands inside the bras of female reporters. Shoes are removed. Jackets are removed. Purses must be left outside. Is this a Canadian courtroom? It is, in fact, a Canadian courtroom asked to rule on the internal politics of another country."

Despite consistent harassment by the authorities, a large contingent of Indians from both sides of the border had gathered in Vancouver; they were coordinated at the Indian Center by Steve Robideau and Russ Redner, who was out on parole on the Oregon charges. "Man, we had skins layin' all over the place there at the Center," Robideau says, "and we had a big march every day down to the court; we kept that courthouse full of Indians. We held ceremonies, using the pipe, we had sweats every day, and we discussed Canadian problems with the people; we really pulled the Indians of Canada together, which is one reason the authorities came down so hard on us. At the court, they had strip searches every day, yanking off medicine bags, pushing people around. And the people were polite, there was no need for that." When Edgar Bear Runner and Louis Bad Wound came to Vancouver to testify for the defense, their hotel-room door was kicked in after midnight by police who pretended to ransack the room for marijuana; this episode was by no means unique.

At Peltier's extradition hearings, pleas to the Canadian government by lawyers, friends, and family that the FBI was engaged in a systematic repression of AIM and that Peltier's life would be in danger if he was denied political asylum were countered by the Wisconsin "attempted murder" charge, which propped up the weak Oglala evidence. But the fatal blow to his hopes of avoiding extradition were two surprise documents in which a firsthand witness identified Peltier as the unassisted killer of Coler and Williams. In two affidavits dated February 23 and March 31, 1976, this witness declared that she had accompanied Peltier to Oglala in May 1975; that Peltier "and others began planning on how to kill either FBI, U.S. Government police or BIA agents who might come into the area. Peltier was mostly in charge of the planning. I was present on the day the FBI agents were killed. I saw Leonard Peltier shoot the FBI agents." She also said that on the day in question, Peltier had hollered, "Here they come!" at the appearance of the agents' automobiles; that Peltier or Ricky Little Boy had shoved a gun into her hands; that subsequently she had heard shots, after which she found herself with a woman named Madonna Slow Bear down beside the cars, where she saw Peltier, Robideau, Jimmy Eagle, and one other unidentified Indian; that one of the agents was lying face down and bleeding; that the second agent, who was leaning wounded against the side of the car, threw his handgun aside, saying, "I surrender," to Peltier, who held a gun on him; that she tried to pull away but was forced to watch by Madonna Slow Bear, who grabbed her by the hair and yanked her head around in time to see the agent's body jump as it was hit by Peltier's bullets; that she now broke away from Madonna Slow Bear and ran up to Peltier and pounded him on the back, telling him to quit; that she then ran to the creek, where Ricky Little Boy was in charge of the horses, and forced him at gunpoint to give her a horse; that she then traveled on horseback to her car, which Peltier had told her to hide in the trees for the getaway after the ambush. (In a separate interview on February 24, the witness declared that she had simply run off, firing a shot at Ricky Little Boy when he pursued her; there was no mention of horses.)

The affidavits, presented on May 11 by Paul Halprin, a prosecuting attorney for the Canadian Department of Justice who was representing the United States, came as a complete surprise to the defense, which according to ethical trial procedure should have been notified of these documents in advance. In another surprise affidavit, an FBI agent claimed to have found in the open trunk of Coler's car a .223 shell casing, apparently ejected by the killer's rifle during the executions, which had since been matched by an FBI ballistics expert to an AR-15 rifle that other witnesses had apparently associated with Leonard Peltier.

Two days later, John Trudell spoke for the stunned defense, describing how AIM had been provoked by the FBI into violent responses so that its leaders could be killed, jailed, or otherwise "neutralized," thereby eliminating all Indian opposition to usurpation of valuable Indian lands. Other Indians testified to the defendant's long history of service to his people, and finally Peltier himself took the stand in an attempt to persuade the court that he was not a criminal but the victim of the ruthless quest for minerals and money, that he was in effect a political prisoner who deserved political asylum. In a letter written from Oakalla in April, he had said in part, "The only thing I'm guilty of is trying to help my people. For this, it's very possible I'll spend the rest of my life in prison, if I'm extradited. I don't say that because I'm guilty but because I know that I can't get a fair trial in South Dakota."

On June 18, the hearings ended with the announcement of Mr. Justice W. A. Schultz's decision. When Peltier stepped into the dock in clanking chains, he was greeted with shouts of encouragement; when Justice Schultz entered, the crowd fell silent. There was terrific tension and suspense, according to Steve Robideau. "Everybody tried to get into the room that day. First we walked in with the drum—they forced us out. Then we walked in without it, but a cop grabbed the medicine bag of a guy named Big Bear, who blew it and threw a punch at him; I intervened, but it took me a little while to straighten that out. Finally, things calmed down again, and we got the people settled.

"When they brought Leonard in, the people rose as a gesture of solidarity; we stood up and sat down with Leonard Peltier. When the judge came in and asked Leonard to stand for the verdict, we *all* stood, because the Indian people were being sentenced, too. Well, the judge got mad: When I tell a defendant to stand, I don't mean everybody! Now clear the court! So people groaned and began singing the AIM song, and nobody was in a big hurry to leave; when we didn't move fast enough, we got pushed and shoved through the narrow exit in the rear of the gallery by the cops. So a fist flew, and they sailed into us; they were slugging our women with their sticks, same as the men." Once the court was cleared, Justice Schultz decreed that sufficient grounds for extradition had been presented; he was not authorized to sign the extradition order, which was the duty of the Minister of Justice.

For the next few months, Peltier's attorneys would appeal Schultz's decision. The defense testimony had persuaded Canada's Minister of External Affairs[15] to call for an "urgent investigation" of FBI misconduct in the case, but there was no longer much question of which way the wind was blowing.

CHAPTER 12
THE TRIAL AT CEDAR RAPIDS
June–July 1976

You Christians, you are a lost people with no identity to this land, the only God you have is your technology which will destroy you because of the greed it demands. . . . I have no fear of your materialistic power and your brutality cannot harm me, it will only separate you further from your spirit which will bring me closer to mine. My love for my People and the land is my strength and that is something you will never be able to touch because it is a power you do not understand.

Darrelle Butler (*Rogue River Tuni*)

I do not regret the part I played and received ten years in prison for, on the contrary, I would have thought less of myself if I had not done that which I am obligated to do, so that my people may live. Moreover, I would not hesitate to do it over again if and whenever the need arose. My only pain is in knowing that my people and family still suffer from our government manipulations and control over their lives, and the lives of our future generations. The struggle of my people continues, and will continue until liberation is achieved.

Robert Robideau (*Ojibwa*)

In January 1976, Bob Robideau had been transferred from Kansas City to the Pennington County Jail in Rapid City to await trail with Dino Butler in the federal district court of Judge Andrew Bogue.

While in the Rapid City jail, Butler and Robideau were subjected to continual harassment, including confiscation of their religious objects. On April 19, several hacksaw blades were discovered in their cellblock. For some reason, five FBI agents—J. Gary Adams, William Wood, Dean Hughes, Frederick Coward, and David Price—were invited to join in a search of the cells by Sheriff Melvin "Mel" Larson and three of his deputies, including Donald "Don" Phillips,* who had worked so successfully with Price on the murder conviction of Dick Marshall, just two weeks before. An excerpt from the 302 report signed by all five agents indicates the thoroughness of this operation:

> Located in the cell of ROBERT EUGENE ROBIDEAU in cellblock six by Special Agent (SA) FREDERICK COWARD, JR.:
>
> One white envelope, approximately ten inches in length.... On the outside of the white envelope was the name "BOB" written in ink. Inside the white envelope was a blue card. On the outside of the blue card was printed "With Love to My Wife On Our Anniversary." This was an American Greeting Card. Also located by SA COWARD in the cell of ROBERT EUGENE ROBIDEAU was a yellow envelope approximately the same size as the aforementioned white envelope. This yellow envelope was addressed to Mr. ROBERT E. ROBIDEAU, 302 Kansas City Street, Rapid City, South Dakota 57701, from Mrs. A. ROBIDEAU, Eagle Butte, South Dakota 57625. Inside the yellow envelope was a yellow and green card with a boy and girl osculating.

Although the two cells that were searched housed sixteen inmates, it was determined by this large body of men that only Robideau, Butler, and two other Indians associated with AIM had been attempting to escape; all of their personal property and clothing was now confiscated.[1] The informer who reported Butler and Robideau's participation in the escape plan was a black man named Marvin Bragg, a.k.a. Ricky Walker. Bob Robideau, who was certain that he and Butler were going to be

* In FBI reports, local officers (but not agents) are identified in this friendly way by their federal colleagues.

convicted and who does not deny their intention to escape, recalls Bragg as "just a little guy, maybe five foot two, and he was a real terror there in Rapid; had more than ten rapes, and most of 'em pretty weird, involving old women. A real sad figure—everywhere he went, he was getting beat up, especially after he snitched on us, because rapists and snitches, well, cons just don't go for that shit, and Bragg was both. But he had a good personality and a real good sense of humor, and got along with everybody who didn't know too much about him. I liked him. He was going with an Indian woman at that time, and I guess it was her that threw them hacksaw blades in through the window. It was just a small jail, maybe fifty inmates, and breaking out would have been pretty easy, but somebody on the upper tier had snitched on us. Bragg was serious about escaping, but he was facing up to eighty years, and when the shit came down, he just switched sides and pinned it all on us, to save himself."

Bragg himself later acknowledged that he had been visited in his cell by Agents Price and Coward, with whom his attorney had advised him to cooperate; he informed them that the planned escape involved only the four AIM Indians in the jail. While he was at it, he also gave a statement (to Agents Coward and Hughes on April 23) that he, too, had heard Jimmy Eagle's boasts, the year before, about participating in the killings at Oglala.

⊡

In April, WKLDOC, arguing that anti-Indian prejudice in Rapid City precluded any possibility of an objective jury, successfully appealed for a transfer of the trial out of South Dakota. Two days after the great escape attempt, Butler and Robideau were transferred to the state penitentiary at Sioux Falls, where they were placed in "punitive segregation"—solitary confinement and cells stripped bare of everything but bunk and toilet. On May 7, they were moved to Cedar Rapids, Iowa, where Robideau stood on his legal right not to be fingerprinted all over again without consulting his attorney. As a result, the deputy "grabbed me and threw me against the wall, kneed me between the legs, and said that he was going to take my fingerprints if he had to 'beat the shit out of you,' whereupon he threw me to the floor and proceeded to do just that." Robideau again requested permission to telephone his attorney; the request was refused: "I then relented to the situation and allowed

[him] to take my fingerprints." Robideau required five stitches where his head struck the concrete floor, and the state ombudsman later determined that Sheriff's Deputy Donald Wharton, a 6′5″ 225-pounder, had used "excessive force." Sheriff Walter Grant denied this; Don had merely displayed poor judgment in trying to get the job done without help, and Walt planned no disciplinary measures. Both Butler and Robideau later complained of death threats from their warders, saying that they feared for their lives while in this jail, and meanwhile their attorneys had discovered that Cedar Rapids was 98 percent white, and that relatives of the late Jack Coler lived in the area.

For its part, the government made the most of this promising situation. The FBI warned local law-enforcement personnel that carloads of AIM terrorists were descending on the town, and on May 11, U.S. marshals visited every office in the Federal Building, telling folks to prepare for shooting incidents and the seizure of hostages and advising them of the precautions to be taken; the frightened citizens were assured that U.S. marshals on the roof would be on the lookout for marauding Indians. On May 24, Rapid City police, reporting a huge cache of Indian armaments left over from Wounded Knee, tore up a vacant lot with backhoes, exposing three spent shotgun shells for their day's work.

> Analysis of facts surrounding A.I.M. leads one to the conclusion that this is one of the most violent and extremist-oriented organizations yet encountered by the United States. . . .
>
> The movement seems to be changing and appears to be more concerned with perpetuating itself rather than conducting large, costly, violent confrontations. Confrontations keep their leaders in court and sap energy and funds.
>
> An additional danger exists in that other radical terrorist and extremist groups, both foreign and domestic, see in A.I.M. a powerful ally for their release of destructive violence against the United States. The assistance of such groups, whether through funds, manpower, weapons, political philosophy or instigation to violence, can be a pertinent threat to the welfare of the United States government and its citizenry of the first magnitude.
>
> Due to the A.I.M.'s violence potential, which is frequently directed toward local and state governments and police officers, timely dissemination of specific intelligence information affecting their agencies, is of the utmost importance.[2]

For the next month, as the trial got under way, Cedar Rapids was rife with rumors of renegade activity. On June 18, AIM's plans to "blow out the candles on America's birthday cake" in this Bicentennial Year were cited in an FBI publication called *Domestic Terrorist Digest,* which also warned of an Indian caravan to the Little Big Horn on June 26, the centennial of Custer's defeat. (In the first memorial ceremony ever held for the warriors who died there one hundred years before, Chief Frank Fools Crow placed a wreath upon the ground. "I was the real leader of the group," the old man said, "although AIM spokesmen did most of the talking.") On June 21, a report allegedly emanating from Connecticut police intelligence stated that a terrorist affiliation of AIM, the Brown Berets (a Chicano activist group, already defunct), and SDS (Students for a Democratic Society, also defunct) had hatched a plan "to kill a cop a day," using "various ruses" to "lure law-enforcement officers into an ambush." According to the nationally distributed teletype, RUDOLFO "CORKY" GONZALES, A LEADER OF THE BROWN BERETS, REPORTEDLY HAS A ROCKET LAUNCHER AND ROCKETS EITHER IN HIS POSSESSION OR AVAILABLE TO HIM ALONG WITH EXPLOSIVES, HAND GRENADES AND TEN TO FIFTEEN M-16 RIFLES WITH BANANA CLIPS.

On June 22, the FBI released another four-page teletype under its own byline; it was distributed to law-enforcement agencies on the same date, oddly enough, as the "kill-a-cop-a-day" alarm, but held up another day before release. This report said that some two thousand AIM "Dog Soldiers"* trained in "the Northwest Territory" by June Little, "who is expert with explosives," and using automatic weapons cached by Sam Moves Camp in Charlie Abourezk's house in Porcupine, were to proceed from the International Indian Treaty Council on the Yankton Sioux Reservation to the Rapid City house of AIM sympathizer Renee Howell (who still wonders how she would have fitted them all in). From there, these two thousand Dog Soldiers would fan out across the state to assassinate the Governor, blow up various state and federal dams, plants, and law-enforcement centers, take unspecified "action" at Mount Rushmore, "burn" farmers, snipe at tourists on the highways, and otherwise spoil all the fun of the Bicentennial celebrations. The Dog Soldier Teletypes were denounced by Senator Abourezk, who said that the mention of his son was part of an FBI "smear campaign" in

* Members of traditional warrior societies.

retribution for the younger Abourezk's criticism of FBI and BIA actions and policies on the Lakota reservations: "It smacks of a total setup that these unfounded, unverified reports are given such widespread distribution."

On June 30, in Rapid City, Sheriff Larson announced that all local, state, and federal law-enforcement agencies had been "beefed up" and all leaves canceled for the Bicentennial celebration. Asked if the alarmed patriots of the region could celebrate America's birthday without worrying about violence, the sheriff said, "We have no concrete evidence to indicate otherwise."[3] In truth, not a single sliver of hard evidence supported the lies and propaganda being aimed at the Cedar Rapids jury by the U.S. Marshal Service, the U.S. Attorney's office, and the Federal Bureau of Investigation of that sadly eroded institution, the U.S. Department of Justice.

Meanwhile, down on the reservation, the BIA Superintendent was expressing concern about a new AIM Citizens Committee in Oglala, which was said to have announced that "any police officer coming into Oglala Housing would be shot": the FBI was warned to stay out of Oglala between June 24 and 27, when AIM planned a memorial ceremony for Joe Killsright Stuntz. The leader of this committee, said the BIA report, was "Wallace Little, Junior, a.k.a. June Little, who recently suffered the loss of a hand and an eye while experimenting with explosives," and its members included Edgar Bear Runner and Sam Loud Hawk. One source of all this information was John Stewart, alias Daryl Blue Legs, the fat and friendly fellow who had turned up in Oglala in early June 1975, about two weeks before the shoot-out, and had spent a lot of time hanging around the Jumping Bull land, ingratiating himself with the inhabitants. Stewart, whose extensive jail record included a conviction for first-degree manslaughter, was one of those who had spread the story that Anna Mae Aquash was an informer; he was also rumored to have known more than he should about her death. In the spring of 1976, his estranged wife, Dorothy Brings Him Back, showed WKLDOC attorneys a note sent to Stewart at her address which read in part, "I have to talk to you—Dave." Because the handwriting looked familiar, Bruce Ellison compared it to initialed FBI 302 forms, and in his opinion, the "D" is identical to those made by David Price. In a letter to Dorothy in this period, Stewart said he was in jail in Rapid City, doing time for one of his AIM brothers; he gave her a telephone number for leaving messages that turned out to be the local number of the FBI. A month later, he turned up on the list of prosecution witnesses for the trial of Butler and Robideau.

⊡

"When they first found Anna Mae, they thought it was me for a while, because I was underground," Nilak remembers. "I had to notify people that I was okay. I'm not going to say where I was, because a lot of people who helped me at that time never did learn my right name. But I will say that I had to hitch rides for a couple of thousand miles up and down the country to get to Bob and Dino's trial. Bobby and Dino were scheduled for trial in Rapid City before Judge Bogue, and I knew I had to be there: if it was before Bogue, they would be convicted. I'd expected more organized Movement support toward their trial. It wasn't that anybody wasn't supportive, it was more that they had so many people going to court so many different places all at the same time. They had the Meanses going to trial in Dakota, they had Banks fighting it out in Oregon and California. I mean, they just had everybody going to court all over the country. Or in jail. Or dead. You know, they really smashed it up there for a while."

The trial opened on June 7, 1976. "They were having a big old parade that day . . . and the police were so paranoid they locked up the whole jail. The headlines at that time were that the Governor was asking for National Guard support during the trial, the feds had psyched them up so bad, and *that's* where we were going to get our jury. The citizens were more concerned that no damage happen to their person, place, or thing, because they were just psyched out—totally psyched out. So we went out into the community and explained that our people were only there to be supportive, that there was a certain code of conduct that we still go by and abide by, and what *they* could expect during the trial."

When the two thousand Dog Soldiers failed to show up, and the rest of the great scare campaign turned out to be lies as well as nonsense, the citizens of Cedar Rapids began to observe the Justice Department stage directions with more skepticism, and perhaps some resentment, as well; they also began to look at AIM with a fresh eye. It was noticed by both press and public that those Indians attending the trial had established a camp outside of town where neither drugs nor alcohol was permitted; instead, sweat lodges were set up and sanctified by sacred-pipe ceremonies, performed each day. Since their sovereignty claims contested

U.S. jurisdiction, the Indian people in the audience refused to stand up each morning for Judge Edward McManus; so did Dino Butler and Bob Robideau. But the many Indians who came to court as well as those seen in the streets were neatly dressed, clean, courteous, and quiet, and the defendants, in long braids and beaded shirts, made a good appearance. Every morning, two traditional stone pipes wrapped in cloth and buckskin and fitted with eagle feathers and wild sage were brought to the defense table, where the defendants filled them with red-willow kinnikinnick and tobacco; Indian witnesses for the defense swore to be truthful on the sacred pipes instead of on the Bible. (As Selo Black Crow explained to Marlon Brando, a visitor at the trial, swearing on the pipe was originally part of a purification ceremony before going to war, in which Indians were always prepared to die. "Today is a good day to die because all the good things of my life are here"—a Lakota war cry sometimes attributed to Crazy Horse—reflects the spirit of this ceremony.)

Judge McManus—called "Speedy Eddie" by the Indians since the conviction of Crow Dog, Camp, and Holder in his court in one week flat—allowed only a single day for the selection of the jury, for which he was sharply criticized by one of Butler's attorneys, William Kunstler, and an attorney for Robideau, John Lowe. Aware of potential local prejudice against "radical sharpie lawyers from the East," Kunstler had dropped his flamboyant courtroom style, remaining almost sedate throughout this trial; in this, he was complemented by Lowe, a more conservative attorney from Charlottesville, Virginia, whose copious knowledge of the details of the case was a great asset to the strong defense team.[4]

Both Butler and Robideau admitted that they had been present at Oglala at the shoot-out and that they had exchanged fire with the doomed agents in the course of "defending our women and children," but both men denied having murdered anyone. No Indians were guilty, the defendants claimed; a whole community had defended itself against an illegal invader. "We are innocent, and I know that many people know that we are innocent," Robideau declared, in oblique reference to the numbers of people at Oglala on the fatal day.

"The U.S. government is out to make political scapegoats of Bob and I," Butler said, in an opening statement to the court. "We are members of a sovereign nation. We live under our own laws, tribal and natural. We recognize and respect our own traditional and elected leaders. The treaties that were made between Indian nations and the United States government state that we have the right to live according to our own laws on the land given to us in the treaties. That the laws of the United States government shall not interfere with the laws of our nations.

"When a person is charged with committing a crime in your society, they are not brought to our society to be tried. We feel we are being deprived of our sovereign rights guaranteed us by the treaties, by being forced to go on trial here in this United States courtroom. The United States Constitution says the treaties are binding; yet by our being here today the United States Constitution and the Indian treaties are being violated by the United States government. We are not citizens of this society, but you, ladies and gentlemen of the jury, are. You have sworn to do what the United States government has never done for Native American people of this country. You have sworn to protect us, respect us as your equals. You have sworn to be unbiased and impartial toward us. You have sworn to give us a fair trial in the United States courtroom of justice.

"This trial concerns all people and their rights. We must all work together to remind the United States government that their government is for the people."

⊡

The senior prosecutor was Brigadier General (U.S. Army Reserve) Evan Hultman, a former Attorney General of Iowa who once ran for Governor of his state; his most prominent assistant was Robert Sikma. An intelligent but inarticulate man, Hultman tripped over a wire during the interrogation of his first witness, knocking over a water pitcher as the jury laughed; because of his often garbled speech, he never quite managed to undo this early impression of buffoonery.

Hultman's first witness was Special Agent J. Gary Adams, a hulking man of six feet six inches, who described in detail the grim events of June 26, 1975, from the time of his last sight of his friend Ron Williams at midmorning in Pine Ridge village until the eerie encounter with Williams's green car in the twilight woods down by White Clay Creek. On cross-examination, Adams acknowledged having reported that red pickup truck which, according to his radio transcriptions, he had seen departing from the Jumping Bull area at 12:18, a few minutes after the agents must have died. It was now apparent that none of the defendants had departed in that truck, which had therefore become an annoyance to the prosecution.

Adams told Kunstler that he could not recall seeing armed goons in the area, although many had been present on that day; that he had not known that Dennis Banks was living on the place; and that William Janklow and the state police were justified in coming to Oglala, since the state had jurisdiction on the reservation in a "white-on-white" situation, and the agents' attackers were of unknown color.

SA Dean Hughes had also been unaware of the presence of Banks or the AIM group on the Jumping Bull land, and so had SAC Joseph Trimbach, the FBI man chastised during the Wounded Knee trial by Judge Frederick Nichol.[5] Kunstler questioned SAC, Minneapolis, about office discussions of counterintelligence programs against AIM, reminding him that a team of three men in his office had received numerous telephone calls from FBI informer Douglass Durham during the Banks-Means trial. The tall, silver-haired Kunstler's repeated references to that trial, in attempting to demonstrate the pattern of FBI misconduct, were successfully objected to by the small, red-haired Hultman, who at times evoked laughter with his dogged phrase "incompetent, irrelevant, and immaterial."

The early FBI reports that both agents had been "riddled by bullets" were explained away by a pathologist, Dr. Robert Bloemendaal of Rapid City. "My initial impression, and this applied to both agents, I thought they were shot more times . . . than when I got everything put together." In his opinion, the bullet that splayed in its passage through the trunk lid and almost severed Agent Coler's right arm at the elbow was the first wound received by the agents, and accounted for the blood splashes and smears on the rear bumper of Coler's car. Elongated blood drops on the dead man's trousers suggested that Coler moved around for a little while, then sat down, perhaps faint with shock and loss of blood. Meanwhile, Williams had received a "superficial" wound in the foot, probably while kneeling, and another bullet passed through his arm and then his side; the second wound occurred before he ripped his shirt off, since the shirt had corresponding perforations, "so that there is no question in my mind that Agent Williams took that shirt off and applied it to Agent Coler's arm." Because of the gunpowder on Williams's palm and the broken fingers of his right hand, Dr. Bloemendaal concluded that Williams, in a last defensive gesture, had raised his hand in front of his face and that the muzzle was put right up against it; passing through the hand, the bullet expanded, blowing a big hole in the mouth and nose area. "That hole measured roughly two inches long and roughly one inch wide," said Bloemendaal, displaying the photographs to the jury. "Involved the upper lip, the nose, the cheek here, and it is just a big hole where a loss of tissue is there. It is a deep hole and you can see down into it a ways." This wound was immediately fatal. Then the gunman finished off the dying Coler, who, to judge from the blood splashes, was lying face up beside the car, in all probability unconscious. The first shot, grazing the forehead, was too high to kill him outright, and apparently realizing this, the gunman shot him through the head a second time—an unnecessary precaution since, in Dr. Bloemendaal's opinion, he would have died of massive hemorrhaging from his first wound "in a matter of minutes."

At least as damaging to the defense as the gory photographs was the testimony of two witnesses who had been members of the AIM group at Oglala. ("I didn't know Norman's last name even when I got to Cedar Rapids," Nilak says. "So when I saw the witness list, saw Wish and Norman from Arizona, I couldn't believe it. I said, It's *got* to be them! But I still couldn't believe it. Wishie wasn't that strong, but Norman was; when *he* got up there on the stand, it tore me in half. I love Norman, I'm always gonna love him, you don't stop loving somebody, but . . ." Nilak's voice trailed off unhappily, and she squinted. "It's scary what they can do to people, what they *did* to people.")

The first to testify was Wilford Draper, aged nineteen, who describes himself somewhat wistfully as a silversmith and painter, "self-employed in the arts and crafts." He stated, among other things, that at Oglala he had not lived down at the camp because "Leonard Peltier was carrying firearms with him" and he was "afraid of Leonard Peltier." On the morning of June 26, said Draper, he had seen Peltier leave the camp in the red-and-white van about 9:00 a.m.; he did not see the van again until it returned to Tent City around 1:30 or 2:00, after the shooting was all over. He also declared that Peltier, Robideau, and Butler had been absent from the camp when the shooting started; that they habitually carried the very weapons that the government ballistics people now claimed to have linked to the killings; and that, on the second night of the escape, Peltier had said just what was needed to establish the premeditation required to convict these men of first-degree murder: "That night we were walking to Morris Wounded's house I heard Dino and Leonard and Bob talking about the agents. Leonard said something like 'I helped you move them around the back so you could shoot them.' Maybe he was talking about Butler and Bob. I don't know who he was talking about that night."

Unlike all other Indian witnesses for the prosecution, Draper did not hesitate to supply the names of Indians who gave help to the fugitives on the escape, relating at one point: "We walked from the scene of the murder, from the tent area, to Noah Wounded's house. From Noah Wounded's house we walked to Morris Wounded's house a mile north of Pine Ridge. And from Morris Wounded's house, Luby and her husband took us in their car to Bear Runner's residence in Porcupine." While he was at it, he also implicated Jimmy Eagle's brother Leon as one of the horsemen who had given them directions during the escape, and identified Ted Lame as the shirtless man met on Highway 18 who "took us to his uncle, Noah Wounded."

Under cross-examination by the defense, "Wish" Draper acknowledged without hesitation that he had lied to the grand jury in January and also as a prosecution witness in this trial; that when he had been apprehended in Arizona in January, he had been thrown against a car, then handcuffed and strapped for three hours in a chair while being threatened with a first-degree murder charge, until he finally agreed to supply useful testimony about the killings; that before the trial, he had told the defense attorneys that Peltier, Robideau, and Butler were all in camp when the shooting started; that he knew little or nothing about guns; and that most of his damning testimony on this subject was based on instruction from the FBI agents at the time of the grand-jury hearing, and also by Assistant U.S. Attorney Robert Sikma.

Q: Who told you that it was not a Thompson?
A: Sikma.
Q: He told you that it was an AR-15? Didn't he?
A: Yes.
Q. And that is where you got the information from, isn't that correct?
A: Yes.
Q: Did he tell you the names of all the other guns as well?
A: No. Some of the agents did at Sioux Falls when I was testifying.

Draper also said that the FBI had promised him exoneration on the ResMurs charges as well as an education and a new start in life in return for his cooperation; since he now claimed that he had been hiding in the woods during the shoot-out, the establishment of premeditation was the most useful contribution he could make.

> Q. It is your expectation after you have finished testifying here that any legal problems you have in the criminal area will be taken care of, is it not?
>
> A: Yes.
>
> Q: I have no further questions.

Here Lowe took over from William Kunstler.

> Q: Mr. Draper, I ask you this carefully. Look at the jury if you choose. I would like to ask you if you can give the jury any guidelines for determining when you are telling the truth and when you are lying.

Norman Brown, brought to Cedar Rapids as a prosecution witness, had tried to get in touch with his former comrades. "They took me to a courthouse, and I asked this one officer, Can I give Dino and Bob some medicine? What kind of medicine? Peyote. I told them it's not drugs, I told them it's medicine. They wouldn't let me do that for them. They started making fun of me then. They always made fun of me. They always made fun of my scars and the sun dance."

The young Navajo, who was obviously proud that he had sun-danced with his friends Leonard and Dino, related his impressions of the shoot-out, acknowledging that all of the AIM men and boys except Wish Draper had been involved in shooting at the agents, and that Leonard Peltier had been fast-firing a weapon that "looked like an M-16." Although admitting that he did not know where Peltier was when the shooting started, he placed none of the suspects closer to the agents than the line of junked cars on the slope near the Y-crossing below the green shack, at least one hundred fifty yards away—almost as far away, in fact, as the cabins from which the other Indians were firing—and in nothing he said did he implicate the defendants in the final execution of Coler and Williams. In fact, he denied what he had said to the grand jury—that he had seen the three down near the agents' cars and that later he had heard three shots. No, Brown said now, he did not even learn that the agents were dead until days afterward, when the group arrived in Porcupine.

The boy's testimony also made it clear that although the AIM camp was aware that attack from goons or the FBI might come at any time, and had therefore posted guards, the people in the camp that morning were taken by surprise by the noise of shooting; at no time, he said, had he ever heard any talk of "ambush." Nor had he heard the incriminating exchange between the three defendants on the second night of the escape as recounted by Draper, even though the fugitives, moving through the dark, had remained close together. Since Draper himself said he had heard no talk of "ambush," the evidence of premeditation in the killings hung precariously on that one vague and unsubstantiated scrap of conversation that he claimed to have overheard on the escape. Therefore, the defense expected that the firsthand witness to the killings, whose affidavits had been used a few weeks earlier in the Vancouver hearings on Peltier's extradition from Canada, and who had also implicated Robideau and Butler, would now be put on the stand to clinch the case.

By a curious coincidence, this crucial witness was none other than that Myrtle Lulu Poor Bear who had been "supplied" by the FBI to the state of South Dakota as a prosecution witness against AIM leader Dick Marshall in the killing at Scenic; as in Marshall's case, she had claimed in her Peltier affidavits that she had been Leonard's confidante and girl friend. But during discovery procedures in this trial, the defense had learned of the existence of an earlier affidavit in which this person stated that she had left Oglala the day before the shoot-out and was therefore not a firsthand witness after all. Since this affidavit was in exactly the same format as the others, the defense meant to demonstrate that it, too, had been prepared for use in Vancouver but was then withdrawn in favor of the later versions.

At the last minute, the prosecutors decided not to call Myrtle Poor Bear as a witness. The defense team, which was all prepared to blast her testimony to pieces, was incensed:

> MR. KUNSTLER: They don't want to call her because they know she is a fake, but they have put us in the position of having worked all weekend on this witness and I think they should be required to call this witness to the stand. This is part of the offensive fabrication.

MR. SIKMA: She is not a fake. . . .

MR. KUNSTLER: Put her on the stand and we will show you. She is an FBI fake. Just as they did in the Means-Banks trial. That is why they are reneging about calling her.

MR. HULTMAN: You have seen the record and what the record shows.

MR. KUNSTLER: They know it is a fake, too. Part of our defense is fabrication by the FBI. That is why this witness becomes so crucial. That is why they don't want to call her.

MR. HULTMAN: I object to this. There is no showing of any kind. It is a bald statement of counsel and we have been getting—

MR. KUNSTLER: Put her on!

But the U.S. attorneys would not produce Myrtle Poor Bear, and they also withdrew the personable rapist Marvin Bragg and John Stewart, a.k.a. Daryl Blue Legs.

Despite the letter to his estranged wife in early May saying that he was in the Rapid City jail doing time for his AIM brothers, Stewart had informed Agents Price and Hughes on May 14 that at about 8:00 a.m. on the morning of the shoot-out, Leonard Peltier, Jean Day, the Butlers, and "an Indian male I know only as 'Wish'" had come to Dorothy's residence in Oglala Housing.

> Peltier was wearing an unknown type of pistol in a shoulder holster. They asked for food, so I and my wife . . . fed them. These individuals then took a bath in my house. These individuals left about 10:00 a.m. or 10:30 a.m. and indicated they were returning to their camp at the Jumping Bulls. These individuals left in a red and white van, and I observed Leonard Peltier driving this van. About five minutes after Peltier and his group left Jimmy Eagle came to my residence driving a white car, a 1959 or 1960 Chevrolet. Eagle asked where Peltier and them guys went. Eagle bragged around and said, "You people should get ready, something is going to happen." Eagle then laughed. Then Eagle left in this white Chevrolet and indicated he was going to the camp at the Jumping Bulls.

Later that day, Stewart said, while driving toward Pine Ridge with his former wife and son, he was waved down by an Indian on horseback who told him that some "boys" who were down there in the bushes needed a ride out of there; shortly thereafter, he drove Peltier, "Wish," the Butlers, and a young Indian named Cris Westerman to Noah Wounded's house, and six days later, on July 2, he drove the same five people from the Bear Runners' place in Porcupine to Crow Dog's Paradise on the Rosebud Reservation. During this drive, Stewart related, Peltier mentioned that his gun had jammed during the shooting, and Westerman said his rifle got so hot that he burned his hand on the barrel; Peltier said, "That pig didn't have a chance," and Westerman said he didn't think any of the Oglala people would turn them in.

Perhaps because much of this account conflicted sharply with the accounts of his fellow witnesses, Draper and Brown, the U.S. attorneys decided against using Stewart, whose effectiveness might have been compromised in any case by his most recent trouble with the law, caused by the rape of a Pine Ridge woman the previous winter. Instead, they produced a white man named James Harper, who had shared a cell in the Cedar Rapids jail with Dino Butler and five others. "My occupation is shoemaker," Mr. Harper said. "I am presently being held on a fugitive warrant from the State of Texas and prosecution in Wisconsin on theft by fraud."

Q: Did Mr. Butler discuss with you the events involving the summer of 1975, and the killing of the FBI agents? . . .

A: He said he was afraid that Jimmie Eagle was going to be a witness against him and a man named . . .

Q: Did he mention any other witnesses?

A: Norman Brown, Norman Charles, Myrtle Poor Bear, a guy named John Stewart. . . .

Q: What if anything did he say he would do if he confronted these witnesses?

A: In his words, exactly, he said he was going to waste them.

Q: Did he tell you in any way about who would take care of you if you assisted in—

A: Yes. I asked him, you know, about money and finances and he said that he wasn't really concerned about money, I wouldn't have to be either, he had a lot of people behind the AIM movement that were well off, moneywise, and influencewise, and he mentioned a man by the name of Avidarius [Abourezk] or something to that effect, he said that this was the son of a powerful politician. . . .

Q: Did he speak about the events themselves, about the date that the FBI agents were killed?

A: Yes. He said that on the night of June 25th Wilford Draper had come to the Jumping Bull Hall residence and let it be known that FBI agents and another Government agent had stopped them and questioned them concerning Jimmie Eagle's whereabouts, that they had a warrant for his arrest and Draper told Butler that they could expect them to come to this Jumping Bull residence to seek his capture. Butler said they had a meeting, the brothers, and some members of the AIM movement. He named a few. Norman Charles, Norman Brown, Leonard Peltier and some other Indian brothers were at a meeting and they decided when and if the agents did come to apprehend Jimmie Eagle they were not going to let it happen without fighting. They were tired of being harassed and nobody was going to be taken off the reservation without first putting up a fight, which led into the incident of June 26th. He said they posted a spotter up by Highway 18 and one over by Oelrichs, walkie-talkies. . . . These spotters were instructed to let them know if any Government cars or suspicious vehicles were seen entering the Jumping Bull Hall residence, let Butler know by walkie-talkie and they would prepare their show of force and this is what happened around 11:30. The spotter up around Highway 18 said agents' cars was approaching, two of them. He said it was a 1972 Chevrolet and a green Rambler, I believe, and they each had an agent in the car. They got ready for them, put their guns out the windows and when the agents drove in with the car, into the area, one of them got out of the car, one of them was speaking on the mike, they were pulling up to this area and one of the brothers panicked and opened fire and the agent hollered he was under fire and they needed assistance, and everybody started firing at them.

Q: Did he say what happened?

A: Yes. He said that after numerous rounds of ammunition had been fired at the agents that one agent was hit and knocked down. I believe he was—Butler said he was hit in the head and the second agent was hit and knocked down and after both of them were rendered helpless they went out, he and the other brothers, and approached the agents down, and still conscious to an extent, and that this agent had pled for his life by saying "I have friends who are Indians," and, "I have a family. I don't want to die." Butler said, "We wasted him anyway." That after they had done this they searched the cars and retrieved a weapon out of the trunk, an agent's .357 and a SWAT jacket, I believe he referred to it as, and that they returned to the house. Upon returning to the house they again loaded their weapons and got ready for anyone else that might come into the residence. . . .

Q: Did you have any conversation with Butler about the type of area, as far as the terrain is concerned?

A: Up to that point I hadn't talked to him about the terrain, no. He did bring up the terrain later when I asked how they were able to get away without being seen by the agents there and he said they were able to effect their escape by the knowledge that Edgar Bear Runner gave them as to where the agents were and they went down a ravine, creek bed, and some tree lines and that during the course of this another Indian identified to me as Leon Eagle had come on horseback and gave them additional information on escape plans and brought food in, by horseback.

Q: Did he state about how many people were at the area at the time of the shooting?

A: Government agents or Indians?

Q: People that were with him.

A: At the time of the siege when they were shooting against the agents, from talking to him, I would say probably 15 or 20. By name there was eight or 10 identified to me.

Q: Did he mention the fact that there were people other than men there?

A: Yes. He said there were a few sisters present.

Q: Have you been made any promises by the Government in exchange for your statement?

A: Only protection for myself and my family. I haven't been made any other promises whatsoever.

Harper said he had also learned from Butler that one of the agents had come to the Jumping Bull property alone, earlier that morning, and was ordered to leave after having been told that he had no right to be there; that the group had automatic weapons; that Butler had a plan to kill Judge Andrew Bogue; that the motor home pulled over in Oregon was used by AIM for transporting weapons and explosives.

In cross-examination by John Lowe, the self-assured Harper was eager to be of service:

Q: Would it be fair to say that being in the clutches of the law enforcement agencies and the courts at this point, that you would not mind at all having some help from anybody that might be in position to give you help with regard to those charges?
A: Yes. That is correct. . . .
Q: You mentioned that you used the name Hardin to get into the Army. Is that correct?
A: That is correct.
Q: And that is the only time you have ever used that name?
A: No. I have used it several times.
Q: Told many police officers your name is Hardin?
A: Yes.
Q: And you lied to them.
A: Certainly.
Q: And you lied to them because you didn't want them to look up your record under Harper.
A: That is correct.
Q: How many times would you say you have lied to police officers with reference to your name?
A: Probably every time I have been arrested.

Similarly, when Kunstler asked him if at other times in his life he had also lied "to get something you wanted," Harper said cheerfully, "Numerous times in my life."

Like Louis Moves Camp in St. Paul, James Harper had filled in the missing pieces in the government case, including the ambush that would serve as motivation, and he also dragged in a number of people whom the FBI wished to see incriminated, or made credible. Yet as the prosecution's final witness he turned out to be a very doubtful choice. To start with, it seemed inconceivable that Dino Butler would reveal such dangerous secrets to some white jailbird and potential snitch as soon as this man turned up in his cell. (At one point during Harper's account, Butler called out, "Liar!") Also, his account collided with those of two other government witnesses, Draper and Brown, who had denied any knowledge of the presence in the camp of Myrtle Poor Bear, Harper's witness to the killings. As to the content of the story, did the prosecution expect the jury to take seriously—for example—the statement that the ambushers had a spotter with a walkie-talkie radio stationed at Oelrichs, thirty-five miles away from what Harper referred to as the "Jumping Bull Hall residence" (and well out of walkie-talkie range), when Draper and Brown had made it clear that most of the AIM people were still getting up when the shooting started? As somebody said, it was not much of an ambush if nobody was ready.

⊡

An early witness for the defense, which began on June 22, was John Trudell, who had organized the political approach of the Indian support group, including a Citizens Review Commission to present evidence that the jury might not hear. Now AIM's national chairman, Trudell was the most effective speaker in the Movement, and his wife, Tina, a young Paiute-Shoshone woman, was a leader in the fight for water rights on her own Duck Valley Reservation in Nevada.[6]

"Life on Pine Ridge was no different in 1975 than it was in 1890—it was the Wounded Knee massacre all over, except that they were taking the people out one at a time," Trudell says today. "If somebody is going to commit homicide on you, you have to shoot back; that was my opinion at Farmington in 1975. I meant that people should defend themselves, not just take it anymore; *how* they defended themselves, I left up to their own judgment of the situation. Those guys at Oglala, they were representing the same office as I was. I try not to tell people to do what I'm not willing to do myself. If we were *planning* a shootout at Oglala, I would have been there." (A few weeks after the Oglala fight, Trudell himself had been arrested in Duck Valley during the course of the water-rights dispute: "We had 'em scrambling in Nevada, you can believe that! So they had to nail us." Trudell was jailed for assault with a deadly weapon, but the charge was thrown out for want of jurisdiction. Remembering this, he laughs, exclaiming, "I was innocent, man! I got into this argument in the trading post, and the guy coming at me around that counter was a hell of a lot bigger than I was, so I just shot my gun in the air, you know, to grab his attention.")

"Indians are united in thought," Tina Trudell told the press during the trial. "They want happiness for their own people. They don't pray for new cars, but that everyone gets along together to live in happiness. . . . If we didn't have technology, we wouldn't need it. Technology has brought with it pollution, competition, nuclear waste, greed. . . . It has bred . . . people whose only concern is their check." For her two children and a third not yet born, her dream was that they "not grow up in fear, that they could trust people at their word, that we would be a society of truth."

On the day of the shoot-out at Oglala, Trudell and his wife and child were returning from Norman, Oklahoma, to their home among Tina Trudell's people on the Duck Valley Reservation; hearing the news of the shoot-out on the radio ("I knew this was going to be bad trouble for our people"), Trudell had detoured north to Custer to consult with Dennis Banks. Trudell provided for the court a general statement of purposes of the Movement, whose national leaders he identified as Banks, the Bellecourts, Russ Means, and Herb Powless. Of the status of American Indians, he said bitterly, "We are statistics that everyone has heard about, the unemployed, uneducated, alcoholics, welfare recipients. We have been the study of many Congressional studies and investigations, all types of studies, but yet we as statistics still remain—our situation has remained the same for a century. So we have grouped together behind our religious beliefs, our respect for human rights, our beliefs that we are entitled to human rights as well as everybody else. Our functions have been to educate our own people and to try and educate the white Americans as to the fact that we exist yet today. I mean when you look at A.I.M., [this is] who we are. We are the descendants of Geronimo, Crazy Horse. We are the indigenous people. We are concerned about what is happening to our people now, because, you know, we don't like to be a statistic. . . . To respect the Creator we must show respect, we must respect ourselves. Too many times we have seen our people in a condition where we don't see . . . even self-respect."

> Q: Does the American Indian Movement believe in self-defense if native Americans are attacked?
> A: Yes.

Kunstler soon got down to his principal line of questioning, which was intended to expose FBI misconduct.

> Q: And who was Annie Mae Aquash?
> A: She was a 30-year-old woman from Nova Scotia, Canada, and she had been with AIM for quite a while and she was very much respected and she was close to a lot of people that were within the AIM group.
> Q: Is she alive or dead?
> A: Annie Mae is dead.
> Q: When did she die?

A: She died in February of this year.

Q: And how did she die?

MR. HULTMAN: If it please the Court, I object to this on the grounds it is incompetent, irrelevant, immaterial . . .

THE COURT: Sustained. . . .

Q: And prior to her death, did you have a conversation about David Price with Annie Mae Aquash?

A: Yes, we did.

U.S. Attorney Hultman objected again, and the testimony was continued out of the hearing of the jury.

THE COURT: Mr. Trudell, Mr. Kunstler asked you about this conversation you had with Annie Mae Aquash and the Government has objected to it on the grounds it is hearsay, and I have sustained the objection. Mr. Kunstler wants to make what is known as an offer of proof here. He wants to offer to the Court what your answer would have been if I would have let you testify. You understand?

THE WITNESS: Yes.

Q: Mr. Trudell, did you have a conversation with Annie Mae Aquash with reference to David Price?

A: Yes, I did. . . .

Q: And would you indicate for the record what she said to you and what you said to her.

A: She told me that she had been arrested at Crow Dog's and . . . Price saw her and when he saw her he shined the flashlight on her and when he saw who she was he said, "There you are. We have been looking for you," and that is all the conversation that took place there. They took them all to Pierre and she said during her interrogation by Price and another agent . . . that Price had told her that he knew that she knew who shot those agents, and that she could—should cooperate, and if she would, she would get a new identity, and she would get a new place to live. . . . She cussed at him and he told her that if she wanted to have that attitude he would see her dead within a year. . . . The last time I saw her was the first—very first part of October, I believe—in Los Angeles. She told me at the time that she would go back to court and then the next time I saw anything, I saw her on TV in Oregon, three days before she was to appear in court, and she had been arrested with Kamook Banks and Russell Redner and Kenneth Loud Hawk in Oregon and that was the last time I ever saw her. She went back . . .

THE COURT: South Dakota.

THE WITNESS: Yes. And she was still in custody as far as I knew at the time. And I got this message that . . . Annie Mae was in trouble and could I help her. I couldn't because they had a warrant for my arrest in Nevada on a charge that later was dropped. I could do nothing about it. The next time I—Dennis told me she had been shot in the back of the head. He told me this in February, about the 25th or 26th of February.[7] He told me this in California. This is when he was out on bail out there. . . . I know it was within two days or so after they had found the body and I knew nothing about that.

MR. KUNSTLER: February 24th.

THE WITNESS: I was sitting in the car with Dennis and he said, "You know they found Annie Mae—" No, he said it this way. He said, "You know that body they found? That is Annie Mae." I didn't know about a body. Then he said that . . .

THE COURT: Getting back to what she said again, about what Price told her. What was it Price told her?

THE WITNESS: He told her if she wanted to have that attitude, that— They had made an offer to her.

THE COURT: All these promises!

THE WITNESS: . . . wanted to have that attitude that he would see her dead within the year. It was not a— He didn't say he would see her charged or anything, because they couldn't charge her because she was here in Cedar Rapids at Crow Dog's trial on the day of that shooting.

A few days later, Kunstler took this matter up with Agent Price, whom some of the Indians, at least, had suspected of involvement in the killing:

Q: Do you know a woman by the name of Annie Mae Aquash?

A: I interviewed a woman who is also known as Anna Mae Pictou, Anna Mae Aquash.

Q: That is the same woman, isn't it?

A: To my knowledge it is.

Q: When did you interview her in connection with this case?
A: I never did.
Q: Did you talk to her?
A: I have talked to her.
Q: And when you talked to her was it in an attempt to get information about this case?
A: No.
Q: Did you mention this case to her at all?
A: I would have to review my interview, but I don't remember that I did.
Q: Didn't you tell her that if she didn't cooperate with you she would be dead within a year?
A: No, I did not.
Q: You never said those words to her at all?
A: No, I didn't.
Q: If you did, you would, of course, say so?
A: I didn't say those words.
Q: If you did, you would tell us here?
A: I did not say those words.
Q: I am not asking those questions. If you had made such an expression to her, a potential witness, you would admit it under oath, wouldn't you?
MR. HULTMAN: I object. The question has been asked and answered three times.
MR. KUNSTLER: He hasn't answered it.
THE COURT: Can you answer that question?
THE WITNESS: I am telling the truth, and I did not say those words and if I had said those words I would say I said those words.

At this point, Dino Butler leapt to his feet and shouted, "Say them!"

Q: Do you remember when you spoke to Annie Mae Aquash?
A: Yes.
Q: When was that?
A: I talked to the girl who identified herself as Anna Mae Aquash, I believe, on September 5, 1975. . . .
Q: And with reference to Annie Mae Aquash on that day, is it your testimony that you had no discussion with her about the shooting at Oglala?

A: I remember I was specifically interested if she could help me with the murder of Jeannette Bissonette . . .

Q: When you spoke to Annie Mae Aquash about the murder of Jeannette Bissonette, did you at any time during that discussion, discuss the events of June 26th of 1975?

A: Not that I remember.

Q: Never came up at all? That is your testimony?

A: As far as I can remember it did not come up.

Q: By the way, Jeannette Bissonette was killed on the Pine Ridge Reservation, wasn't she?

A: Yes. Three months to the day before the agents were killed.

Q: Was anybody indicted for her crime?

A: Not yet.

Kunstler established that it was Price who had interviewed Poor Bear, Bragg, and Stewart, all of whom had been withdrawn as witnesses in the trial. But when he brought up the name of Louis Moves Camp, Hultman asked if he could approach the bench. The following exchange took place out of the hearing of the jury.

THE COURT: What is this about?

MR. HULTMAN: Your Honor, this is clearly an attempt to get into the record a matter that is incompetent, irrelevant, immaterial, that has to do, from my reading of the background on the Means-Banks trial to which counsel continually keeps referring to, has to do with a matter that took place during the course of that trial that has no bearing, no competency, no relevancy to this, and serves to prejudice the jury.

MR. KUNSTLER: We want to show this man fabricated testimony. That he has suborned perjury with witnesses in Indian trials involving A.I.M. people before. That he was the principal agent that produced witnesses they don't dare use now, produced witnesses that were to be used in this trial. John Stewart, Myrtle Poor Bear, Marvin Bragg, who was one they didn't produce on the stand, and that this man is notorious for producing fabricated evidence. They have put a witness like Harper on the stand and we are permitted to show, I think, under the rules of evidence that this is the way they prepare and work on witnesses, that they deliberately suborn perjury and use perjurious witnesses.

A late surprise witness for the defense was Mrs. Thelma Hess, James Harper's erstwhile landlady, who became disturbed after reading his prosecution testimony in the paper, and got in touch with the defense.

Q: Mrs. Hess, during the time that Mr. Harper was out of custody, while he was still living at your house, and working, apparently, with your husband, did Mr. Harper have occasion to comment to you anything about this case where two Indians were accused of killing two FBI agents?

A: Yes, he did. He watched all the news, watched newspapers, constantly talked about other states that—where he heard things on them. He knew the people's names. Even briefed me on it. Even the people I didn't know. He would say, "Now listen to this," he was studying night after night, and would say that this was cool, this person would waste that person, things like that, and he seemed to be studying it and what he thought was a real cool case . . . not only on this case, on other cases. Constantly.

Q: Was he reading a book at the time he stayed at your house?

A: Yes. Something about a Manson case.

Q: The Manson case out in California?

A: Yes. Where there were a lot of murders and that.

Q: You contacted one of the attorneys for Mr. Butler and Mr. Robideau this morning, didn't you?

A: I called the Roosevelt Hotel and asked for somebody on the defense side, yes.

Q: Why did you do that?

A: Because I had been trying—well, the other day I didn't know anything about this case, and I didn't know anything about James Harper's testimony until another person asked if I had read Jim Harper's statement and I went back and found the paper and read it and in Jim's wording, and that, wasting this person and wasting that person. I recognized this, these were the things that he told me; that if he ever got picked up that he would waste somebody. He didn't care who it was, whether it was a jailer or an inmate. In fact, he said, "Hopefully I can find somebody that is a no-account in that jail, a queer or a rapist." Wouldn't make any difference whether they were wasted or not. He even told me that he would give information on anything. He said he didn't care how close a friend who it was, he was going to hurt. . . . That then he could get the Federal agents interested in the Texas case. He was going to turn state's evidence against other people. This is what his intent was. He said he would have to have attention to get people to listen to him so he could deal with them.

Q: You are here under subpoena, are you not?

A: I am.

Q: Thank you very much.

THE COURT: Do you want to cross now or wait until after lunch?

MR. HULTMAN: I would rather wait. I never knew such a person existed.

⊡

Senator Frank Church (D, Idaho), chairman of the Select Committee on Intelligence, told the court that the committee had found cases in which the FBI had released false information not only to discredit but to cause violence to targeted organizations. Next day, Crusade for Justice leader Corky Gonzalez described the national police bulletin, so oddly similar in timing and intent to the Dog Soldier Teletypes, which said that "myself . . . Corky Gonzalez, was involved in setting up terrorist groups in association with A.I.M. . . . to kill a cop a day on July 4th, and I was in custody of a rocket launcher, rockets, M-16s, and hand grenades. This went out across the country." In fact, the kill-a-cop-a-day bulletin was aired again on KWTV in Denver on July 1—two weeks before the Cedar Rapids jury reached its conclusion—and on national television the next day.

On the basis of the Dog Soldier Teletypes and other evidence, the defense now wished to subpoena FBI Director Clarence Kelley.

MR. KUNSTLER: This is a very complex issue of how COINTELPRO—

THE COURT: Come to the bench.

(Out of the hearing of the jury the following proceedings were had:)

THE COURT: What is your theory on this?

MR. KUNSTLER: . . . Harper's testimony . . . is the kill-a-cop-a-day situation. That is the direct tie. . . . The counterintelligence program of the FBI which infiltrated many of these groups was a program to destroy the American Indian Movement . . . [with]

deliberate provocation, discreditation, creating situations where you have confrontations and pushing them, and all this was done with the cooperation with local police by the FBI. . . . We think it is directly leading to the 26th of June, 1975.

MR. LOWE: . . . This ties in with evidence where Clarence Kelley admitted, or the FBI, at least, admitted in the Church report they had deliberately planted false information, let's say about the Black Panthers in Chicago. Tell the police there were weapons, dynamite, and grenades at a certain location. Warn them to go in with no knock, and maximum surprise, so that they wouldn't sustain casualties, knowing that the information was completely false . . . to create confrontations, shootouts and intragroup rivalries, deliberately planting false information.

We believe . . . the agents in this case were given that kind of preparation for the group staying at the Jumping Bulls. That is why the map with the bunkers written on it, part and parcel of this psyching up. They were thinking there was an armed camp, perhaps thinking they were planning ambushes and all kinds of things. When any agent had any contact with these people they would shoot first at the slightest sign of hostility and ask questions later. . . .

MR. KUNSTLER: The agents said they believed it, on the stand. I think it was Gary Adams or Hughes. They believed that the whole warrant situation was set up to lure them in so they would then be shot. Look at it, the false reports to the police. To lure in agents and law enforcement so they could shoot one a day in every state in the union. I know it is far-fetched and crazy, the things they talk about, but that is what the police believe.

You will remember from the testimony in this record that Ron Williams was following a truck and he said that the truck was filled with armed Indians, and I think that is pretty clear how the confrontation began here, because the agents are psyched out by this program. I think the American Indian Movement is psyched out. So are the Brown Berets, Corky Gonzalez's group, and this is part of a long range plan. Mr. Kelley admitted it did not end in 1971. He admitted that to the Church Committee. It goes on now. It is all part of the same plan.

Judge McManus, like Judge Nichol, had initially been sympathetic to the government's case; he was now so suspicious of the FBI's performance that he granted the motion to subpoena Kelley, the first Director of the FBI ever to serve as a witness in a court trial. Director Kelley, just three weeks after AIM had been singled out for Bureau attention in the FBI's *Domestic Terrorist Digest,* expressed surprise that his men should regard AIM Indians as "terrorists." "It is my very definite knowledge," he said, "that the American Indian Movement is a movement which has fine goals, has many fine people, and has as its general consideration of what needs to be done, something that is worthwhile; and it is not tabbed by us as an un-American, subversive, or otherwise objectionable organization."

Asked if there was one shred of evidence in FBI files to support the Dog Soldier Teletypes, Kelley answered, "I know of none. I cannot tell you." Depending on his emphasis, this answer is somewhat ambiguous, like David Price's "I did not say those words." A few months earlier (March 17, 1976), Kelley had announced that a "search of our central records reveals no information concerning the establishment of counter-intelligence disruption programs against the American Indian Movement," which was still reeling from the disruption caused by Douglass Durham, and might well have suffered bloody retribution had the Dog Soldier Teletypes been taken seriously.

In regard to COINTELPRO, Kelley stated that this program had been terminated in 1971, although the Church Committee had concluded that FBI counterintelligence was still going on; as is evident from the Dog Soldier Teletypes as well as from Gonzalez's testimony, only the name "COINTELPRO" had been discontinued.

Mr. Kunstler pressed Mr. Kelley about the paramilitary operation that the FBI search on the reservation soon became:

> Q: What I'm trying to refer to is that agents, and there has been testimony in this record, agents on the Pine Ridge Indian Reservation have, among other things, M-16's, automatic weapons, they have bullet proof vests, there are Army type clothes issued, jackets and so on. That is somewhat different than agents normally have in, say, Cedar Rapids, or New York or Chicago, isn't it?
>
> A: Yes. That is different.

Q: And that is due . . . to the fact the reservation is essentially considered to be more dangerous than Cedar Rapids, Iowa?
A: More dangerous perhaps to FBI agents, two of whom have been slain.
Q: Hundreds of native Americans have been slain, too, haven't they?

Here Mr. Kelley lost his composure, and his voice rose:

A: There have been many Americans slain but two FBI agents were slain, too, and I think they have reason to be really concerned about their own lives!
Q: One of the reasons for equipping them this way is that there is a fear that strangers who come into isolated areas on the Pine Ridge Indian Reservation who are not known to the people there, might themselves come under attack out of fear. Isn't that correct?
A: I don't care who it is that comes in! If they are threatened they have the right to protect themselves!

Having made the defense attorney's point, Director Kelley was excused without further questions.

⊡

In his summation for the defense, John Lowe reminded the jury that Wish Draper's damaging account of the alleged conversation between Peltier, Robideau, and Butler during the escape from Oglala was the only firsthand testimony they had heard that these three had killed the agents, and that it should be considered in the context of Draper's other statements, which had been shown to be coached or fabricated: "The Government desperately needed some kind of a statement like the one attributed to Leonard Peltier on the way to Noah Wounded's. Their case was almost non-existent without that. Harper, perhaps, would substitute. We destroyed Harper. I don't think there is any question [about that] in anybody in the courtroom."

Lowe also pointed out that there was very little meaningful evidence against Butler, Robideau, and Peltier that did not incriminate the younger men as well. In his opening statement early in the trial, Lowe had said:

> The closest Mr. Robideau and Mr. Butler had been placed by any of the witnesses is 200 yards away by some vehicles and that is Norman Brown who said that they were taking up defensive positions there and firing. . . . In fact, I think that it is fair to say the evidence of the Government shows . . . if at all, that Norman Charles or Joe Stuntz were the ones that were on the scene when the shooting started and if anything, those two people were involved. And I point out Norman Charles is not even an indicted person in this case.

In his summation, he took up this point again:

> Two very important characters in this case are Mike Anderson and Norman Charles, and you haven't heard much about them from the Government for reasons known best to the Government. They are not charged. Apparently they are teenagers that were on guard up by the houses, the white houses there, and had weapons with them, apparently, and there has been testimony given they were firing.

In his own summation, William Kunstler also turned to this troubling point: "When you consider possibilities and probabilities, think of the fact that Norman Charles was found in the car in Wichita. . . . Think of Joe Stuntz, he had the FBI jacket on, and think also that Mike Anderson was also in . . . that car in Wichita and was the one who, according to Government witnesses, had the .44 Ruger with him. . . . There is virtually no evidence on how these agents died."

Prosecutor Hultman acknowledged that the final sequence of events remained unknown:

> What happened next? There is some question and unfortunately nobody knows. . . . I think it is almost incredible to think that two agents down there in the middle of an open field with a pistol and shotgun are going to take on people up here in this woods and houses. If that is a reasonable conclusion, you certainly draw it.
>
> What was then seen? Robideau and Butler are coming down this road and they have weapons. We still don't know where Mr. Peltier is. But then the eyewitness said he saw the three of them. Where? Right there. And what were they doing? They were firing rapidly. That is the exact words of this witness. It is interesting to take a

> look from that point to this point with the weapons that these men had, with the weapons that when they get back here they clearly do have, and to draw any conclusion but to the fact that at this moment there were three men, some of which were semiautomatic weapons, there were four here that we know of, and that with the pouring of the fire into the two men in the open, with the most guns available, with two pistols and a rifle and a shotgun, and I say to you, from that point on if there was any question up to that time, there is not much question of any self-defense going on from that point forward. The only question of any self-defense going on at that point is two men trying to save their lives!
>
> So I say to you, if there was any question in anybody's mind at any time during this trial as to whether the elements of this crime were proven, it is at this point in time that somebody, and that is two agents, have been murdered in cold blood, because at that time they couldn't even defend themselves. . . . They didn't go somewhere else. They were at their cars trying to the best of their ability to stay alive.

Despite his remarkable use of the language (Lowe had referred to it irritably as "gibberish," and a number of witnesses were unable to make head or tail out of his questions), Hultman had made some telling points. No one could doubt that the defendants had participated in shooting at the agents; that the agents had been seriously outnumbered; that somebody approached and killed two wounded men, at least one of whom was no longer able to defend himself; that the armed group of which the defendants had been leaders was seriously implicated by its possession of the dead men's weapons. With all these points clearly established, the prosecutors (and the FBI) felt they could not lose. But in its eagerness to establish premeditation and thereby exact the maximum penalty, the government counted too much on the doubtful testimony of Draper and Harper. It *did* seem incredible, as Hultman said, that the two agents would take on a whole compound full of Indians unless they had no choice (or unless an important piece of the story was still missing); yet the "ambush" theory of the killings seemed incredible, too, even with the kill-a-cop-a-day scenario and Harper's tale thrown in.

The government's circumstantial evidence against the two defendants was also tenuous, despite the bureaucratic paper storm that whirled it up. The only fingerprint of any significance—a print of Bob Robideau found on the driver's-door handle of Williams's car—merely confirmed what the defendants themselves had never denied, that they had moved Williams's car down to the camp by the creek. As for the weaponry, it was established that the .44 Ruger was the source of the bullet fragment found in Williams's side; it was not the death weapon, however, nor was it made clear to anybody's satisfaction who had actually used it during the shooting. As for the AR-15 taken from Robideau's burned car outside of Wichita—and singled out at Peltier's extradition hearing, a few weeks before—the FBI had suggested that although it was too damaged to be test-fired, it could be linked by a less definitive test to the controversial .223 shell casing theoretically ejected during the killings into the open trunk of Coler's car. The ballistics evidence, in short, was a lot more notable for quantity than for quality.

Even if the jury had decided that Butler and Robideau had participated in the executions, there was still the intricate question of self-defense. On July 11, Judge McManus, instructing the jury on all pertinent matters affecting their decision, emphasized the law on "self-defense," pointing out before he did so that the term "deadly force" means force that is likely to cause death or bodily harm.

> In order for the defendant to have been justified in the use of deadly force in self-defense, he must not have provoked the assault on him or have been the aggressor. If the defendant was the aggressor, or if he provoked the assault upon himself, he cannot rely upon the right of self-defense to justify his use of force. One who deliberately puts himself in a position where he had reason to believe that his presence will provoke trouble cannot claim self-defense.
>
> The circumstances under which he acted must have been such as to produce in the mind of a reasonably prudent person, similarly situated, the reasonable belief that the other person was then about to kill him or the Indian women and children or to do them serious bodily harm. In addition, the defendant must have actually believed that he or the Indian women and children were in imminent danger of death or serious bodily harm, and that deadly force must be used to repel it.
>
> Even if the other person was the aggressor and the defendant was justified in using force in self-defense, he would not be entitled to use any greater force than he had reasonable grounds to believe and

> actually did believe to be necessary under the circumstances to save his life or avert serious bodily harm.
>
> In determining whether the defendant used excessive force in defending himself or the Indian women and children, you may consider all the circumstances under which he acted. The claim of self-defense is not necessarily defeated if greater force than would have seemed necessary in cold blood was used by the defendant in the heat of passion generated by an assault upon him. A belief which may be unreasonable in cold blood may be actually and reasonably entertained in the heat of passion.

In its five days of deliberation, the jury informed Judge McManus twice that it was "hopelessly deadlocked" and wanted to quit without coming to any decision. A defense motion for dismissal of the charges was fought hard by the prosecution, which was confident that it simply could not lose. Refusing to declare a mistrial, McManus sent the jury back to think again.

Kunstler and Lowe became convinced that the jury would remain deadlocked and that a mistrial would eventually be declared, but as the days passed, they grew uneasy. The Indians, on the other hand, seemed confident that all would go well. "The last time I saw Anna Mae in California," Trudell remembers, "she talked a lot about the rain, and how much she liked it, and how she would always visit me through the rain. Later I realized that she knew she was going to die, but there was something else that became clear at the Greenwood sun dance which I went to during the trial; it rained there while I was sun-dancing, and in that rain, Anna Mae was telling me that Dino and Bob were going to be set free." Also, the defendants had received word from Selo Black Crow and the young medicine man Sam Moves Camp that if there were four thunderstorms while the jury deliberated, all would go well. The first storm occurred on the day the jury went out, and the third on the eve of the verdict; when the fourth occurred early in the morning of the final day, Dino Butler, at least, went into court in the full confidence that he and Robideau would be acquitted.

On July 16, 1976, the jury came back into the courtroom; no one looked upset and a few people were smiling, which the nervous defense team took as a good sign. Then the foreman stood and announced four verdicts—two for each defendant on the two separate charges of murder. WKLDOC aide Candy Hamilton describes the courtroom as stunned and hushed after the first verdict of "not guilty" and joyous after the fourth.[8] "The entire defense table burst into tears and embraced each other," says Bruce Ellison. Kunstler was astounded by the "historic" decision, praising Judge McManus for "a mystical standard of fairness," and John Trudell granted the jurors "all the respect I could ever give anybody." Chester Butler, Dino's father, said, "If there was any justice in the world, I knew they would be found innocent. My son told me he didn't kill anybody, and he has never lied to me."

The "historic" verdict—almost unprecedented in cases of armed combat between law-enforcement officers and poor people—was completely unheard of in the case of Indians. A determining factor, as it turned out, was the testimony by Norman Brown and others about the constant dread that pervaded the atmosphere on Pine Ridge Reservation, a point confirmed by William Muldrow of the U.S. Commission on Civil Rights. "A great deal of tension and fear exist on the Reservation," Muldrow had testified. "Residents feel that life is cheap, that no one really cares about what happens to them. . . . Acts of violence . . . are commonplace. Numerous complaints were lodged in my office about FBI activities." Muldrow concluded that by the summer of 1975 conditions at Pine Ridge had become so fearful that traditional Indians as well as AIM members felt obliged to carry weapons at all times. Although the commission's report had been ignored by the Department of Justice, the jury—mostly workers from a local electrical plant who were familiar with the FBI–AIM controversy because of Crow Dog's trial in this town the year before—realized that almost any response might have been justified under the day-and-night pressure of such an existence. In the words of the foreman, Robert Bolin, "The jury agreed with the defense contention that an atmosphere of fear and violence exists on the reservation, and that the defendants arguably could have been shooting in self-defense. While it was shown that the defendants were firing guns in the direction of the agents, it was held that this was not excessive in the heat of passion." The jury did not believe that the charge of "aiding and abetting" in the killing had been established by Draper, Harper, or anybody else; it also suggested that it might have voted for acquittal *even if the direct participation in the killings alleged by the FBI had been proven*, which Bolin said that the jury never believed: "The government just did not produce sufficient evidence." Although the alleged FBI misconduct had not been a crucial factor in the verdict, the jury was unanimous about James Harper; as Bolin observed, "Not one single person believed one single word of what he said." (The disillusioned Harper was to sue the U.S. Attorney's office and the Justice Department for breach of contract, saying that assistance with his many career problems had been implicit in his negotiations with the FBI agents and Robert Sikma.)

For the U.S. attorneys and the FBI, the vote for acquittal was made all the more bitter by its obvious popularity in Cedar Rapids; before the verdict, the white community had organized a spontaneous march on behalf of the defendants, and the courtroom audience—not all Indian, by any means—burst into applause when the verdict was announced. Robert Sikma, who had spent ten months putting the case together, left the room before the reading of the verdict, and Evan Hultman sat heavily for a moment, then departed quickly. Next day, according to the local paper, "One of the South Dakota FBI agents close to the case had tears in his eyes as he walked down the federal building hall."[9]

The town seemed proud of this rebellious verdict by its hometown jury. A long-standing local prejudice against Indians, and against AIM especially, had been offset by fair press coverage and the good impression that the Indians had made, at least by comparison to the FBI and its crude police-state tactics; and the acquittal, in the words of the Cedar Rapids *Gazette* on June 19, "devastated FBI morale." Norman Zigrossi moaned, "The amount of time we spent on that case—oh God! But the System beat us."

Much credit was due to Nilak Butler and Tina Trudell, who had worked hard throughout the trial to offset the hostility in Cedar Rapids that had been pumped up by the agencies of the U.S. government. ("Nilak was very young and naive when she first showed up on the res back in '74," Bob Robideau says. "You could still see a lot of city in her. But after Oglala, she understood the threat to the Indian people, and she went to work.") "In Cedar Rapids," Nilak says, "people were really paranoid, really scared, but their attitudes *did* change. That community became a lot more aware of what is going on, and they were appalled at the illegalities in that trial. Even though the guys were acquitted, it was still not a fair trial, I still do not believe in justice for Indians within the court system of the United States. I have to look at how many people they killed on Pine Ridge, so how can we call anything much of a victory at this point? I have to look at what they are doing in the Black Hills, raping the earth. I have to look at what they are doing in the Southwest, raping the earth, killing the people. So we cannot claim victory yet. Not yet."

Robideau, serving a ten-year term in Leavenworth, and Butler, completing a two-year sentence on the weapons charges stemming from the Rosebud raid, were returned to prison. Upon his release a few months later, after the arms conviction was reversed and the "escape" charges in Rapid City had been dropped, Butler assisted the Trudells in organizing the Minnesota Citizens Review Commission on the FBI. Says a young activist who worked with them: "Dino was one of the people who put together those first hearings on the FBI in 1977, and when he testified, he looked straight at the camera for an hour and never blinked—there was no way to stop him. And people cried. Dino is incredible. He's like Dick Marshall; you know right away that he is telling the truth. He comes across as incredibly gentle. He's small, but there's some sort of spiritual strength—and I say that as a very nonspiritual person—so that you feel you're with someone very big."

"Bob and I knew we were right that day," Butler told the commission. "The Grandfathers were with us, and we walked out of the area safely with three women. We stood up against the violence of the U.S. government to protect Indian lives. We are not guilty and the people who helped us are not guilty.

"You know, I don't mourn the death of those two FBI agents. I don't say they had it coming to them, but they have been running over people down there too long. They are part of a system that has killed a lot of our people. And maybe that is the way it was supposed to be. If you believe in a god, if you believe in a creator, you know that these people aren't supposed to act that way, not supposed to come into homes, tear these homes apart, threaten little babies, search little babies, make little kids get on the ground with M-16s pointed at their heads. . . . If you believe in the Creator, if you believe in a god, you know in your heart that this ain't right. And you know that this stuff has got to be stopped, and that these people have got to be punished. They will be punished not by us, not by anybody on this earth. They will be punished by the Creator. And that's why I am here today. That's why I am walking here and that's why I am talking here. We were right that day.

"Sacred feathers, whistle bones, eagle feathers, pipes, and stuff like this, they violated these things. . . . That is why those agents died. It wasn't because we killed them, it's because *all* of those agents were being punished. They walk around and cry about me and Bob being acquitted. They say we shouldn't be acquitted, you know. That we are evil, cold-blooded killers, and they cry. They say that there was an agent walking down the halls of the federal courthouse in Cedar Rapids who had tears in his eyes. Now they are knowing a little bit about what it is to suffer. If they learn how to respect people and everything, then there need be no more suffering amongst them like that, there need be no more agents dying, Indian people dying."

CHAPTER 13

THE TRIAL AT FARGO

March–April 1977

We may have been happy with the land that was originally reserved to us. But continually over the years more and more of our land has been stolen from us by the Canadian and U.S. governments. In the 19th century our land was stolen from us for economic reasons because the land was lush and fertile and abounded with food. We were left with what white society thought was worthless land. . . .

Today, what was once called worthless land suddenly becomes valuable as the technology of white society advances. White society would now like to push us off our reservations because beneath the barren land lie valuable mineral and oil resources. It is not a new development for white society to steal from nonwhite peoples. When white society succeeds it's called colonialism. When white society's efforts to colonize people are met with resistance it's called war. But when the colonized Indians of North America meet to stand and resist we are called criminals. What could be more clear than that to treat us as criminals is a farce? We are an Indian nation and the governments of Canada and the United States and the dominant white society they represent have made war against our people, culture, spiritual ways and sacred Mother Earth for over 400 years.

Leonard Peltier (*Ojibwa-Sioux*)

The federal case against James Theodore Eagle was abandoned a few weeks after the verdict at Cedar Rapids, despite all the people, including himself, who allegedly claimed he had participated in the killings. On August 9, 1976, "Director Clarence Kelley conferred with U.S. Attorney Evan Hultman, prosecutor in the RESMURS trials. . . . Present were Associate Director Richard G. Held [and others]. . . . USA Hultman stated that the RESMURS case on James Theodore Eagle was weak . . . and all present concurred with the Director and USA Hultman that this case be dismissed, so that the full prosecutive weight of the Federal Government could be directed against Leonard Peltier."

Richard Held—now second in command of the FBI—had been promoted on July 20, not long before the vanquished Hultman had been summoned to Washington. This was the same man who in 1967, on the Rosebud Reservation, had concluded that there was "insufficient evidence" to support Jancita Eagle Deer's charges against William Janklow; he was also that Held who as SAC, Minneapolis, administered COINTELPRO activities in the region (and may or may not have signed his Christmas cards to Judge Fred Nichol), and who as SAC, Chicago, was a chief FBI observer at Wounded Knee and the first signatory on the ultimate report on "paramilitary law enforcement"; in 1974, he was made head of IS-1, the Internal Security Section, and he returned to Pine Ridge in this capacity during the ResMurs investigation, remaining on the reservation for three months, although most people never knew that he was there. An old friend of Clarence Kelley, Held was transferred from Chicago to Washington, D.C., in 1976, while his part in the FBI cover-up of its own role in the Black Panther murders in Chicago was being investigated, and in 1977 his agents were harshly criticized by the Seventh Circuit Court of Appeals for obstruction of the judicial process and other misconduct in that ugly case.[1] Held's long history of counterintelligence expertise is inseparable from his anti-AIM activities, which suggests that for the FBI any AIM case was political, just as Peltier's defenders had always said.

Throughout the Cedar Rapids trial, Leonard Peltier had simply been included in most of the descriptions of events, and no good evidence that his actions had differed in a meaningful way from those of the defendants had been brought forward; had he been tried with Butler and Robideau, it seems almost certain that he would have been acquitted. But now, because of the strange collapse of the case against Jimmy Eagle, he represented the FBI's last chance to obtain a conviction in the killings of the two agents. Knowing this, his defense attorneys fought desperately to block his extradition from Canada, while the Justice Department applied extraordinary pressure to obtain it, assisted by a thunderous report on AIM from Senator James Eastland's Senate Subcommittee on Internal Security (the same report cited by R. D. Hurd in protesting the reduction of Crow Dog's sentence), which appeared in September 1976, just prior to Peltier's appeal hearing in Canada.

In April 1976, Douglass Durham had appeared before this subcommittee, damning AIM as a Communist-infiltrated organization involved in international terrorist activities, including gun-running between the U.S. and Canada; Durham took advantage of this occasion to name Judge Frederick Nichol as a Communist dupe. Durham stated that at Wounded Knee the AIM people had hung a man from a cross and beaten him for six hours in full view of the U.S. marshals; and that AIM Camp 13 in California had been a "guerrilla camp" where George Aird had been "scalped" and dismembered. Scarcely a year after his talk of a "necessary social protest movement," Durham told the committee that AIM was "a frankly revolutionary organization . . . committed to violence . . . and has Communist ties with Cuba, the Soviet Union, and China." These opinions on AIM were so agreeable to a professional flag-waver of Eastland's stripe that the Senator did not bother to solicit any others; thus Durham's ideas formed the substance of the report. No one listened to Senator Birch Bayh (D, Indiana), who denounced his own committee for issuing a "totally unacceptable" report on the basis of "the unchallenged testimony of one solitary witness." Both hearing and report, Bayh said, "seem to have no other purpose than to discredit . . . the American Indian Movement."[2]

The prosecution and trial of Leonard Peltier took place at an unlucky time, when congressional sentiment was turning heavily against the Indians. In the East, the Passamaquoddy tribe of northern Maine was making a huge land claim based on the Indian Trade and Intercourse Act of 1790, and other tribes were making claims as well; in the Pacific Northwest, the Boldt decision in regard to the fishing-rights treaty had been upheld by the Supreme Court, causing new outbreaks of bitterness and violence. On February 2, 1976, just a few days before Peltier's capture, anti-Indian groups in Washington state, Montana, and South Dakota ("South Dakotans for Civil Liberties") had joined forces in an Interstate Congress for Equal Rights and Responsibilities (ICERR), which intended to fight what it perceived as federal discrimination against the white majority. The public outrage focused by this angry bunch was identified by Senator Mark Hatfield (R, Oregon) as "a very significant backlash that by any other name comes out as racism in all its ugly manifestations."[3]

During Peltier's appeals, Canada's Minister of Justice had presumably familiarized himself with all the evidence, including the early affidavit signed on February 19, 1976, by Myrtle Poor Bear, in which she said that she had left Oglala before June 26 (and therefore had not been an eyewitness); this contradictory document, turned up by the defense during the trial in Cedar Rapids, had been unlawfully withheld from both Peltier's attorneys and the court during the hearings in Vancouver.[4] But apparently the Minister of Justice was more impressed by the requests of his American colleagues than by the dictates of justice itself. Offering the Cedar Rapids verdict as proof that the defendant would be given a fair trial, he signed the order to return Leonard Peltier to the United States. Not until April 1978, with Peltier safely out of Canada, did a British Columbia Supreme Court judge comment, "It seems clear to me that the conduct of the U.S. government involved misconduct from inception."[5]

In 1876, fleeing to Canada, Sitting Bull had said, "What law have I broken? Is it wrong for me to love my own? Is it wicked for me because my skin is red? Because I am Lakota, because I was born where my father died, because I would die for my people and my country?" One hundred years later, from a Canadian prison, Leonard Peltier had spoken in similar terms, and now that he was being returned to the United States, his supporters recalled Sitting Bull's fate.

Peltier was removed from Vancouver to Rapid City on December 16, 1976. "They brought a helicopter right into the prison; all the people were outside on vigil, weeping," says Steve Robideau. Originally the case was assigned to the federal district court in Sioux Falls, where Judge Nichol would have presided, but when Nichol excused himself, he was replaced by Judge Paul Benson, a former Attorney General of North Dakota and a Nixon appointee, whose bias was clear two months before the trial. In January 1977, carrying out Judge Benson's warrant, the FBI broke down Angie Long Visitor's door and jailed her as a material witness, in what her lawyer, Kenneth Tilsen, calls "an outrageous violation of due process." On February 17, a few weeks before the trial, the Justice Department, having investigated the South Dakota activities of its own FBI at the request of the U.S. Commission on Civil Rights, concluded that the Bureau was conducting itself just as it should.

After a preliminary hearing in Sioux Falls, on January 14, the trial was removed by Benson to his own hometown of Fargo, North Dakota, not far north of the Wahpeton government boarding school where Leonard Peltier, at the age of eight, had his first intimate experience of racism. Fargo, on the Minnesota line, has been steadfastly anti-Indian since the Sioux uprising around nearby New Ulm in 1862,[6] and as in Vancouver and Cedar Rapids, the FBI was furnishing the local police and media with an ample supply of unsubstantiated rumors about armed Indians descending on the town to interfere with the processes of justice and perhaps with the innocent townsmen into the bargain; the citizens were counseled to lock up everything that was not nailed down, their wives and daughters included, and inevitably the twelve white jurors were impressed by round-the-clock SWAT teams of big marshals, there to protect them from Peltier's blood-crazed associates and perhaps encourage a right-thinking verdict. Carted from place to place in a bus with taped windows, the jurors were met regularly each day at the courthouse door by a SWAT team that would burst out and surround them before hurrying them inside, out of harm's way. But in general the Department of Justice avoided such heavy-handed tactics as the Dog Soldier Teletypes, having learned to its cost in Cedar Rapids that the public from which the jury would be drawn was not so stupid as it had supposed.

Although the government still maintained that the presence of the AIM camp had nothing to do with the agents' visits to the Jumping Bull land, it had decided to ease off on the "ambush theory," which was simply too lumpy for a jury to swallow. Quite apart from the unlikely premise that the Indians had set up a shoot-out in their own front yard, with three pregnant women and a number of young children living in cabins within yards of those "sophisticated bunkers" that turned out to be fallen root cellars and horse shelters, the ambush theory had been destroyed by two of its own witnesses, Draper and Brown, who established in passing that most of the treacherous ambushers were scarcely out of bed when the shooting started.

For its part, the defense abandoned the equally improbable proposal (advanced at Cedar Rapids by both John Lowe and William Kunstler) that there was no real proof of a close-up execution, that perhaps the two agents had been killed by long-range fire from unknown assailants shooting from the general direction of June Little's cabin, where a number of shell casings had been found. In fact, Elliott Taikeff, who was primary counsel for Peltier, abandoned the self-defense approach that had won in Cedar Rapids, acknowledging from the outset that first-degree murder had occurred, as opposed to a shooting that turned out to be fatal.

Mr. Taikeff, a New York lawyer who prided himself on precise use of the language, seemed much more than a match for Evan Hultman. "The general there, he really helped our case in Cedar Rapids," says Bob Robideau. "It wasn't just that nobody could understand him, it was the *way* he spoke; you couldn't keep your attention on it; and when he was done, you could hardly remember what he was talking about. When they put him on again at Fargo, we just couldn't believe it." But Hultman was much more effective at Fargo than he had been at Cedar Rapids, avoiding behavior that made him appear foolish while making the most of a "folksy" manner that comforted these very conservative rural jurors—mostly Lutherans of Scandinavian ancestry, with long faces and a long ruminative memory of the nineteenth-century massacres in Minnesota. In general, the jury seemed ignorant about Indians, or prejudiced, or both; in any case, it was openly suspicious of "East Coast Jewish radical lawyers" and their "East Coast sarcasm," which the harsh-spoken, sharp-tongued Taikeff—cool and quick as a snake with witnesses—seemed to personify. John Lowe, who assisted him, seemed less aggressive in this trial, apparently to avoid conflict with the domineering Taikeff, who often seemed less considerate of his associates than of the prosecutors and Judge Benson—so much so that out of the hearing of the jury he was called "Ellie" by his opposite number, U.S. Attorney "Curly" Hultman (who had not felt encouraged to address William Kunstler as "Bill").

In the opinion of the defense, prosecutor Hultman had both judge and jury squarely on his side. "At Fargo, they had it all under control," Bob Robideau says. "We knew they were going to get Leonard before that trial even started." His cousin Steve Robideau agrees. "The cold black spirit in that courtroom," he says, shaking his head. "I've been in many courts and I've never known anything like that; it was all the evil spirit behind that trial coming out. Even Judge Benson had to ask the marshals to go do something about the heat—all the people were wearing blankets—but they couldn't get any warmth in there no matter *what* they did."

"Leonard—well, he's a strong man," Nilak Butler says. "He's strong. He didn't think he could get a fair trial, especially after the illegal way they extradited him from Canada. And I thought, Gee, he'll be really messed up when I see him, but he wasn't. He'd joke around, you know, really high spirits. But he did not think he could get a fair trial, and he was right. The jury we had there—my God!"

After more than a year in prison, almost all of it in solitary confinement, without exercise, Peltier was pale and heavy and uncertain; at 5′11″, he was normally a husky 180 pounds, but "in December, before I left Vancouver, everyone was sending me in food, and I guess I got up to well over two hundred!" Nevertheless, he did his best to encourage his defense team—"Here was Leonard on trial for murder, and he was trying to cheer *us* up!" says Bruce Ellison, who was legal assistant to Taikeff and Lowe and who had recently met Peltier. Peltier had let his hair grow long, and he came to court in bright ribbon shirts—red, black, green, and blue—made by Indian supporters all over the country, which he wore with a bead-embroidered brown suede vest, fresh jeans, and boots. Except to wave or smile at his friends, he sat quietly throughout the trial, listening and taking notes; the only time he became upset was when Ernie Peters, who fiddled habitually with his medicine pouch, was accused by the prosecutors, then by the judge, of attempting to signal or intimidate the Indian witnesses.

As in Cedar Rapids, the AIM support group at the trial was impeccable and strict in its behavior; even Steve Robideau's "Auntie Alvina," the defendant's mother, was sent away from Fargo after she forgot herself and shouted at the U.S. marshals. And once again, the AIM support was coordinated by John Trudell, accompanied by his two children and his pregnant wife. Trudell's effectiveness was a subject of concern to the FBI:

> TRUDELL is an intelligent individual and is an eloquent speaker who has the ability to stimulate people into action. TRUDELL is known as a hardliner who openly advocates and encourages the use of violence although he himself never becomes directly involved in the fighting. . . . TRUDELL has the ability to meet with a group of paci-

> fists and in a short time have them yelling and screaming "right-on." In short, he is an extremely effective agitator.

One day during the lunch recess, with the jury sequestered and nobody around, a U.S. marshal gave Trudell an arbitrary order to leave the corridor outside the courtroom. Insisting on his rights, Trudell refused, at which point he was threatened with arrest. When the volatile Trudell told this lawman to go fuck himself, he was sentenced to sixty days for contempt of court.

Judge Benson ruled right from the start that evidence would be almost entirely limited to the events of June 26, 1975—that the suspect affidavits used in Canada, the historical background of Pine Ridge violence, the persecution of AIM by the FBI, the verdict at Cedar Rapids, together with all testimony from that trial, were inadmissible as evidence in his court. The effect of these rulings became clear with the very first prosecution witness: the defense was forbidden to impeach Agent Gary Adams for glaring contradictions in his testimony at the two trials. At Cedar Rapids, for example, Adams had confirmed his own report that a red pickup truck had fled the Jumping Bull land at 12:18; at Fargo, he denied having made that report, asserting that the only departing vehicle he recalled was a pickup driven on and off the property by Wallace Little, Sr., an hour later. Despite its emphasis in the early period of the ResMurs investigation on the significance of the red pickup truck and/or red International Scout, the Department of Justice was now pretending that this vehicle was some sort of "phantom" conjured up by the defense to distract attention from the red-and-white Chevrolet van associated with Leonard Peltier, and Benson denied all defense efforts to enter the FBI's own radio transmissions into evidence.

Reduced to discussing Adams's zeal in pursuing the Oglala suspects—he traveled to Arizona, Kansas, and the state of Washington to serve his subpoenas, although local agents could have done this for him—attorney Taikeff found himself hobbled by the U.S. Attorney's objections, which Benson sustained throughout the trial. The cross-examination of this critical witness fizzled out in an *ad hominem* interrogation that may well have evoked sympathy for the huge agent, who was visibly moved by his own account of his friend's terrified last moments.

Q: Do you have any feelings that perhaps you might have done more to assist your fellow agents on that day?

A: No, not necessarily.

Q: What do you mean by "not necessarily"?

A: I feel I did all I could.

Q: Did you at any time in the first hour that you were there make any effort to get down into that area?

A: No, I did not.

Q: Do you feel, sir, some sense that it is very important that you see to it that there is a conviction in this case because maybe you didn't do everything that you could have done on that particular afternoon? "Yes" or "No."

A: Yes.

MR. TAIKEFF: I have no further questions.

Russell Means left Fargo in disgust on the first day of the trial, after a shouting match with Taikeff over what Means perceived as his "sucking up" to the judge instead of going after Gary Adams hard enough. "You have to *hit* 'em! 'Aren't you the one who came in there without a warrant and gave that old man a heart attack by busting the door in?'[7] 'Overruled!' 'Sorry, Judge!'—but keep on *hitting* 'em! I've had eleven trials, and we won ten of 'em by taking the offensive; the only one we played defensively put me in jail!"[8]

"The only question is, did the defendant participate . . . that's what this trial is all about," Taikeff told the court. "The government doesn't have to prove first-degree murder, we concede first-degree murder." This concession was part of a defense effort to stipulate to the gory photographic evidence—permit it, that is, to go on the record uncontested rather than expose the jury to such material. But this tactic was fought hard by the skinny, dark-haired Robert Sikma, and although Judge McManus in Cedar Rapids had limited the number and display of the red and repetitious death-scene photographs, which might have unfairly prejudiced the jury, Judge Benson decided in favor of the prosecution on the grounds that the relevance of this evidence outweighed the prejudice. Therefore, although the same pathologist who testified at Cedar Rapids agreed with the defense that a verbal description would suffice, the whole set of photographs was brandished before the jury over and over, to make sure that as much blood as possible was wrung from these awful exhibits. In addition, a second expert from Los Angeles, Dr.

Thomas Noguchi, ran the jury through the whole raw business one more time.[9]

The next major witness—and the one whose testimony did Peltier the most damage—was young Mike Anderson, who had been arrested by Gary Adams in Albuquerque on February 1 for violation of his Wichita probation. Held in reserve for Peltier's trial, Anderson's testimony was apparently designed to replace that of Norman Brown, which had been sworn to on the Bible before the grand jury, then recanted on the sacred pipe at Cedar Rapids.

Speaking throughout in a dull, unhappy way, the desperate and badly frightened boy said "I don't know" as often as he could get away with it, and contradicted himself, as well as Draper and Brown, over and over. Before the shooting, he related, he had gone up the hill to have breakfast at the Little cabin, and while he was up on the roof, on watch, the red-and-white van that had left the AIM camp earlier that morning returned to the property, pursued by the two agents; the three men in the van, he said, were Peltier, Joe Stuntz, and Norman Charles.

Q: The three came back in the red and white van you say?

A: Yes.

Q: And what if anything happened following their coming back in the red and white van? Just tell us in your own words.

A: They stopped over at Little's place and started talking; and I was sitting on top of the roof and then those two FBI agents' cars were coming. So they all hopped in the van and went down the hill. . . .

Q: All right. And it was at that time you say that you saw the FBI cars come; is that right?

A: Yes.

Q: And what if anything took place at that time?

A: He just asked June Little if Jimmy Eagle was around.

Q: And what if anything then happened?

A: Well, I guess they seen the orange pickup going down that way and they followed it.

Q: Now, when you say "orange pickup," is that the red and white van to which—

MR. LOWE: Objection, Your Honor. That's objectional, it's an outrageously leading question and I object and ask that the jury be instructed, and counsel be admonished. He knows very well what he's doing.

THE COURT: The objection is sustained. . . .
Q: (By Mr. Hultman) Mr. Anderson, tell us what the car was—
A: The orange and white and red and white van, that was going down the hill.
Q: (By Mr. Hultman) And had you seen that car before?
A: Yes.
Q: And whose car was that?
A: Leonard Peltier's.
Q: All right. Who was in it at this particular time?
A: Peltier and Charles and Stuntz.
Q: All right. Now, where did they then go?
A: Down the hill.
Q: And where did they go from there?
A: They parked beside the fence.
Q: All right. What if anything did you see next?
A: I saw everybody hop out.
Q: And what if anything did you see next?
A: FBI agents went down the hill.
Q: All right. What if anything did you see next?
A: I don't know.
Q: Did you hear anything?
A: Yes.
Q: And what did you hear?
A: Gunfire. . . .
Q: All right. Did you, what if anything did you do next?
A: I just ran back around and went back down to Tent City.

At "Tent City" (which had never been called that by its inhabitants), Anderson grabbed a rifle and returned to the white house, from where he witnessed the same scene described by Norman Brown to the grand jury but repudiated at the Cedar Rapids trial.

Q: Did you see any individuals down at the agents' cars at any time?
A: Yes.
Q: And tell us who it was you saw at the agents' cars.
A: Butler, Robideau and Peltier.
Q: And did they have weapons with them?
A: Yes.
Q: Would you tell us starting with Mr. Peltier what kind of a weapon he had?

A: AR.*
Q: And how do you know it's an AR?
A: Because of the handle.
Q: Had you seen that weapon before?
A: Yes.
Q: And where had you seen it before?
A: Down in the tents.

Anderson declared that he himself had never shot at any people, only at targets such as Jumping Bull Hall and official cars. (The other boys who testified for the government never shot at a soul, either; Wish Draper claimed he was hiding in the bushes, and Norman Brown, who was apparently skilled enough to shoot out tires at long range with a .22 and presumably could have shot at heads instead, had refuted his earlier testimony, declaring now that he and Anderson had been sent away by Joe Stuntz before the killings.) Unfortunately for Anderson, both Draper and Brown had mentioned at Cedar Rapids that on the escape, at least, Anderson had carried this group's .44 Ruger, bullet fragments from which, found in Williams's body, were the only ones definitely traced to a specific weapon. Although this testimony doesn't mean much (Brown said that Anderson had started out the day with a .22, and there was also testimony that Stuntz had fired the .44), it may have been used by the FBI agents to coerce his testimony, but more likely, as with the other young Navajos, it was simple terror that made Mike talk. During cross-examination, Anderson granted that he had been threatened while in jail in Wichita by Agent Adams, who told him that the FBI knew all about his involvement at Oglala. (SA Victor Harvey, who assisted Adams in breaking down Anderson and Brown, testified that Mike had denied for quite a while that anyone had been shooting at Coler and Williams except Stuntz and Charles; it was only later that he came to see that he might have been mistaken.)

Q: And what happened at the end of that hour?
A: Well, I was refusing to talk until Gary Adams said, "If you don't talk, I will beat you up in the cell."
Q: Gary Adams told you that?

* Armalite Corp.: this lightweight plastic Vietnam weapon and its copies have improved the U.S. balance of trade all over the Third World, and are often seen in the hands of teenage revolutionaries on the evening news.

A: Yes.
Q: And the other agent was present when he said that?
A: Yes.
Q: And did that make you afraid?
A: Yes.
Q: And did you understand that you would get beat up if you didn't give him the answers that he wanted?
A: Yes.
Q: And did you then give him the answers that you understood he wanted?
A: Yes. . . .
Q: Did you believe that Special Agent Gary Adams was capable of hurting you if you didn't do what he wanted?
A: Yes. . . .
Q: Did the FBI tell you that they would try to help you on your charges in Wichita arising out of the exploded car?
A: I don't remember.
Q: Have you ever been prosecuted on those charges?
A: No.
Q: In fact, those charges have been dropped, haven't they?
A: Yes.

Anderson mostly avoided naming other Indians against whom the FBI might wish to build a case, and he acknowledged the constructive efforts of Leonard Peltier.

Q: You had some disagreements with Leonard Peltier over the question of your drinking, didn't you?
A: Yes.
Q: Would it be fair to say that Mr. Peltier is, was trying to get people to stop drinking and was complaining when they did drink?
A: Yes.
Q: Would it be fair to say that he was trying to help you to straighten out on that?
A: Yes.
Q: Do you think he was looking out for your welfare and trying to help you?
A: Yes.

Q: Was he doing that with other people also?
A: Yes.

Again and again, the unhappy boy contradicted his prior testimony, saying that the first time he had actually seen the agents' cars was not when Coler and Williams drove up to the Little cabin but after they were dead. He also said that he believed in his traditional religion, and when he acknowledged that he had not sworn on the sacred pipe before testifying for the U.S. government, the implication was that he had felt no obligation to be truthful.

Mike Anderson's story about breakfast at the Little cabin and the pursuit of Peltier's red-and-white van by the two agents rather neatly fits the radio transmissions of Ron Williams, but it is nowhere to be found in a long affidavit of seven pages that Anderson gave to the FBI on the day after his arrest in Albuquerque on February 1, 1977, in which he reported that Peltier "didn't like me too well anyhow because I usually drank when I went to Oglala. I recall that he ran Frank Black Horse away from the camp because he drank too much"; that "Leonard Peltier left the tent area in the red-and-white van on the morning of the shooting"; that "June Little was in the vicinity of the Jumping Bulls when the shooting started"; that "I could see Peltier, Dino Butler, and Robideau standing over the Agent with rifles in their hands" (he said nothing of this kind in Wichita); that "I believe Bob Robideau drove the green car to the area of the tents"; that the escape group had been helped by Leon Eagle and Ted Lame; that Edgar Bear Runner had brought food to them while they were camped at his father's place in Porcupine.

> On the morning of June 26, 1975 . . . Dino Butler, Bob Robideau, Jimmie Zimmerman, and I, together with the girls, were getting ready to eat. We were approximately a half mile away, south of the Harry Jumping Bull residence, in the tree area. I heard about four shots coming from the vicinity of the Jumping Bull residence. I didn't know what was happening. Dino, Robideau, and myself all picked up guns and ran to the top of the hill to see what was going on.

By trial time, only a month after this affidavit was taken, this camp-breakfast account (which resembles the one given in Wichita) had been replaced by the rooftop version of events involving the "orange and white and red and white van." And this leads to another disturbing question: Did Hultman know about this prior affidavit when he elicited the second, much more damaging version from Mike Anderson on the witness stand?

Anderson was not strongly cross-examined on the critical discrepancy in his breakfast accounts. "They scared Mike, and he just lied," Ellison says. "He wasn't even where he said he was during the shooting, and we couldn't put June or Wanda on the stand to deny his roof story without implicating them. So his testimony did Leonard a lot of damage, and everyone knew it, and after the trial, Mike kind of hid out, because he wasn't too popular."

⊡

Among those who unwittingly denied the rooftop story was Wilford "Wish" Draper, who testified that Mike Anderson was in camp when the shooting began; he supported Anderson's statement that Peltier had been carrying an AR-15 on the fatal day, but acknowledged on cross-examination that there were several AR-15s around the camp. Draper also admitted that fear of goons ("people who . . . do the dirty work for the BIA police of Pine Ridge Reservation . . . all hired by Dick Wilson") and not fear and disapproval of Leonard Peltier was the real reason he had lived up at the cabins rather than down in the AIM camp. Like Norman Brown, he admitted that much of his grand-jury testimony had been false, and again he denied any knowledge of Myrtle Poor Bear.

> Q: And would it be fair to say that you continued to be worried that your own testimony might put you in a position of being prosecuted, would that be fair?
> A: Yes.
> Q: Did there come a time when the Government agreed not to prosecute you if you would testify?
> A: Yes.

Norman Brown also appeared at Fargo, much against his will. "Right after the trial at Cedar Rapids," he said later, "Robert Sikma told me that they were going to use me again—We'll be looking for you—and I told them, I don't think so. And they said, We'll be looking for you.

And I said, For what? And he said, We will be looking for you, you'll have to talk. So after that . . . I danced the sun dance at Crow Dog's, and then after that I went over to Canada, started staying there. Scared to go home because they threatened me that if I didn't talk at Leonard's trial, . . . they would . . . put me in jail."[10]

> Q: You went to the sun dance for the first time when you were 13 years old.
> A: Right.
> Q: Is there any connection between the first time you go to a sun dance and becoming a man?
> A: No, it's not. . . . You don't do that just because you become a man. We thank our Creator, we *thank* Him. Like if we offer Him tobacco or a horse or something, it's already His. We offer ourselves. We belong to ourselves but we're His children and these are our own bodies so we offer Him all we have got, offering ourselves to Him so that, you know, we can live in harmony and have a good understanding of nature.
> Q: From your contact with Leonard Peltier, would you say that he is a spiritual man?
> A: Right.

As a prosecution witness at the Fargo trial, Norman Brown acknowledged that Peltier had carried an AR-15, but he would not repeat his earlier statements that he had seen Peltier down at the death scene. When Hultman reminded him of what he had said to the Sioux Falls grand jury on January 13, 1976 ("I saw Dino Butler, Leonard, and Robideau near the car"), the boy said coolly, "Are you trying to tell me *I* saw them down there? It was the agents who said I saw them. It seems like you are calling me a liar. I have just sworn on the sacred pipe." Asked sarcastically if he had sworn on the sacred pipe before his testimony to the grand jury, Norman Brown said he had not. Brown seemed to impress the Fargo jury with his truthfulness, and the defense attorneys felt that his overall testimony as a prosecution witness in both trials did the prosecution a lot more harm than good. "Norman actually *helped* us at Cedar Rapids," Ellison says, "and he did his best not to hurt us much at Fargo." The defendants forgave Brown for his actions, understanding that he was young, frightened, and coerced; however, he is no longer considered an AIM warrior.

"Those guys surprised everybody, testifying like that—Wish, too—they seemed so strong," Jean Bordeaux remembers. "Mike and me were in Wichita jail together, shared the same mealtimes and exercise. By the time he saw me there, he had already talked, but he pretended he hadn't, and told me not to say nothing, no matter what." Jean, a young woman of twenty, paused a moment, as if reluctant to speak about her boyfriend of those long-ago June days down by White Clay Creek: "I know Norman thinks what he done was wrong, so now he's working real hard for his people." At the sun dance after the Cedar Rapids trial, at Green Grass, South Dakota, Brown "really sacrificed," as the Indians say, "piercing" and making flesh offerings to Wakan Tanka.

⊡

After appearing before the grand jury in December 1975, Angie and Ivis Long Visitor had been set free. For a time, they eluded the authorities, and they did not testify at Cedar Rapids. Ivis, humiliated because he had talked, remained in hiding, refusing to cooperate a second time, but in January 1977, his wife was seized as a material witness for Peltier's trial after FBI agents kicked her door down. This outraged Ivis's mother, Roslynn Jumping Bull. "The FBIs wanted my son to witness, but he didn't want to do it. . . . They say he has to testify. One of them told my daughter-in-law that even after the Leonard Peltier trial was over, he's going to go to jail if they ever catch him, he's not going to get away with it. . . . Right now they said Pine Ridge people are telling each other that whoever tells where my son is, they're going to get seven hundred dollars."

At the grand-jury hearing in Rapid City in November 1975, Angie Long Visitor had testified that when she went outside at the sound of shots, she saw Joe [Stuntz] and Norman [Charles] (she knew none of the last names of the outside Indians) "just laying there" by the woodpile west of her little green cabin, and that Bob [Robideau], wearing his brown cowhide vest and a dark-blue stocking cap "ski mask" with eyeholes, was standing by the old wrecked station wagon nearby. In her appearance at Peltier's trial, she said, "We seen a red-and-white van" that she recognized as a car belonging to Sam Loud Hawk and used by Leonard [Peltier], who had repaired it; this van was parked at the Y-fork in the pasture road just uphill from the line of junked cars from which (Brown and Anderson had said) Peltier, Robideau, and Butler had fired at the agents. She also said that she saw one of the agents kneeling by his car and shooting. "Me and my husband and kids ran across the field and went down to the little road that goes to the highway. . . . There were a lot of cop cars going by."

Cross-examined, Angie Long Visitor related how when she returned to the compound a few days later, she had seen one of her children's dolls in the green cabin, cut almost in half by automatic fire, and also the pictures on her grandparents' walls, shot in the face and through the heart. Although her statements had done little harm to Peltier, they did serious injury to her own self-respect. On the stand, she wept almost continually in fear and shame, her voice all but inaudible. "There were so many bullet holes in those pictures," she murmured to the court, so softly that John Lowe said he could not hear her. "There were so many bullet holes in those pictures," she repeated.

⊡

In her interview on June 28, 1975, Angie Long Visitor had mentioned a "Leonard LNU" among the people who lived down in the woods below her house; Peltier's full name headed the suspect list just three days later. The explanation for this—or so it appeared—was an extraordinary sighting made by SA Frederick Coward of the Rapid City SWAT team, the same sharp-eyed operative who would subsequently spot that "osculating" couple on the valentine in Bob Robideau's cell.

Arriving from Rapid City about 1:20 p.m., Coward had been dispatched by Adams to the Pumpkinseed house, about half a mile southwest of the Jumping Bull compound, together with Agents Skelly and Breci, the BIA SWAT-man (and off-duty goon) named Marvin Stoldt, and several other Indian policemen. In the course of the afternoon, Stoldt was alerted that four men were fleeing the Jumping Bull compound, headed for the creek. Using a telescopic sniper sight mounted on a rifle, he saw only a blur of running figures; seizing seven-power binoculars from someone else, he clapped them on these figures fast enough to identify the last Indian in line as Jimmy Eagle. At this point Coward, summoned to the window, used the telescopic sight to identify Leonard Peltier in the same group.

For some reason, Coward failed to mention any sighting of either Peltier or Eagle in his 302 report on his own activities for that day; nor does Peltier's name appear in a 302 report of an interview with Stoldt prepared by Coward and Breci two days later:

> On June 26, 1975, at approximately 3:45 PM, SA FREDERICK COWARD, JR. and MARVIN STOLDT were inside the PUMPKIN SEED residence on the north bank of the White Clay Creek at Oglala, South Dakota.
>
> While in this position, STOLDT advised that he observed four Indian males run from the HARRY JUMPING BULL's residence, traveling west and running down into the creek bottom.
>
> STOLDT at this time stated that he, with the use of his binoculars seven-power, focused on these four Indian males. Upon doing so, STOLDT stated that the last Indian male in the group appeared to be JIMMY EAGLE. STOLDT stated that this individual appearing to be JIMMY EAGLE was wearing a black shirt and black pants.

On the stand at Fargo, Coward decided that the "28" must be a typographical error, since he recollected interviewing Stoldt on June 26; at another point he said that although Stoldt had mentioned the Eagle sighting when it occurred, and that they had discussed this exciting news during a car ride later that day, he had not actually taken down Stoldt's statement until September 4—a very curious statement in itself, considering the significance of the event.

Marvin Stoldt, who later took the stand as a reluctant witness for the defense, became irritable when asked to remove his big one-way shades so that the jury could have a better look at him. Stoldt asserted that his own participation in these talks was "highly impossible"; he did not recall any car ride with Coward, nor any discussion of identifications with Coward on June 26, or on June 28, either, for the good reason that they had not seen each other or communicated in any way from the time Stoldt had left the Pumpkinseed house on June 26 until September 4. "Maybe he saw *me,*" Stoldt snarled, "but I never saw *him.*"

In stubborn unwillingness to take responsibility for anything he might or might not have said or done or seen or even thought on June 26, 1975, Stoldt responded "It's possible" or "I might have" or "That was two years ago, you know" to every question, until Judge Benson remarked with some asperity, "This witness seems to be totally unable to state definitely one way or the other!" And perhaps this Stoldtish trait of owning up to absolutely nothing, true or false, accounts for a few of the inconsistencies in the Stoldt-Coward accounts, which were not completely reconciled until September 11. On that date, Coward transcribed his September 4 interview with Stoldt, emerging with a serviceable version in which Stoldt claims that he, too, identified Leonard Peltier:

> At approximately between 4:30 and 5:00 p.m., STOLDT observed four individuals running from the rear of HARRY JUMPING BULL's house towards an open plowed field. STOLDT stated he saw all four individuals with rifles. STOLDT continued and stated he saw a tall Indian male in this group with long hair and by the way this individual was built and the way he moved and because he has seen LEONARD PELTIER in the past, thought that this was the same individual. According to STOLDT, running directly behind this individual was a person who he has known and identified as being JIMMY EAGLE.
>
> STOLDT stated that during the first statement he had given to the FBI a few days after the shooting of the Agents, he told the Agents then, one of the Agents being Agent COWARD, that he saw JIMMY EAGLE in the group that he had just identified but was not absolutely positive during the first interview. STOLDT continued and stated, But since then I have continually thought about what happened on June 26, 1975, and at this time and during this interview he was positive in his own mind that JIMMY EAGLE was the individual that was running behind the person who appeared to be LEONARD PELTIER.
>
> STOLDT, referring back to the window where he was located while the four individuals were running across the field, stated that he called Agent COWARD who was also in the house to quickly come over to the same window and observe the activity. STOLDT stated that he pointed out to Agent COWARD what he was seeing and observed Agent COWARD also look out the window at the individuals running. STOLDT stated he then left the window, went outside of the house and told Agent SKELLY what he had seen.

Before the grand jury Stoldt would declare that he had seen these running figures between 2:00 and 3:00 p.m.; now he and Coward had apparently agreed that they had seen Peltier running from the cabins between 4:30 and 5:00, although other accounts, and on both sides, including the 302 of Agent Adams, place Jimmy Zimmerman at the edge of the open field at about 3:00, well *after* the AIM group—which had already been down in the camp at least an hour—had apparently headed away toward the south, down White Clay Creek.

Apart from all the inconsistencies, the identifications raise a number of other questions. Note that Agent Adams, observing the meeting between Joanna LeDeaux and "three or four Indian males" through a similar rifle scope, made no attempt at individual description, although no more than three hundred yards away; it is an estimated eight hundred yards—a good half mile—between the Pumpkinseed cabin and the Jumping Bull compound. Just how, then, did Coward (and Marvin Stoldt) identify Leonard Peltier at such a distance, since even assuming that they knew he was in the area, there is no reason to believe that either man would have recognized him face-to-face, far less running away. Not Coward but Stoldt claimed to have seen him "in the past" (as Coward notes in the September 11 report): how was it that not Stoldt but Coward was the first to recognize him?

In any case, an expert on telescopic sights, who conducted his test in the presence of a defense attorney and an FBI agent, assured the court that he could not make out facial features at that range, even when observing a familiar person, standing still and facing him, on a bright day; Stoldt himself, using what was probably the same rifle sight, had said he could make out almost nothing until he switched over to binoculars. Yet Judge Benson scoffed at the defense suggestion that Coward's feat be tested in the field by both judge and jury, assuring the jury that the defense was wasting its time. (After the jury retired, prosecutor Hultman would tell a reporter that Coward's testimony was "totally unbelievable."[11])

Even if the jury had believed Agent Coward—and it probably did—his testimony established almost nothing, since the sighting did not tend to show that Leonard Peltier had participated in the killings or even in the shooting, but simply that he was among those on the Jumping Bull property that day. Since Peltier himself has never denied this (despite the point made by his attorneys that no hard evidence of his presence on June 26 was ever produced), one has to ask why the FBI invited doubt and even ridicule by letting this man claim to have recognized—through a hastily raised rifle scope, in summer haze—a running stranger a good half mile away.

Agent Coward described how the agents met twice every day between June 27 and June 30 to work out a consistent theory of the case, during the course of which his sighting of Peltier had been discussed. Yet Agents Waring and Skelly, who followed him to the stand, could not recall hearing Peltier's name in those first days. (SAC Zigrossi said the same thing when talking to the defense attorneys, although he changed his mind once on the witness stand.) Like Coward, Waring described the numerous conferences with his fellow lawmen to discuss suspects and theories of the case; and like Coward, he claimed, not persuasively, that a typographical error accounted for the seeming discrepancies in his own eight-page 302 of June 26. As it turned out, the *first* four pages of this document were dictated *later* (on June 30) to a different secretary, apparently on a different typewriter, as if—Taikeff suggested—Waring had revised the first part of his report to fit the scenario of Peltier's guilt that was being worked out at all these agents' meetings. It is in these controversial four pages, for example, that Waring recalls hearing Williams refer on the radio to a number of Indians in a "red-and-white vehicle"—by inference, the van associated with Leonard Peltier. No "red-and-white" vehicle had been reported by anyone else; all other listeners had heard "red" vehicle or "red" pickup, Scout, or jeep. But as in Coward's case, efforts by the defense to place this disjointed 302 into evidence were contested by the government, supported in both cases by Judge Benson, who plainly resisted the idea that one or more agents had lied: as he repeatedly made clear, it was not the FBI that was on trial in his court but Leonard Peltier.

The case for the prosecution was concluded by the Royal Canadian Mounted Police. Corporal David Golden Doll, a member of the squad that arrested Peltier at Smallboy's camp in February 1976, reported that Peltier had asked a Cree elder "to pray with him, to his grandfather and the elder's grandfather, both of them to pray to grandfathers. Following that he asked him again to say another little prayer. Following that, before he was escorted out, the elder asked him a question. He asked him what would have happened had he seen the police coming, and Mr. Peltier replied that he would have blown us out of our shoes, consequently resulting in a further question by the elder, 'Do you mean to say you would have opened fire with my grandchildren and other children present?' And he said, yes, that was his life that he was defending."

Oddly, this damaging exchange does not appear in Doll's first official report, or even in his second. In fact, it is nowhere to be found in the files of the Canadian police, nor was it used in the extradition hearings in Vancouver, despite its obvious suitability on that occasion; it turns up like a dead mouse more than a year later, during Peltier's trial. Even Lynn Crooks, the husky, balding Assistant U.S. Attorney with the bristling mustache who assembled most of the case against Peltier, appeared embarrassed that such vital and dramatic evidence had emerged in casual conversation during the lunch break, just before this witness took the stand. Like the unsubstantiated charge, made in earlier testimony, that the defendant had shot at a state trooper in Oregon; like the charge of "attempted murder" in Wisconsin, what this officer claimed he had overheard gave another dash of color to the prosecutor's portrait of Leonard Peltier as a hardened cop-killer who would murder two agents in cold blood as quick as look at them.

Corporal R. C. Tweedy was the last witness for the prosecution. "Mr. Chuck Tweedy" (as he was called by Crooks, who seems to have been on fraternal terms with all these Mounties) was one of the arresting officers who escorted Peltier from Hinton to Edmonton on February 7, 1976; during this journey, if Chuck Tweedy is to be believed, the defendant confided in this cop—whom he had never seen before in all his life—that the two agents had been killed because they had come to arrest him on the Wisconsin charges. Asked if he himself had shot the agents, Peltier told Mr. Tweedy, "No, but I know who did."

Peltier says he just chanted a simple prayer with an elder named Yellow Bird; he flatly denies the damaging remarks attributed to him by Mr. Golden Doll and Mr. Tweedy.

⊡

On April 6, 1977, after its twenty-fifth witness had appeared, the United States rested its case against Leonard Peltier. Before the defense presented its first witness, some lengthy colloquies took place at the bench as to the relevance of its proposed testimony in regard to both Anna Mae Aquash and Myrtle Poor Bear. Defense attorney Taikeff shortly accepted the prosecution position that the Anna Mae Aquash episode was "irrelevant," a concession that upset all of his colleagues. (According to one defense witness, Taikeff dominated the defense team by "bullying and snarling at the other attorneys—it was a very ragged atmosphere.") John Lowe and the others felt strongly that the fate of Anna Mae and the handling of her death, especially as it affected Myrtle Poor Bear, reflected the whole pattern of FBI misconduct on which the case for the defense was based. And this feeling was reinforced when, after considerable pressure from the defense (sustained for once by Judge Benson), Hultman finally agreed to reveal the identity of the two agents who had prepared those Poor Bear affidavits.

MR. HULTMAN: Well, your Honor, one, I resist, and two, I think the matter is now moot; and thirdly, I do not know, standing here, but I want, one, the Court to know that I resist that particular motion; and two, I feel that it is a moot matter; and three, if the Court does make such a ruling, I will, of course, proceed accordingly to make inquiry. . . .

THE COURT: I think that in fairness to the defense you should reveal the names. I don't know that it has any relevancy. . . .

MR. HULTMAN: Your Honor, what I have been able to find out at this point is that the affidavit itself was prepared—and correct me because I have not talked to Mr. Halprin; that during the period of time itself there were two agents that assisted, and I am not sure what part each of the three individuals play; but the three individuals, two in addition to Mr. Halprin, would you identify the two agents—Agent Woods [*sic*] and Agent Price.

Called to the witness stand, David Price recalled that he had first met Myrtle Poor Bear in 1974 in connection with a shooting in her home village; that he had seen her next in January or February of 1976, at which time she had been removed from home and placed in various motels for her own protection. "She was in a great deal of danger," said Agent Price, "due to the information she was furnishing us on another matter." This other matter—though Price now denies it—was apparently the Dick Marshall murder case. During the investigation of this matter, Poor Bear had "volunteered" her information about the shoot-out at Oglala. In addition to the fact that in both cases she claimed to have been confidante to the AIM murderers, there were other interesting similarities. For example, both culprits were apparently tortured by the memory of what they had done. "I'll never forget the look on [his] face," Marshall told her; Peltier revealed that his deed "makes him sick when he thinks about it." More interesting still, her stories in both cases precisely fitted prosecution theories of the crimes.

In Rapid City, on February 19, 1976, Price and his partner, William Wood, took down the first of her affidavits, which was primarily concerned with the planning phase of the ambush; for some reason, Price did not ask who the other planners were. On February 23, these two prepared the second affidavit, a word-for-word copy of the first except that the sentence "I left Jumping Bull Hall at this point and did not return" has been replaced by "I was present the day the Special Agents of the Federal Bureau of Investigation were killed. I saw Leonard shoot the F.B.I. agents." Unaccountably, the standard field report, or 302 form, for the first affidavit—there are 302s for all four of the other Poor Bear interviews and affidavits—is now missing. The following day, the witness was interviewed by Agent Edward Skelly, possibly because Agents Price and Wood were elsewhere; this was the day that Anna Mae Aquash's body was discovered. Skelly (who was never informed by his FBI colleagues that they had already interviewed this critical witness not just once but twice) was told by Poor Bear that in addition to the Madonna Slow Bear who had forced her to watch the executions, a local youth named Ricky Little Boy had been present on the scene before, during, and after the events described; therefore he must have witnessed the two killings. Yet Skelly admitted at Peltier's trial that he had never asked Poor Bear for further information on this important witness, not even a physical description. Like Price's lack of interest in who planned the ambush, Skelly's indifference to the two eyewitnesses who might have corroborated Myrtle Poor Bear's story indicates the true opinion of this evidence held not only by the agents but by the U.S. attorneys, who, far from calling Slow Bear or Little Boy as witnesses, never bothered to interview them at all.

Myrtle Poor Bear also revealed to Agent Skelly that, two nights before the shooting, when her boyfriend Leonard Peltier was absent, she had been raped by Jimmy Eagle and about eight others, including Dino Butler, all of whom wished to "get even" with Peltier, whom they disliked. (In her other case, she had confided to Agent Price that she had been raped by Dick Marshall and some of his friends.) Under the Major Crimes Act, the FBI has jurisdiction on the reservation in a rape case, but Skelly never got around to questioning Eagle or Butler, both of whom were immediately accessible, nor did he ask for the other culprits' names, although all of these rapists were presumably Oglala suspects. In fact, he made no investigation whatsoever. As he said, "She was bound and determined she was not going to give me any other information," quite possibly because no other information had been provided her.

The third affidavit was prepared by Price and Wood on March 31, following consultations with Canadian Department of Justice prosecuting attorney Paul Halprin, who wanted more details about the killings in preparation for Peltier's extradition hearings; the agents spent two days with Poor Bear in a motel in Sturgis, South Dakota, emerging with the more damaging version of the events that enabled the U.S. Justice Department to triumph in the courts of Canada.

⊡

In her statement to Skelly, Poor Bear had said that Butler and Robideau had also participated in the killings. Yet though their trial went on for two months after her evidence was presented in Vancouver, the government did not use this witness at Cedar Rapids, presumably because her testimony might be more persuasive to FBI agents and prosecuting attorneys than it would be to more objective people on a jury. And though she was listed as a prosecution witness, she was not called at the Fargo trial, either.

In his opening statements to the court, defense attorney John Lowe—who had anticipated that Myrtle Poor Bear would be called by the prosecution—had dismissed her as a "witness whose mental imbalance is so gross as to render her testimony unbelievable." Despite an FBI teletype to the Director a few weeks earlier which specified that "the Special Prosecutor considers Poor Bear an important and necessary witness and he fully intends to use her as a witness during the Peltier trial," Hultman had decided not to call her after all; as assistant prosecutor Crooks explained to her, the trial was "going all right" without her help. To add to the confusion, Poor Bear herself, who had refused at Cedar Rapids as well as at Fargo to have anything to do with the defense attorneys, decided that she was going to change her testimony.

"After she attempted to move to the defense side," Peltier recalls, "I talked to her on a phone from the next room, and asked her why she had done something like this to me. After speaking with her for a moment, I knew she did not write those statements against me." ("She is a poor, sick woman," he has said since. "I have no bad thoughts for her. She was a pawn to them, and they used her like they have used so many Indian people."[12])

Learning that the defense would call his erstwhile "important and necessary" witness, Hultman dismissed her as "mentally unstable." Furthermore, he hotly contested the relevancy of any testimony she might make in open court, a position in which he was supported by Judge Benson. "With reference to Myrtle Poor Bear," the judge said, "she not having testified in the government's case, I can see no relevance in the matter of her testimony in connection with the extradition proceeding." Benson could not or would not see that the two FBI agents who had prepared her testimony in two separate cases, and who knew her well, were at least as aware as Hultman that their witness was unqualified, and that under those circumstances their exploitation of her to ensure Peltier's extradition had been a flagrant example of the misconduct on which the defense had built its case. Having decided in the first days of the investigation that Peltier was guilty (the defense declared), the FBI had constructed evidence to fit that theory, and meant to see him convicted by fair means or foul. Once Peltier had been returned to the United States, there was no point in putting that witness on the stand, where her instability might undermine the jury's confidence in the integrity of the U.S. attorneys.

Neither Madonna Slow Bear nor Ricky Little Boy, the two people Poor Bear had named as co-witnesses to the killings, had ever heard of Myrtle Poor Bear. Madonna Slow Bear testified out of the presence of the jury that until the previous evening, on the plane from Rapid City to Fargo, she had never seen this woman in her life. And it was also out of the presence of the jury that Poor Bear told the judge that all three of the damning affidavits had been composed by Price and Wood, whom she had come to know so well that in her testimony she referred repeatedly to both men by their first names. In her pitiable account, Poor Bear admits that she had not been at Oglala after all, but at home in Allen, sixty miles away; she had never laid eyes on Leonard Peltier before his trial. Stating that AIM had promised her protection if she would simply tell the truth, she declared that she had signed those affidavits only because "Dave" and "Bill" had threatened her and her young child with harm; it was also "Dave" and "Bill" who had rehearsed her intensively for this trial in a motel room in Kansas City. Among other tactics, the agents had cited the mysterious murder of a young woman on the reservation, showing Poor Bear pictures of the corpse and suggesting that she could also be executed with impunity, since everyone would think that AIM had done it. Like Angie Long Visitor, the plump, unprepossessing Poor Bear was in tears throughout her interrogation, which at one point had to be interrupted while she regained her composure.

The questioning of Poor Bear was designed by the defense as an "offer of proof" to Judge Benson as to why this witness's testimony was relevant, and why it should be heard in open court, before the jury.

MYRTLE POOR BEAR, being first duly sworn on the sacred pipe, testified as follows: . . .

Q: What is your name?

A: My name is Myrtle Poor Bear. . . .

Q: Do you know a person by the name of Leonard Peltier?

A: No. . . .

Q: Did you ever see him in your life?

A: No.

Q: Were you ever at the Jumping Bull area on the Pine Ridge Reservation?

A: No.

Q: Did you ever live with Leonard Peltier?

A: No. . . .

Q: Last night did you tell me you were frightened?

A: Yes, I did.

Q: What were you frightened of?

A: I don't know. I am scared of the Government.

THE COURT: What was her answer?

MR. TAIKEFF: I don't know. I am scared of the Government.

Q: (By Mr. Taikeff) Did anyone from the Government ever say anything to you to make you afraid?

A: The agents are always talking about Anna Mae.

Q: What did they say about Anna Mae?

A: Oh, they just would talk about that time she died.

Q: What did they say about it? You can tell the Judge, it is all right.

(Counsel confer.)

MR. TAIKEFF: May counsel approach Your Honor?

THE COURT: You may.

(Whereupon the following proceedings were had at the bench:)

MR. TAIKEFF: Your Honor, I would ask that your Honor briefly advise her that she is under oath and that you want to hear what she has to say providing it is the truth and that she has nothing to fear by telling the truth.

She is very frightened, Your Honor. She told me last night she is afraid that she is going to be killed, and that's why she is so upset at this particular moment.

MR. CROOKS: Yes, I suspect that she *is* afraid she is going to be killed. It sure isn't from the FBI. . . .

MR. SIKMA: I spoke with this witness about a year ago . . . she was afraid to go back to her home because the people from the Wounded Knee Defense-Offense Committee had been hounding her ever since she made a statement. She testified in another case they had threatened to take her life on a number of occasions. She was afraid to go back and said that the only way that she would be able to go back is if she would agree to say that the FBI had forced her to say what she said.

MR. TAIKEFF: Why don't you indict those people instead of just talking about it? That's a serious violation of Federal criminal law. . . .

Shortly thereafter, Mr. Taikeff resumed his questioning:

Q: What did [the agents] tell you about the American Indian Movement?
A: They told me that they were going to kill me.
Q: Did Mr. Wood ever say anything about the subject of getting away with killing people?
A: I think he did.
Q: Do you recall what he said?
A: He said that they could get away with killing because they were agents. . . .

Myrtle Poor Bear was cross-examined by Lynn Crooks, who wore dark glasses. . . .

Q: Well, didn't you tell me that Bill Wood was your friend?
A: No, I don't remember. . . .
Q: Didn't you also say that Dave Price was your friend?
A: I don't remember.
Q: You don't remember having told me that?
A: No.
Q: All right. What about the interview that I had with you in Rapid City, didn't you tell me that Leonard Peltier was standing over the bodies and he was pointing the gun toward the agent who had just fallen?
A: I don't remember.
Q: Well, are you saying you don't remember or that you didn't tell me that?
A: I don't know. . . .

Q: Bill Wood has never beaten you or threatened you at any time, has he?

Can you answer that question?

A: No.

Q: David Price hasn't beaten you or threatened you at any time either, has he?

Can you answer that, Myrtle?

A: No. . . .

Q: You said earlier you didn't know Leonard Peltier before walking into the courtroom, isn't that right?

A: Right.

Q: Myrtle, why was it when you walked into the courtroom that you gave Leonard Peltier a big smile?

A: I don't know.

Q: You just picked him out as a person you wanted to smile at?

A: Probably.

Q: Has anybody threatened to do something to you if you did not change your story?

A: No.

Q: Nobody even suggested it?

A: No. . . .

Q: Why were you signing these affidavits?

A: I don't know.

Q: Well, did Bill Wood threaten to harm you or hurt you if you didn't sign?

A: (No response.)

Q: Can you answer that question?

MR. TAIKEFF: Your Honor, I'd like the record to reflect a 45 second pause measured by the courtroom clock between the last question and the following question.

Q: (By Mr. Crooks) Can you answer the question, Myrtle?

A: I was forced to sign both of these papers.

Q: By whom? . . .

A: They said one of my family members was going to be hurt if I didn't do it. By Dave Price and Bill Wood. . . .

Q: And is this the same Bill Wood that you told me in Rapid City was a good friend of yours? . . .

A: He's not a good friend.

Q: You didn't consider Bill Wood a friend?

A: No.

Q: Do you consider him a friend now?
A: No.
Q: Did you ever consider him a friend?
A: No.

When Taikeff concluded the interrogation in what is known as redirect examination, Myrtle Poor Bear was clear and emphatic.

Q: Do you remember Mr. Crooks, that's the man with the dark glasses, asked you a couple of times this afternoon about whether you ever were threatened by Agent Price or Agent Wood. . . .
A: Yes, I remember.
Q: Do you remember that when he asked you that question you remained silent for a very long time every time he asked you that question?
A: Yes.
Q: Why did you remain silent and not answer his question?
A: Because they *did* threaten me.
Q: Miss Poor Bear, will you please tell us whether Agent Price ever threatened you.
A: Yes, he did.
Q: What did he say to you?
A: He told me that they were going to plan everything out and if I didn't do it I was going to get hurt.
Q: Did anybody else ever say that to you from the FBI?
A: Bill Wood.

Still out of the hearing of the jury, the prosecution and defense teams gave arguments before Judge Benson.

THE COURT: I am concerned that much of her mental imbalance may arise from fear. I think the record is not at all clear as to where that fear arises from. . . .

MR. TAIKEFF: Where did Myrtle Poor Bear come from? Can you imagine with what your Honor has heard so far about the practices and procedures of the FBI that a witness such as Myrtle Poor Bear, who was not only an eyewitness to the killings according to those documents, but was privy to the planning, the advance planning, would suddenly walk in or appear in the life

> of the FBI and give an affidavit directly and immediately to be sent to Canada, and there would not be a 302 as thick as I am tall detailing everything she could remember about anything since the day she was three years old? . . .
>
> It is not possible. . . . There must be a 302. There must be some explanation of where she came from. There must be an explanation of why they say there is no 302. . . .
>
> No wonder there is no 302 any longer in existence, your Honor, because that 302 was prepared like any other document in connection with Myrtle Poor Bear and had to be gotten rid of because it was something they couldn't live with.

But Judge Benson, ignoring the cynical exploitation of an incompetent witness in two separate cases, determined that Myrtle Poor Bear's false affidavits, like all the rest of the coerced and fabricated evidence in the ResMurs trials, were "irrelevant."

> THE COURT: The Court noticed that this witness was under obvious great mental stress. Her testimony was interrupted at least three times by an emotional reaction of some kind. The Court is also aware of the extreme difficulty that was encountered in attempting to bring her back into this court at the request of the defendant.
>
> The Court observed that she had a complete lapse of memory on cross-examination relating to recent events.
>
> The Court also is taking into consideration the fact that this witness was not used in the presentation of the Government's case . . . the three FBI agents who interviewed her were not used in the presentation of the Government's case: Mr. Wood, Mr. Skelly and Mr. Price.
>
> And the Court concludes that credibility of this witness for any purpose is so suspect that to permit her testimony to go to the jury would be confusing the issues, may mislead the jury, and could be highly prejudicial. . . .
>
> The offer of proof is denied. . . .

Judge Benson later refused a defense request that the jury be given Jury Instruction #19, which reads as follows:

> Testimony has been given in this case which if believed by you shows that the Government induced witnesses to testify falsely. If

> you believe that the Government, or any of its agents, induced any witness to testify falsely in this case . . . this is affirmative evidence of the weakness of the Government's case.

☐

Another controversial person who testified out of the jury's hearing was Jimmy Eagle. Gladys Bissonnette, who accompanied her grandson to the trial, was so exhausted by the deaths and fear and pain and trouble that had descended on her family since the day she had spoken so bravely after Wounded Knee that she dreaded her grandson's appearance as a defense witness and refused to let him appear without a lawyer; in fact, she had convinced herself that WKLDOC was an FBI front outfit, since one of its lawyers had defended David Sky, who later became an FBI material witness. Ever since Oglala, the FBI had seemed anxious to pin something on Jimmy's brother Leon, and perhaps the old lady imagined that Jimmy's appearance for the defense would only invite more trouble for both boys.

Refuting Mike Anderson's statement that he had frequented the AIM camp with his girl friend Wilma Blacksmith, Eagle denied that he had ever been there; nor had he been present at Oglala on June 26; nor had he boasted of participating in the killings to the four felons whose accounts were prepared by Agents Hughes and Coward, Price and Wood. On the contrary, he said, his attorney had warned him to keep his mouth shut, since snitches were likely to turn up in his cell.

> Q: What did Agent Gary Adams say to you when he came to see you?
>
> A: He come in and asked me to sit down and it was him and another agent there at the time, I told them I refused to talk to them. He said, "We ain't asking you to talk, we're asking you to listen." That's when they brought up the thing about June 26th.
>
> Q: What did they say about June 26th?
>
> A: He said, "You know you're in a lot of trouble, don't you," and he went on to say that how much time I'd be facing, how long I'd be behind bars. He said, "We know you wasn't there but we think you could help us by linking a few things together for us," and then he went on to say, "Your brother's in a lot of trouble," and I said, "Who?" He said, "Leon. He was out there

with those guys in Oglala." . . . The other agent got up and he said, "Well, we could help you in any way you want. We'll get you out of here." He was referring to the jail. And he also said, "We could help you with your financial problems."

Q: Did he tell you what would happen to you if you refused to help him?

A: I would be in jail for quite a while and I'd be indicted on a charge of murder.

Despite Stoldt's sighting and Mike Anderson's account, despite Harper and Stewart, Clifford and High Bull, White Wing and Bragg, Adams himself would say at Fargo that he had never seen any good evidence that Jimmy Eagle was present at Oglala on June 26, 1975; for whatever reason, the government had decided that—his own boasts notwithstanding—he hadn't really been there after all. Eagle's strange history might well have affected the jurors' opinion of FBI dependability, but as in the case of Myrtle Poor Bear, Judge Benson determined that this youth's account of FBI misconduct would only confuse them. (To the defense, it seemed appropriate that Benson, during Eagle's testimony, referred to himself as "the Government" when what he had meant to refer to was "this Court.")

Two of Eagle's accusers had been brought to Fargo as potential witnesses for the defense. ("At that time we were convinced that Jimmy Eagle wasn't at Oglala, and we wanted to get them to admit that the FBI made up stories to incriminate him," Ellison says.) For reasons never satisfactorily explained, Marvin Bragg and the double child-murderer Marion High Bull were actually placed in the same holding cell as Leonard Peltier. Perhaps it was hoped that these good felons would inspire the defendant to open his heart to them, as Eagle had done; more likely, however, the hope was that Peltier would attack them, and thereby worsen the reputation for violence that the FBI had gone to such pains to establish. Apparently, both of his new cellmates inclined to this second theory. Bragg declared later that when Peltier was brought in, he just scooted right around that man and departed from the cell, crying out for other accommodations. The frightened High Bull was not fast enough, and was obliged to while away the evening in earnest discussion—so he said—of the possibility of changing his proposed testimony to something more acceptable to the defendant.

Once they were safe, both men complained that Peltier had threatened them; he had also passed the word along the cell tiers to Marvin Bragg that if the rapist didn't change his story, his long-suffering wife would be harmed as well as himself. Both denied that anybody had encouraged them to provoke the violent threats by the defendant, and both swore that they had spoken nothing but the truth, so help them God. However, in "offer-of-proof" testimony (once again, out of the jury's hearing) Bragg acknowledged having benefited from a concurrent sentence on his three rape convictions (other rapes, assaults, and burglaries had been forgiven), apparently due to his public-spirited effort to see justice done; he also confided his high hopes of an early parole from his two recent sentences on charges of murder.

Among the witnesses scheduled to appear for the defense was Chief Frank Fools Crow, whom Taikeff eventually rejected. "He told me the reason was that Chief Fools Crow was getting senile," Peltier recalls, still somewhat mystified. Even more mystifying was the rejection of Mike Anderson, who had done Peltier more damage than anyone else and was therefore in a position to do him the most good. "Mike Anderson was called and came back to testify for me with the encouragement of his mother and his brother Larry. . . . All our defense witnesses are first interviewed by our investigators, and one of them told me Mike was going to be a good witness for me.[13] Sure, he was a little scared because of threats, etc., but she felt he was going to be good. After she was finished, she called Elliott in, and it could not have been five minutes later he came out and said, No good, he's scared and will destroy us. Our investigator could never understand why Elliott did this, or why he rejected Chief Fools Crow's testimony. . . . As for the comment of Mike destroying us—to this day I don't know what the hell he meant because there is nothing truthful Mike could have said that would have destroyed me or anyone at Oglala that day."

⊡

An elusive phenomenon throughout both ResMurs trials was the red Scout, jeep, pickup, and/or "vehicle," originally associated with Jimmy Eagle, then with the unidentified Indians being pursued by Williams and Coler, then with the person or persons unknown who departed the Jumping Bull land immediately after the agents' deaths. As will be recalled, FBI stenographer Linda Price (David Price's wife), recording

Ron Williams's radio transmissions in the Rapid City office on the morning of the shoot-out, heard Williams say, "We're following a red vehicle, you want to keep an eye out for it." At 12:18, three or four people in the Rapid City office, taking down the transmissions from Oglala, heard Adams report a red pickup leaving the Jumping Bull area.

Yet in the first weeks after the shoot-out, the description of this vehicle, then its very existence, became shrouded in mystery. As William Kunstler had pointed out at Cedar Rapids, "The FBI waited almost two weeks before announcing that there was such a pickup truck and that there had been a chase by the agents of the pickup truck." After Butler and Robideau were acquitted and the government dismissed charges against Jimmy Eagle, the confusion—if that is what it was—increased, as the red pickup, closely followed by Eagle's "red International Scout," disappeared into the sunset and Leonard Peltier's red-and-white Chevy van came into view.

Since no "red pickup" could be linked to the defendants, the defense lawyers had been happy to agree with the early FBI theory of events in which a red pickup had been chased onto or across the Jumping Bull land by Coler and Williams just before the shoot-out and had then departed. But as we have seen, Agent Adams was now saying that what he meant by this red pickup was actually a red-and-white pickup operated by Wallace Little, Sr., that drove on and off the property an hour later (also carrying away persons unknown) and that neither had anything to do with the red-and-white *van* that had actually been chased onto the farm by the doomed agents. In support of this theory was the controversial two-part 302 of Agent Gerard Waring, who alone among all those people who were listening to Williams's last transmissions, heard "red-and-white" rather than "red." There was also the confused testimony of Mike Anderson, who said that the "orange pickup" he had mentioned as the vehicle occupied by Stuntz, Charles, and Peltier and pursued down the hill by the two agents was actually an "orange and white and red and white van." These changes from red to red-and-white were crucial to the effectiveness of witness Draper, who stated that Leonard Peltier had driven his red-and-white van away from camp about 9:00 that morning, and that this van was present once again when Draper emerged from hiding in the woods in the early afternoon, and also to that of Angie Long Visitor, who said she saw Peltier's red-and-white van parked at the Y-fork below the green shack. (Under the circumstances, it is interesting that the FBI, intent on the red pickup, Scout, or jeep, paid little or no attention to the red-and-white van until at least three months after the shoot-out.)

When the smoke cleared, however, the prosecution was still stuck with the 302 of Linda Price, which was supported by FBI stenographer Ann Johnson's recollection, as elicited at Cedar Rapids, not by the defense but by Assistant U.S. Attorney Robert Sikma:

> Q: What was the general nature of the radio transmissions, what was being said between 11:55 and 12:10 p.m.?
> A: There was a general background of what had been happening, of the agents being fired at, and what was being done.
> Q: O.K. What happened at 12:06?
> A: Adams was receiving fire.
> Q: And what happened at 12:10, approximately 12:10 p.m.?
> A: An ambulance was called to go down there.
> Q: O.K., and what happened at about 12:18 p.m.?
> A: Adams was on the scene and he had been receiving fire.
> Q: And what else happened?
> A: He said that he saw a red pickup leaving the Jumping Bull Hall area, and the Pine Ridge Police were instructed to stop this pickup.

For the prosecutors, it was important that these unwelcome recollections be blurred or otherwise discredited in the jury's mind. Therefore, it was now revealed that these ladies had been "assisted" in their stenography by Resident Senior Agent George O'Clock, the suggestion being that those nice girls back at the office had confused things and should not be taken too seriously by the jury. At Fargo, Johnson dutifully declared that she did not really recall that stuff about the red pickup anymore, nor could she refer to her own notes on the actual transmissions, since she had destroyed them several months earlier—after Cedar Rapids, that is, and before Fargo. (SA George O'Clock has also suffered a lapse of memory. "There were times when I was away from the radio," he says today. "I don't recall hearing about that red pickup.") And as with Coward and with Waring, Judge Benson forbade the defense to place in evidence the stenographers' 302s, which make no mention of any "assistance" from Mr. O'Clock.

⊡

Closing arguments began on April 15, 1977. In his summation for the prosecution, Assistant U.S. Attorney Crooks returned to what he called "perhaps the most important piece of evidence in this case"—the controversial .223 shell casing, supposedly ejected from the killer's rifle during the executions into the opened trunk of Coler's car. The government's position was that this shell casing went unnoticed by whoever gathered up the incriminating shells after the killings (the government said it was the killers, suppressing evidence, and the defense said it was the government, which was eager to suggest that the agents had scarcely fired a shot). However, it also went unnoticed by the five FBI agents who scoured the death scene that same day, while the bodies lay there in the sun, and it is nowhere mentioned on the list of items in the July 1, 1975, 302 report of Agent Cortland Cunningham, head of the FBI Firearms Division, who performed a systematic inspection of the car on June 30, after Agent Winthrop Lodge had checked it out for fingerprints. Nevertheless, Agent Cunningham had signed that affidavit which was used at Peltier's extradition hearings in Vancouver, claiming "I found one .223 cartridge case in the trunk which I took into my possession and placed it in an envelope marked 'Items recovered from trunk, Jack R. Coler automobile.'" At Fargo, Cunningham acknowledged that he had not found this casing after all; he said that Agent Lodge had found it, and had given it to him later. Sure enough, the casing turns up on the last page of the notes Lodge said he took while inspecting this automobile on June 30; why notes were taken on this car and this car only (Lodge also inspected the Williams car and the red-and-white van) was not explained. Like Coward, Waring, and Cunningham before him, Agent Lodge felt obliged to adjust his testimony throughout, claiming at one point, for example, that everything in Coler's car had been turned over to Cunningham, and at another that "not everything was turned over to Cunningham." During cross-examination, both agents were helped with their multiplying difficulties of recollection by helpful interjections from Judge Benson. For example, when attorney Lowe demanded to know whether Cunningham was aware that he had made a false statement under oath on that affidavit used in Canada, the agent said vaguely that "the significance of that paragraph at the time I signed the affidavit was not apparent to me." (Was he suggesting that the affidavit had been prepared by his superiors?) Pressed for a simple yes or no, the witness was assisted off the hook by Benson, who decreed that the question had already been answered.

Even if this elusive casing was legitimate evidence, it had to be linked to a gun of the right caliber, and the gun that the government came up with was the damaged AR-15 rifle taken from Robideau's exploded station wagon outside Wichita. An FBI laboratory report of October 31, 1975, on the analysis of four weapons collected from the exploded station wagon on the Kansas Turnpike, made clear that none of the ammunition components recovered at Oglala could be associated with this gun; apparently the same was true of the AR-15 with the obliterated serial number recovered at Rosebud, and the third AR-15 found in the motor home in Oregon two months later. Not until January 19, 1976, would ballistics expert Evan Hodge (who had signed the October 31 report) discover that the crucial casing could be linked to that Kansas Turnpike weapon after all—a theoretical conclusion only, as Hodge admitted, since unlike the Rosebud and Oregon weapons, this AR-15 with firing mechanisms and upper barrel partially melted and otherwise damaged by explosion and flames could not be test-fired. In short, it was as difficult to *disprove* that .223 casing's connection to the damaged gun as it was to prove it. Anyway, the government announced that the Wichita AR-15 had been the murder weapon, and the Hodge report was in good time for the affidavit he signed under oath to help secure Leonard Peltier's extradition.

Hodge accounted for the delay in his diagnosis by saying that although he had received that crucial cartridge case from Rapid City on July 24, 1975, he had not gotten around to testing it until late December, perhaps January, despite the ferocious urgency of the ResMurs investigation. Since this critical casing and another fired by a .308 were the only ones found near the bodies that could have come from the high-velocity weapon(s) that caused the deaths, this delay seems remarkable, to put it mildly.

Judge Benson ruled that the defense, in its summation, was not to point out the strange timing of all these ballistics reports; presumably he felt that the suspicious attitude of the defense attorneys might confuse the jury, causing it to wonder if the Cunningham and Hodge affidavits had any validity at all. Once again, the judge seemed to have usurped the jury's legal responsibility to decide the true facts of the case.

Reading the trial transcript, it is hard to understand why the defense did not hammer at the weak connection between the wandering shell casing and the busted gun, and the still weaker connection between this gun and Peltier. Wish Draper, for one, had associated "an AR-15" with others in the group, and Evan Hodge himself had testified that at least three AR-15s were involved in the shoot-out on that day; in addition, numerous AR-15s were carried by BIA police and others involved in the assault upon the compound. It was also interesting that no .223s were found among the cartridge casings at the junked-car–tree-line location from where Peltier was said by every witness to have been shooting.

Both sides now agreed that Coler and Williams had been killed at point-blank range by one or more high-velocity weapons. Among the weapons located by the FBI, those in this category included—in addition to Coler's own rifle, by no means an unlikely possibility—the Springfield bolt-action .30-06 deer rifle collected at the June Little cabin and two British Enfield .303s, one of them found down in the AIM camp and the other allegedly used by Norman Charles. Casings from the latter weapon were found not only in the compound but near the tree line and at the Little cabin (and in demonstrating the case that might be made against other suspects, the defense went so far as to suggest that in apparently moving from one location to another, Charles would have passed close to the agents, which is not necessarily true). In trying to focus the guilt on the AIM suspects, the government ballistics charts and maps seen by the jury ignored what Agent Hodge referred to as "a whole lot of ammunition components" that were never connected to any identified gun. Since almost every weapon used by the agents and the AIM group had been identified, who was doing all the shooting? And why—despite all the evidence of people fleeing the Jumping Bull area in early afternoon in red pickups and gold autos, as well as on foot—were these shooters scarcely mentioned, not only by the prosecution but by the defense? One may suppose that the ResMurs defendants and their attorneys were anxious to avoid incriminating other Indians, and that the prosecution had good reasons for not doing so; even so, there was something unexplained, something disturbing in the avoidance of this whole area of investigation that was simply allowed to disintegrate, like that red pickup that the prosecution was dismissing as a "phantom."

The massive and brain-numbing ballistics testimony in the trial transcript fails to establish Peltier's presence at Oglala, far less his identity as the killer, and evidently prosecutor Crooks feared that the jury might perceive this, to judge from his emotional evocation of the bloody killings and his rabble-rousing denunciation of the defendant, neither of which had much to do with the hard evidence. (A few days earlier, he had also denounced the defendant's attorney, calling Taikeff "an idiot" on the court record.)

> It is obvious that both of our two most important witnesses, Norman Brown and Mike Anderson, would have been defendants in this case along with Leonard Peltier and perhaps should have been. I think it's also obvious why they were not. As I said, our best two eyewitnesses are dead, Jack Coler and Ron Williams. They can never testify.
>
> In short, we needed witnesses. There's no question about it. The evidence for instance does not indicate that Mike Anderson or Norman Brown initiated these killings, or that they fired the fatal shots. The evidence on the other hand indicates that Leonard Peltier was not only the leader of this group, he started the fight, he started the shootings, he executed these two human beings at point blank range.

The evidence indicates no such thing; there was no evidence for these last three statements whatsoever.

> . . . There was one individual who was most responsible, and I think the evidence without any question proves and establishes beyond any doubt that that was the man seated over there (indicating) in the blue shirt and the vest, Leonard Peltier. . . .
>
> Apparently Special Agent Williams was killed first. He was struck in the face and hand by the bullet, as I have demonstrated, probably begging for his life, and he was shot. The back of his head was blown off by a high-powered rifle.
>
> Leonard Peltier then turned, as the evidence indicates, to Jack Coler lying on the ground helpless. He shoots him in the top of the head. Apparently feeling that he hadn't done a good enough job, he shoots him again through the jaw, and his face explodes. No shell even comes out, just explodes. The whole bottom of his chin is blown out by the force of the concussion. He dies. Blood splattered against the side of the car. Special Agent Adams arrived, a

> good friend of Ron Williams. I think that was obvious from his testimony. You will recall that he was very emotional, and I think understandably so, especially from looking at his involvement in this case. He came under fire immediately. . . .
>
> The tragic part, or perhaps the fortunate part, if he had gone a little farther, he probably would have seen Leonard Peltier standing over the bodies. . . . Had he gone any farther, we would have probably had three dead agents instead of two. . . . Everyone that came near this area was shot at including, I believe, there is testimony of an ambulance team coming in. Everyone drew fire. Passerbys on the highway drew fire from this blood-crazed bunch.

Crooks spoke angrily of the "senseless, brutal, cowardly murders" of "two young, relatively handsome young men . . . killed in the performance of their duties" and of "human lives unique in God's creation." Among his many misstatements of the record, he told the jury that Mike Anderson had said that Peltier had gotten out of the red-and-white van and started shooting at the agents, when Anderson had said nothing of the kind. "The agents are now dead," Crooks intoned, "the sniveling coward that shot them has fled." Since the jurors were instructed not to take notes and were not to consult the more than five thousand pages of trial transcript, they could not retain pertinent details of the complex and lengthy arguments; and since Judge Benson had also forbidden direct quotations from the transcripts during summations, it was difficult for the defense to show what Crooks was up to. An experienced prosecutor who knew just what he was doing, Crooks took full advantage of this situation, and John Lowe's demand for a mistrial based on "grievous mistakes" in Crooks's argument was dismissed by Benson, who paid no attention to Lowe's pleas that the court admonish the rampaging prosecutor or warn the jury that much of what this Assistant U.S. Attorney was telling them was simply untrue.

Comparing the behavior of Lynn Crooks and Robert Sikma with that of R. D. Hurd in the trial of Banks and Means, a lawyer familiar with both cases says, "In my opinion, Hurd knew what was going on, and didn't stop it; Crooks and Sikma took an active role in the preparation of false evidence." Old-fashioned Americans who prefer to think that United States attorneys should maintain some sort of standard of integrity, even if the FBI does not, might well feel ashamed of the crude cynicism of these men, and dismay that their behavior is sanctioned and even commended by their superiors. Like Hurd before him, Crooks was to be honored by the Justice Department for his "outstanding performance" in this trial.

⊡

Although the defense had prepared two weeks of testimony, about four fifths of it was disallowed, so that after fifteen days of prosecution evidence the defense found itself limited to just two and a half days in open court. By this time, attorney Lowe, in the face of impending disaster, was already devoting his main effort to getting material on the court record that might later be used as the basis for an appeal.[14]

In his summation, having acknowledged that first-degree murder had been committed, Taikeff contested the idea that it had been committed by Leonard Peltier, for which there was virtually no evidence:

> Mr. Crooks said that it is unfortunate that Anderson and Draper and Brown couldn't be prosecuted, they participated in these murders; but it was necessary to give up the privilege and the experience of prosecuting them in order to get the leader.
>
> Well, Norman Charles didn't testify for the Government. How come he is not sitting over there with his lawyer? It's very interesting. Norman Charles doesn't testify for the Government. We don't know why. . . . We have a lot of evidence of Norman Charles. . . . I also call to your attention that Joe Stuntz was found in an FBI jacket which came out of the car of one of the agents. . . . When did he put that jacket on? Was he one of those people with a .44 magnum who went down there? . . . That's the one identifiable bullet in one of the agents, a .44 magnum. And Joe Stuntz has the jacket on.

Taikeff also returned to the enigma of the red pickup:

> Why the great sensitivity about the red pickup? Did that red pickup carry away the people who killed the agents? Did that red pickup carry away people who were directly involved? They went out at 12:18. That is a very significant fact because that is within minutes, just a few minutes of the time by which it is fairly certain that both agents had died.
>
> If you recall, and it's perhaps a very subtle point, why did Mr. Sikma keep asking these witnesses questions which used the word

"vehicle" in spite of the fact they kept answering him with the word "pickup"? . . .

Anderson was on the stand. Anderson who was on the roof of Wanda Siers' residence, the tan and red residence, Mr. Hultman was questioning him. Mr. Hultman said, "What if anything then happened?" Answer: "Well, I guess they seen the orange pickup going down that way and they followed it." . . .

Next question by Mr. Hultman: "Now when you say orange pickup, is that the red and white van?" What kind of a question is that? When someone says orange pickup they mean orange pickup, they don't mean red and white van. . . .

Why did Mr. Anderson refer to it as the orange pickup? How did he convert on the stand a red and white van into an orange pickup? . . . "The orange and white and red and white van that was going down the hill." So now it was both orange and red and white and it was a van all in a few seconds. The conversion was made right there in the courtroom. . . .

Taikeff repeatedly returned to the contradictions in the testimony of Mike Anderson:

Anderson, when shown a photograph of Jimmy Eagle, said, "Yes, he was there with his girlfriend, Wilma, who was cooking." So not only does Anderson by some magical process place Jimmy Eagle at Tent City, but he is there with a girlfriend by the name of Wilma and she is cooking that late morning meal. How come nobody mentioned Wilma? Norman Brown, Michael Anderson . . . Draper, nobody mentioned Wilma, the provider of the food. Strange, isn't it? And then again . . . if Anderson, when he was interviewed, was in a position to say who was in Tent City preparing breakfast, because that's where everybody was when the shooting broke out, then how could he be on Wanda Siers' roof unless he has the capacity to fly? He may have the capacity to lie but he doesn't have the capacity to fly. . . .

Can you explain except by saying there is something terribly wrong here? You are asked to do a very, very serious task. Either way, just to return a verdict in this case, is a monumental act. Can you do so with comfort and assurance? . . .

Adams, the first witness for the Government, testifies the official investigation revealed nothing to indicate that Eagle was present

> on 6-26. Then how does it happen that Eagle is spotted through a telescope at a half mile? How does it happen that a witness who testified here that he saw Leonard Peltier down by the cars with two others—Michael Anderson—says that Jimmy Eagle was in Tent City with a woman named Wilma? How do those things happen?

In the end, it was Judge Benson's determination of what the jury should or should not see and hear that became the deciding factor in the trial. While permitting reference to Peltier's past "crimes" (for not one of which had he been tried, far less convicted), and permitting the unrestrained brandishing of gory pictures of the agents' corpses, "bullet-riddled" by this "blood-crazed bunch," not to speak of several weeks of testimony that was mostly immaterial even when not perjured or coerced, Benson forbade the defense to cite the evidence and verdict in the case of Butler and Robideau, and ruled all reference to COINTELPRO and most references to FBI misconduct inadmissible. Due to this judge's apparently biased exercise of his discretion, the jury was never troubled by the strong evidence of fabrication in the many contradictory 302s, or by the manipulation of Myrtle Poor Bear, or by much other evidence tending to show that Leonard Peltier was being railroaded into prison. Denied evidence of the whole pattern of fabrications that had laid the foundation for this trial, the jury had no way of knowing that the evidence against Peltier was essentially identical to the evidence against the two men already acquitted, and no way of sorting out the parade of prosecution witnesses, the hodgepodge of hollow circumstantial evidence, the charts and diagrams and table load of dangerous weapons that were brandished by the prosecutors for fifteen days. What *was* clear was that two white men, frightened and outnumbered, had been brutally killed, and that this Indian and his associates had been caught with the victims' guns; this damning circumstance, reinforced by those awful red photographs, ensured the prosecution's victory in "United States of America versus Leonard Peltier."

"With a hanging judge," one lawyer says, "counsel has to choose between defying the bench, making the judge mad, goading him into actions and decisions that can be used as basis for a later appeal, or trying to bring him around through reason and courtesy to a fairer point of view. There was no hope of that with Benson. He gave the defense a continuous series of adverse rulings, right from the first cross-examination of Gary Adams. Not only did he sustain almost all prosecution objections; he undermined the defense over and over by accusing it in the jury's hearing of wasting the jury's time in its cross-examinations. If I had been counsel, I would have approached it in a different way. The crucial point was that Peltier was no more and no less innocent than Butler and Robideau, and I would have hollered to the jury about the Cedar Rapids verdict even if Benson had jailed me for contempt."

In its deliberations, the jury requested to hear over again (the request was denied) that exciting part of the prosecution testimony about how Peltier, in the course of his arrest at Smallboy's camp, told a Cree elder that if he had known those visitors were cops, "he would blow the (blankety-blanks) out of their (blankety-blank) shoes." The campaign to make a cop-killer out of this "sniveling coward" seemed to have worked.

On April 18, 1977, after six hours of deliberation, the jury returned with a verdict of guilty on two counts of murder in the first degree.

⊡

Before the sentencing, on June 1, Leonard Peltier addressed the court; he had prepared the speech himself, with consultation on the precise wording. Although he started out in a calm voice, he became outraged as he proceeded, and before he finished, Judge Paul Benson had gone steak-red in the face. Bruce Ellison says that the court clerk, taking the speech down, sat all hunched up as if warding off the blow of Judgment Day, and that tension in the court grew so intense that he expected the angry U.S. marshals to launch a bodily assault on Peltier at any minute.

> There is no doubt in my mind or my people's minds you are going to sentence me to two consecutive life terms. You are and have always been prejudiced against me and any Native Americans who have stood before you; you have openly favored the government all through this trial and you are happy to do whatever the FBI would want you to do in this case.
>
> I did not always believe this to be so! When I first saw you in the courtroom in Sioux Falls, your dignified appearance misled me into thinking that you were a fair-minded person who knew something of the law and who would act in accordance with the law! Which meant that you would be impartial and not favor one side or the

other in this law suit. That has not been the case and I now firmly believe that you will impose consecutive life terms solely because that way you think will avoid the displeasures of the FBI. Neither my people nor myself know why you would be so concerned about an organization that has brought so much shame to the American people. But you are! Your conduct during this trial leaves no doubt that you will do the bidding of the FBI without any hesitation!

You are about to perform an act which will close one more chapter in the history of the failure of the United States courts and the failure of the people of the United States to do justice in the case of a Native American. After centuries of murder . . . could I have been wise in thinking that you would break that tradition and commit an act of justice? Obviously not! Because I should have realized that what I detected was only a very thin layer of dignity and surely not of fine character.

If you think my accusations have been harsh and unfounded, I will explain why I have reached these conclusions and why I think my criticism has not been harsh enough. First, each time my defense team tried to expose FBI misconduct . . . and tried to present evidence of this, you claimed it was irrelevant to this trial. But the prosecution was allowed to present their case with evidence that was in no way relevant—for example, an automobile blowing up on a freeway in Wichita, Kansas; an attempted murder in Milwaukee, Wisconsin, for which I have not been found innocent or guilty; or a van loaded with legally purchased firearms and a policeman who claims someone fired at him in Oregon state. The Supreme Court of the United States tried to prevent convictions of this sort by passing into law that only past convictions may be presented as evidence. . . . This court knows very well I have no prior convictions, nor am I even charged with some of these alleged crimes; therefore, they cannot be used as evidence in order to receive a conviction in this farce called a trial. This is why I strongly believe you will impose two life terms, running consecutively, on me.

Second, you could not make a reasonable decision about my sentence because you suffer from at least one of three defects that prevent a rational conclusion: you plainly demonstrated this in your decision about the Jimmy Eagle and Myrtle Poor Bear aspects of this case. In Jimmy's case, only a judge who consciously and openly ignores the law would call it irrelevant to my trial; in the mental torture of Myrtle Poor Bear you said her testimony would shock the conscience of the American people if believed! But *you* decided what was to be believed—not the jury! Your conduct shocks the conscience of what the American legal system stands for!—the search for the truth by a jury of citizens. What was it that made you so afraid to let that testimony in? Your own guilt of being part of a corrupted pre-planned trial to get a conviction no matter how your reputation would be tarnished? For these reasons, I strongly believe you will do the bidding of the FBI and give me two consecutive life terms.

Third, in my opinion, anyone who failed to see the relationship between the undisputed facts of these events surrounding the investigation used by the FBI in their interrogation of the Navajo youths—Wilford Draper, who was tied to a chair for three hours and denied access to his attorney; the outright threats to Norman Brown's life; the bodily harm threatened to Mike Anderson; and, finally, the murder of Anna Mae Aquash—must be blind, stupid, or without human feelings so there is no doubt and little chance that you have the ability to avoid doing today what the FBI wants you to do, which is to sentence me to two life terms running consecutively.

Fourth, you do not have the ability to see that the conviction of an A.I.M. activist helps to cover up what the government's own evidence showed: that large numbers of Indian people engaged in that fire fight on June 26, 1975. You do not have the ability to see that the government must suppress the fact that there is a growing anger amongst Indian people and that Native Americans will resist any further encroachments by the military forces of the capitalistic Americans, which is evidenced by the large number of Pine Ridge residents who took up arms on June 26, 1975, to defend themselves. Therefore, you do not have the ability to carry out your responsibility towards me in an impartial way and will run my two life terms consecutively.

Fifth, I stand before you as a proud man; I feel no guilt! I have done nothing to feel guilty about! I have no regrets of being a Native American activist—thousands of people in the United States, Canada, and around the world have and will continue to support me to expose the injustices which have occurred in this courtroom. I do feel pity for your people that they must live under such an ugly system. Under your system, you are taught greed, racism, and corruption—and most serious of all, the destruction of Mother Earth. Under the Native American system, we are taught all people are Brothers and Sisters; to share the wealth with the poor and needy. But the most important of all is to respect and preserve the Earth, who we consider to be our Mother. We feed from her breast; our Mother gives us life from birth and when it's time to leave this world, who again takes us back into her womb. But the main thing we are taught is to preserve her for our children and our grandchildren, because they are the next who will live upon her.

No, I'm not the guilty one here; I'm not the one who should be called a criminal—white racist America is the criminal for the destruction of our lands and my people; to hide your guilt from the decent human beings in America and around the world, you will sentence me to two consecutive life terms without any hesitation. . . .

If you were impartial, you would have had an open mind on all the factual disputes in this case. But you were unwilling to allow even the slightest possibility that a law enforcement officer would lie on the stand. Then how could you possibly be impartial enough to let my lawyers prove how important it is to the FBI to convict a Native American activist in this case? You do not have the ability to see that such conviction is an important part of the efforts to discredit those who are trying to alert their Brothers and Sisters to the new threat from the white man, and the attempt to destroy what little Indian land remains in the process of extracting our uranium, oil, and other minerals. Again, to cover up your part in this, you will call me a heartless, cold-blooded murderer who deserves two life sentences consecutively. . . .

Finally, I honestly believe that you made up your mind long ago that I was guilty and that you were going to sentence me to the maximum sentence permitted under the law. But this does not surprise me, because you are a high-ranking member of the white racist American establishment which has consistently said, "In God We Trust," while they went about the business of murdering my people and attempting to destroy our culture.

To this address, the flustered judge retorted, "You profess to be an activist for your people, but you are a disservice to Native Americans." With that, he administered the harshest punishment at his disposal, sentencing Peltier to two consecutive life terms in federal prison. The defendant turned and exchanged a long look with his father, Leo Peltier, with whom he had never been close; both men looked stricken by the knowledge that it was now too late to make up for lost time.

⊡

Leonard Peltier was sent directly to the high-security penitentiary at Marion, Illinois, a very unusual procedure for a first-time convict except in "political" crimes. In December 1977, his conviction was appealed by a new team of lawyers[15] before a panel of three federal judges in St. Louis, one of whom, William Webster, had already learned from attorney General Griffin Bell that he was to be nominated as the new head of the FBI. Judge Webster, who is said to be a man of intelligence and integrity, has a poor reputation in the field of civil rights, and was already noted for his anti-AIM opinions in a WKLDOC suit against the FBI in 1973, in the Means-Wilson election scandal in 1974, in fighting the reversal of Wounded Knee nonleadership convictions in the appeals court, and in upholding the severe sentence administered to John Trudell during Peltier's trial. Despite his high position on the bench, he was a member of two clubs in St. Louis that excluded women as well as blacks; one of these is known as The Mysterious Order of the Veiled Prophets.

Apparently Webster saw no impropriety in a future FBI head sitting in judgment on an appeal based on FBI abuses, for he did not remove himself from the case until the nomination had been made public. Therefore his opinions were familiar to the other two judges, who were retained when another panel was convened; by this time—the defense believes—the damage to Peltier had been done. The appeal was heard by the new panel in April 1978, and in September of that year, it was denied.

Before the appeals court, the defense contended that Peltier's extradition from Canada had been illegal, since it was based on "false affidavits . . . obtained by the government through coercion and deceit and known by the government to be false." U.S. Attorney Evan Hultman argued that "the jurisdiction of the trial court over the defendant is not affected by the manner in which his presence before the court was obtained."

> JUDGE [DONALD] ROSS: But anybody who read those affidavits would know that they contradict each other. And why the FBI

and Prosecutor's office continued to extract more to put into the affidavits in hope to get Mr. Peltier back to the United States is beyond my understanding.

MR. HULTMAN: Yes.

JUDGE ROSS: Because you should have known, and the FBI should have known, that you were pressuring the woman to add to her statement.

MR. HULTMAN: Your Honor, I personally was not present at that stage. I read the affidavits after they had been submitted, so I want this court to know that . . .

JUDGE ROSS: The Government—

MR. HULTMAN: And I don't excuse, by my remark just now to Your Honor, I don't in anyway excuse what the court has just indicated. Your Honor, I have trouble with that myself, and Your Honor, that is the exact reason which I did read these affidavits. . . . It was clear to me her story didn't check out with anything in the record by any other witness in any other way. So I concluded then, in addition to her incompetence, first, that secondly, there was no relevance of any kind. Absolutely not one scintilla of any evidence of any kind that had anything to do with this case. And it was then that I personally made the decision that this witness was no witness. First of all, because she was incompetent in the utter, utter, utter ultimate sense of incompetency . . . there was not one scintilla that showed Myrtle Poor Bear was there, knew anything, did anything, et cetera. . . .

JUDGE ROSS: But can't you see, Mr. Hultman, what happened happened in such a way that it gives some credence to the claim of the—

MR. HULTMAN: I understand, yes, Your Honor.

JUDGE ROSS: —the Indian people that the United States is willing to resort to any tactic in order to bring somebody back to the United States from Canada.

MR. HULTMAN: Judge—

JUDGE ROSS: And if they are willing to do that, they must be willing to fabricate other evidence. And it's no wonder that they are unhappy and disbelieve the things that happened in our courts when things like this happen.

MR. HULTMAN: Judge Ross, I in no way do anything but agree with you totally.

JUDGE ROSS: And you try to explain how they get there is not legally relevant in this case, and they don't understand that.

MR. HULTMAN: I understand, Your Honor.

JUDGE ROSS: We have an obligation to them, not only to treat them fairly, but not give the appearance of manufacturing evidence by interrogating incompetent witnesses.

MR. HULTMAN: Your Honor, I agree wholeheartedly.

Even so, the court of appeals held that since the defense had not claimed that the Poor Bear affidavits were the only evidence that brought about the extradition, its arguments were beside the point; the fugitive warrant from Wisconsin might have sufficed. It also accepted the government's position that since the defense was unable to prove any conspiracy between Jimmy Eagle's cellmates and the FBI, "it didn't matter" whether or not those convicts had been lying (which the government now granted might have been the case). Finally, "while the more prudent course might have been to allow the defense to present the evidence," the court affirmed Judge Benson's decision to withhold the Poor Bear and Eagle testimony from the jury:

> The evidence was only minimally relevant. Neither Jimmy Eagle nor Myrtle Poor Bear testified as a government witness against Peltier. Furthermore, Peltier made no showing that the integrity of the government's evidence against him was in any way tainted by the Myrtle Poor Bear and Jimmy Eagle episodes.
>
> Peltier argues that the evidence was relevant to show bias on the part of government witnesses Anderson, Draper, and Brown. He argues that Poor Bear's and Eagle's testimony, if believed by the jury, might have caused the jury to speculate further as to whether the knowledge Anderson, Draper, and Brown testified to was implanted in their minds by coercive F.B.I. interrogation.
>
> It is true that "[e]vidence tending to show a substantial reason for bias or interest in an important witness is never collateral or irrelevant. It may be * * * the very key to an intelligent appraisal of the testimony of the [witnesses]." . . . However, Eagle's and Poor Bear's allegations of F.B.I. harassment, even if true, shed very little, if any, light on the credibility of other witnesses, since the trial court allowed full inquiry into the dealings of Anderson, Draper and Brown with the F.B.I. In light of the full presentation to the

> jury of F.B.I. actions which might have caused bias on the part of these three witnesses, the testimony of Poor Bear and Eagle would only have been cumulative.
>
> Peltier also argues that the Poor Bear and Eagle testimony was admissible to show the intention of the F.B.I. to bring about his conviction, no matter what the cost. The issue is a more difficult one. As we stated earlier, Peltier's theory of the case was that the F.B.I. framed him by manufacturing evidence and inducing witnesses to testify in accordance with its theory of the murders. The Poor Bear and Eagle testimony was certainly consistent with that theory. However, we do not find an abuse of discretion on the part of the district court in excluding the evidence.[16]

In its conclusions, however, the court noted that "The use of affidavits of Myrtle Poor Bear in the extradition proceedings was to say the least, a clear abuse of the investigative process by the F.B.I." Why the defense request for a new trial was denied, under these circumstances, seems somewhat mysterious, since as Judge Ross had pointed out, "If they are willing to do that, they must be willing to fabricate other evidence"—in other words, if the government is willing to present coerced or fabricated testimony, why would it hesitate to present fabricated circumstantial evidence as well? With that query in mind, the rickety ballistics evidence purporting to link Peltier to the killings becomes even more suspect than before.

The appeal attorneys had also shown that during Peltier's trial the prosecution had bludgeoned the jury with his past crimes—illegally, according to the defense, not only because he had never been tried or convicted of those "crimes" but because the Federal Rules of Evidence provide that "Evidence of other crimes, wrongs, or acts is not admissible to prove the character of a person in order to show that he acted in conformity therewith." This rule also provides, however, that such evidence is admissible for such purposes as proof of motive, and the prosecution argued that "the defendant's knowledge that he would be taken into custody and returned to Milwaukee to stand trial for attempted murder tended to show why Peltier reacted with deadly force when followed by the FBI agents." The court of appeals agreed. Therefore, it seems bitterly ironic that one month later, in January 1978, prior burglary charges against Peltier were dropped in Oregon, and he was acquitted of the "attempted murder" in Wisconsin, in both cases because the police witnesses involved had been discredited. With Peltier serving two consecutive life sentences, the obsolete charges, once so useful in "neutralizing" an AIM leader by making him a fugitive from justice, were now just cluttering up justice's books. "As a native person," Peltier wrote in a letter from prison, "I stand before your courts with no defensible legal status, in my own land."

Eventually Peltier filed an appeal (as a political prisoner) to Amnesty International, which had sent an observer to Vancouver and to Fargo.

> This is the last appeal I will make. If you continue to feel that my act of protecting my People was the act of a dishonorable and dangerous man, an act that the Amnesty Committee cannot see as worthy, then I condemn your Amnesty Committee for condoning illegal government acts of terror directed against the People. . . .
> I hope your decision will be guided by your conscience and the Great Spirit. Thank you for hearing me.

But Amnesty International finally refused to become involved—regretfully, according to one Amnesty official—because its bylaws rule out cases that involve armed violence. A few years later, however, it published an analysis of this case that was highly critical of the U.S. government.[17]

On January 10, 1979, a round-the-clock vigil sponsored by the Leonard Peltier Defense Committee was begun outside the Supreme Court in Washington, D.C.; this vigil, led by John Trudell, Crow Dog, and others, continued night and day for fifty-five days, through bitter weather that included some of the worst storms in the city's history.

On February 11, in zero-degree temperatures, a protest march demanding a Supreme Court review of Peltier's case was harassed by dozens of police, many of them in riot gear, and the next day, the Supreme Court refused to hear an appeal of the Fargo sentence, offering no explanation of its decision. "After all, it's their court system, it's all one government," one attorney said. "There is so much FBI illegality here that they can't afford to have a new trial. They know he'd be found innocent. This is a case that's not going to go away."[18]

BOOK III

CHAPTER 14

THE ESCAPE

Lompoc Prison and the Los Angeles Trial

Crazy Horse saw nothing, knew nothing but treachery from the white man. He felt himself above dealing with men who knew no honor. As by all such men Crazy Horse was sincerely hated and feared. To get rid of him was the dearest wish of many, both white and Indian. . . . He represented the last stronghold of a weakened and all but subjected nation, so against him trickery and treachery was concentrated and finally prevailed.

Luther Standing Bear (*Lakota*)

In 1978, during the Fourth of July barbecue in the prison yard at the federal penitentiary in Marion, Illinois, Leonard Peltier was approached by another inmate, named Robert Hugh Wilson, who informed him that his life was in danger, since he, Wilson, had agreed to kill him. By reputation, Wilson, a heavy-set bank robber of 235 pounds, was a very dangerous man; according to his copious prison records, he had "assaulted every officer who has ever attempted to apprehend him, and is considered to be the most dangerous individual apprehended in this [Chicago and northern Illinois] district."

Robert Hugh Wilson, born in 1923 in Oklahoma of an Oneida mother and a Choctaw father, was chosen to recite the Gettysburg Address on the local radio station at the age of three and had a good record as a boy in school. But career opportunities for Oklahoma Indians were (and are) extremely limited, and he embarked early on unlawful enterprises, making a specialty of robbing banks. As time went on, he adopted a variety of aliases, none of which suggests his Indian heritage; under religion, the records record "None." To a probation officer in 1970, however, Wilson described himself as "a short fat American Indian, highly sensitive; I like the country [as opposed to the city] and people." He was also an inveterate reader, with a special liking for T. S. Eliot, and a quirky humor; his aliases included "Arvin Ignance Cohen."

On April 30, 1975, with a companion named Donald Richardson, Wilson escaped from Oklahoma State Prison, and on June 3, he wounded a police officer while evading arrest after an armed robbery in Oklahoma City, in which he was assisted by Richardson and Steven Berry. All three were caught within the year—Wilson and Berry were seized in Illinois on April 6, 1976—and Wilson and Richardson were sent to Marion. Despite the affection for people noted above, there is no record of any visitors to Wilson, who has two daughters as well as an ill wife.

Wilson, who was in his fifties, had a history of painful back trouble from degenerative discs, and he was in the prison hospital when on March 17, 1978, he was approached by a Dr. J. R. Plank, who suggested that he help out the head guard, or chief correctional supervisor, R. M. "Max" Carey, by informing on the activities of Leonard Peltier. Angrily, Wilson ordered Plank to leave. A few days later (March 23), he made a routine request for transfer of his medical records to Oklahoma, where he expected to be returned shortly for trial. (In addition to the twenty-five-year term he was already serving, he was charged with seven felonies, including bank robberies, auto thefts, and the near-fatal shooting of the police officer in Oklahoma City. Because of his previous record, he was technically subject to seven life sentences in prison.) On March 27, Dr. Plank returned to his bedside to inform him that, despite his condition, he was being transferred from the hospital to solitary confinement in "the Hole."

For the next six weeks, a wheelchair and all medical attention were denied him, despite repeated written pleas for help. His pain was such that, on May 5, when he fell down while trying to negotiate the twenty feet between his cell and the shower, he could not get up. On May 10, the head guard visited his cell. According to Wilson's diary for that day, "Carey asked me if I was ready to cooperate with him in return for medical treatment. I told him we could talk about it if he would get me some medical treatment right away." On May 12, he was given a cursory examination, and on May 15, he was returned to the hospital, although medical treatment was still being withheld.

The following day, the Indians' cross-country protest march called the Longest Walk,[1] from Alcatraz to Washington, D.C., arrived in Marion. Largely organized by Dennis Banks, the three-thousand-mile walk across the country, in protest against new anti-Indian legislation and the mass removal of traditional Navajo people from the Big Mountain region of Arizona, had arrived outside the prison walls, where a demonstration was staged on behalf of Peltier and other political prisoners (among them Rafael Miranda, the Puerto Rican activist, who had been helping Peltier with his public letters and teaching him a good deal about law and language). Leonard Crow Dog (as a convicted felon) was refused admittance, but John Trudell, Ernie Peters, and a few others were permitted to visit Peltier, whose notoriety and growing stature as leader and martyr were increasingly embarrassing to the U.S. government. The very next day, Wilson says, he had a visit in his hospital room.

> COMES NOW ROBERT HUGH WILSON, WHO UPON HIS OATH DEPOSES AND SAYS: That on May 17, 1978, I was a prisoner of the United States confined in a hospital room at the United States Penitentiary in Marion, Illinois; That on the afternoon of May 17, 1978, Chief Correctional Supervisor R. M. Carey unlocked the door to my room and entered. Mr. Carey was accompanied by a well-dressed stranger in a light brown suit and diagonal striped tie. The man accompan-

ying Mr. Carey appeared to be in his late thirties, about six-feet tall and 170 pounds, very erect posture, nearly blond hair with blue eyes. The stranger said that if I would cooperate in "neutralizing Leonard Peltier" he would see to it that I received immediate medical treatment, and, after I cooperated with him he would get me paroled from the federal prison system to my Oklahoma detainer; I asked the stranger who he represented and what he meant by "neutralizing" Leonard Peltier. He replied that he was a person who had the power to do what he promised. As to what he meant by "neutralizing Leonard Peltier," he said that I would have to weigh that for myself, but that according to my record I was not averse to "going all the way" when faced with a desperate situation. I asked what he meant by "going all the way" and Mr. Carey interrupted saying that I was wasting their time if I was going to play dumb. The stranger asked me how it felt to know I would never make it through the Oklahoma trial alive. He said that shooting a police officer in Oklahoma was a charge that would bring down the wrath of all Oklahoma City law enforcement officers on my head. He said that if I did not cooperate, he would personally see to it that I would not survive the trip to Oklahoma. On the other hand, if I would cooperate, he said he would guarantee my safety in Oklahoma by having me held in the federal prison at El Reno, Oklahoma during the trial and never having me in the custody of state authorities without the presence of two United States marshals. I stated that I lived in terror of the trip, and I would do almost anything to stay alive, but what they were asking me to do could get me a life sentence. Mr. Carey laughed and said, "for a man who just received three life sentences in Texas, you worry too much about a life sentence." The stranger then said that if anything happened to Peltier and an inmate was acting in self-defense, no court would give the inmate a life sentence. I said, how could I know they would keep their end of the bargain, and more important, how could I know they even had the power to promise parole. I pointed out that the Captain of the prison guards (Mr. Carey) obviously did not have the authority to promise a parole, and on top of that I did not even know who the stranger was nor who he represented, and most important of all the Parole Board was not famous for granting paroles to freshly convicted murderers. The stranger said there were a good many ways for me to fulfill my task and if I agreed to act for them he would explain a simple procedure whereby I would be able to neutralize Leonard Peltier without even seeming to be involved. I asked him what that procedure might be and he said that I must first agree to cooperate. I told him that I would cooperate only on the condition that they advance me something tangible so I would know they had the power to keep their end of the bargain. The stranger asked me if I wanted money. I told him that the only thing I wanted was to have the charges in Oklahoma City dismissed so I would not have to go to trial there. . . . I said if I could have immediate medical treatment, a promise of parole from the federal system and the seven indictments in Oklahoma dropped before I cooperated, I promised to kill Leonard Peltier in front of the control center on any day he designated. Mr. Carey and the stranger both laughed. Mr. Carey turned to the stranger and said, "It looks like I wasn't wrong when I told you he's your boy." The stranger told me that the first thing they had to do was get me to establish the utmost trust between myself and Peltier. He said the quicker we could get my back well the quicker I could get back into population and go to work. He suggested I use my talent for writing administrative remedies to represent the Indians in getting a culture group started. This would help build the strong bond necessary for the next step. He instructed me to tell Leonard that I had access to several home made zip guns. He said he would furnish three such weapons which would appear to be in operating condition, but they would actually be inoperable. He said they could not be tested in the prison, and they would be kept "hidden" until shortly before the time of the "escape." He told me to urge Leonard Peltier to escape by playing on his patriotic feelings. He said I would be furnished with wire cutters capable of cutting through the fence and concertina wire, hacksaw blades, material for making dummies and anything within reason in order to get Leonard Peltier out to the fence preferably at night. He said that I would not be expected to take part in the "escape" because of my age and bad back. He said that once I lured Leonard Peltier out to the fence he would be taken care of. I told the stranger that I would rather just kill Leonard Peltier than to go through all that deceit and treachery. The stranger replied, "That is exactly what you'll have to do if this plan doesn't work. Don't even think of playing us for fools because, at this point, it's Peltier's life or yours. We don't accept backing out or betrayals. You are now committed to this with your life. If you betray us you will die. If

> you perform honorably you will be rewarded even more than our agreement. If you tell about this conversation it will be our word against yours and you won't be believed. When you have things in hand and it is imperative that you see Carey, submit a sealed letter requesting an interview regarding a personal problem. Never mention *anything* in the interview request. Take your time. Don't try to move too fast, and don't hold any serious conversations with Peltier about escaping until you are certain you have his trust." Mr. Carey and the stranger left my room.

In his diary for May 17 Wilson wrote:

> This is too fucking heavy to even think about. I don't know what to do. If I tell Leonard and he wants me to expose it, they'll probably kill me. If I refuse to act they can get somebody else and we won't even know who. I'll just have to get back into population and dump the whole thing in Leonard's lap.

Wilson doubted that the stranger had sufficient influence to remove what amounted to seven life sentences, especially when one charge involved the near-killing of a policeman. But treatment with drugs, hot packs, and liniment began that very afternoon, and on May 24, the Marion records control supervisor was notified by the Oklahoma County sheriff that the state had removed detainers on Wilson and that the warrants in his case should be returned.[2] On the first of June, he was informed that his return for trial was no longer scheduled; Wilson's diary for that day reads: "I guess I'm committed now." At the end of the month, he was discharged from the hospital, and in the prison yard on the Fourth of July, he found his chance to talk to Peltier.[3]

According to Wilson, Peltier was visibly upset by the news that Wilson was supposed to kill him, and asked Wilson to pretend to cooperate so that he would not be replaced by an unknown enemy. Meanwhile, Wilson acted on the blond-haired man's suggestion that he join the Indian "culture group" that was trying to practice traditional culture and religion, and he resumed the name Standing Deer, given to him, he says, by his grandfather. Because of his intelligence and his organizing skills, Standing Deer was soon chairman and spokesman for the group. In mid-September, he was notified that all the Oklahoma charges had been dismissed.

> On November 9, 1978, at approximately 2:00 p.m., I was leaving the office of Supervisor of Education, R. L. Williams, when the stranger who was with Mr. Carey on May 17, 1978, called me into a classroom. He was alone. He appeared to be angry. He wanted to know what I was doing to keep my end of the agreement. I told him that I had been vigorously representing Leonard Peltier and the other Indians in trying to win religious freedom in Marion prison; that I was certain that I enjoyed Leonard Peltier's complete trust; that I had been preaching escape as the patriotic duty of a warrior; that Leonard wasn't interested in any zip guns; that it would soon be early winter with dense foggy mornings making escape more feasible; and, finally, that these things take time, and he, himself, had said that I should not rush things. He replied that they were just about out of time and so was I. He told me that they had come to a decision that Marion has so much security that planning a successful escape was just about impossible, therefore, unless I had firm plans to neutralize Peltier they intended to move both me and Leonard Peltier to a less secure prison in California where an escape attempt would be hard to resist. He said I would be going to Leavenworth in December. Leonard would go to USP Lompoc about 60 days after I got to Leavenworth. I would not go to Lompoc until they had another Indian situated in Lompoc who would help me to neutralize Peltier. He said the Indian I would meet in Lompoc enjoyed their complete trust, and he would also be watching me to be sure I performed. He said he did not know how long I would have to be in Leavenworth, but he wanted to hold me there until both Leonard Peltier and the assassin were in Lompoc. . . . I asked why I couldn't just go ahead to Lompoc. He replied that he wanted me on ice for a while so that Leonard Peltier would welcome me with open arms when I got to Lompoc. He said he further did not want me at Lompoc until the other Indian got himself established. I agreed to go along with him once again.

(R. M. Carey flatly denies the conversations with Wilson and the blond-haired stranger: "Why would I or any FBI agent want to put out a contract on Peltier?"[4])

On December 21, Standing Deer was sent to Leavenworth, as promised. The journey aggravated his bad back, and on Christmas Day, following a dispute over his medication, he threatened one of his new guards. At a disciplinary hearing two days later—which he could not attend because a wheelchair was denied him—he was sentenced to solitary confinement in the Marion Control Unit, a notorious "behavior modification" prison-within-a-prison that is known to convicts as "the end of the line," the worst "hole" in the whole country.

Standing Deer had already served a three-month term in this unit, a clangorous metal zoo of 6 x 6 x 8-foot cell boxes with steel-slab beds where captive humans were (and are) subject to pseudoscientific experiments and "character invalidation" techniques devised by a certain Dr. Edgar Schein.[5] Marion, which opened in 1963, replacing Alcatraz as the highest-security prison in the country, appears to have been the first penitentiary where this Schein's unsavory experiments were put into practice.

> For me, existing for three months in the Control Unit was the most nightmarish experience of my entire life. To wake up day after endless day in a tiny 6′×8′ sealed-tomb tiger-cage completely destroyed my will to live. I would have killed myself, but 24-hour-a-day deadlock solitary confinement produced so much apathy that even suicide required more interest than I could muster. . . .
>
> Until the Control Unit, the worst mental pain I had ever known was when my brother died. Imagine the worst you ever felt in your entire life. That's how I felt every single minute when I was in the Control Unit.[6]

Before Standing Deer could be transferred to Marion and the Control Unit, he was visited by the associate warden of Leavenworth, Ray Lippman, after which this notorious felon, just recently sentenced to "administrative detention" (the Hole) for yet another manifestation of his "assaultive" personality, was awarded the first job of his prison career as a clerk in the office of Leavenworth's chief correctional supervisor, with access to all prison documents and free run of the prison. (In his job application, Standing Deer states that his typing of thirty-five to forty words per minute, although slow, was accurate, with good spelling, and that his reputation for violence had been "grossly exaggerated"; the seven "incidents" that had taken place in prison, he explains, had been mostly of a verbal nature.) At the same time—also for the first time in his prison career—he asked for and received a change of cell in order to be near his old bank-robbing partner, Steven Berry.

"He's kind of a loner," says Bob Robideau, who was in Leavenworth when Standing Deer turned up in early 1979. "He never associated with anybody much except his partner there, Steve Berry. Berry's a white man, big, over two hundred pounds, who broke him out of jail back in Oklahoma, but Standing Deer is the leader, you see that straight off. When he come to Leavenworth he was on the same block as me, on the first tier, and he sent word that he was a friend of Leonard, so I went down a couple of times to talk to him. Heavy-set, roly-poly personality, but not fat, and he's got a good sense of humor, which is why him and Leonard got on so good." Robideau was astonished when this tough old con told him about his new job in administration. "Later I thought it was kind of funny that he never told me about the plot, never even mentioned it, although Leonard must have told him I was okay; maybe he just didn't see where talking would help. Standing Deer has lots of guts, he's always standing up for the rights of prisoners and firing off letters of protest to the authorities, what he calls 'administrative remedies.' But he's doing a lot of time, and I guess he's learned not to say nothing when he don't have to."

On February 23, 1979, Leonard Peltier passed through Leavenworth on his way to Lompoc, which lies just inland from the coast in the Santa Ynez Mountains, north of Point Conception, in California. He arrived at Lompoc on April 10, two days before the Oklahoma City prosecutors made a formal motion to dismiss all outstanding charges against Robert Hugh Wilson (the decision anticipated in the Marion records seven months before). At Lompoc, Peltier met Archie Fire Lame Deer, who was establishing a sweat lodge: "I'm afraid they are trying to kill me," he told Lame Deer. "They are trying to set me up." (This was the worry that Lame Deer would mention to me a few weeks later, at Point Conception.)

On or about May 11, a federal prisoner named Charles "Chuck" Richards came through Leavenworth, also on his way to Lompoc: Standing Deer was convinced that this man was the second assassin. An Oglala Lakota from Pine Ridge, and a well-known goon from a goon clan so unusually brutal that it was known to the traditionals as "the Manson family," this Richards had been one of the gang responsible for the death of Byron DeSersa; probably because his wife, Saunie, was Dick Wilson's daughter, he had not been prosecuted in the DeSersa killing. Subsequently he had assaulted Lieutenant Pat Mills of the Oglala police, holding a shotgun to Mills's head before Mills had knocked the shotgun away in a desperate maneuver.[7] Despite his record, which included two prior convictions for felonies involving violence, Richards had gotten off with a three-year sentence in Leavenworth, from where he was transferred to Lompoc after a brief stay.

Standing Deer wrote immediately to a Peltier admirer in Seattle (prisoners are not allowed to correspond with one another), advising her to warn Leonard of Richards's arrival at Lompoc, which had occurred on May 24.[8] Calling himself "Richardson" because his own name was so notorious on Pine Ridge, Richards had befriended Peltier before the warning was received, playing basketball and talking and eating meals with him on several occasions. In this same period, Peltier was suddenly transferred from his usual work detail on the grounds of Archie Fire Lame Deer's sweat lodge, directly beneath Guard Tower 4, to a secluded area as far from the view of any tower as a prisoner could get without escaping.

When Peltier learned "Richardson's" true identity, he broke all contact with him, alarmed at how close he might have come to his own enemy. Already the Lompoc prisoners, under the direction of Bobby Garcia, were making sure that Peltier was accompanied by two bodyguards wherever he went, but one night, seeing another inmate knifed before anyone could move, Peltier realized that his friends could not save him from anyone who really meant business. With the encouragement of an "outside man," Roque Duenas, his old Northwest Coast associate from his Seattle days, he began to consult with Bobby Garcia, who had a prison reputation as an escape artist.

Bobby Gene Garcia was born in 1946 in a camp for migrant farm workers near Scott City, Kansas. When he was eighteen, he and his brother and father managed to extricate the family from the brutalizing migrant life by opening a garage in Tucumcari, New Mexico, where Bobby Gene worked as mechanic as well as manager. On November 9, 1966, in a confused state of mind that followed a whole series of personal reversals—the separation of beloved parents, the illness and jailing of his brother, the desertion by his young wife because he was investing all his earnings in the new garage—he shot and killed his flirtatious sister-in-law in a wild argument, then killed the guard at the local jail just twenty minutes later in a bungled attempt to set free his sick brother before turning himself in for the first killing. At his trial, seeing his young wife sitting there pregnant by another man, he went to pieces. "Fourteen months of dreading the death penalty had strained my emotions beyond caring and my reaction was immature and suicidal," he wrote later. "Drowning in self-pity and guilt, I wasn't aware of much of what was happening, but I would stare at the jury with the most hateful expression on my face, as if that would be enough to condemn me to death. I thought that by getting sentenced to death, it would punish Dolores for betraying my trust; a wounded heart does many stupid things. My execution was scheduled for March 28, 1968, but it was postponed and finally commuted to life in 1969."

Because New Mexico's jails could not hold him, Garcia was transferred to Marion, where he spent his first four or five months in the Control Unit; eventually he was given so much time in solitary that he could not handle people when he was returned to the general prison population: "I had been locked up in isolation too long." Besides an Indian named Alan Iron Moccasin and an Inuit, Joe Komok, Garcia's only friend in Marion was Victor Bono, who in 1975 filed a celebrated prisoners' suit against the Marion authorities, in specific protest against the horror of the Control Unit; thanks to Bono, the lightless "boxcar" cells, declared unconstitutional as cruel and unusual punishment, have since been modified. Nevertheless, Bono's suit was denied in 1978, despite criticism of the Control Unit's police-state techniques from many authorities, including U.S. District Judge James Foreman of St. Louis: "In several instances," the judge commented, the Control Unit "has been used to silence prison critics. It has been used to silence religious leaders. It has been used to silence economic and philosophic dissidents." Ralph Aron, a former warden of Marion, agrees: "The purpose of the Marion Control Unit is to control revolutionary attitudes in the prison system *and the society at large*" (emphasis added)—a remark to which every American, red and yellow, black and white, might pay attention.[9]

After two years in Marion, Garcia was returned to New Mexico, where he escaped again from the state prison; he was returned to Marion in 1976 and sentenced to two straight years of isolation. ("If you believe my punishment has been enough—Help Me!" he cried in a public letter to his judge and New Mexico's Governor Apodaca.) Inevitably he suffered a complete breakdown, after which he was transferred, in January 1979, to Lompoc Federal Correctional Institution. "It was the best prison I have ever been in in all the years I have been in prison," he said later. "You could spend a lot of time in the sunshine, walk around the yard . . ."

While in Lompoc, Garcia received word from Alan Iron Moccasin, telling him to set up bodyguard protection for an incoming convict named Leonard Peltier. "I saw this fellow which I thought was a Mexican which turned out to be Leonard Peltier," Garcia remembered. Accosting Peltier in Spanish and receiving minimal response, he said, "I thought you were a Mexican. You sure *look* like a Mexican." And Peltier said, "Well, that could be a compliment, because as far as I am concerned, Mexicans are Indian people."

Garcia, a shy untrusting man whom Peltier remembers as having no friends and being "in a total shell," was won over by this easy remark and the warmth behind it. "I don't make too many friends," he said, "and me and Leonard became good friends. He was teaching me about the Indian religion, my Indian heritage, things that I didn't know that I should be proud of, and I come to like the man."

Another convict who became attached to Peltier was Dallas Thundershield, aged twenty, from Little Eagle on the Standing Rock Reservation, who arrived in Lompoc not long after Peltier himself. The two had met briefly in 1974, at the first International Indian Treaty Council meeting at Standing Rock, and the young Lakota was working hard to relearn the traditional ways; he had brought his sacred medicine and tobacco bundles with him to Lompoc, and was taking part in the sweat-lodge ceremonies run by Lame Deer. Inspired by Peltier, he wrote the letter of exhortation to his people that is quoted in the Introduction to this book.

Peltier says that "Dallas had gray eyes and was light-complected, but he was real traditional, even when I met him as a kid back on Standing Rock in 1974. He was real stone Indian, all the way. He used to talk about the poverty and drinking back there in Little Eagle, and he wanted to see some changes made when he got home."[10]

On the evening of July 20, about 8:30 p.m., Peltier and Garcia found excuses to leave an Indian meeting in the prison auditorium, then started fires in their cells to distract attention from their escape. At the last minute, they were joined by Dallas Thundershield. ("I tried to talk him out of it," Garcia recalls, "because he only had a few years to do in prison, and he was inexperienced at everything.") The three used keys manufactured by Garcia to reach the roof of J Unit cellblock; from there, they jumped, running along past the laundry building and the prison industries in the bright light under Tower 4, and "hitting the fences" not far from the back gate. The tower guard yelled at them, but for some reason he did not fire until the fugitives were almost beyond shotgun range. His shots were answered by what turned out to be diversionary fire from outside persons who had positioned themselves near the northeast corner of the prison, where a service road ran along a tree line; one of these people gave a Mini-14 rifle to Peltier as he ran past.

"Bobby went over the first fence," Peltier remembers. "I followed right behind him, Dallas, too; the second fence is higher than the first fence and Bobby climbed up [and] was cutting the wires on the second fence and I was holding his legs. And in the meantime this guy in this tower started shooting and Bobby fell down and I asked him, I says, Are you all right? He says, Yeah. And I say, Well, I'm going. So I just climbed the fence and Dallas gave me a shove and I just went . . . right over the fence.

"In the meantime this guy was still shooting, so when I hit the ground, I realized that I had to get close to this powerhouse to get behind cover. . . . Dallas was right there behind me, then Bobby was right behind him. Then I lost Bobby, I don't know where. I lost him someplace, and me and Dallas headed for the trees. In the meantime there was a vehicle coming at a very high rate of speed . . . I remember we looked and we seen the headlights coming. . . . Dallas was there alongside of me and we got to the trees and Dallas was to the right of me. And we had been running, been running very hard, so we were kind of out of breath a little bit, and we stopped there for just a second. In the meantime, the guy in the van, or pickup, whatever it was—I guess I don't actually know what it was because all I seen was headlights—and he—I heard somebody holler, All right, come on out from behind those trees!"

W. H. Guild, engineer, powerhouse:

> At about 9:45 P M I heard #3 tower firing his shotgun, I went out to see if I could be of assistance. I saw inmates in between the fence. I then locked the power house and drew a 38 revolver and took the power house truck toward the delivery entrance. I saw two inmates running toward the tree line. I drove the truck toward the treeline until I could see both inmates. I stopped the truck and yell halt several times. At that time they stopped, but then started running again. I fired two rounds and one fell. I called and told him not to move. At that time Mr. Blackburn arrived to give assistance.

> Also Mr. Graves arrived with a flashlight. At that time we saw that the inmate was wounded. At that time I returned to the power house.
>
> The .38 Revolver that was issued to me was SER. #445497.

D. A. Blackburn, correctional officer, fence patrol #1 E/W:

> I heard someone calling for assistance east of my present location. The Officer, Mr. Guild, was stating that he had a man down and he was hurt. When I reached his location, I observed Officer Guild standing over a white male, with long black hair, 6-0 feet, approximately 180 pounds. I asked Mr. Guild if he was okay, and he replied he was not hurt. I then attempted to question the man about the extent of his injury. He told me he hurt and could not move his legs. At that point I recognized the man as being Dallas Thundershield, one of the inmates who resides in "J" Unit. I continued to reassure him that he was going to be okay and that help was on the way. Within approximately two or three minutes after my arrival the subject started to go into convulsions and at one point stopped breathing. At this time I advised Mr. Guild that I was going to direct the staff coming to assist to our location. As I started to walk back toward the delivery access road, I heard and observed a man running east of my location in a westerly direction along the south side of the tree line. I identified myself and ordered the man to stop. He ran approximately 15 feet further and knelt behind a large tree with his back facing me. I told him that if he moved I would shoot and ordered him to raise his hands. He complied with my orders and remained sitting in a squatting position. I walked to a position to where I was parallel to the tree and approached the subject, shotgun in hand. When I reached the tree I ask the subject to stand and walk away from the tree in a southerly direction or toward the institution. He walked out approximately 15 ft. when I directed him to lay face down with arms spread. He again complied without saying a word.
>
> Within minutes, Officer Graves and Lt. Hutson arrived at my location.

Graves and Hutson had heard over the radio that two men had been apprehended near the tree line by the service road on the east side of the prison boundary. There they found Blackburn guarding a man lying arms spread, face down on the ground. On the far side of the tree line, the powerhouse engineer, a former prison guard named William Guild, stood with his handgun pointed at another prostrate figure.

E. D. Graves, special officer:

> I then approached the subject and conducted a brief search for weapons. No weapons were found to be on his person nor in his reach. The subject was lying with his head pointing in a northerly direction. I questioned the subject to determine if he was conscious but received no audible response. I checked the carotid area to determine any pulse and was unable to feel any pulse. No breathing was determined. I then checked the subject's pupils with a flash light and received no response from same. The pupils were dilated and the eyes lacked luster. The subject was warm to the touch.

John B. Hughes, correctional officer:

> At approximately 10:30 p.m. I was engaged in making a search of the area in a northerly direction from the Institution toward the F.C.I. Firing Range. As I was proceeding toward the Range at a point about 75–80 yards east of the Sewage Pond #1 I was alerted by a voice saying *"This is Garcia. I'm unarmed. Don't shoot."* Or words to that effect. While a light was held on Garcia, who was laying in knee deep grass, I approached him and put the flexible emergency handcuffs on the suspect, after performing a frisk search of his person.

Lieutenant Greg Hutson, correctional supervisor:

> At approximately 9:50 p.m., I returned to the individual being detained and asked him his name and what unit he was from. He said his name was "Rocky" and that he was not from here. We searched "Rocky" and found a .45 caliber magazine with ammo in it, inside his right rear pocket.
>
> About 9:55 p.m., Graves then informed "Rocky" of his rights, and "Rocky" acknowledged he understood his rights, but refused to answer questions. When Graves asked Blackburn where he first saw this man, Blackburn pointed to a large tree, where Graves

> shined his light and found a .45 caliber automatic pistol. A wallet was found on his person which contained a Washington state driver's license, giving the name of the person as Roque Orlando DUENAS. Duenas was subsequently removed from the area.
>
> The outside agencies began arriving and a coordinated search effort was initiated. A picture of the downed person was brought to the area of one Dallas THUNDERSHIELD, 03301-073J, with the downed person identified as Thundershield. Shortly afterwards, we were informed the third person, who was still missing, was Inmate Leonard PELTIER, 89637-132H. At approximately 10:45 p.m., Dr. Hudson arrived and officially pronounced Thundershield dead.

In his report, Guild is at pains to say that his weapon was "issued" (he does not say who issued it) and furnishes its serial number for good measure; tower guard R. Hodgkinson states that he issued it, and Officer Graves, too, makes a point of establishing where the weapon came from as well as Guild's right as a powerhouse employee to use it. Graves goes so far as to declare that he "stepped through the tree line and saw Bill Guild pointing an institution-issued .38 caliber revolver at a male subject"—a very keen observation indeed at such a chaotic moment in the night, and a very prudent one, as well.

L. D. Mahan, unit officer, "J" Unit, E/W:

> This officer was notified by Control at 11:45 Pm that inmate THUNDERSHIELD #03301-078 had been released to Death during an escape attempt.

Thundershield, #03301-078, had been "released to Death," according to the coroner's report, because of "exsanguination [due to] perforation of superior vena cava [as a consequence of] gunshot wound to posterior chest."

9:28 P.M.	Smoke alarm #14 H Unit—fire put out 9:36 P.M.
9:41 P.M.	Escape attempt #3 tower—reported approximately 3 inmates scaled fence.
9:41 P.M.	Escape procedures put into effect.
10:00 P.M.	Thundershield reporting missing from J Unit. Peltier and Garcia reported missing from H Unit.
10:45 P.M.	Thundershield J to deceased

11:09 P.M. Official count verified
11:09 P.M. Garcia 02002-136 apprehended from escape status and placed in I Unit.
11:55 P.M. Peltier 89637-132 still on escape status.

21 July 79/SATURDAY MORNING

12:00 AM All assigned personnel present for duty.
1:20 AM Inmate BLACK CLOUD #1021-288(J) placed in I-Unit—investigation. —All official counts verified.
6:00 AM Escape search continued for escaped prisoner.
6:18 AM Mr. Meckus completed fence repairs.
7:00 AM Dining Room opened for coffee and rolls.

At approx 9:05 P.M. 07-21-1979 a Mr. Simmons called and stated that he had been called from the F.C.I. Lompoc to make the notification to a Mrs. Simmons being Thundershields mother of her sons death. Mr. Simmons stated that Mrs. Simmons had passed away approx one hour before he had gotten there. Apparently from a heart attack.

CHARLES RICHARDS, Prison Number 05295-073, was interviewed at the Federal Correctional Institution (FCI), where he is an inmate. . . . RICHARDS reported he is a Sioux Indian from the Pine Ridge, South Dakota, reservation. RICHARDS placed himself in the Administrative Detention Unit at FCI on July 15, 1979 after hearing rumors that he would be stabbed. RICHARDS advised he did not know about LEONARD PELTIER's escape in advance and added that he did not get along well with PELTIER at FCI. RICHARDS stated he is married to SAUNIE RICHARDS, nee Wilson. Her father is RICHARD WILSON, who was the former Tribal President at Pine Ridge, South Dakota, who had opposed the American Indian Movement (AIM). RICHARDS stated his wife was at the Inmate Hospitality House at Lompoc, and was advised by another inmate's wife that PELTIER had remarked that "RICHARDS was a government agent sent here to kill me." RICHARDS noted that he had conversed with PELTIER about three times at FCI since May 1979.

RICHARDS stated he had heard vague rumors that other Indians were supposed to get him, and as a result, he was locked up in protective custody for safety reasons.

Chuck Richards was transferred out of Lompoc shortly thereafter.

⊡

The day after the escape, radio and TV alarms and a new "wanted" poster were issued; the poster's warning that Peltier might be carrying an automatic rifle (he was not) was an invitation to nervous law officers to shoot him on sight. California AIM issued a call for young Indians to flood the area in order to confuse the search, as Peltier, equipped with Forest Service maps, headed north and east. In the July heat, to travel the dry hills and brush-choked gullies was exhausting, and he was weak with hunger five days later when he thought he saw melons (they turned out to be pumpkins) in an unguarded vegetable patch in Orchid, a small village in Santa Barbara County, about fifteen miles from Lompoc. "I kept looking at the house to make sure that nobody was there, kept observing it. And the only thing around there that was moving was a couple of old dogs. So . . . I decided to go down there and get myself a melon and go back into the hills and wait until it got dark and cross the highway. And when I went down to the melon patch, all of a sudden I heard a vehicle moving and I heard some gunshots, so I looked up and I seen this guy hollering, Hey! and shooting at the same time. So I ran back to where I was hidden and I heard his vehicle come up . . . by where I was laying, and I heard it stop and I was sitting there, I was watching him come walking up, walking around behind me, and when he came behind me he had his rifle up, not down, he had it pointed at me. I had my rifle behind me, and I pointed back at him. I told him, I says, Better drop your rifle, I says, please, I says, I don't want to kill you.

"So he threw his rifle down. I told him to step away from his rifle, and I walked over to his rifle and emptied it, and then I just threw it aside. And that is when he said, I suppose you are going to kill me now. And I said, No, I'm not a killer. I am not going to kill you. He said, I'm just a working man. And I said, Well, I'm a political prisoner. I don't go around killing people for no reasons at all. In fact, I haven't killed anybody.

"He showed me his ID and he had thirty dollars in his wallet, so I took that and gave him his wallet back and I told him, I said, I would tie you up, but at your age something might happen to you, you might have a heart attack or something, so I am going to give you a break and all I am going to do is take your boots and hope that gives me a little bit of time to get away from here."

Peltier acknowledges that he was angry at this man for shooting at him over a pumpkin, and he also knew that with nobody around, killing the man and taking his truck was his best chance for escape from the Lompoc region. But he did not harm him, and as soon as Peltier had left, the bootless farmer, Jerry Parker, hotfooted it to a telephone and reported the theft of his truck to the sheriff's office in Santa Maria, at the same time announcing his suspicion that this pumpkin thief might be Leonard Peltier, whose description had been widely broadcast ever since the escape.

A short time after Parker's call, his broken-down truck was found abandoned, not two miles from where he had last seen it. A teenage boy told Detective Bruce Correll of the Santa Maria Police Department that the truck had roared past him so fast that he thought "a crazy man was behind the wheel"; Correll speculated that the driver had thrown the clutch trying to shift down at high speed, starting uphill. (Peltier says the clutch was shot and the truck got stuck in second gear.) He also speculated about the driver's frustration, since the truck was plastered with its own cargo of tomatoes. (Peltier says the vegetables were thrown around on the rough ride.) But other would-be witnesses confused the search party, and not until early afternoon did the police conclude that the fugitive would not take flight across this open country carrying a rifle, nor would he give the rifle up; in all likelihood, he was somewhere within a one-mile radius of the abandoned truck. Footprints were located in a nearby field that matched the prints found in Parker's garden, and the hunt was on; in fact, Correll changed into hunting garb for the occasion. With Correll's group was Special Agent James Wilkins of the FBI, who had taken charge of the search on the night of the escape, five days before.

The trail crossed a ditch that the fugitive had taken in full stride, then climbed toward a eucalyptus grove on the top of a hill; a posse of more than twenty-five men spread out over the dry hills in groups of four. As his group started uphill, Correll remembers hearing himself yell, "We're coming up to get you, Peltier!"

From this point forward, the group was led by a young detective named Bill Turner, a Vietnam combat veteran; Turner, who was tracking, had the squad move from tree to tree, with two men covering him. On the hilltop, they came upon a place with a view of all the valley where someone had recently been lying, and here they slowed, moving carefully through thick poison oak and brush until, a short way down on the far side, they saw a man awaiting them under a tree. "That's when the adrenaline started flowing," Correll told a reporter for the Santa Maria *Times,* which published his excited account of the capture. "The information that we had on him was that he had a very explosive character, that he would not be taken alive. Every other time they caught him there was a shoot-out. Up in Canada, South Dakota. From what we heard, they just massacred those two FBI agents who tried to take him in."

The lawmen ordered Peltier not to run, at which point, according to Correll, the Indian began his "death chant" (Peltier doesn't have a death song, which is very rare now even among elderly traditionals). "It was something like *whoo-oo-oa,"* Correll told the press, "a very eerie sound." Then Peltier, expecting to be killed, said, "I have done my death chant, I'm an Indian, and an Indian is not afraid to die." (Peltier denies all this stuff, too.) With Correll and Wilkins covering, Turner moved in and put handcuffs on Peltier, and the hunt was over.

Near the fugitive, covered by branches, was the Mini-14 carbine and a clip of ammunition, and his captors asked him why he hadn't shot it out. Peltier said, "Maybe I could have gotten one or two of you, but I'm not a killer." Apparently Correll believed this, since he told the reporter about the pumpkin man's surprise at Peltier's reluctance to use his gun. "The story we got was that Parker asked him, You going to kill me now? and Peltier said, Naw, you're just a working man, like me. He told him he was an American Indian political prisoner, and the whole time Parker thought the guy was going to kill him. But he didn't and that was his biggest mistake." (That Parker was so sure Peltier would kill him suggests the effectiveness of those "armed and dangerous" broadcasts, not only on ordinary citizens but on law officers such as Correll whose lives would be risked in making the arrest.)

Although equipped with rifle, binoculars, and maps, the captive seemed very tired and disoriented after traveling without food for five long days. Handcuffed and searched, he was taken to the nearest house, where his tattoos were checked to make certain of his identity. Correll said that he had teased the prisoner. "I expected you to be a better woodsman," he said. "Your trail wasn't very hard to follow." And Peltier said, "Don't underestimate yourself, man. We need people like you back on the reservation." Peltier's wry response amused Correll. "Of course he was probably jerkin' me around," the lawman said.

Agent Wilkins's memories of the day are less convivial, to judge from the tight-lipped tone of his report, which does not record any rhetoric or death songs.

> Approximately 75 yards to the south of the dry creekbed, and at approximately 4:30 p.m., an individual was observed lying in the brush. This individual was immediately ordered to "freeze" and to place his hands over his head. He was heard to say "Okay, you got me. Now go ahead and kill me." He was advised that he was not going to be killed unless he did not follow instructions and made any move toward his weapon. He was handcuffed by Detective TURNER, and upon his face being revealed, Special Agent JAMES R. WILKINS immediately identified him as LEONARD PELTIER. He was removed from the brushy area to an open clearing where he was advised of the identities of the arresting officers. He was also advised of his rights orally by Special Agent WILKINS. PELTIER advised he understood his rights, but declined to answer any specific questions regarding his possible possession of a weapon.
>
> It was noted at the time of his arrest that PELTIER was wearing levis, a denim jacket, a black t-shirt and white tennis shoes. He was also wearing leather gloves. It was noted that he had a pair of binoculars around his neck and was in possession of a glass water bottle, a red address book, and several maps.
>
> PELTIER was questioned regarding his physical condition and he advised he was "Okay, but tired." . . . He was removed from the field to the first residence to the east for a closer examination and search. PELTIER was accompanied in the vehicle by Detective CORRELL and Special Agent WILKINS.
>
> Upon arrival at the residence, a check for tattoos revealed a "rose" on his right shoulder and LEONARD on his left shoulder. These were known tattoos and confirmed his identity.
>
> At that location, PELTIER's handcuffs were loosened by Detective CORRELL and he was given a cigarette and a drink of water by Special Agent WILKINS.

Peltier denies that the agent ever offered him the cigarette and water; his account of the capture, which emerged at his November trial in Los Angeles, differs markedly from that of Wilkins.

> A. . . . I was laying there and I could hear them. I couldn't really see them yet but I could hear them coming up real close. And

when I finally did see them they walked within ten feet of me, twenty feet at the most.

Q: Did you have your weapon there?

A: Yes.

Q: Could you have shot them if you wanted to?

A: I was looking at them and I was thinking Jesus, these guys, you know, if I wanted to, I could have wiped out two or three of them! . . .

Q: Would there have been anything then in your own mind that would have been between you and escape if you had in fact wiped them out?

A: Well, yeah, it would have drew all the officers into that area and I could have easily split out of there.

Q: In other words, there was nothing?

A: It would have been a diversion.

Q: You could have escaped if you had shot these people, is that what you felt?

A: Yes. . . .

Q: Start from the point that you believe they discovered your position.

A: Well, when they walked by me there was kind of a ridge . . . and up on top there was kind of an open area. They had walked up there and just kept on going. So I stood up and watched—or I laid there for a little while; I guess I laid there too long because when I stood up and started to try to look over the ridge, or edge, whatever—ridge, I guess you want to call it—I seen them coming back. So I, when I got down, I made some—some dry leaves made some noise. They said, somebody said, "There's somebody down there." And I just laid still and then they—somebody threw a piece of dirt, and I still didn't move. And, finally, so I guess one of them spotted me and said, "There he is." And I heard them come, surround me. And that's when Wilkins came on to the right. Turner was at my back and then—

Q: What was Mr. Turner doing?

A: Mr. Turner was putting the handcuffs on me.

Q: Did you resist in any way?

A: No, I didn't.

Q: All right.

A: He kept saying, "Don't move." He was very nervous, he was extremely—he was shaking, voice was quivering.

And Wilkins put the gun in my face, he says, "You punk, you killed my friend," he says, "I'm going to blow your fucking head off."

I told him, "Go ahead."

And Turner says, "I ain't going to be part of no killing."

And that's when Mr. Wilkins moved back.

Q: Mr. Peltier, directing your attention to the 20th of July, in the evening, was your purpose in fleeing the institution to avoid confinement?

A: No. For fear of my life.

To Detective Correll, Peltier had expressed astonishment that he had survived the capture, especially when an FBI agent was present. "I don't think he understands, even now, why we didn't kill him," Correll reflected. "There was so much the Indians were saying about an FBI conspiracy to do him in."

Peltier was booked at the sheriff's office on charges of armed robbery and auto theft; Agent Wilkins also booked him on "an outstanding federal arrest warrant for escape from a federal prison." He was later charged with conspiracy, assaulting a correctional officer (a stray bullet had whistled past an Officer Whitlock during the escape), and using firearms in commission of a felony.

Officer "Pete" Graves, who came to pick up the prisoner in Santa Barbara, reported that no questions were asked of Peltier on the drive back to Lompoc and that "the only remark Peltier voluntarily made was that he was tired and hungry." The next day he was flown back to Marion. According to Agent Wilkins, who spoke to him just prior to the flight, the prisoner, asked how he was feeling, said, "Sad. You should have killed me."

Both Garcia and Peltier claim that they saw Thundershield shot, and they also say that ex-guard William Guild, who acknowledged that the two fugitives had stopped after he first yelled at them, did not wait for the prisoners to start running again before he started shooting; Dallas Thundershield had been shot down where he stood. "That guard yells at us, Step out of there with your hands up! Well, I was only a few yards from Dallas, and I seen him step out away from the trees with his hands up. I was looking the other way, looking for a way out, when I heard the shot; when I looked back, I seen the dust rising, that's how hard he fell. He was laying there face down, his hands still up." He held his hands up to demonstrate. "They killed him in cold blood. Bobby and Roque seen it, too."

"That guy Guild come up in a truck that had very bright lights," Duenas remembered, "and from the moment he jumped out, he was yelling, Halt! Step out here! He wasn't excited, though, he seemed relaxed—in fact, he was the only one of all them guards that wasn't excited. Because of them bright lights, there was a deep shadow behind my tree; he never seen me, but I never took my eyes off that guy for a minute. Dallas was just beyond me—I was kind of between him and that guard—he was out in the open and he wasn't running; he seemed kind of confused, and it seemed like he was hurt and stumbling a little. Coming over the fence, he fell on top of Leonard and Bobby, and maybe he sprained his ankle, I don't know. Anyway, I was watching the guard, but I was *aware* of Dallas, know what I mean? He wasn't running. He was just kind of shifting his weight, like, as if he had fallen and was just getting up. The guard kept yelling, and then he fired—didn't hardly seem to aim. Bobby said he thought he heard two shots, so maybe one missed, but I only heard the one. Dallas had his hands up and he went right over. Then Guild was yelling for assistance, and another guy with a riot gun come up; him and Guild stood over Dallas, and the second one turned away, saying to Guild, I don't know if I can keep my supper down. Dallas died in a couple of minutes; I never heard him say a word, all I heard was his last breath, like a sigh of relief."

Asked in court if he could have shot William Guild, Leonard Peltier said, "If I wanted to, I could have easily shot him . . . I was probably only 20 feet from him." Although fleeing for his life, he had shot at no one, not at Guild, not at Parker, not even at the lawmen who—he thought—intended to execute him on sight.

Peltier's attorneys now believe that someone had tipped off the authorities that Peltier was "going over the wall"; and they do not believe that the tower guard, Hodgkinson, using a shotgun, could have shot at three fugitives, climbing two fences and cutting wires, without getting a pellet in any one of them, unless the idea was to let them get outside the fence, where Guild was ready. Nor do they believe that Hodgkinson "issued" that gun to Guild by dropping it forty feet, at night. On the witness stand, the powerhouse guard admitted that he knew just where the fugitives were headed, and that he went right to the spot. After shooting Thundershield, Guild handcuffed the dying boy while he lay there in convulsions, never checking him for life signs—it was Graves and Blackburn who did that—after which he went back to his job.

"That guard was there, and he was ready," Bruce Ellison says. "He didn't know about Dallas, who decided to join at the last minute, and it looks like the wrong long-haired Indian got shot."

Archie Fire Lame Deer, who had held a sweat-lodge ceremony for Duenas on July 18 and breakfasted with him on the day of the escape, was interrogated by the FBI and denied any foreknowledge of the event. (The following year, when I asked him a few questions about Dallas Thundershield, there was a slight pause on the telephone. Then Lame Deer said, "It's ironic you called today to ask me that. I was just over at Lompoc yesterday to pick up that boy's things to be sent home! I'm looking at his owl feathers and eagle feathers, his tobacco bag and choker, right this minute!" He sighed. "Dallas was spiritually strong even before he came to Lompoc and met Leonard. It was Dallas who taught Leonard some of our Lakota songs.")

On July 27, 1979, Dallas Thundershield, twenty years old, was buried in the Good Shepherd Cemetery near Little Eagle.

In its exhaustive preparations for Peltier's escape trial, the FBI interviewed large numbers of people, among them the guard in charge of Peltier's cellblock, who stated that Peltier "appeared to be happy. He knows of no reason why Peltier would have been forced to escape from prison other than a desire to be free." This testimony, taken on August 17, nearly a month after the escape, seemed intended to counter the defense that Peltier's attorneys seemed certain to present: that he had attempted to escape because he feared for his life.

On September 4, Standing Deer (who had been fired from his office job at Leavenworth on the very day of the escape, despite a recent memo in his record about the "very high quality" of his work) got a message to Peltier and his attorneys:

> I received word from the folks in California that you want me to testify at your trial. I realize that you promised never to reveal that the United States had hired me to help kill you because you thought that I would lose my life if they ever found out what I told you. However, it seems obvious to me that they decided to use Chuck Richards to neutralize you instead of me, so it is unlikely

> that they will allow me to live very much longer anyway. I would rather go to my death knowing that at least their murderous scheme has been exposed than to carry that knowledge with me to the grave. . . .
>
> I release you from your vow of silence on this matter. I don't think it can hurt me to make this information public at your trial. . . . Let me know something as soon as possible. . . .
>
> In the spirit of Crazy Horse, Anna Mae, Joe Stuntz, Buddy Lamont & Dallas Thundershield, Robert
>
> P.S. We fasted from July 30 to Aug 8 and gave flesh for all the people, for Dallas & You & Bobby Garcia & Roque Duenas & all those who have given their lives and freedom in our struggle for nationhood & sovereignty.

Leonard Peltier's trial opened in the U.S. District Courthouse in Los Angeles on November 14, 1979, after U.S. marshals, booting shrines and breaking religious objects as they made arrests, broke up a prayer vigil outside the building; among those badly beaten in the fray was Bob Robideau's old comrade Nacho Flores, former coordinator of California AIM. The prosecution was handled by Assistant U.S. Attorneys Lourdes Baird and Robert Biniaz, who took almost a month to present the government's case; because of restrictions laid down by the judge, the defense was finished in three days.

⊡

Judge Lawrence Lydick, appointed to the bench by his old law-firm partner Richard Nixon, had denied the prosecution's pre-trial motion to prohibit evidence supporting the coercion-and-duress defense that was Peltier's one hope for acquittal; for some reason, he reversed himself on this critical point after the trial was well under way. That defense was invalid, Lydick ruled, because (a) the defendant had not tried to escape from Marion when he first heard about the plot to kill him; (b) he had not reported the plot to the prison authorities; (c) he had failed to turn himself in to the police upon escaping from Lompoc Federal Correctional Institution. That an escape from the highest-security prison in the land had never succeeded; that reporting the plot to those he thought wished to kill him was absurd; that turning himself in, after his escape, to the people from whom he was fleeing was suicidal—these points were all ignored by Lydick. He ruled that the coercion-and-duress defense would not be permitted, and neither would testimony concerning the assassination plot by the twelve federal prisoners whom the defense was prepared to call, including Standing Deer, his erstwhile partner Don Richardson, and David Owens (who had offered to testify that in January 1979 he had overheard a conversation between Standing Deer and the associate warden of Leavenworth, Ray Lippman, in which Lippman made clear that he knew about the plot to murder Peltier).

Both Owens and Richardson are white men, and both took the same risks as Standing Deer in testifying in the defendant's behalf. The remarkable loyalty to Peltier shown by these men was expressed in a different way by Bobby Garcia, who was asked in court why he had risked his life to accompany the escape, then given himself up to divert attention from his friend.

> A: Well, because I wanted to make sure that he made the escape good. I had escaped before and . . . this was his first time in prison. I didn't think he could make it by himself, so I helped as much as possible. I wanted to make sure that I could draw fire in case it was necessary.
>
> Q: Now, when you say "to draw fire in case it was necessary," what do you mean by that?
>
> A: Well, Leonard has a lot to give to the people. I don't. And he's a good man. . . .
>
> Q: What experience did you have that would be of any assistance to them?
>
> A: I had escaped twice before, not from Lompoc, from other penitentiaries, from New Mexico, and I thought my, call it experience, would enable Leonard to make good his escape. . . . Because all the men around that area would come toward me and I would occupy them . . . while Leonard could make his escape. . . . I have nothing to give to my people. I got a lot of time to do, and Leonard, you have to talk to the man before you can understand, before you can know him. The way he explains things to you, he makes it so clear. And he gives you a sense of unity, a sense of worth. What can you say? What more honor can you give a man than that?
>
> Q: Than to be willing to give up your life?
>
> A: Yes.

Asked on the witness stand if he had any particular skills, Robert Hugh Wilson, "Standing Deer," answered, "Writing administrative remedies and robbing banks." Although forbidden to mention it, he inserted the assassination plot into several answers, all of which were ordered stricken from the record by Judge Lydick. Eventually the judge became so incensed by this witness's seeming inability to comply with orders that he was half up off the bench, looming over the unrepentant felon in the witness chair. Accused by defense attorney Lewis Gurwitz of attempting to intimidate the witness by "sticking your face in his," Lydick denied this, adding, "We don't think he is intimidated."[11] At this point the witness himself turned a cool gaze upward.

"You frighten me, Judge," Standing Deer said.

"I can tell," said Judge Lawrence Lydick.

Leonard Peltier, taking the stand, referred to the fear for his life that inspired the dangerous escape attempt from Lompoc, and Judge Lydick threatened the defendant with contempt of court if the subject of the assassination plot came up again. When Peltier remarked to the jury that restrictions like these on his defense had brought about his murder convictions at Fargo, Lydick intervened again, at which point Peltier, refusing to participate further in his own "railroading," walked off the stand in disgust.

Peltier, who had been quiet and courteous throughout the Fargo trial, realized that once again he had no chance, and at one point exclaimed, "Farce!" in open court; he repeated, "Farce!" more loudly when the judge demanded to know what he had said. Lydick, very angry, ordered him not to direct any remarks to the court except through counsel. Peltier whispered to his lawyer Bruce Ellison, who came forward to the bench. "Mr. Peltier wishes to inform you," Ellison told Lydick, "that this whole trial is a farce."

"Lydick was even worse than Benson," Ellison says. "Neither of them wanted to believe what they were hearing about the FBI and the government, so they refused to listen. Judge McManus in the Cedar Rapids trial didn't want to believe it, either, but he recognized his duty to hear the evidence with an open mind, which Benson and Lydick were not able to do."

Lewis Gurwitz, representing Duenas, came to the same conclusion. "Every single day," he said, "I was in there slugging it out with a judge who refused . . . to listen, even *listen,* or accept the possibility that anything we alleged could have happened. That was his position, in my opinion: It's impossible that this could ever happen, and therefore I don't want to hear anything about it, and I don't want any witnesses talking about it."

On February 4, 1980, Leonard Peltier, acquitted of conspiracy and assault, was sentenced to five years for escape plus two years for possession of a weapon by a felon; the seven years were added to his two consecutive life terms. Bobby Gene Garcia, who had given himself up, received five years. Both men received the maximum sentences allowed by law. In a letter to supporters from Los Angeles County Jail, Peltier said, "Given the full facts of this trial, I am of the fixed opinion that no American jury would have convicted us. Instead I believe they would applaud the action that we took." Subsequently he was returned to the Marion Penitentiary with a recommendation from the Lompoc authorities that he be placed for an "indefinite" period of time in the Control Unit.

Roque Duenas was acquitted on charges of assault and of smuggling arms into the prison; a jury deadlock on the charge of aiding and abetting in the escape ended in a mistrial, and the government, rather than try him again, accepted a plea bargain: Duenas pleaded guilty to aiding and abetting, with the understanding that he would receive a prison sentence of two years. Judge Robert Takasugi, who immediately released him on probation—Duenas had already spent eight months in jail—expressed the conviction that he was not dealing with "a common criminal but a man with very deep human dimensions" and a true commitment to the Indian struggle. "I see no sin there," the judge said. "In fact, any person who does not possess empathy and concern for the way the Indian has been exploited and mistreated, in my opinion, is a moral dwarf." Judge Takasugi also expressed "very deep concern" about possible misconduct by the government in the Peltier case, citing especially Standing Deer's affidavits; he was eager to know, among other things, if the seven charges against Wilson in Oklahoma had actually been dismissed; if it was unusual for Wilson with his maximum-security classification to have been transferred to Leavenworth, then Lompoc (the same might have been asked about Peltier himself); if Wilson had actually been given that clerk's job at Leavenworth, and if he had been fired on the day of the escape. Takasugi was assured by prosecutor Biniaz that the alleged assassination plot had been thoroughly investigated by the Justice Department's Office of Professional Responsibility, which had found "absolutely no merit" in Wilson's charges.

Since the trial, however, the official records that support Standing Deer's statements have been verified by a Los Angeles *Times* writer named Bill Hazlett, a former combat infantry sergeant in the Korean war and a veteran police reporter with many friends in the law-enforcement profession. Though by no means a liberal, Hazlett was disturbed by what he had learned of the alleged plot to assassinate Peltier, and also by the uneasiness of the government attorneys: "I don't know for certain why the government is so jumpy about the Peltier case, but I do know this jumpiness is what got me to wondering about just what was going on."[12] The Los Angeles *Times* sent Hazlett east to Oklahoma, where he discovered that Robert Hugh Wilson's account of the dismissal of seven serious charges on his record was entirely true.

"Standing Deer is a tough, con-wise prison inmate who tried to use the system to his advantage, which I don't think is necessarily wrong, faced with the situation he was in," Hazlett says. "Somehow, I do believe most of what Standing Deer says, because of the fact that he didn't know about the seven-month delay in the actual dismissal of the felony charges in Oklahoma . . . and because of the way Larry Puckett reacted when I tried to question him about the case in Oklahoma." Puckett, a former assistant district attorney who signed the motion to dismiss the charges against Wilson, told Hazlett he could not recall being contacted by any government agent in regard to Standing Deer's case, nor could he explain the delay between the time Wilson and the Marion authorities were told that the Oklahoma charges had been dismissed and the actual dismissal, nearly seven months later. (In the opinion of attorney Gurwitz, the delay was an insurance of Standing Deer's cooperation: "Once the charges were dismissed they could never be refiled because the statute of limitations had run, so they held on to them for a while to keep Standing Deer in line.") Puckett attributed the decision to dismiss the charges to Wilson's back problem, which would complicate his return to Oklahoma for trial; since this convict had so much prison time in store for him, including three life sentences in Texas, Puckett said, "it didn't seem worthwhile to add to the expense and time just to add to his sentence." Yet prison records showed that despite his back problem, Wilson had been sent to Texas for trial in 1977, and they also showed that Donald Richardson, his partner in the 1975 bank robbery that resulted in the wounding of a police officer, had been returned to Oklahoma, tried, and sentenced to thirty-five additional years, although already facing more than a century in state and federal prisons.

Increasingly disturbed, Hazlett extended his researches to four other states, then continued east to Washington, D.C., to discuss his findings with old acquaintances at FBI headquarters and to hear the Bureau's explanation of the strange story. "I've always been a welcome guest back there in Washington, you know; used to get letters from J. Edgar Hoover and Clarence Kelley commending me for stories I had written concerning the FBI. But when those guys found out I was looking into this Peltier case, I couldn't even get up to the second floor. I mean, there's got to be *something* fishy here, because they stonewalled me entirely; they don't want to discuss this case at all." Hazlett's inquiries resulted in a five-part series of almost thirty thousand words, but despite all the time and money that went into it, the *Times* decided not to run it after all.

⊡

The comparative lenience with which Roque Duenas had been treated fueled the suspicions of those who were already saying that he had cooperated with the government. Even before the escape from Lompoc, Duenas was among the Movement people who had fallen victim to "informer" rumors. There was speculation, for example, that Duenas was the one who tipped off the FBI in November 1975 about the AIM fugitives in the motor home on the Oregon highways and who had led the authorities to Smallboy's camp when Peltier was arrested a few months later. But Dennis Banks names someone else as the Oregon informer, and a prominent leader in the fishing-rights struggle in the Northwest attributes the stories about Smallboy's camp to a woman in the Peltier defense group whose mistakes Duenas had criticized and who was also jealous of Roque's long friendship with Leonard. (Peltier himself says that "the person who was responsible for our arrest was the old man Yellow Bird who we learned later was paid for his work by the R.C.M.P.; because of this traitor, Smallboy's camp nearly split up. The camp schoolteacher said she understood the purpose of the camp was to help Indians, not to turn them in to those who Indian people consider our enemies.") But when Black Horse and Peltier were arrested, Duenas was suspected once again, and "the rumors spread, and the worse they got, the harder Roque worked to dispel them. Then the last debacle, trying to help Peltier escape—just romantic bullshit. I suppose he had the fantasy that if he could get Peltier free, then all the rumors against him would go away. Needless to say, the rumors did not stop."

One reason the rumors did not stop was what someone who suspected him refers to as "certain disconcerting unanswered questions" in regard to official behavior prior to and during the escape. Although visitation rights at Lompoc were very lenient, and although Duenas, an old friend of Peltier from the 1970 Fort Lawton days and after, had no prison record, the authorities denied him visits with Peltier after mid-June 1979, then ignored the fact that Duenas had promptly arranged to visit another prisoner at the same time and in the same visitation room in which Peltier met with a young Nez Perce woman named Carlotta Kaufmann.[13] On the last such visit, on July 18, Duenas left behind his wallet, which contained bills of sale for a .45 automatic and a .223 Mini-14 carbine, both of which were later identified as weapons brought along for the escape. Apparently untroubled by its contents—which were noted—the prison authorities returned this wallet to two women who came to claim it on July 19 without even asking for these people's names; this was later interpreted as foreknowledge of the escape, and increased the suspicion that Peltier had been set up. Duenas's friends, including Peltier, assume that this was just carelessness on both sides, but for other members of the West Coast group, "it was just too sloppy. Roque has been with us a long time; he's family, you know, and we trust him. But we just can't work with him no more."

When I talked with Duenas in New York, in the winter of 1981, he identified himself as "a Chichimeca Indian from Texas."[14] Since his friends considered him a Chicano, I wondered if it was Peltier who had given him this pride in his Indian origin, as he had also done for Bobby Garcia. "They put me in a cell next to Bobby by mistake in the L.A. County Jail, and I had a real good talk with him," Duenas told me. "I believe he was really sincere about wanting to learn about Indian culture; he was just beginning to learn."

Duenas brought up of his own accord his reputation as an informer. "I've had the finger pointed at me," he said, and shrugged. "Many of us have. That's what the Man has done to us, sowed all that mistrust. But you know something? It don't really bother me no more. I just do my work, do what has to be done to help the people. And after a while, people get to know who does what he says he is going to do, and who is just talking."

While in New York, Duenas was interviewed by a reporter for an article on Peltier; in the article a "friend" of Peltier was quoted as saying, "I think Leonard may well have killed those guys—he's capable of it."[15] Once again, rumor implicated Duenas as the source of this damaging remark, but the reporter says emphatically—and persuasively—that this "friend" was not Duenas. A strange, thin, haunted man with eyes that looked somehow lost behind his glasses, Roque struck me as earnest and well-meaning; he *did* say something very indiscreet (not about Peltier), but he seemed to speak out of naive inability to hide what had come into his head, not to cause trouble. A few months later, the news came that he and his nephew had drowned when their salmon-fishing boat apparently overturned in rough weather off Narrows Point in Puget Sound.[16] The younger man's body was recovered—it had a large bruise on the forehead, caused by a blow—but Roque Duenas disappeared, trailed by dark rumors to the end.

CHAPTER 15

THE REAL ENEMY

Those people will wander this way . . . they will be looking for a certain stone. . . . They will be people who do not get tired, but who will keep pushing forward, going all the time. They will keep coming, coming. . . . They will travel everywhere, looking for this stone which our great-grandfather put on the earth in many places. . . . These people will not listen to what you say; what they are going to do they will do. You people will change: in the end of your life in those days you will not get up early in the morning, you will not know when day comes. . . . They will try to change you from your way of living to theirs. . . . They will tear up the earth, and at last you will do it with them. When you do, you will become crazy, and will forget all that I am teaching you.

Sweet Medicine (*Cheyenne*)

With the near-destruction of the American Indian Movement, the Indians realized that the real enemy in the new Indian wars was not the federal and state bureaucracies and their hostile agents; what threatened them most was "the corporate state," that coalition of industry and government that was seeking to exploit the last large Indian reservations in the West. By the mid-1970s, according to the Federal Energy Commission, Indian lands had already produced nearly $4 billion worth of oil and gas, coal, uranium, and other minerals, and the corporate state did not intend to allow Indians to get in the way.

> The authorizing legislation creating the Department of Energy allows the director of the agency to enter into a pact with the Department of Defense to seize unilaterally and hold areas of strategic mineral significance if such action is justified as being in the "national interest." For Indian nations that have enough energy resources to make a difference in the future direction of this country, such a stipulation is equivalent to a threat to call out the cavalry again . . . for Indian nations to defy the national policies of the U.S. government and multinational corporate interests is to defy the two most powerful forces on the face of the earth. To do so is to invite possible military intervention. For most Indians, it would not be the first time. During the 1973 Arab oil embargo the U.S. government made contingency plans to intervene militarily in order to secure "our" oil in the Mideast because it was in the "national interest." So if the *Wasi'chu* government talks about using military intervention to secure "our" oil in an area halfway around the world, what is it going to say about securing "our" coal and "our" uranium right here in Indian Country?[1]

By the time the North Central Power Study appeared in 1971, the Northern Cheyenne nation in Montana had begun to question the effect of the coal leases on its lands; fifteen miles north of the reservation, at the great strip mine and power plant called Colstrip, huge green machines were overturning the broad rangelands of the old buffalo country, and even "progressive" Indians perceived that the destruction of their sacred lands could only lead to the destruction of the Cheyenne as a people, as their prophet, Sweet Medicine, had warned them more than a century before. New lease applications were resisted, and on March 5, 1973—perhaps inspired by the confrontation at Wounded Knee—the Cheyenne Tribal Council voted unanimously to cancel all existing leases, and sued the Department of the Interior for betrayal of its trust responsibilities in encouraging the leases in the first place. Although these cancellations were fought by the mining companies, the Interior Department was forced to support the Cheyenne, who also challenged the construction of further power plants in the region on the grounds of deteriorated air quality caused by the Colstrip operation, and have since demanded that the Interior Department protect their water by forbidding strip-mining within fifty miles of their boundaries. In all these matters, the Crow nation has followed their lead, and so have Montana ranchers, irate citizens, and eventually, the state government itself. Realizing that the Yellowstone River, on which the state largely depends, might run dry in drought time if the proposals in the study were carried out, the state issued a water permit moratorium in 1977 that brought the headlong rampage of the strip miners under control.

The companies, insisting on their leases, continued their efforts to divide the reservations through bribery and coercion while exhausting the Indians' limited resources in court. Meanwhile, the industry stuck to its plan to encircle the Black Hills with thirteen coal-fired plants, producing ten thousand megawatts apiece; more than sixty additional plants were under consideration. Also proposed was a nuclear-energy "park" of as many as twenty-five reactors, with attendant water-reprocessing and disposal grounds, fed by exploration holes, mines, mills, and the deadly hills of processed ore, or mine tailings that erode and leak and blow downwind in eight states of the West.

The waste and ruin of precious water throughout the western states is a calamity that few public servants have yet found the courage to deal with. The lakes and streams of the Black Hills, and the tilted rock layers that ensure that much of the rainfall restores groundwater to the great aquifers, have provided abundant water for the agriculture and tourism on which until recently these states' economy had been based. Now the energy industry was seizing this water, which is required in immense amounts in all phases of its operations; the water level in the deep Madison Formation (which underlies much of southern Alberta and Saskatchewan as well as all the northern Plains states) is expected to sink at least a thousand feet in mining regions. In 1977, the Interior Department's final environmental impact statement endorsed the North Central Power Study's grand designs for this "national sacrifice area," despite an acknowledgment that mining and power-plant development on the proposed scale would devastate some 188,000 acres and inflict damage that was probably irreparable on the water, land, and life of the Great Plains. A doomsday smog of sulfur, nitrogen, and ash would shroud the big skies of the mountain states even at night, and carry eastward in an acid rain all over the country, while toxic waste and runoff from the huge earth-busting operations would sink into the aquifers and sour the disappearing creeks and prairie sloughs across thousands of square miles. Even the impact statement specified that reclamation, if any, "would be hampered by the severe climate, limited rainfall, short growing season, and . . . nature of surface materials" in the region. Also, Indian people would lose their "special relationship to the land," as the land itself shifted to "mineral extractive use." On the other hand, the Indians would be compensated by exchanging their "isolation" for "a closer relationship with American society" in "the mainstream of American life." This hypocritical "mainstream" talk, an echo of the nineteenth century, was denounced by the AIM leaders as "cultural genocide."

Under the banner of national defense and "energy independence," the same old entrenched and greedy interests were eating away at the heart and spirit of the land, but now resistance had begun to spread through the Rocky Mountain states and eastward into Minnesota. The Western Shoshone had been joined by many whites in the Great Basin MX Alliance, which was fighting the proposed destruction of vast tracts of their Utah and Nevada land for the absurd MX-missile railroad. The Utes in Colorado and Utah were fighting to protect their land and water rights; in New Mexico, the Navajo were threatening to cancel energy-industry leases on the Navajo Mine and the Four Corners Power Plant (the pollution from which was the only man-made creation that was visible to the voyagers to the moon), while the Laguna Pueblo, beset by cancer and crippled infants, were reconsidering the lease on the largest uranium strip mine in the world. In the dirtied light of the once brilliant Southwest, with contamination everywhere and spreading, even those people who had rushed to profit were starting to realize that red-man problems were white-man problems, too: that destruction of the human habitat, and the sickness that followed, would make no distinctions of human color. But South Dakota, which Indians call "the most racist state in the Union, even worse than New Mexico and Arizona," was also one of the poorest, and not until recently did red men and white finally join forces in a desperate fight to protect their future and their children from the multinational conglomerates, which had demonstrated everywhere a cold avoidance of responsibility toward the local people and the long-term economic stability of these doomed regions. As Ted Means said not long ago, "In ten years, there will be nothing left for us to fight over."

In addition to federal and Indian territory, 700,000 acres of state land had been signed over to the energy domain by 1978, when Attorney General William Janklow became the Governor of South Dakota. To no one's surprise, he had received the full support and financial endorsement of the energy corporations; in fact, this support was organized and led by his friend Jeremiah Murphy, attorney for the Union Carbide Corporation, which was involved in every phase of the nuclear cycle, from exploratory mining in the West to the weapons laboratories at Oak Ridge, Tennessee, and had been awarded $10 billion in contracts by the Department of Energy for 1978–83. In January 1979, in his very first week in office, the grateful Janklow abolished South Dakota's Department of Environmental Protection, assigning its duties to the Department of Natural Resources, which sponsors energy development; four months later, he issued a remarkable "gag order" on any comment from people in state government on energy issues, presumably because so much of it was adverse. As in Montana, even the bureaucrats were starting to realize that for want of water, not uranium or coal, the great energy consortiums would abandon the Black Hills in no more than thirty years, by which time all irrigation, all significant agriculture, would have ceased.[2] Already the Bureau of Reclamation and the Army Corps of Engineers were allocating Missouri River water to the energy corporations at a rate well above the level of replacement, as mining exploration spread east and west from the Black Hills; the Powder River in the great buffalo country claimed by Red Cloud had been assigned in such a way that industries had permits for more than seven times the amount of water that actually flowed there. The dispensation of the precious water necessitated the violation of prior water rights of the Lakota, Cheyenne, Crow, Arikara, and other Indian nations of the Missouri River Basin—easily arranged, since the Bureau of Reclamation supervises the BIA.

Ironically, the shadow of the energy empire in the northern Plains fell very close to the old boundaries of what was once the great Lakota territory. In a few decades, perhaps less, a dry, poisoned, and eroded waste would transform this gold-green country, and to no good purpose: the uranium to be produced far exceeded all domestic nuclear demand.[3] Despite all the patriotic rhetoric by politicians and energy executives, the uranium was not intended to resolve the pumped-up and immensely profitable "energy crisis" but to add to the grotesque accumulation of weapons for the formerly unthinkable World War III. In the clamor of so-called "serious" discussion of "nuclear options," "limited nuclear war," and other half-cocked concepts by men of stunted imagination and no vision, it was difficult to forget the great destroying fire of Indian prophecy.

In January 1979—the same month that Janklow abolished South Dakota's Department of Environmental Protection—Indian and white people joined forces in an inspired environmental group called the Black Hills Alliance, dedicated to educating the people of the state about the dangers of nuclear mining and milling, water depletion and contamination, and other environmental problems; it would also support the Lakota land claim to the Black Hills, which might help to delay the mining rampage by tying up the companies in court. The Indians in the Black Hills Alliance had mostly been organized by the Means family, and one Alliance leader was Russell Means's cousin Madonna Gilbert, former state coordinator of AIM, a tough-minded energetic woman whose lively smile was rarely seen when she first worked with white people in the Alliance; now they teased her as "the meanest of the Means." Though mainly concerned with the AIM survival schools, which teach her people to adjust to the realities of the white economy without losing the power of traditional culture, she is also a founder of AIM's sister organization, Women of All Red Nations (WARN), which helped to hold AIM projects together in the violent years when the Movement's leaders were dispersed. "Indian women have had to be strong because of what this colonialist system has done to our men," she told me in April 1980, when I visited the Alliance office in downtown Rapid City. "I mean, alcohol, suicides, car wrecks, the whole thing. And after Wounded Knee, while all that persecution of the men was going on, the women had to keep things going."

The Wounded Knee confrontation in 1973 had intensified the Lakotas' bitter feelings about white people, and the years that followed made it clear that in the multinational energy corporations and the government they faced a single monolithic enemy. "We were thinking about something like the BHA about a year after Wounded Knee, when all those whites came in to help as lawyers," Gilbert says. "After the shoot-out down at Oglala, we knew for sure that there was a bigger, broader problem behind all these local issues; there was a hell of a lot more going on than disputes between longhair Indians and redneck ranchers. Janklow got elected Attorney General as an 'Indian fighter,' out to wipe out AIM; when he ran for Governor, a lot of Indians registered and voted for the first time in their lives, and when he *still* won by a landslide, we knew the kind of racism we had to deal with. But soon Janklow began to lose support even with white ranchers, and we realized that, for the first time in history, we might be able to work with white people in a common cause."

The Black Hills Alliance, joined by WARN (but not AIM, which is still a red flag to most white South Dakotans), was supported by a whole range of environmental, anti-nuclear, and anti-powerline coalitions. "The spirit is fantastic around here," says Madonna Gilbert. "I come in here, you know, and I just feel *good*!" As she says this, her face lights up in a great smile. "And it's not just what BHA is accomplishing; I'm thankful that I've found a way to fight the whole damned syndrome of Indian existence."

⊡

While in Rapid City, in April 1980, I drove down to Pine Ridge with Bob Robideau, who was recently out on parole from his sentence in Leavenworth; while in prison, Robideau had an excellent work record in the machine shop and attended night courses, acquiring two years of college education. "Most commendable," said the judge who reduced his ten-year sentence in 1979.

A taciturn, lanky, light-skinned man in his early thirties, Robideau was dressed in a red shirt, leather vest, jeans, boots, and a black cowboy hat with a buffalo-nickel hatband from which his long black hair fell straight down between his shoulder blades; he is near-blind in one eye from the explosion on the Kansas Turnpike, and he speaks quietly, with laconic humor, often directed at himself, and a lot more firmness than his wary manner might suggest. "This is the first time I've visited the res since 1975," he told me as we drove southeast out of Rapid City; he wanted to visit his friend Ted Means and also the grave of Joe Killsright Stuntz, killed at Oglala.

Robideau's mother came from Turtle Mountain; his father, Bill, was originally from the White Earth Reservation in Minnesota. In the 1940s, this Ojibwa family was relocated in Portland, where Bob was born in 1946. Many relocated Indians, the Robideaus among them, became migrant farm workers; they were never accepted by the white culture, and those who made it home to the reservations often found that they were not quite trusted anymore as traditional Indians.

Like many children of these uprooted families, Robideau was in trouble very early. "I started young, but I did it more for adventure than for money. Except to use in a robbery or something, I never stole but one car in my life; I took a Renault Dauphine when I was twelve and just drove her off into a swamp. The only other one I ever took was because I had to get home and I couldn't figure out any other way to get there."

In 1959, his cousin Leonard Peltier traveled west to join his mother's people; Leonard did not live with his mother but just camped there occasionally, having already begun the highway wandering that is so much a part of Indian existence all over the country. Not long after his arrival, Leonard accompanied Bill Robideau and his wife on a visit to their son, Bobby, who was now a reform-school student at McLaren, Oregon. "Instead of a visit," Robideau recalls, "they took me straight on south to California, and we never went back. I don't know whose idea it was—probably mine. Anyway, that's when I first began to associate with my cousin Leonard. We did a lot of migrant work—Gurneyville, Stockton, Santa Rosa Valley—and meanwhile we were learning a lot from my dad, who was a good welder and a carpenter. No politics then—just drinking and hell-raising. The year after he came out there—he was fifteen then—Leonard bought his first car, a '50 Chevy; he was real proud of that old car.

"When I was eighteen, I tried an armed robbery of a supermarket. I wasn't very impressive in my size, so I took along a cousin who weighed two hundred pounds, and also a busted sawed-off shotgun. Well, the manager was the only one knew how to open the safe, and he got away from my cousin while I'm in the back, so my cousin took off, too, never letting me know. I wind up trying to get the butcher to open up the cash registers, all the time looking out the door for the cops, and finally I decide I better go. When I get outside, I see this car idling, and it's the manager. As soon as I start across the road, that car starts after me, trying to run me down. Luckily, there was a little hill there, and I ran up as fast as I could run, and his bumper's just tapping the backs of my legs, you know, when he finally stalls out. But they caught up with me anyway," Bob Robideau said, with a short laugh like a snort of disgust. "I sure never made my livelihood off my criminal activities, because I kept getting caught."

Between the ages of eleven and eighteen, Robideau was convicted of seven burglaries and two armed robberies, but "in all them times I got in trouble, I never hurt anybody, and I never got charged with assault; it was that busted shotgun that put violence on my record. Leonard was the only one of us that never had no violence on his record—oh, I mean, he'd get into fights, maybe misdemeanor stuff, but nothing serious. And Dino Butler's not a violent person, either; I've never heard of Dino even getting mad except just once, when an Indian hit him in a bar for no good reason. He just sat there on the floor a minute, really astonished, and then he got up and just shredded that guy. Dino's not an aggressive person or a bully. That one time he ever got into real trouble, he was provoked into it, but he got two years for assault with a dangerous weapon all the same. That's when we first met, in the Oregon State Penitentiary, in 1968; those were the days when you had to walk lockstep everywhere, even to meals, single-file on a red line, until finally the cons almost destroyed the pen and they had to get rid of the warden."

In the penitentiary, Robideau read Camus and Dostoevsky ("I was doing time, so I could relate to *Crime and Punishment*"), and in 1973, he got out on a school release to Oregon State University. But when he went home to Portland on a pass, he was stopped by police while driving his cousin's car. "I was wearing a black cowboy hat and braid," he says, "and it was very obvious that I was not part of the System." Since he was not supposed to be driving cars, and since his cousin's car was unregistered, his school release was revoked, and rather than return to the penitentiary, he traveled south a second time to California, where he hid out for a month at the Box Canyon camp that was taken over by AIM the following year. From there he went to South Dakota, joining his cousins Jim Robideau and Leonard Peltier at the huge sun dance at Crow Dog's Paradise that took place in the dramatic months after Wounded Knee. It was here that Robideau joined AIM ("I had never participated much before because I was always doing time"). He was assigned to the security patrol guarding the sun dance from the local goons.

From Rosebud, Robideau headed north to his father's place on the Fort Totten Reservation in North Dakota, where he found work laying water pipe. "Me and my dad never got to do much together because I was always locked up, and now he was paying me more attention than his girl friend could handle. So I took off again, heading south by way of Rapid, where I picked up a friend of mine named Nacho, who was coordinator for California AIM. We went back to Box Canyon—I didn't know where else to go—but I didn't get along good with Grandfather Semu,[4] who was running the camp there before AIM got it; I thought he was a charlatan, and he thought I was some kind of a hit man, out to get him, so he persuaded Nacho to get me the hell out of there. I went to Seattle—I was running out of places where I felt safe—and hooked up with Leonard and Jim again, and pretty soon we took off for the Dakotas."

"The West Coast group," as it became known on Pine Ridge, was answering a national call to all AIM members to attend the funeral of Pedro Bissonnette in October 1973. "We're all first cousins in that group," Robideau said. "You'll find that many AIM groups are family-oriented, like the Meanses; that way, you know everybody and you trust them, you're not afraid of FBI infiltration. And that was my first serious involvement with the American Indian Movement; I was amazed that everybody was armed and ready. AIM was asked to investigate that death, and we learned that Pedro was just taken out and shot. At the funeral, there were guns all over the place, and they were setting up security against the goons—I didn't even know who the goons were! And sure enough, the goons started coming in, and we was catchin' 'em by the fistful, and I guess we kind of took out on them goons a lot of the anguish over Pedro's death. Some of 'em got pretty messed up, too, but none of 'em got killed—not to my knowledge." Mimicking this favorite phrase of FBI agents on the witness stand, Robideau grinned, then became serious again. "Pedro wasn't big, but he was a real good fighter, very spirited; he could beat anybody on Pine Ridge. That kind of spirit was just why they wanted him out of the way; I mean, everybody just *knew* they killed him. And you know who did the autopsy that tried to cover it all up? The same guy who did Joe and Anna Mae! Anyway, the people were so upset about that death that they were ready to stage another Wounded Knee right there.

"With all the tension between local families, they made our West Coast group responsible for security during the four days of the funeral. Most of us had been brought up in the cities, we'd had a rough life of poverty and jail, we were outsiders, and we were militant—no bullshit involved. We set up a perimeter around the area, right there across from Calico, and the BIA set up another perimeter right around *us*. Both sides put up guns and wouldn't move. So on the third day, there was some shooting, and a couple of BIA cops got dusted when a bullet hit their windshield. The shooting was pinned on Leonard because his car in his own name and title was involved; that was the first clue they had that he might be on Pine Ridge.

"Leonard and Jimmy Robideau were in charge of our group from the West Coast, but Leonard was a leader before that; his problem was that he was always underground, dodging the law. The feds had had their eye on him ever since the Trail of Broken Treaties, and then there was that frame-up in Wisconsin; Leonard was later proven innocent, but they didn't get around to that until 1978, when they had already sent him up for life. Then Leonard's car, at least, was involved in that little episode at Pedro's funeral. So he had a history of cop trouble, and the cops don't care that he was innocent; if they can make a cop-killer out of him, they have their excuse to shoot him when the chance comes.

"The truth is, Leonard is anything but violent; anybody who knows him will say the same. In fact, he'll go out of his way to avoid trouble—I know because I'm just the opposite, I'm headstrong. When trouble comes down, I always want to get it on right there, get into action, but Leonard always cools things out: Hold it, he says. Let's think about it. Leonard is pretty up front; if he thinks something, he'll tell you, and people don't always like that. But if there is any way of getting around trouble, he will take it. He's a very likable man, you know, very warm; he comes right out, shows you who he is straight off—nothing stiff about him.

"When he was eight, Leonard was taken from his folks and sent to the government boarding school, but after the age of twelve he was on his own. Sometimes he lived with us but mostly he wandered; he went all over, got to know a lot of people, tried to help out, and everybody liked him. He was a real promising leader, but because of harassment, because he was hiding, he couldn't organize; it was the U.S. government which through its actions created a leader who is now well known all over Indian country.

"You can't help liking Leonard; even his enemies like Leonard. At Fargo his guards liked him so much they would run out and get him pizza and Cokes! (Once I suggested to Detective Bruce Correll, who assisted in Peltier's capture near Santa Maria, that he, too, kind of liked this desperate cop-killer; it was right there between the lines in the Santa Maria *Times*. For a moment, Correll seemed startled by the idea, but then he said, You know something? I *did*. I really did!)

"Leonard was popular everyplace, even before the Trail of Broken Treaties; he always stuck up for his friends, and he always helped people—*everybody* knew him. The only reason people remember me is because I travel with him: Oh yeah, *that* guy—he's the quiet one. And Dino—he's *super*quiet!" Robideau laughed a little, then said seriously, "I'm quiet. But I was given leadership because people know that I will do what I say I will do." For a moment Robideau stopped speaking. From the brown distance came the glint of the huge auto dump at Scenic, on the northwest border of the Badlands, a decrepit settlement which rose from the pale emptiness of the cold spring Plains.

"After the funeral, Leonard went back to Seattle; him and Nacho and Roque Duenas were working with Chicano people, and during that time, as I recall, they got in trouble on illegal-weapons charges, trying to support a protest by Kootenai Indians. As for me, I went to Rapid, I was living in the AIM house with a bunch of Wounded Knee people—Russ and Ted Means, Lorelei, Madonna Gilbert and Milo Goings, and my wife, Andrea. Me and Milo was bodyguards for Russ Means. Milo is a great big guy, six foot four or five, I guess, who was very strong at the time of Wounded Knee; he made a lot of supply trips in and out of there with Oscar Bear Runner, who probably made more than all the others put together, and he was the first person who was wounded. Anyway, everybody was still upset about Pedro, what was done to him could be done to any of us at any time."

⊡

Scenic, South Dakota, is a near-ghost town of thin weathered buildings just north of the Pine Ridge Reservation. A faded 1906 sign on its old Longhorn Bar reads: NO INDIANS ALLOWED: LAKOTA IYUSKINYA—UPO. ("No Dogs and Indians Allowed" was another sign that was once popular in South Dakota.[5]) The sign is an antique, and Lakota dollars if not Indians are welcomed in the town's main place of business; when I came through here the year before, the Indian customers were all sitting in the rear.

The Longhorn is low and dark and stale, with thick sweet sawdust on the floor and dirty walls crusted with dog-eared mementos of the frontier era; the owner, Halley Merrill, a bushy big-bellied old man with a yellowed beard, was presiding over the store next door, where "western" wares cover high windowless walls and the counters are stuffed with Indian crafts and pseudo-Indian novelties of foreign make, their colors fading as they await the rare, stray visitors to the Badlands.

The Lakota say that Halley Merrill charges Indians a fee to sleep his liquor off in one of the abandoned cars in the auto graveyard out in back, and that occasionally one of his customers freezes to death. "Things haven't changed much since the old days," Robideau commented. "Scenic is a pretty racist little place, and there aren't too many Indians who want to drink here." The walls of the men's room in the rear where it was claimed that Martin Montileaux was shot down by Richard Marshall are painted a dark red, like clotted blood; they are scarred by holes and knife cuts and initials, and an ancient message, "Curly and Bill passed by."

⊡

Beyond Scenic, the road enters the Badlands National Monument, an eerie moonscape of eroded rock parted here and there by stretches of rangeland that trail off southward across the reservation line. This desolate region, known as the Gunnery Range, forty-three miles by twelve, was taken from the Indians for bombing practice by the Army Air Force during World War II and never returned. The forty-two families suddenly evicted were homeless and uncompensated for six months, through a long winter; they were promised that their land would be returned to them, but they had nothing in writing to back up their claim. Although the Department of the Interior tried to retrieve the land in 1944 (reminding the War Department that an astonishing one thousand Pine Ridge Indians had volunteered to serve in World War II), the government refused to act until 1963, at which time less than a third of the 382,000 acres originally taken by condemnation in the federal courts was returned to the reservation. By coincidence, perhaps, this was the year that extensive negotiations with the Tribal Council for mineral rights to the remaining land got under way.[6]

In the early 1970s, as uranium exploration spread north and east from the Black Hills, sophisticated satellite devices contributed by NASA and the NURE (National Uranium Resource Evaluation) program of the U.S. Geological Survey located rich deposits of uranium (and molybdenum) in the Badlands region southwest of Scenic, on the reservation,[7] but the exploration remained so stealthy that in 1973, when the

Pentagon equipped a large paramilitary force to deal with the Wounded Knee occupation (which at the outset, at least, differed little in intent from many other AIM occupations around the country), few people wondered if the government's interest in the region had any source other than the FBI's well-known hysteria about left-wing groups. The Oglala themselves perceived the confrontation as a renewal of the century-old campaign to suppress all efforts toward self-determination, and in truth there is little if any overt evidence to support the now widespread belief that the government response was a show of force aimed at protecting mineral interests in the region. Yet the government attitude did not relent after Wounded Knee, and for two years afterward, Senator Abourezk and others who were trying to improve federal practices on the reservation in order to reduce the violence were increasingly mystified that their best efforts were being ignored.

Then, on the day before the Oglala shoot-out, in clear violation of the Fort Laramie stipulation that three quarters of the adult men must approve any transfer of Lakota territory, Dick Wilson agreed to cede to the Department of the Interior a large tract of tribal land, including a sacred place of the Lakota people called Sheep Mountain. This transfer was officially approved by the Wilson Tribal Council on January 2, 1976. Wilson's actions merely completed Tribal Council negotiations with the government that had been started by his predecessors, notably a 1968 agreement whereby the Badlands National Monument was permitted to expand across 76,200 acres of tribal lands: "Congress has by Public Law 90-468 authorized the additions to Badlands National Monument . . . consisting of lands within the exterior boundaries of the Pine Ridge Indian Reservation . . . which will be held by the United States in trust for the Tribe." Technically, the Oglala still owned the land and technically the Park Service had jurisdiction; but why would the Park Service want this arid wasteland that attracts no visitors? And why does the agreement specify that "the Tribe does not have the right to develop minerals on land reacquired under Public Law 90-468"? The reason is—or appears to be—that those mineral rights are very valuable. "The government knows this," Dino Butler said in 1977. "That's why all this is happening out there. They knew this before Wounded Knee; they knew this before the BIA takeover. But the Indian people didn't know it yet." Understandably, many people now believe that the disruption of the time period 1973–76 was instigated by the Wilson administration—and U.S. agents using that administration—to distract the people from these and other agreements being made about their land.[8] As Senator Abourezk exclaimed to the press after the Oglala shoot-out, "They [the government] have an interest in keeping this thing stirred up."

A joint report by the Geological Survey, the Bureau of Mines, and the BIA, based on surveys made in the same year as "the Wilson agreement," concluded that "numerous potential pay zones" and "relatively shallow drilling depths . . . combine to make the Pine Ridge Reservation an attractive prospecting area" for oil, gas, uranium, and gravel.[9] None of these agencies of the Department of the Interior paused to ask whether these "pay zones" would be "attractive" to the rightful owners of the land, whose welfare and health were not considered, despite the imminent threat to both, and apparently none of them—least of all the BIA—wished to see the mineral wealth of Indian country drawn to the attention of the Indians themselves. Instead, the government continued to combat the resurgence of traditional Lakota spirit, led by the American Indian Movement, which had openly identified itself with national liberation movements all over the Third World. An intensified harassment campaign against AIM reached its height in this same period, after which almost all of the AIM leaders were scattered, in hiding, or in jail. Not until after the conviction of Leonard Peltier, in April 1977, did the full extent of energy operations in the region become apparent; in May, when TVA revealed its extensive leases near Edgemont, in the southern Hills, twenty-five huge corporations had already staked claims in the Black Hills and the surrounding plains.

In recent years, exploratory leases on Pine Ridge land have been sought by Union Carbide, which already has one of the largest leaseholdings in the region, including land just north and south of the reservation. In regard to the uranium deposits on Pine Ridge, a Union Carbide spokesman says, "We don't think there is much uranium there, but . . . we haven't ruled it out." A more objective source at the South Dakota State Surface Mining Licensing Office comments, "Of course they won't tell us exactly what they have learned, but the first thing they do is take a water sample: if the water sample shows a relatively high level of radioactivity, then they know that the uranium is there somewhere, and they explore to find it. I know that the water samples from Pine Ridge showed a considerable amount of uranium, one of the highest. They know it's there. It's one of the prime spots."[10]

⊡

The nightmare years of the Wilson regime eventually ended, but the desperation of the Oglala people, and the bitterness between its factions, continued. It was 1975, Dennis Banks believes, when AIM lost most of its support from the Oglala "because the killings continued and the people had been through too much; they just didn't want any more trouble." After Al Trimble came into office, in April 1976, a great celebration was held at Wanblee by his supporters; a new era of peace had come at last. The goons dispersed, the shooting and house-to-house fighting all but ended, and for the first time in years, people could travel on the reservation without fear of violence. AIM supporters were given good jobs in the tribal administration, and the following year the BIA police were disbanded and replaced by local officers elected by their own people out in the districts. But increasingly, Trimble was slandered and threatened by the Wilson faction (especially when he tried to move the tribal government away from Pine Ridge village, to Three Mile Creek, near Kyle) and he was also let down by traditional Indians and AIM people he had put into office; too many exploited their jobs as opportunities for absenteeism, special privilege, and petty graft, thereby discrediting the first constructive Tribal Council administration in many years.[11] In 1978, Trimble was defeated by another BIA bureaucrat named Elijah Whirlwind Horse, who soon replaced most of the AIM people with the Pine Ridge faction, including many of the old faces from the Wilson days; this trend was continued two years later by Stanley Looking Elk. Already the Lakota warrior spirit, restored by Wounded Knee and fired by Oglala, had been weakened by an illusory prosperity, while for the majority of the poor, elderly, and unemployed, the hopeless conditions had changed little if at all.

Among the traditionals who had turned away from AIM was Chief Frank Fools Crow, who had signed the declaration of June 1, 1975, that invited AIM to return to the reservation. "Even the questionable attention collected by AIM has given a much-needed boost to the Indians' dignity and self-esteem," Fools Crow told his biographer in 1976. "The traditionalists do not like violent tactics, so we do not support AIM anymore. But they have accomplished things that our passive methods did not accomplish."[12]

As Ted Means says, "We had no positive or definite strategy, especially for those who participated in Wounded Knee. We provided no plan for the people, and we suffered for it. A lot of people who had that fire within them, that commitment and energy, began to turn it in other directions because we had no strategy for them. Of course, we also got our name used wrongly by a lot of people who would be drunk and raise hell and then claim they were AIM. I think it hurt us most with the old people, because that respect that we had from them in 1973 is just now beginning to come back."[13]

⊡

At Porcupine, the Thunder Hawk house, where the local survival school is located, lies below the road, surrounded by a fence. Ted Means, a husky, mustachioed man wearing a red wind band and white T-shirt, was playing with his children in a fenced-off yard as we drew near. Recently Means had been released from prison on orders from Judge Nichol; a few weeks after this visit, his conviction on courthouse-riot charges stemming from the trial of Sarah Bad Heart Bull was overturned.

Getting out of the car, Robideau pointed at the gate, a zigzag arrangement designed to halt cattle and slow down anything going through. "You got a stopper there, Ted," he said approvingly. "Yup," Ted Means said. "Lets you draw a bead on 'em before they get in too close to the house." Both men grinned. Although the two had not seen each other in five years, their greeting was spare and laconic, in the Indian way.

Means led us inside the house and gave us coffee while he spoke to Robideau about the Gunnery Range. Robideau had not introduced me to Means because Indian people rarely make introductions, preferring to let people get the feel of one another naturally, and so for a long time they talked as if I were not there. Thousands of acres were still under tight military control, Means was saying, and the Air Force refused to give them back, even though they were no longer in use. Therefore the Indians suspect that the region is seriously contaminated, not only by unexploded ordnance but by the dumping of nuclear and chemical wastes. "There's *something* going on up there at that bombing range," he said. "There's *got* to be! We knew that even at the time of Wounded Knee. I mean, why did the *Pentagon* get so excited over an Indian demonstration? Christ, they had the Eighty-second Airborne and everything else out here, and FBI activity all over the res, and that was before one person had been hurt." (His wife, Lorelei, agrees. "I believe they're dumping nuclear wastes or toxic chemicals on Indian land," she says. "A guy—a white guy—got over the fence up there at Sheep Mountain, and they were on him in two minutes with jeeps and M-16s and dogs. What are they so jumpy about if nothing is going on?")

Lorelei Means ran the clinic at Wounded Knee with Madonna Gilbert and was also a founder of WARN (Women of All Red Nations); she was now a student nurse at Pine Ridge Hospital, where Indian Health Service statistics had shown that the rate of miscarriage in a recent period was over six times the national average, with high numbers of cleft palates, bone cancers, and other ailments often caused by low-level radiation in the environment. The Janklow government, facing a uranium-development referendum in November 1980 which would give voters some choice about uranium mining and milling in the state, was not eager to hunt down the precise sources, but radon-contaminated water in the Cheyenne River and/or the Oglala and Arikara aquifers (from uranium bore holes in the Black Hills), the suspected dumping of nuclear wastes on the Gunnery Range, and irresponsible agrarian use of dioxin poisons by the ranchers who leased Indian land were all suspected. Pine Ridge would also be affected by the proposals of the North Central Power Study, since the reservation was downwind from the main power-plant complex in Montana and Wyoming and would be crossed by no less than four of the huge and dangerous high-power lines that would carry the output of these plants to Omaha and Des Moines and St. Louis.

WARN was also publicizing the poor health care that Indians receive through the Indian Health Service, including IHS "voluntary" sterilization programs—WARN denounced them as "genocide"—in which sterilization was commonly performed without the patient's knowledge, far less consent.[14] Like most of the fifty-one hospitals that the government maintains for Indians, Pine Ridge does not meet the government's own minimum standards, and many Indians will not send their sick there.

"The hospital would like to get rid of Lorelei," Ted Means said proudly. "She's too mouthy. WARN is trying to determine the causes of all these spontaneous abortions, birth defects, and cancers, but the studies will take a lot more money, which we don't have. The EPA and [Senator] McGovern's office are whitewashing the whole thing; they say our water's okay, and it isn't. McGovern's office was reassured over the phone by the Indian Health Service people there at the hospital, and he accepted it; the local press questioned hell out of the WARN report, but nobody ever questioned the IHS.

"The water situation in this state is really critical. Maybe eighty percent of the water in South Dakota is Indian water, and they want it all for energy development, and they don't want to hear about contamination. The government is willing to sacrifice everyone here, not just Indians anymore but *everyone,* and just for thirty years of energy. People come to us with tears in their eyes, with deformed babies, babies with holes in their heart, asking us what they can do; this is starting to happen more and more." Means sat stone-still at his kitchen table for a little while, then said in a low voice, "Every successful revolution has been inspired by this sort of offense against the people. Except for Wounded Knee, Oglala, and a few other episodes around the country, we have not fought back—that's going to turn around." This was the old AIM rhetoric of the early 1970s, and Ted Means knew it, for after a moment, he sighed. "It's hard to organize the people around anything except money, especially when the press is telling them that everything is okay. The government has done one hell of a good job in colonizing us. They give a guy a pickup truck and a six-pack, and he's satisfied. The Indians are satisfied to be miserably comfortable." When I remarked that this wasn't true only of Indians, that the whole population of the United States had been reduced from citizens to consumers, Ted Means looked my way for the first time, and I noticed that he has a chin scar. "We've been programmed to accept defeat," he said, unsmiling; and Bob Robideau grinned briefly, saying, "Some of us have been de-programmed."

Means got up and poured more coffee. "These tribal chairmen," he said to me, disgusted, "they got no business negotiating for us on Fort Laramie. Our Treaty wasn't made with tribal councils! Those people are just negotiating with their own side, and if we allow them to run free, they'll sell us out." The Cheyenne River Tribal Council was working to divide the people, much as the Pine Ridge Tribal Council did eight years ago, in order to undermine Indian resistance to energy development, which is now spreading all the way east into Minnesota. (At Cheyenne River, twenty-nine companies had already filed for exploratory rights for oil and natural gas, and Sidney Keith, whom I had spoken with in Eagle Butte the year before, had lost the job at the Indian Health Service hospital which he had held for twenty years because he resisted Tribal Council policies in regard to mine leases on Indian land.)

"They're getting a lot of local problems going, just like they did here in Pine Ridge, to divert attention from what the companies are up to. Things are starting to simmer, and they're going to boil—the water shortage, energy pollution, everything—and there's going to be a showdown. I mean, what do you do when you get backed into a corner, man? And maybe another showdown is what they're after, just like '73 and '75." Ted Means was still looking at me when he said this, and I appreciated his polite use of the word "they."

⊡

From Porcupine, we headed south on the high open rolling plains. "Looks like a big reservation, don't it?" Robideau said. "But most of it's owned or leased by white people, the same as Rosebud." Many traditionals had lost what was left of their land in the early 1950s, when a BIA resolution carved the common rangeland into fenced grazing units that the poorer Indians were unable to manage under the discriminatory regulations; the units soon came under the control of the wealthier mixed-bloods and white ranchers who had promoted that resolution in the first place. As of today, about half of the Pine Ridge Reservation, with the encouragement of the BIA, has been sold off or leased on terms far more beneficial to the lessors than to the people whose best interests the BIA is mandated by law to represent.

On Porcupine Butte, the road passes a sign: CHIEF BIG FOOT SURRENDERS. The sign marks the place where Big Foot's doomed band of Minnecojou, having crossed one hundred and fifty miles of winter Badlands from Cherry Creek on the Cheyenne River to sanctuary under Red Cloud at Pine Ridge, was intercepted by soldiers of the Seventh Cavalry, who escorted the half-frozen Indians down this long hill to Wounded Knee Creek.

> Big Foot, though not a famous chief as was Spotted Tail, Red Cloud and Crazy Horse, yet he with Chief Hump exerted much influence in their day among the Indians of the Great Sioux Nation. He was a wise chief, mild mannered and always very considerate of the personal rights of his band. He was for peace, and on several occasions acted as peacemaker when rival bands were about to go on the warpath with each other. . . . From the account that the Indians give of him, he took the duties of chief very seriously, and was of the old type of chiefs, who lived prior to the ones that were

before the public at the end of the nineteenth century; for example, Sitting Bull, American Horse and Short Bull.[15]

"I am going to a certain place and when I get there I will lay down my arms," Chief Big Foot told the Blue Coats. "You meet us out here on the prairie, and expect me to give you my guns out here. I am a little bit afraid that there might be something a little crooked about it, something that may occur that wouldn't be fair. There are a lot of children here."[16]

> The soldiers met us near the Porcupine Butte, and after they talked to Big Foot we went on to Wounded Knee Creek. . . . The next morning we were getting ready to break camp when the Indian men were ordered by the soldiers to come to the center of the camp and bring all their guns. After they did this, the soldiers came to where the Indian women were and searched the tents and the wagons for arms. They made us give up axes, crowbars, knives, awls, etc. About this time an awful noise was heard and I was paralyzed for a time. Then my head cleared and I saw nearly all the people on the ground bleeding. I could move some now, so I ran to a cut bank and lay down there. I saw some of the other Indians running up the coulee so I ran with them, but the soldiers kept shooting at us. . . . My father, my mother, my grandmother, my older brother and my younger brother were all killed. My son who was two years old was shot in the mouth that later caused his death.
>
> We had ten horses, harness, wagon, tent, buffalo robes, and I had a good Navajo blanket. All this property was lost or taken by the Government or other people. I had a hard time in my life and you can see that I am having a hard time now. It is cold weather and this is an old house and I suffer from the cold. . . . Is the Government going to pay for what they did to us?[17]

⊡

Big Foot and the more than two hundred men, women, and children shot down in the December snow lie in the mass grave on top of the small hill to the west, with Buddy Lamont, killed in 1973, buried nearby. The bodies lie in a Christian cemetery because the Holy Rosary Catholic Church acquired the hill and built a church beside the common grave and sanctified it; right after the siege, in 1973, the church was burned down by arsonists unknown, allegedly to spare tourists the sight of a house of God shot to splinters by federal bullets. These creekbeds and gullies, used for escape in 1890 by the few survivors, were used again in 1973 to bring in food and arms and medical supplies to the defenders. Although the historic marker on the road has been changed successively from WOUNDED KNEE BATTLEGROUND to WOUNDED KNEE TRAGEDY to WOUNDED KNEE MASSACRE, this has not placated the Lakota, to judge from the number of smashed bottles at the base of the sign.

Somewhere in these rolling hills, within a night's walk of Wounded Knee, is the unmarked grave of Crazy Horse. "My lands are where my people are buried," said "the Strange Man" of the Oglala, recognized by red men and white alike as the greatest war leader in Indian history.

> Crazy Horse was a small man, dark in complexion, with fine brown hair which he wore gathered in a knot in the center top of his forehead. Through the knot was thrust some slough grass worn for magic purposes. On the occasions that I saw him he wore but one feather of the spotted eagle at the back of his head. Crazy Horse was very modest and retiring in nature, but was beloved for his bravery. Eight horses were shot from under him at various times but he was never even wounded, for the reason that he was a great medicine man as well as a great warrior. Other chiefs were very jealous of my brother-in-law and they brought about his death. His parents and my sister took his body from Fort Robinson and buried him close to Pine Ridge. Later, however, they removed the body secretly and buried it in some white sand cliffs near Porcupine Creek. The parents and widow continued to guard the body, refusing to reveal the burial place, and to this day no one knows where his body lies.[18]

Here and there along the road into Pine Ridge, trucks and cars sat stalled, hoods up in symptom of defeat, and many dead cars, scavenged for their parts to keep one live one going, sat in their final resting places in the yards, often as many as six to a small house. In the bare spring light, surrounded by old stubble, mud, and tin and plastic litter, the tarpaper cabins had the makeshift air of foremen's shacks on shut-down construction projects.

On this Sunday morning, the streets of Pine Ridge were empty of almost everyone but weary drunks. As Peltier says, "The alcoholics are the Indians that people notice, because so many are downtown, hanging around the bars; they draw attention to themselves, one way or another. There are many, many families, a whole lot of Indian people, who never touch liquor at all. Sure, there's a lot of drinking among Indians, but it's amazing that there isn't more, considering how depressing those reservations are, with nothing going on, and nowhere to go."

Before the coming of the whites, the Plains Indians knew nothing of hard liquor, and the rotgut whiskies, or "firewater" (often spiced with tobacco juice and pepper), with which they were plied by dishonest fur traders and others led to so much violence and disruption that Congress passed laws in 1851 prohibiting the sale of spirits to the native peoples. For the next century, bootlegged liquor greased the way for the unscrupulous, Indian as well as white. In 1934, the Indian Reorganization Act, permitting the use (though not the sale) of liquor on the Indian reservations, released it as a destructive force against the entire people. In 1953, in conjunction with the termination legislation under President Eisenhower, the Indians were given full rights to buy liquor. Rosebud soon adopted liquor ordinances, but Pine Ridge remained dry, and bootleggers such as Richard Wilson prospered; in the early 1970s, when Wilson became president of the Tribal Council, Pine Ridge village passed a liquor ordinance, and for a few years Robert Ecoffey of the BIA police (whose report first connected Jimmy Eagle to the red International Scout) was the proprietor of an "unofficial" drive-in liquor store. Under Al Trimble, the liquor store was closed, but these days there was talk of opening it again, despite the fact that alcohol causes almost all Indian arrests and is the leading cause of death on the reservation.[19]

In recent years, the people of Pine Ridge have been mainly serviced by a white man's store just across the south boundary in White Clay, Nebraska, which offers the Indians a wide selection of cheap spirits, beer, and drastic views of splayed white women in girlie magazines. In 1974, this small store in a dead hamlet on a lost county road owned up to net profits of $200,000, and presumably the Longhorn Bar in Scenic, on the Rapid City road, does a lot better. Because there are very few cafés, no movie houses, and no public transportation in all the 4,500 square miles of the reservation, the relief provided by these establishments is badly needed, and alcoholism at Pine Ridge, where 70 percent of the people are unemployed, is approximately five times the national average. The suicide rate among teenagers is twice that among whites of the same age—the village has a "crisis center" for would-be suicides—

and the life expectancy among Pine Ridge Indians averages forty-four years, or about thirty years less than among white Americans—and this in a people who, in the old days, commonly lived for a hundred years or more. Anna Mae Aquash, who studied this problem, saw it as a direct consequence of inferior food, which is all that most families can afford; the median family income is less than one half the amount below which white families are considered to live in poverty. And all of these shameful statistics are true despite the fact that government agencies (in 1976) claimed to be spending $8,040 every year on each Pine Ridge family (as opposed to a median family income of less than $2,000). To judge from appearances, all this money goes to BIA Indians and the well-fed white bureaucracy; the "Sioux Nation Supermarket" is owned by white people, and the neat suburban houses of the whites are almost the only decent housing in Pine Ridge village.

"We were poor," says Madonna Gilbert, "but at least we grew our vegetables and used the land; these welfare Indians, even the ones that still own land, they don't grow gardens anymore, they just wait for the lease check to come in, then spend it all on clothes and booze." The previous day, Madonna had gone to Eagle Butte for her cousin's funeral—"forty-five years old, and hemorrhaged to death because of alcohol." She shook her head. "The only way that Indians are going to make it is by getting back to an independent spirit, in our own sovereign nation. At least at Pine Ridge there has been a little progress. Over the years, when we were talking about self-determination, the Tribal Council laughed at us—sovereignty, too. But sovereignty is what we're going to get, and I notice they're not laughing anymore."

⊡

We took the north road past Pine Ridge Hospital, where Anna Mae Aquash was autopsied twice; past the hidden cabin on the hillside north of the road where I had visited the year before with medicine man Pete Catches ("This nation—I can't say *my* nation because they stole it away from me. They cheated and lied, and broke every treaty, even the sacred treaty that protected the Black Hills"); past the grave of Red Cloud ("They made us many promises, more than I can remember, and they never kept but one: they promised to take our land, and they took it"); past the log building called Calico Hall, where in 1973 the decision was made to go to Wounded Knee. Then Highway 18 headed north and west through a spare rangeland, crossing the bends of White Clay Creek and rising again to level off on a flat mesa; to the south rose the soft sandhills of Nebraska, and off to the north the high white bluffs stretched away into the Badlands toward Sheep Mountain.

At the end of a dirt lane that turned off westward, a compound of small cabins came in view. We drove slowly down the rutted track past Jumping Bull Hall, which stood in last summer's long brown grass, the worn wood wind-slotted and chinked with hard spring light. At the corner of the road, where it turns back south along the bluff into the compound, stands the Little cabin; under the closed window of the cabin, a child's body, still as the cold earth, lay with its face turned away on the April ground.

As the car idled, we stared at the small form, then at each other, then back again; the body did not stir. Leaving the car, I caught the movement of a hand at a twitched curtain. All the inhabitants could see was a white stranger, and the man who came around the corner of the cabin looked wary and hostile; the child stirred, yawning. Then Robideau got out, nodding in greeting, and I trailed the two into the cabin where Ron Williams and Jack Coler had noticed the American flag hung upside-down, where Mike Anderson said that he had breakfast on June 26, 1975, where Joanna LeDeaux had left her car before walking alone along the bluff, staring down at that Colorado car with the blinkers flashing, and the white torso and green shirt of two human bodies lying dead still in the hot summer grass.

Robideau greeted Vickie and Steve Little, whose older brother had been living in this place on June 26, 1975; Vickie Little is the widow of an Apache AIM leader named Angel, killed in a car crash in Arizona not long after the shoot-out at Oglala.

"Haven't seen you for quite a while, Bob," Vickie said. "What *you* been doin'?" And Robideau said, "Time."

Although Bob Robideau had not been back since that long early-summer day five years before, there was no mention of the shoot-out or its consequences. Instead, they chatted and laughed about old friends, and after a while I went to the door and gazed out over the land. The cabin perches on the bluff edge, overlooking the pasture, and the Jumping Bull compound, also on the bluff, sits in an open grove of trees, some two hundred yards away to the southeast. At the bottom of the pasture is the dense river wood that follows White Clay Creek toward the AIM camp, which was located perhaps a quarter mile to the southeast. On the far side of the creek, the open rangeland rises to low buttes that overlook the dry plains of Nebraska, sloping southward to the Niobrara River. This is the Lakota country to which Red Cloud and Spotted Tail wished so passionately to return.

"The Chief Spotted Tail sprang up, walked toward him, waving in his hand the paper containing the promise of the Government to return them to White Clay Creek. . . . 'All the men who come from Washington are liars, and the bald-headed ones are the worst of all. . . . You have but one thing to do here, and that is to give an order for us to return to White Clay Creek!' "[20]

We went over to the compound and walked around for a little while, not saying much; perhaps Bob was remembering that early afternoon when death surrounded him, and I didn't feel like nagging him with questions.

He gazed at the silent cabins, one red, one green, one white. "Nobody here now," he said after a while, contemplating the mangled car that had been hauled into the yard and abandoned next to an old stove; it was by this car that Angie Long Visitor had said she'd seen him. Nearby stood a white washing machine black-pocked with bullet holes. "The family tried to come back in here, but the house was all shot up and busted; then Grandpa Harry got killed by a truck, just a few months ago, ran right over his car up there near Lone Man's. Other people tried to live here, too, I heard, but they just didn't like the feel of the place."

Robideau turned his gaze from the wrecked car and looked about him: there was a winter stillness here, and I wondered what was going through his head. How different this scene must have been on that hot summer morning, the yells and bullet whine and crack of rifles, the whack of slugs through the thin metal of the cars. "That log cabin was where Banks was living; he was gone that day. The feds come here claiming they was after Jimmy Eagle, but we think they was after AIM." He shrugged. "We knew Jimmy Eagle, but he never come around, unless maybe he showed up in that crowd for the Jumping Bulls' anniversary, right after we come here from Farmington. I didn't know the Oglala people the way Leonard and Dino did—I stayed mostly in Porcupine—and it's true that I didn't know Eagle at the time. But I know him now, and I just don't remember him being here that day. I had heard that he was here a few days earlier, and if you knew him, you would know that he was capable of telling all them stories in the jail whether he was here or not. He's got bad attitudes and a real kid mentality, he's a boaster and a bullshitter, too; he's just running his mouth off *all* the time. Here he was, already in heavy trouble, and he just talked himself right into an indictment for murder."

(Still serving a six-year sentence for the shooting of James Catches on May 17, 1975, Jimmy Eagle was paroled in 1977, but in October of that year, he shot his uncle almost fatally in a drunken argument over some car keys. In 1978, he was freed from the Pine Ridge jail by his girl friend, Wilma Blacksmith, who turned up armed with a .22; the angry authorities arraigned his grandmother, Gladys Bissonnette, on charges of aiding and abetting an escape as well as harboring a fugitive. He has since been recaptured, imprisoned, and released.)

In his first statement to the FBI, Mike Anderson had said that Jimmy Eagle and not Robideau was down at the agents' cars with Peltier and Butler. "I don't know why Mike named Eagle and not me. But I had developed a pretty good relationship with Baby Aim, so I guess he felt reluctant." Robideau sighed. "They let those three kids tell a lot of lies to cover up their own part in the shooting," he said a little later, without either contempt or resentment. "But we were all kind of surprised and disappointed, especially by Norman; of all those boys, it seemed like he was the strongest. We liked Norman, and when he comes up for the sun dance, we don't let nobody bother him, but we can't trust him anymore.

"We liked Mike, too—we called him Baby Aim not because his big brother was an AIM leader but because he seemed like the baby of the group, even though he wasn't the youngest. We'd tease Mike a lot, and he'd go stomping off, then come bouncing back; he handled it real good. But we know now that he fell right there in Wichita, first time they questioned him, though I guess it took them quite a little while to break him down; they scared him and made him feel isolated, that was their tactic.

"After Leonard's trial, Mike went underground, and nobody could find him for a while, I guess. After what he said at Fargo, there was really a lot of pressure on him, especially being Larry's younger brother—Mike grew up on AIM. So when he got himself killed in a car wreck a year later, down in Arizona, we wondered if it wasn't guilt that caused it."

("I liked Mike, you know," Leonard Peltier says. "I was close to his brother, and I just liked the guy; we'd joke around, he was like my own little brother. Sometimes I had to discipline him because of that drinking and raising hell, because we were there to provide safety to the people and we had to set an example. One time the people were saying that one of our kids shot out some windows, and the elders came to me, and I came down on that pretty hard." He sighs. "During my Los Angeles trial, Larry Anderson came in, and we had a pipe ceremony, and I asked him what happened to Mike. Larry told me that Mike was being chased by BIA cops when he cracked up; they said he was speeding, raising hell, throwing beer cans around, but Larry wondered if there might not be some other reason they were after him." Peltier shrugged as if to say, In this damned case, it's hard to know *what* to believe.)

As if sensing an unspoken question, Robideau said, "Norman Charles is still up in Washington somewhere. There never was no suspicion that he talked, and we know that they tried hard to make him do it. Anyway, they had already cracked them other three, and most likely they just thought they had enough; Norman Charles turned out to be too much trouble." Here Robideau shook his head with a weary grunt. "After Cedar Rapids, I became convinced that the court is just a stage, and the side that sets the stage right, and has the best actors, is going to win; the evidence is less important than the way it's presented. And at Fargo, of course, we couldn't present it at all."

Robideau turned his collar up in the stiff raw April air. "We wasn't up here when they first showed up. We had our camp about a quarter mile down." He pointed southeast, along the wooded creek. "When we heard the shooting, we come running up here, keeping to the woods"—he pointed again—"then coming up one by one along that cattle fence while the rest fired at where the agents were, to keep their heads down. By that time, most of the women and children had taken off across the fields.

"I remember Angie and her family came running by, saying, What're we gonna do! And I told them, Just get out of here." Reminded of Angie's testimony that he had been wearing a ski mask on that day, Bob managed a sour grin. "Yeah, I was wearing it for a little while that day. In the summertime I used to use it as a cap to keep my hair down when it got too windy to wear my cowboy hat, and that day I decided to pull down the front. I was brought up on West Coast city streets, you know, and my first instinct when trouble comes down is to hide. But after a while I felt ridiculous; everybody else had their face showing, so I put it up again."

Robideau jerked his chin at the pasture road that came down under the bluff from the Little cabin. "That's where them agents got it," he said, expressionless. "They come in right down there. Before we knew it, the whole area was surrounded, all along the roads and over there across the river—everywhere! There's just no way they could have got so many guns out here so fast unless they were looking for a shoot-out in the first place."

He circled a small green shed near the east wall of the small farmhouse, which was riddled with big holes; a young apple tree beside the shed was in fresh blossom. That morning, he said, the rifle he was carrying was next thing to useless, and he took the .44 Ruger from Joe Stuntz, sending him back down to the camp for a .30-30 Marlin deer rifle. "That's the gun Joe died with, and that's where Joe got it," he said, pointing at the ground beside the shed. "He was firing down into them trees." Bob nodded, as if some missing piece had fallen into place. "Norman Charles had his brother-in-law killed right beside him, and maybe that's one reason they decided not to put him on the stand; it might not look good to draw too much attention to the fact that an Indian also got killed at Oglala.

"Pretty soon, we decided to leave, and went down to camp. But somebody never got the word to Joe and Norman Charles, I guess, and I think it was Draper went back up to tell them; by that time the feds had come up there through the woods, and there was an exchange of fire in which Joe was killed." Agent Hughes's testimony about heavy fire received hours later in the assault on the green shack "was just a lot more hype," Robideau said. "By the time they launched their big attack, and shot this place to pieces, there was nobody home; they accused us of escaping in broad daylight."[21] (During his trial, Robideau acquired a grudging respect for the big red-haired balding Hughes: "He was pretty cool; there was something dangerous about him. They had him up there on the stand for a long time—days!—before they cracked him even a little." Of David Price he remarks sardonically, "He's a real clean-cut gung-ho fed who really enjoyed his job with the native people.")

"Anyway, there was nobody in them houses. Even when that white woman [Joanna LeDeaux] come in there, the women and children were all gone, and most of the men, too. What they could have heard was Wishie's .22 pistol, which he fired off by accident on the escape; we gave him hell. Anyway, we headed down into the woods again, and followed the creek south, then went through that culvert under the school road over there. They had us pinned down for a while in a little clump of cottonwoods; then we went way up over there under that mesa.

"Running uphill, Norman Brown blew the muzzle on his gun, firing back down at the roadblock—must have jammed the barrel down into the mud along the way. That gun was finished; we just left it in the crotch of a tree. The law says now that they searched the whole escape route, but I guess them guys didn't like getting too far off the road, because when Dino came back here a year and a half later, that evidence was still in that tree crotch, out in plain view." Robideau mentioned the canteen that was shot right off the hip of Norman Brown. "Them bullets were close, man." He held up thumb and forefinger to make an inch. "Those guys were right on target and shooting hard. Why nobody was hit I'll never know." He grunted. "Maybe Norman seen that eagle after all."

Robideau pointed at the white sandstone monuments and pine bluffs to the eastward. "Spent the first night up in there, and the second day, too, because we figured they expected us to move. Later we heard there was a whole Search-and-Destroy outfit running around the res—National Guard jeeps, helicopters, spotting planes, and all—but we saw just one helicopter in the distance; they never come near us. The third night, we took off eastward, headed for Manderson, except we hit Pine Ridge instead." Robideau laughed. "We studied them lights for a long time, until somebody said what we all knew: Hell, that ain't Manderson! And a good thing, too, because Manderson was just where they was laying for us. So we got into Pine Ridge and hid out, and the next morning a busload of FBIs pulls right up to the door. Oh shit, I thought, it's on again. But the people in the house give some good answers and the feds took off.

"While I was in Pine Ridge, I attended Joe Stuntz's funeral; among the warriors, I was the only one who went." Five years later, Robideau raised his eyebrows, mildly puzzled by his own rashness; the funeral was bound to be swarming with agents, and any one of the numerous people being questioned—over five hundred were eventually interviewed—might have identified him as one of those who took part in the shoot-out. "By that time, you see, my whole frame of mind had changed. We were sure they would kill us the first chance they got, and we were in a drastic state of mind. But that day at the funeral, I wasn't even worried—careful, sure, and I kept away from all the cameras, but I wasn't concerned. I realized this during the escape: there was no reason to fear anymore, 'cause you *know* what's going to happen, so you straighten up and do what has to be done. It's kind of a good feeling, like breathing in fresh air. I had accepted death. Maybe you'll think I'm crazy, but knowing I was sure to die was a kind of freedom, it really was—relaxing, man!" Bob Robideau laughed and I did, too, understanding better now why this thin man, so diffident and unassertive in appearance, seemed so confident in everything he said.

⊡

On the edge of the plateau a few miles to the southeast, overlooking the ranch of Wallace Little, lies Joe Stuntz's grave, which Robideau had never seen. We walked out onto a bluff with a broad prospect of the Badlands and stood for a long time in silence before three simple unmarked mounds; the graves were decorated with dull plastic flowers and the four small bright-colored flags of the four directions. In one grave lies June Little's brother Jim. On September 10, 1975, the same day as Robideau's arrest near Wichita, Jim Little had been stomped to death in broad daylight by four goons in Oglala Housing, who attributed the killing to an argument over some spurs; three of the four men involved eventually served short terms for manslaughter.

On a rough base of cinder blocks is a plaque that reads: "In honor of our brothers who have given their efforts here for the Lakota, June 26, 1975." After a little while, Bob cleared his throat. "Joe was one of our West Coast group. Big guy. Didn't say too much—real easygoing, quiet, never got excited. Even in a real heavy situation, he'd just *be* there."

After the Oglala shoot-out, Joe Killsright's body had been removed to Pine Ridge Hospital, where it was turned over to a Rapid City coroner. Dick Wilson signed an order that no wake or burial of this AIM Indian could be held on the reservation, but the order was contemptuously ignored; the body was brought back from Rapid City by Evelyn Bordeaux and another woman (in the vengeful climate, no Oglala male wished to be implicated) and placed on a rack on the Jumping Bull property while people passed by, paying their respects. The funeral took place right in Pine Ridge, and Joe Killsright ("He would like to be remembered by that name," Peltier says) was buried in a traditional ceremony on Little family ground on June 30; in Los Angeles, the following day, the FBI Director gave American flags to the families of the two dead agents.

"Joe Stuntz was learning the spiritual way," Dino Butler says; "he wanted to be a spiritual man someday. Joe Stuntz was a very quiet man. He never had very much to say. I had a lot of respect for him. . . . He never seemed to want to be out in front, you know, but he was always there when trouble started. He was never afraid to face up to trouble when it happened. . . .

"If we were in the wrong that day, these sacred things wouldn't have helped us. We would not have been taken care of. I know Joe Stuntz died there, but in the Indian way, there has to be sacrifices. That is part of our religion. We always sacrifice and we are stronger afterwards if we survive. . . . This is why Joe—it was time for him to go. It could have been any one of us. When it's time—my time—I hope that I can go like Joe; I hope that my death, my passing, will give life to others."

Beside Joe Stuntz lies Anna Mae Aquash, who "was kind of like Joe," Bob Robideau said. "She was always easy, even in a tight situation. She was the only woman in our group who really learned how to use weapons—ballistics and everything; she really wanted to learn. She had worked with the women, but she got frustrated by the lack of action."

"We had a sweat lodge in our camp," Dino Butler says. "We went to ceremonies. Anna Mae was there. Joe Stuntz was there. Jimmy Little was there. A lot of people were there who will never be there no more, you know; they're dead now. I won't say they are dead. They are gone. To Indian people there is no such thing as death. When we pass over into the spirit world, our body returns to the sacred Mother Earth and becomes a part of her. . . .

"I used to go for walks with Annie Mae. We used to talk about her children up in Canada. We used to talk a lot about a lot of things. When I was in jail she came to me a couple of times in my dreams, you know. And I know that she is still watching. She's still taking care of us, you know. She is still around. Joe Stuntz is still around. A lot of spirits of our ancestors come back and let us know that they are there helping us. We know we are right. We are just as right as our ancestors who stood up against the United States government, against these white folks, and fought for what they believed in. They knew it was right, and we are just as right as our ancestors."

⊡

Robideau turned from the graves, and we walked back to the road. "Mainly Anna Mae was pretty serious, but she was likable. She didn't crack jokes or anything, the way Leonard did, but she liked to laugh. That's the way Indians are: in a serious situation, someone will say something and they'll laugh hard to cool things out before going back to being serious again."

Anna Mae Aquash was completely trusted by the West Coast group, and to this day serves all her people as a symbol, but one gets the impression that many Indians still wonder who she was. Although both were in Wounded Knee during the siege and both worked later in survival schools, Madonna Gilbert says that she scarcely knew Anna Mae and seems rather unwilling to discuss her—possibly, I thought at first, because the Oglala women, out of loyalty to Kamook Nichols, had disapproved of "Dennis's West Coast woman."

Bob Robideau has a different explanation. "We think people are quick to be jealous. It's true that AIM people all over the Dakotas were being harassed and jailed, and probably they didn't want to get involved. All the same, not one Means came to Joe's or Anna Mae's funeral, for example, even though they were right here on the res, and they gave the Oglala group no support at all until the time of the Cedar Rapids trial, when their own people began to notice they were holding back. Then they began to help a little; they really didn't have much choice. We think the Means women are the jealous ones—they want all the attention and support money for their own group. Also, they didn't care too much for Leonard because he wouldn't take orders from Russ the way most people did, wouldn't let Russ push him around. And maybe the Bellecourts are jealous, too. During the Los Angeles trial, I called up Vern Bellecourt and Herb Powless and asked them how come they weren't giving Leonard any support, and they asked me who the hell I thought I was, talking to the AIM leadership like that." Bob grinned that wry grin, shaking his head. "Banks didn't support us, neither. Even at the time of Cedar Rapids, we had to send his statement back three times to get an effective version; he just kept writing about himself and his own problems in California. Dino won't even speak about him anymore. I was never tight with Dennis the way Dino and Leonard were, so I didn't feel hurt; him and me can still talk about it, and I know he regrets the way he acted. Leonard's cooled off, too; he knows we have to work with Dennis, and he let Dennis visit him at Lompoc. But if Leonard had been out of jail when Dennis let me and Dino down like that, it might have been a very different story.

"Anyway, that lack of support is where the trouble started. Dennis is out of it in California, and we don't get along too good with the Means no more. We cooperate with them, but we don't actually work together, because we don't agree with some of Russ's ideas on where the Movement is going. The West Coast group is autonomous now, and so is the Means' Dakota AIM; the few AIM groups that are still going are all autonomous. Of course, the Movement has always had autonomous groups; there was never any real direction from the national office, because it wouldn't do no good to tell any local Indians what to do, and everyone knew it—except the big things. We still get together for the big things, like the national conventions and Pedro's funeral and the Black Hills Gathering that's coming up here in July."

Headed west on Highway 18, we were silent for a little while. It was possible, of course, that the lack of support for the West Coast group mentioned by Robideau came about not through jealousy but through the suspicion that the group might have killed the agents, which not all traditional Indians by any means believe was justified. One AIM leader, asked if Leonard was capable of violence, evaded the question with the statement "All Indians are capable of violence; we had to be in order to survive." Another (who deplored the "violent element" in AIM) claimed to have heard from Pine Ridge people that Peltier was responsible for the killings, and did not think that "a man of violence" should become a hero for Indian children. This person conceded that Leonard's guilt could be mere rumor, which is epidemic on the Indian reservations; she scarcely knew Peltier personally, she said, because "Leonard was always outside helping build the sweat lodge, or taking care of something else."

Eventually Bob remarked, "They killed Anna Mae because they knew she was one of us and wouldn't talk." But later he said, voicing his thoughts during the long drive to Rapid City, "The FBIs didn't kill her—not directly, at least." He did not explain this, and I did not question him. In the feudal atmosphere of the Wilson years, almost any goon or AIM-supporter on Pine Ridge might have found a reason for taking the life of Anna Mae, and probably no one really wants to know who did it.

In all likelihood, most people feel, the original suspicions about Anna Mae were spread by Douglass Durham, who tried to discredit anyone he did not control, and these rumors intensified when David Price questioned her in March 1975; apparently Price was working with John Stewart, who may have started the rumors in Oglala. But despite occasional suggestions to the contrary in lurid articles on this case, no one I have talked to makes the serious claim that David Price killed Anna Mae Aquash; all seem to agree that, whoever was responsible for the death, it was an Indian who pulled the trigger. It is sometimes said that Lakota medicine men, making their own Indian-way investigations, had received that message in the sweat lodge: an Indian had killed Anna Mae at the direction of two white men, and sooner or later the names of the killers would come out. As Red Cloud remarked of Spotted Tail's death, ". . . an Indian did it. But who set on the Indian?"

⊡

A few months later, on the long Dakota roads between Cheyenne River and Pine Ridge, I passed through the white twisted land that lies south of the White River—"up in the Badlands," said the woman who answered the telephone of Roger Amiotte, describing the gully where that Indian woman's body had been found. In early July, the draw down through the pale eroded hills was parched, and the yellow flowers of arrowhead balsamroot, the scattered song of the western meadowlark on the hot gusts, intensified an emptiness of wind and death. Dusty junipers, gaunt willows, and poor cottonwood along the draw were evidence of the water here in winter, and perhaps the killer thought that the small body would be sucked into the culvert or picked apart by coyotes before being discovered, since the few travelers who crossed this wasteland would have no reason to stop, far less to wander off the road. In any case, he was too confident or drunk or scared to hide the body, which was discovered by a man on horseback, tending fences.

Not far to the south, Route 44 led west through Wanblee, where Byron DeSersa was gunned down. At the litter of government housing known as Kyle, a road turns south toward Allen, and wondering if Myrtle Poor Bear were still in this area, I knocked at the door of Russell Means, who was sure to know what had become of her.

In the years since Wounded Knee, Means has been involved in eleven cases, and he has been tried four times in the white man's courts. In October 1975, he waived his right to a South Dakota jury trial after his attorneys had spent two weeks and dismissed two hundred candidates without coming up with twelve unbiased people. Given a sentence of four years for defending himself in the courtroom riot at the trial of Sarah Bad Heart Bull, he eventually spent one year in the state prison at Sioux Falls, much of it in Senator James Abourezk's office on the prison work program. "Judge Richard Braithwaite, who convicted me, he was busted this year for shoplifting," Means says, "except in his case it was called a sickness, and he is receiving treatment instead of serving time." (Judge Braithwaite was replaced on the bench by the up-and-coming R. D. Hurd, a personal friend of William Janklow, and the man commended by the Justice Department for his "superior performance" in losing the Banks-Means trial for the government.) Between 1974 and 1976, Means survived three shootings, in two of which BIA Indians were involved; in 1978, he was stabbed by a white man in state prison. "That knifing was set up," he says. "That was the first time in history that there were no guards around at recreation."

While in prison, Means decided on a fresh start for AIM's South Dakota chapter, which would now be called "Dakota AIM." Although he calls himself "an Oglala patriot" rather than a leader, he manages to remain in the public eye, and he still has a taste for controversy and altercations. Many Indians as well as whites, including some with a high opinion of his abilities, consider him arrogant and overbearing—the very personification of those attitudes that other Indians resent in "the Mighty Sioux," whose tendency toward self-assertion is alien to most Indian groups. ("No man will dispute what I say. I am a Lakota," Red Hawk said. "The Lakotas are superior to all others of mankind."[22]) As Vine Deloria, Jr., has ironically observed,

> The Sioux, my own people, have a great tradition of conflict. We were the only nation ever to annihilate the United States Cavalry three times in succession. And when we find no one else to quarrel with, we often fight each other. The Sioux problem is excessive leadership. During one twenty-year period in the last century the Sioux fought over an area from LaCrosse, Wisconsin, to Sheridan, Wyoming, against the Crow, Arapaho, Cheyenne, Mandan, Arikara, Hidatsa, Ponca, Iowa, Pawnee, Otoe, Omaha, Winnebago, Chippewa, Cree, Assiniboine, Sac and Fox, Potawatomi, Ute, and Gros Ventre. This was, of course, in addition to fighting the U.S. Cavalry continually throughout that period.[23]

From what I had heard, I hadn't expected to like Means much, and at our first meeting in the Rapid City airport, two months earlier, I didn't. Seated beside me in red wind band, earrings, bone neck choker, and embroidered vest, he remained aloof from a lively discussion of mining-

and water-pollution issues led by his bright tough sister-in-law Lorelei Means. Instead, mouth set in a hard twist, he fixed me with a rigid gaze that bored into my temple for five minutes, until at last he broke into the talk, demanding loudly and accusingly, "What are you doing here?" Taken by surprise, I accounted for myself, which filled me instantly with irritation. Today, on the other hand, he welcomed me into his house and gave me coffee and answered my questions incisively all morning.

"Russ is a psychological terrorist, at least in public," one Indian says. "Until he has control of the situation, he is always trying to throw strangers off balance, and he usually succeeds. But when you're alone with him, and he doesn't have to prove anything, he's great—warm, intelligent, and a lot of fun to be with." For the moment, at least, I agreed. Means is often reckless in his speech, but that recklessness had power behind it that was badly needed by his people. The week before, in a friend's kitchen in Minot, North Dakota, a young horse rancher and Vietnam combat veteran—by reputation, the last cowboy in North Dakota who knew how to break a horse—had expressed the local dislike and suspicion of AIM in general and the Dakota AIM leader in particular; from what he had seen on television and read in the local newspapers, this Russell Means was just a loudmouth and a hip-shooter who said any damn thing that came into his head. Because the rancher had spoken without anger, I tried to explain the Fort Laramie Treaty and the environmental background of the struggle, the nightmare years on the Pine Ridge Reservation, and AIM's fight, led by Russell Means, to restore the "spirit of Crazy Horse" to the Lakota: the United States governments, one after another, had failed the Indian people in every moral and legal obligation. He listened carefully, nodding his head. And when—just *because* he had really listened—I conceded that Means could be abrasive, he shrugged his shoulders, saying quietly, "Well, I don't know. From what you tell me, the Indians probably *needed* a fella like Russ Means, especially back there a few years ago when they were trying to get things started." Hearing this, I realized there was hope.

In his present conciliatory mood, Means wished to heal over some of the ill feeling of the past. "Dennis Banks and I have *never* had a split," he said at one point. "It was Dennis Banks who invited me into the Movement, and we were very good friends; he made some mistakes, but I'll always admire and respect that man. We chose different paths, that's all." He took a deep breath before he said, "I never made a public statement against Dennis Banks. And I never made one against Dickie Wilson, or Janklow, either—you don't condemn children."

In 1967, when Means was employed by the Rosebud tribal government, he was friendly with Janklow, who had taken his first job after law school as head of the Legal Services program on the reservation. "I never knew the prejudice against Indians in this state!—that's what Bill told me. He was a great guy, humorous and fun to be with, and he had a lot of humanity. I remember Christmas 1967, when he dressed up as Santa Claus and he drove around in a blizzard delivering presents to the poorest people, the ones living in tarpaper shacks and tents and car bodies. He drank pretty heavy, and Indians were always dropping by his house to get some of his liquor, and I guess it was alcohol behind the rape of Jancita Eagle Deer.[24] He did it, all right. I knew Jancita—that really ruined her life. But rape of an Indian girl by a white man is common in South Dakota, and because nothing is done about it in the courts, the great majority of the cases aren't reported; Indian women don't like to talk to white men about what one of their kind has done to them.

"Anyway, Janklow was interested in politics right from the start, and he soon realized there wasn't any future in Indian law or working with Indian people—that's what he told me over the phone in 1969, when I called him from Cleveland, asking him to stay on where he was and help us out. The truth was, he didn't *like* Indian people, and he only kept that benevolent attitude, that idealism, until he learned the realities of Indian law. From my personal experience, he was a good man, but he's been corrupted by the power that he always wanted, and he turned against us. Not that he attacked me; he made Banks his scapegoat instead. It's only lately that he's spoken out against me; the man needs a target these days." For a moment, Russ Means's handsome face curled with disgust. He showed me a paper that he planned to read two weeks later at the Black Hills Survival Gathering,[25] a huge demonstration designed to educate the public about the damage being done by the energy industry to the Great Plains region; the Gathering would also support the Lakota treaty claim and a uranium-mining referendum that would go before the voters in November.[26] "In this state," Means said, "every government that has ever been elected has been backed by the mining companies. Janklow went from raping young girls to raping Mother Earth."

⊡

Russ Means said that Myrtle Poor Bear might still live in Allen, although he had not seen or heard of her in several years; he suggested that I accompany him and his family to an Oglala giveaway being held that day—July 4—down near the Nebraska border, where people from Allen could tell me what had become of her. In the noon heat, we stopped for gas at Swett, and unaware that Means had sworn off alcohol after leaving prison, I offered to pay for beers in the station store. "I don't drink," Russ said shortly, in the manner of a man who has disapproved of drinking all his life.

At the giveaway, where a crowd of local Indians sat under a shade in a big circle, a man from Allen said that Myrtle Poor Bear came and went but that "there was no use talking to her; she's so far gone on alcohol that she don't make any sense, and she needs it so bad that people have got scared of going near her." He shrugged unhappily. "Her sisters have married Mexicans, I hear." Means introduced me to the mother of Dick Marshall, who felt sad that Dick and Cleo had split up and that Cleo will no longer permit their child to visit the prison. "I got a lot of trouble in my house," Mrs. Marshall said, "with my old man dead three months ago and Dick gone away; I just got to get along as best I can." Of Myrtle Poor Bear, she spoke without bitterness. "She's kind of sick, I guess," Mrs. Marshall said, making a vague hand gesture around her head.

"The FBI used a young girl from our community," Cleo Marshall has said, "and everything she said was false. The girl lived in the same village, and in two years, we had about three contacts with her. I couldn't understand why the FBI would use this girl who had so many problems, who is pitiful. Sometimes I say I hate the FBI. I do. You hope someday these things will stop—people will stop using other people. It's hard to hate. I try to look at the FBI . . . to see if maybe I can have some respect for them, but what I see them doing on Pine Ridge to our people—I can't find respect for them." In the opinion of this young woman (who says she was told by the FBI that her husband would not go to prison if she helped the Bureau to prosecute Russell Means), "We are fighting the government. Who do you turn to when you are fighting the government?"

I told Means how impressed I was by the forgiving attitude toward Myrtle Poor Bear—and even toward Wilson and his goons—on the part of people whose lives had been so damaged. "Those goons have families," he explained. "Anyway, AIM doesn't take retribution on anyone. We're dedicated now to fight to regain Indian sovereignty, starting with the Oglala and spreading out, and when you're involved in a liberation struggle, you don't make war on your own people."

Hearing this, I remembered something Bob Robideau had said. "Even the goons aren't so hated, really, because being goons was the only way they could find a job, have something to do. They grew up here and everybody knows them, knows what they been up against—Wilson, too. Everybody knows him for a drunk, just a petty crook, doing the dirty work for the real criminals who paid him off."

CHAPTER 16

ANOTHER IMPORTANT MATTER

Myrtle Poor Bear and David Price, 1976–81

The U.S. government won't obey the laws its own Congress enacted, so it's up to us, the people with respect for land and life, to join hand in hand.

Richard Marshall (Lakota)

A reservation Indian is already well-prepared to go to the penitentiary. Before he gets there he has already practiced being in prison. And even off the reservation, many Indians are still having a barbed-wire attitude—I try to teach my children and my people to get rid of the barbed wire mind.

Leonard Crow Dog (Lakota)

On April 12, 1978, Richard Marshall's appeal of his life sentence was denied by the South Dakota Supreme Court, which cited Myrtle Poor Bear's worthless testimony in support of its decision; the very same day, U.S. Attorney Evan Hultman, defending Leonard Peltier's conviction in St. Louis before the Eighth Circuit Court of Appeals, admitted that Poor Bear "was incompetent in the utter, utter, utter ultimate sense of incompetency."

This young woman's medical record, which she released in an effort to undo the damage after both of her alleged lovers had received life sentences, seemed sufficient cause all by itself for two new trials. Poor Bear had been arrested repeatedly for alcoholic episodes, and she was hospitalized eleven times between July 1963 and July 1976, claiming two rapes, three falls from horses, nervous disorders due to a husband who wished to take her child away, and many other calamities. In addition, she had made well over a hundred outpatient visits to various clinics in the region. Her father, with whom Myrtle has lived all of her life, says that she was very sick as a small child, apparently from typhoid fever contracted from drinking contaminated water. "Since she was a little girl, Myrtle lived in her own fantasy world," he says. "She always made up stories. She is a good girl, generous . . . but ever since her fever, the one that almost killed her, her mind is like that."[1]

According to cousins with whom she had actually spent the day and night of June 26, 1975, this small heavy-set unprepossessing woman considered herself an AIM person on the basis of attendance at one AIM meeting in July of that year at Dick Marshall's house in Allen; sometimes she imagined that she had been Jimmy Eagle's girl friend at the time of Oglala. Her sister Elaine says that Myrtle was forever lying and hallucinating, and that the family expected it; that she was never raped or thrown from a horse, had never lost a boyfriend at Wounded Knee, had never had a husband (or any other man) who threatened to take away either of her two illegitimate children. Since Myrtle's school principal in Allen,[2] who was consulted by Agent David Price, was well acquainted with this pathetic history, one can fairly assume that Price and Wood were aware of it, too.

Despite the poor opinion of her faculties expressed by lawyers for both the defense and the prosecution, Myrtle Lulu Poor Bear had been employed as radio dispatcher in the BIA police office in Pine Ridge when she first came to the attention of David Price in 1974. ("Myrtle is *not* stupid," one lawyer says. "She is a person of average intelligence, but she is a weak woman, very easily confused, and very suggestible, which is just the kind the FBI likes to work with: 'You *were* there, weren't you, Myrtle?' And after a while, she actually believes it herself.") In her job in Pine Ridge, Poor Bear had been readily accessible to the agents, and Wood says he talked with her three or four times in January 1976. On January 30, the agents reported to Elaine Poor Bear that Dick Marshall and "other guys" had raped her sister, beating her badly in the process, and that Myrtle had been taken to the hospital at Martin. Elaine Poor Bear told the agents that she did not believe this, and there is no 302 or medical report to support the story.

Motel bills, signed receipts, and other documents established that Poor Bear was in custody of Agents Price and Wood between February 19 and February 23, which were also the dates of her first and second affidavits in the Peltier case. SA Edward Skelly, to whom Myrtle was delivered on February 24, says that Price and Wood did not inform him that they had already interviewed her twice, nor that they had already obtained two affidavits in the Peltier case, nor even that she had been in their care for several days. His own interview took place on the same day that the body of an unidentified woman turned up in the Badlands.

For most of February 1976, Myrtle's whereabouts were unknown, and her family became extremely worried. When rumor spread through the reservation that the body of an unidentified young woman was lying in the morgue at Pine Ridge Hospital, Elaine Poor Bear and her sister Darlene Cross feared that it might be Myrtle. Since they had no car, they were taken in the local ambulance from Allen to Pine Ridge, where they viewed what later turned out to be the body of Anna Mae Aquash. Myrtle turned up in Pine Ridge and was taken home, but she soon disappeared again; this time she was gone for weeks. On April 1, she telephoned Elaine to say that the authorities wished her to testify against Dick Marshall. "They are making me do it," she told Elaine, and on April 2, she did. Marshall was found guilty of murder four days later.

David Price has acknowledged that when he and Wood first interviewed Myrtle about Peltier, on February 19 and February 23, they were already talking to her on "another important matter." On March 16, at the pre-trial hearing, when both sides are obliged to disclose all their witnesses, no mention was made of Myrtle Poor Bear, who was not officially "supplied" to Sheriff's Deputy Donald Phillips until March 22.

On the basis of Poor Bear's recantation, and her manipulation by the FBI, Kenneth Tilsen made a series of post-trial appeals based on the assumption that Price's other "important matter" was Marshall's alleged role in the Montileaux killing.

> The FBI had no reason to be involved in the Richard Marshall case at any time. It is unthinkable that they would be talking to a witness in a State prosecution for murder and not divulge that fact to any State police or prosecutorial authorities. It is apparent from the facts that, unless serious perjury has been committed by FBI Agent Price, State prosecutors deliberately failed to disclose to counsel or the court the existence of Myrtle Poor Bear as a witness when ordered to do so by the court on March 16, 1976. . . .
>
> It is most unlikely that the State authorities have no evidence of a contact or statement from Myrtle Poor Bear before March 22, 1976. It is most likely that exculpatory statements in the possession of State authorities have been withheld from the defense in violation of the court's orders in this case.[3]

In post-conviction hearings (March 1979) Price claimed that the other "important matter" was not the Montileaux killing but Marshall's alleged terrorist activities, as specified in this FBI report:

> . . . a source contacted SA PRICE and indicated that Ms. POOR BEAR had provided the source with information regarding a list of people to be killed on the Pine Ridge Indian Reservation. The source also indicated that Ms. POOR BEAR had stated that she wished to be contacted by SA PRICE. Thereafter, on January 15, 1976, SAS PRICE and WILLIAM WOOD met Ms. POOR BEAR and the source near Allen, South Dakota . . . this information provided by Ms. POOR BEAR concerned plans by RICHARD MARSHALL and others to engage in various violent activities, including the murder of specified individuals, bombings, and arson.

Pursuing the question of the manipulation of Myrtle Poor Bear by the FBI, Tilsen asked Agent Skelly if he had noticed that Myrtle Poor Bear was distraught and started to cry during Skelly's interview. Skelly said, "Yes sir, if that's what it says on there." William Wood was even more elusive, taking shelter in such statements as "I don't believe that is within the guidelines I was given to answer, sir." In fact, he could scarcely recall anything. "I couldn't get a good reading on Wood," Tilsen reflects. "He seemed to go his own way pretty much; I didn't feel that he was just Price's helper, which is the feeling that Ron Williams gave me in St. Paul."

Tilsen also interrogated Price, who was elusive and aggressive simultaneously.

> Q: In fact, Mr. Price, did you have a picture of the body of Anna Mae Aquash?
> A: Sir, pictures were taken of Anna Mae Aquash in an effort to identify her.
> Q: Did you show those pictures to Myrtle Poor Bear?
> A: Sir, I believe I showed pictures to a large number of people.
> Q: Including Myrtle Poor Bear?
> A: Sir, I can't say I have a specific recollection.
> Q: Did you carry the pictures on you during the period of February 24th and March 22nd?
> A: The dates you are talking about, February 24th, I don't personally remember when the body was found.
> Q: Assuming it was found on the 24th, and the pictures were taken a day or two thereafter, which the testimony will show, if I have to, did you carry the picture during this period of time?
> A: During this period of time, I had pictures available, whether I carried them, I do not know whether I carried them.
> Q: If the family testified that they did not know where she was during the immediate time, and in that period, and the week following February 24th, do you know where she was, Myrtle, that is?
> A: At this particular time, do I recall where she was in February of 19—
> Q: February 24th, and the week after, and the seven days thereafter, which would not be covered by any of the motel bills that we have?
> A: Sir, I don't recall at this time . . .
> Q: After the death of Anna Mae Aquash, did you and Myrtle discuss Anna Mae Aquash?
> A: Yes, sir.

Q: And Myrtle was there and you showed her pictures of Anna Mae Aquash?
A: I don't recall showing them, if I did.
Q: But you did discuss Anna Mae Aquash?
A: I don't recall.

In May 1977, Canadian prosecutor Paul Halprin filed suit against Peltier's Vancouver lawyers, who had suggested at the extradition appeal hearings in September–October 1976 that Halprin had known about the first Poor Bear affidavit, which contradicted the ones actually used, and was therefore guilty of unethical behavior, if not fraud. Halprin declared that he had been unaware of the existence of the first affidavit until just prior to the appeal hearings, and according to the finding of the Canadian court, "He was shocked that the United States government and the F.B.I. had suppressed this evidence. . . . It is clear beyond all doubt that the plaintiff had no knowledge whatsoever of any suppression of evidence, or of any misconduct on the part of anyone." On the other hand, a long memo from the FBI to the U.S. Attorney General's office in May 1979 notes that Halprin went to South Dakota to confer with Robert Sikma (who had been present when Price and Wood were preparing the third affidavit) on the "available evidence against Peltier. . . . It was upon Halprin's recommendation, with concurrence of special prosecutors Evan L. Hultman and Robert Sikma, that only Myrtle Poor Bear's second and third affidavits were used in the Peltier extradition."

Like Halprin, Hultman has denied this, telling Judge Ross of the Eighth Circuit Court of Appeals (April 12, 1978) that he had not seen the affidavits until "after they had been submitted . . . after they had gone to Canada." Without question, somebody is lying. Were the prosecutors involved in the suppression of evidence, or was the FBI trying to implicate them in order to blur its own role in the matter?[4]

In the period between the conviction and the sentencing of Leonard Peltier (April 18 and June 2, 1977), Myrtle Poor Bear continued to repudiate her testimony in regard to Peltier and Marshall. In sworn statements made in Canada on May 11, she stated that in early February 1976, Agents Price and Wood had come to Allen and suggested to her that she had been present at the Scenic shooting; that on February 23, they had questioned her again "in a mean and cruel way" by threatening that her little girl might come to harm and that she herself would be identified to AIM as an informer.

> I remember Dave Price and Bill Wood, the two FBI agents, telling me about Anna Mae Aquash. Dave described her body to me. He said that from what he heard she had been burnt and her clothes were put back on her and that after her clothes were put back on her she was shot. At this time the body had not been identified and Dave said "If I think I know who she is?" He showed me several pictures of the body and said to me that if I don't co-operate this is what may happen to me.
>
> The two FBI agents constantly reminded me of what happened to Anna Mae Aquash. And every so often the FBI agents showed me pictures of Anna Mae Aquash's body and I was really scared. The FBI agents would also ask me if I was able to sleep at nights and they would usually put these questions to me after they had shown me the photographs of the FBI agents' bodies and the body of Anna Mae Aquash.
>
> Bill Wood said that all the way along he knew that the body that was found at Pine Ridge was Anna Mae's body but that he had had her hands severed from her body and sent to Washington for identification in order to verify his own observations.

Subsequently, Myrtle said, she was kept in a Belle Fourche hotel with "Mary Ann Montileaux, or Mottlow" (a.k.a. Marion Poor Bear), who coached Myrtle on details of her story and who told her that she, too, was being coerced to testify against the AIM people, although she had no real reason to believe that Marshall had done the shooting.

Poor Bear's incompetence makes the foregoing somewhat suspect, yet it seems unlikely that all this was made up. And if it *is* true that William Wood knew Anna Mae's identity, his partner must have known it, too, since it was Price who took those grim pictures that were shown to Myrtle Poor Bear (he does not really deny it) during the preparation of her final statements against Marshall and Peltier.

In the Peltier case, Poor Bear said, the affidavits that she signed had been presented to her as protective-custody-release documents, with a paper over the statement she was signing; she had never read them until she went to Fargo for the trial. "They said I had a lie detector test," she remembers sadly, "and I never had one.

"I was kept from my family for a long time, I couldn't telephone. . . .

I was visited by Dave Price or Bill Wood every other day with pictures of the dead agents and Anna Mae. . . . I was forced to look at those pictures mostly every other day, to remind me of what would happen if I didn't do what they wanted me to do."

Since then, Myrtle has continued to repudiate her testimony in both cases. "I'm not afraid," she says, in a high sweet childlike voice. "They're always coming around, they threatened me, they come to my home with three cars and machine guns, but my family protects me very well, I'm pretty safe around them."

She recalls how her Indian people "looked away from her"; that, she says, is what hurt her the most. According to her friends, Myrtle was very upset that both sides dismissed her publicly as "mentally incompetent"; she wishes to cooperate, but she dreads having to appear in court ever again.

Despite all the new evidence presented at Marshall's post-conviction relief hearing, a South Dakota court[5] discounted the argument that without Poor Bear's testimony the Marshall jury might have arrived at a different verdict; a motion for a new trial was denied. In finding that conviction would have been probable in any case, the court ignored the fact that the testimony against Marshall supplied to South Dakota by the FBI was the only significant difference in the cases against Marshall and Russell Means, who was acquitted on the identical charge a few months after Marshall's conviction. As for Poor Bear's repudiation of her testimony, it was asserted that recantations were always very suspicious. Citing Peltier's case, the court expressed concern about the behavior of Agents Price and Wood: "Their conduct in some instances seems inappropriate and inconsistent," said the court, in judicious understatement. However, the agents' evident manipulation of the crucial witness did not strike Judge Merton Tice, Jr., as grounds for a new trial, and neither did prosecutor Hultman's admission to Judge Ross that Poor Bear's testimony in the Peltier case was worthless: in fact, Tice dismissed this admission by a U.S. Attorney as "a personal opinion to which this court can give little if any weight."

⊡

In late October 1980, I traveled to St. Paul, Minnesota, to discuss the Marshall case and other matters with Kenneth Tilsen. The last of the founding lawyers of the Wounded Knee Legal Defense/Offense Committee, dissolved in 1977 ("Millions of dollars and four years of a lot of people's lives went into that group"), who still works closely with the Indians, Kenneth Tilsen is a small husky balding man with a short grizzled beard, bright intense eyes, and fierce energy. Born in North Dakota farm country, he is a tough blunt composite of populist and conservative for whom any transgression of the Constitution is a grave offense; he was a campus radical at the University of Minnesota in the early 1950s and has been battling against the excesses of "the System"—the Vietnam war included—ever since. He also maintains a local practice. "I'm kind of an anomaly, I guess, an old-time lawyer; I still take a lot of little cases, and I've worked in this same building for thirty-one years." Throughout most of that period, Tilsen has contested the selective justice that Americans receive because of the political nature and the right-wing bias of the FBI.[6]

I asked Tilsen to comment on a rumor that an Indian who had recently died was actually the man who shot Martin Montileaux in Scenic; that his identity had been known to Dick Marshall from the start; and that Marshall had refused to cooperate with the white men in sending another Indian to jail. Among traditionals, such behavior would be taken for granted, and it had occurred to me that Leonard Peltier might have chosen the same course. In neither case could the convicted man establish his own innocence without incriminating someone else; and while for Marshall and Peltier there was always hope of new evidence or a new trial, for those whose proven guilt exonerated them there would be no hope at all. Though he did not deny it, Marshall's lawyer refused to confirm this rumor or even comment on it, saying that any discussion of such evidence could jeopardize any future appeal.

Although my account of the Peltier case openly argued the position of traditional Indian people and their allies in the American Indian Movement, it seemed important to interview certain individuals, such as U.S. Attorney Evan Hultman, who was the prosecutor in both Res-Murs trials, and Special Agent David Price, who was involved in events on Pine Ridge from the time of the Wounded Knee occupation in 1973 until he was recalled to FBI regional headquarters in Minneapolis four years later. Fairly or not, Price had come to personify the most cynical abuses of the FBI's regressive attitudes toward Indians, and it seemed important to hear his side of the story. I also wished to talk to Douglass Durham, and hoped that Ken Tilsen might have a lead on him. But after his service as a John Birch lecturer, Tilsen said, the informer had apparently disappeared, and as for Price, "he was here in Minneapolis, but they've transferred him again, down to Rochester, Minnesota." Tilsen, who has dealt with Price since the time of Wounded Knee, and knows most of the Indian people Price has dealt with, had no patience with my speculations on this man's blind obedience to the System. "In my opinion, David Price is one of the most corrupt and vicious agents in the FBI. I said this to two hundred agents in 1979, from the steps of the FBI Building in Washington, so you may as well quote me. Anyway, you can forget it. They don't let Price talk to anybody, and believe me, a lot of people have tried; there was a guy here not long ago from the L.A. *Times,* good tough reporter, hired a car and drove all the way down there, hoping to catch Price off guard—he struck out, too."[7]

One evening, on a restless impulse, I picked up the telephone and called Rochester information. No David Price was listed; there was a "D. F. Price," however, and I asked the operator to try that number. The woman who answered was not friendly, nor did she inquire who was calling when I asked for Mr. Price. There was a brief pause before she said shortly, "Just a minute," and in that pause I could hear young children's voices in the background; in this friendly heartland of mid-America, her hesitation was a warning that D. F. Price might be the man that I was looking for. Then a man's voice said, "Yes?" in the same guarded way. I had an instinct not to ask, "Is this Special Agent David Price?" in case that flared him, but to come on instead in a no-nonsense manner that an FBI man would appreciate: I-know-you're-in-there, Price, so-come-out-with-your-hands-up—that sort of tone. Without civilities, I said something like "Mr. Price, I'm not a reporter but I *am* a writer, doing a book on the Pine Ridge situation in the 1970s, and I really feel that your side of the story should be heard, since in everything I've read so far, you come out badly."

This time there was no mistaking a tense pause; the man taking a deep breath down there in Rochester was David Price, and I held the phone away in anticipation of a loud "click" in my left ear. I could still hear children, happily engaged, and their heedless voices made the reasons for this call, and the games of the weary adult world, seem sad and empty. Then the suspense was broken by a sort of sigh.

"I got worked over extremely heavily, to say the least," the voice said. "I've just had too many ringers thrown at me." The voice died off. "Look, I don't know you." The tone had hardened, as if "the bad cop" had interrupted "the good cop" in an interrogation. "Probably I shouldn't speak to you. Where are you calling from? Whose house are you in?" I said I was calling from a hotel, and gave him the name in case he wished to check it. I also warned him that my sympathies in the Pine Ridge confrontations lay with the traditional Indians. "The Indian situation *deserves* sympathy," Price assured me, reverting to a soft and thoughtful tone, "but it's hopeless. All the FBI was trying to do was to stop the Indians out there from killing each other."

A moment later, he was guarded again, repeating that he did not know me. I identified my most recent book, and he said, "Oh, you wrote *The Snow Leopard?*" as if he were familiar with it, which I felt certain he was not. Something odd was going on here; I began to feel guarded myself. *Why* was he talking? Also, he seemed quite aware that I was in touch with the Peltier Defense Committee and its attorneys, and that I would know whom he was talking about when he warned me that I was "dealing with people who will lie to you to your face. And you'll have to play it their way if you want a story other than the death of two agents and a lot of sadness on the Indian reservation. That's all it's about—murder!"

Again, Price reverted to a reasonable tone, saying, "The Bureau hasn't always benefited by its no-comment policy. I feel somebody has to tell the truth about this thing; if we all stand around and say, I'm not going to get burned by those guys, then the truth doesn't come out. I hope you're going to be objective." I told him I would do my best to present his views fairly.

At one point, Price interrupted himself to say, "Excuse me, I have a little girl here," going on to explain that it was his wife's birthday, for which he himself had baked the cake. Feeling increasingly disoriented and depressed—we might have been Minnesota neighbors discussing feed prices or tractor insurance; instead, we were strangers, political antagonists, "enemies"—I apologized for intruding on the festivities. He had his excuse here to hang up, but instead he muttered that it was all right, and resumed talking. I kept expecting Linda Price to rescue him, but she never did, and after a while, I didn't hear those children anymore.

It was now clear that, for whatever reason, Price was eager to talk, but more than once in the early part of the conversation, I thought I had lost him, as a question or comment caused his high boyish voice to rise still higher. "There's no use talking!" he would cry, in what sounded like genuine despair. Then the "good-cop" voice was back again, rueful, disillusioned, and confiding.

"Most agents are stupidly idealistic—we all think we're here to help somebody. You keep getting burned by that belief, and some of us give up on trying to help. We're not world-beaters, we're just guys; we come to do a job, making it safer for other people, and we leave." He sighed. "So I'm an idealist, okay? All agents are idealists, or we wouldn't be in this.

"Like the case of Jeannette Bissonnette. Parked with her boyfriend on Jim Wilson's land, four miles from Jumping Bull Hall, three months to the day before the shoot-out. Somebody fires into the car, not the husband, not the wife—just shooting into a car that happened to be on Jim Wilson's land! They thought the car belonged to Jim. I was very unhappy about Jeannette Bissonnette's death, and the caliber of people who would shoot blindly into a car—"

I had never heard that Jeannette Bissonnette had been parked on Jim Wilson's land, or that the man who stopped to help her was her "boyfriend"; these details seemed calculated and insidious, like the unidentified "Leonard" in Myrtle Poor Bear's account of the party at which Dick Marshall had allegedly confessed to killing Montileaux. I interrupted Price to say that this account of Jeannette Bissonnette's death was supposition.

"That *happened*!" Price said sharply. "My supposition is correct!"

I didn't challenge this, and in a little while, "the good cop" said, "I liked the Indians, okay? My *own* feelings. I liked the Indians; they're very human. That's why I got the flak—I had a lot of Indian friends, and I got well known. And when things go wrong, and you've got a guy like me who's supposed to be so bad, why then they hang this thing on him, and that thing on him, too. I still have friends there, but I'm not going back; I didn't accomplish anything. And I don't think it's part of an FBI agent's duty to accomplish *nothing*!

"It's just what I say—it's sad. And that's got nothing to do with race, it's *booze*! I'm not saying the Indian reservation hasn't got happiness, good times, but the alcoholic rate speaks for itself. I have never said the AIM was bad. I've said that if it gave the Indians pride, it would be good. It hasn't! Look at them! You can go down there and look for yourself. You know that liquor store down there in White Clay, across the Nebraska line? You can pitch all the federal money you want into Pine Ridge, that's where it's going—unbelievable amount of cases sold, phenomenal! Enough to make every man, woman, and child on the reservation an alcoholic! And ninety-nine percent of the crimes on Pine Ridge are alcohol-related. People get drunk, half-kill each other, and next day they say, He's my friend, I won't testify. Well, you're not going to change that world. Maybe killing a cop is the only way they can strike back at society, but it isn't the fault of the poor cop. *I* didn't hurt Indians! The two guys who are dead, *they* weren't guilty of harming Indians!

"Those Indians in Tent City, they weren't Pine Ridge people. The women and children, sure, but what Sioux men were there? There were no local men at all—not one of 'em came from the reservation. Peltier, Robideau, and Butler—all fairly not-nice guys, right? And this is what it filtered down to—people who were killing to kill. They had contingency arms caches, the opportunity presented itself, and they did it. Otherwise, what were they doing in there?"

I suggested that they were defending the local Oglala people from harassment by the goons. When Price questioned that word, as if ignorant of its meaning, I reminded him that the goons themselves had used this acronym (for "Guardians of the Oglala Nation"), and suddenly he cut me off in a mean, hard voice. "Don't tell *me* about the goons and the AIMs," he snapped. "I know more about the goons and the AIMs than you *ever* will, even when you're through writing this book you're pretending to write!" Before I could deal with this, he switched tones again, saying, "I'm not going to go trying to defend the goons. But you try and find someone on the Indian reservation with a broken nose done by an FBI agent. If you can find one Indian on that reservation who says he got hit, he got shoved—" I said I had heard that Jack Coler was pretty aggressive, and that he had shoved someone in Oglala that same morning. Price said that he hadn't known Coler, but that he doubted this story very much.

Price referred to "the mythical red Scout" linked to Jimmy Eagle, but later he declared that the red Scout was *not* mythical, "there were maybe two guys in it." He would not explain further. "Ron was on that property earlier; he said, I'm looking for Jimmy Eagle and I'll be back. A classic mistake! They were ready for 'em! I was on the radio when Ron was talking to Adams—the trouble was, I was sixty, seventy miles away."

I asked his opinion of the suggestion made at Peltier's trial that Gary Adams might have saved the agents' lives if he had shown a little more persistence, and David Price made noncommittal noises: "All *I* know is, I was too damned far away.

"We know Coler had his rifle cased, unloaded, in the trunk. He gets out, he gets his arm hit, through the trunk, by a heavy-caliber bullet; there's a quarter inch of arm left, hanging from the elbow, and he goes down—no danger to anybody.

"Ron Williams is over by his car, wounded in one arm—his gun arm—and one leg. Ron runs over, strips off shirt, fixes tourniquet—think what it's like to be fired at by thirty guys when you're doing that! He never fires at anybody; he's not doing *anything*. He can't anyway; he's left-handed, and that arm is wounded. Three, four, five men walk up to him; one of 'em's Peltier, and two others are the ones who beat the rap. He's just standing there, and he says to 'em, This guy's got a wife and kids, let him get to the hospital."

Price would not tell me who reported this account, which corresponds roughly to the one attributed to Jimmy Eagle.

"So Ron took a .223 round, and because he put his hand up, it blasted all four fingers all over his face—what was left of his face. He drops dead. They shoot Jack—Jack would have died, anyway—and that's the end of Jack. Then they shoot both of 'em when they're already dead. Ron didn't have a *face*! Here are two men, just trying to do a law-enforcement job—!

"And now some people try to make Peltier a hero. I never saw any courage there." Price's shrill voice, which had been genuinely outraged, turned matter-of-fact again. "An Indian told us that they turn 'em over, so that they're face down. That way, they don't go to heaven. They took the guns and they left. It happened that way! It did! You have at least two, three eyewitnesses. And Peltier kept Coler's gun as a souvenir.

"Ron could have deserted Jack, run for the swamp; he had one chance for life, and that was desertion, immediately, without one second's thought. Maybe there wasn't time, but anyway, that wasn't in his character.

"Don't take it from me, because I'm supposed to be this heinous villain; ask somebody else who knew Ron Williams. Go to Rapid City, ask his neighbors; ask George O'Clock, who was Resident Senior Agent in Rapid; Ron was like a son to him." Price sighed. "Ron can only be described as a gentle, gentle person, one of the few gentle, gentle people. He wasn't tough, but his morals were such that he couldn't desert. No, you're not going to come up with a bad guy."

(I later spoke to O'Clock, now retired, who sounded kind and fatherly over the telephone; he called me "Pete" as soon as he had caught my name. Mr. O'Clock described Ron Williams as "a member of the family, a second son to me. Ron was just an outstanding young man, mentally, morally, and physically. He was concerned about people, and he made friends easily. Ron was a sincere lad who just enjoyed life, an outstanding lad.")

"I don't think either of 'em knew what they were doing in there; that's not a criticism, but that's the way I see it," Price was saying. At the mention of Coler's map (the one showing "bunkers" at the Wallace Little ranch), he was incredulous. "What map? What? I never heard of it! I didn't dig his pockets out—all I did was roll him over and help put him on the stretcher—but I never saw any *map*!" It was in his car, I said; the government never contested this. "Coler's briefcase had a piece of classified information in it, but no *map*!" David Price said.

I came at the point another way, suggesting that agents could be conditioned by what they were told by their superiors about "terrorists" and "bunkers" and so forth, which might have explained the large numbers of armed men, the support teams and sniper teams and SWAT teams flown in from all over the country, the helicopters and airplanes . . . in short, the overkill—

"*Overkill!?*" Price's voice went shrill again. "Read my 302! We're not out there to die, or get medals! The idea is not to go down there and have a shoot-out but to get the job done effectively! Two hundred to thirty is lousy odds! In Detroit, with an officer down, two thousand to one would be more like it! Even then, we never *did* have control—they got away, remember? We didn't catch anybody, not *no*body, do you realize that? Why? Because the distances out there are bigger than here! If Ron hadn't gotten off those radio transmissions, we might never have known *what* happened! That's a big reservation!

"I mean, why did they stay and shoot it out with us? They could have gotten away easily in the first hour! It took me an hour just to get around behind them! And they knew we were coming; they had Ron's car down there, and the radio going full blast. They *planned* that escape!" Clearly the Indians' escape after the shoot-out (for which Edgar Bear Runner was somehow held accountable) was still an embarrassment to the FBI.

I reminded him of the Indians' contention that they had not fled because they feared for the safety of the women and children, and to my surprise, Price seemed to acknowledge that this was a possibility. "I could hear the women and kids crying and screaming—they were scared. Ron Williams had helped one of those women in her daughter's rape case, a thirteen- or fourteen-year-old—no big deal. Nobody seriously hurt." (Hearing this, I recalled somebody's observation that around Price's witnesses—Moves Camp, Poor Bear, John Stewart, Marvin Bragg—there is usually an overtone of rape, which is apt to be a "big deal" to the victim.) "The daughter was living there in Tent City. There's the sad thing: Ron thinking he's helping, and now he's dead. She wouldn't help us as a witness. The rape case went to trial after his death, and we lost.

"Anyway, there wasn't much firepower into the ranch. We were down this hill—a hundred yards straight down—and we couldn't shoot into the cabins. The only reason there were bullet holes in the houses—it was done on the assault, because we thought there was someone shooting from inside, where we found the weapons caches after the escape."

At one point, Price attributed the escape to the good sportsmanship of the law-enforcement officers: "The discipline there was really something. You don't shoot somebody in the back when they are running—that's why they got away." On the other hand, he kept reverting to the idea that the escape had been planned in advance, and so had the killings; he still argued the ambush theory that the prosecution itself had all but discarded in the Fargo trial, and he went beyond it, referring to some cold-blooded left-wing conspiracy for which he refused to supply details. "Their cause was dying on the vine," he said, "so they decided, It'll make the front page nationwide if we kill an FBI agent. The planner was not an AIM leader, not even an Indian, but you'd better stay away from that; you have to be careful, I'll tell you that. If they thought you'd write something . . . I just don't know. It's not their game plan not to have you write what they want." At another point, however, Price advised me, "Dig in, find out who's behind Oglala. You've got to be on their side or you'll be in extreme danger. *Who* planned the idea and knew it would be page one, nationwide? You'd really have a problem, you'd be in real danger, but it would be fun if you really looked into it. Talk to Ted Lame; you'll find him if you're talking to the shooters."

Repeatedly—and despite his earlier insistence that outside Indians had been responsible—Price referred to "thirty" men involved in the

Oglala shoot-out. "They all should have the same penalty," he said. "But there are discovery procedures for prosecution witnesses, so that the defense can pressure these potential witnesses and figure out who the informers are. If there *are* any," he added quickly. "And by the time it gets to court, your witnesses have chickened out. This legal system can be beat, with money, radical attorneys—it can be beat. They have good attorneys.

"We couldn't put a conspiracy case together on *anybody,* but we proved who did it, how the final shooting occurred. You'll be surprised to hear that it wasn't me who put together the Peltier case, but I'm content that we got the right guy. Butler and Robideau, who beat us in Cedar Rapids, they were right down there with Peltier, we know that. That's *another* example of the jury system, which I'm not against, but I don't think *anybody* could stomach that Cedar Rapids verdict!"

At the mention of Myrtle Poor Bear, Price was instantly wary. "I'm not going to go into the Myrtle Poor Bear mess," he said, "but they certainly did beat that poor little girl up enough. It's an amazing process that *we* end up the villains." A little later, when I returned the conversation to this subject, he evaded it again, and eventually I tried a third time, certain now that he would not hang up: I wondered aloud why he had used a self-evidently incompetent witness, on the basis of whose testimony two men were now serving life terms.

"Myrtle? Who never testified? Did she testify at Fargo? No!" And the Dick Marshall case? He became shrill again: "I didn't *care* about that case!" Like the alleged rape by Louis Moves Camp in River Falls, Wisconsin, which never happened because no charges had been brought, "Myrtle Poor Bear doesn't really count, because Myrtle Poor Bear never really *testified* to anything!" How about the extradition affidavits, how about— "Okay, she testified in the Dick Marshall case, and I think she told the truth!"

Earlier that day, I had watched two videotapes of Myrtle Poor Bear, speaking out against her exploitation by the FBI in the year after the trial of Leonard Peltier. With her waddle walk and puffy face, her wheeze, she seemed almost a caricature of the depressed reservation Indian reared on sugared food, TV, and beer. The unlucky young woman with the child's sweet voice seemed less "incompetent" than confused; she got her facts mixed up in answering questions, and appeared to be making up details as she went along, according to what she thought might be expected of her. And having seen her in these calm unthreatening interviews (on the witness stand at Fargo, she had cried throughout), I found it impossible to believe that Dick Marshall or anybody else had made her privy to a "list of people to be killed on the Pine Ridge Reservation," or that Price and his partner, William Wood, had not known immediately that she was unfit to serve as a witness in two trials that could (and did) send men to jail for life.

Perhaps Price sensed that I was unpersuaded, since he later returned to the subject of Myrtle Poor Bear of his own accord. "Poor Myrtle has to live with those people, afraid and pressured. She just couldn't stand up to Peltier and Butler—that's understandable. She's a scared little rabbit; she got hurt a lot by those people." But now, discussing Poor Bear on his own initiative, Price sort of snickered. "Poor Myrtle," he said. "She ain't the prettiest critter who ever walked the face of the earth." Once again, he made that mirthless sound. "You can bet Bill Wood and I, we never let ourselves be alone with her, not for one minute, in case she'd later say we tried to do something. Myrtle needed protection from the U.S. marshals for a long time, and Myrtle's not always fun to take care of. Those female marshals became her only friends."

Getting nowhere on the manipulation of Myrtle Poor Bear, I asked Price how it was possible that he had not recognized Anna Mae Aquash on the day that her body was discovered. "Her face was pure black with exposure and dehydration," he exclaimed, "and she had no eyes! *You* try to identify a girl you've only seen twice in your life, and the second time only because she identified herself! The only reason I was interested in Anna Mae was because she was living with that AIM bunch out at Ted Lame's place when Jeannette Bissonnette was killed, and shell casings found in the Bissonnette murder matched up with one of the guns used at Oglala!

"We'd *love* to know who killed Anna Mae! We're still investigating. But where do we go? If you were me, wouldn't *you* like to know who killed Anna Mae?" A little later, he said, "If *I* were gonna look, I'd look heavily at Selo Black Crow's place near Wanblee, only a few miles from where she was found." (Price did not mention the two raids he had led on Black Crow's place before and after the Oglala shoot-out, nor the fact that his former partner, William Wood, was still harassing Black Crow, whose wife had reported a hit-and-run victim in the area before the body was found; like Price, Wood was intimating that Black Crow knew something about the death. "Selo never done it," Bob Robideau had told me flatly when I mentioned this. Asked if he meant that Black Crow wasn't capable of it, Bob shook his head. I could see that he wasn't going to answer any more questions.)

It is very noticeable how often the names of certain people who were never prosecuted—Ted Lame, June Little, Selo Black Crow, Frank Black Horse—turn up in FBI accounts, as if the incantation of these names might produce enough evidence to take them to court. At one point, Price said, "We were looking for Black Horse; we thought he was at Oglala—an Italian from Cleveland! Ran off to play Indian and kill agents! A crumb!

"The actual events are very sad," Price said again. "It is only murder. I personally don't think I belong in any book—the little I did! I'm just another agent in the FBI, I'm not in on the big things like ABSCAM. Without the allegations, I would be nobody. Peltier, too. You're not going to do good by working up Peltier into a hero, because he isn't. I don't really think Peltier deserves much attention: his character—he's just a grub! I don't class him as an important big killer; maybe he was just the lucky one who held the gun. Peltier can write words, ghost-written maybe, that make him sound worthwhile, but he still did what he did, and he's just a crumb.

"Read the ResMurs file if you want the truth; Peltier's lawyers received twenty-six thousand pages of it, two or three weeks ago.[8] It won't tell you character, it won't tell you courage, but it *will* tell you what really happened. The Bureau is a strange critter, but it never cheats on its paperwork; it will tell you just how inept we can be." Price also said that I should look at the autopsy pictures of Coler and Williams, read the ballistics reports, and check out his own 302 report for that day. "If you want to play it fair, you've got a lot of work. But you'd better be careful." Once again, this man was warning me.

Returning to a touchy subject, I suggested something to the effect that a man like Jack Coler, with his official maps of nonexistent "bunkers," might be conditioned by fear of "terrorists" to nervous and aggressive behavior, that field agents might be caught in the middle between extreme actions inspired by official propaganda and an appropriate response to a local situation. William "Rusty" Calley, for example, who might have lived out his life harmlessly as a Miami gas-station attendant had the Vietnam war never occurred, became the Monster of My Lai— "Who?" Price said. It appeared that he had never heard of Lieutenant Calley. (Earlier he had astonished me with the statement that he had never heard of Douglass Durham, who did so much to disrupt AIM during Price's period on Pine Ridge.) "Anyway," Price said impatiently, "I'm not caught in the middle." He had never received any inquiries from his superiors about his actions? "I'm under supervision all the time," he said. "Everything I do, the Bureau knows it the day I do it."

I wondered how soon the Bureau would know about this phone call, how long before a new entry under my name would appear in those gigantic Bureau files. Because ever since the first few minutes of our conversation, I had been feeling paranoid myself. Why was Price telling me so often that I had to be careful, that I could expect harm from "them" if I told the truth? Was this his way of threatening me on the Bureau's behalf? More important, why was this man talking to me at all, when he had refused so often to talk to others? Was it because he wanted to get his own views on the record, in the fear that the Bureau would respond to unwelcome publicity by making him the scapegoat for its abuses on Pine Ridge? Or was he talking to me on orders from his superiors, who had somehow learned about this book, and were feeling out my attitudes and my intentions?

Throughout, Price had shifted with unsettling speed from soft-voiced sentimental reflections about the plight of Indians in general and Myrtle Poor Bear in particular ("Poor little Myrtle! Poor, poor little girl . . .") to paranoia, sarcasm, and anger, together with desperate interjections such as "I gotta quit talking to you, it won't do any good!" But eventually I knew that he had never intended to hang up; in fact, it was I who ended the call just three minutes short of three hours after it had begun, not because I had lost interest but because, from the start, we had spun in circles, returning obsessively to the same topics, only to veer off again, until finally I was too spaced out to continue.

To judge from his speech, David Price is not a stupid man, but one whose intelligence is severely limited by preconceptions—either that, or he is a liar who not only believes but is angered and moved by his own lies. Despite his awful sentimentality—about Myrtle Poor Bear, about the idealism of his fellow agents—his outrage about Ron Williams's death is genuine; and he does not whine about his villain's role, but seems to accept it in the line of duty. Despite the great amount of evidence of his misconduct, Price acknowledges nothing wrong in his own actions. "There's no reason for me to get upset about absurd allegations," he declared at one point. "I know the allegations; if you write it up on allegations, you'll be writing a lie!"

Toward the end of the call, Price suddenly said, "You're the first guy I ever talked to."

"I know that," I said. "Why?"

"I knew I'd hear from you," he said. "They sent me the article." Two weeks before, as it turned out, there had been a news item in the Rapid City *Journal* about a proposed book and film project on the Peltier case; word of this piece had been sent on to Price, perhaps by Wood. "The Bureau hasn't always benefited from its no-comment policy," Price explained again. "You can play word games if you want, to quote me out of context; if you want to play fair, then you better be careful." I told him again that I would do my best to quote him fairly, and the conversation came to an unhappy pause.

"Probably I shouldn't have talked to you," he said quietly, sounding gloomy and bitter, and I felt sorry for him. Like Myrtle Poor Bear and Angie Long Visitor, like the young Navajo boys bullied into testifying against their leaders, like many others on both sides whose lives have been corrupted to ensure the victory of the United States over Leonard Peltier, this man on the other end of the wire was only another casualty of the new Indian wars, and he would be soiled for the rest of his days by deeds done in the belief that the end justified the means, whether or not he ever pays a formal penalty. However, there was no sense trying to talk about it. In easing the conversation to an end, I said, "You don't have any Indian problems down there in Rochester, I guess." And Price retorted, "I may have when you people get through; some nut may decide to go after my wife and children."

Hanging up, I felt disturbed that the man regarded wrongly as the villain of the tale had turned out to be a family man, a maker of birthday cakes; I could still hear the diminishing voices of his children, whose play had ended with a stranger's call that had taken away their father from the party. How odd it was to hear this man, accused of threatening the frightened Poor Bear with harm to her child, expressing concern for the safety of his own family; yet his concern was natural, and the irony had no flavor at all.

⊡

Despite serious criticism of his agents' use of Indian witnesses by Judge Nichol, Judge McManus, and Judge Ross, FBI Director William Webster had ordered no meaningful inquiry in regard to abuses by his men in South Dakota. In a long letter of response to questions by Arthur Flemming, chairman of the Commission on Civil Rights, the Director stated that only one agent had been present at the death scene of Anna Mae Aquash; that the suggestion that the hands be severed was made by a different agent; and that the hands were placed in the custody of a third.[9] Thus, it appears, three different agents—none of them prominent in the ResMurs case—shared the responsibility for this murky episode. There was little mention of Price or Wood, whom Webster seemed to exonerate of all misconduct.

As for Poor Bear, "All affidavits were voluntarily furnished and taken in good faith," Webster declared. "At the time the three affidavits were furnished, it was believed that she was totally reliable and mentally stable. The inconsistency between the first affidavit and the second two affidavits is believed to be the result of Myrtle Poor Bear's initial reluctance to fully cooperate because of her legitimate fear for her personal safety."[10] Unfortunately for Webster's argument, the Freedom of Information Act documents recommended to me by David Price show clearly that Poor Bear herself did not share this fear of vengeful AIMers and WKLDOC harassment, which Robert Sikma used repeatedly as an excuse to hold her in custody. According to an FBI teletype of March 21, 1976, the informant "insisted" that she "did not want anyone protecting her" and that she desired to return home; even so, she was not released until April 17, and Sikma attempted to take her back into custody just four days later. Another document reveals that on March 4, two weeks after the first affidavits were taken, prints of her fingers and her palms were compared with the hundreds of unidentified prints recovered on the Jumping Bull property; the entirely negative results, which even the FBI regarded as "significant," did not deter the authorities from extracting the third affidavit from this person on March 31, "in good faith" or otherwise, and using this suspect eyewitness account to ensure Peltier's extradition from Canada.

⊡

During his tenure in Rapid City, the Special Agent in Charge of the Oglala investigation, Norman Zigrossi, told WKLDOC's Bruce Ellison that if any evidence was forthcoming that any of his men had abused their positions, those men would be gotten rid of that same day. When Ellison cited the numerous complaints that the Oglala people had made against David Price, Zigrossi said he regarded Price as "a model agent." What is alarming here is not that Zigrossi is wrong but that he is right; according to the value system of the FBI, Price is indeed "a model agent," in the same way that "Doug" Durham was a model informant, who carried out his job faithfully and well; in the same way that Richard G. Held was a model head of the Internal Security Section in charge of those "anti-terrorist" counterintelligence activities that used to go under the name of COINTELPRO, and therefore became Associate Director of the FBI. What these men did right is precisely what is wrong with the FBI, and with the Justice Department, and with a government of quick-stepping bureaucrats and politicians for whom truthfulness and integrity have been reduced to an aspect of public relations. As Dick Marshall says, "The U.S. government won't obey the laws its own Congress enacted, so it's up to us, the people with respect for land and life, to join hand in hand."

⊡

Kenneth Tilsen has a lot of respect for Marshall, and full confidence that one day he will be exonerated. "At the time he went to prison, Dick was still pretty young and wild, and always in and out of trouble; now he's a tower of strength. In fact, he's the Indian leader there; he's fought for the prisoners' rights and he's given them something to live for. Almost single-handed, Dick has wiped out 'huffing,' or glue sniffing, which was epidemic among the inmates. Back in '78, when Russ Means spent nearly a year in that state prison, there was a rally for Dick and Russ and for prisoners' rights, and during this rally a white convict put a knife in Russ; this guy had already stabbed a black inmate in some federal prison, and had had to be transferred. Anyway, there was a near-riot there between the races, and Dick had the strength and influence to stop it. Even the warden knows how valuable he is. He tells people how much he likes Dick, he even says that Dick is doing Russ's time in the Montileaux killing, he's made him a trustee. This summer, Dick was permitted to go home for his father's funeral, and also to sun-dance, and now he's been put on a prison farm because of his good behavior. We think this has been done to isolate him, cut his influence with the other inmates, make them think that Dick Marshall has sold out to the authorities.

"A lot of AIM people have really grown while they were in prison—look at Leonard. That guy was just one of the warriors when he was around here for the Banks-Means trial, and probably at the time of Oglala, too; it is only in prison that he has developed into a real leader. And Bob Robideau. There's a guy who has spent more time in than out, all the way back to reform school, and all for petty offenses; the only major conviction he ever had was the one in Kansas. But Bob will never go back to jail for a petty offense, only for something important that he believes in. That goes for Dino, too—in working for their people, even in prison, these guys have found meaning in their lives."

A few weeks earlier (September 9, 1980), Tilsen had presented arguments before the South Dakota Supreme Court, appealing the circuit court order denying Dick Marshall a new trial. A few months later (May 20, 1981), the state Supreme Court turned down the appeal. In his vigorous dissent, Chief Justice Wollman declared that, in addition to the numerous contradictions in the evidence, he was persuaded that had the jury been aware of evidence not available to the defense at the time of trial—Poor Bear's medical history, her conflicting affidavits in the Peltier case, and her proven incompetence as a dependable witness—it might well have voted for acquittal. "Moreover, there are the statements of Mr. Hultman, who all but stated that Myrtle Poor Bear was lying." Commenting on Judge Tice's dismissal of Hultman's statement as "a personal opinion to which this court can give little if any weight," Judge Wollman said, "I am not disposed to take lightly statements made by a United States Attorney before a panel of judges in a United States Court of Appeals. I would hold that the circuit court erred in not granting a new trial."

Under the circumstances, Marshall's defenders refuse to abandon this case. "The stark reality of Richard Marshall serving a life sentence for murder based on the testimony of this witness ought to offend the sensibilities of every jurist," Kenneth Tilsen says.[11] (Even Halley Merrill of the Longhorn Bar and his daughter Twila, both of whom testified against Dick Marshall, have written letters in support of a commutation of his sentence.) And since Marshall's continuing appeal is essentially based on FBI misconduct involving the same witness whose false affidavits ensured Leonard Peltier's extradition from Canada, the outcome of his case is bound to affect Peltier's own chance for a new trial.

CHAPTER 17

FORKED TONGUES

The Freedom of Information Act and the New Evidence, 1980–81

They spoke very loudly when they said their laws were made for everybody; but we soon learned that although they expected us to keep them, they thought nothing of breaking them themselves. They told us not to drink whisky, yet they made it themselves and traded it to us for furs and robes until both were nearly gone. Their Wise Ones said we might have their religion, but when we tried to understand it we found that there were too many kinds of religion among white men for us to understand, and that scarcely any two white men agreed which was the right one to learn. This bothered us a good deal until we saw that the white man did not take his religion any more seriously than he did his laws, and that he kept both of them just behind him, like Helpers, to use when they might do him good in his dealings with strangers. These were not our ways. We kept the laws we made and lived our religion.

Plenty-Coups (*Crow*)

Although convinced that Leonard Peltier had been tried unjustly, I still lacked any strong sense of his innocence. The brutal nature of the agents' executions and the fact that Peltier and his men had eventually been caught with the dead men's weapons made me resist the Movement propaganda according to which "AIM Warriors at Oglala were defending the Native People against Genocide," as if the killings had somehow been sanctified by the sacred pipe. With the passage of time, the events of June 26, 1975, were being portrayed in the bright proud colors of Crazy Horse and the days of Lakota glory, when what had happened at Oglala was not glorious at all but sad and ugly. Three young men had lost their lives and the death list was still growing, quite apart from the many surviving victims whose lives had been contaminated and stained.

On the other hand, the Peltier case, like that of Sacco and Vanzetti, had historic reverberations that went far beyond what happened at Oglala. The federal agencies had encouraged the conflict between Indian factions, and the traditional Indians had been fighting for survival, and in the stark light of those medieval years down on Pine Ridge, talk of guilt or innocence in the inevitable shoot-out seemed beside the point: whether or not he had killed the agents, Leonard Peltier deserved a new trial, not only because of dishonest proceedings at Vancouver and Fargo and Los Angeles but because of accumulating evidence that the authorities had wanted him out of the way whether he was guilty or not.

In early 1981, former U.S. Attorney Evan Hultman told a reporter, "There's no doubt in my mind that Peltier shot the agents. He was the enforcer on the Reservation—everyone knew that."[1] If there is any good evidence for that assertion, it was never brought out at the trials, nor does it appear in the twelve thousand pages from the ResMurs file which Peltier's attorneys eventually obtained under the Freedom of Information Act (FOIA) in late 1980 and 1981. (Although this case was officially "criminal," not political, the Bureau refused to release six thousand additional pages, said to be "classified . . . in the interest of the national defense or foreign policy, for example, information involving intelligence sources or methods.") The ResMurs file is a monument to bureaucratic zeal, but it does not show that "Peltier shot the agents"; what it shows is how much effort was devoted to constructing a case in support of a preconceived idea of one man's guilt.

"The one individual that appears to have been identified by more witnesses than any other is FBI fugitive Leonard Peltier," SAC Richard Held reports to Washington in one of these documents in the very first days of July 1975—but who *were* all these witnesses? Excepting Angie Long Visitor's "Leonard LNU," the only immediately available evidence of Peltier's presence at Oglala *on June 26* (Peltier's fingerprints were found in the AIM camp; so were those of Anna Mae Aquash and many others who had not been present on that day) was the Pumpkinseed sighting by Agent Frederick Coward, which no one seems to have taken seriously—not prosecutor Hultman, not Coward's superiors, and not even Coward himself, if the fact that he did not write it up in a 302 until September 11—more than two months after the event—is any evidence. The one person who seemed to take it seriously was BIA Officer Marvin Stoldt, who was never called as a witness for the prosecution.

A clue to the FBI's real estimate of these critical identifications by eyewitnesses (at a time when no other eyewitnesses had been produced) is the fact that in spite of the feverish hunt for suspects that raised hell on the reservation for ten weeks, Held's assistant in the field, SAC Norman Zigrossi, asserted at Fargo that he had never heard of Marvin Stoldt, far less discussed with him the crucial information that gave whatever credibility it had to Coward's sighting. One can only conclude that there was no reason for Zigrossi to consult with Stoldt, since verifying those sightings was beside the point. Among the FOIA documents is a government memo dated April 6, 1977 (or about two days before defense testimony began in the Fargo trial): the memo is addressed to U.S. Attorney Hultman, and its subject is an FBI test conducted that day of the rifle scope used by Coward on June 26, 1975. This test (made at an outside temperature of 38 ° F—a temperature at which the mirage factor is far less distorting than it would be on a hot and hazy day) could not vindicate the sighting, and the memo implicitly casts doubt on Coward's identification. Since this memo turned up in the work files of Hultman's associate Lynn Crooks, it is conceivable that Hultman never saw it; but if either man saw it, why didn't he share its potentially exculpatory contents with the defense, as he was obliged to do by law?

The reason is—or appears to be—that those Pumpkinseed sightings were needed to shore up a weak case in the government's huge dogged effort to make sure that its last suspect did not "beat the rap." And perhaps there was also a tactical decision: with an all-white jury, rather than just trust to luck with a bunch of sullen Indians who were clearly on the witness stand under duress, why not let a clean-cut hawkeye lawman pin that cop-killer right at the scene of the crime, where he belonged? Because in the absence of any better evidence than Held's unsupported statement about witnesses, or the Coward sighting, it must be assumed that the FBI *knew well in advance* that their Wisconsin fugitive was with an AIM group somewhere in Oglala, and that Coler and Williams (perhaps innocent of their real mission: "I don't think those guys knew what they were doing down there," says David Price) were checking out suspected sites of the AIM camp, under cover of the search for Jimmy Eagle. But since to acknowledge this after the event was also to acknowledge a miscalculation that caused the death of two of their own men, it seemed easier to the FBI to stick with the cowboy-boot story while "rediscovering" through Held's ghostly witnesses and an incredible telescopic sighting and the fantasies later attributed to Myrtle Poor Bear the presence of a suspect who the agents knew had been there all along.

At Fargo, Agent Skelly had acknowledged that he had been assigned to Peltier's case when that fugitive warrant was issued in Wisconsin; he was on Pine Ridge at least as early as February 25, 1975, when he interviewed the legal team assaulted by Dick Wilson and his goons at Pine Ridge airstrip. Unless the FBI had reason to believe that Peltier was present on Pine Ridge, why was Skelly in South Dakota in the first place? Yet neither Skelly nor SA Gerard Waring could recall any mention of Peltier's name during the numerous agents' meetings in the first days of the ResMurs investigation. This is very odd indeed, since the FOIA documents reveal that on May 30, 1975, an Indian woman identified Peltier from a photograph as one of the outside Indians present on Pine Ridge, and since Officer Stoldt had informed the grand jury in November 1975 that he had seen Peltier a few miles north of the Jumping Bull property "approximately a week" before the shooting.

> A: I stopped a car with about seven Indian people in it, and he was in that car. He had at this time Federal warrants on him, but my orders were not to try to take him alone. I was by myself. I requested a back-up unit. It was refused. He got away from us. . . .[2]

Q: Why did you think they refused the back-up unit?
A: Well, fear. The only one that could respond to me at that time ... gave me the excuse that he couldn't assist me because he didn't have a spare tire.

Somewhat belatedly, Stoldt would claim that he had seen Peltier as well as Eagle in the line of four men running from the back of the Jumping Bull house between 2:00 and 3:00 in the afternoon of the shoot-out; Peltier, whom Stoldt said he recognized first, was the third man in line, with Jimmy Eagle bringing up the rear.

Q: How long was Mr. Peltier in your view?
A: Approximately a minute and a half....
Q: How long was Mr. Eagle in your view?
A: Oh, maybe two minutes....
Q: What did you do when you saw those people running in a southeasterly direction?
A: I immediately brought this to the officers' attention who I was with.... At this time I was with Fred Coward and Ed Skelly and another FBI agent by the name of Vince.

Presumably Skelly was aware of this grand-jury testimony, and surely he knew of the official teletype sent to Washington on June 29, which described sightings of Peltier by Coward as well as by Stoldt. Moreover, Skelly's own lengthy 302 report for June 26 includes the following:

> At approximately 3:45 PM, SA COWARD and Officer STOLDT advised SA SKELLY that they had seen some movement or activity to the rear of the JUMPING BULL community. SA SKELLY then relayed this information via Bureau radio to SA ADAMS. The information consisted of the fact that SA COWARD and Officer STOLDT had observed four Indian males running toward the east bank of the creek. SA COWARD almost immediately stated that one of the individuals appeared to him to be LEONARD PELTIER, who is a known Federal fugitive, wanted by Wisconsin authorities for attempted murder of a police officer. The Federal warrant which was issued was for Unlawful Flight to Avoid Prosecution. SA COWARD furnished this information after having scanned the four individuals through the use of a scope mounted on his .30-06 rifle.

Why, then, did these agents say that Peltier's name did not come up in the early meetings, unless the Bureau wished to camouflage the fact that this AIM fugitive had been "targeted" by a prior assumption of his guilt, long before any good evidence had been obtained? Why was the whole AIM group "targeted," *long before it was caught with the agents' weapons*? From the government point of view, there were at least four excellent reasons: first, they were AIM men, including a well-known AIM fugitive, and AIM itself had been targeted for three years; second, as "armed terrorists," they were likely suspects against whom a strong case might be built; third, there was (apparently) insufficient evidence on which to build a case against any of the local Indians, including Eagle; and fourth, even if such evidence existed, it was important to disguise the fact that a whole community, not just a few "outside agitators," was rejecting the oppression of the U.S. agencies and the Wilson government. Presumably the first (known) witness, Angie Long Visitor, found it easier to mention strange Indians from off the reservation whose last names she didn't even know than to betray men of her own Oglala people, and perhaps it was hoped that other Oglala witnesses would come forward as long as they knew that no Oglala suspects would be prosecuted. Some such promise almost certainly was made, since the FOIA documents show clearly that right from the start, the FBI had a number of serious suspects besides the four who were indicted for the murders.

As will be recalled, David Sky was the first suspect arrested; he was identified by a tracking dog as a member of the escape party, and allegedly told friends in Porcupine, "You should have been there, it was fun." What is now revealed is the opinion of the polygraph examiner that David Sky "has at least a guilty knowledge and was probably present at and participated in the shooting of Agents Coler and Williams." Also, an undisclosed informant who claimed to have been an eyewitness saw "David Sky and an Indian named 'Snag' . . . from Oklahoma open fire on WILLIAMS and thereafter pulled [*sic*] WILLIAMS from his car." Finally, David Sky and Cris Westerman were identified as members of the escape party by Mike Anderson and John Stewart, respectively (the defense does not deny that David Sky was there).

Ted Lame was identified by a Lucy White Dress as one of those involved in the shooting, and fingerprints of Lame, Sam Loud Hawk, and Dave Hill, among others, were recovered from the ResMurs scene (which is not proof they were present on June 26). A female witness told the FBI that Russell Loud Hawk "had gone into the Jumping Bull residence with horses in order to get his sons out of the area. Both Sam and Kenneth Loud Hawk are allegedly the sons of Russell." Another witness saw June Little and Jerry Mousseau "go right into the area carrying a small satchel." Another reported hearing "through the grapevine" that "Melvin Lee Houston, Jimmy Eagle, Dusty Nelson, and Kenny Loud Hawk were involved." Another saw Sam Loud Hawk running from the scene. Yet another, observing the firefight from a distance, thought he had identified Eagle, Nelson, and Sam Loud Hawk (who had been involved with Jimmy Eagle in the shooting episode the month before). This last witness also reported that during a firefight between the Indians and the BIA police, he saw "one of the Indian males fall to the ground from what he assumed was a result of gunfire." One of these men wore an undershirt and the other a "fatigue-type jacket."

In addition to this handy eyewitness account of Joe Stuntz's death in Coler's SWAT jacket, this man relayed rumors about local Indians, including two of the Loud Hawks, who had been involved in the shooting. (Perhaps one reason his account never emerged in the ResMurs trials was that the important psychological advantage of establishing that Joe Stuntz died in Coler's SWAT jacket was outweighed by the incrimination of local Indians, which tended to weaken the government's weak case against the defendants.) He also felt "confident that he saw Richard Little at the scene of the shooting and during the time the shooting was taking place talking to some girl. He heard later that Little had supposedly been seen at a road block later on so maybe he is wrong but he does not believe so. He again said he is confident in his own mind that he saw Richard Little at the shooting."

This opinion about Richard Little's presence at the shooting could not have surprised SAC Richard Held, who had prepared the following brief 302 on June 28, just two days after the shoot-out:

> During the course of an informal meeting with RICHARD and BEAU LITTLE, in the presence of Agency Administrative Officer and Acting Agency Superintendent KENDALL CUMMINGS, a comment was made concerning the shooting of two FBI Agents on June 26, 1975. RICHARD LITTLE then volunteered the comment that he had seen the entire thing from start to finish but that he will not make available at this time the details of his observations.

Both Mike Anderson and Norman Brown told the FBI that Beau Little (David Sky's brother) was present at Oglala; what was not revealed was that Beau Little had been "identified as an individual leaving the crime scene immediately after the shooting of the agents." Richard and Beau Little also appear in later 302s in connection with the proliferating red vehicles, and so does Richard's brother June, who was identified as one of the passengers in the 1974 Ford red pickup with white top driven on and off the property about 1:30 p.m. by Wallace Little, Sr.; the second passenger was not Wanda Siers, as reported by Mike Anderson (Siers and her children had fled the place much earlier), but another man, apparently Jerry Mousseau, who, with June Little, was identified by several witnesses when the pickup passed through the BIA roadblock at the intersection of Routes 18 and 35. (While coming and going, Little, Sr., was commanded to stop by the BIA police, and both times this spirited old man ignored the order. One of the Indian policemen later told the FBI that Mr. Little had made a second expedition into the area about twenty minutes later, emerging this time with a young woman, and that once again he had refused to stop. On June 30, two FBI agents who invaded Wallace Little's land—a team of five others remained outside the fence line—in search of his son June were confronted by his huge nephew Bruce, or "Beau," who waved them off, bellowing that they were trespassing on private property. Then Wallace Little himself "advised that he did not wish to have agents on his land, that he would have to have a purification ceremony because agents had previously been on his land. He advised that his son, WALLACE LITTLE, JR., was not at home.")

Another suspect was James War Bonnet, "armed and extremely dangerous," whose fingerprints were found on an explosives manual allegedly picked up in the AIM camp and whose white Chevrolet was found only fifty feet from the bodies of the dead agents. (Apparently this is the same white car that the FBI wished to associate with Jimmy Eagle through John Stewart, who was willing to testify at Cedar Rapids that Eagle had shown up in Oglala Housing in this car a few minutes after Peltier had left, promising exciting action out at the Jumping Bulls'. Its location would seem to lend support to the Stewart story, but Peltier says that it had been there nearly a week; ordinarily this white car was started by being rolled downhill from the plateau, and when it had failed to start, it had been abandoned.) War Bonnet, a Vietnam veteran, had been arrested on March 1, 1975, and charged with possession of a .223-caliber Heckler and a Colt AR-15 semiautomatic rifle; he "is knowledgeable in the use of explosives and carries a gun with him at all times." A witness who spoke to him after the shoot-out told the FBI that "Jimmy War Bonnet was 'scared to death' and very excited when talking about the killing of the two FBI agents."

And there are others; Price's repeated figure of "at least thirty" does not come out of thin air. A suspect list of twenty-nine names, dated July 23, includes all the male residents of the AIM camp except Brown and Draper, as well as several other "outside" Indians, among them Frank Black Horse, Cris Westerman, and Dave Hill, and also a few such as Steve Robideau who seem to be listed on general principles rather than because of any evidence that they were present in Oglala on that day. All of the local men already cited were also on the list, with the exception of Richard Little and Jerry Mousseau, who later became an Indian policeman; in fact, he was the jailer in Pine Ridge in 1978, when Jimmy Eagle was set free by his .22-toting girl friend, Wilma Blacksmith.

In addition, there were certain people, such as Herman and Homer Thunder Hawk and Jimmy Harjo (all suspected of cooperation with the FBI), who had visited the camp and were acquainted with its members, although apparently not present on that day. Any one of these people, and many others, could have come forward and provided testimony against the outside Indians in return, perhaps, for immunity for local families, and almost certainly one or more did, to judge from details that were provided to Myrtle Poor Bear and other potential prosecution witnesses.

None of the foregoing material is intended to implicate those mentioned—the FBI documents have already done that—but simply to emphasize the agents' knowledge that no one man or even one small group was responsible for what happened at Oglala. On April 21, 1976, five months after the murder indictments were handed down, an FBI memo sent to Director Clarence Kelley specified that "Numerous individuals, some of which have not yet been positively identified, were involved in the deaths of Williams and Coler." Another FBI teletype of June 28, 1976, circulated at the time of the Butler-Robideau trial, acknowledges "a possibility that subjects involved in RESMURS escaped . . . and have, in fact, never been fully identified." It is also true that a number of suspects, all of them Oglalas from Pine Ridge, *were* fully identified, and that not one of them was ever prosecuted. A few weeks after the Cedar Rapids acquittal, Kelley, Hultman, Held, and others, conferring in Washington, D.C., decided to drop the "weak" case against Jimmy Eagle, so that "the full prosecutive weight of the Federal Government could be directed against Leonard Peltier."

Until they obtained the ResMurs files under the Freedom of Information Act, Peltier's attorneys had assumed that the U.S. government dropped its case against Jimmy Eagle because it really had no case at all; that Eagle had been indicted on the basis of false "confessions" reported by prison snitches because he would not cooperate in naming suspects. Eagle, it was said, did not even frequent the Oglala area—hence the derision with which mention of Eagle's girl friend, Wilma, "the provider of the food," was greeted by Peltier's defense counsel at Fargo. In November 1975, Agent Adams was told by Hazel Little Hawk that Jimmy had spent the entire day at the Pine Ridge house of his grandmother Gladys Bissonnette: Adams himself declared at Peltier's trial—the Pumpkinseed sightings notwithstanding—that he himself had seen no evidence of Eagle's presence at Oglala on June 26. Yet on August 11, 1975, as it turns out, Adams was told by an eyewitness that Jimmy Eagle had been on the Jumping Bull property during the shoot-out, and the documents show that the FBI took his alleged participation very seriously. According to a lab report, "five latent fingerprints on an inner carton of a Winchester Super x .30-06 cartridge box containing 20 spent cartridges from Tent City have been identified as finger impressions of Eagle." A local resident named Michael Rooks told Coward and Stoldt that he had seen Jimmy and Leon Eagle down near the lake "before the early part of May" (or about the time some guns were supposedly stolen from Rooks's house); later that spring, he had also seen these brothers "at the Harry Jumping Bull residence." On June 28, Herman Thunder Hawk, surrendering himself in the cowboy-boot case, told the agents not only that Jimmy Eagle had participated at Oglala but that he might have been wounded in the shoot-out. On July 2, the BIA police reported that "Hawk may have been involved with Jimmy Eagle" in the killing of the agents. The same day, two SWAT teams in helicopters descended on Selo Black Crow's place, searching for Eagle; as FBI documents make clear, Eagle was considered "a primary suspect from the outset" and "a known suspect." Small wonder, then, that Richard Held himself presided over this youth's reception at the Rapid City jail on July 9 and took charge of his clothes as "evidence" on July 15, twelve days before his boasting was reported. Even the "false" story must be reappraised in the light of the heretofore unavailable report of a polygraph test administered to his cellmate Gregory Dewey Clifford, which concluded that Clifford "was truthful when he said that he . . . heard Jimmy Eagle brag of his involvement in the shooting of two FBI agents, June 26, 1975." Herman Thunder Hawk told the agents that he, too, had heard his old confederate brag about the killing; there was also yet another listener, whose identity has not been revealed.

Whether or not he participated in the killings, Jimmy Eagle was no stranger to Oglala, and his role in the story seems a lot more complex than is generally acknowledged by either side. Wilma Blacksmith's family is very close to the Jumping Bulls, and Eagle's associates in the community included the Loud Hawks and the Littles and John Star Yellow Wood, or "Dusty Nelson," who was staying at the Little cabin. Of particular interest in this regard is a 302 dated March 11, 1975, describing the questioning of Eagle in regard to a recent assault with a dangerous weapon in Pine Ridge. Except to wonder why this first of four separate assault cases in which this youth was involved in just five months had never been mentioned at the trials, I did not pay much attention to this report until I noticed the site of the interview and the identity of the interviewer. "JAMES EAGLE was contacted at a residence just west of Jumping Bull Hall in Oglala, South Dakota." The one residence that fits this description is the June Little cabin, which suggests why the agents looking for Eagle came to that cabin three months later. As on most of the FOIA documents, the names of the interviewing agents are blotted out, but in this case, one of the two is visible. The name is "SA RONALD A. WILLIAMS." Thus it appears not only that Williams knew how to reach June Little's house when BIA Officers Ecoffey and Little Bird escorted the agents there on June 25—in which case the Indian police (whether they knew it or not) may have been present not as escort but as backup—but also that Williams was familiar with Jimmy Eagle. Therefore, the episode later that afternoon, when Williams and Coler took Anderson, Charles, and Draper into BIA headquarters to see if one of them might be Jimmy Eagle, must be regarded in a different light: either Williams, a longtime veteran on Pine Ridge, had forgotten in three months what Eagle looked like, or he confused him with one of the three boys from the AIM camp—not at all likely, since Eagle is heavy-set, even chubby, whereas all of the other three were small and slight. And if Williams *did* know what Eagle looked like, then in detaining these three on a pretext, he seems to have been checking out those outside AIM Indians down in the woods behind the Jumping Bulls', just as people said.

On June 26, while monitoring the FBI frequency a few minutes before noon, Rapid City headquarters heard Williams "mention the name Jimmy Eagle and something about chasing a red jeep." In the same period, according to a teletype, "SA HUGHES heard over the Bureau radio the voice of SA WILLIAMS and SA WILLIAMS was talking to another unnamed agent that he thought he saw JIMMY EAGLE in a red jeep." (If Williams recognized Eagle on June 26, why had he been unfamiliar with his appearance on June 25?) Subsequently Hughes heard Williams say he was "under fire by unknown individuals from the jeep at that location." At the very least, these reports suggest that Eagle might have been involved in the start of the shoot-out, though not necessarily the finish. A FOIA document of related interest is the 302 for June 26 prepared by SA David Price:

> While SAS HUGHES and PRICE were en route to Rapid City, SA WILLIAMS was heard to say on the Bureau radio words to the effect that "He's supposed to be in a red Scout." Later SA WILLIAMS was heard to say, "That looks like a red Scout over there." Another comment was heard to the effect that "There's a lot of people around." Shortly after this either SA COLER or SA WILLIAMS stated on the Bureau radio, "They're getting in the red Scout." Shortly after this, a voice believed to be SA WILLIAMS stated, "There are three men getting out of the red Scout with rifles. They're shooting at us."

Price's insistence here on the "red Scout" (as well as the emphasis on the number of people around, and the "three men getting out of the red Scout with rifles") is very interesting. Similarly, BIA Officer Robert Ecoffey, in an interview of July 9, presumably refers to the same vehicle when he says, "I went back to where Eastman and Glenn Little Bird was and advised them and Dave Price of what I found. I also found the red International which the agents chased into the Jumping Bulls res. James Eagle was supposed to be in that red International." These sentences had at one point been blotted out. Neither report was made available to the defense at Fargo, perhaps because both emphasized the red International Scout, which no longer suited the prosecution's case.

To judge from the occurrence of these vehicles in report after report, FOIA and otherwise, the FBI attached great significance to the red Scout in which Jimmy Eagle had supposedly been seen and also to that "red pickup" that SA Gary Adams had observed as it left the Jumping Bull property at 12:18, a few minutes after the execution of the agents. (Apparently nobody came forward to identify the red pickup and its occupants—or not, at least, in documents that have surfaced—for the good reason that no one could do so without incriminating other local people or acknowledging his or her own participation.) Reports of red cars go back to the previous March, when BIA officers visited the Pumpkinseed residence, where Judy Pumpkinseed had noticed a red International Scout after hearing shots fired in her direction. The BIA officers also

> noticed a red International Scout parked in the area where the FBI Agents were later shot. (   ) stated that their two BIA police cars chased this red International Scout to the residence of RICHARD LITTLE. (   ) estimated that there were four or five individuals in the truck at this time and they did not shoot at the BIA officers. (   ) stated that their units discontinued the chase when the International Scout pulled into LITTLE's residence.

The only one of these "individuals" identified in the report was Jimmy Eagle.

On April 10, in Rapid City, Leonard Peltier and June Little were seen riding in the back of a red-and-white Ford pickup.

On June 25, BIA Officer Ecoffey, assisting Agents Coler and Williams, noted "a red pick-up with a white stripe parked at the Wallace Little residence." When they subsequently went to that residence, the vehicle was gone, and they were informed that Jimmy Eagle had "just left in the red pick-up."

On June 26, within a half hour of the departure of the red pickup at 12:18 p.m., Richard Little turned up at the FBI-BIA roadblock in "a red Ford Ranchero" (a farm-country model with a sedan cab and short pickup body that might be confused with a red pickup). An hour later, a BIA officer saw Richard Little follow Wallace Little's red-and-white pickup once it had left the Jumping Bull property.

On June 27, a red pickup was "spotted" at Mount Rushmore.

On June 28, local resident Michael Rooks stated that "he has seen June Little driving the red Scout . . . on several occasions."

On June 28, an interview was obtained from a youth named Rayford Featherman, who was married to a Jumping Bull granddaughter and delivered groceries to the old couple every day; he turned over to the FBI seven rifles that (he said) had been removed from the Jumping Bull house after he had returned there with his wife's grandparents that first evening. (This was the "arms cache" mentioned to me by David Price.)

> The story in Oglala about the events of June 26, 1975, are that the men in the red Scout are body guards for DENNIS BANKS. He advised that he knows that there have been several people living near the JUMPING BULL residence and they live south of the residence. This group has been there about one month and includes four men and four women, but recently one of the women left for Cedar Rapids, Iowa. Of those staying near the JUMPING BULLS, he knows only one name and that is "DINO" whom he has seen hauling water for the group in the red Scout vehicle. DINO is described as an Indian male, age 31, 5′8″ tall, slender build, dark complexion, dark shoulder-length hair.

On June 29, an agent reported the discovery of a number of Ron Williams's personal effects ("One pair of rolled blue socks . . . one pair of yellow underwear with blue stripes . . . one pair of red-and-white-striped underwear . . .") "at the base of a hill and approximately 200 yards to the east of a line of cars which included one red Scout jeep." On July 2, an inventory of items found in that vehicle—"an International Harvester Scout, red in color"—included a newsletter addressed to Wallace Little, Jr.

On July 1, in Los Angeles, Director Kelley referred to "the fact that some subjects or possible subjects were leaving the area in a red pickup and this red pickup has become the subject of some concern in this investigation."

On July 3, a Bureau teletype referred again to "the red jeep" in which Jimmy Eagle had reportedly been seen riding.

On July 9, *The Washington Post* cited the importance of the "red pickup" that the agents had chased onto the Jumping Bull property.

On July 9, Bruce "Beau" Little, or Little Sky, being served with a subpoena for a grand-jury hearing on the ResMurs case scheduled for July 14 in Rapid City, was pursued from a "gravesite overlooking the WALLACE LITTLE, SR. ranch . . . down the driveway to the WALLACE LITTLE, SR. residence. At the bottom of the hill, BRUCE LITTLE stopped momentarily to speak to WALLACE LITTLE, SR., driving a red Ford pickup."

On July 12, "WANDA SIERS was located exiting from the RICHARD LITTLE residence driving a red Jeep pickup truck. . . . Upon motioning by Bureau agents, Siers stopped her vehicle in the driveway of WALLACE LITTLE, SR. residence on the east side of Route 18."

On July 12, agents observed "a red jeep pick-up truck" near the Weasel Bear house in Oglala.

All these red Scouts or "jeeps" may well have been the same utility vehicle, in general use in the Little–Jumping Bull community, and found parked in the line of junked cars near the Y-fork after the shootout. However, it would be hard to confuse the short-bodied jeep-like "Scout" with a red pickup truck (though a "red jeep pick-up truck" turned up in two reports). To add to the confusion, the unidentified witness who claimed he saw Richard Little at the scene of the shooting was himself driving "a red-colored pickup"; Wallace Little, Sr., owned a red-and-white Ford pickup (probably the one in which Peltier and June Little rode on April 10 and also the vehicle that entered the Jumping Bull property at about 1:30 p.m. and carried away persons unknown); and the people in the AIM camp used a red-and-white Chevy Suburban van, belonging to Sam Loud Hawk, which had been repaired and put back into service by Leonard Peltier.

In contrast to this abundant evidence concerning the red pickup and red Scout (or "jeep"), scarcely a document makes any mention of the red-and-white van except as the getaway vehicle found in the camp. Yet by the time of Peltier's trial, the van had replaced those other vehicles (and Jimmy Eagle had been retired as well). The prosecuting attorneys went so far as to insist that the red pickup was a "phantom" and the red Scout a "junked" vehicle; it was almost as if the prosecution, not just the defense, had been denied all access to the inconvenient evidence in numerous FBI reports, one of which stated that the Scout "started easily and was found to be operative." The line of junked cars in which the Scout was located was just below the Y-fork where the red-and-white van was now said to have halted, causing the agents to pull up down in the pasture; more interesting still—despite its protected position in the line of cars—this Scout contained "approximately ten bullet holes," while the red-and-white van had none.

The FOIA documents reveal that the evidence against Peltier (and the red-and-white van) in those early weeks was minimal by comparison to the evidence against Eagle (and the red Scout). Unless a valid first-hand witness identified Peltier as the killer but refused to confirm this on the witness stand, the only reasonable explanation of the conduct of the ResMurs investigation was a political decision to give immunity to local Indians and blame the whole mess on "outside AIM agitators," even to the extent of dismissing the "weak" case against Jimmy Eagle, who had a known propensity for violence, who had already been charged in his angry young life with beating, stabbing, shooting, assault, destruction of property, and cruelty to animals, who had been placed at the scene by several witnesses, and who had boasted of participating in the killings, according to not one witness but five.

⊡

An FBI teletype of July 27—the same day that Eagle's boasts had been transcribed—which deals with the ResMurs information on Frank Black Horse, also includes this fascinating paragraph: MICHAEL ANDERSON APPEARED AS SCHEDULED BEFORE FEDERAL GRAND JURY, RAPID CITY, SOUTH DAKOTA. SUBPOENA FOR ANDERSON'S ARREST AS MATERIAL WITNESS WILL NOT BE ISSUED AT THIS TIME. Other suppressed documents reveal that a subpoena was served on Anderson on July 9 through his brother Larry, and that "Mike appeared as scheduled before a federal grand jury." Apparently Mike was released after the hearing, and apparently the agents stayed in touch with him, since it was Mike who told Gary Adams on August 11 that Jimmy Eagle had participated in the shoot-out. As already indicated, the Bureau had a report that Peltier and his men were present at Crow Dog's Paradise at the time of the sun dance, and possibly it depended on Mike Anderson to keep it informed of the group's movements during August.

Bob Robideau was astonished that Mike Anderson "fell" as early as July. "He never got out of our sight long enough!" Robideau exclaimed when I mentioned the FOIA document; he thought that another Oglala suspect named Robert Anderson—a white man whose fingerprints were located on the scene—might possibly have been confused with Mike. But the suspect list of July 23 included all the names of Peltier's group except those of the other two young Navajos: these two names—and these two only—were also omitted from Mike Anderson's statement to the FBI in Wichita two months later.

"They could have convened the grand jury in Pierre, which is only an hour away from Rosebud," Bruce Ellison says. "They could have brought a plane into Mission, had him back on the res in about four hours." Peltier just shakes his head; he speculates that some FBI informer must have approached Mike while the group was at Crow Dog's, and threatened him unless he cooperated. "We're pretty shocked. We just don't know how it could have happened, how he could have got away long enough to do it. We're trying to get hold of that grand-jury transcript, but they're not going to give it to us; if that statement had done them any good, it would have showed up in the trials. Anyway, it sure looks like it happened."

Inevitably, Peltier's defenders must suspect that this frightened boy was the unknown informant who gave whatever credibility it had to the government's case, and that fear of exposure as well as fear of prison accounted for his desperate performance on the stand at Peltier's trial. Yet it is clear that the AIM fugitive from Wisconsin had been singled out for prosecution even before Anderson was subpoenaed for the grand-jury hearings in July.

As the Rapid City FBI office reported to Washington on July 17, one of the primary goals of its investigation was to "develop information to lock Peltier and Black Horse into this case." To this end, apparently, the red Scout would be discounted, and Jimmy Eagle with it, in favor of a vehicle that could be associated with Leonard Peltier. By late September 1975, Rapid City was reporting that Norman Brown had identified the white-over-red 1966 Chevy van as the one chased onto the property by the doomed agents—a claim entirely unsupported by the FBI's own interviews with Brown or by any statement that Brown made, then or later. It is also missing from all interviews and statements made by Mike Anderson prior to the rooftop tale of the "orange and white and red and white" vehicle that the special prosecutor elicited at Fargo. Like the Myrtle Poor Bear affidavits and the Coward sighting, the red-and-white van came into prominence because of the absence of good evidence that could "lock Peltier" into the case.

The documents cited above are by no means the only ones that would justify an appeal for a new trial. Others cast light on the disputed connection between the damaged AR-15 rifle recovered from Robideau's exploded station wagon on the Kansas Turnpike and the .223 shell casing allegedly found in the trunk of Coler's car, which—keeping in mind that no evidence or testimony associated Peltier with that particular AR-15 in the first place and that even FBI expert Evan Hodge acknowledged that at least three AR-15s were involved in the shootout—represented the sum total of the ballistics evidence against him.

To repeat the opinion of Hultman's associate, Lynn Crooks, that casing was "perhaps the most important piece of evidence in this case." The court of appeals referred to it as "critical evidence against Peltier," and said that a "crucial question in this case was whether the .223 casing found in Coler's trunk was fired from the AR-15 found in Wichita." As will be recalled from testimony at the Fargo trial, an FBI Lab report of October 31, 1975, signed by Evan Hodge, stated that this casing could not be linked to that damaged AR-15. Not until months later, after strangely delayed tests, did Hodge arrive at the opposite conclusion; his report appeared on February 10, 1975—just four days after Peltier's capture—in good time for an affidavit prepared for Peltier's extradition hearings in Vancouver.

The extreme suspicion with which Hodge's tests were regarded by the defense turns out to have been well founded. Among the FOIA documents is an earlier Bureau teletype to the Director concerning an FBI Lab report of October 2, 1975, a copy of which was sent to Agent Hodge. ".223 CASINGS NOT IDENTIFIABLE WITH AR-15 RIFLE LOCATED IN VEHICLE WHICH EXPLODED ON KANSAS TURNPIKE SEPTEMBER 10, 1975. LABORATORY REQUESTED TO COMPARE ALL .223 CASINGS WITH AR-15 RIFLE (SERIAL NUMBER OBLITERATED) LOCATED AL RUNNING'S PROPERTY SEPTEMBER 11, 1975 AND SUBMITTED TO LABORATORY SEPTEMBER 15, 1975." Presumably, "all .223 casings," in the urgent ResMurs investigation, meant just that; and obviously the negative tests made with the AR-15 found on the Running property were repeated with the third AR-15, recovered in Oregon on November 14.[3] (Interestingly, a Bureau teletype of November 17, requesting analysis of this weapon, inserts an assumption of Peltier's guilt between two other passages that have been—for national security reasons?—blotted out: "PAST INVESTIGATION HAS INDICATED AN AR-15 AND A RUGER .44 MAGNUM HAVE BEEN USED BY BUREAU FUGITIVE LEONARD PELTIER DURING PERTINENT RESMURS PERIOD AND THAT AR-15 MAY BE ACTUAL WEAPON UTILIZED BY HIM TO KILL COLER AND WILLIAMS." That the Oregon AR-15 did not work out as the murder weapon either did not prevent Peltier's indictment for the killings a week later.)

The urgency of the October 2 teletype, and the urgency of all the FOIA documents relating to the ammunition components and the weapons, make it more difficult than ever to believe that the only .223 casing found in the immediate vicinity of the bodies—which as we have seen was missing from the original list of ammunition components found at the scene, and missing from the original charter-jet shipment of "important evidence" components sent to Washington in early July—was *also* missing from the "all .223 casings" submitted for testing; that not until "about the end of 1975, beginning of 1976" did Hodge finally get around to his second test with the Kansas rifle. The firing-pin test that would have been definitive, Hodge said at Fargo, was simply not possible on the damaged gun recovered on the Kansas Turnpike, but by removing the bolt from this half-melted rifle and test-firing it in another AR-15, he was able to make an extractor test that "positively identified" the casing from Coler's car trunk as having been loaded into and extracted (but not necessarily fired) from the Kansas weapon. Until this theoretical connection had been made, of course, there was no point in proceeding to the even more theoretical connection between that particular AR-15 and Leonard Peltier.

In order to make these connections, however, Hodge's final formal report in February 1976 had to ignore another document of October 2, 1975, in the form of a cable from the FBI Director to the Rapid City office which preceded the "all .223 casings" teletype quoted before. Among other things, this cable transmitted a lab finding that the Kansas Turnpike AR-15 "contains a different firing-pin than that in the rifle used at the ResMurs scene"—that is, in the rifle that fired that critical .223 bullet. This fact (which could not have been determined without the definitive firing-pin test on the damaged gun that Hodge had told the Fargo jury was not possible) blows away the last shred of credibility attached to that "most important piece of evidence," which had such a peculiar history in the first place. In effect, the ballistics evidence against Leonard Peltier is worthless. As Peltier says, "They just manufactured a murder weapon—it's as simple as that."

The FOIA documents also reveal considerable discrepancies in the findings of the pathologists Bloemendaal and Noguchi, among which Bloemendaal's opinion—which Noguchi was called in to contest—that the bullet that killed Williams was probably *not* from a high-velocity weapon is the most significant, since it suggests two different weapons and two different killers. Finally, there is additional evidence, if any were needed, of the dishonest origins of the 302s and affidavits furnished by a good half-dozen special agents of the Federal Bureau of Investigation, whose purpose it was not to investigate but to "lock Peltier . . . into this case."

In a pre-trial hearing on February 14, 1977, special prosecutor Evan Hultman assured Judge Paul Benson (and the defense) that "there has been literally total disclosure in this case." Hultman told the court, "I am saying very straightforward and honestly, your Honor, that there is very little if anything to my knowledge . . . by way of evidence [that has not been made available to the defense]. In fact, all the documents, literally all the 302s literally are within their possession right now." Did Hultman believe this? If so, it appears that many documents were withheld from the prosecution.

In the light of the FOIA documents, Mr. Hultman's statement to a reporter in 1981 that "If I knew the FBI was doing that stuff [faking evidence] I'd go after those sons of bitches just as hard as I went after Peltier" is as perplexing as his conclusion that the case against Jimmy Eagle was a weak one. It is in this interview that he says, "There's no doubt in my mind that Peltier shot the agents. He was the enforcer on the Reservation—everyone knew that." Hultman's "everyone" brings this argument full circle to Held's statement about all those witnesses—who were they? If even one genuine witness had been willing to testify, would Myrtle Poor Bear have turned up in this case at all? Or Bragg? Or Harper? (Was the hidden witness poor Mike Anderson, who contradicted himself left and right, who was humiliated before his comrades, his elder brother, and his people, and who died under obscure circumstances within the year?) Considering the ambiguous—and at times farcical—nature of much of the testimony he had to deal with in two ResMurs trials and an appeals court hearing, Hultman's conviction that "Peltier shot the agents" can only reflect a stubborn and uncritical acceptance of the FBI's prior assumption of Peltier's guilt, and also a tolerance of the Bureau's attitude that this AIM Indian's conviction would justify even such means as coercion and perjury and ruined lives.[4]

Predictably, the U.S. Justice Department sees no significance in these

FOIA documents. "There is simply no new evidence," declares Lynn Crooks, denouncing Peltier's appeal for a new trial as "ridiculous."[5]

At least by comparison with his associates, Sikma and Crooks, Evan "Curly" Hultman won a certain respect from his opponents, who granted him a mild interest in truth and justice. As special prosecutor in both ResMurs trials, he was better qualified than anyone else to answer certain disturbing questions, and my hope was that since he was no longer a U.S. Attorney, he might be persuaded to check my material for accuracy as well as bias and offer some general conclusions on the case. In a friendly telephone conversation, Mr. Hultman agreed to an interview, suggesting, however, that I send my questions in a letter before coming to see him in Waterloo, Iowa. I asked Mr. Hultman some tough but not antagonistic questions, concluding my letter as follows:

> I'm persuaded by our talk on the telephone that you will understand what I am getting at here—the erosion of ethics and even morality in agencies and institutions that all Americans would like to hold in highest respect and esteem. . . . What I really need is your honest opinion and insight, as a uniquely qualified observer of one of the most complex and interesting trials of our time. Needless to say, if you feel you cannot answer some of these questions candidly, that is understandable; but if *all* of them go unanswered, then they are going to be left hanging in the book, and I cannot believe that the U.S. Justice Dept. or its agencies will emerge the better for it, although I intend to be fair as possible. In the *People* article, you declared that if you thought "those sons of bitches" (interesting choice of epithet, I thought, for working colleagues whom, on the record, at least, you seemed to endorse) had been fabricating evidence, you would go after them just as hard as you went after Peltier; yet you *know* they fabricated evidence, isn't that true? Without meaning to play the Devil's advocate here, I suggest to you respectfully, not impertinently, that your duty as a leading citizen of your state, a former U.S. Attorney, a brigadier general in the U.S. Army Reserves, etc. etc. and most of all to yourself, requires you to be candid about the background of this case, and its implications for the good health of American justice. Whether Leonard Peltier is guilty or not cannot be determined fairly by a jury if the FBI and the U.S. Attorney's office and perhaps even the federal judges are in agreement that the end—the desired convic-

> tion—justifies unfair means. And whether Leonard Peltier is guilty or not, that seems to me an unavoidable conclusion, not only from the evidence of the Fargo trial but from the FOIA documents that have come to light since.

Mr. Hultman decided that my questions were asking him "to re-try and defend the government's case in a news or literary forum," which, as he pointed out, he had no obligation to do: he declined to answer them. "In my professional and personal opinion," his letter concluded, "I truly believe that Leonard Peltier had a fair trial and is guilty of the charge."

CHAPTER 18
IN MARION PENITENTIARY

I have tried to make it clear that there was no "Indian outbreak" in 1890–91, and that such trouble as we had may justly be charged to dishonest politicians, who through unfit appointees first robbed the Indians, then bullied them, and finally in a panic called for troops to suppress them. From my first days at Pine Ridge, certain Indians and white people had taken every occasion to whisper into my reluctant ears the tale of wrongs, real or fancied, committed by responsible officials. . . . To me these stories were unbelievable from the point of view of common decency. I held that a great government such as ours would never condone or permit such practices while . . . standing in the relation of guardian to a race made helpless by lack of education and of legal safeguards. At that time, I had not dreamed what American politics really is. . . . It appears that they are anxious to pass on their religion, but keep very little of it for themselves.

Ohiyesa (*Lakota*)

The old Lakota was wise. He knew that man's heart, away from nature, becomes hard; he knew that lack of respect for growing, living things soon led to lack of respect for humans too.

Luther Standing Bear (*Lakota*)

In February 1980, after the Los Angeles trial, Leonard Peltier was returned to Marion, where he was placed immediately in solitary (the Isolation Unit). After two weeks, he was transferred to the general prison population, due to a letter-writing campaign by his supporters that apparently persuaded the authorities not to invite an overdue investigation; since then, he has been threatened repeatedly with the Control Unit, and his friends believe that his life is still in danger. In the opinion of Peltier's old Milwaukee associate, Herb Powless, who served a three-year term in the federal penitentiary at Terre Haute, Indiana, for his AIM activities, "The U.S. government and its law-enforcement agencies would like to see Peltier dead; not because he is guilty of anything but because he is a symbol of the free spirit of our Indian people, a spirit that has been passed on from generation to generation, from grandmother to grandmother, to the yet unborn. This spirit the white man is blind to because it is inbred; it is the spirit of the soul, it is the spirit of caring and sharing and of being willing to give up your life if necessary."

Whatever the degree of his guilt or innocence, Leonard Peltier had this "Crazy Horse spirit" and seemed to inspire it in other people, even a tough, sly convict such as Robert Hugh Wilson (Standing Deer). At first I had doubted that a long-term inmate with a painful back condition, so vulnerable to retribution, would expose his keepers as he had tried to do at the trial in Los Angeles; the very act of confiding the plot to Peltier, after all, could have been part of the plot itself, intended to scare this man into an escape attempt that would cost his life. On the other hand, one must ask why—if Standing Deer was lying—a dangerous "cop-killer" with a maximum-security classification was suddenly transferred to a minimum-security "correctional institution" such as Lompoc.[1]

Standing Deer's actions and statements, like the hard-nosed reckless candor of this letter, speak for themselves:

"I've wondered myself what there is about Leonard that made me unable to participate in his murder. I had seldom deliberately acted against my own interests up to that point in my life. I have killed men before and there is nothing in my personal code that prohibits killing. I would say there are two reasons that Leonard survived: 1) I have spent most of my life trying to be accepted by my own people, and 2) I have always hated policemen since I was old enough to think, and the idea of cooperating with them was repugnant to me.

"I started life as an American Indian. I spoke Choctaw and Oneida before I spoke united states. My grandmother on my father's side spoke only Choctaw. She held me when I was an infant and sang songs in Choctaw and talked to me in Choctaw. I spoke to my mother's mother in Oneida. This felt good and I was happy with Indians. My mother's people were in Wisconsin and my father's people were in southeastern Oklahoma. I don't know when my mother started teaching me united states but I was reading it when I was 3½. I read Lincoln's Gettysburg Address over an Oklahoma City radio station at this age.

"My mother wanted to make a freak out of me. She forbade my brother and sister and me from speaking our native language. She would not let us discuss our grandparents or the clan. She always spoke of them with scorn. She wanted us to hate everything Indian and to think of ourselves as white people. I was beaten by my father to get all the Indian out of me. I don't know how they did this, Peter, but when I was about six years old we were driving in the country near Shawnee, Oklahoma. I was in the car with my father, mother, brother and sister. I looked out the window and saw two Indian boys running and I hollered in surprise, Look, there go some Indians! I really didn't know our skins were as dark or darker than the boys running beside the car.

"We lived in a white neighborhood and went to a white school. My mother and sister were both color-struck. I was lighter-skinned than my brother, therefore I was better. My father was an auditor for the united states Indian Service. USIS was the agency before the BIA. My father graduated from Haskell Institute at Lawrence, Kansas. Somehow all his friends were white. I was taught to fight anyone who called me an Indian. I was taught to beat them until they agreed to call me an 'American.' I beat people until I was about 15 years old and by then my brother and me were so well known in northwestern Oklahoma City that everybody knew we were 'Americans.'

"I caught on when I was about six—shortly after the incident of seeing the Indian boys—that it was all sick and that for some reason I was being required to hate a part of myself that I remembered was good (memory of my grandparents) so I kept up the charade because I was too desperate to be accepted and approved by my mother to go against it, but I knew it was something I had to get away from.

"I escaped for the first time when I was 12 years old. I went to southeastern Oklahoma where my father's people were. It was a great feeling but I was recaptured after two weeks and returned to Oklahoma City. I escaped again when I was 15 years old and went to Wisconsin with my mother's people. The consensus in both Oklahoma and Wisconsin was that my parents were crazy. I couldn't have agreed more heartily with that determination. From 15 to 17 I ran away from home several times always going where there were some Indians. I was never accepted around Indians who weren't relatives because I did not know how to act. I no longer remembered the language or customs. I was an outsider. I married a white girl in 1951 and lived in Oklahoma City where I had several arrests for possession of stolen property and minor offenses.

"In 1963, I received my first prison sentence. I was sentenced to ten years in Leavenworth for Interstate Transportation of Counterfeit Securities. I served from 3/28/63 to 2/11/70 in Leavenworth. On 11/30/71 I was charged with Armed Robbery and Larceny of an Auto in Oklahoma City. I was sentenced to 25 years in the state penitentiary. On July 27, 1973 I was involved in a 21 million $ riot during which the state prison was burned to the ground. I was on deadlock solitary confinement for a year during which time my 5′ x 8′ cell door was never opened. On April 29, 1975 I took over a bus when the guards were attempting to transport me and I was on escape until April 6, 1976. I was recaptured in Chicago. It was on June 3, 1975 that a police officer in Okla City was shot following a robbery and I was accused of the shooting. This resulted in seven indictments being filed against me, each carrying a possible life sentence. These were the charges that Capt Carey and the stranger had dismissed in the Peltier case. I was tried and convicted of a $40,000.00 bank robbery in Indianapolis and sentenced to 15 years. I was tried for interstate transportation of stolen jewelry in Chicago and sentenced to 10 years concurrent. I was tried and convicted for a $279,000.00 jewel robbery in Houston and given three concurrent life sentences. I am indicted on a $51,000.00 bank robbery in St. Louis which is pending along with several other bank robberies. The FBI has written on court documents 'considered by the FBI to be the most dangerous individual ever apprehended in Chicago.'

"So when I was approached by Carey and the other man I had just returned from trial in Houston where I got three life sentences. I have never cooperated with the police in my life, but because of the physical suffering I was going through I talked with them. After thinking it over I thought I had a chance to actually get free. When they offered to parole me to Oklahoma, that is the same as setting me free. I can escape from Oklahoma. I hated myself for going along with them because of my hatred for police. But I didn't know Leonard Peltier from a sack of apples and if that would get me to Oklahoma I was willing to kill him.

"When I got on the yard with Leonard on the 4th of July, 1978, I had intended to start trying to get close to him. It had occurred to me to tell him, but I had never seriously considered doing it. Leonard was hypnotic in his talking that day. I saw in him everything I could never be. He was loved by his people and he was dedicated to them. I saw my life as a lie and I knew that I was being offered a chance to redeem myself with my people by giving them the gift of this man's life. I knew I would die if I betrayed the united states but I knew I wouldn't want to live if I didn't. So I told him. That decision has caused me a lot of misery but I can't say I regret having made it.

"My grandfather named me Standing Deer when I was very small. I took my name Standing Deer back when I came back to my people."

Standing Deer's courage in risking the anger of the authorities can scarcely be overestimated, and the same loyalty to Peltier was displayed by Bobby Garcia, who apparently sacrificed his own chance to escape. In drawing attention to himself that night at Lompoc, Garcia must have known that he might be returned to the Control Unit at Marion, which he had told Peltier he would not survive. Peltier describes Garcia as "a no-bullshit person, but not hard; he is as gentle as he is potentially violent." In prison, Garcia became a painter and a poet, and his poetry is full of yearning for that sunlight that made him so happy when he got to Lompoc.

Morning Song

Oh! Heart. You are my eyes for
    I can not see through steel
and concrete walls.

Oh! Sun who caresses and warms
    me in my dreams. Shine on
    her your Sunshine for I give her
        My heart with all my sorrow

The breeze is walking in the valley
    and caressing all the flowers

> This is the first morning song in the
> world and I am listening to you
> from deep in my heart . . .
>
> Oh Sun, caress me![2]

This poem was written on February 11, 1980, after Garcia's return to the Control Unit. A few weeks later, he and Standing Deer were transferred to the federal penitentiary in Terre Haute, where for some reason they were placed in the same cell.

> Bobby and me were cellies from March 12 to April 17, 1980. I have no idea why they put him in my cell when there were six other units and over 600 other cells available. My guess is they hoped we might kill each other. Any two men living in a cage nine feet long and six feet wide might be tempted to, but if there was a distrust it could be magnified under those conditions to paranoia. Unfortunately for the correctional criminals, there was no distrust between us and instead of eliminating any of their problems (if that *was* their purpose) we created more by demanding our religion and organizing a strong Indian group. On April 17, they kidnapped Bobby and took him to Marion. They returned him to Terre Haute on May 29th but they put him in a unit clear across the penitentiary from my unit. They refused to let us live in the same unit—much less the same cell—from that time on.

On August 1, in the course of a transfer to another prison, Standing Deer says, he was attacked by a deputy sheriff and a prison trusty, and had to wrest a knife from his jailer's hand. Back in Terre Haute, "Standing Deer walks the prison yard with Bobby," as Standing Deer wrote in one of his more oratorical public letters, "and together they await what fate the united states has in store for them. Death at the hands of the government will be the inevitable reward for exposing the government conspiracy to assassinate Leonard Peltier."

Standing Deer was not the only one who felt endangered. Defense witnesses Don Richardson and David Owens, in transit from Los Angeles, were repeatedly beaten by their guards in the Hole at Leavenworth, and Richardson was brutally beaten again in the Marion Control Unit on April 28, 1980, when ten guards who had put down a food-tray-throwing protest selected five of the offenders for special attention, taking them one by one into another room for truncheoning. Afterward, these five sought the aid of lawyers of the church-supported Marion Prisoners' Rights Project, in Carbondale, which filed a class-action suit against the Marion authorities on their behalf. "The guards have said we attacked them," said one of the plaintiffs, who claimed he was left in his cell for three days before being hospitalized for cuts and bruises on his back, head, and legs. "But look, no man in his right mind would dare attack a goon squad in Marion when his hands are handcuffed behind his back. No man would be crazy enough, I don't care if he's a lobotomy case. You're standing up against somebody who's a tank; he's armed and he's ready to hurt you." This agitated convict, whose name was Jack H. Abbott, said repeatedly that he wanted to take a lie detector test to prove the truth of what he was saying; he also said, "Yes, I hate them. I don't have no love for these people who do this . . . to me. I'm in prison, I understand where I'm at. I'm not going to go out there and take off on a guard, especially a dozen armed guards."[3]

"We work with some difficult people here, and we expect that from time to time they will make these allegations against us," explained Richard G. Phillips, the warden's executive assistant, and the man with whom I had to deal for permission to visit Peltier; this permission could be denied while the inmate was in solitary, and Phillips appeared to be doing his best to keep Peltier out of reach. Ever since his return from Los Angeles, in February 1980, Leonard had been one of the few among more than four hundred inmates in Marion Penitentiary who were denied "contact" visits in the regular visitors' room, even when he was not in solitary in the Hole.

> 3/6/80 I went before the Committee, and they said the sentence I received in L.A. was only a recommendation, and another hearing will be pending in about six months: in the meantime I stay in the Hole, or as the Committee likes to call it, "Administrative Detention" (smile). . . .
>
> I have someone here who wants me to be her old man. She shaved her legs today and said feel them. I said Get the hell out of here (smile) What a world. . . . Tell everyone to write! And I love them! And I miss them!
>
> 3/20/80 No matter what punishment they dish out to me I'll always keep my sense of humor and keep laughing. I made myself a promise a long time ago. They will never take that.

3/26/80 Mail tonight . . . some literature asking for funds to support John Anderson for President. Ha! Ha! Ha! (Christ. Forgive me. Forgot myself there.) . . .

4/14/80 [in regard to a family member who wished to be appointed "national coordinator" of the Leonard Peltier Defense Committee] No one! And I mean *no one* is appointed to anything. They earn their leadership. They must think I'm weak or stupid. Razor knows how I am dedicated to the struggle and not even my own mother will get in the way from keeping me working until liberation is won. I have not come this far to let my family disrupt our work now. . . .

4/22/80 I received my Control Unit Hearing papers yesterday . . . still an indefinite sentence. I imagine Bobby has received his also. . . . Conditions are getting worse instead of better down in the Control Unit. . . . Beatings are becoming a regular thing in there and here in the Hole. . . .

8/11/80 As you know, my Dad . . . brought my daughter Lisa, and Hey, I'm not saying this with any bias because she's mine, but is she ever beautiful. She's got my dad, her grandpa, wrapped around her little finger and also me. . . . I spoke a couple of days ago with some Mexican bros that came from t.h. [Terre Haute] and said Bobby was doing good; Standing Deer was just through the other day, going to Leavenworth for a trial. . . .[4]

In this same period, assisted by the Carbondale attorneys, Peltier and other members of the inmate Advisory Council formed a "Law Project" to advise prisoners of their legal rights in prison. On September 7, his name appeared at the head of a list of over three hundred convicts who were petitioning (under the American Indian Freedom of Religion Act of 1978) to hold sweat-lodge ceremonies and a sun dance, and when, on September 15, a prisoners' strike occurred in the prison industries because of beatings by guards and other offenses, the Law Project was blamed by R. G. Phillips for this "work stoppage." Eventually Peltier was convicted of inciting a riot (which never occurred) and running an illicit business (the Law Project); on these administrative convictions, he was returned to solitary for another thirty days.

By keeping Peltier shut up in the Hole, Phillips was able to obstruct or prevent visits by people such as myself who might be sympathetic to his cause. We were corresponding, however, and on November 25—the same day that Nilak Butler and Archie Fire Lame Deer presented his case before the Fourth Bertrand Russell Tribunal in Rotterdam (which accepted the case and will present it before the World Court in 1983)—Leonard wrote an excited letter about some of the FOIA material being turned up by his Washington, D.C., attorneys. "In an ordinary criminal case this would be an automatic reversal and a new trial would be ordered. Unfortunately for myself . . . this is a political case . . . and I am willing to bet my life the Government will not order a new trial or even consider the legal issue." Clearly, he was trying hard not to get his hopes up. "I fully realize and understand that none of this is a guarantee it will get me released from prison, which I cannot truthfully say is not my main concern."

⊡

On December 1, Bobby Garcia was removed from the general prison population in Terre Haute. "Nobody has been able to learn why he was locked up, but I fear for his safety," Standing Deer wrote to a Law Project attorney named James Roberts two days later. "I tried calling you but they said all the lawyers were tied up in St. Louis, so I tried to call Bruce Ellison, Lewis Gurwitz, Dennis Banks, Russell Means, and Archie Fire Lame Deer but I couldn't find anybody. . . . I would appreciate it very much if you would attempt to contact warden Ray J. Lippman here at Terre Haute and see if they have decided to kill Bobby."

Another inmate, named Fidel Ramos, who lived and worked in Garcia's cell unit and spoke to him at some length every day, was also concerned about Garcia's sudden removal from the unit, for which there seemed to be no reason:

> At this time Bobby Garcia was doing legal work and research on his case pertaining his transfer from the New Mexico State Penitentiary to the Control Unit located in the Federal Facility at Marion. . . . Also during this time Bobby was preparing a painting. He was very involved in this painting and did not show any emotional instability.
>
> On the morning of December 1, 1980 after Bobby Garcia had completed his work assignment, Mr. Robert Perdue (Unit Manager U4M) called Bobby and was having a discussion with him. During

> this conversation there were no indications that the discussion being held was hostile. . . . At this time Bobby was placed in segregation.

On December 13, Bobby Garcia was found dead in his cell in Terre Haute's N-2 Unit, located in, but not a part of, the prison hospital. ("N-2 is completely isolated from the rest of general population and only the extremely sick-minded guards are selected for duty in this death chamber. . . . It was the habit of the guards to ask the question, 'Are you still alive?' each time they counted at night."[5]) Prison authorities said that they did not know how long he had been dead, but according to an inmate in the unit at that time, the guards could readily have heard the death throes of Garcia, since their office was just across the corridor. Herb Powless, who spent time in that cellblock during his stay in Terre Haute, says that it had twenty-four-hour TV scanning, no sheets, and an hourly cell count; nevertheless, the official report claimed that Garcia had died of self-inflicted "fractures of the neck and secondary strangulation," caused by hanging himself from the neck on a twisted sheet from the low bars of his cell window.[6]

Apparently to silence any rumors, all other prisoners were removed from N-2 Unit after the death and scattered out to other prisons; these transfers occurred after Standing Deer had organized a black-armband demonstration in the prison yard.

> There was an evil tension in the mess hall and there were more guards than was usual. All the prisoners were talking about Bobby and wanted to know what we should do. When I got back to my unit I got together with my friends and suggested that we wear black armbands until Bobby was returned to Mother Earth. . . . Eight of us began cutting up black tee shirts and other black materials for armbands. We put the word out to the entire prison and at breakfast on December 14th there were many people with black armbands. By the evening meal there were men of all races honoring Bobby.
>
> On Monday, December 15th, two guards came to my quarters and told me the Chief Correctional Supervisor wanted to see me. When I got to the CCS office there were two men present. One man said his name was Martin K. Riggen and the other was named

Inman. They said they were FBI agents and both flashed their buzzers. I told them I did not want to be interviewed but Riggen told me they were "investigating the possible murder of Bobby Gene Garcia." I believed them (I told you I was in shock, or something). They asked me what I knew about it and so I told them . . . about the threat Lippman made on Bobby's life in November. I told them about Bobby's trouble on December 1 with Unit Mgr. Perdue. When I slowed down Riggen said: "There is absolutely no connection between this suicide and the Peltier case. You are hysterical. What you need is a good old-fashioned lobotomy."

I left the CCS office and returned to my cell after talking shitty to them.

On the night of the 15th the Indian brothers had a drum and prayer ceremony for Bobby's spirit. The drum could be heard over much of the prison.

About 8:00 a.m. (12.16.80) four guards came to my cell and told me that I was wanted in the hospital on a small matter. They escorted me to the hospital and down the elevator to the basement where Lt. Mustain and other guards were waiting with handcuffs, belly chains and leg irons. I was chained and put in a vehicle and driven straight to Springfield.

The psychologist admitted that I was sent to Springfield simply to get me out of Terre Haute following Bobby's death. He was the only staff member that even acknowledged there was a person named Bobby Gene Garcia. Michael McGrath, the white man who was in N-2 was transferred to Marion and the 12 Cubans who were on N-2 were also transferred out of Terre Haute.

Standing Deer had no doubt at all that Bobby Garcia had been murdered, and he didn't mind saying so in a letter that he knew would be scrutinized by prison authorities.

Ray Lippman, the warden of Terre Haute, lied about the reason Bobby was locked up on Dec. 1, 1980. He lied about why Bobby was transferred to N-2 on Dec. 12, 1980. He lied about the reasons the 13 prisoners in N-2 were in N-2. He lied about why the 13 prisoners were transferred following Bobby's murder. He lied about why I was kidnapped and brought to Springfield on Dec. 16, 1980. Ray Lippman was the associate warden in charge of custody at

> Leavenworth in Jan. of 1979. David Owens' affidavit showed that Lippman had knowledge of the conspiracy to assassinate Leonard. . . . Please acknowledge receipt of this.
>
> In the spirit of Crazy Horse,
> *Standing Deer*[7]

Because of the implied threat by the FBI men, Standing Deer feared that he might be subjected to a lobotomy in the medical facility at Springfield, Missouri ("for major surgery and nut cases," Bob Robideau says), but he was soon transferred to the Lewisburg (Pennsylvania) Penitentiary with his brain intact, to judge from his energetic letters. "He's an old con, and he's careful, he knows how to take care of himself. But so did Bobby," says attorney Roberts, whose investigations have convinced him that Garcia did not take his own life. Apart from the near-impossibility of persisting in self-suffocation when the hands are not tied and the feet can touch the floor, the autopsy revealed eight different drugs in Garcia's system, mostly barbiturates, two of which were "contra-indicated"—that is, not to be prescribed at the same time. All this suggested that Garcia had been drugged into a stupor and then hanged, and his friends demanded a coroner's inquest to lay the foundation for a charge of murder.

On December 18, Bobby Gene Garcia was "returned to Mother Earth" in Colorado, in traditional ceremonies conducted by Leonard Crow Dog; the funeral had been arranged by Leonard Peltier. When he got the news, five days before, Peltier was sitting in the dining hall with Alan Iron Moccasin, who was also a good friend of Garcia. "Naturally our first response was of disbelief that he would take his own life: no one will ever make me believe otherwise than that [the officials] had some involvement, either directly or indirectly. When I returned to my cell, I layed on my bunk and said to myself, The dirty bastards murdered him." Peltier made a public statement that was circulated by his Defense Committee: "In case something happens to me, I want you to know that I have no intentions of committing suicide. Never! Nor do I need any drugs for any illnesses. If something happens to me, it will not be by my own hands."

And Standing Deer wrote in an open letter: "I know Bobby didn't commit suicide and they know I know. . . . I am refusing all food and drugs I can't identify. The doctor removed me from the medication I can identify and I am afraid of being poisoned or incapacitated to the point I won't be able to defend my life. . . . The door to my cell is steel and it completely sound-proofs the cell. If they intend to kill me, this is the best place."

On December 12—the same day (and the same hour) that Bobby Garcia was transferred to the N-2 Unit at Terre Haute—Marion executive assistant R. G. Phillips presided over a long interrogation by U.S. Attorney Michael Hursey of a prison informer who was volunteering certain incriminating information on the Law Project attorneys. These Communist-oriented agitators, this man said, had smuggled marijuana to Leonard Peltier and other prisoners while fomenting the "work stoppage" that has since become the longest work strike in federal prison history.

> A: . . . drugs were getting into I-unit [solitary] and I seen Peltier when he would come back from a visit . . . he would have some. . . . He used to always turn me on. He used to always give me some. . . . All he has to do is say strike and they're down. They compare him with Crazy Horse. I mean legitimately he's a hero through a world of people.
>
> Q: What is the relationship between Leonard Peltier and the Marion Prisoners Rights Project staff?
>
> A: . . . these lawyers, through . . . some of the main Communist attorneys, and, you know, the wealthier radicals in this country, Marlon Brando, people like that, you know, they endorse him as far as they can go. . . .
>
> Q: There are three inmates I want you to focus on, Leonard Peltier and two others. . . . Do you have reason to believe that they are what is termed contacts for the Marion Prisoners Rights Project?
>
> A: No, not Peltier, not Peltier, but . . . if something was already going and the Indians come to him and say what are we going to do about this, then he would just say yes or no one way or the other.
>
> Q: Have you been promised anything by the government, or specifically the Bureau of Prisons, in exchange for your cooperation here today?
>
> A: No, but I expect protection. I didn't up until recently. As a matter of fact, I'm very concerned about that because they've got me in a spot where I can't even get a weapon. If I get a weapon to defend myself, and they know I'm going to be

armed. If they put me around some more prisoners, the guards are just going to know I'm going to be armed and I can't wait on the defensive because when it comes, it comes, and there's only one shot, and if somebody brings it to me to kill me, I got to bring it to them. I can't be put in that position. That was the original reason why I got out of H-Unit [the "Boxcars" in the Control Unit]. . . .

Q: Has the presence of Richard Phillips, Chief of Classification and Parole, U.S.P. Marion, during the course of this testimony of yours influenced your testimony in any way?

A: No, it hasn't; no.

MR. HURSEY: May the record reflect it is now 1:55 P.M., December 12, 1980.

On the basis of this document, which came to 116 pages, the Law Project was barred from the penitentiary ten days later, but in mid-January, during appellate-court hearings in Chicago, the document was unsealed, at which time the informer was removed from Marion for his own safety. At these hearings, one lawyer[8] charged that the Marion authorities had put most of his words in "the mouth of a pathetic and demented twenty-year victim of their own vicious and backward penology," and whether or not the judges agreed, they restored the Project's visitation rights in Marion.

Meanwhile, two guards had declared (in the Philadelphia *Inquirer* and the St. Louis *Globe-Democrat*) that beatings did indeed take place at Marion, just as the striking prisoners had claimed ("A lot of lieutenants and guards think the way to handle a tough situation is with a beating," said James Laswell. And Vernon Henry said, "I'd rather leave most inmates alone with my wife than I would the people who run this place.") This unwelcome publicity, followed quickly by the court order for restoration of visitation rights to Law Project attorneys, may have encouraged the authorities in a more lenient attitude toward Peltier, since permission for my own visit was now granted.

Media interest in the case was growing fast, due to increasing attention from Washington, D.C. Most of the senators who had spoken up for Indians in recent years—Abourezk, McGovern, Bayh, Church—had been "targeted" and crushed by the dead weight of "the Moral Majority" that had swept President Reagan into power, but a number of young congressmen were trying to help. After Garcia's death, Congressman Ron Dellums had issued a public letter to prison authorities, warning that Peltier and Wilson must be protected; the House Judiciary Committee under Don Edwards was considering hearings on FBI behavior on the reservations, and Congressmen Toby Moffett and Wyche Fowler had endorsed a petition by Peltier supporters for presidential commutation of his sentence. ABC-TV and *People* magazine were seeking interviews, and so was actor Robert Redford, whose interest in the story was intensified by the environmental issues in the background of the case.

In his trial at Fargo, Peltier's attorneys had not had access to the FOIA documents. Even so, Peltier feels they were giving him "poor representation . . . [but] I knew I was in trouble and maybe there was still some hope of them beating the case, so I kept my mouth shut. . . . My life was at stake, and that is just what it cost me, my life—because as every prisoner believes, the day I entered prison, I died." When his sentence was appealed before the Eighth District Circuit Court in 1978, his primary counsel was William Kunstler; subsequently, Michael Tigar and John Priviterra, in Washington, D.C., prepared the appeal that the Supreme Court refused to hear the following year, and also secured the FOIA documents that would be the basis of his appeal for a new trial. The appeal would be presented by Bruce Ellison, in association with Kunstler and Lewis Gurwitz.

A young soft-spoken lawyer of Jewish background who has moved permanently to the Black Hills from the East, Ellison wears his hair in a long Indian braid as a token of his fierce endorsement of the cause of the traditional Lakota people. For a long time after his arrival in South Dakota, a few days after the shoot-out at Oglala, he received overt threats on his life, and when I first knew him, I was wary of a certain weakness for conspiracies and unwarranted conclusions; since then, I had learned that the violent circumstances on Pine Ridge would have been very difficult to exaggerate, and that Ellison had usually been right.

⊡

On February 21, 1981, I accompanied Ellison across the brown-and-yellow riverlands of southern Illinois, heading west from the old coal-mining community of Carbondale through tired farm country and blackish lumpy wastes of reclaimed mining land where only poverty grass has been able to take hold. Entering a "Government Reservation," the country road became a sweeping drive, and a small stone plaque, discreet as any headstone, identified these well-mowed premises as "U.S. Penitentiary—Marion." The institution itself was hidden from the public by the winter woods, and its bristling glint and strange hard lines, when finally it came in view, made it look like a crashed space lab, now abandoned. Under a flat sun and a watery blue sky, a silver light glanced off the concrete ramparts, as if the whole twenty-six-acre complex were made of steel; over windowless walls, a water tower loomed like a blue mushroom cloud on its long steel-blue stem, and guard towers like pylons jutted at random, dominating unseen yards full of captive men.

While still a considerable distance off, the car was challenged by a big slow voice that seemed to descend on us out of the sky. "Can we help you?" the Voice demanded, with an edge suggesting that if the small car proceeded one foot farther, it might be incinerated by laser beams of retribution. When Ellison offered up our names to an intercom device beside the road, the Voice conveyed electronic disappointment. "Ain't you supposed to have a *Redford* with you?" it inquired. Ellison informed it that Redford would be arriving in perhaps two weeks. "Is that the *actor* Redford?" Bruce said it was. "Oh boy," the Voice said, in sepulchral tones.

In an admissions building not unlike a tourist information center, we were greeted politely and signed in by a friendly fellow American in a fine sports jacket, who beckoned us through a security door at the end of the red carpet on the gleaming floor. Marion is proud of its sophisticated electronic surveillance, which includes this device so sensitive to metal that belts and boots must be removed in order to get past. Beyond the scanner, the guard at a heavy locked steel portal admitted us to a glassed tunnel, and the tunnel passed through a huge rolling wave of electrified barbed wire that explains why not a single inmate has "gone over the wall" since this place replaced Alcatraz as the nation's highest-security prison, in 1963.[9] Inside the wire is a moat of tight-mowed grass, then the concrete walls of the inner prison, which is entered through a second electronic portal of thick steel. Beyond this door is the visitors' area, which resembles a waiting room in a municipal airport, or perhaps a bus station—big junk-food machines, sallow rest rooms, and a "lounge" of shiny orange-and-white plastic tables and chairs, monitored by two guards with hip radios and occupied by a few inmates and their visitors. A black convict sat in contented quiet, holding hands with his family; two middle-aged white ones with cropped hair and tattooed arms played cards with middle-aged lady friends or wives, and a younger white man with a beard sat with his girl; though these two scarcely spoke, there was something she was trying to get across, and vice versa.

Ten days before our visit, Peltier had been returned to the Hole on a sixty-to-ninety-day sentence for alleged participation in a riot (the cell doors in his unit had been closed, he says, before the prisoners were ordered to return to their cells, and not realizing this, the guards had been panicked by what looked like mutiny, and launched a wild attack with clubs and tear gas in which three of their own men were hurt). Since coming to Marion, he has spent almost two thirds of his time in solitary; in the year since his return here, nine months have been spent alone, despite the fact that he has tried to be a polite and cooperative prisoner. Even when he has not been in solitary, his privileges have been severely curtailed, particularly in regard to the number, duration, and conditions of the few visits he has been permitted; these special restrictions, in his friends' opinion, are intended to break this prisoner down. ("We say, the Spirit of Crazy Horse, and spiritually, this is who Leonard is; spiritually, you are not going to defeat this man," says Ernie Peters, who saw him in Marion at the time of the Longest Walk. "But he is a man like you are, like I am, with certain needs, and physically, he can deteriorate in those years in prison, that's what worries me.") Peltier's own family had been forbidden "contact" visits—in effect, the privilege of physical greeting and sitting together at these shiny orange tables and sharing poor food from the big dispensers near the rest rooms. Only his attorneys, who must confer with him privately—or as privately as the bugged interview booths permit—and journalists, who might give the place bad publicity if forced to communicate by telephone through a glass panel or mesh screen, are permitted to sit with him in a small booth with glass windows, locked from outside and watched by a guard. The excuse given is "security," although all prisoners must submit to a strip-and-"cavity" search after each contact in the visitors' room, in the vain attempt to keep drugs out of the prison.

Soon Ellison was taken to this booth, and after a while, a guard was sent for me. When I came through the door, "a large Mexican-looking person" in a blue headband that held long hair neatly in place stood up in the booth and smiled a warm welcome through thick glass partitions, remaining standing until I was turned loose in the booth and the door was banged shut and locked behind me. We shook hands, sat down, and looked each other over.

Leonard Peltier was dressed in a white shirt with maroon shoulders, white prison fatigue pants, and sneakers. Upright on his chair, hands on his knees, like someone on his very best behavior, he seemed shy at this first meeting, but there was "nothing stiff about him," as Bob Robideau had said. At five feet eleven inches, he is loose-muscled in his movement, with coarse black hair, deep shadowy brown eyes, a Zapata mustache, a scar on his left cheekbone, a slight puffiness from starchy food, and the pasty skin of a man who has spent four and a half years indoors (on later visits in the spring and summer, when he wore a T-shirt, I noticed buffalo-head and war-shield tattoos on his upper arms).

Peltier has a husky voice and a warm easy laugh. He likes to tease and be teased, and he laughs infectiously at his own mishaps, but there was none of that loose, back-slapping affability that reports of his sociable and joking ways ("Leonard will bullshit you right out of the room!") had led me to expect. He was open and friendly but also watchful and contained, as any man might be in the knowledge that, barring a new trial, he will not be eligible for parole until the year 2015.

Leonard knows that the increasing attention to his case will make the authorities more careful how they handle him; he also knows that this publicity might precipitate some preventive move, and so he still fears for his life. Understandably, such topics make him restless. I noticed that he smoked a lot (he had given it up when I went back to see him in August), and although he never once complained or showed the smallest indication of self-pity, his face at moments had a desperate look that made his seeming ease and laughter more affecting. At one point, he referred to the former guard captain, "Max" Carey, as a "wild man," notorious for his brutality; prison officials of this sort, Peltier says, make life miserable not only for the prisoners but for the guards, who are exposed daily to the convicts' resentment, and many of the Marion guards were now asking for transfers. "Some of them are pretty decent people," Leonard said, "just trying to do their job, but others are here for a different reason; they're real animals, and they never let up on you. They're really working on me now, man, poking me along with them goddam sticks, trying to get something started." Ellison warned him that he must be especially careful these days, and he nodded. "I know what these people are capable of, so I'm doing my best to keep quiet, just get along; I might be the next one hanging from a sheet."

Leonard is grateful to Bobby Garcia and Standing Deer, who came to his assistance at such risk; in his modest way, he does not regard their actions as a tribute to himself but as "the old convict philosophy: the Man is your enemy, and everybody else is your comrade who is not a snitch. They put that label 'dangerous' on Standing Deer, same as they did me, but Standing Deer's just a regular old dude, he ain't no more dangerous than I am. He's got guts, and he is *smart*, and he pesters them about his rights—what he calls 'administrative remedies,' " Peltier recalled, with that good laugh of his, "and that's the real thing that's 'dangerous' about him. Socially we get along great: he always had ways that seemed very comical and had me smiling and laughing. When it comes to the convicts' code, Standing Deer is real strong, and Bobby was, too; they never let nobody go poking them with a stick, they jump right in their face, guard or no guard. And that's why Bobby stuck by me. We got nobody else to turn to; all we got is one another." Peltier sighed, and gave a tired grin. "Well, the heat's on now, and even Standing Deer is worried; I hear that guy is really thin, down somewhere near one hundred pounds—that's how bad they got to him, over in Springfield. I have only admiration and great respect for Standing Deer. It takes more than just being a man to come forward as he has done, knowing his life is no longer worth a wooden nickel."

⊡

Before leaving Marion after my first visit, I asked Peltier if he knew Jack Henry Abbott, a fellow inmate and the author of a brilliant and chilling review of a book on death-row prisoners that had appeared a few days earlier in the *New York Review of Books.*[10] Peltier, who is generous and uncritical in almost all his references to other people, actually reared back in his seat, for this Abbott was the very man who had given the damaging story about the Law Project to the authorities. "He's a punk and a snitch!" Leonard exclaimed. "He got our lawyers banned from the prison, and he got me put back in the goddam hole!" Until recently, Abbott had been known as a hard-core convict who had led in the fight for prison reforms throughout the federal system; it was Abbott, in fact, who had denounced the guards and asked for a lie detector test after the severe beatings in the Control Unit the previous April. But when, in the months following the beating, an expected parole after nineteen years in prison was deferred yet again until August 1981, this desperate man began to come apart. Denouncing the Project lawyers as left-wing agitators who got convicts in trouble, he denied that he had been beaten in the Control Unit, and withdrew from the class-action suit brought by Don Richardson and the other victims of the beatings. On December 12, 1980, in the course of the long interview supervised by Phillips, he declared repeatedly that his life was in danger, saying "I've got to get out, I've got to get out of prison."

Peltier said that Abbott was no longer in Marion, having been transferred the month before for his own safety after the contents of the "snitch document" became known; wherever he was now, he would probably soon be released, since he must have made a deal with Phillips, and since the authorities could no longer protect his life.

Although such a deal was subsequently denied by the prison spokesmen, Abbott himself was apparently convinced that he was going to be freed, to judge from two letters written to a New York editor on December 25 and December 29, shortly after the interview with Hursey and Phillips. In these letters, Abbott says that he is soon to be transferred to Utah State Prison, and that he expects a favorable parole hearing within sixty days. For reasons that did not become clear until after the "snitch document" emerged in the January court hearing in Chicago, Abbott was very anxious that his whereabouts be kept secret, knowing that his life would not be worth much in the prison systems, and he requests that Marion Control Unit should be identified as his address. He repeats this request in the letter of December 29.

On January 16, Jack Abbott was moved to the maximum-security unit of Utah State Prison and locked up in solitary for his own protection.[11] In anticipation of parole in August, Abbott was to be released to a New York City halfway house in June. A few days after his arrival in New York, I heard from Standing Deer, whom I had asked for a professional opinion.

> I've never heard anything bad about him until Leonard's report. I know he has been abused about as much as any prisoner I know. In all I have heard about him he has always been in the forefront of active resistance. . . . It is likely that Leonard's put-down is appropriate because I have heard Jack is expecting to be released on parole this summer and . . . it would seem that parole would be an extremely remote possibility. Unless he did bargain his way into the hearts and minds of the correctional criminals. . . .

On June 18, after visiting Marion, I skimmed through the damning 116-page interview in the Law Project offices in Carbondale, Illinois. By this time, Jack Abbott had made his media debut on *Good Morning, America!* and was already an existential hero as well as a literary "event" in New York City. Reading this desperate betrayal of the code that had given such meaning as it had to his dark life, one had to feel sorry for him, since the news of this document was bound to emerge to spoil the well-deserved celebrity of his book. "Jack was shaken and embittered after that beating last April," said one of the young lawyers named by Abbott, "and the authorities picked up on it, they knew he was vulnerable. The Control Unit broke him, that's all."[12]

A few weeks later, Abbott was told that rumors were circulating about a "snitch document." Very upset, he acknowledged to friends that he had testified against the Law Project attorneys, but he denied any disloyalty to his fellow convicts. According to a mutual friend, "Abbott was terribly anxious to get in touch with you when he heard you were involved with Leonard Peltier. He seemed very, very agitated about it, there was something he wanted you to do, because he felt that Peltier was a great leader, but too naive to defend himself from those lawyers properly, something like that." On July 17, Abbott tried to reach me on the telephone; I was away that day, and we never spoke. At daylight next morning, he took the life of a young waiter in an all-night restaurant who had told Abbott that he could not use the employees' toilet, since that was against the law.[13]

Jim Roberts of the Law Project, whom I ran into in the entrance to Marion on August 6, had no doubt that Jack Abbott had paid his way out of prison. "First they beat the hell out of him, then they threaten him in the Control Unit with a lot of heavy people, one guy particularly, who he thought might kill him. I think they broke him. Phillips knew just who he was interviewing, and that under the circumstances, nothing Abbott said could be depended on, but they used it anyway. Hell, this guy is schizoid, totally bent out of shape after all these years, and the authorities know it. But they got what they wanted, and they send him back to Utah, and he's out on the street within five months. Well, *nobody* goes from the Control Unit to the street, not in five months, not without making a deal."

News of the deal emerged in the press a month after the killing, by which time Standing Deer had satisfied himself that Peltier was correct. "I learned that Abbott told lies on James B. Roberts, the lawyer near Marion who represents Leonard and others. He did that in September of 1980 . . . I guess that's what his parole was based on. If a prisoner becomes a quivering, snivelling jellyfish, the authorities imagine him to be rehabilitated." In the same letter, Standing Deer said he could not meet with me as planned because he was afraid of Terre Haute's new warden, who had known him at Marion in 1978. "I must keep a low profile or he will have his correctional officers kill me. I am very afraid of that man. . . . I have to live out my life here and I must try to survive . . . I know you understand. Take care, brother. In the Spirit of Crazy Horse. Standing Deer."

Although Standing Deer said he would be glad to respond to future questions, he did not answer my next letter, and I knew I should not write to him again.

As a man whose life may well depend on strict adherence to the convict's code by himself and others, Leonard Peltier has no use for the men who break it. "I know a lot of guys whose lives have been threatened; you don't snitch unless you want to snitch," he said when I visited him in August. "I mean, snitching is bad enough, but you don't go *making up* lies, the way Abbott did." Upset and scowling, Peltier was silent for a few moments, while his own sense of forgiveness got the better of him. Then he looked up at me, shaking his head. "I liked Abbott when I first met him. I did. I liked Abbott. I thought he was a good, solid con until he did that, and I guess he was. But I think this place will drive you mad. My own personality has changed a hell of a lot since I been in prison; I noticed that myself. I find myself back in the cells acting like I'm somebody real *bad*, you know? And *that's* not me! That's never been me! Sure, I'll fight you in a minute if you *attack* me, but just to go around *looking* for it, *acting* like you're tough?" He shook his head again. "I'll lay down in my cell and I'll think, *That's* not me, why am I acting that way?"

One answer might be his instinct to protect himself from danger that may come at him at any time, from any quarter; he has no doubt that the new trial that he seeks threatens the state. In fact, he believes that he will be dead within five years, even if he is granted a new trial and set free. "He really believes that," Ellison says, "and I agree. I told him today that if he *does* get a new trial, they may try to kill him before he gets to court—he knows that himself. And in here, it would be pretty simple; they could just get some nut in the Control Unit to take him out. If Marion explodes, the way it's bound to do, with the last of the decent guards getting out of the place while there's still time, a riot could cover anything they want to do. I told him he's got to be careful, extra careful. But they'll get him anyway."

On a subsequent visit, in May 1982, I asked Peltier if he still thought he would be killed. Because of his hopes for a new trial, based on the FOIA documents, Leonard looked more lean and optimistic than I had ever seen him, but he had not changed his mind about his chances. "That's not pessimistic, you know," he said. "That's just reality. Right now I sincerely believe that the main reason they haven't already hit Dino and Bob is because they have me where they want me. But if I go free—" He shook his head. "Dino especially, because he's been out a lot longer than Bob, and he spoke out against the System as soon as they let him go." He paused again. "I'm not worried about it anymore; you can't live, being worried all the time. I can't *do* nothing about it, so I'm just gonna live day by day—otherwise, I'll *really* go to pieces!"

Leonard laughed. "I've had more than my share of fun, you know," he concluded, as cheerfully as a man on vacation taking time out for a beer. The courage and life-spirit of this man, under such circumstances, made my temples tingle with admiration. As Steve Robideau says, "That guy is amazing; he keeps us *all* going."

⊡

As a rule, Leonard Peltier speaks kindly of Myrtle Poor Bear and of the young Navajos who testified against him—"I understand what they had been through; they were just kids, they were alone, and those people filled them with terror." (But another day, as if tormented by his fate, he burst out against these boys with a growl of pain: "Little bastards! Just told lies to save themselves! I don't understand how those kids could stand up and tell lies like that!") Of Dennis Banks, whose public support of the Oglala group when they most needed it was so reluctant, Peltier says slowly, "Dennis had a lot of charisma, and he was intelligent and sincere. As far as I'm concerned, he's still one of the most effective leaders in the country. He's got faults, sure, we all have, but he taught me a lot, and I still have a lot of love and respect for that man."

Banks himself, asked his opinion of his former comrade, seems tentative, noncommittal: "Leonard was just getting into it, listening to everybody, but he didn't have a complete grasp; even after he gets out of jail, he'll have a lot to learn before he can assume a real leadership position." And Russ Means, too, seems more enthusiastic about Peltier the Dog Soldier than Peltier the leader: "He's a good tough bro, man, a regular skin; if you've got Leonard for a friend, you've got something." Until recently, neither Banks nor Means appeared willing to grant Peltier the stature that other Indians wish to give him; he was only a warrior at the time of Oglala, after all, and his leadership, they seem to say, derives from notoriety and the Indian people's need for another Crazy Horse rather than from proven ability and real experience. Peltier himself would agree with this—in fact, he worries that his people have made him something he is not, and that if he gets out, he can no longer be just good old Leonard.

Peltier's admirers do not agree: John Trudell, for one, has referred to Peltier as "this generation's Geronimo, this generation's Crazy Horse." If Leonard lacks the commanding style and articulate intelligence of Means and Banks, he is rich in traditional leadership qualities such as courage, generosity, humility, and a sincere willingness, proven over and over, to put the interests of his people ahead of his own. What comes from him is warm simplicity, a playful openness, a disarming lack of that arrogance and selfishness which many Indians still associate with the AIM leadership. Perhaps it is true, as Bob Robideau suggests, that the U.S. government created this leader who is now well known all over Indian country, but he has become a real leader nonetheless.

"At times I feel that everything has been a waste, but you know, I would not change my life with anyone on earth," Leonard has said. "It's been a hard life certainly, one filled with poverty, more than enough for any one family, but I have a heritage and culture everyone in the world would like and wants to be and that's Indian."[14]

Archie Fire Lame Deer says, "Leonard Peltier is a sun dancer, and that is one of the most honored things to be in our religion." And Dino Butler says, "I sun-danced with Leonard Peltier in 1975 in South Dakota. A sun dance is a sacred religious ceremony of the Red Nation. It is a ceremony to give strength to our people, through our sacrifices. It is a ceremony to help our people, to help the sick and the weak and the ignorant. We danced for four days in this ceremony together, me and Leonard Peltier. You do not dance for yourselves, but you dance for your people. Your people includes all life, whether they walk, swim, crawl, or fly. He represents the truth, unity, bravery, the Red Nation, the Red Way of Life. He represents the pipe to us, represents our prayers . . . represents our people, represents life, which knows no death."

"I know Leonard Peltier," Leonard Crow Dog told me. "I respect this man. When he lived here with us, he waked in the morning, he took part in spiritual ceremonies. He was sincerely committed to the land, to our unborn and our future generations, and to the hope that all tribes will be united. He worked for his people—not just for AIM but for everyone who believes in the spiritual way."[15]

(In January 1982, the national leadership of AIM met in San Francisco. It was the first meeting in years, and it was a great success, according to Dennis Banks, who no longer sounded like the isolated, wary, brooding man I had spent an evening with in San Francisco the year before. "There was no yelling and no screaming." Dennis laughed, pleased by how peaceable the meeting had been. "This was the first time I can remember when Russell and I could really discuss Movement activities. Bill Means was there, too, and Clyde and Vernon Bellecourt, and Janet McCloud from the fishing-rights fight up in Washington state, and Phillip Deere, our Creek spiritual leader from Oklahoma—a lot of important people from around the country came back in. Not long after that, Bob Robideau called up to say that the people in Peltier's group were with us, too." Russ Means, passing through Los Angeles after the AIM meeting, spoke out strongly for Peltier, who with Herb Powless had been made a national co-director of the reconstituted AIM, which intended to take an increased responsibility for native peoples all over the Americas. "We discussed what is happening to Indian people in El Salvador and Guatemala and Nicaragua," Dennis said, "and what we could do for Leonard and Dick Marshall and Dino Butler. And finally we asked Clyde Bellecourt to put the national office in Minneapolis back together: the American Indian Movement is alive again!")

⊡

On our first visit to Marion, Bruce Ellison had repeated what he had told me once before: "I don't want to know who killed those agents, and I don't ask. But I do know Leonard didn't kill them; I don't think it, I *know* it." I asked him why, if that was true, a statement of innocence had been made so rarely by the defense attorneys at the trials.

"Because the attorneys didn't know," Bruce said. "We just didn't know at Cedar Rapids, or at Fargo, either, and these guys never once tried to persuade us. I know Bill Kunstler thought they killed the agents, but he believes that they were innocent whether they did it or not."

Of all Indians that he has worked with, Ellison respects the West Coast group the most. "They're honorable and they're consistent and they're real strong about drinking—no bullshit episodes. I just like working with them."

We discussed the likelihood, in the light of the new evidence, that Leonard was doing time for one or more young Indians who were being protected by the Oglala community; apart from the damning circumstantial evidence of the West Coast group's possession of the agents' weapons, the government had had a much stronger case against at least two and perhaps as many as six others than it had had against Peltier, Robideau, and Butler. "In the appeal," Ellison said, "we'll simply point out the evidence already in possession of the government which it ignored or suppressed to avoid prosecuting local Indians. We'll call no witnesses, offer no new evidence, that tends to incriminate others. We didn't do it at Fargo, and we're not going to do it this time, either. Leonard wouldn't permit it."

"I never killed them agents," Leonard said toward the end of our first visit, looking me straight in the face, without a blink. "I never even *fired* at them, not directly; I just kept shooting over their heads, trying to keep them from firing at *us*." He was restless once again, as a man is apt to be when stating a truth that he knows may not be believed.

When the guard came to the booth to escort me out, Leonard stood up to shake hands. "Even if you can't help me," he said, "I hope your book will help my people. That's what I'm in here for, and that's what I'm working for, and that's what's most important. But it's also important that you know I never killed them agents." We were both aware that a man who hoped for a new trial could scarcely say anything else, and anyway, my personal opinion of his guilt or innocence was of no importance: what was important not only to Peltier but to all Indians (and all Americans) was that this man receive a fair trial in the U.S. courts.[16] Nevertheless, I told Leonard I believed him, and I did, and I do.

CHAPTER 19

PAHA SAPA

The Treaty, the Supreme Court, and the Return to the Black Hills

Right now, today, we who live on the Pine Ridge Reservation are living in what white society has designated a "National Sacrifice Area." What this means is that we have a lot of uranium deposits here, and white culture (not us) needs this uranium as energy production material. The cheapest, most efficient way for industry to extract and deal with the processing of this uranium is to dump the waste by-products right here at the digging sites. Right here where we live. This waste is radioactive and will make the entire region uninhabitable forever. This is considered by industry, and by the white society that created this industry, to be an "acceptable" price to pay for energy resource development. Along the way they also plan to drain the water table under this part of South Dakota as part of the industrial process, so the region becomes doubly uninhabitable. The same sort of thing is happening down in the land of the Navajo and Hopi, up in the land of the Northern Cheyenne and Crow, and elsewhere. . . .

We are resisting being turned into a National Sacrifice Area. We are resisting being turned into a national sacrifice people. The costs of this industrial process are not acceptable to us. It is genocide to dig uranium here and drain the water table—no more, no less.

Russell Means (*Lakota*)

On April 4, 1981, a caravan of twenty cars, carrying sacred pipes, sweat-lodge materials, tipi poles, cold-weather equipment, stoves, and food, departed from Porcupine, bright red flags waving, and traveled through Rapid City to Victoria Creek Canyon, about twelve miles southwest of Rapid City, in the Black Hills. Here a camp was established on federal land, in what was perceived as the first step in the reclaiming and resettlement of Paha Sapa.[1] The legal basis of this action was the "undisturbed use" of the Black Hills guaranteed to the Lakota in the 1868 Treaty, as well as the American Indian Freedom of Religion Act of 1978 and a federal law (1897) relating to the free use of wilderness sites for schools and churches.

On a day of light snow, the Indians set up tents in a canyon bend, where striking red cliffs rose to the ponderosa pines on the spring sky; there was good running water here, and a small pond. Naming the camp for Raymond Yellow Thunder, the man from Porcupine killed in Gordon, Nebraska, in 1972, Dakota AIM proposed to the government a permanent alternative-energy community for which it would ask federal cooperation, and on April 6, spiritual leader Matthew King filed a claim with the U.S. Forest Service for 800 acres of surrounding forest. Asked by the excited press if he thought the Indians would be allowed to stay, King declared, "This is our land!"

A Forest Service spokesman blustered, "We have the legal muscle and the law-enforcement muscle to evict them very quickly," and Sheriff "Mel" Larson conferred with the FBI. For want of a better plan, two vanloads of heavily armed agents showed up at the camp gates, apparently in a show of force; asked to state their business, they said, "Turkey-shooting." Other armed agents in camouflage costumes were seen prowling the rimrock and high pines, on the lookout for suspicious signs of terrorist activity around the cook tent. But unlike Wounded Knee, the Camp Yellow Thunder "occupation" had the support of many whites right from the start, not only those in the Black Hills Alliance, which served the camp as a communications center, but the American Friends Service Committee, several church groups, and many private organizations and individuals across the country. With so much attention from the media, the authorities decided upon an indulgent attitude, not wishing to risk bloodshed on color TV; Russell Means, who had moved to Yellow Thunder from "that BIA concentration camp at Kyle," had made it plain that the Indians would not go without a fight.

Dakota AIM's dramatic move revived the spirits of the traditionals, whose Black Hills land claim had been stifled by the courts. In 1977—more than a quarter century after the claim was filed—the U.S. Court of Claims had finally affirmed the Indian Claims Commission conclusion that no valid agreement to cede the Black Hills had ever existed, the "abrogation" of 1877 notwithstanding, and that the Hills had been taken without compensation, as the Indians said. "The Dakota nation" was promptly offered $17.5 million, the estimated value of the area in 1877, and a modest fraction of the more than $1 billion worth of gold removed from the Black Hills by the Homestake Mine, which to this day accounts for half of U.S. gold production.

The traditional Lakota refused this ignoble offer, having maintained throughout that Paha Sapa was not for sale; they demanded the return of the Hills themselves. The tribal-council chairmen of the seven Lakota bands, persuaded that they could do better, refused it, too. In 1979, the Court of Claims, holding the federal government responsible for "the most ripe and rank case of dishonorable dealing in our history," decided that the Lakota were also entitled to 102 years' interest, or a total of $122 million. This much-improved offer—more precisely, a judgment—advertised as the largest settlement ever offered by the Indian Claims Commission, worked out to approximately the equivalent of a secondhand car for each eligible Indian (about sixty thousand people) for land that is estimated to contain billions of dollars in uranium, in addition to gold, copper, molybdenum, and other precious minerals.[2] The Justice Department, protesting that the payment was too high, appealed the decision before the Supreme Court on the basis of its archaic *Lone Wolf* decision of 1903, in which it was held that Congress had plenary power over Indians and could, in effect, abrogate treaties with Indians at will; the Justice Department also cited the *Tee-Hit-Ton* decision of 1955, which had catered to the termination mood in Congress by removing all constitutional protection from "Indian title" or "aboriginal title" lands (that is, territories inhabited by an Indian nation before the advent of the Europeans)—in no way applicable to this case, since title to the Great Sioux Reservation had been signed over by the U.S. government itself.

The Sioux tribal councils were attracted by the larger settlement, but the traditionals continued to hold out for the return of the Black Hills; more than three fourths of Paha Sapa, or about 1,320,000 acres, was classified as federal or state land (mostly national forest), which could be returned to the Indians without causing hardship to private citizens. The traditionals' views were ignored, however; it was only because the award had been contested by the Justice Department that the case was turned over to the Supreme Court.

In June 1980, when the Court of Claims judgment was affirmed by the Supreme Court,[3] it was contested by traditionals of the "Oglala Sioux Tribe of Pine Ridge Reservation." (As "Sioux," they were not endorsed by Dakota AIM or the Means family, for whom the word "Sioux" represents *wasicu* values. "Sioux sold the Black Hills; the Lakota did not sell," says Russell Means.[4]) This group, led by Louis Bad Wound, sought a temporary restraining order prohibiting the government from paying out any part of the award; the request was denied in September 1980. Meanwhile, Washington attorney Arthur Lazarus continued to press for a monetary settlement, even though his own contract with the Oglala Tribal Council had expired in 1977 and had not been renewed, despite his urgent request to be reinstated. Acknowledging that the majority of the people he wished to represent would have preferred land, Lazarus—who was claiming as a fee over $10 million of the Indians' money—expressed great satisfaction with the Supreme Court decision. On May 20, 1981, he and two associates were awarded $10,595,493—the "nothing short of sensational result" of what Lazarus himself hailed as "a unique accomplishment in the annals of American jurisprudence." The case had been won by the wealthy lawyer and lost by his poverty-stricken clients, and for once, Dakota AIM and the Oglala Sioux Tribe joined forces, threatening a malpractice suit in contesting this immense payment to a lawyer who had "prosecuted the claim for money without proper authorization and without the understanding and consent of the Dakota people." The Indians' complaint, put in the form of a motion before the Court of Claims, was speedily dismissed without hearing or explanation, and on this sordid note, a claim first filed in 1923 came to an end.[5]

Al Trimble, who was head of the Tribal Council when Arthur Lazarus was fired, does not excuse the lawyer's misrepresentation of his clients or the massive fee, but he points out that for many years Lazarus and his firm had done honorable and competent work that had the full support of the tribal councils; most of the people in those days wanted money. Many of the older Indians who now repudiate the money and are holding out for the return of the Black Hills "were pretty shifty characters back in '49, '50; they sold off a lot of our land, and I can still remember all the talk about 'getting our Black Hills money.' The AIM people have to be given credit for renewing the people's awareness of what the Black Hills meant."

Under the auspices of the International Indian Treaty Council,[6] founded by AIM in 1974 (and a non-governmental organization of the United Nations since 1977), the Lakota had presented their treaty case to the United Nations in Geneva and to the World Court at The Hague, where international law maintains that, except as an act of war, treaties between nations may not be altered without mutual consent. But the United States no longer recognizes the sovereign status of the Indian nations (recognition of Indian sovereignty would require an act of Congress, which seems most unlikely[7]) and will not accept outside jurisdiction in domestic issues. Still, World Court judgments are binding on the U.S. government, and a favorable decision in European tribunals would increase the chances for international recognition that the traditional Indians now seek.[8]

"They're listening to us in Europe now," Madonna Gilbert says. "We're going there again and again, and we're going to give them the hard facts; we're not going there just to play Indian, in beads and braids."

⊡

Among those stirred by the return to Paha Sapa was Chief Frank Fools Crow, now ninety-one, who had withdrawn his spiritual support of AIM just a few years before. When certain members of the Oglala Tribal Council dutifully deplored the "occupation," Chief Fools Crow said he was reminded of those Indians who betrayed Crazy Horse. "The government is always making laws, so many laws, every day new laws. Then they break every one. They use the law to cheat people, but that is not the Indian way. We have one law, God's law: to live on this earth with respect for all living things, and to be happy with what God has given to us." Matthew King agreed. "Respect is very important," this elder said. "Respect is our law—respect for all living things. That means we cannot harm the earth or the water because we have respect for the place of those things in the world. We could not kill all the buffalo because that shows no respect for why the buffalo are here. . . . Heart, body, mind and soul all together with the world: that is the Indian way to live. You see, these hills are our church; the rivers and the wind, and the blossoms and the living things—that is our Bible. Nature is God,

God is Nature. Our whole life, our government, our religion, comes from watching these things."[9]

But in a dispute over tactics, Madonna Gilbert and Lorelei Means had withdrawn the support of WARN from both Camp Yellow Thunder and the Black Hills Alliance, causing a hard break in the Means family. Then Oglala Sioux Tribe attorney Mario Gonzalez (who as Rosebud tribal judge, in 1974, had disbarred William Janklow from practice on the reservation) questioned the precedent that had been set by filing a claim to a restricted part of Paha Sapa, since this seemed to acknowledge federal ownership of Indian land; Bill Means retorted on behalf of AIM that the laws meant nothing anyway, and that Camp Yellow Thunder was a traditional alternative to the ruinous programs of the BIA and a first step in the ultimate return to Paha Sapa.

This position was endorsed by Vine Deloria, Jr., who called the Yellow Thunder idea "a realistic alternative to all existing federal programs for American Indians. It builds directly on the innate strengths of the traditional element of each tribe which has long been neglected and shunted aside in favor of assimilationist groups which promised much and delivered little. . . . Indian people everywhere see in this effort the first and best means of returning social and community institutions to the hands of the traditional Indian people. For that reason this project is one of the most progressive proposals to be received by the federal government in the last century of Indian relationships."

The Black Hills occupation had excited all seven bands of the Lakota nation, and in June, the traditional elders at Standing Rock announced their intention of establishing a ceremonial sweat lodge and spiritual center at the beautiful site of ancient petroglyphs in Craven Canyon, in the southern Hills. Reversing itself, the Oglala Tribal Council announced that it, too, wished to establish a camp in the Black Hills. While few believed that this would really happen, it was felt that an implicit endorsement by a tribal council of a political action by Dakota AIM was sure to reverberate all over Indian country. Al Trimble, now director of the Indian Center in Rapid City, was not so sure: "There's something very unhealthy about this Tribal Council move, in my opinion; they're up to something. Stanley Looking Elk [the Tribal Council president] worked closely with Wilson in the old days, and he tried to give Wilson a job when he got in office; he still works closely with the Wilsons, and he's still trying to get some of those goons reinstated.

What is particularly pitiful is that conditions are rapidly returning to what they were before Wounded Knee. The BIA is still undercutting any tribal attempt at independence—they're even trying to restore the BIA police force—and a lot of the same old faces are still there. Anyway, it's going to take more than camping permits and agreeing to be good little Indians before anybody is going to pay this Tribal Council 'occupation' much attention."

⊡

One hot early morning in late June 1981, Russ Means hailed Bob Robideau and me in the streets of Rapid City, laughing and talking even before he reached us; he had just come in from Camp Yellow Thunder, dressed in a rough shirt and rubber boots. "We're back in the Black Hills," he shouted, "and now the goddam Tribal Council wants to get in, too! Eight years ago they were shooting at us—*now* look!" He laughed gleefully as he shook hands, and Bob laughed, too. "There's solidarity in the Oglala people for the first time in years! Did AIM do its job or didn't it?" Means demanded, and Robideau said easily, "We did it, man."

I wondered if the job were over. The organized violence seemed to have subsided, yet the violent deaths went on and on and on. The previous Christmas, their old partner Milo Goings had been killed in a knifing by his woman; with Ted and Bill Means among his pallbearers, he was buried at Wounded Knee, where he had been the first Indian casualty in 1973. ("Milo was pretty quiet most of the time," Bob said, "but when he got drunk, he went kind of crazy.") In March, their old friend Evelyn Bordeaux, who had been in the Means party on the night of the shooting in the Longhorn Bar, who had opened her Rapid City house to the West Coast group and carried Joe Stuntz's body from the Rapid City hospital back to Oglala, had died in a head-on collision with a drunken driver in the northern Hills. In the past fortnight, Ted Means's eleven-year-old daughter, Kimberly (the child he had been playing with in the yard of the Porcupine survival school when Bob and I had visited the year before), had been run over by another drunken white man while participating in the "Run for Freedom" marathon on behalf of Dick Marshall and other Indian prisoners in South Dakota. A few days later, Hank Means had confessed participation in a robbery-assault that ended in the death by heart attack of a respected local priest who had supported the Black Hills Alliance, and because he was Russell's oldest boy, the local papers were making the most of an already unpleasant case.[10]

Despite his exhilaration about the occupation of the Hills, Means looked haggard and unshaven, but when I ran into him a few days later, he was dressed up in his Russ Means outfit and was clearly his old free-wheeling self again. The previous day he had led a shake-up of the Black Hills Alliance that had eliminated all but one white person from the board, and when I said I thought it was too bad that the Alliance had lost its biracial balance, he snapped harshly, "I've been in this from the start, so there's not a goddam thing you can tell me about it!" Well, I said, we weren't going to have much of a conversation if I couldn't express my opinions. Russ laughed cheerfully, switching gears, and went right on handing out the word as if nothing had happened. "Indian people recruit and organize through example," he informed me. "If you want to be an Indian, you have to *act* Indian, not just talk Indian. The Tribal Council occupation, if they go through with it, is a natural continuation of what we started, so we strongly support it: it's going to wake up tribal councils all over the country. The Indian people *had* to take this action, because as far as the U.S. government is concerned, the Black Hills negotiations are all over, finished; that was clear as soon as Lazarus got his payoff. They've delivered the money to the Interior Department to distribute, and they've washed their hands of the whole thing. The only legal recourse we have left is the international courts. But meanwhile, we are back in the Black Hills—we're *there*, man! And we have them in a bind: the only way they can get us out is wipe us out!"

⊡

The Tribal Council "occupation" was scheduled to take place on the anniversary of the Custer battle, in the Wind Cave National Park in the southern Hills; it was from Wind Cave, according to one legend, that the Lakota first appeared in Paha Sapa. The following day, June 26, a commemoration ceremony would be held in Oglala in honor of Anna Mae Aquash and Joe Killsright Stuntz.

John Trudell, who came in from California for this ceremony, has worked hard for Peltier's Defense Committee in trying to raise public support for a new trial. In his view, this case represents "the death of the Constitution," and like many Indians, he believes that the government agents intend to have Leonard Peltier assassinated. For Trudell, at least, this assassination talk is not just "the usual radical propaganda." On February 11, 1979, he burned an upside-down American flag on the steps of the FBI Building during the vigil for Peltier in Washington, D.C.; twelve hours later, Tina Trudell, her mother, and the three Trudell children were burned to death in an arsonist's attack upon their house on the Duck Valley Reservation in Nevada. There is no evidence that the two events were connected—in fact, there is no evidence of any kind, since the FBI made no investigation, despite clear jurisdiction under the Major Crimes Act—but as in the case of Anna Mae, the atmosphere of anti-AIM violence encouraged by the FBI may well have given courage to the unknown killers.

Like many AIM Indians, Trudell wears a red (or black) wind band, jeans, and vest, and he also wears a small bone necklace, black-rimmed spectacles, and a weird psychedelic shoulder tattoo of a grinning death's-head crowned in feathers, inscribed "Candy Man." He is small, brown-haired, olive-skinned, with a kind of feral restlessness, intensified by relentless eyes in a shaman's wise quick face. While considering joining Bob Robideau and me on a trip south to observe the Tribal Council's invasion of the Hills, Trudell parodied a stoned AIM warrior asking directions from the state police—"Hey, man, I got the guns and bombs here, man, so like, where is the goddam *camp* at?"—and this cool humorous style, together with his charismatic mix of born-again Indian, spirit talk, and anti–white man fervor, has made him a model for Indian youth, which would like to restore the traditional spirit without "going back to the blanket" of the past. He is also a kind of angry jester for the rich revolutionaries of the entertainment world, although Trudell himself is not jesting.

"When I got sent up for sixty days, that time in Fargo, I was approached by another inmate, some guy I didn't know, and he started talking about my public statements. You can't go around talking that shit, he says, you'd better get out of the country. You don't know these crazy bastards—they could kill your wife and children. Well, I was suspicious of that guy's so-called warning even at the time; *that* was a message John Trudell was supposed to *receive*!" Sitting on a river rock in the Black Hills' Dark Canyon, arms wrapped around his knees, he was quiet for a moment, then spoke in a different voice. "I know who did it, and I know how they did it. What I still don't understand was *why*; it was so unnecessary. But it *was* arson, and it *was* deliberate—an assassination.

Those people did a terrible thing; they should think a long, long time about what they did. I'm not mentioning any names, but they will be dealt with, you can count on that."

After Tina Trudell's death, when Peltier escaped from Lompoc prison, Trudell, Dino Butler, Steve Robideau, and others went to Canada for a Peltier rally and, because they feared for their "political and personal rights and safety," decided to ask for political asylum. "We knew the prejudice was just as bad up there," Trudell admits, "but we decided on it as a political gesture." Trudell and Butler remained in Canada until Peltier's trial in Los Angeles, and since then, both men had avoided staying anywhere for very long, or letting people know where they were going. Trudell no longer had reason to doubt that somebody might wish to "neutralize" him, and as for Butler, "They'll be gunning for Dino for the rest of his life because they think he killed two pigs and walked away."

⊡

A few months earlier, I had gone to California to see Butler, who with Bob Robideau and Trudell had set up a Peltier Defense Committee office in Los Angeles. But Butler had not been seen for several weeks, and Robideau would only say that he was "underground" somewhere in the Pacific Northwest. From Los Angeles I went to San Francisco to see Dennis Banks, then to Rapid City to meet Nilak Butler. Nilak had not yet arrived, but Steve Robideau, who had opened a Defense Committee office in Rapid City, had sent a message suggesting a visit to his house, which has no phone: "Tell him not to eat before he comes," the message read, "and ask if he eats dog."

A tall, soft-voiced man who is now in spiritual training ("When you work with alcoholism, you have to replace it with something, and for Indians, the best thing we can offer is spirituality"), Steve is open and friendly, anxious to communicate, but his brother Jim, who turned up while we were talking, studied me for a long while before he spoke. Jim Robideau was at Wounded Knee and spent several months in prison for the Custer riot, and on that bitter February evening, well below zero with white winds of snow whipping in over the Plains, his face looked hard and guarded; he shifted restlessly, as if hearing some disturbing sound he could not locate. Finally, however, he settled down, and accepted a good supper. "The Peltier case is just one case," he said, describing the material he is assembling on anti-Indian practices in the courts. "If you took all the Indian cases in this state, you'd find that the pattern is the same."

In recent years, Steve Robideau has been running sweat-lodge ceremonies, and he served as informal spiritual leader during Peltier's court appearances, starting in Vancouver; this year he would lead the memorial service for Anna Mae Aquash and Joe Stuntz to be held at Oglala on June 26. He has also been taking correspondence courses in his spare time, and needs only four credits to complete a college degree in Indian studies. Leonard, he said, had been learning the spiritual way ever since 1973, when he had joined most of the AIM leaders in their first sun dance, and he has been teaching other Indians in prison. Thinking of Leonard, Steve smiles his soft-eyed smile, shaking his head. "Leonard was always ready to do something for Indian people in trouble, even when he's in bad trouble himself—Hey, he says, we can't let 'em get away with *that*! He was always ready to do *anything*; if he couldn't find no other way to help, he'd go cut their wood!"

Listening, Jim Robideau laughed out loud for the first time, a wide-open laugh that banished his guarded expression. "Yeah," Jim said, "he's really *like* that, man!"

Steve Robideau said we would not know Butler's whereabouts until Nilak turned up in Rapid City, and John Trudell, whom I spoke with next day on the phone, knew nothing, either; he believed, however, that Dino would be accompanying him to New York sometime in March. But Dino never reached New York, nor did Nilak show up in Rapid City; she returned to Vancouver, where, on February 23, 1981, Dino and his cousin Gary Butler, aged twenty-three, had been arrested by the Vancouver police. A wild car chase had followed an attempt by the police to detain the Butlers for questioning—it was alleged, briefly, that the Indians had their eye on a local bank—and supposedly the Butlers had fired at their pursuers with the .357 Magnum handguns that were located in their car, which was demolished when it crashed and overturned. In a near-miracle, the two men escaped almost unhurt from the flattened wreck, but they were seized two blocks away and jailed in Oakalla Prison on charges of attempted murder of the pursuing officers as well as weapons charges and negligent driving.

On the day after the arraignment in Vancouver, the state authorities in Oregon announced the pending indictment of both Butlers for the murder of Donald Pier, a Georgia-Pacific lumber company employee killed in Toledo, Oregon, on January 21; the year before, Pier had been among several men investigated on complaints by Indians of Butler's Tututni band that he had been looting traditional graves and selling the artifacts. A month after the death, the Oregon state police were still acknowledging that they had no good leads to the killing, having stated repeatedly that there were no local suspects and that outside people seemed to have been implicated. The Butlers were never mentioned, far less accused, until they were arrested on the Vancouver charges, but the fact that they had been traveling well armed, and that they had fled when the Vancouver police approached them, encouraged the Oregon authorities to name them as the only suspects in Pier's murder.

"Of course they split when those pigs started looking them over!" Nilak Butler said when she met me in the spring at Vancouver airport. "Gary was wanted on escape charges in Oregon, and anyway, they don't need no excuse to bust someone they want as bad as Dino. Those guys *had* to run; they had no choice." Since then, she said, they had been jailed without bond, awaiting trial. The police had dropped the early allegation that these "dangerous criminals" had been "eyeing a bank" when first approached (which leads to the question of why they were approached at all); apparently their Vancouver offenses were being minimized to remove obstacles to extradition to the United States, or so it appeared to their attorney, Judi Gedye. "We don't know why the Oregon authorities are lying low since they first announced their indictment, unless it's because they haven't got much of a case; so far, they haven't actually indicted Dino and Gary nor filed for extradition. All they did was make a fuss at the time of the Vancouver charges to influence the atmosphere up here; they really got the police and the authorities hyped up about dangerous killers, just as was done in Peltier's case, and they're going through all that leg-chain stuff all over again. But the prosecutors also know that after the Peltier case, all that fabricated evidence, people up here are better educated; the public might assume that U.S. evidence in the Pier killing is fabricated, too. They'll have to put together an airtight case to get away with extradition a second time. Even if they can't put a case together, the U.S. authorities may go through the motions of indicting the Butlers and filing for extradition when the trial comes up here in Vancouver, just to help the local prosecution with publicity."

Nilak is small and ebullient, in braids, with a round pretty face that she can turn squinty-eyed and mean when something upsets her; she is articulate and fiercely loyal to the struggle of Indian people in general and to a certain Tututni Indian in particular. At supper in a Chinese restaurant downtown, she filled me in on Dino's situation, and afterward we continued our discussion on a bus ride to East Vancouver, where the Butler support group is located. On the bus, an excited young man asked us, "Are you talking about the Butlers? I saw them arrested on TV! One of 'em was this good-looking guy, *strange*-looking, he had something in his eyes, some kind of *power*!" Nilak winked at me and nodded. "Dino," she murmured. The young man said, "It really got to me. And when they took him into the police car, he looked back at the camera, and I *saw* something"—he frowned, groping for the word—"some kind of deep resignation . . ."

A tall handsome young woman who is carrying Butler's child was cooking fish for young Butler supporters perched on scavenged mattresses that filled the hall and doorways of the small apartment. "When people hear my name these days, they think I'm Dino's *sister,*" Nilak said later, rolling her eyes, but there was no note of bitterness or complaint. "Dino and I, we're not together anymore, but we *work* well together, and we'll always be partners, no matter what; we've been through too much to let anything personal get in the way." She was silent again for a few moments, then burst out resentfully, "That's what people don't understand about us, and that's why I hate it when people talk of a feud between Kamook and Anna Mae. I lived with those two women, and there was no such thing, it was all exaggerated by people who didn't know jack shit. Kamook and Anna Mae were both strong women, *very* strong women, and they still trucked together after that, and they got busted together, too. Sure, Kamook was upset, that's natural, but she never let on about it, never laid it on the rest of us; she took care of her feelings by herself."

The next morning, Nilak drove me to Burnaby, just east of Vancouver, where Oakalla Prison sits like an old-fashioned dark red-brick fortress on a long slope overlooking the Fraser River Valley and the dark rainy mountains of British Columbia; she would wait in the prison parking lot while I was inside. "Any message?" I said, and Nilak smiled sleepily, with a big yawn. "Hello-o-oo," she said softly to the man in prison.

On the wallboard behind the guard at the outside gate was a warden's memo ordering a thorough search of today's visitor to Darrelle D. Butler. In the visiting room, a small well-made Indian in green prison fatigues took my hand limply and did not look me in the face. There had been warnings that this silent man might not talk to me at all, and for a time he just stared down at the table. His long braid and thin mustache gave him an old, Asian look; the round unblinking eyes and sad expression conveyed the appearance of "deep resignation" observed by the young man on the bus, but there was also that stillness of someone who knows where he is going and does not look back.

Dino Butler had no real reason to trust me, and his wary silence was intensified by the presence of a big prison guard who stood over us, arms folded on his chest, alert for the first sign of evil doings. But after ten minutes or so, the guard withdrew from the room and did not come back, and we both relaxed, and gradually Butler began talking of his own accord, describing his childhood and the drinking that had led to most of his arrests, his prison experience, his redemption by AIM, together with some reflections on Oglala, arriving eventually at his present troubles, which could put him in prison for the rest of his life.

"After I got out of jail, back in '76, I avoided getting involved with my Tuni people—the white man spells that 'Tututni,' but my grandmother told me that the old people called themselves 'Tuni.' The law was on the lookout for me after Cedar Rapids, and if I went to my people, they would be hassled and disrupted at a time when the last Indians in the Rogue River country—there was some small tribes there and we got terminated, and our good timberlands got terminated, too—were trying to reorganize themselves and get back a little land for what they were calling the Siletz Confederacy.[11] Anyway, I kept hearing about this white man over in Toledo who was boasting on the job about the easy money he was making robbing graves, maybe six hundred dollars every time he went out. He was working for this big lumber company, and he didn't know that the guy he was boasting to was married to one of our people. Then two elders caught another white guy digging and confiscated his equipment and filed a complaint with the police. There was an investigation, but the local police did nothing, or the state police, either, so the grave robbing continued. Maybe the pigs themselves got in on it—we think so. Anyway, this guy from Toledo was one of those investigated, and now the police are saying that he had promised to give back all the things he stole, and that the two medicine bundles they found in the back of our car were part of what he intended to give back; that's their excuse for trying to hang this thing on me and Gary." Butler sighed. "Well, I feel that the spirits are with me still, or we wouldn't have got out of that car alive; and Gary's learning the spiritual path, and he's fasting now to protest the leg chains and all the rest of the harassment. Those chains just represent their hatred for the Indian people."

Although Butler makes no secret of his detestation of the looting of Indian burial grounds by greedy whites, his feeling of outrage and anger on this subject is shared by Indian people all over North America[12] and is no evidence of any participation in Pier's death. Having no right to ask if he had any knowledge of the killing, in which three men were reportedly involved, I asked instead for his first impressions of the former Kelly Jean McCormick. Butler fixed me for several seconds with those round dark eyes, as affection for Nilak and warm mirth softened his gaze; then a delighted grin burst on his face, the first time he had smiled since we met. "I think she fell head over heels in love with me!" he said, and laughed aloud, so infectiously that I burst out laughing, too. I warned him that Nilak was right outside the prison, that I would ask for her side of the story, and he laughed some more, nodding his head, as if he could just hear her indignant response, and could hardly wait. ("Oh-h, *sick*ening!" Nilak sighed, when I reported Dino's answer to my question; she was blushing, amused, and a little angry all at once. "We have two different memories, for sure!" Lost in those memories, this talkative person was silent most of the way back to Vancouver.)

When the guard came for him, Butler stood up and shook hands, looking me full in the face for the first time. In the corridor, as he turned the corner toward the cells, he stopped short, turned halfway around, and gazed back for a long moment through the glass window of the closing door, as if to seal our meeting, as if to say, *We have trusted you: now be responsible.* Whatever it was, the small figure in the prison corridor with the big guard starting to agitate beside him was sending word, and I recalled what Leonard had once said about Dino, that somehow they communicated best when sitting face-to-face and saying nothing.

Two months later, I received a wry letter from Oakalla. "All of a sudden we have been declared a high security risk and that's why the quick change in our custody and treatment. We are up on death row where Peltier was held, our doors are not only locked in the conventional way but have chains welded on and padlocked. I heard five different versions of why I might be here, and as lies go, they make no sense at all. The reason we're here is, we never gave them any reason in six months to put us here, so they created the lies . . . to subdue our spirits and morale. We are not allowed religious ceremonies, and everywhere we go, we have to wear shackles on our hands or on our legs, if not both. Incidentally, we have refused to walk into their courts with their shackles of hate and racism, so they choose to drag us in and out. . . . So that's how it goes nowadays for me, nothing out of the ordinary. . . . Take care. Dino."

⊡

Headed south for Pine Ridge on June 23, Bob Robideau followed the open rangeland road that leaves the highway at Hermosa, curving southeastward and crossing the Cheyenne at the frontier of the Badlands desert country assigned nearly a century ago to the Oglala. Though he doesn't say so, it seems clear that Bob feels most at home in South Dakota, where he made his commitment to the Indian people in 1973; he would like to find a home in the Black Hills.

A mountain bluebird crossed the road where it turned to dirt and gravel, and a little farther on, a prairie falcon. Crossing dry plains between lines of silvered posts, our way descended to a green feather of cottonwood where White Clay Creek flows into the White River. Red Shirt Table, Lone Man's, then Oglala; a solitary store and a few cabins lie scattered out from the green water tank that marks the brown and treeless tract called Oglala Housing. Bob pointed at the turnoff by the store, which sits out on the decrepit county road known as Highway 18. "That's where them BIA cops pulled us over, on our way back from Colorado late that August," he said. "I told everybody to get their guns ready, and I remember Mike Anderson saying, Leonard ain't gonna like this, and I said, Leonard'll like it fine. But I was able to persuade the cops that we were strangers, just looking for an old friend there in Oglala Housing, and so a shoot-out was avoided."

Heading east, Bob turned off at the junction of Highway 18 with the loop road, the BIA "school road," that circled back west around the shoot-out area. He stopped where it crossed the narrow culvert under the road—closed off now by spiderwebs and weeds—through which the group had escaped into the open hills after the shoot-out: it was hard to believe that people crouched among these scraggy cottonwoods had gone unseen by the cars passing on this road. At the Pumpkinseed house, from where Coward and Stoldt had made their fabulous sighting, we tried out a pair of good binoculars on the people convening at the Little cabin across White Clay Creek; we could make out no one.

Then we followed the school road out to Highway 18 east of Oglala and returned to the Jumping Bull property by way of the dirt track across the pasture.

At the Little cabin, in a kitchen full of people, Ellen Moves Camp laughed with pleasure at the sight of Robideau; she makes no secret of her admiration for the outside Indians who risked their lives here on Pine Ridge. "There's so many things that still come back to me about that day! Grandpa Harry was down there at the corrals loading them steers at five-thirty that morning, and I remember Little Joe saying how he would stay home that day and wash his clothes; he never got the chance. And later Grandpa Harry said he found a lot of blood down the hill a ways that couldn't have come from anyone but Joe; they must have dragged him up there to where Grandpa and Grandma seen him, which is why he had all them leaves and sticks stuck in his hair." I had heard this tale before, and so had Bob, and when we did not comment on it, Ellen Moves Camp, who is lively and humorous, shrugged and sighed; it didn't matter. "Two days before that, I warned Leonard that something was going to happen; I seen too many of them people standing in bunches and shooting guns around."

Her son, Sam Moves Camp, the young medicine man named in the Dog Soldier Teletypes as a co-conspirator, said, "There are four qualities very important to the Indian people—bravery, generosity, fortitude, and knowledge—and Leonard had all of 'em. He's a fine man!" Everyone nodded, and two people repeated, "A fine man!" And Ellen Moves Camp said, "Leonard was never a troublemaker; he always tried to stop trouble before it got started. He took a lot of time, and he saw all sides; he was never a vicious man. Leonard is truly big-hearted, kind-hearted." Bob Robideau nodded without comment, and Sam Moves Camp said to him, "Mom was fasting for you guys, and praying; that's how she felt about it."

"Well," Ellen said, "the AIM people stood up for us until our own men could stand up for themselves. And the West Coast bunch didn't drink, and they didn't fool around; they were hard core, and we knew that we could count on 'em."

As she spoke, a handsome Indian in a red shirt who had gone outside when we arrived reappeared in the doorway; he paused there a moment, as if uncertain about entering, and Ellen Moves Camp said, "Here's the hard core now." Despite the sardonic harshness of her tone, her expression was affectionate and sad; she watched the man in the red shirt come to the table and stick out his hand. "I'm Louie Moves Camp," he said; he glanced at his mother and his brother, who were looking away ("My people looked away from me," Myrtle Poor Bear said), and then he said, "I'm helping my people now, best way I can."

In the silence, Louie Moves Camp chattered rapidly about Arco Oil Company attempts to acquire leases on reservation land. But nobody commented, and he said bravely, "I'm an Indian by the way I look but not by the way I act; I drink and I use drugs and I don't like people." When the silence continued, he said in a strange voice, "It used to be an honor for an Indian to go out and steal horses; now they throw you in jail." At this, everyone laughed hard, to put Louie at ease; he was doing his best, and his persistence showed courage. But soon he got up and went out again, and he did not come back.

"Even the goons call themselves AIM people now," somebody said.

"Instant AIMers!" Ellen exclaimed, setting out coffee cups.

"Well, they have a pipe, and they are praying—it's a start." Sam Moves Camp sighed. "And maybe their children will take it on from there." Though he gazed down at the table, I had the feeling he was speaking to me. "Our main problem is to forget the past, help people improve—don't call another man a thief or rapist. We don't agree with the priests here, who won't bury a bootlegger; their job is to pray for them, not to refuse them." Moves Camp raised his eyes to mine. "One of these days, everything will turn; it's slow but it's coming. For the last two years, here in Oglala, we have had sun dances again. We have to re-educate the people to Indian way: don't choose this table over this man"—he rapped the table—"because you can make another table but you cannot make this man again. The white man will learn, too, they say, but we're not supposed to teach him everything at once, he must redevelop in a natural way."

⊡

At Oglala Housing, Russell Loud Hawk, an alert wiry man with a worried expression, verified an interesting story about the day of the shootout that had been told to me by Dino Butler. "Cora Shellwoman was that old lady's name. She's dead now, but she told me twice that there was a lot of activity in the hills up around her place that morning and that those armed men just stood around waiting for something; and she said they left there fast, soon as the shooting started." Russ Loud Hawk shrugged, as if to say, If you don't wish to believe this, that's up to you.

In the room with Loud Hawk were his son Sam and two Indians from Camp Yellow Thunder. One was a dark lanky Indian with long wild hair and a dead eye and a broad mouth set in an involuntary grimace; a metal arm hung down from his left shoulder. This man had come home in one piece from hard combat in Vietnam, only to nearly lose his life after a car crash in 1974; his left arm and an eye had been lost in an explosives accident here in Oglala two years later. Reminded of Nilak Butler's story of the car crash, he made a harsh sound that might have been a laugh. "They drove me up to somebody's trailer, and they were in there drinking beer while I was outside in the cold, bleeding to death. *That's that June Little, they said. Let him die.*"

Beside June Little sat a heavy-set silent Indian who watched me with no sign of expression; this was Kenny Kane, a Means lieutenant jailed after the Sioux Falls courthouse riot, and one of the Indians accused with Robideau and Butler of the hacksaw-blade escape attempt from Rapid City jail in April 1976. Kane and Little had come to see the Loud Hawks about the proposed occupation at Wind Cave National Park by the Pine Ridge Tribal Council. The Tokala, or Kit Fox Warrior Society, a full-blood group restored in 1977 in a religious ceremony led by Harry Jumping Bull, to resurrect and maintain the dying Lakota language and traditions, had been reactivated after the Camp Yellow Thunder occupation, and Russ Loud Hawk, who was now Tribal Council representative from the White Clay District, was making sure that the council participated in this last desperate fight for the Black Hills. June Little doubted that council president Stanley Looking Elk would defy the warnings being issued by Governor Janklow, who had tried to laugh off the Camp Yellow Thunder occupation ("Just a bunch of kids camping out") but had told the media that any attempt at a second occupation would be stopped; Little believed that the entire Oglala community, Grandma Jumping Bull included, should abandon this spiritless government housing and move into the Hills, with or without Tribal Council participation.

"I'm going to take Stanley up there this afternoon," Russ Loud Hawk said, "and pick a site, and try to figure out the best way in." He looked worried again, shaking his head. "I'll have more trouble with the FBIs over it. They're still after me about the shoot-out, you know, trying to prove that I went in there with horses and took my boys out."

I didn't ask whether he did or not, and he didn't volunteer the information, and in a sudden silence, Sam Loud Hawk, a big quiet man who had not spoken, left the room and went into the kitchen.

"We still think about Leonard here, and pray for him," Russ Loud Hawk told Steve Robideau, breaking the silence. "And the spirits say that he will get out of prison. But Indian troubles are not over; we still have a very long way to go." The men nodded, and fell silent again. Then June Little spoke, looking at no one. "Skins have a lot to relearn," he said, "a *lot*. We got too far away." Although they knew that Steve Robideau would not have brought here a white man whom he did not trust, Steve himself was still an outside Indian, and anyway, the local people were suspicious and afraid of too much close attention to Oglala. As late as May 1977, FBI agents had visited June Little to question him about the death of Anna Mae, in an ongoing campaign of harassment against Oglala suspects whom, for one reason or another, they had not brought into court. According to the FBI report, Little had become "abusive," telling them not to return without an Indian policeman who had jurisdiction. Now he stretched out his long legs, gazed at his boots, then said in a low matter-of-fact voice, "Whatever the *wasicus* did, it's going to come back on them."

⊡

June 25, the anniversary of the Custer battle, was a day of high clouds and bright sun. From Hot Springs, in the southern Hills, the road led north into Wind Cave National Park, a rolling grassland that flows down into Buffalo Gap from the dark ridges of ponderosa pine on the east slope of Paha Sapa. The grazing animals, the hawks, the yellow coneflowers and sweet clover, the sego lilies, bellflowers, and wild rose, made one wonder how this country must have looked in the lost days when the first Lakota came to it across the Plains.

> The various entrances to the Hills were very rough and rugged, but there was one very beautiful and easy pass through which both buffalo and Lakota entered the Hills. Every fall thousands of buffalos and Lakotas went through this pass to spend the winter in the Hills. *Pte ta tiyopa* it was called by the Lakotas, or "Gate of the Buffalo." Today this beautiful pass is denuded of trees and to the white man it is merely "Buffalo Gap."[13]

Pronghorn antelope wandered near the road, and a car full of young Indians drove off into the meadow for a better look at an old solitary bull bison, up to his knees in the rank grass. No Indians would show up at Wind Cave before afternoon, even if Stanley Looking Elk did not lose his nerve, everyone said. "You know Indians," Bob grinned. "Take 'em all morning to get it together." But by early afternoon more than one hundred people were already at the site, on an open hillside near a tract of pine by the buffalo corrals at the north end of the park. To the music of transistor radios and Lakota drums, tents of every shape and size were being set up within walking distance of a portable latrine, and Looking Elk, a round-faced man with close-cropped hair and a certain resemblance to Dick Wilson, sat on a camp chair near a trailer, laughing uneasily and shaking his head, as if still unable to believe that a tribal council had invaded a national park without a permit. "First they promised us there would be no police, but of course them white-man promises never meant too much, so we snuck up on 'em Injun-style, took 'em by surprise! If Russ Loud Hawk was a woman, now, I would have kissed him!"

"Stanley almost had a heart attack," Loud Hawk said later, his boyish face lit up by a fine smile. "He *said* so! Because that night when we come up here to look things over, there were cops all over the place on the main roads, and we had to figure they were getting set to stop us. So I decided to take the people in real early, using the dirt roads up through Buffalo Gap, the buffalo trails and cattle trails that have been there since the old days. About fifteen cars came up over the hills, we was in here around about seven a.m. And sure enough, there was a big bunch of state police and sheriffs, even FBI—we really took 'em by surprise! They were facing the wrong way, toward the main road!" Loud Hawk laughed in real delight. "Well, they didn't know what to do. There we were, already on federal land, and they realized that the state had no authority to move us out."

The Oglala Tribe intended to remain in the Black Hills after its two-week permit had expired, in order to force a hearing in federal court on its right to be there. (While campaigning in South Dakota, Ronald Reagan had said, "We will honor all treaties"; instead, the Reagan administration, while doing its best to prop up the nuclear and armaments industries, had eliminated over four hundred jobs on the job-poor Pine Ridge Reservation and gutted the funding for social services such as the crisis center for would-be suicides.) The following week, the Wind Cave site was named Crazy Horse Camp, and June Little, Kenny Kane, and others moved over from Camp Yellow Thunder to make sure that Looking Elk didn't lose his nerve. "We're not in the Hills for a weekend or a month—we are here to stay,"[14] said Ivan Star Comes Out to "a Deputy Assistant Secretary of the Interior for Indian Affairs"[15] sent out from Washington to try to head off an embarrassing confrontation with the government. "You can't help us," this well-meaning man with Choctaw blood was told by elder Matthew King, who waved a cane at him. "You know that. You are part of the government. I don't believe anything you say."

CHAPTER 20
RED AND BLUE DAYS

The white people have to surrender their arms to the Great Spirit.

This purification is coming real soon, and all the guns and gold will melt. The holy spirit, the atom, the power of god, will melt those guns and tanks and poison gasses they create. . . . They will be standing by themselves. . . . When the time comes, there won't be no amnesty.

We're going back to the beginning of time. . . . I have no fear, I have no slightest fear whatsoever. Even if I have to face death like Chief Big Foot, it's very beautiful.

We hold the key to eternity, where it is beautiful and it is everlasting for everyone. That's where we're going. We're going home. And finally, we will be back in the Great Spirit's hands again—Grandmother's arms again. She'll cradle us in her arms again.

Wallace Black Elk (*Lakota*)

At Oglala, on June 26, 1981, the people prepared the feast and give-away that would take place after the memorial for Joe and Anna Mae; there would also be a naming ceremony for the baby born in recent weeks to Steve Robideau and his young Oglala wife. At the Little cabin, a fire pit was filled with wood, and a caldron heated, and soon a red pickup truck arrived with a dead cow on the bed. The cow was skinned out by a crowd of cheerful amateurs armed with dull knives, while others fetched wood and hauled water for the cooking fire; then the cow was axed and hacked into ribs and quarters. At a table set up among the small trees west of the cabin, Roslynn Jumping Bull and Angie Long Visitor worked side by side, carving the beef into small pieces, and Ellen Moves Camp, directing the butchery, called out to Bob Robideau's former wife, "Come on, Andrea! Be a nice little Indian woman and help with all this meat!"

In the hot dry sun, Jean Bordeaux walked hand-in-hand along the bluff with Nilak Butler, who had come all the way from Vancouver for the memorial. In Vancouver, trying to tell me of Jean's mother's death in March, Nilak had become flushed and upset three months after the event. "Evelyn was returned to the earth on the first day of spring, in Rosebud—she went home."

Steve Robideau introduced me to Leonard Peltier's pretty children by a former Oglala wife named Audrey Shields; next month, this little boy and girl would enter the steel doors of Marion to see their father for the first time in four years. ("When I was younger," Leonard says, "I thought it was a lot of fun running around like that, shaking off all those wives. Now I'm older, I realize I hurt a lot of those women, and I feel very bad about it, I really do. I think about them all the time now, especially the ones that had my kids.")

Emerging from the outhouse, John Trudell found himself confronted by a knot of people. "Okay, folks," he yelled, "office hours are over!" and everyone laughed. Trudell took his infant daughter from her Lakota mother and patted her asleep upon his shoulder; observing him, Steve Robideau said, "My brother John lost five people, and he's still working hard—that's *strong*. And you know what Tina was working on when she was killed? Water and water problems! And that is what's starting to happen all over now—problems with water."

From the south side of the Little cabin, the whole area of the shoot-out could be seen. On the lower edge of the hill pasture where it meets the river wood along White Clay Creek, young Indians were stripping timbers for the cooking fire from what was left of the old Jumping Bull corrals. Sitting quiet in the hot prairie grass up on the bluff, hearing the grasshoppers' wild ringing that must have filled the taut silences between shots at this same hour of the same day, six years before, I tried once again to sort out all the accounts and piece together what had actually taken place. The FOIA documents, still coming in, had clarified government methods and conclusions and made it plain that Peltier had been railroaded into jail. Yet the two critical events—how the shoot-out with Coler and Williams actually began, and how it finished—remained almost as obscure as they were that day when Edgar Bear Runner and the BIA Superintendent walked down this slope to that unmarked grassy flat where the bodies lay.

If—as the government tried to suggest—Agents Coler and Williams chased Sam Loud Hawk's red-and-white van onto the property, then the "lot of people around" referred to early in the agents' radio transmissions might have been onlookers in Oglala Housing, where the van had been driven earlier that morning. More likely, they were near the Little cabin, which before the shoot-out served as political, cultural, and social center for AIM activities in the White Clay District; here the traditional people would convene for sovereignty discussions, sweat-lodge preparation, and other matters. "There was never no 'ambush,' " Leonard says. "There were *always* a lot of people around, coming and going, and a lot of 'em visited our camp. Not that just anybody could drive in there to the Jumping Bulls', even though the security wasn't obvious, know what I mean? But one time two guys stayed two days and I never even knew it. And there were people living there whose names have never been mentioned, not even in the FOIA documents."

When we talked in Vancouver, Dino Butler had proposed a theory of how the shoot-out actually began. "This is just my opinion, and I can't prove it, but I really think this is what happened. The FBI knew we were organizing the Oglala people toward independence, toward sovereignty, which meant resistance to the mining leases. They wanted to clear out the last pocket of real resistance on the reservation, but they didn't know exactly where we were—it could have been Ted Lame's, the Jumping Bull place, maybe Wallace Little's. They knew Joe was one of us because they'd seen him at Custer for more than a week as a bodyguard for Banks, and that morning they spotted him in Oglala Housing when he went down there for a shower. They trailed the van back to Jumping Bulls', but they still didn't know just where the camp was, so after a while they started a little provocation; maybe they *wanted* to invite a warning shot, because they had people all around that area waiting to come in and back them up. So it sounds like they were ready to go in and wipe us out; all they needed was the excuse of that first shot. Anyway, those two agents ran into a lot more firepower than they expected, and when the backup people heard all that shooting, they just didn't go in until they got more reinforcement, and by that time, it was too late."

Peltier agrees with Butler's theory. "In fact," he says, "it was me who assigned Joe to be Banks's bodyguard, now that I think of it. Anyway, we knew we were a big threat to the government, being in that area, and we knew that they knew why we were there, because all we talked about to the Oglala people was self-sufficiency, the need to farm our own lands, the different stages on the way to sovereignty; this was our conversation with everybody."

Though Butler had been careful not to say so, Leonard told me that he was also in the van that went down that morning to Oglala Housing. "We were getting ready to go to Cedar Rapids on the support group for Crow Dog's sentencing the next day, but something was wrong with the ignition on the van—it didn't always kick over—so about nine-thirty, I took it in to a guy called Ears in Oglala Housing. And I was under the van when these two cars came in real fast, screeching around from house to house. And Ears says, Look at that! If any skin drove around here like that, they'd bust his ass! What the hell gives them pigs the right to come into our community and go squealing around like that! So anyway, Ears located a crossed wire—I felt like an idiot that I never found it—and after them agents left, we stood around a little while and bullshitted about a big deer he had seen a few times, and how to hunt it, and then we went on back to the farm. We weren't gone from Jumping Bulls' more than a hour, hour and a half, and we must have been back another hour before we heard the first shots."

Despite Mike Anderson's unwilling testimony that "the red and white and orange and white van" had been pursued onto the property just prior to the shooting, Peltier's contention that the van returned at least one hour earlier is supported by the government's own witnesses, including Norman Brown, who said he was with Joe Stuntz down in the camp when the shooting started. Lawrence "Doley" White Eyes testified at Cedar Rapids that he had been interrogated by the agents in Oglala around 10:00 a.m. (he also told a WKLDOC attorney that one of the agents had "pushed him around," but apparently he was too scared of retribution to testify to this in open court), or about the same time that Peltier and Ears saw the agents' cars go "squealing around" the housing. Also, John Stewart was prepared to testify that Peltier and others in his group had left Dorothy Brings Him Back's house at about 10:30 a.m. and that Jimmy Eagle had turned up sometime after, alerting them to the showdown that would soon occur. Stewart's tale fits the story told at Cedar Rapids by James Harper, according to which one agent came earlier to the Jumping Bulls' and promised to return when told to leave.

(In his controversial "double" 302, Agent Gerard Waring reported that Williams and Coler had left the Hacienda Motel in Gordon about 9:25 a.m. Since Gordon is twenty-five miles from Pine Ridge, this did not leave much time to go fifteen miles beyond Pine Ridge to Oglala, "squeal around" Oglala Housing, question Doley White Eyes and perhaps others, visit the Jumping Bull land, and still arrive back in Pine Ridge before 11:00 a.m. But as already noted, Waring's account conflicts on key points with all other 302s that have come to light, including a FOIA document [June 30, 1975], not turned over to the defense at Fargo, in which another agent states specifically that Williams left Gordon about 8:30 a.m., and Coler, about 9:00.)

At Cedar Rapids, neither side pursued the question of whether or not the agents had made an earlier visit to the Jumping Bull property on the morning of June 26, but evidence of such a visit crops up here and there in the accounts, and an FBI summary sent to special prosecutor Hultman on January 14, 1977, indicates that before Peltier's trial it had become part of the official version of events. According to this account, the agents arrived at Doley White Eyes's residence between 10:15 and 10:30 a.m. and stayed for "no more than five or ten minutes."

> Thereafter they drove to the HARRY JUMPING BULL property . . . where they stopped at a house where WANDA SIERS and WALLACE JUNE LITTLE, JR lived . . . shortly after 10:30 a.m. They probably remained there for five minutes or less and, thereafter, drove to the Pine Ridge Indian Police Office, where SA COLER [*sic*: it was Williams] was observed at 11:00 a.m.
>
> Sometime after 11:15 a.m. and no later than 11:50 a.m. SA WILLIAMS reported observing and following a red-and-white vehicle. Between 11:30 AM and 11:50 AM, both of their vehicles and the

> Agents were observed near the bottom of the hill below the WANDA SIERS residence. Also in this time frame, WILLIAMS radioed that three men were getting out of a red Scout with rifles.

This document (not released to the defense until the fall of 1981) raises a lot more questions than it answers. Was Mr. Hultman (and the jury) supposed to assume that this "red-and-white vehicle" (apparently derived from Waring's 302) was none other than Peltier's red-and-white van? Was it *also* identical with the "red Scout"—very different in appearance—from which the three men emerged with rifles? And precisely who observed the agents and their vehicles "near the bottom of the hill below the Wanda Siers residence" between 11:30 and 11:50 a.m.? There is no evidence of any such observation—or not, at least, in the documents released so far—which leads one to suspect an unidentified informer whose report may be the basis of other documents as well. Finally, this report skirts the nagging question of why the agents traveled twelve miles back to Pine Ridge village, only to turn around shortly thereafter and drive to Oglala for the second time that morning. In the absence of a definite answer, I arrived at an explanation of my own.

By June 1975, the FBI was unquestionably aware of Peltier's presence on Pine Ridge. Therefore it seems likely that the agents identified not Joe Stuntz but Peltier himself—or at least his van—in Oglala Housing, and that they decided that backup units would be necessary before any attempt at an arrest was made. Having trailed—but not chased—the van out to the Jumping Bulls', Agent Williams might have proceeded to Pine Ridge, twelve miles farther east, to coordinate support, leaving Coler behind on Highway 18 to make sure that the van did not leave the farm; whether or not Coler and/or Williams entered the property, this would explain why Williams separated from Coler, and also the midmorning return into Pine Ridge. (Several FOIA documents reveal that the FBI did not consider their radio communications "secure," and Williams may not have wished to reveal his urgent plan on his car radio.) There he conferred briefly with Hughes and Price at 11:00 a.m. On his way out of town a few minutes later, Price observed Coler coming in, and another FOIA document records a subsequent interview with both Coler and Williams in the Law and Order office of the BIA with an officer whose name is blotted out but who may be identified by other details in the report as either Glenn Little Bird or Robert Ecoffey, probably Ecoffey.

> ( ) stated that during this conversation, he told Agents WILLIAMS and COLER not to go out to the JUMPING BULL community alone and that they should wait for a couple of units to assist them . . . he finished his conversation with Agents WILLIAMS and COLER, at which time he and his partner ( ) left the Law and Order office . . . and . . . drove to Batesland, South Dakota, to check out the burglary report. ( ) added that both he and ( ) left prior to Agents WILLIAMS and COLER. ( ) advised that he thought Agents WILLIAMS and COLER were going to wait for his return and that both Agents WILLIAMS and COLER would accompany him and his partner ( ) along with another unit to the JUMPING BULL community.

To date, the activities of Coler and Williams in the period between this interview and the first radio transmissions are unaccounted for. The Indian police must have departed from Pine Ridge shortly after 11:00 a.m., since they had traveled twenty-six miles east to Batesland and had already checked out the burglary report when they heard the distress calls on their radio and took off for Oglala. In addition to headquarters radios, a number of BIA and FBI automobiles were tuned in that morning to the FBI frequency, yet no communication between the two agents was reported until shortly before 11:55, at least three quarters of an hour after they were last seen in Pine Ridge—a very long time to be out of contact with a working partner on a search, unless the two were together in the same car, or had left their cars, perhaps to talk with someone. The alternative explanation is that the two *were* in communication, and that the transmissions that led up to the shoot-out have been suppressed.

On July 9, 1975, *The Washington Post* described an exchange between Williams and Coler "in which one agent advocated pursuit of a red pickup truck. The other told his partner to make sure the gas tank was full." An FBI spokesman (Clay Brady) at Pine Ridge confirmed that "they were after a truck" and said there was "no particular reason" that the truck incident (which emerged in a federal affidavit justifying the arrest of David Sky) had not been announced earlier. "The South

Dakota law enforcement communications department tape-recorded the conversation between the slain agents prior to the shoot-out and recorded their plea for help after the gunfire began. South Dakota Attorney General William Janklow, whose office oversees the law enforcement communications network, confirmed that the state did record the FBI communication but declined to say what was on the recording. He said the FBI had asked him to keep the information confidential."

Why was the FBI unwilling to release these tapes, which would have resolved all the conflicting versions of the transmissions? What do these tapes reveal? Why were the defense attorneys told later by the state police (prior to the Cedar Rapids trial) that no such tapes had ever existed, even though the state Attorney General had "confirmed" their existence? Who is lying here, and for what reason?

Assuming that those tapes do not exist, or reveal nothing—assuming, in short, that the radios were silent—then Williams and Coler, in the same car or separately, must have stopped somewhere to speak with someone. And if so, there is some reason to suppose that that someone was the old Eagle-spotter Marvin Stoldt, whose SWAT team just happened to be on maneuvers in the area on the day of the shoot-out, and who, as it turned out, was "the first unit to respond there for assistance," according to Stoldt's own testimony to the grand jury on November 24, 1975. Is Stoldt saying he was there ahead of Agent Adams? Was Stoldt's five-man SWAT team the group of armed men waiting in the hills that was reported by old Cora Shellwoman? Was it this group, perhaps, that observed the agents and their cars "near the bottom of the hill below the Wanda Siers residence" between 11:30 and 11:50, and were they carrying out this surveillance after consultation with Coler and Williams?

Linda Price heard Agent Williams say, "We are following a red vehicle, you want to keep an eye out for it." If "we" was Williams and Coler, then who was "you"? Could "you" have been Stoldt and the SWAT team? Or was it BIA Police Chief Del Eastman, whose location just prior to the shoot-out is not recorded? (If Mrs. Price's memory is accurate, this transcription makes it almost certain that the chase began *outside* the farm, since "you" was presumably not hidden on the premises.)

If Stoldt's unit *was* the first on the scene, then, like Gary Adams, he arrived well before the death of the two agents. By his own account,

Stoldt "approached up in my police unit, up to Jumping Bull Hall, trying to get down in there. . . . I drove up as far as Jumping Bull Hall and there were people beginning to shoot at me. I was receiving heavy rifle and pistol fire from that area . . . so I requested assistance. I was told to pull back. . . . I think that order probably came from Del Eastman, he was in charge at this time."

Just a week later, on July 2, 1975, Marvin Stoldt quit the BIA police for good; not long thereafter he moved away to Denver. Queried about this strange circumstance by a grand juror, Stoldt claimed, not at all persuasively, that he had left the BIA police because "those two agents were my friends." He went on to say that he had known beforehand of a buildup by "militants," under cover of the Jumping Bulls' anniversary, and had warned his superior "to be leery of that particular area," but Eastman "didn't check far enough into it, I would say." Stoldt indicated that, in addition to his grief and exasperation, he had been persuaded to depart by "threats," although the source and nature of these threats was not made clear.

On June 26, 1976, during the Cedar Rapids trial, Stoldt was approached in Denver by a private investigator hired by the defense team, which had learned that the government had discarded the man who spotted Eagle (and Peltier) as a prospective witness for the prosecution and was curious to find out why. Stoldt told the investigator "that he had been acquainted with the two FBI agents who were killed (called them by their names), that they (BIA) had worked with the FBI on other matters prior to this incident, that these two FBI agents were known to him as being arrogant and abusive, that they (BIA officers) were to serve as a backup unit to the two FBI agents, that the FBI agents were aware of the explosive atmosphere which existed at the time and in fact were pre-warned about the same. Mr. Stoldt expressed that it was his belief that the FBI was testing the situation at Pine Ridge, that he (Stoldt) knew that 'there would be trouble.' That they heard the distress call (radio) come over the air from the two FBI agents, that they (SWAT team) were unable to assist the two FBI agents because of the heavy gunfire."

Two days after this report was written, the investigator told the defense team over the telephone that Stoldt had referred to Coler and Williams as "bad-asses," and that Stoldt was very frightened, saying that his life was in danger from both sides, but particularly from the FBI. On July 7, the investigator telephoned again to say that Stoldt would not answer additional defense-team questions, or talk at all, except to repeat that he now feared for his life.

In 1977, Stoldt was subpoenaed by the defense to appear at Fargo, where, to judge from the extreme evasiveness described earlier, he was still frightened. Defense attorney Lowe had promised that Stoldt would produce "some surprises," but on the stand, as we have seen, this stubborn witness refused to cooperate, taking refuge so often in "I would rather not answer" that the defense gave up on him very quickly. However, he denied having criticized the agents; all he had said was, "I told them they'd get in trouble if they went down there." Asked whether he thought the two were "troublemakers," Stoldt said, "I'd rather not answer that." He did say, however, that he had been warned that making an arrest in that community would be very difficult, and that (despite sworn testimony to the contrary by Trimbach, Adams, Hughes, and others) the FBI knew all about the AIM camp on the Jumping Bull land, which was "common knowledge."

Stoldt's testimony, very interesting despite itself, encourages still more interesting speculations. He acknowledges warning Coler and Williams: when and where did he do so, and under what circumstances, since the two agents seem to have operated as a team for less than twenty-four hours, from the period after 4:00 p.m. on June 25, when they set off for Oglala in search of Eagle, until approximately 12:10 p.m. the next day, when they were killed? Thanks to BIA Officers Ecoffey and Little Bird, the late afternoon of June 25 is well accounted for (though the agents' 302s or even rough notes for that day, if any, have never emerged): did Coler and Williams encounter Stoldt that evening when they took Charles, Draper, and Anderson into Pine Ridge for identification? Or did they meet him the next morning after their brief visit to Pine Ridge, in that period when their activities are still a mystery, at least to those not privy to those tapes? In that case, what did the agents say to Stoldt, and Stoldt to them, and why was he so certain they would "get in trouble down there"? Who appointed Stoldt's SWAT team as a "backup" in case of trouble, and why were those BIA roadblocks in place so quickly—no later than 12:18, when Adams reported the departure of the red pickup? Why is there no (known) report about this crucial meeting during which Stoldt says he warned the agents—assuming that it took place at all? And finally, why did the agents *require* warning, since the explosive atmosphere in the Oglala community had been well known since March?

Taken together, Stoldt's accounts bear out the reservation view that with the contempt for Indians that characterized FBI operations on Pine Ridge, Coler and Williams ignored the advice of the Indian police, invited a warning shot through nervous or aggressive behavior, then shot it out in the expectation of immediate support. And in fact, their backup units arrived in good time, only to retreat again in the face of gunfire from an unknown number of AIM "terrorists" and local Indians, not wishing to get killed on a white man's errand. If this account is roughly accurate, and if Stoldt was held accountable for the retreat, it might also explain his sudden "retirement" from the BIA police and his move to Denver.

⊡

Bob Robideau, in vest and cowboy boots, long black hair blowing, moved restlessly from group to group, settling nowhere; finally he squatted on his heels against the cabin side, gazing out over the river woods of White Clay Creek. Sensing something, I intruded on his privacy, asking him what his feelings were, being back here on Jumping Bull land on June 26. Bob gave me a brief wary look, then let a silence hang on this stupid question, which he recognized as an effort to smoke him out. After a time, he said shortly, "I don't feel no different. Why?"

After many days together, in California as well as South Dakota, this man and I understood each other pretty well. For Leonard's sake, as long as there was hope of a new trial, he had to be careful about what he told me, and trust to my good sense in what I wrote; once that trust was established, he had been as candid as he could be under the circumstances, which had changed considerably with the appearance of the FOIA documents. The Defense Committee and the attorneys felt that the time had come to tell the truth about Oglala, or at least most of it, and Bob (and Leonard and Dino, too) had been speaking much more openly about the shoot-out than he had fourteen months before, on that cold April day when we first visited this property.

"I was on security the night before," Butler had told me in Vancouver. "It was a very long night with a lot of rain, and I was tired, so I slept late; I remember the young girls were cooking pancakes. Norman Brown came and woke us when he heard the shots, and he ran up ahead of me. By the time I got going, and came up out of the woods, the Long Visitors were already on their way out, and I told them which way to go; they were hurrying toward the road, maybe a mile across that field, and the way they were moving, even with the kids, that distance could not have taken them more than ten minutes. Later they said that a car came along right away and picked them up, and that just down the road toward Pine Ridge, there was a big van parked, and someone was handing out weapons to white lawmen. So that was already happening within fifteen minutes after they left the compound!

"By the time I got up there, Adams and the BIA cops had already arrived, and the two Normans were shooting in their direction. There was a lot of automatic fire coming from the cars, and Norman Brown got pinned down by the outhouse; I could hear the bullets whack into the wood. Norman hollered at me that they had him trapped, so I let off a clip to keep their heads down while he ran for it; I was shooting an M-1 .30-06 with a top clip that day.

"At that time, them agents could still have got away without any trouble." Saying this, Dino had seemed vaguely regretful that they had not done so. When I mentioned the reported cross fire that might have held them there, the trial evidence that one or more people were shooting at them from around June Little's cabin, he shook his head. "There was no one shooting at them from June's cabin. All those shell casings over there were old ones, used for target shooting a few days before. So the agents could have gone back out that way, but they didn't. And the reason they didn't was because they thought that people were coming in there quick to back them up."

When I repeated this account to Robideau, he nodded in confirmation. He was silent a moment, as if making a decision, then spoke out quickly in a flat even tone, as if he wished to get something over with as quickly as possible. "Leonard was down there by that big elm near where them junked cars used to be. He never moved from that place during the shoot-out. I was up there by that old car past the green shack. Dino was over by that woodpile, Joe and Norman Charles were near him, and another guy and another guy whose names are not going to be mentioned, they were here and here—hell, there were Indians all over. What we couldn't understand was why them two men stayed right where they were, down in that field; they couldn't have picked a worse position in the first place. The least they could have done was backed them cars down into the woods—that would have been easy. Or at least run for those corrals, where they had a little cover. They didn't even *try* to take cover; the most they did was kneel down alongside their car. The rest of the time they just stood there, right out in the open. Of course, we was quite a ways away,* but even so, it's just amazing that they lasted as long as they did.

"I remember that one of 'em was trying to get into the car for some reason, probably the radio; by that time, I had taken that .44 from Joe, and when I let off a clip of five, that agent raised his rifle and let go at me."

I didn't ask him who had fired the first shot. By his own account and those of others, he had not been up there when it happened, and knowing this man's instinctive discretion, I felt it was conceivable that he had never asked and did not know; if he *did* know, and the truth would have helped Leonard, he would have told me. Not counting Poor Bear, the only known firsthand account was still Mike Anderson's rooftop story, but in the light of Anderson's earlier versions (in September 1975, in Wichita, and February 1, 1977, in Rapid City; what he told the grand jury in July 1975 is still unknown), there was no good reason to believe it.

On the other hand, the evidence suggests—to me, at least—that Coler and Williams had indeed been chasing one or more vehicles, and that whether or not those being pursued stopped at the Y-fork above the junked cars (not wishing, apparently, to lead the FBI cars either down toward the camp or up into the compound), the agents pulled up in that vulnerable place down in the pasture because they heard a warning shot or came under fire; if there is another persuasive explanation of the location and position of their cars, I cannot find it. (According to one report, the two cars had been pulled up in a defensive V, with the agents between them, using the engine blocks for protection; this isn't true, according to Robideau, who says the two cars were one behind the other, headed almost in the same direction.) Not that this means much in terms of Peltier's guilt or innocence, since even if it could be shown (it never was) that the red-and-white van was the vehicle in question, and that Peltier was driving it again just before noon—or even that Peltier emerged from the car and started shooting—no connection has ever been established between this event and the executions of the agents perhaps fifteen minutes later.

In the absence of any contradictory account from the defense—from the start, there has been total silence on this subject—it seems probable

* It was approximately 150 yards from the cabins—and also from Peltier's position—to the agents' cars.

that the Indians started the shooting. *Why* they did so, of course, is another matter; no onus is necessarily attached to the first shot. Perhaps the beginning of the fatal episode was trivial ("Maybe those guys in the truck got themselves chased because they flipped those two agents a bird," one Indian girl says, elevating a finger. "That's all it would have taken, the way things were"), but whatever the details, there seems to be no doubt that the agents repeatedly invaded hostile territory, sparking an impulse to drive off these hated intruders who had already been warned away at least once before. I imagine a wind of anger and a yell, a warning shot. When Coler and Williams stopped short in the pasture, someone may have fired in grim fun, not yet deadly serious, and instead of retreating, the agents fired back, without even improving their exposed position. And by the time they realized that the situation was out of control, that the backup cars—if they heard them come—had already retreated, long-haired figures were running here and there along the rim, shooting down at them from more vantage points than they could cover. In a few wild minutes, Coler had received that shocking wound, and Williams could not or would not desert him—the details, the degree of bravery, the precise order of events are lost. But a tension that had been gathering on Pine Ridge for almost a century burst like the lightning in the huge black skies of the summer thunderstorm the night before, and three men died.

With both agents wounded and one down, Robideau says, he ran down the slope to the edge of the tree line where Peltier was stationed and suggested that they take the two as hostages; cars were already arriving on Highway 18, they would soon be surrounded, and some sort of bargaining power was needed if they were going to survive the day. When Peltier agreed, Robideau went back up to fetch Butler, after which the three made their way down through the thick woods, then northward in the cover of the neck of trees, not far from the agents' cars; unable to see any sign of the agents ("Their heads never showed above the windows") but covered by the Indian guns on the rim above, they began to make their way toward the cars, taking advantage of the scattered cover of small trees.

Bob gazed at me like a poker player raising his eyes over his cards. It was now, he said, that a red truck "came down the road fast from somewhere up around this cabin. At the cars, it slowed down, maybe even stopped, though I never heard anyone get out; we couldn't see, because the truck was on the far side of them cars, but we heard the shots. Then the truck took off again up the hill, got the hell out of there."

Taken aback by this unexpected story, I stared at him; he didn't flinch. I asked why the defense attorneys had not revealed this, since SA Adams's report of the red pickup that fled the area at 12:18 seemed to confirm it. "We discussed it," Robideau said calmly. "But there was no way to prove it, not without getting them others into trouble, and anyway, it was decided that it was better to keep us out of the area of the cars entirely, not only because of aiding and abetting [even minor involvement in the commission of a crime could invite prosecution on this charge] but because it might have been too hard for a jury to believe what really happened."

When I grunted, still a little dazed, Bob said, "You see?"

How had that truck escaped through the BIA roadblock?

"Hell, there was people passing through them roadblocks all day long. They didn't really have 'em set up right, and we think that's because them agents jumped the gun before the rest of 'em were ready."

I supposed aloud that Williams must have thrown his gun down (Price had said he was wounded in his gun arm) before stripping off his shirt without unbuttoning it and trying to tie a tourniquet on Coler; perhaps he had waved that white shirt first in sign of surrender. Robideau shrugged. "I never seen no sign of surrender," he said. "But of course that could have happened while we was down there in the woods; maybe that's why we never seen their heads show in the windows of the car when we were creeping up there, trying to get the drop on them. If I had known they had surrendered, I would have hollered for a cease-fire; we would have taken them prisoners, taken them hostage, like I said."

Asked what the group would have done with two hostages who were probably bleeding to death, and who certainly could not have been taken along on an escape, Robideau gazed at me, unblinking. "I don't know," he said, after a while.

Trying to ease a sudden tension, I suggested that for a jury there would be a big difference between wounding the agents in a long-range exchange of fire and going down there to finish off the helpless men. What I wanted to hear, I guess, was some sort of moral disapproval of the "execution," because try as I would to understand the event in historical and sociological perspective, it was still horrifying in terms of the live victims (". . . a voice yelling for help, sounds like a scream. This voice was vague and appeared to be quite a long way off".[1]) I could not get Ron Williams's last minutes out of my mind—that panic, apparently intensified by the sight and sound of his maimed partner, which was so painfully evident on those radio transmissions ("Come on, guys! Come on, guys!"), the knives of terror in heart and temple as the depthless hole of the rifle muzzle rose before him, as his hand flew up before his face in the shocked realization that he was about to be killed *right now* by another man as crazed and frantic as himself. The long black hair, the sweating forehead, the wild eye squinched by the rifle stock—*NO!*—as Jack Coler, mercifully unaware (the experts say) of what was happening, sat slumped against the car, the light already fading from his eyes as the barrel of this gun or another turned toward him. As it had so many times before, this recurrent scene or something like it fled through my mind in that long moment while Robideau and I considered each other.

But Bob had no intention of claiming innocence for himself or for his partners; as in Dino's case, his wonder that the agents had not fled while there was time had carried an overtone of vague regret, but he was not going to let either of us off the hook by making excuses. In fact, he looked at me as if I were just obstinate; from the Indians' viewpoint—and increasingly from my own—any talk of innocence or guilt was beside the point. All the Indians who were here that day were warriors, and the nameless figures in the red truck were no more guilty than he and Dino and Leonard, because no Indian that day was guilty; the only thing that might have been questioned was the judgment of those men, and Robideau refused to question even that. "None of us was innocent," he said finally, referring to the three who were finally prosecuted. "We fired on the agents and we hit the agents: we participated. But we didn't kill them."

According to one veteran police reporter, Bob Robideau has "the eyes of a killer; I been around guys like this for a long time and I know the eyes of a killer when I see 'em." Perhaps what he is referring to is a kind of lidded ex-con look that reveals nothing; once Bob relaxes, his eyes open wide in disconcerting youthfulness. He has a good sense of humor and laughs at himself often, never attempting the mildest excuse for messing up in the course of his youthful burglaries, and taking complete responsibility for such fiascos as the badly fitted tailpipe that caused the near-fatal explosion on the Kansas Turnpike. He gives an impression of bare honesty even when, to protect others, he is not telling the truth; that you suspect he may be lying does not bother him, since he knows that you know that he has no choice. It is not "the eyes of a killer" that one sees but a certain deadliness of intent that makes one wonder if his cousin Leonard is only referring to Robideau's thin build when he refers to him as "Razor."

("Bob's got his faults, we all do," Leonard says, "but there's one thing we learned about him after all these years: if he says he'll do something, he's gonna do it. He speaks right out, he's very blunt, and he doesn't worry at all what the person thinks about him, but he's not someone who speaks rashly. Everybody that's met Bob through the years all like him; I've never run into anyone who said, I don't like that guy, I don't like his attitudes. The same goes for Dino. They're quite a lot alike in many ways. They're both very quiet and sincere, and they're both dedicated to the people's struggle. With them, it's not a romantic thing, the way it is with a lot of people, and they're still gonna be there when the going gets rough.")

After a pause, I asked if those men in the truck had finished off the agents so that there would be no witnesses, no one left to point a finger at the Indians who had participated in the shoot-out. Robideau shook his head. "I don't think they did it to eliminate witnesses. I think they just did it out of years of pent-up frustration and rage about not being able to do anything about the hopeless kind of lives that they were leading on this reservation." For the first time since I had known him, Bob Robideau, in a very controlled way, was upset and angry; his body was restless, and his voice had taken on a subtle thickness. "I've never killed anybody in my life," he said, "and I hope I never have to, because I hate the idea. But if I have to, I can do it, and I could have done it that day. We were just sick of being pushed around; we didn't care about them agents. They were shooting at us, and we shot back."

⊡

We went down the hill from the Little house, on the pasture road toward the corrals which the agents had descended that day to the place they died. A great blue heron lifted on slow summer wings out of White Clay Creek, and the noisy killdeer cried—*kee-dee, kee-dee*—from the fields near the Pumpkinseed cabin on the far side of the trees.

The old corrals were sagging with disuse. "Everything's grown up quite a bit," Bob said, inspecting the narrow neck of woods that he and Leonard and Dino used as cover in trying to sneak up behind the agents. Then he walked out, as he had six years before, to the foot of the steepening slope below the cabin where the white-over-tan Colorado car and the green Rambler had sat in the dead heat of midday summer. From this low place, all the two agents could have seen was the silvered wood of the root cellars in the long grass of the ridge line, and the dark doorway of the leaning outhouse on the bluff, and the shivering dark leaves of the trees that shaded the Jumping Bulls' white cabin, and the silhouettes of long-haired figures running down the hot pale sky of the Dakotas.

Everywhere, wild roses were in bloom. "Lots of sage here now," Bob said. "We had it pretty well picked clean when we was here, had to go all the way to Lone Man's for it." Near the Y-crossing between the green shack and the woods stands a big elm with a depression all around the base of the trunk where Peltier had lain during the shoot-out; not far downhill from this tree, inside the wood edge, is another large elm—very likely the one climbed by Eastman and Waring when they first saw the Colorado car. On this tree is tacked a weathered blue tin sign, #13—EXQUISITE, that advertised some unknown long-gone product.

Asked where the red pickup truck had come from, Bob glanced at me, then shrugged his shoulders. "There you go with them questions again," he said. I pressed him a little: had he seen it earlier? "Could have been up around the houses. I wasn't too aware of what was going on up there; from the time I come up from the camp, I was concentrating on them two guys down in the pasture. And I stayed pretty much over there on the south end, by the green shack; I never went among the houses until after them agents were dead. Anyway, the first time I saw that truck was when it started coming down the hill. Those other people up on the hill—so far as I know, they never saw who was in the truck because it cut back up the hill way over this side of the Jumping Bulls' and then went out."

When the red truck had gone, the three men crossed the pasture to the agents' cars. A shotgun was leaning against the rear bumper, and there was a rifle on the ground. "I didn't really look at them two bodies, but I noticed they was laying right beside each other by the left-side rear wheel of the car. While Dino and Leonard was searching 'em for weapons, I was gathering up whatever I could find. On the green car, in front, the radio was still going strong, and we could hear what was coming down on us. I figured we would have to leave here quick, and that we better know just what the FBIs were up to. I don't think I even asked Dino and Leonard; I just loaded the guns in the backseat and got in that car and drove straight ahead up over this hill and down toward our camp, flat tires and all. By that time there was a lot of cars arriving on the highway, and them guys up there was running around, trying to cover all sides; probably they never noticed me drive off. Draper was already down at camp, and I assigned him to listening to the radio while I headed back on up the hill to tell Leonard and Dino that there was law coming at us from all over, that we better get out while we still had a chance. Not that I really thought we had a chance."

Butler, Robideau, and Peltier were still down at the cars when Joanna LeDeaux entered the property. "I first seen her up there by that woodpile," Bob remembered, "and she started coming down the hill past them old root cellars; she got down maybe fifty feet before we waved her off. We were headed that way"—he pointed—"toward the Y-fork and our camp, so she kind of angles down across the slope to meet us. I guess maybe that was when I was moving that green car on its flat tires. Anyway, I seen Leonard get angry. Leonard don't get excited too often, but when he does, you can see it from a long way off."

(In his own account of the silence after the killing, when he and his partners had approached the bodies, Leonard had grunted, his face colorless. "I felt we were all dead," he said somberly. "I was feeling crazy because there were still women and children up there in June's cabin. When Joe come down there to the cars, I said to him, I think they're gonna kill everyone here. That's when I told him, This is the day to be a warrior, but all I could think of was, We gotta get *outa* here, or we're dead, too. So I was running back and forth, making sure that everybody was moving out; we knew what was coming. And all of a sudden I look up and see this *white* woman!" In a long pause, he shook his head, as if still stunned. *"Shock!* Where in hell did *she* come from! I had known her, you know, before she moved over to Porcupine a few weeks earlier; she was living right close to us for a while in Russ Loud Hawk's old house when we were living at Ted Lame's, and we became friends. I went over to investigate when she arrived, check out who she was, and I . . . stuck around." Leonard grinned, a little sheepish, then shrugged his shoulders. "I was going around with Jean Day, too—I was just . . . *happy!* But that day of the shoot-out, I got pretty excited—I did. I couldn't take it in—what was she *doing* there? Here was this white woman up there on the hill screaming, Stop! Stop! Stop *what*? What the hell's she talking about? I mean, this was a while after they were killed. Joe was back up there, and I hollered to him, Get her *out* of here! I wasn't trying to hurt her or nothing, she knows that, it was just shock. It was no use trying to explain to her what really happened, because it wouldn't do no good; no matter *how* it happened, they were going to kill us, and we all knew it.")

"When I got back up to the compound," Robideau said, "I seen this woman over by the cabins, and I went on over. She was asking if anyone on either side needed medical attention because there was an ambulance out on the road. Leonard was all hyper after what had happened, same way I was, and he calls over, *No!*—kind of rough, you know—No, nobody needs medical attention! And he told someone to get her out of there. But I guess she had looked over the edge of the hill on her way in, and she wanted to go down there and see if them agents needed medical assistance. She started to insist, and he got mad, yelling, Nobody down there needs medical assistance, because they are dead! What we need here now is ammunition! And that was the truth; our bullets were almost gone."

("Joanna said she wanted to help get the women and children out," Butler remembers. "All the women and children in the cabins had gone, so I took her down to our camp in the woods because I was worried about Nilak and the kids. I hollered around, but there was no sign of them; I guess that was when Nilak was off exploring for an escape route. So I sent Joanna back while I did some reconnoitering on my own. Leonard was angry that she was in there in the first place; I guess he figured that this white woman was the last thing we needed at a time like that.")

Nobody tried to explain to LeDeaux that they had not killed the agents, Robideau said; she had seen them down there at the cars, and even if they had felt like accounting for themselves, they did not really expect to be believed. However, he told her that everyone was upset and that she should not take Leonard's anger personally. "She understood that, but she was pretty upset, too, and I had to cool things out a little. I said, Look, it's okay, but there's nothing you can do, so just get out of here. Some of them Oglala women didn't like her so much—there was some kind of a personality problem—but she never said one word to the feds about who she had seen in there, or what, even though she spent eight months in jail.

"Leonard was still very distracted, and when he saw I was carrying one of the agents' revolvers, he asked me to try it out, although I told him it wouldn't carry very far unless I fired it up in the air. After we looked the situation over, we headed back down to the camp, leaving Joe and Norman Charles behind to keep an eye on everything until we got organized. Then Mike and Norman Brown come in, and Wishie took off up the hill to tell Joe and Norman Charles we were ready to go. Leonard still had this idea that we were going to make a run for it in the van; I think that was part of the same crazy state of mind that made him yell like that at Joanna LeDeaux."

I mentioned the account of SA Dean Hughes, in which the Indian who was hit was apparently wearing a white shirt; this seemed to confirm what some people had said, that Joe Stuntz had never put on that FBI jacket in which the agents said they found him. Yet the FOIA documents include reports from at least three people who saw him wearing it before he died. One of these people, accompanied by a deputy sheriff, had "gone up on a butte to observe the firefight":

> About 2:30 p.m. he saw an Indian in a green jacket killed. The Indian in the jacket and another man in a white T-shirt were shooting toward an area where he knows that Bureau of Indian Affairs officers were located at the time. The man in the green jacket was firing what he believes was an automatic weapon. When he was struck, this man dropped immediately to the ground. . . . The man in the white T-shirt dropped his own weapon, picked up the automatic weapon, and left the scene. He said he understands the FBI recovered a shoulder weapon by the dead Indian but said this is not the weapon the man was actually using.

On July 3, an unnamed Indian who lived near the Jumping Bull property informed the agents that he had been mending fence on the morning of June 26 when he heard "quite a lot of shots," both shotgun and rifle or pistol; when he left to go check on his family, "he could hear a voice yelling for help, sounds like a scream. This voice was vague and appeared to be quite a long way off, coming from the direction of the gunshot sounds." Subsequently he led some (unidentified) lawmen to "a hill . . . across from the shooting scene where he could see a man in a white T-shirt and another in a dark-colored coat standing by a green shack. Both of these men were shooting at something. As he watched, he saw the man in the dark-colored coat go down. He is not sure whether the second man was shot or if he knelt down to check on the man on the ground."

"Joe put that jacket on," Bob said. "Him and Norman Charles come down after the shooting. Norman found that rifle clip they took off him the day before, and Joe took that jacket."

("I seen Joe when he pulled it out of the trunk and I looked at him when he put it on, and he gave me a smile," Leonard remembers. "I didn't think nothing about it at the time; all I could think of was, We got to get *out* of here! And you have to know Joe: he wasn't smiling because he picked up the jacket, he was *always* smiling. You look at Joe, and he'll smile at you—that's the way he was, especially with me, because I was always joking with him, wisecracking." Remembering Joe Stuntz, Leonard smiled himself. "You would have loved him if you could have gotten any words out of him. Joe was a very gentle guy." Asked why they had taken the agents' guns and why they had never gotten rid of them, Leonard stopped smiling. "We took them because we didn't have real weapons," he said, "and it never occurred to us to get rid of them because it never occurred to us that we might be taken alive.")

It was Norman Charles who was wearing a white shirt that day, and who probably dove down when he was shot at, making BIA Officer Gerald Hill think he had hit him. The Indians do not believe that Hill killed Joe; they believe he was killed by SA Gerard Waring, drilled through the forehead by the only man in Hughes's squad with a sniper scope, and that the FBI gave Hill credit for the kill—he boasted of it to Gary Adams—because, from a public-relations point of view, it looked better to have that Indian killed by an Indian.

⊡

We walked along the grassy slopes west of the old fields on the plateau which have not been planted since the elder Jumping Bulls moved away; along this bluff the Long Visitors had fled, and Jimmy Zimmerman, hands high, had first been spotted from the highway. Off to the northeast was a high white butte, called Onogazi, or "Last Stand," according to Sam Moves Camp, who came down the hill to join us: Onogazi had been the refuge of Red Cloud's people, who retreated up there, fearing the worst, after news came of the massacre at Wounded Knee.

> We were going back to Pine Ridge [from Wounded Knee], because we thought there was peace back home; but it was not so. While we were gone, there was a fight around the Agency, and our people had all gone away. . . . We crossed White Clay Creek and . . . soon we could hear many guns going off. So we struck west, following a ridge to where the fight was. It was close to the Mission, and there are many bullets in the Mission yet. . . . While we were over at the Mission Fight, they had fled to the O-ona-gazhee and were camped on top of it where the women and children would be safe from soldiers. . . . Afraid-of-His-Horses came over from Pine Ridge to make peace with Red Cloud, who was with us there.
>
> Our party wanted to go out and fight anyway, but Red Cloud made a speech to us something like this: "Brothers, this is a very hard winter. The women and children are starving and freezing. If this were summer, I would say to keep on fighting to the end. But we cannot do this. We must think of the women and children and that it is very bad for them. So we must make peace and I will see that nobody is hurt by the soldiers."
>
> The people agreed to this, for it was true. So we broke camp next day and went down from the O-ona-gazhee to Pine Ridge, and many, many Lakotas were already there. . . .
>
> I did not know then how much was ended. When I look back now from this high hill of my old age, I can still see the butchered women and children lying heaped and scattered all along the crooked gulch as plain as when I saw them with eyes still young. And I can see that something else died there in the bloody mud, and was buried in the blizzard. A people's dream died there. It was a beautiful dream.
>
> And I, to whom so great a vision was given in my youth,—you see me now a pitiful old man who has done nothing, for the nation's hoop is broken and scattered. There is no center any longer, and the sacred tree is dead.[2]

At a grassy knoll just at the wood edge, the slope falls off steeply to the cottonwood flats along the creek. "Here's where I left that car," Robideau said over his shoulder, and kept on going down into the woods. In the cool shade of the big cottonwoods, in long fresh grass, he uncovered the old hearths where Dino's tipi and the cooking fire had been located. Sam Moves Camp offered us a handful of wild currants and showed me a plant called "kidney tea," good for the stomach; wild grape and poison ivy grew where sunlight pierced the heavy leaves of summer. By the creek bank was the stone circle where the small sweat lodge had stood; the skeletal lodge frame of cottonwood saplings, splayed and sagging, had been almost reclaimed by underbrush and humus. Across the creek, the wood margin was narrow, letting in sunlight from the fields that ascended gradually toward the school road.

Along the creek the pale clay mud was crisscrossed by the sharp prints of raccoons, and near the water was a tree gnawed long ago by beaver. I told Sam about the big footsteps in the creek heard on the night before the shoot-out by Jean Bordeaux and Jimmy Zimmerman and Norman Brown, and he nodded, saying, "That was a sign, a warning."

"There is your Big Man standing there, ever waiting, ever present, like the coming of a new day," Pete Catches had told me two years earlier, here on Pine Ridge. "He is both spirit *and* real being"—he had slapped the iron of his cot for emphasis—"but he can also glide through the forest, like a moose with big antlers, as if the trees weren't there. At Little Eagle, all those people came, and they went out with rifles and long scopes, and they couldn't see him, but all those other people at the bonfire, he came up close to them, they smelled him, heard him breathing; and when they tried to get too close, he went away. He didn't harm no one; I know him as my brother. I wanted to live over there at Little Eagle, go out by myself where he was last seen, and come in contact with him. I want him to touch me, just a touch, a blessing, something I could bring home to my sons and grandchildren, that I was there, that I approached him, and he touched me.

"It doesn't matter what you call him; he has many names. I call him Brother, Ci-e, and that's what the Old People would call him, too. We know that he was here with us for a long time; we are fortunate to see him in our generation. We may not see him again for many many generations. But he will come back, just when the next Ice Age comes into being."

On our return, Bob paused at the top of the hill, hands in hip pockets, and gazed around the Jumping Bull land, as if there were something he could not quite remember. Then he shrugged his shoulders and walked on. "At the Black Hills Survival Gathering last summer, we seen some of them people who were here that day. They just nodded to us, and kept on moving—didn't want to stop and talk about old times. Nobody talks about it much, even me and Dino, and that's probably best—only particular incidents, if there was something funny about it that we didn't understand. Maybe it's distasteful to us, or maybe because there is no *need* to talk. We were there, we seen it, we done what we had to do—why talk about it?"

⊡

When the work was finished, the women changed into fresh clothes, and everyone went over to the gravesite, which lies a few miles down the road on Wallace Little's property, overlooking the Little ranch in the valley below. From here there is no sign at all of the "bunkers" discovered by the FBI investigators in early June 1975. ("The Black Elk family had a burial up there along about that time," June Little says, shrugging contemptuously, "and that fresh grave was probably what them feds was looking at.") As the mourners gathered, a fast-food wagon pulled in among the cars to sell the Indians a few sticks of water ice in the dry heat; the glistening confection came in patriotic colors, a hard chemical red-white-and-blue.

The previous day, a fence had been erected, setting off the AIM warriors' graves from those of the Little family. Roslynn Jumping Bull said that the remains of Little Joe and Anna Mae would probably be moved to the Jumping Bull land, where the community felt that they belonged. "We'll have to talk to the medicine men first, of course, because it has to be done right," she said; the medicine man Billy Good Voice Elk, who had buried Anna Mae and assisted at Joe's burial as well, would be here today. A good-natured person who likes to laugh, Mrs. Jumping Bull regrets all her angry words when the place was ruined and her family harassed by the U.S. government after Oglala, and like almost everyone in this community, she feels grateful to the young AIM Indians who stood up for the local people on that day.

"Joe was a real good person," Jean Bordeaux sighed, "the same way Anna Mae was a good person, and Tina Trudell; they gave everything to everyone and never asked questions, never complained, as if taking care of other people was what they were there for. It's funny how people like that are always the ones to get killed."

Bare to the waist, his feather-tipped braids bound with ribbons of red and blue—the red of the day and the blue of *skan,* the sky—Steve Robideau welcomed the people, and Billy Good Voice Elk gave a ceremonial invocation in Lakota. With three other Lakota singers, long black hair blowing against the white bluffs of the Badlands, the medicine man commenced a sad high chanting song to the hard pound of the Plains drum, while Robideau made the ritual purification, taking the sacred pipe from its rack before the ceremonial fire and lifting it to the blue sky in the four directions. In the midday sun, in the good scent of dried cow dung and fresh grass, the transparent flame of the small fire made the green earth around it dance and shimmer, as a meadowlark sent its sliver of sweet song down the south wind. The wind quickened the red, black, white, and yellow flags at the corners of the graves, and the green flag that honored the earth Mother: the red flag represents the east, and the sun rising, and the spirit of day; the black flag is west, land of big mountains and dark weather and the sacred rain, of evening and darkness and the spirit of death; the yellow is south, the warm soft winds, the warmth that brings growth and harvest; and the white is north, the home of the giant Waziya whose icy breath brings cold and death, and the purifying snows that turn the autumn browns to green again when the land awakens in the spring.

> O You, sacred power of the place where the sun goes down, where we shall journey when that day comes to us. . . .
>
> Hee-ay-hay-ee, Tunkashila, Wakan Tanka, Grandfather, Great Spirit! Give to our people your red and blue days, that they may walk the sacred path in a *wakan* manner!
>
> O You, Grandmother and Mother Earth from which we have come, You are *wakan,* nourishing all things, and with You we are all relations.[3]

Robideau spoke of the sacrifices made by Joe and Anna Mae, and also by Dallas Thundershield and Bobby Garcia, who had paid with their lives for trying to help Leonard, and also by the family of John Trudell. He offered the latest news of Leonard and Dino, who sent greetings from prison,[4] and told of the fight against uranium contamination of their land and life by the Dine nation in the U.S. and the Dene in Canada, of the Six Nations people and many others now struggling for sovereignty, and of the support that Indian peoples of the Americas were receiving in the tribunals and world courts of Europe; and he spoke of the patience needed by reborn Indians such as himself, who were "lost in the cities and want to come back home."

John Trudell also talked about those Indians who had wandered away from their people's traditions and from the healing spirit and power of the earth. Moving restlessly, lifting his hands, he exhorted the gathering to give up the greed of the white man's way that had corrupted them, and return to the spirit of sharing and self-sacrifice that Joe and Anna Mae had died for. He warned the people of the ten years of trouble that were sure to come, trouble of the kind that their grandparents had known, because "this government is our enemy. It is owned by the money-makers, and they don't care about us, and that is the reality. They want to assassinate us; they did it to our ancient ones, and they are doing it again today by different methods. If we are to continue to survive, to endure, we must keep our spirit connection to our people who came before us; in this earth is where our power lies.

"The next generation, their spirit will be more strongly connected to the earth than ours. Many of us were lost out there; we made many mistakes, we became dependent on the white-man poisons, alcohol and chemicals, and it weakened our spirit power. But our little ones, they will have their power with them. This is what we want the young ones to understand: we do not engage with the U.S. government over ownership of land, because 'owning' land is white-man talk and white-man values; we engage with the U.S. government over the natural creation. We are a part of the natural world, and the white Americans are the enemies of the natural world."

Across from me in the circle of silent Indians stood a white woman named Candy Hamilton, a friend of Anna Mae and, for a time, a permanent WKLDOC aide on the reservation, where she has good friends; Candy had come all the way from North Carolina for this occasion, and as Trudell spoke of the white enemies, I wondered what she might be thinking. Earlier I had mentioned to Bob Robideau how disturbing it was to feel oneself—as I did at times—part of an unwanted and despised group, not just a stranger but an intruder, a *wasicu,* even an "enemy," and we had agreed that if all white people were exposed to this experience, race problems in America might diminish quickly. "White people just can't handle being disliked," Bob said, and burst out laughing.

Nilak Butler, dressed in a long skirt, was offering a message from Dino, which concluded:

> June 26, 1975, was the day I became a red man. It was the day that truth was born in my mind and heart, uniting me with my spirit and the spirits of all our ancestors. It was the day I learned about life without death. There was no fear in me for the first time in my life, and I knew I could never die, for the fear of death no longer limited my perception of life, which is everlasting. That is what my brother Joseph taught me that day, and I know he has not been lost in the past but awaits me in the future.
>
> I know that I can continue on no matter what burden I must carry. I will always stand with honor and dignity in the dust of my ancestors upon Mother Earth amongst my people—all people. I shall never be defeated by our enemy—that is my freedom. That is what Annie Mae taught me.
>
> We must always fight for what we believe in. We must never tire in our fight. It does not really matter how we fight, what matters is what we are fighting for. It is our right to live: that is our first right. That is why we fight for our unborn, for it is through them that our nations live on. If we have to shed blood for them—the unborn—it is only right. As it was right on June 26, 1975.

Despite her tough talk and fierce squint, Nilak is gentle, easily moved; though her voice never faltered, she was flushed with emotion as she finished reading and strode away from the sacred fire with her head high. She is "a brave-hearted woman," as the Lakota say, and a generous one. "I wish I could do some of Leonard's time for him," says Nilak wistfully, "I really do. And a lot of people feel that way, because he really stood up for us that day."

Cecelia Jumping Bull, now nearly eighty, came to the fire in a blue shawl and print dress and black laced shoes. Standing straight and still, the old lady spoke strongly to her people in their native tongue, which not all of them understood; her words were translated by Melvin Blacksmith, who told me later, "I am Grandma's son in the Indian way." Mrs. Jumping Bull thanked everyone for coming from so far to honor Little Joe and Anna Mae. "Six years ago, these boys lived on my land. I used to talk to them every day, especially their leader, Leonard, warning them that they must be very careful." The old lady described her return from Gordon, Nebraska, on that summer evening just six years before, how young girls at the roadblock up the way toward home had told her and Grandpa that their house had been shot up, and how, arriving at the ruined house, they had found a big crowd of armed white men "standing around the body of Little Joe in three circles like you are standing now. I became angry. My thoughts went back to World War Two, when my son got killed for America, got killed for these people who ruined my house and killed this boy. When the ambulance came to take him away, I told them he had died for his people, and they treated me roughly. . . . I have a right to be proud because I took care of these boys. I'm getting old now, and when I am gone, I hope that the people here today, and the AIM people, will bury me, and honor me." In this way, the old woman talked for a long time in the soft harmonies of her language, standing stone-still without once shifting her feet, hands folded on her breast as she gazed outward toward the high white monument of Onogazi, on the southern rampart of the Badlands.

In another quadrant of the circle, Bob Robideau stood beside his former wife. We met each other's gaze without expression. Although respected here, he had not spoken to the gathering, and somehow I felt certain he would not.

Earlier that afternoon, he had nodded toward a high ravine in the white hills to the northeast, where dark-green pines, black in the summer sun, rose to a point on the blue Dakota sky. "That's where old Noah Wounded's cabin was. Back up in there, maybe an hour's walk. When I come in, Leonard was sitting there with the old man, and he says, Noah wants a picture of a buffalo; can you do it? Because Leonard knows I've been drawing since I was five. So I looked at that old man a minute. Then I said I could, and he gives me an old raggedy piece of paper and a broke-up pencil, and I made the picture. Old Noah's dead now; I often wonder what he did with it." Bob paused to consider his words carefully, making absolutely certain that I understood. "You see, I didn't do that buffalo picture just because he *wanted* it. I did it because I realized that that buffalo was very significant to that old man in some old-time way."

NOTES

Although this book argues and supports the cause of the traditional Indian people and their allies in their long struggle with the U.S. government, I originally wished it to include as many views as possible on both sides of the question. I discovered, however, that federal judges, prosecutors, and law-enforcement personnel are rarely willing to comment on a case that is still being contested; also, their essential views are everywhere throughout the text, in field reports, memos, trial transcripts, court rulings, and many other documents, and any attempt to balance the argument with "official" comment would sink an already long book under the weight of rhetoric and repetition. For a concise summation of the federal case in *United States* v. *Peltier*, the reader is directed to the findings of the Federal Court of Appeals for the Eighth Circuit, September 14, 1978 (Vol. 585, Federal Reporter 2nd, p. 314); for a defense of the FBI position, to "Inquiry Concerning Indian Matters" (18 pp.), FBI, January 5, 1982.

⊡

Book I mainly concerns the historical, political, and economic background of the fatal shoot-out at Oglala; this information, which is critical to a true understanding of the events, comes from many sources, which are not always in agreement (sources for more controversial quotations and statements may be found in the chapter notes). I am particularly grateful to the authors of the following books and publications, all of which are highly recommended to the reader who wishes to investigate various aspects of the story in more detail:

Akwesasne Notes. BIA: We're Not Your Indians Anymore (Rooseveltown, N.Y., 1973).

———. *Voices from Wounded Knee* (1974).

Akwesasne Notes. Various issues, 1968–82.

Deloria, Vine, Jr. *Behind the Trail of Broken Treaties* (New York: Delacorte, 1974).
———. *Custer Died for Your Sins* (New York: Macmillan, 1969; Avon, 1970).
———. *God Is Red* (New York: Grosset & Dunlap, 1973).
Eastman, Charles A. (Ohiyesa). *From the Deep Woods to Civilization* (Boston: Little, Brown, 1916).
———. *Indian Boyhood* (New York: Dover, 1971).
———. *The Soul of an Indian* (Boston: Houghton Mifflin, 1911).
Erdoes, Richard, ed. *Lame Deer: Seeker of Visions* (New York: Simon & Schuster, 1972).
Mails, Thomas E., ed. *Fools Crow* (Garden City, N.Y.: Doubleday, 1979).
Neihardt, John G., ed. *Black Elk Speaks* (New York: Morrow, 1932).
Standing Bear, Luther. *Land of the Spotted Eagle* (Lincoln, Neb.: University of Nebraska Press, 1933).
Steiner, Stan. *The New Indians* (New York: Harper & Row, 1968).
Talbot, Steve. *Roots of Oppression* (New York: International Publishers, 1981).
Walker, J. R. *Lakota Belief and Ritual* (Lincoln, Neb.: University of Nebraska Press, 1980).
Witt, Shirley Hill, and Steiner, Stan. *The Way* (New York: Vintage, 1972).

Additional information, quotations, and epigraph material were taken from:

Andrist, Ralph K. *The Long Death* (New York: Macmillan, 1964).
Brown, Dee. *Bury My Heart at Wounded Knee* (New York: Holt, Rinehart & Winston, 1971; Bantam, 1976).
Brown, Joseph Epes, ed. *The Sacred Pipe: Black Elk's Account of the Seven Rites of the Oglala Sioux* (Norman, Okla.: University of Oklahoma Press, 1953; Baltimore: Penguin Books, 1971).
Bourke, John G. *On the Border with Crook* (Lincoln, Neb.: University of Nebraska Press, 1971).
Highwater, Jamake. *The Primal Mind* (New York: Harper & Row, 1981).
Jackson, Helen Hunt. *A Century of Dishonor* (1881; reprint ed., Minneapolis: Ross & Haines, 1964).
Johansen, B., and Maestas, R., eds. *Wasi'chu: The Continuing Indian Wars* (New York: Monthly Review Press, 1979).
McGregor, James H., ed. *The Wounded Knee Massacre from the Viewpoint of the Sioux* (Rapid City, S.D.: Fenwyn Press, 1940).

McLuhan, T. C., ed. *Touch the Earth* (New York: Promontory Press, 1971).

Oyate Wicaho (Porcupine, S.D.: various issues, 1980–81).

Sandoz, Mari. *Crazy Horse* (Lincoln, Neb.: University of Nebraska Press, 1971).

Schmitt, M., and Brown, Dee. *Fighting Indians of the West* (New York: Scribner's, 1948).

U.S.. Commission on Civil Rights. *Indian Tribes: A Continuing Quest for Survival* (Washington, D.C.: U.S. Government Printing Office, 1981).

References to additional sources, including government publications and documents, are included in the chapter notes.

CHAPTER NOTES

INTRODUCTION

1. Jackson, *A Century of Dishonor,* pp. 30–31.
2. Indians are not among the nine ethnic American groups (including Puerto Ricans and Mexicans) discussed in Thomas Sowell, *Ethnic America* (New York: Basic Books, 1981).
3. Articles by the author on transgressions of Indian land appeared between 1978 and 1981 in *Audubon, Geo,* the *Nation,* the *New York Review of Books, Newsweek, Rocky Mountain Magazine,* and the Sunday magazines of the *New York Times, Washington Post,* and Miami *Herald.*
4. Highwater, *The Primal Mind,* p. 196.
5. See the description of "red and blue days" in Brown, ed., *The Sacred Pipe,* pp. 19 and 54.
6. For a discussion of Wakan Tanka, see Walker, *Lakota Belief and Ritual,* pp. 69–119.
7. *Rugaru* is not an Ojibwa word; possibly it is a corruption of *loup-garou,* or "werewolf," which French Canadian trappers may have called this spirit-being.
8. Eastman, *Indian Boyhood,* p. 183.
9. Chief Frank Fools Crow, quoted in Mails, ed., *Fools Crow,* pp. 119, 122, and 124.
10. "The Lakotas, as a whole, were devoted to their religious ceremonies, those of high class taking upon themselves the duty of observing very

closely religious etiquette. . . . So when one came to a place that had been dedicated to Wakan Tanka it was considered sacred and no one would trespass upon the ground. The Sun Dance poles which were allowed to stand from year to year were never desecrated. Children coming upon a pole would at once become quiet and respectful, while older people often stood in silent reverence for a moment or so." (Standing Bear, *Land of the Spotted Eagle,* pp. 155–56)

11. John Fire Lame Deer, quoted by Richard Erdoes in conversation with the author, May 1982.
12. Standing Bear, *Land of the Spotted Eagle,* p. 43.
13. The bull-necked portrait of Crazy Horse on the U.S. stamp ignores all known descriptions of this small, light-skinned man by those who knew him.
14. John Fire Lame Deer, quoted in Erdoes, ed., *Lame Deer,* pp. 93–94.
15. Neihardt, ed., *Black Elk Speaks,* pp. 232–34. Ben Black Elk served as translator for his father during the preparation of this book.

BOOK I

1. THIEVES ROAD

1. Originally a native animal, the horse became extinct in North America during the Pleistocene, then returned to this continent with the Spanish. Many of the Spanish horses escaped during the Pueblo Indian revolt that overthrew Spanish rule in 1640; the horses spread northward, reaching the peoples of the northern Plains in the late eighteenth century.
2. Standing Bear, *Land of the Spotted Eagle,* p. 43.
3. Early Lakota dates are from "winter counts" of the Flame, the Swan, and others (compiled by Sandra Le Beau for Cheyenne River Sioux Reservation, 1973).
4. Red Cloud, quoted in Schmitt and Brown, *Fighting Indians of the West,* p. 3.
5. The Fetterman Fight and the Hayfield Fight, respectively.
6. William Tecumseh Sherman, another veteran of the Seminole wars, was named for the great Shawnee leader who tried in vain to rally the Seminole, Sioux, and many other nations in a great confederacy to resist the relentless encroachments of the whites. "Each year our white intrud-

ers become more exacting, oppressive, demanding, and overbearing. Wants and oppressions are our lot. Are we not being stripped day by day of the little that remains of our ancient liberty? Unless each tribe unanimously combines to give a check to the avarice and oppressions of the whites, we will become conquered and disunited and we will be driven from our native lands and scattered like autumn leaves before the wind." (Tecumseh [or Tecumtheh], 1812)

7. Red Cloud, quoted in Schmitt and Brown, *Fighting Indians of the West,* p. 62.
8. Commissioner Francis Walker, quoted in Witt and Steiner, *The Way,* p. 60.
9. This description of Custer is from Colonel (later Brigadier General) D. S. Stanley, in a letter to his wife, quoted in Andrist, *The Long Death,* p. 243.
10. Fast Bear's speech to the commissioners, 1875.
11. See Walker, *Lakota Belief and Ritual;* Eastman, *The Soul of an Indian.* While the term *wasicu* was in use in the nineteenth century, Walker suggests that it derives from *wa,* or "white," and *sicun,* or "medicine," as in the powerful "white medicine" of the white man's firearms and liquor; Eastman translates *wasechu* as "rich"; for both there is a connotation of spirit power. As Eastman remarks in *Indian Boyhood,* p. 239, "In some things we despised them; in others we regarded them as *wakan* (mysterious), a race whose power bordered on the supernatural." Perhaps Walker's informants were being polite, or perhaps "the greedy one" (John Fire Lame Deer says "the fat-taker") is a more recent variation.
12. Bourke, *On the Border with Crook,* pp. 247–48 and 244.
13. The Dakota east of the Missouri became known as the Yankton Sioux; the Santee Sioux were the remnant Dakota bands in Minnesota.
14. One account suggests that it was Spotted Tail who deterred Little Big Man from a violent action. See Andrist, *The Long Death*, p. 247.
15. The adviser was Colonel John Gibbon, quoted in Andrist, p. 269. Custer answered ambiguously, "No, I won't."
16. Deloria, *Behind the Trail of Broken Treaties,* p. 64. Another great defeat was in the protracted, expensive, unpopular, and inconclusive Seminole war in Florida.
17. Red Cloud, quoted in Eastman, *From the Deep Woods to Civilization,* p. 100.
18. See Mari Sandoz, *Cheyenne Autumn* (New York: Hastings, 1975).

19. Standing Bear, *Land of the Spotted Eagle,* p. 179.
20. *Congressional Record,* 1880, quoted in Johansen and Maestas, eds., *Wasi'chu,* p. 24.
21. This account was given the author by Richard Erdoes, who is completing a book on the Crow Dog family. Ohiyesa (Dr. Charles Eastman) has a different version of this dramatic story (in *The Soul of an Indian*): "The cause of his act was a solemn commission received from his people, nearly thirty years earlier, at the time that Spotted Tail usurped the chieftainship. . . . Crow Dog was under a vow to slay the chief, in case he ever betrayed or disgraced the name of the Brule Sioux. There is no doubt that he had committed crimes both public and private, having been guilty of misuse of office as well as of gross offenses against morality; therefore his death was not a matter of personal vengeance but of just retribution." See also *Indian Tribes,* pp. 139–40.
22. Quoted in *Indian Tribes,* p. 140.
23. Andrist asserts that this last hunt was led by Sitting Bull and his Hunkpapas; see *The Long Death,* p. 334.
24. Spotted Tail, quoted in McGregor, ed., *The Wounded Knee Massacre,* pp. 18–19.
25. Little Wound, American Horse, and Lone Star, speaking in 1896, quoted in Walker, *Lakota Belief and Ritual,* p. 68.
26. Among those quoted are Senators Teller and Pendleton. Senator Dawes's remarks are from an address to philanthropists in 1885. On this subject, see Talbot, *Roots of Oppression;* Andrist, *The Long Death;* and the works of Vine Deloria, Jr.
27. See Standing Bear, *Land of the Spotted Eagle,* p. 124.
28. Much more than two thirds was lost in Indian Territory, to which many of the eastern tribes had been removed after 1831; there the swindles were given a huge impetus by the "Red Land's" wealth in coal and oil. Among those who profited most heavily was Dawes Commissioner Pliny L. Soper, the official defender of the Indians as U.S. District Attorney for the northern Indian Territory, who was also chief attorney for certain oil and railroad corporations; Soper's profitable accommodation of special interests with his own has been emulated by unworthy government officials ever since. A suit by a Kiowa chief (*Lone Wolf* v. *Hitchcock*; see Deloria, *Behind the Trail of Broken Treaties,* pp. 144–45) contesting the allotment and the great land grab was dismissed in 1903 by the Supreme Court, which held that dealings with Indians were a political matter, not a judicial one, and that Congress had plenary power

over Indians, including the right to alter or ignore treaties as it saw fit. This precedent has been used to justify ruthless dealings ever since. In 1907, what was left of Indian Territory was merged with the new state of Oklahoma (from a Choctaw word meaning "Red-Earth-Colored People").

29. Sitting Bull, quoted in Witt and Steiner, *The Way,* p. 20.
30. Deloria, *Behind the Trail of Broken Treaties,* p. 65.
31. Eastman, *From the Deep Woods to Civilization,* pp. 110–13, 193.
32. "The subjugation of a race by their enemies cannot but create feelings of most intense hatred and animosity. Possibly if we should put ourselves in their place, we might comprehend their feelings. . . . Suppose this vast continent had been overrun by sixty millions of people from Africa, India, or China, claiming that their civilization, customs, and beliefs were older and better than ours, compelling us to adopt their habits, language, and religion . . . and we realized that such a conquest and the presence of such a horde of enemies had become a withering blight and a destroying scourge to our race: what then would be our feelings towards such a people?" (General Nelson A. Miles, "The Future of the Indian Question," *North American Review,* January 1891; quoted in Mails, ed., *Fools Crow,* p. 29)
33. Although Red Cloud protested the treatment of his people to the end, he stopped well short of the open defiance and contempt expressed repeatedly by Sitting Bull, who told a white audience in 1883, "I hate all the white people. You are thieves and liars. You have taken away our land and made us outcasts." (Brown, *Bury My Heart at Wounded Knee,* p. 401)
34. See Walker, *Lakota Belief and Ritual,* p. 10.
35. Red Cloud's farewell address, quoted in Ibid., p. 137.
36. Fools Crow on Black Elk, quoted in Mails, ed., *Fools Crow,* p. 45.
37. Ibid., pp. 67–73.
38. This rare Indian agent was John Brennan, known to the Oglala as "Longneck." (See Mails, ed., *Fools Crow.*)
39. See Deloria, *Behind the Trail of Broken Treaties,* for extensive historical material on the Lakota reservations.
40. Mails, ed., *Fools Crow,* p. 113.
41. Standing Bear, *Land of the Spotted Eagle,* pp. xv, 229, and 245. Luther Standing Bear was a remarkable man, educated at Carlisle Indian School, who later became a movie actor in Hollywood; his beautiful books were prepared and edited by his niece Warcaziwin (May Montoya Jones).

42. See Deloria, *Behind the Trail of Broken Treaties,* pp. 16–17. The anthropologist Oliver La Farge, who helped prepare Collier's reforms, was eventually disappointed by their consequences. Other anthropologists, including those who genuinely liked Indians, were finding themselves increasingly unwelcome on the reservations, where a people already treated like children resented being treated like guinea pigs as well. "There are many, many books dealing with their history; biographies have been written of their great men," Clark Wissler wrote of the "Sioux" in 1940. "What more should a people want?" (*The Indians of the United States* [Garden City, N.Y.: Doubleday, 1940]) In an anthropologist who had visited Pine Ridge and written several papers on this people (and who had edited James Walker's research over many years for the American Museum of Natural History), such foolishness is remarkable, and Wissler was by no means alone. The fatuity of all too many scholars, with their talk about the "clash of cultures" (as if the annihilation of the older culture could not be helped), their cold absorption in their data to the exclusion of the real human beings all around them, made them even more disliked by Indians than the missionaries whose contamination of the culture they so deplored.
43. Indian Reorganization Act, quoted in *Indian Tribes.* See note 13 to Chapter 11 of the present book.
44. Indian Claims Commission statement by Senator Arthur Watkins (R, Utah).
45. Mundt statement, quoted in Deloria, *Custer Died for Your Sins,* p. 58.
46. House Concurrent Resolution 108, the "Termination Resolution" (1953), also provided for the sale of liquor to the Indians. The first Indians to be terminated included Ute and Paiute bands in Senator Watkins's home state, together with relict groups in Oregon and California that still persisted on small tracts of land; more than one hundred small bands were eventually terminated. But the Klamath in Oregon (terminated in 1958) and the Menominee in Wisconsin (1961) "voted" to be relieved of well over a million acres of productive forest. As it turned out, the Klamath forests had been coveted for years by the Weyerhaeuser Timber Corporation, which had gained the sympathetic ear of an Oregon Republican named Douglas McKay, considered—until 1981—the most destructive Secretary of the Interior since Albert Fall of Teapot Dome, in the Harding administration. The Menominee, who had invited trouble by successfully suing the BIA for mismanagement of their forest resource a few years earlier, lost their land in an orderly

process, personally supervised by Claims Commissioner Watkins, in which less than 10 percent of the adult population turned out to vote. The Menominee (an Ojibwa name meaning "People of the Wild Rice") had been one of the relatively prosperous Indian nations, paying for almost all of their services with the proceeds from their own sawmill; these people lost not only their land base but all federal support, including health care, and were soon in a state of utter ruin. What was left of their lands was returned to the fragmented tribe in 1974, under the Menominee Restoration Act. (For details on termination and the Claims Commission, see Deloria, *Custer Died for Your Sins*; also, *Indian Tribes.*)

47. Eastman, in *Indian Boyhood* (1902), quoted in Highwater, *The Primal Mind,* p. 196.
48. Frank Fools Crow and Charlie Red Cloud led the delegation that met with Collier: see Mails, ed., *Fools Crow,* p. 147.
49. Vine Deloria, Jr., letter to the author, May 1982.
50. See the case of Mrs. Hildegard Catches, cited in Talbot, *Roots of Oppression,* p. 149.

2. THE UPSIDE-DOWN FLAG

1. John Pittman, "Wounded Knee and the Indian Future," quoted in Talbot, *Roots of Oppression,* p. 75.
2. President Lyndon B. Johnson, "The Forgotten American," Special Message to Congress, March 6, 1968, quoted in *Indian Tribes,* p. 6.
3. Richard Oakes and the other "new Indian" leaders were also involved in a number of protest occupations of treaty territories or surplus federal land by the Pit River nation of northern California and other groups. These occupations were more flashy than effective, yet they served to organize young Indians from all over the country.
4. Mad Bear Anderson had previously organized his Six Nations people in a fight against state and federal seizure of their New York State land in the late 1950s; the protest had culminated in a march before the White House and an attempted citizen's arrest of the Secretary of the Interior. This outrageous gesture was seen by the startled authorities as "Communist-inspired," especially when, not long thereafter, Mad Bear went to Cuba with a delegation of Miccosukee Indians, who were fighting the Everglades Reclamation Project, and "recognized" the Castro govern-

ment on behalf of the first Americans. See Edmund Wilson, *Apologies to the Iroquois* (New York: Random House, 1966).

5. Proclamation quoted in McLuhan, ed., *Touch the Earth,* p. 164.
6. Deloria, *Behind the Trail of Broken Treaties,* p. 41.
7. Fort Lawton was named for Captain H. W. Lawton, U.S. Army, who accepted the surrender of the Apache war leader Geronimo. Eventually the occupation was called lawful by the federal courts, and Fort Lawton is now the Daybreak Star Cultural Center, operated by United Indians of All Tribes.
8. Although Richard Oakes's killer had quarreled with him a few days before the shooting, he was charged with manslaughter instead of murder, and acquitted of this charge in March 1973. See Deloria, *Behind the Trail of Broken Treaties,* p. 46, and *God Is Red,* p. 35.
9. The Twenty Points (and the government response) are quoted in *BIA: We're Not Your Indians Anymore,* pp. 63–90.
10. Carter Camp, quoted in Ibid., p. 11.

3. TO WOUNDED KNEE

1. Yellow Thunder story: Severt Young Bear, in *Voices from Wounded Knee,* p. 13.
2. Dick Wilson, quoted in *BIA: We're Not Your Indians Anymore,* p. 34.
3. For additional comment on missionaries, see Deloria, *Custer Died for Your Sins,* Chapter 5.
4. From Dennis Banks's opening statement at the trial in St. Paul, 1974.
5. Ellen Moves Camp, quoted in *Voices from Wounded Knee,* pp. 31 and 14.
6. Carter Camp, quoted in *The New York Times,* March 1, 1973.
7. Ellen Moves Camp, Wilbur Riegert, and Rachel Hollow Horn, quoted in *Voices from Wounded Knee,* pp. 39 and 155.
8. Report to Pentagon of Colonel Frank B. Oblinger: see "Army Tested Secret Civil Disturbance Plan at Wounded Knee, Memos Show," *The New York Times,* December 3, 1975.
9. From John Adams's account in *Voices from Wounded Knee,* pp. 51–52.
10. Lorelei Decora, quoted in Ibid., p. 56.
11. See the testimony of Colonels Warner and Potter at Wounded Knee trials in St. Paul, Minn., and Lincoln, Neb., where the illegality of an Army presence without Congressional action or Presidential executive order was made clear. Haig's efforts to disguise the source of military

equipment—it was Haig and General Creighton Abrams, with President Nixon's approval, who directed that Warner and Potter and their staffs should wear civilian clothes—were exposed by Army records, and the colonels admitted under cross-examination that military equipment, including weapons, had been transferred to civilian vehicles and driven to Wounded Knee by soldiers in mufti; abandoning his early claim that the Army men were present as "observers," Warner acknowledged ordering the FBI agents and U.S. marshals to follow the Army's "Rules of Engagement" prepared for civilian disorders. (See Martin Garbus, "General Haig of Wounded Knee," *Nation,* November 9, 1974.)

12. Dick Wilson proclamation in *Voices from Wounded Knee,* pp. 125–26.
13. Kenneth Tilsen, quoted in Ibid., p. 128.
14. Russell Means, quoted in Ibid., p. 136.
15. Wayne Colburn, Stan Holder, Ellen Moves Camp, and Clyde Bellecourt, quoted in Ibid., pp. 150, 148, and 151; Gladys Bissonnette, quoted from St. Paul trial transcript.
16. McGovern, quoted in *The Washington Post,* April 22, 1973.
17. Arvin Wells, in *Voices from Wounded Knee,* pp. 241–43.
18. Dennis Banks, quoted in Ibid., p. 248.
19. This figure was very much increased by the widespread investigations and prosecutions in the years to follow. A civil-rights suit based on the illegal military presence at Wounded Knee was brought by the traditional people against Alexander Haig and several others; after eight years, this suit—denied, appealed, reversed, bogged down in endless procedural disputes, mostly involving jurisdiction over high personages—was eventually transferred from the Washington, D.C., courts back to South Dakota, where it is still pending.

4. THE WOUNDED KNEE TRIALS

1. Some of the most militant "Indians" at White Oak (and also on the Trail of Broken Treaties) were federal agents; see Deloria, *Behind the Trail of Broken Treaties,* p. 57.
2. Russell Means, quoted by John Adams in *Akwesasne Notes,* Early Summer 1975.
3. Quoted by Richard Erdoes, in conversation with author.
4. Fools Crow, quoted in Talbot, *Roots of Oppression,* p. 76.
5. Hurd remark from a tape by Kevin McKiernan, 1974.

6. Ibid.
7. Ellen Moves Camp remarks, Ibid.
8. Judge Nichol's statement about the FBI was quoted in *The New York Times,* September 17, 1974; the longer statement is from his memorandum decision of October 9, 1974.
9. Other federal judges who tried Wounded Knee cases were Van Sickle (Bismarck, N.D.), McManus (Cedar Rapids and Council Bluffs, Iowa), and Urbom (Sioux Falls, S.D., and Lincoln, Neb.). Judge Urbom agreed with Judge Nichol that the Army presence at Wounded Knee had been illegal.
10. Judge Urbom pointed out that treaties were placed "by the Constitution of the United States on no higher plane than an Act of Congress, so if a self-executing treaty and an Act of Congress be in conflict, the more recent governs." Relations with Indians were the exclusive right of the executive and legislative branches of government, beyond the province of the courts. "Perhaps it should be otherwise, but it is not. . . . In summary, the law is that native American tribes do not have complete sovereignty, have no external sovereignty, and have only as much internal sovereignty as has not been relinquished by them by treaty or explicitly taken by act of the U.S. Congress."

    Criteria for sovereignty have been defined by the National Lawyers Guild as (a) a permanent population; (b) a defined territory; (c) an effective government; (d) a capacity to enter into relations with other states. The Oglala Lakota met all these criteria in 1868, and still meet them today.
11. Pedro Bissonnette was arrested in the company of white AIM supporter Harry Shafer, who turned out to be an FBI informer. Bissonnette's statement is quoted in *Voices from Wounded Knee,* p. 259.
12. Don Holman's report turned up in testimony before the Minnesota Citizens Review Commission on the FBI, February 1977.

5. THE NEW INDIAN WARS

1. See Richard O. Clemmer, *Continuities of Hopi Culture Change* (Ramona, Calif.: Acoma Books, 1978).
2. "According to a 1975 report of the Federal Energy Commission, Indian lands have already produced over $2.7 billion in oil and gas, $187 million in coal, $349 million in uranium, and over $434 million in zinc,

copper, phosphate, and limestone. Yet, in the Navajo Nation, the coal companies are receiving an average net profit of $2.26 per ton while the Navajos receive only 15–20¢ per ton for their non-renewable resource." (Talbot, *Roots of Oppression*) These figures have improved somewhat with the rise of Tribal Chairman Peter MacDonald and the emergence of the Council of Energy Resource Tribes (CERT), but only a few Navajo have prospered; despite the enormous wealth under their lands, the great majority of the people live in dire poverty.

3. Jancita Eagle Deer's school principal was Kay Antoinette Lord; her doctor was John Crockett; the BIA investigator of her case was Peter Pichlin.
4. These BIA reports cannot be verified, since the government refuses to release them.
5. Gridley attested to this statement in an affidavit of May 22, 1976.
6. This account of Anna Mae Aquash's activities at Wounded Knee is adapted from Johanna Brand, *The Life and Death of Anna Mae Aquash* (Toronto: James Lorimer, 1978).
7. Durham later said that he was inside Wounded Knee for only about five hours, on March 20, 1973.
8. Mark Rosenbaum of the American Civil Liberties Union, in conversation with the author, February 1981.
9. See the account in the *Nation,* December 24, 1977.
10. Governor Lucey and Colonel Hugh Simonson of the National Guard deserve most of the credit for avoidance of bloodshed; they also persuaded the Alexian Brothers to deed the all-but-abandoned property to the Menominee.
11. The coroner in Jancita Eagle Deer's death was Dr. Donald Larsen.
12. For a fuller discussion of the Janklow incident, see pp. 108ff. The information on Delphine Eagle Deer was contributed by Richard Erdoes and Leonard Crow Dog.
13. See pp. 108ff for an account of the Janklow incident. For a detailed (though speculative) account of this whole story, see Paula Giese, *Secret Agent Douglass Durham and the Death of Jancita Eagle Deer* (Minneapolis: Anvil Press, 1976); also, Brand, *The Life and Death of Anna Mae Aquash.*
14. Other accounts also refer to a CIA connection:

    "In September 1974, Durham attempted to involve AIM in relief operations in Honduras (Belize) following a severe hurricane in that country. Durham wanted Dennis Banks to use his interest in reservation lands to fund a team of medics to be parachuted into the country by the Foundation for Airborne Relief of California. AIM learned the organization was a CIA front and the idea was abandoned. Next Durham wanted AIM to put up $30,000 to fund a plane chartered from Flying Tiger Airlines. When a worker in the AIM office pointed out that the airline had close ties to the CIA, this plan too was dropped. Durham finally succeeded in getting the Defense Department to provide a plane and a special crew.

"Exactly what Durham's intentions were in these manoeuvres remains unclear. AIM had just begun to make contact with native people in South America. In many of these countries, the CIA had been active in propping up dictatorial regimes. Had Durham been successful, AIM funds would have been spent in a mission that would have linked AIM with the CIA and discredited it in the eyes of South American Indians, as well as native people in Canada and the United States." (Brand, *The Life and Death of Anna Mae Aquash,* p. 101)

15. The name of this agent was Ray Williams, not to be confused with SA Ronald A. Williams.
16. John Adams, in *Akwesasne Notes,* Early Summer 1975, p. 14.
17. The charge of "criminal syndicalism"—in effect, union activities leading to worker control over the means of production—had last been filed in 1918, against Eugene V. Debs.

6. THE U.S. PUPPET GOVERNMENT

1. The final vote was 1,714 to 1,514.
2. The Wounded Knee defendant was Bernardo Escamilla.
3. Wilson's statement is quoted in the Rapid City *Journal,* April 4, 1975.
4. Trimble is quoted in an article by Cheryl McCall, Pacific News Service, June 13, 1975.
5. Russell Means is quoted in *The New York Times,* April 22, 1975.
6. Lorelei Means is quoted by Cheryl McCall, Pacific News Service, June 13, 1975.
7. Janklow is quoted in *Akwesasne Notes,* Early Summer 1976.
8. FBI, "Responsibility on the Pine Ridge Indian Reservation, South Dakota," June 16, 1975.
9. ". . . OPINIONS OF THE SACS WHO WERE ON THE SCENE: SACs Richard G. Held, Chicago; [and others] . . . furnished their observations regarding

the Wounded Knee Special. In essence, they advised complete confusion existed as there were a number of DOJ [Department of Justice] representatives on the scene, each issuing conflicting orders. There was no coordination between the agencies other than that provided by the FBI, nor was there any advance planning done. . . . The military did not realize in many cases that they were there to assist and not direct the FBI. SAC Held at the time advised FBIHQ to have any success at Wounded Knee it would be necessary to withdraw the 'political types' and make it an FBI operation under FBI direction and leadership. . . . Should we in the future become involved in another situation similar to Wounded Knee where Special Agent personnel are deployed that the entire operation be under the direction of FBI officials. . . . It was reported in the initial phase of Wounded Knee that the militants were in possession of an M-60 machine gun and AK-47s (Communist automatic assault rifles), which could result in heavy casualties. It was necessary to convince the decision makers that APCs were necessary for the protection of the Special Agents and U.S. Marshals. . . . If such an incident occurs in the future or an incident similar to Wounded Knee and the FBI is involved, the FBI will insist upon taking charge from the outset."

10. FBI, "Law Enforcement on the Pine Ridge Indian Reservation," June 5, 1975.
11. Richard Wilson, quoted in *The New York Times,* July 6, 1975.
12. Buffy Sainte Marie, Harry Belafonte, Kris Kristofferson, and Rita Coolidge were among those involved in the school benefit.
13. The Tututni band has since joined with other remnant coastal groups in what is called the Siletz Confederation.
14. Roslynn Jumping Bull, quoted in *Rolling Stone,* April 7, 1977.
15. Chief Frank Kills Enemy, quoted in *Oyate Wicaho,* December 1980.
16. Means and Tom Poor Bear were acquitted in a non-jury trial in 1976.

BOOK II

Most of Book II is directly based on conversations, tapes of conversations, and correspondence with people involved in the events of June 26, 1975, and the long aftermath that concluded with Leonard Peltier's trial in the spring of 1977; additional material comes from the Minnesota Citizens Review Commission Hearings on the FBI (1977), FBI field reports, trial transcripts, and newspaper and magazine accounts, as well as tapes, interviews, and articles by Kevin McKiernan.

7. THE SHOOT-OUT I

1. Bob Robideau's account is from a letter to WKLDOC attorney Jack Schwartz, June 11, 1976.
2. Ibid.
3. Ibid.
4. Nilak Butler's accounts in this chapter come mostly from a tape made by Paulette d'Auteuil.

8. THE SHOOT-OUT II

1. Teddy Pourier is a descendant of Baptiste "Big Bat" Pourier, famous half-breed guide and interpreter to General Crook; numerous present-day Indian families in the northern Plains (including the Peltiers and the Robideaus) have the French names of nineteenth-century trappers and traders.

9. THE "RESERVATION MURDERS" INVESTIGATION

1. Vernon Bellecourt and Richard Erdoes, in New York, received frantic telephone calls from Gladys Bissonnette and others, expressing the hysteria, fear, and shock that swept the reservation with the huge invasion. At least one of these calls, Erdoes believes, came in *before* the shoot-out.
2. Testimony of Ethel Merrivale, tribal attorney, in the ResMurs trial at Cedar Rapids.
3. The FBI's public-relations man was Thomas Coll.
4. *Columbia Journalism Review,* September–October 1975.
5. Cited in *Newsweek,* July 7, 1975.
6. The petition was reported in *The New York Times,* June 30, 1975.
7. The white ranch hands were Robert Dunsmore, fourteen, and Jerry Schwarting, twenty-three.
8. Indians suspect that Herman Thunder Hawk had been an FBI informer

since November 1974, and that possibly he "set up" the cowboy-boot episode in the first place.

9. Edgar Bear Runner, quoted in the Rapid City *Journal,* July 14, 1975.
10. There was also a full-fledged white suspect named Robert Lewis Anderson, who had also been at Wounded Knee, whose fingerprints were found in the camp, and who had a close resemblance to Bob Robideau.

10. THE FUGITIVES I

1. The two agents who interviewed Dino Butler were Olen Victor Harvey and Charles Kempf.
2. Quoted by Richard Erdoes in *Akwesasne Notes,* Early Spring 1976, p. 13.
3. Interview with Candy Hamilton, September 1975.
4. Quoted in the Rapid City *Journal,* October 14, 1975.
5. David Price suggests that a shell casing recovered at the Little cabin could be matched to a Springfield rifle recovered near the site of the Bissonnette killing; in a government document obtained under the Freedom of Information Act, this rifle is linked (very inconclusively) not to Peltier but to Melvin Lee Houston, one of the young AIM warriors then living at Ted Lame's.
6. The Long Visitors' attorney was Gregory Gaut.
7. The court-appointed attorney was Ron Olinger.

11. THE FUGITIVES II

1. Trooper Clayton Kramer, as quoted by AIM warrior Russ Redner.
2. The reporter who interviewed Anna Mae was Ken Matthews of the *Idaho Statesman.*
3. FBI report on AIM, 1976.
4. The Wanblee ambulance driver was James Charging Crow.
5. Dr. Shanker, quoted by Kevin McKiernan in the Minneapolis *Tribune,* May 30, 1976.
6. Dr. Peterson, quoted in *The Washington Star,* May 24, 1976. Subsequent remarks come from a conversation with the author, October 1981.
7. Tilsen, quoted by Kevin McKiernan in the Minneapolis *Tribune,* May 30, 1976.
8. Interview by McKiernan in the Minneapolis *Tribune,* May 30, 1976.

9. Norman Zigrossi, quoted in *Rolling Stone,* April 7, 1977. In an unpublished interview with William Hazlett, Zigrossi vehemently denies making these statements; he also denies that Anna Mae's identity was known.
10. Mary Lafford, quoted in Brand, *The Life and Death of Anna Mae Aquash,* p. 163.
11. Nogeeshik Aquash quoted in *Akwesasne Notes.*
12. Frank Black Horse has since been released and may still be in Canada.
13. Canada's Indian Act (and, incidentally, South Africa's Bantu Reorganization Act) is similar to the Indian Reorganization Act of 1934.
14. The director of Oakalla is H. B. Bjarnason.
15. The Minister of External Affairs was Allen MacEachen.

12. THE TRIAL AT CEDAR RAPIDS

1. The other two Indians were Kenny Kane and Alonzo Bush, brother of AIM member Tony Bush.
2. This is from the same FBI report cited in note 3 to Chapter 11 of the present book.
3. "It is immaterial whether facts exist to substantiate the charge. If facts are present, it aids in the success of the proposal, but . . . disruption can be accomplished without facts to back it up." FBI memo, quoted in *Counterintelligence: A Documentary Look at America's Secret Police* (Chicago, 1980).
4. The defense team also included Lewis Gurwitz and Bruce Ellison.
5. See p. 90.
6. The Duck Valley water dispute was one of many on Indian lands, including reservations of the Utes in northern Utah, the Crow in Montana, the Lakota in South Dakota, and several tribes in the Southwest.
7. Asked in 1981 if he had gotten the dates wrong when Banks told him of Anna Mae's execution (February 25 or 26 was well before the identity of the body and manner of its killing had been announced), Trudell shook his head. "Banks just had this feeling, this intuition about it, that's all." Banks says the dates must have been confused.
8. Candy Hamilton, as related to WKLDOC attorney James Leach, as related to the author.
9. Quoted in Cedar Rapids *Gazette.*

13. THE TRIAL AT FARGO

1. FBI behavior in this case, including the role of Richard G. Held (his son, Richard W. Held, is also an FBI official), is under investigation by the People's Law Office in Chicago.
2. Quoted in Brand, *The Life and Death of Anna Mae Aquash,* pp. 108–109.
3. Leading the backlash were the people of the state of Washington, whose Republican Congressman John Cunningham, in 1977, sought to abrogate all treaties, terminate all federal relationships with Indians, and break up the reservations once and for all with a legal device that he entitled the "Indian Equal Opportunity Act." Another Washington representative, Lloyd Meeds, proposed complementary acts to limit Indian jurisdiction on their own territories and to compel them to trade or sell their fishing rights to others. Though none of this primitive legislation passed, it was taken seriously by many conservative congressmen who resented federal interference in state matters.

   It was true that, having signed the treaties, the federal government tended to protect the Indians in regions in which—unlike the Black Hills—it did not have much to lose. But in the absence of a responsible and consistent Indian policy based on obligation rather than expedience, a firm national policy that could survive the changes of administration as well as tremors in the public mood, the Departments of Justice and the Interior began to weaken on the Boldt decision of 1974, and the irresolute President Jimmy Carter, instead of enforcing the decisions of the courts, sent out a "task force" with instructions to come up with some sort of innocuous solution. However, the fishing-rights decision, based on three years of comprehensive study, was all but unassailable, even by a reactionary Supreme Court; in an opinion of July 2, 1979, which made only a few concessions to white interests, the Court reaffirmed the much-vilified Judge Boldt. See the account in *Indian Tribes: A Continuing Quest for Survival* (Washington, D.C.: U.S. Government Printing Office, 1981), Chapter 3.
4. The Canadian Minister of Justice at the time of Peltier's appeals was Ron Basford.
5. The British Columbia Supreme Court judge was R. P. Anderson.
6. The death of five settlers killed by restless Sioux whose Minnesota lands were being taken without recompense began a wild fortnight of massacre in which hundreds of whites and an unknown number of Indians lost their lives. Of the eighteen hundred Indians seized for punishment,

all but thirty-eight were eventually pardoned by President Lincoln. The thirty-eight said to have been ringleaders were hanged at Mankato, Minnesota.

7. The old man was James Brings Yellow, in Oglala.
8. Eleven cases have been filed against Russell Means. All but four were dismissed or settled before trial.
9. As the star-struck coroner of Los Angeles, Dr. Noguchi lost his job for a while as a consequence of "inappropriate smiling" at the prospect of performing the autopsy on Robert Kennedy; he has since been much censured for inappropriate speculations about the controversial circumstances surrounding the deaths of actors William Holden, Natalie Wood, and John Belushi, and was suspended a second time in March 1982.
10. WKLDOC affidavit, 1977.
11. Reporter Kitty Bell, *Victims of Progress,* Fall 1977.
12. Peltier's comments on Myrtle Poor Bear quoted in *New Age* and *Akwesasne Notes,* respectively.
13. The investigator was Cathy Bennett of the Jury Project.
14. Letter to the author from John Lowe, November 9, 1981.
15. The lawyers were William Kunstler and Michael Tigar.
16. Federal Court of Appeals for the Eighth Circuit, September 14, 1978.
17. See note 4 to Chapter 17 of the present book.
18. The attorney quoted here is Lewis Gurwitz.

BOOK III

Book III is derived from personal conversations and correspondence with many of the principals and participants in the events of 1977–82, together with trial transcripts, newspaper and magazine accounts (including sections of a series originally prepared by Bill Hazlett for the Los Angeles *Times*). Many of the government documents were obtained by Peltier's attorneys after November 1980 through the Freedom of Information Act; these documents are presently the basis of an appeal for a new trial.

14. THE ESCAPE

1. At one point or another, the Longest Walk, protesting new "backlash" legislation, attracted an estimated thirty thousand Indians—the largest gathering of Indian people in this century—but dissension and power struggles within its ranks dissipated its impact.
2. The records control supervisor was Bonnie Streed; the Oklahoma County sheriff was Lieutenant Larry Hayes.
3. "The first months I spent with Leonard Peltier in Marion prison were the most important days of my life. Leonard re-centered my life. He put me in touch with my roots and started me on the road to recovering the humanity that had been buried most of my life under the conditions of wasichu greed." (*In Total Resistance* [Leonard Peltier Support Group, 1980], p. 41)
4. Carey, quoted in *People,* April 20, 1981. Carey retired not long after Wilson's affidavits became known; he was tracked down by reporter Jim Calio after prison authorities refused to reveal his whereabouts.
5. Edgar Schein is a former Hollywood psychiatrist and sometime associate of Los Angeles coroner Thomas Noguchi, who testified for the prosecution in Peltier's trial; Noguchi permitted Schein to perform "psychological autopsies" on the cadavers of celebrity suicides such as Marilyn Monroe. Apparently Schein was so excited by Korean and Vietnamese brainwashing techniques used on American prisoners of war (which he had studied under Dr. L. J. West) that he advocated their use on civil prisoners at home.

   In 1962, in an address to Bureau of Prisons personnel in Washington, D.C., Schein instructed the assembled wardens that "In order to produce marked changes of behavior, it is necessary to weaken, undermine, or remove the supports of the old attitudes. I would like you to think of brainwashing not in terms of politics, ethics, and morals, but in terms of the deliberate changing of human behavior by a group of men who have relatively complete control over the environment in which the captive populace lives." These changes could be brought about by "isolation, sensory deprivation, segregation of leaders, spying, tricking men into written statements which are then shown to others, placing individuals whose willpower has been severely weakened into a living situation with others who are more advanced in their thought reform, character invalidation, humiliations, sleeplessness, rewarding subservience, and fear." (Cited in "Breaking Men's Minds," an undated [c.

1978] publication of the National Committee to Support the Marion Brothers)

6. *In Total Resistance,* p. 44.
7. Pat Mills was a member of the group under SA Dean Hughes that had managed to kill Joe Stuntz at Oglala.
8. The correspondent was Ramona Benke.
9. Judge Foreman and Warden Aron, quoted in "Breaking Men's Minds."
10. Thundershield, convicted on a rape charge, convinced Peltier that he had been framed by a jilted girl friend; the girl friend accepted Dallas's collect call and, as Leonard listened, expressed regret for what she had done.
11. The defense lawyers were Bruce Ellison, Lewis Gurwitz, and Wendy Eaton, assisted by deputy federal public defenders Rudy Diaz and Karen Smith.
12. Bill Hazlett, in letter to the author, May 9, 1982.
13. The two were married on December 21, the last day of the trial, in civil and Indian ceremonies, but the marriage has since dissolved.
14. The Chichimeca are an ancient people who preceded the Aztecs.
15. Roque Duenas was interviewed by Jim Calio for an article in *People* magazine, April 20, 1981.
16. Duenas and Kevin Henry apparently drowned on October 1, 1981, although Duenas's friends suspect foul play.

On March 20, 1981, Peltier's escape conviction was overturned by the Ninth Circuit Court because "denial of the right to cross-examine a prosecution witness [SA James Wilkins] to show bias constitutes reversible error." (The defense had claimed that Wilkins was a personal friend of the late Ron Williams and that—as Peltier had testified—Wilkins had threatened to kill him at the time of his arrest.) The defense contention that the escape attempt had been "entrapment"—that is, abetted by the authorities in order to set up an assassination—had been dismissed by the appeals court as "bordering on frivolous"; nevertheless, it was pointed out that no review had been permitted of defense evidence in regard to the assassination plot at Marion, and in ordering a new trial, the jurists recommended that, should the defense present sufficient advance proof of a plot by government agents to kill Peltier, "the court should allow him to present to the jury a defense based on duress." This defense was precisely what Judge Lydick had forbidden, and represented a crucial change in Peltier's favor.

The government appealed this decision, offering to show in a supplemental hearing before Lydick that the denial of right to cross-examine Wilkins was a harmless one that would not affect the verdict. This petition was granted, and a rehearing took place on January 12, 1982.

Agent Wilkins, called to the stand, denied that he had ever known or worked with Ronald Williams; he also denied that he had threatened Peltier's life, admitting, however, that he had pointed his rifle at Peltier's face. Wilkins said that he had joined the FBI in order to make the world a better place, and that the FBI was not only a fine organization but the best investigative agency in the whole country.

Defendant Peltier described once more the circumstances of his capture, including Wilkins's alleged statement to the effect that "One of those agents was a friend of mine, you punk, I'm going to blow your fucking head off." Wilkins, called back to the stand, denied this statement, but then, in an extraordinary spontaneous admission, made after the government attorney had turned away, he blurted out that what he had *really* said was "Was this [the rifle muzzle] the last thing Coler and Williams saw before you killed them?" ("The Great Spirit must have dragged that right out of him," Russ Means commented, when told about the episode by Bob Robideau.) At the trial in 1979, Wilkins had specifically denied any such statement. What he had said, in the opinion of the defense, was certainly a clear indication of bias, and therefore grounds for a new trial. The decision on this trial is still pending.

15. THE REAL ENEMY

1. John Redhouse, quoted in Johansen and Maestas, eds., *Wasi'chu,* pp. 12 and 13.
2. See Peter Matthiessen, "High Noon in the Black Hills," *New York Times Sunday Magazine,* July 13, 1980.
3. U.S. Department of the Interior, Bureau of Reclamation, *Water for Energy: Final Environmental Impact Statement* (1977).

   "Nearly all the uranium requirements and nearly all the global changes created by nuclear energy to date are due to military uses." (*Science,* August 1978)
4. Paul Semu Huaute, a Chumash medicine man.
5. Deloria, *God Is Red,* p. 25.
6. See Jacqueline Huber et al., *The Gunnery Range Report* (Oglala Sioux Tribe, 1981).

7. See map on p. 37 of *Status of Mineral Resource Information on the Pine Ridge Indian Reservation* (BIA Report No. 12, 1976).
8. See Huber et al., *The Gunnery Range Report.*
9. Department of the Interior, *Status of Mineral Resource Information.* A Federal Trade Commission report in 1975, noting that "The BIA has occasionally been less vigilant in the protection of Indian interests in mineral leasing than it should have been"—and calling this failure "inexcusable"—emphasized that the mineral wealth in Indian lands was "considerable, both in absolute terms and as a percentage of total resources."
10. Quoted in *New Age,* January 1981.
11. "It should be recognized that the pro-full-blood, pro-traditional, and pro-AIM positions that I took and maintained were little understood or appreciated by my mixed-blood relatives and friends I grew up with, many of whom work for the government or otherwise believed themselves to be of station and position superior to the full-bloods and traditionals. It has cost me friendships of my lifetime, while not necessarily gaining me friends and allies from the side I stuck my neck out for. I am not sorry for this because I believe I followed the right course." Al Trimble to the author, June 1982.
12. Fools Crow, quoted in Mails, ed., *Fools Crow,* p. 216.
13. Ted Means, quoted in *Oyate Wicaho,* December 1980.
14. These charges of genocide are supported by a report released by Senator Abourezk in 1976, which found that 3,406 women and 142 men had already been sterilized by this IHS program in South Dakota, Oklahoma, Arizona, and New Mexico alone.
15. James H. McGregor, *The Wounded Knee Massacre from the Viewpoint of the Sioux* (Rapid City, S.D.: Fenwyn Press, 1969), p. 14.
16. Chief Big Foot, quoted in Ibid., p. 95.
17. Mrs. Rough Feather, quoted in Ibid., p. 119.
18. Iron Horse, quoted in Standing Bear, *Land of the Spotted Eagle,* p. 180.
19. See Selo Black Crow, "The Flood: How Alcohol Is Drowning the Great Sioux Nation," in *Oyate Wicaho,* February–May 1981.
20. Jackson, *A Century of Dishonor,* pp. 183–84.
21. This opinion is supported by a BIA spokesman quoted in *The New York Times,* June 27, 1975, who said that only about twelve shots had been fired from the compound all afternoon; by this time, however, there seems to have been random firing from unknown locations all around the area.

22. Walker, *Lakota Belief and Ritual,* p. 137.
23. Deloria, *Custer Died for Your Sins,* p. 29.
24. For a more complete discussion of this matter, see pp. 108ff.
25. The complete text of Means's paper (which harshly repudiates the Marxism that AIM's enemies like to associate with the Movement) may be found in *Mother Jones,* December 1981.
26. In November 1980, the anti-nuclear referendum was defeated. But in a rural conservative state, beset by poverty and racial strife, the referendum won 49.2 percent of the vote in the face of a well-organized propaganda war waged by the mining companies, and the Black Hills Alliance and other groups intensified their efforts, taking the companies to court for infractions of the weak state environmental laws and persuading at least six of the multinational corporations to abandon exploration efforts in South Dakota. A growing awareness on the part of the public that western South Dakota was already the site of the largest land-based concentration of nuclear weaponry in the world, with Air Force installations, including 150 missile silos, scattered across more than 14,000 square miles, intensified resistance to the MX missile railroad-deployment system, refused by Utah and Nevada but welcomed to South Dakota by Governor Janklow, whom the mild-mannered Senator McGovern once described as "the biggest dud ever to inhabit the State House."

16. ANOTHER IMPORTANT MATTER

1. Myrtle Poor Bear's father, in the Post-Conviction Relief Hearing of March 12, 1979.
2. The school principal was Robert Riggs.
3. Kenneth Tilsen's statement is from the March 12 hearing.
4. In a letter to the author of April 15, 1982, Tilsen says, "It seems to me that the conflict between Halprin's testimony under oath in his libel trial and the FBI report which indicated Halprin and Hultman were the moving parties in that episode is so sharp and so bizarre that it . . . cannot be passed over lightly.

   "It strikes me personally as odd that Halprin, in response to a very generalized attack on his integrity, would put himself in the position of taking the witness stand and committing absolute perjury. Furthermore, we have Hultman's assertions before the Eighth Circuit that he knew absolutely nothing about the affidavits until they had been returned to him from Canada and that he read the affidavits after they had been submitted. Hultman is, and has been, a politician all of his life, as well as a trial lawyer. . . . When taken together with Halprin's testimony and the fact that Halprin was the moving party in an effort to clear his name, it seems more likely that both Halprin's and Hultman's stories are true and thus the FBI memorandum is a fabrication. The implications of an FBI memorandum created to justify conduct that several courts have criticized are to my mind most significant."

5. The Seventh Judicial District Circuit Court.
6. Tilsen's statement about the FBI appeared in *Quaere,* Vol. 3, No. 1, September 1976: "Most Americans still cling to the notion that the system of justice in the United States is essentially fair and that the laws are applied equally to all persons. If some are persecuted and others not, most persons seem to hold the view that this results primarily from chance. . . .

   "The evidence . . . does not point to mistakes or excesses within the F.B.I. so much as it points to a police organization with its own political bias, judgments, and goals, which is designed to function and does function to achieve those goals consistent with its own vision of what is correct and proper for our country. . . . Furthermore, it is essential . . . that we recognize that the F.B.I. plays a critical role in decisions as to who gets arrested, prosecuted, convicted and imprisoned. In making or influencing these decisions, the political outlook of the FBI dominates its actions. The result is that justice in the United States is neither fair nor equal."
7. The reporter was Bill Hazlett. See above, p. 596.
8. The twelve thousand pages actually received in 1980–81 were considered sufficient for an evidentiary hearing by Peltier's lawyers, who are still fighting to obtain the withheld documents.
9. The three agents Webster mentioned in connection with Anna Mae Aquash were Donald Dealing, Thomas Greene, and John C. Munis, respectively.
10. The FBI statement on Myrtle Poor Bear is from a letter from Director William Webster to Dr. Arthur Flemming, head of the U.S. Commission on Civil Rights, August 7, 1979. Most of these arguments reappear in an eighteen-page "Inquiry Concerning Indian Matters," issued on January 5, 1982, in response to questions from the Senate Judiciary Committee, the actor Robert Redford, and others.

11. Tilsen's statement about Richard Marshall is from the Appellant's Reply Brief before the Supreme Court (South Dakota), March 14, 1980.

17. FORKED TONGUES

1. Evan Hultman, quoted in *People,* April 20, 1981.
2. Peltier denies this: "I was never once stopped on that reservation in all the years I was there." Marvin Stoldt and Lucy White Dress (who allegedly identified him from the poster or photograph) are both unknown to him.
3. Since this rifle, rather than the Wichita AR-15, was the only one with a flimsy link to Peltier, it might have confused the Fargo jury, which may explain its unaccountable absence from photographs of the Oregon weapons used in the trial.
4. In a comprehensive report issued in October 1981, Amnesty International discussed at length the FBI's role in the Peltier and Marshall cases, which revealed "at the very least, some disrespect for the law on the part of the FBI. In *Peltier,* the Court of Appeals held that the more prudent course might have been to allow the defense to present Myrtle Poor Bear's evidence to the jury; in *Marshall,* the judge felt some 'concern.' Considered together, these two cases give rise to sufficient doubt about the integrity of the FBI in these matters to warrant further examination. . . . Amnesty International . . . wonders what conclusion should be drawn when a federal government agency (the FBI) . . . appears willing to fabricate evidence against its 'targets' and to withhold information which, according to law, should have been disclosed. It is, moreover, clear that the FBI have abused their power by producing false evidence and infiltrating the defense teams of people indicted on serious charges." *Proposal for a Commission of Inquiry into the Effect of Domestic Intelligence Activities on Criminal Trials in the United States of America* (Amnesty International Publications, 1981)
5. Crooks is quoted in *Newsweek,* July 19, 1982.

18. IN MARION PENITENTIARY

1. Since Peltier's escape, Lompoc has been upgraded to a maximum-security penitentiary.

2. Bobby Garcia poem quoted in *In Total Resistance* (Leonard Peltier Support Group, 1980), p. 60.
3. Jack Abbott, quoted in the *Evansville Courier,* May 17, 1980.
4. From letters to Paulette d'Auteuil, 1980.
5. Fidel Ramos, letters to Law Project attorneys, December 1980.
6. An inmate named Haneef Shabazz, a.k.a. Beaumont Gereau, wrote a letter to the lawyers on December 18, and another in late February, when more facts were known: "[Bobby] was brought to N-2 around 1:00 p.m. on December 12th, and as he passed my cell we shook hands as my food slot in the door was still open from the noon meal. At this time Bobby looked relaxed and normal and there was nothing strange about his appearance and seemed to be strong as usual. . . . That night I did not hear any strange noises or sounds of a struggle [but] . . . there was an unusual lot of movement on the range that entire night between the hours of 12 midnight and 6:00 a.m. This same night was his last night alive. They found or rather pronounced him dead at 6:00 a.m. in the morning, the exact same time that they usually start feeding in N-2. So you see if any commotion was made, everyone would think it was just the pigs in the process of getting breakfast ready. For this reason, none of us in the first four cells saw when Bobby's body was taken out."

   Meanwhile, Fidel Ramos had been finding out all he could, although he and Shabazz were inviting the same retaliation that appeared to have befallen Bobby Garcia: "During our continued research of Bobby Garcia death, I had received some vital information from an inmate that was working in the hospital N-3, that he was able to briefly talk to a Cuban that was housed in N-2 during the time of Bobby's death. The Cuban had related to the inmate working in the hospital that he saw Bobby Garcia arguing with the officer and that Bobby had hit the officer. The officer had left and returned shortly afterwards with some more officers and went into the cell that Bobby Garcia was in. He heard some noise, then it was quiet and the officers left. The Cuban said that Bobby did not hang himself and that he was murdered. Shortly after Bobby Garcia's death this Cuban was removed from N-2. . . . Since then this individual has been transferred to another facility, whereabouts is not known. . . .

   "Bobby Garcia was a strong and sincere man who had taught me a lot during the period of time I got to know him. Personally I know for a fact that Bobby Garcia did not take his life, the prison officials took his life."

7. Letter to author, April 21, 1981.
8. The lawyer was Michael Deutsch of the People's Law Office, Chicago.
9. Designed to contain up to five hundred "adult male felons who are difficult to manage and control," Marion is "the only six in a system which rates security from minimum to maximum on a scale of one to six," according to a spokesman for the Bureau of Prisons. "It has the toughest security in the whole federal prison system." (Mike Aun, interviewed by Bill Hazlett of the Los Angeles *Times*)
10. Abbott's book review appeared in the February 17, 1981, issue of the *New York Review of Books.*
11. At a parole hearing on April 8, the chairman of the Utah Board of Pardons took note of testimonials on behalf of Abbott's literary talent from Norman Mailer and two editors in New York City. The testimonials, solicited by Abbott, may or may not have been his own idea; they seem to have had very little to do with his release, which was already in the works, and apparently they were meant to camouflage the deal already made.
12. The lawyer was Jackie Abel.
13. The murder victim was Richard Adan. Abbott was recaptured in Louisiana on September 23, 1981, and returned to New York City; for his own safety, he was kept in isolation from other prisoners while awaiting trial. In January 1982, he was tried for murder in New York Criminal Court, and in April was sentenced to fifteen years in prison.
14. From a letter to Al Trimble, June 4, 1981.
15. Crow Dog: conversation with the author, June 1982.
16. On April 20, 1982, Leonard Peltier's attorneys, Bruce Ellison and John Priviterra, filed an application to the U.S. District Court in Fargo, North Dakota, to vacate the judgment against their client and grant him a new trial; the application, which would be reviewed by Judge Paul Benson, was "based primarily upon previously undisclosed evidence recently obtained from the government in a still pending federal action filed under the Freedom of Information and Privacy Acts" and would emphasize three main points: the suppression of potentially exculpatory evidence, the knowing use of false evidence, and the failure to disclose evidence of the presence and involvement of others. "The government's manipulation and falsification of the evidence deprived petitioner of due

process of law. . . . We have not asked for dismissal of an indictment . . . we ask only that a new and fair trial be granted." (See *United States of America* v. *Leonard Peltier:* Motion to Vacate Judgment and for a New Trial, April 20, 1982.)

19. PAHA SAPA

1. The move into the Black Hills was given urgency by a court decision of a few weeks before to place under the jurisdiction of the state of Montana that stretch of the Big Horn River that flows through the Crow Reservation, which had been Crow territory long before the coming of the white man; even Custer's old allies were no longer exempt from the new Indian wars.

   "We had always fought the three tribes . . . anyway, and might as well do so now . . . not because we loved the white man who was already crowding other tribes into our country, or because we hated the Sioux, Cheyenne, and Arapaho, but because we plainly saw that this course was the only one which might save our beautiful country." (Plenty-Coups, in Frank B. Linderman, *Plenty-Coups, Chief of the Crows* [Lincoln, Neb.: University of Nebraska Press, 1962], p. 154)
2. According to the *Engineering and Mining Journal,* November 1979, an estimated $8 billion worth of uranium lies beneath the soil of South Dakota, most of it in the Black Hills.
3. "The purpose of the suit was to regain as much of the sacred land as possible and a money award, while distasteful, is still a means to that goal. Per capita distribution and the subsequent expenditure of over $100 million on consumer goods, however, would be a clear signal that the Sioux people have adopted the white man's wasteful ways, and demand everything now in defiance of their responsibilities to coming generations. . . . It would be tragic if, after the long struggle to recapture our dignity and sacred lands, the magnitude of our victory obscured our vision of ourselves." (Vine Deloria, Jr., in the Los Angeles *Times,* June 25, 1980)
4. Russell Means, quoted in *Oyate Wicaho,* December 1980.
5. As of summer 1982, the award by the Court of Claims has not been paid except to the attorneys, due to continuing resistance by most of the Lakota to this money settlement.

   Having failed in its suit to recover 7.3 million acres of the Black Hills and $11 billion in past damages (the Supreme Court refused to hear the case in January 1982) the Oglala Sioux Tribe joined forces with former Senator James Abourezk, the Native American Rights Fund, the Indian Law Resources Center, and other attorneys, individuals, and organizations in an effort to develop new strategies for the recovery of at least part of Paha Sapa; a first step in this program was a suit against the Homestake Mining Company for a settlement based on a fair share of profits made illegally on Indian land.

6. The International Indian Treaty Council was put together by a Cherokee named Jimmy Durham, who split with AIM in 1979 after sharply criticizing the behavior of certain Indian leaders on the Longest Walk. The Means women give him little or no credit, but Russ Means says, "He was fantastic; he was my main man. It was Jimmy who got the Indian Treaty Council going; he did all the groundwork. He was also responsible for that Geneva conference in 1977 [Geneva Conference on Discrimination against Indigenous Peoples of the Western Hemisphere]. If it wasn't for him, we wouldn't be anywhere near where we are with the UN today."
7. On February 9, 1982, Senator Thurmond announced a new bill that would deny all future Indian land claims based on the 1790 Non-Intercourse Act—the basis for most Indian land claims in the East—and a few weeks later, Secretary of the Interior James Watt, concluding that "American socialism had failed the American Indian," said that the Reagan administration would "like to see them liberated" (Los Angeles *Times,* February 28, 1982); once again, the Indians were faced with termination.
8. See Robert T. Coulter et al., Indian Law Resource Center, Washington, D.C., various reports, especially Annual Report, 1981, pp. 26–29.
9. Fools Crow and Matthew King, quoted in *New Age,* July 1981.
10. Hank Means pleaded guilty and was sentenced to twenty to forty years in prison.
11. The Siletz Restoration Act of 1977, signed by President Jimmy Carter in September 1980, returned 3,600 acres of timberland to the Confederacy from the Bureau of Land Management.
12. Chief Joseph's skull now ornaments a dentist's living room, and AIM, as early as 1971, was protesting archaeological digs in Minnesota. See Deloria, *God Is Red,* p. 35. See Sidney Keith, on pp. xxxiii–xxxiv of the Introduction to the present book.
13. Standing Bear, *Land of the Spotted Eagle,* p. 43.

14. In September, with the onset of cold weather, and a government promise that talks "on the issue of the return of the Black Hills" would be held once the Indians were back on the reservation, the campers were happy to disband. Once again, the U.S. broke its promise; no talks took place, and in early November a group of young White Clay full-bloods of the Tokala (the Kit Fox Warrior Society, re-established in 1977 by Harry Jumping Bull) joined other traditionals in setting up a winter camp on Flynn Creek, about seventeen miles southeast of Custer; on November 15, a large force of state police and Custer County sheriffs broke up the camp and took its occupants to jail.

Meanwhile, Dick Wilson, deploring the administrations of Trimble, Whirlwind Horse, and Looking Elk, announced his candidacy for president of the Tribal Council; he wished to institute clean government, legalize the sale of liquor, take law enforcement out of the untrained hands of locally elected officers from the districts and restore it to the BIA police, and abide by the wisdom of the U.S. courts in their money settlements for the Black Hills. "We cannot be dictated to by a handful of renegades occupying Black Hills lands and representing no one but themselves," he said. In March 1982, Wilson—and Looking Elk—were defeated by Joe American Horse, who declared himself against the legalization of liquor on Pine Ridge; the debate on this subject still continues.

The "renegades" of Dakota AIM were still established at Camp Yellow Thunder, despite orders to disband from the U.S. Forest Service. On August 13, 1981, on behalf of the camp, Bill Means had made a formal request to the secretaries of Agriculture and the Interior that its 800-acre claim be withdrawn from the public domain. On August 24, the Forest Service, which had leased grazing rights on part of the area and sold timber on the rest—road building and logging were scheduled to begin in the spring of 1982—refused the application, which was "not in the public interest." The Indians were ordered to leave the area by September 8, which they refused to do. Wisely, the government decided against the use of force, at least for the time being; although Governor Janklow had assured the press that the Indians would depart "as soon as the snow flies," Camp Yellow Thunder celebrated its first anniversary in the spring of 1982, and (August 1982) is still in the Black Hills. For the moment, the main threat to its existence comes from local whites, one of whom, Clarence Tolleson, died on July 21, 1982, apparently by his own gun, in an accident during an argument outside the camp.

15. The government representative was Roy Sampsel.

20. RED AND BLUE DAYS

1. From an FBI 302 (interview).
2. Black Elk, in Niehardt, ed., *Black Elk Speaks,* pp. 224–30.
3. Adapted from Brown, ed., *The Sacred Pipe.*
4. In March 1982, Dino Butler was sentenced to four years in Canada's prisons; it is believed that Oregon will seek his extradition sometime in 1983.

In 1981, the right-wing businessmen's administration had commenced its reign with trumpeting scare talk about terrorism. Inevitably a Security and Terrorism Subcommittee was assembled by Senator Strom Thurmond (who by no coincidence was also the sponsor of new anti-Indian legislation: see note 7 to Chapter 19 of the present book), although even the Director of the FBI could "find no real evidence of Soviet-inspired terrorism within the United States." Nevertheless, those who coveted Indian resources would damn any resistance as a scheme of "the international Communist conspiracy," and because Indian activists maintain a natural alliance not only with traditional Indian liberation movements throughout the Americas but with native peoples fighting exploitation of their territories all over the world, they were sure to remain a target of oppression. In the 1970s, AIM was considered a "subversive organization" for trying to make the U.S. government uphold its own Constitution and its treaties; in the 1980s, it was sure to be attacked for defending what is left of the Indian lands. For example, "The U.S. has learned that members of a radical American Indian movement are being trained in South Yemen, where P.L.O., East Germans, and Soviet cadres drill members of national liberation movements." This ominous nonsense did not appear in the FBI Terrorist Digest or the John Birch newsletter or even in a political journal but in *Business Week* (June 1, 1981), a voice of the multinational corporations.

When *Business Week* raised the alarm, national AIM was so fragmented and dispersed that the FBI itself scarcely felt threatened, and many Indians who, thanks to AIM, had achieved some measure of identity and self-respect, were repudiating AIM's excesses and mistakes, which the Movement's fiery young leaders had never denied. Dennis Banks and Russell Means, who had drawn national attention to the Indian struggle, were not "real Indians," it was sometimes said, and the violent confrontations of the sort that had put Leonard Peltier in prison had nothing to do with traditional Indian way.

AIM and its warriors were eloquently defended by Janet McCloud, one of the fishing-rights leaders from the Pacific Northwest, a twenty-year veteran of the new Indian wars who was sick of the envy, back-biting, and gossip:

"The greatest beneficiaries of the American Indian Movement are the tribal council leaders who are always quick to seize the opportunities created by the Movement, and to claim unwarranted credit for the positive social changes won for Indian people.

"The tribal leaders and others who denounce AIM justify their actions by pointing out the human weaknesses of individual AIM people, with never a glance at their own.... Indian people can disagree 'til doomsday about which defensive strategy is best, or whether we should even resist. If we continue to disagree on politics, policy, philosophy, and enter into destructive personality clashes, we will lose all....

"And who protects the Indian people now that the FBI has almost destroyed the American Indian Movement? Nobody. Do we see tribal leaders who claim the credit for AIM's labors and sacrifices rushing to protect and defend the Indian people against the onslaughts they face today? ... Few acknowledge that real change only began to take place after the tremendous sacrifices of the young warriors of the American Indian Movement. The beneficiaries of the Movement live in new homes, drive new cars, live longer, have better health, are better educated, have well-paid jobs, etc., while the real warriors lie unrecognized in their graves or in prison cells.

"The American Indian Movement supports the efforts of all tribal leaders and programs that genuinely promote the better health, education and welfare of the Indian people. Neither AIM nor any other organized resistance movement of Indian people begrudges any benefit their people receive; they rejoice at all improvements, this is what they fight for. But the warriors have never grabbed benefits for themselves, and the few who do were never true Movement people. That is how you tell the difference between leaders and opportunists.

"We need our warriors, and where are they? In prisons, in hiding, pursued relentlessly by the FBI, or paroled to one county in one state, unable to travel, or forbidden to talk for or about their people, lest they be imprisoned again? How many Indian people will take the time to send a card or gift to warriors rotting in prisons? . . . It is time that Indian people, those who have received most from the American Indian Movement took some time to count their blessings, to give credit where credit is due. Don't forget the warriors, we may never see their like again." *Oyate Wicaho,* January 1981.

INDEX